Pg 21, 81-121

The Official Guide

Corel PHOTO-PAINT 9

David Huss

Osborne/McGraw-Hill

Berkeley New York St. Louis San Francisco
Auckland Bogotá Hamburg London Madrid
Mexico City Milan Montreal New Delhi Panama City
Paris São Paulo Singapore Sydney
Tokyo Toronto

Osborne/**McGraw-Hill**
2600 Tenth Street
Berkeley, California 94710
U.S.A.

For information on translations or book distributors outside the U.S.A., or to arrange bulk purchase discounts for sales promotions, premiums, or fund-raisers, please contact Osborne/**McGraw-Hill** at the above address.

Corel PHOTO-PAINT 9: The Official Guide

1234567890 AGM AGM 90198765432109

ISBN 0-07-211985-3

Publisher: Brandon A. Nordin
Associate Publisher and Editor-in-Chief: Scott Rogers
Acquisitions Editor: Megg Bonar
Project Editor: Jody McKenzie
Editorial Assistant: Stephane Thomas
Technical Editor: Jennifer Campbell
Copy Editors: Jan Jue, Carl Wikander
Proofreader: Pat Mannion
Indexer: Meg McDonnell
Computer Designers: Roberta Steele, Michelle Galicia, Gary Corrigan
Illustrators: Robert Hansen, Brian Wells, Beth Young
Cover Illustration: Cristina Deh-Lee

Dedication

This book is dedicated to our daughter Grace.
In short, the best daughter any dad
could ever ask for.

About the Author...

In the last seven years I have authored or co-authored nine books on Corel PHOTO-PAINT, which have been translated into six languages. I was seen on CNN and my photo montage with PHOTO-PAINT, titled *Beautiful Lady,* won Grand Prize in the 1997 Corel World Design Contest. During the day I am a technical writer and graphic illustrator for Motorola in Austin, Texas, where I live with my wife of 25 years, Elizabeth. (Note: She isn't 25, our marriage is.) I also write articles in several computer magazines and teach at conferences in both the United States and Europe. In my spare time . . . Who am I kidding—what spare time?

There's the official version of my biography. Now for my favorite: Born on the planet Krypton, David lost his biological parents at an early age and was raised by a kindly couple. He left his home in Smallville and moved to Texas where he pursued a writing career with a great metropolitan book publisher (CorelPRESS—which he mistook for a drycleaner). Where, disguised as a mild-mannered author, he continues his fight for truth (not like Clinton), justice (not like OJ), and the American way (lots and lots of cash).

Contents at a Glance

Contents

Workshops at a Glance

Foreword

With the availability of Corel PHOTO-PAINT 9, Corel offers graphics professionals a premium image editing and bitmap creation product packed with features so that you can create inspiring works of art for print and the Web. Whether you're working only in PHOTO-PAINT 9, or in PHOTO-PAINT in conjunction with other products, you can focus on getting professional results instead of figuring out how to work. Version 9 provides the latest graphics and Internet tools to help boost your creative productivity and offers exciting new features to explore. These new items include Artistic Media brushes with hundreds of options, Internet publishing features, and powerful Web design features to allow you to seamlessly take your graphic creations directly to the Web, or to optimize your files for a variety of file formats for any print opportunity. At Corel, we are excited about PHOTO-PAINT Version 9, and know you will benefit from the design time we have all invested.

In the same way that PHOTO-PAINT 9 provides a powerful solution to enhance your productivity, *Corel PHOTO-PAINT 9: The Official Guide* does the same. In your hands you hold a guide designed to help you make the most of your software tools. This book shows you how to quickly upgrade to the PHOTO-PAINT 9 working environment, demonstrates how to use the new tools and features, and gives excellent guidance on making the most of this great product. Author Dave Huss has included special Workshop Projects throughout the book so that you can follow along to learn about the tools, features, and techniques that he explains. An exciting chapter on creating Web graphics offers a wealth of information to ensure your artwork is optimized for use on the Web.

Corel is excited about the new technologies now available with PHOTO-PAINT 9, and we invite you to follow along in this CorelPRESS™ Official Guide. Dave Huss, along with the PHOTO-PAINT product team at Corel, spent many hours working on the accuracy and features of this book, and we think you'll appreciate our efforts.

The Official Guides to Corel software represent a giant step in the ability of Corel to disseminate information to our users with the help of Osborne/McGraw-Hill and the creation of the CorelPRESS series of books. Congratulations to the team at Osborne who created this excellent book, and to the team at Corel who supported their efforts!

Michael C. J. Cowpland
President and CEO
Corel Corporation
May 1999

Acknowledgments

The acknowledgment portion of a book is like a secret compartment, since generally only those mentioned in it ever read it. It is late in March of 1999 and the book is ready to be put to bed (with milk and cookies of course). It's a little after four in the morning (I do my best writing when everyone else is asleep). After a book is finished, it's pleasant to look back and think about all that was involved to get this book into your hands.

Of course, my family once again must be given thanks for giving up father and husband in exchange for the grumpy old man that I become when writing a book under deadline. As always, my family got to see more of the back of my head than the front.

The creation of a technical book is always a challenge to everyone involved. To have a book ready to ship with the product meant it was necessary to write about things in PAINT during the beta cycle. Now that's entertainment. A typical telephone conversation begins with, "When I move the cursor it changes shape. Is it supposed to do that or is it a bug?" I think we were successful because of the efforts of several people up Ottawa way. Ottawa, Canada, is where Corel is—you knew that, right? First and foremost I must thank Doug Chomyn and Steve Albert, who together head up the PHOTO-PAINT development team and once again endured a ceaseless barrage of questions during the creation of this book. My other PHOTO-PAINT technical wizard is David Garrett, who never ceases to amaze me with what he knows about the product—must be why he does PHOTO-PAINT quality assurance. Speaking of quality assurance, a great big thank you to the following people who read the manuscripts in such great detail that they even caught errors from the previous version of this book. Therefore the golden Fickle Finger of Fate award (I loved *Laugh-In* as a kid) is presented to: Bryan Shearer, Gordana Borovcanin, Guy Gravel, Jasmeet Kambo, Jim Deneumoustier, Neil Takahara, Peng Fang, and Stephan Smygwaty. Before leaving our friends in quality assurance, I'll pass along a safety tip I received from David Garrett: "Never clean your PHOTO-PAINT brushes with kerosene."

A great big thank you—for a giant of a man—goes to Mike Bellefeuille (that's pronounced like "Delphi," but with a "B"). Hey, if I can learn to spell it, you can learn to pronounce it correctly. Mike wears so many hats up at Corel, I'm thinking that investing in a hat company might be a sound financial move. Of course, to the lady who I am convinced can do almost anything—Michelle Murphy—a CD-ROM containing over 10,000 thank yous. I am sad that Corel has allowed her to transfer to their office in her native land of Dublin, Ireland. I will miss her. Of course, I can't be too sad, as she is only a few kilometers from the Guinness brewery.

My thanks to Jennifer Campbell who worked during weekends and part of her family vacation to complete the technical edit so we could get this book completed in time to ship with the product. I felt bad it took away from her vacation, but then how exciting can Idaho be? Just kidding—please, no email from Idaho.

A big thank you goes to Mary Thomas at Motorola (yes, I do have a "day job") who worked things out so I could have time off so this book could get out on time.

Also, thanks go to a mystery author, named Gary, who helped produce Chapter 24, "Creating Elements for the Web." If you feel that there are any errors or you need additional information concerning that chapter, Gary asks that you write to Gary@Exclamations.com with your question, and you'll get a cheerful reply before you know it.

Finally, (it keeps going and going and . . .) I am grateful to my acquisitions editor and friend Megg Bonar who makes the task of getting a book out on time almost fun. The rest of the Osborne team so essential to getting the book completed is Stephane Thomas, who makes sure all parts of the puzzle that make up a complex book project like this one are turned in on time, and Jody McKenzie who has worked tirelessly to make sure both the printed and electronic versions are correct. Once again I would be remiss if I didn't mention a head honcho at the Osborne ranch—Scott Rogers. You've been mentioned.

Last, but surely not least, my daughter Grace (now 18) wanted to remind all of you reading this book she is still looking for a boyfriend. I guess the Boyfriend-in-a-Box I bought her last week didn't work out. So if you are either Prince William or another dashing member of the opposite gender, send her email at my address (davehuss@austin.rr.com). And if you are really interested, remember—I own a gun and have a shovel.

Introduction

So there you stand, looking at a multicolored wall of computer titles, most of which are nearly as thick as phonebooks for major metropolitan cities. You ask yourself, "Will this book help me learn PHOTO-PAINT 9 or will it become another dust collector?" Your puzzlement is understandable. After all, the word "idiot" or "dummy" doesn't appear anywhere in the title. By now you have already looked at the dazzling color inserts and noticed it wasn't the typical collection of award- winning art produced by people with years of experience and way too much time on their hands. Instead you've seen a large collection of images that YOU will create using the step-by-step exercises in this book. If you owned one of the previous editions of the book, you also have noticed that the exercises are different from the previous editions. Yet, you may still hear that small voice in the background (not to be confused with the store announcement of the half-off sale on all organic chemistry textbooks) saying you won't be able to do stuff like that. Let me assure you that you will.

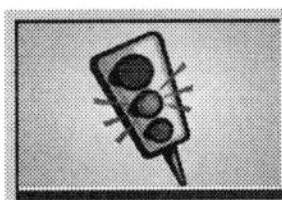

CAUTION: *This book contains exercises and information about digital photo-editing that could be harmful to your non-computer literate status.*

My "day job" (as in "don't give up your day job") for several years involved talking to thousands (OK, dozens) of people every day who began their conversations by telling me how stupid they were regarding their computer knowledge. That is generally just before they hand the phone over to their 8-year-old. These people are not stupid. However, they have come to believe that they are, convinced by a legion of techno-babble-talking computer types, many of whom simply need to date more often. In creating this book I have worked with the following assumptions:

1. You have not received the Nobel Prize recently.
2. Your IQ is higher than that of mayonnaise.
3. You would like to learn to use the computer for something other than Solitaire or Quake.
4. You are not a graphics arts expert, in fact you may even be wondering if graphic art is the stuff they hang in motel rooms and sell by the truckload at "starving artist" sales.

In short, if you want to learn PHOTO-PAINT 9—this book is for you. There is one tiny secret I must share with you if you really want to learn how to use PHOTO-PAINT. It is: READ THE BOOK and DO THE EXERCISES! Contrary to rumors in the computer industry, you cannot learn anything in this book by any of the following methods:

1. *Osmosis*—Keeping the book near you at all times so the knowledge of the product migrates into your mind.
2. *Sleep teaching*—Sleeping with a copy of the book as a pillow hoping that it will somehow jumpstart one or more of your brain cells.
3. *Super Speeder Reader method*—Thumbing through the pages wondering what all of the pictures mean.
4. *Proximity method*—Placing the book close enough to the computer so the PHOTO-PAINT program can make your computer smarter and do what you want it to do.
5. *The musical* Annie *method*—I'll figure it out tomorrow. Bet your bottom dollar that tomorrow, it'll make sense. (Sung to the tune of "Tomorrow.")
6. *The Impress Your Friends technique*—Keeping a copy of this book on your shelf so your friends (or your boss) will think you are really getting into the program. Actually, this technique does work except you never really learn anything, you just impress your friends.

Enough already. Here is the short version. Using PHOTO-PAINT isn't brain surgery; it's electronic finger-painting without the mess to clean up afterward. As I always tell people at the PHOTO-PAINT seminars, if you're not having fun with PHOTO-PAINT, you're probably doing something wrong. Buy the book and then check out that sale of organic chemistry books.

Where did I put the files for the workshop exercises?

Now I remember. At the last minute Corel couldn't fit them in the CorelDRAW 9/PHOTO-PAINT 9 CDs, so we had to put them on the CD containing the electronic form of the book which was shipped with the stand-alone version of PHOTO-PAINT 9. If you don't have the electronic version of the book, CorelPRESS has a coupon at the back of the book for a mighty sweet offer to buy the CD at a very low price. The files are also available for downloading at the web site **www.osborne.com**.

PART I

Introduction and Digital Fundamentals

CHAPTER 1

An Introduction to PHOTO-PAINT 9

You are about to begin an incredible journey into the world of photo-editing and digital wizardry. (Does that last sentence sound like the preview for a new movie?) This was once the exclusive domain of multimillion-dollar computer systems and dedicated graphic artists.

With Corel PHOTO-PAINT 9, you will quickly correct and produce images that can make your desktop projects dazzle. Photo-editing programs have traditionally been labor intensive. They required many hours of tedious effort to manipulate images (removing trees, adding people, changing sky color, and so on). PHOTO-PAINT 9 greatly simplifies this time-consuming process. Just as CorelDRAW enables you to achieve professional computer graphic effects with little effort, Corel PHOTO-PAINT 9 will allow you to reach that same professional level in the manipulation of photographs, paintings, and other bitmap images. The bottom line is that PHOTO-PAINT 9 is fun to work with, period. The fact that you can quickly produce professional results is a bonus. Next, Dave's genuine history of PHOTO-PAINT.

A Brief History of PHOTO-PAINT

Corel PHOTO-PAINT began its life as a software product called Photofinish, created by Z-Soft. It was introduced as Corel PHOTO-PAINT 3 in May 1992. It was, at best, an interesting bitmap-editing package that was very similar to Microsoft PAINT, which Z-Soft also wrote.

When Corel PHOTO-PAINT 4 was released in May 1993, there were many improvements, and only a small amount of the original Z-Soft program remained. PHOTO-PAINT 4 had limitations in the size of the image files it could handle, and the absence of several other key features prevented it from being a first-class product. In fact, it resembled Microsoft PAINT on steroids.

PHOTO-PAINT 5, which Corel originally released in May 1994, showed marked improvement. There were many changes still in progress when the product had to ship. Those changes appeared when the maintenance release (E2) was shipped in September. PHOTO-PAINT 5 began to draw serious attention from the graphics community with its support of objects and layers and its other features.

PHOTO-PAINT 6 entered the world of 32-bit applications, offering a robust set of photo-editing tools coupled with the power of a 32-bit architecture. If all this talk about 32-bit power is confusing, then—to borrow some terms from *Star Trek*—think of 32-bit power as warp drive and 16-bit as impulse power.

PHOTO-PAINT 7, which was released in November 1996, remains a 32-bit-only application that ranks among the best in the area of photo-editing applications. While retaining the general form and structure of PHOTO-PAINT 6, it provided greatly improved speed and functionality over the previous release. During its brief reign as Corel's premier photo-editing application, it won the coveted Editor's Choice award from *PC Magazine.*

PHOTO-PAINT 8, released in November 1997, had as its most notable change the addition of advanced mask functions like Clip Mask and Clip to Parent. Exciting new paint brush controls like Orbits and Symmetry were added. In addition, PHOTO-PAINT 8 marked the beginning of the migration from roll-ups to Dockers.

PHOTO-PAINT 8 for the Power Macintosh was released a few months later. Building on the success of PHOTO-PAINT 8, the product won rave reviews from the Mac community press.

With PHOTO-PAINT 9 the program continues to build on its previous successes. New filters add a whole new range of effects to an already robust package. Many of the improvements in PHOTO-PAINT 9 are "under the hood," meaning they are not new features but performance-enhanced existing ones. PHOTO-PAINT 9 can now directly read a majority of the digital cameras in the market today. Both performance and precision of many of the PHOTO-PAINT tools have been substantially improved.

Before We Get Started

One thing that makes PHOTO-PAINT such a powerful package is that there are so many combinations of tools and functions available. Of course, these qualities also make PHOTO-PAINT confusing for the novice. If you are new to photo-editing programs, I have included a section in this book to help you understand the sometimes-complex world of bitmap images. For the experienced Photoshop user, I have tried to associate Corel names with their equivalent Adobe Photoshop names wherever possible (I am not a Photoshop expert) or appropriate.

PHOTO-PAINT 9: A Premier Photo-Editing Program

Corel PHOTO-PAINT 9 is first and foremost a photo- or image-editing program. It is in the same league as Adobe Photoshop, but it costs hundreds of dollars less. As a photo-editing program, it offers all the features you should expect from a professional photo-editing package, and in several areas you can do more with PHOTO-PAINT 9 than with its main competitor. In case you are wondering why I mention Adobe Photoshop, it's because before PHOTO-PAINT came along, Adobe Photoshop was the unchallenged leader in digital photo-editing. Corel PHOTO-PAINT is not so quietly changing that.

One of the more useful tasks you can perform with PHOTO-PAINT 9 is to take a poorly composed, overexposed, scratchy photograph and make it look as if the photographer did a great job. In Figure 1-1 you may have noticed that the original photograph of a country school in Nebraska (on the left) has scratches and marks on the bottom. These were removed in the restored version (right). No big deal, right? Now compare them again and ask yourself this question. Where did the handrail go? Only you and PHOTO-PAINT 9 will know the truth.

People tend to get excited about all the breathtaking, surrealistic effects they can achieve with photo-editing packages such as PHOTO-PAINT 9. In truth, I get excited, too. But it is the everyday work of making the images in documents look as professional as possible, with the least amount of effort, that makes PHOTO-PAINT 9 such an important addition to your desktop publishing library.

FIGURE 1-1 A simple restoration of a school photo contains an interesting surprise—the original is on the left

Changing Reality (Virtually)

With PHOTO-PAINT 9 and this book, you will learn how simple it is to add people or objects to existing images. You can easily create things that don't exist, as shown in Figure 1-2, or, more commonly, remove unwanted objects like scratches, stains, or old boyfriends, as shown in Figure 1-3. You will even be able to change the way people look. I recently did a brochure for our church. The photo of one of the pastors had been taken several months and over 20 pounds ago. No problem. With PHOTO-PAINT 9 I took off those excess pounds in less than an hour—which is more than the pastor or the diet industry can say.

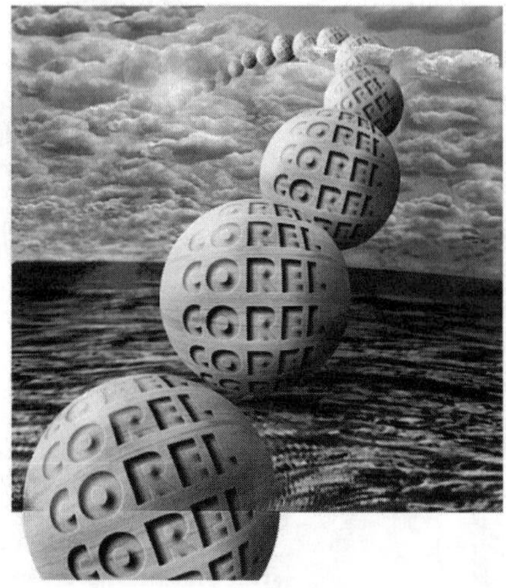

FIGURE 1-2 With PHOTO-PAINT 9 we can easily create things that exist only in our minds

(a) (b)

FIGURE 1-3 Breaking up may be hard to do, but removing a boyfriend from a photograph is simple by use of PHOTO-PAINT 9

Altering people's appearance (removing blemishes, changing hair color, and so on) has been done by professionals for a long time. I knew a guy who was one of the kings of the airbrush (back in the predigital days), and was greatly appreciated by more than one playmate-of-the-month. Now, like my friend, you will be able to change the way people look. The only difference is that PHOTO-PAINT 9 doesn't require an airbrush, long hours, or years of experience.

In Figure 1-4 we have an easy shot. My CorelDRAW counterpart, Gary Priester, wrote a book titled *Corel Studio Techniques.* It's a fantastic book about how to use PHOTO-PAINT and DRAW together and . . . oops. Anyway, we needed a picture of the two of us for the chapters entitled "Back to Back." No sweat. Gary lives near San Francisco and I live in Austin, Texas. So I had a picture taken of me leaning against a tree and Gary has his taken of him just standing there

FIGURE 1-4 Why is Gary (left) smiling? Because he knows he is several inches taller and I am several inches wider

with a smug expression on his face. With PHOTO-PAINT it was easy to put us both in the same picture as well as to make us the same height (Gary is 4 inches taller) and shave about 40 pounds off of me. I am real good at that last part.

What else can you do with PHOTO-PAINT 9? We have been talking up until now about changing existing images, but you can also create original images. If you're not an artist, don't feel excluded from this discussion. Like CorelDRAW, PHOTO-PAINT 9 lets you take clip art and assemble it to make exciting images. Corel has provided an assortment of objects that can be placed together to make a composite image. Using the PHOTO-PAINT filters and its powerful editing tools, you will quickly learn to create all kinds of original images, logos, and what-have-yous (and still maintain your I'm-not-an-artist standing). You can take the background from one photograph and place it seamlessly with another. Figure 1-5 shows how you can make an object stand out by replacing the background. Can you find the can of Coke? It's hidden under his paw—and I wouldn't want to fight him for it.

Of course, there is the fun stuff of PHOTO-PAINT—making really crazy things. I made Figure 1-6 for a CD label I was using to send my screen shots to my publisher. It's just objects and a little fiddling, but it was fun to make it.

FIGURE 1-5 Background replacement enhances the subject

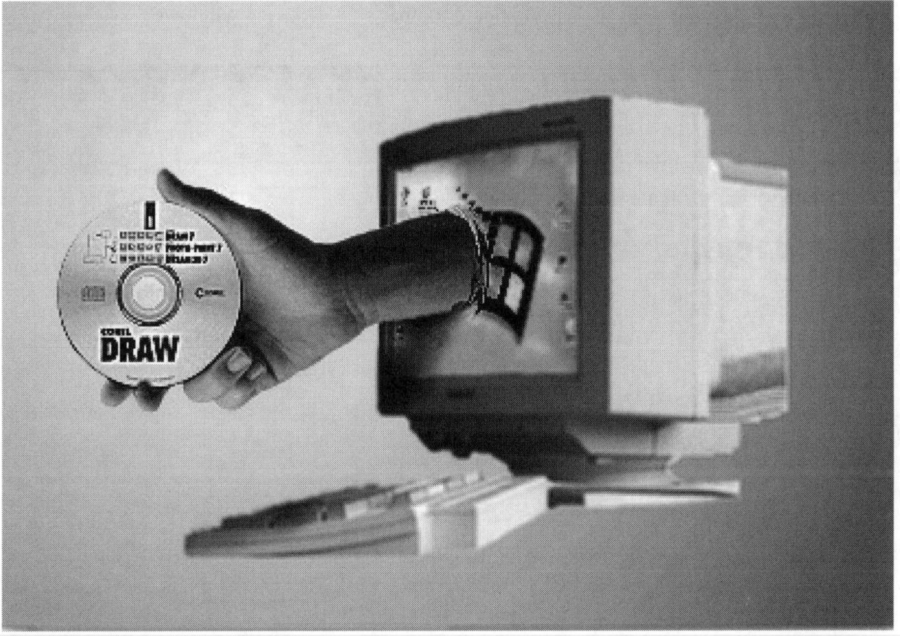

FIGURE 1-6 Safety tip—if you see a hand coming out of your computer, run, don't walk, to the nearest exit

A Quick Tour of PHOTO-PAINT 9

There's a lot of useful information in this chapter, so I urge you to look through it. If you are a first-time user of PHOTO-PAINT, I recommend that you familiarize yourself with (don't memorize) the terms and concepts described in this chapter before you begin to use the program. Time invested here will pay off in later chapters.

Elements of the PHOTO-PAINT Screen

Figure 1-7 shows the Corel PHOTO-PAINT 9 main screen. Your screen may look quite different depending on how it is configured (you'll learn about this in Chapter 3).

The Onscreen Color Palette

The onscreen color palette is used to select the *Paint* (foreground color used by the brushes), *Paper* (background), and *Fill* colors. These three terms are used throughout

Menu Bar
Property Bar
Standard toolbar
Docking windows
Toolbox
Title Bar
Image window
Mask marquee
Guidelines
Rulers
Onscreen color palette
Status Bar
Mask/Mode icons

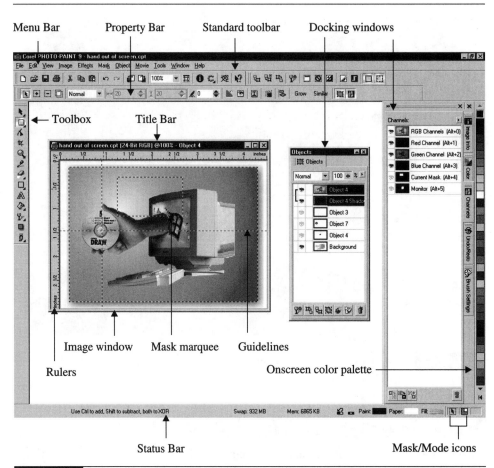

FIGURE 1-7 The main screen in Corel PHOTO-PAINT 9

PHOTO-PAINT, so you should try to remember them. To choose a Paint color—that is, to change the color of a brush—click a color on the palette with the left mouse button. To choose a Fill color, click with the right mouse button. To select a Paper color, hold down CTRL and click the left mouse button.

TIP: *If you don't enjoy memorizing mouse button/keyboard combinations, click and hold the right mouse button over the desired color. After two seconds, release the mouse button, and a pop-up menu (Figure 1-8) appears allowing you to set the Paint, Paper, or Fill to that color.*

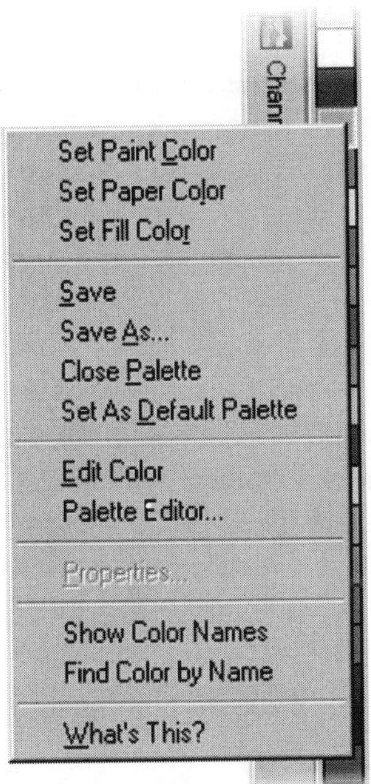

FIGURE 1-8 The Onscreen Color Palette pop-up menu

Onscreen Color Palette Pop-up Menu

In addition to selection of colors, the Pop-up menu allows you to customize the Color palette by choosing Properties.

TIP: *A keyboard shortcut to the Find Color By Name dialog box is to hold down the* CTRL *and* ALT *keys and click on a color in the palette.*

The Menu Bar

Select any menu heading in this bar to access dialog boxes, submenus, and commands. Access is also available by pressing ALT followed by the highlighted or underlined letter in the command.

The Title Bar

The Title Bar displays the application title or the image title (image filename). New in PHOTO-PAINT 9 is that the Title Bar now displays information about the image in the windows. While it's nice to know the title, the important thing about the Title Bar is the background. The background color of the Title Bar indicates whether an image window is selected, which is important when you have several image files open and want to know which one you are about to apply an effect to.

Dockers

The successor to roll-ups, windows called *Dockers* are parked on the side and provide the same functionality as the equivalent roll-up. In PHOTO-PAINT 9, there are more than 12 Dockers listed in the Windows | Dockers pop-up menu.

Rulers and Guidelines

Selecting View | Rulers or the keyboard combination CTRL-R toggles the display of the rulers on the image.

Rulers are important in PHOTO-PAINT because they provide the only visual indicator of how large an image actually is. We will explore why this happens in Chapter 2. For now, be aware that it is possible for a photograph to completely fill the screen and yet be smaller than a postage stamp when you print it. That's why rulers are important. Guidelines are new to PHOTO-PAINT 9 and provide a necessary alignment tool when you're setting up multiple objects in an image. Rulers, guidelines, and grids are explored in Chapter 5.

Toolbars

Toolbars were first introduced in PHOTO-PAINT 6 and are similar to the Ribbon Bar found in many other Windows applications. There are 21 toolbars available by default. Choose Window | Toolbars to see the list. You can also make your own toolbars, which you will learn to do in Chapter 3. I recommend displaying five of them at all times: Standard, Mask/Object, Property Bar, Toolbox, and Status Bar. Buttons on the toolbars provide quick access to commonly used commands. All the functions available on the toolbars can also be accessed through the Menu Bar. The appearance of the Toolbar and the number of buttons visible depend on which tool is selected.

The Image Window

This is the image-display window. The zoom factor of each image window is controlled independently by the Zoom control in the Standard toolbar. The default setting of Zoom—100%—is set in the General page of the Options dialog box (CTRL-J). If you have a medium- to high-performance graphics board in your system, you can choose Best Fit. But for an accurate representation of the image on the screen, you should always use 100%.

TIP: *When you choose a zoom factor that is less than or greater than 100 percent, the image may have a poor appearance. This is a result of the way it's displayed by the graphics adapter under Windows 95 and does not reflect the actual image quality.*

Toolbox/Flyouts

The Toolbox contains all the tools used for image editing. Many of the buttons in the Toolbox have flyouts to allow access to additional related tools. Most flyouts are identical to their toolbar. A flyout is actually a toolbar containing all of the tools in that category.

NOTE: *Availability of a flyout is indicated by a tiny black arrow in the lower-right corner of the button.*

To open a flyout, you can click and hold the cursor on the button for more than a second or click directly on the black arrow. Clicking on any tool in the flyout places the selected tool button at the head of the flyout.

The Status Bar

The Status Bar contains a wealth of information. By default, it is located at the bottom of the screen. Refer to Chapter 3 for information on how to customize the Status Bar for your desktop needs.

Mask and Mode Icons

The mask icons are displayed in the Status Bar. The three icons are the Mask Mode, Mask Present, and Symmetry Enabled icons. The two mask icons are more important than you might imagine. Suppose you try to apply an effect or use a brush stroke, and either nothing will happen, or what happens is not what you expected. More often than not, this is because you have a mask somewhere in the image that is hindering you, or you have the mask in something other than Normal mode. Make a habit of looking for the Mask icon when things don't work as planned.

The Property Bar

The Property Bar is a great productivity enhancement. Most of the common tool settings items now appear on Property Bars, relieving the screen from overcrowding by too many toolbars. Put simply, the Property Bar displays the most-often-used commands for whatever mode is selected by the user.

The Standard Toolbar

The Standard toolbar is enabled by default. The nine buttons of the Standard toolbar are common Windows functions. The remaining buttons of the Standard toolbar will be discussed in greater detail as we learn to use them:

Button	Function
New	Activates the Create A New Image dialog box for creating new image files.
Open	Activates the Open An Image dialog box to open existing files.
Save	Saves the currently selected image. This button is grayed out (unavailable) until the selected image has been modified.
Import	Used to import graphic files into PHOTO-PAINT that cannot be opened with the File I Open command.
Export	Used to make a copy of the currently selected image in another graphics format.
Print	Allows printing of the selected image.
Cut	Cuts (removes) the defined (masked) area and copies it to the Clipboard.
Copy	Copies a defined (masked) area to the Clipboard.
Paste as Object	Pastes (copies) the image in the Clipboard into the selected image as an object. Note: Unlike the Paste *command,* which gives you a choice of pasting as an object or as a new document, the Paste As Object *button* does not give you a choice.

Where to Find Help

Most users don't take advantage of the extensive help features built into products. I can't say for sure why they don't use them, but I can say that Corel has built a lot of help features into PHOTO-PAINT 9. These help features will answer many questions for you without the need to reference either this book or the manual that shipped with the product. Here is a brief summary of what and where they are.

Corel Tutor

It's hard to miss this one—it's one of six possible choices on the opening screen. Selecting Corel Tutor opens the Corel Tutor main menu. This is a step-by-step tutorial that teaches you how to use PHOTO-PAINT 9 to accomplish many tasks in photo-editing.

TIP: *If you cannot find some of the buttons mentioned in this section, there is a good chance their current setting is too large to fit on your display. To change the size of the buttons, select Window | Toolbars and change the Button Size slider so that all the buttons in the Standard toolbar fit the display.*

Context Help

The button with the question mark and the arrow, shown next to the Corel Tutor button, is the Context Help button. Clicking this button changes the cursor to an arrow with a question mark. It remains in this mode until clicked on an item, which brings up the context-sensitive help screen that explains the purpose of the item clicked.

What's This?

Place the cursor on a feature anywhere on a tool or feature inside a dialog box, hold down the right mouse button for two seconds, and release it to produce a small rectangle with the message "What's This?" This provides a brief description of the function selected. The trick to making it work is to click the "What's This?" message box with the left mouse button *after* you right-click the feature.

TIP: *Don't forget to click on the message box that contains the message "What's This?" to access the information.*

The Help Manual

Throughout the book I have included tips to direct you toward the more useful help files. These files provide all the information that you would expect to find in the PHOTO-PAINT 9 reference manual. Speaking of which . . .

The manual that shipped with both the CorelDRAW 9 suite and the stand-alone version of PHOTO-PAINT 9 is an excellent reference. I am not just saying this because this is a CorelPRESS book. The crew that Corel assembled created a robust manual that is a vast improvement over the 48-page insert that was included with the original CorelDRAW 5 release.

Help on the Web

There are several Internet sites that provide answers to questions, including the Corel web site (www.corel.com). Another useful site is I/US home page (www.i-us.com), which also has a wealth of resources available. As Corel PHOTO-PAINT continues to increase in popularity, expect to see an even greater number of resources appearing.

Before finishing this chapter, we need to discuss some hardware requirements that are recommended for those about to venture into the land of PHOTO-PAINT 9.

Setting Up Your System—Do You Have What It Takes?

This is more than just a cute title. Corel PHOTO-PAINT 9 requires some substantial systems resources to work properly. To make sure that you have sufficient system resources, it is necessary to spend a little time understanding what's "under the hood" with the system you already have. (Good news for you techno-wizards: If you already know everything about hardware, go directly to the next chapter.)

Hardware Considerations

The minimum requirement to run PHOTO-PAINT 9 is that you must have Windows 95/98 already installed and running. While the minimum hardware necessary to run

Windows 95 is not insignificant, it is not sufficient for photo-editing. Let's consider some realistic system requirements for using PHOTO-PAINT 9.

RAM

According to Microsoft, it is possible to run Windows 95 on 4MB of RAM (lots of luck). The minimum amount of RAM that you should be using is 8MB, but even that's tight. According to all the computer magazines, Windows 95 runs well with 16MB of RAM. They call it the "sweet spot." It is even said that increasing the amount of RAM above 16MB doesn't provide any significant boost in performance. While this is true for many Windows 95 applications, it is not true for programs that manipulate large bitmap images—like PHOTO-PAINT 9. If you can afford it, I recommend you running with a minimum of 32MB RAM installed. I am running with 348MB RAM while working on this book. The reason for this large amount of RAM is because the price of RAM is low right now, and it was too good a deal to pass up. The performance increase you will realize with additional RAM installed greatly outweighs the dollar/benefit increase you will see with almost any other hardware purchase.

CPU

I recommend a Pentium (P5) system. While working on this book, I am using an Intel Pentium II (300 MHz) processor and it is really fast. How fast, you ask? I can actually finish a photo-editing project before I start. Now that's fast!

The Hard Disk

Your hard disk drive should have at least a 500MB capacity. If that figure gave you a start, take a look at your local computer superstore. In late 1998, 4Gb drives were selling for $189 or less. So how big a drive do you need? After CorelDRAW9 is loaded, you should have at least 50 to 100MB of free disk space remaining. Bitmap images take up a lot of space. So does Windows 95, for that matter. If you are going to be working on a lot of images and not constantly archiving them on tape or floppies, get yourself a drive large enough to handle the load. I am currently using a Seagate 18Gb, and I have already filled up most of it. Scary, isn't it?

That's all for this chapter and the first part. Next we will learn about digital images, resolution, and color. If you think that pixels are mythical winged creatures that fly in the forest, you really need to read Chapter 2.

CHAPTER 2

Learning About Digital Images

As the field of digital imagery expands, many people with little or no background on the subject are getting deeply involved with computer graphics. While there are many books about graphics, most of them assume that the reader knows the terminology and the technical material that serve as the foundation of computer graphics. The end result is a frustrated user. This chapter will try to help you fill in some of the gaps you might have in your graphics background.

Basic Terms in Digital Imaging

Before we dive into computer terms and acronyms, there is something you must first understand: There are many terms in the computer industry that are nonstandard, colloquial, or just plain dumb. This has led to one of my theorems regarding computer terminology: *The only thing that is universally accepted in the computer industry is that nothing is universally accepted in the computer industry.*

I don't expect the Pulitzer prize for that one, but it helps explain why there are so many different terms to describe the same thing in the computer industry. I am also a strong believer in using the terminology in common use rather than the technically correct term. When it comes to communicating ideas, the popular or commonly used term is more important. In this book, I will always try to use the commonly used term (even if it isn't accurate) as well as the technically correct term. Here are a few terms you need to know something about.

Bitmap and Vector Images

Computers can only understand 1's and 0's. When it comes to displaying art on computers, it is necessary to convert the images into something the computer can understand—1's and 0's. There are two ways to display images: *bitmap* (sometimes called "paint" or "raster") and *vector* (also called "freehand").

The photograph of a hamburger shown in Figure 2-1 is a typical example of a bitmap image. The image file is composed of millions of individual parts called *pixels* (picture elements). The color or shade of each part is determined by a numerical value assigned to each pixel. This photograph is small, yet it contains 289,224 pixels. Since each of these pixels requires some number of bits to define its shade or color (some require up to 32 bits), you can see why bitmap files tend to be large. The original image is color and it weighs in at 1.3 megabytes (MB). These bitmap images are displayed by using the pixels in the bitmap image to control the intensity of individual pixels on the monitor.

FIGURE 2-1 A bitmap image is composed of millions of tasty pixels

NOTE: *Adobe refers to black-and-white images as "bitmaps." For the rest of us on the planet, a bitmap is any image composed of pixels.*

The other way to display images involves creating a series of instructions for the output device (a computer display, a printer, and so on) to follow. The hamburger shown in Figure 2-2 from a CorelDRAW clip-art collection is a relatively simple *vector* image. The image contains no pixels. The file it was created from contains hundreds of lines of instructions that define where each line

FIGURE 2-2 A vector image is made of less tasty vectors and curves

segment and curve is to be placed in the image, as well as the type, size, and color of fill for each object. If the instructions were in English, and they're not, they might look like the following:

```
001 Go to row 00, column 00
002 Draw a line (direction 090) to row 00, column 80
003 Draw a circle at row 23, column 22, radius 34
004 Fill circle with a radial fill
```

This means each time the image is opened, the software application (such as CorelDRAW) must read the instructions and create the image on either the display or the printer. The advantage of this approach is that the image can be changed to almost any size. After it is resized, the application re-creates it based on the modified instructions. When a bitmap image is resized, the image is distorted.

Vector images tend to be complex—meaning they may be composed of thousands of individual objects—and yet they have a much smaller file size than their bitmap equivalent. The file containing the hamburger vector image is only 17K (kilobytes). Figure 2-3 shows a comparison of the resulting file sizes of the two hamburgers shown in Figures 2-1 and 2-2.

What have we learned so far? Vector images can easily be resized, and their resulting file size is smaller. If we limited our comparison to the two hamburgers previously shown, it would appear that vector images are limited in their ability to look realistic. Actually, if you are willing to put in the time and effort, vector images can look like photographs—as the entry from the 1996 Corel Design Contest by James L. Higgins III shows in Figure 2-4.

FIGURE 2-3 Which burger is the light burger? The one made with vectors

FIGURE 2-4 Is it real or a drawing? Complex vector drawings approach vivid realism

The complexity of the vector-based image necessary to create the illusion is shown next in a zoomed-in view of a portion of the image as it appears (wireframe view) in CorelDRAW. Corel PHOTO-PAINT only works with bitmap images, so when a vector-based image file (like the "light" hamburger) is loaded into PHOTO-PAINT, it must first be converted, or *rasterized,* to a bitmap as it is loaded.

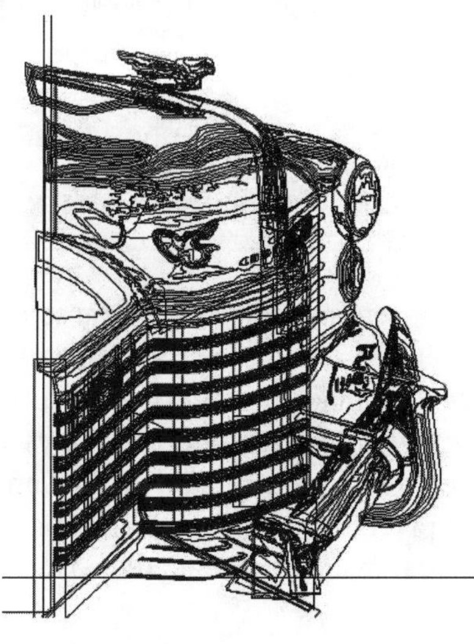

To work effectively with bitmap images in PHOTO-PAINT, it is necessary to understand how these bitmap wonders work. Let us begin by defining our terms.

Pixels

Pixels are not little elf-like creatures that fly through the forest at twilight. As we said before, bitmap images are composed of pixels. A *pixel* is the smallest variable element on a computer display or in a computer image. The term "pixel" is short for "picture element" and is used to describe several different items in graphics. At this point in the chapter, we are concerned with pixels as a way to describe the number of discrete horizontal and vertical elements in an image. The term pixel has replaced an earlier contraction of picture element, called the *pel*. As shown next, a pixel is one of several units of measure in PHOTO-PAINT.

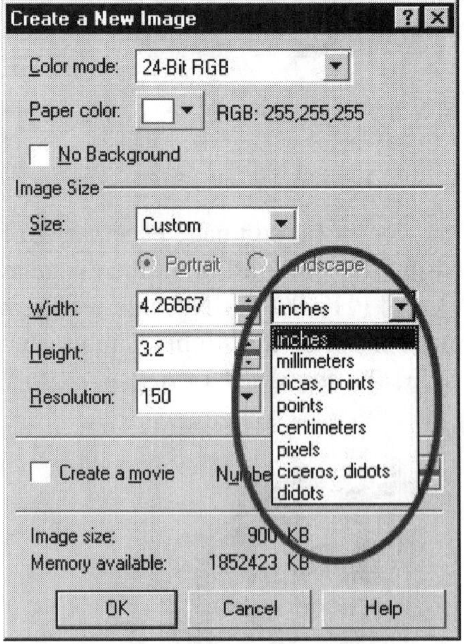

Unlike the other choices—centimeters, inches, and so on—a pixel is not a fixed size. A combination of resolution and the physical size of the image determine the size of the individual pixels that make up an image on a computer screen or on hard copy. For example, your computer monitor displays 96 pixels per inch if it is a Windows-based computer, making each pixel 1/96 of an inch square.

One way to understand pixels is to think of a mural created with mosaic tiles. When you get close to a mural made of mosaic tiles, it looks like someone had a bad Lego day. This is because you are so close that you are looking at individual tiles. But step away a few feet from the mosaic, and the individual tiles begin to lose their definition and to visually merge. The tiles have not changed their size or number, yet the farther back you move, the better the image looks. Pixels in bitmaps work much the same way.

I have created a sample image, shown in Figure 2-5, to illustrate how pixels make up an image. The part of the hamburger surrounded by the white circle on the left has been zoomed in to 1,000 percent and displayed on the right. It shows that as you zoom in on an image, the individual pixels begin to stand out more; the image they produce becomes less and less evident. Returning to our mosaic tile analogy, there are, of course, major differences between pixels and mosaic tiles. Pixels come in a greater selection of decorator colors (more than 16.7 million), and pixels don't weigh as much as tiles. However, mosaic tiles and pixels operate in the same way to produce an image.

Color Depth

What is *color depth?* It is the number of bits necessary to describe an individual pixel color. If a color image has a depth of 4 bits, that means there are 16 possible combinations of bits ($4^2 = 16$) to describe the color in each pixel. In other words, there are 16 possible colors available, or the image has a 16-color palette.

There are several different color depths available with PHOTO-PAINT. They are 1-bit (2 colors), 4-bit (16 colors), 8-bit (256 colors), 16-bit (65K grayscale), 24-bit (16.7 million colors), and 48-bit (281 billion colors!). There is also 32-bit

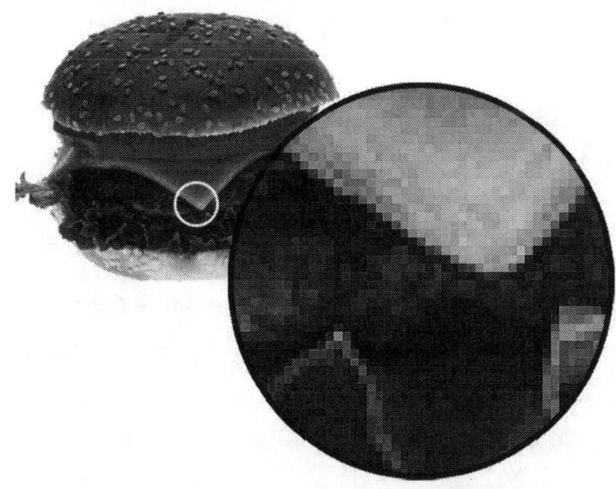

FIGURE 2-5 The pixels that make up the image become apparent at high zoom levels

color, but it is used for prepress and essentially only represents 16.7 million colors using a different type of color model.

The greater an image's color depth, the more shades of color it contains, as shown in Table 2-1. In turn, as the color depth of an image changes, the file size changes. An image whose color depth is 8-bit (which is also called *paletted)* and has a size of 400K becomes almost 1600K when converted to 32-bit CMYK. Color depth is explored in depth (pardon the pun) near the end of this chapter.

NOTE: *PHOTO-PAINT does not support conversion of an image to 16-bit color depth, although it will allow 16-bit color images to be opened and saved as a 24-bit color image.*

All image file formats have some restrictions regarding the color depth that they can accommodate, so it becomes necessary to know what color depth you are working with in order to recognize what kinds of colors and other tools you can use with it. Don't worry about memorizing this information; PHOTO-PAINT already knows these limitations and will only let you use file formats that can accommodate the attributes of the image you want to save.

If color depth is new to you, you may be wondering, "Why do we have all these different color depths? Why not make all the images 24-bit and be done with it?" There are many reasons for the different image types. One of the major factors of color depth is the physical size of the file that each type produces. The greater the number of bits associated with each pixel (color depth), the larger the file size. If an image has a size of 20K as a black-and-white (1-bit) image, it will become more than 480K as a true-color (24-bit) image. If an 8 × 10-inch color photograph

Color Depth	Type of Image	Color(s) Available
1-bit	Black-and-white	2 colors
8-bit	Grayscale	256 shades of gray
4-bit	Color	16 colors
8-bit	Color	256 colors
16-bit	Color	65,000 colors
16-bit	Grayscale	65,000 shades of gray
24-bit	Color—also called RGB color	16.7 million colors
32-bit	Color—also called CMYK	16.7 million colors
48-bit	Color	281 billion colors

TABLE 2-1 Color Depth for the Different Image Types

is scanned in at 600 dpi (don't ever do it!) at a 24-bit color depth, the resulting 64MB+ file will probably not even fit in your system. Not to mention that every operation performed with this image will be measured in minutes instead of seconds. There are other factors associated with the different color depths as well.

While not all monitors are set to display 24-bit color, the ones that can are capable of displaying the full-color detail of 24-bit RGB images, which can contain almost 17 million different colors (16,777,216 to be exact). The result can be vibrant, continuous-tone, photographic-quality display. Nevertheless, 24-bit images pose certain size problems for the World Wide Web—no one wants to spend 10 minutes downloading those really cool images you create. Let's take a closer look at the various types of color depth used in the industry today.

NOTE: *If you're not sure how many colors your monitor displays, try this: right-click on your Desktop and select Properties. A dialog box similar to the one shown next opens, displaying your current monitor settings. This Display Properties dialog box is found in Windows 98, so yours may look slightly different.*

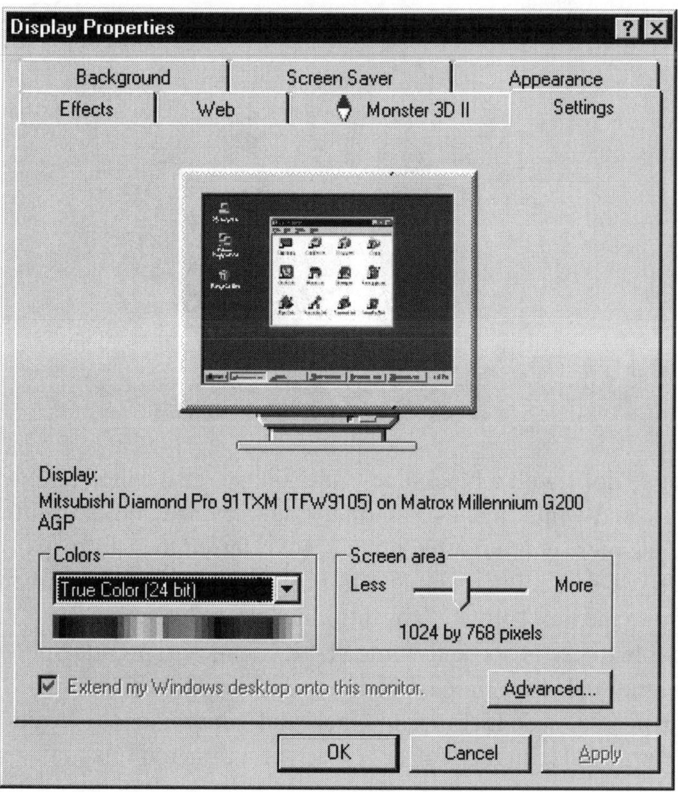

Black-and-White Images

The term "black and white" has caused some confusion in the past because old movies and television shows are referred to as being in black and white. They are actually grayscale, not black and white. Don't try to educate anyone on this subject. Just remember that the old TV shows like "The Andy Griffith Show" and "The Dick Van Dyke Show" are really in grayscale, not black and white.

In real black-and-white images, one bit of information is used per pixel to define its color. Because it has only one bit, it can only show one of two states, either black or white. The pixel is turned either on or off. It doesn't get any simpler than this.

Black-and-white images are more common than you would imagine. The following illustration shows a royalty-free, black-and-white image of a Windows user who has discovered a different way to adjust her display settings. This image was downloaded from http://www.arttoday.com, which contains a wealth of clip art for a small yearly subscription fee. It is common to associate black-and-white images with old Victorian woodcuts, but as you can see next, black-and-white is still in use today. Probably one of the most common forms of black and white now are logos on business cards. They are usually very small, and the business card that you have been asked to scan is wrinkled, stained, and . . . never mind. Where were we?

A lot can be done with a black-and-white image, also called *line art.* Adobe refers to black-and-white images as bitmaps; no one else does. Also, this can be confusing since most photographic images are referred to as bitmaps. To best understand how Corel converts images to black and white, I recommend taking a little side trip to the box entitled "An Introduction to Screening."

It is possible to use black-and-white (1-bit) images to produce photographs that appear to be grayscale by a process called *dithering.* Dithering can be thought of as pseudo-grayscale when it comes to black-and-white images. While dithering can simulate grayscale, quality suffers greatly if a dithered image is resized later.

An Introduction to Screening

Printing is simple. A given spot on a printed page either has ink (or toner) or it doesn't. Printing does not understand shades of gray. Therefore, photographs and other material containing shades of gray must be converted to spots of pure black on a field of white.

The traditional method of doing this is called *screening*. Screening essentially simulates shades of gray by converting light grays (they are like regular grays, but have only half the calories) to tiny black dots on a white background (paper color). Conversely, dark grays are represented by large black dots. Because of the way our eyes work, these dots or, in the case of more sophisticated screening techniques, configurations of dots appear as various shades of gray to the viewer.

A continuous-tone image, like a photograph, after being screened is known as a *halftone*. If you look at a halftone in a newspaper or magazine under a magnifying glass, it consists of a regular grid of dots. The grid is made fine enough so those individual dots are inconspicuous to the viewer. The exception to this definition is the late Roy Lichtenstein, who made a fortune creating large comic-strip panels with the dots very visible.

If an area in the photograph is 90 percent black, the halftone would be a white area occupying 10 percent of the area and black dots filling the remaining 90 percent. If another area is 30 percent gray, there would only be 30 percent of the image filled with black dots while the rest is white. Magnified, this area would look like a checkerboard, but to the viewer it appears as a gray area.

The quality of the halftone image depends both on the fineness of the grid of dots and on the number of possible dot shapes for each dot. Yes, Virginia, the dots come in different shapes.

The printing industry measures the grid of dots using the term *screen ruling*. Screen ruling is equivalent to dots per inch (dpi), but it is measured in lines per inch (lpi). Screened photographs in your local paper are typically 85 lpi, while the halftones you see in magazines are typically 150 lpi. It's not that the newspapers don't like quality pictures; the screen ruling is determined by the paper type and the printing presses used.

Now that you know something about screening, you can understand how PHOTO-PAINT converts images to black and white a little better.

In addition to line art, there used to be three different types of dithering available for black-and-white images: Ordered, Error Diffusion, and Halftone. Not anymore. PHOTO-PAINT 9 has seven ways to convert an image into a 1-bit black-and-white image.

Question: With color printers becoming so common, why would I want to convert an image to black and white? Because many times your work is reproduced on photocopy machines, and converting photographs to black and white using error diffusion offers the best results.

The way to get to image conversion options, shown in Figure 2-6, has also changed in PHOTO-PAINT 9. Notice the pop-up help that appears (if enabled) to tell you exactly what the conversion is doing. Selecting Black And White (1-bit) opens the Convert To 1 Bit dialog box. When you click the Conversion down arrow, a list of seven options appears, as shown here:

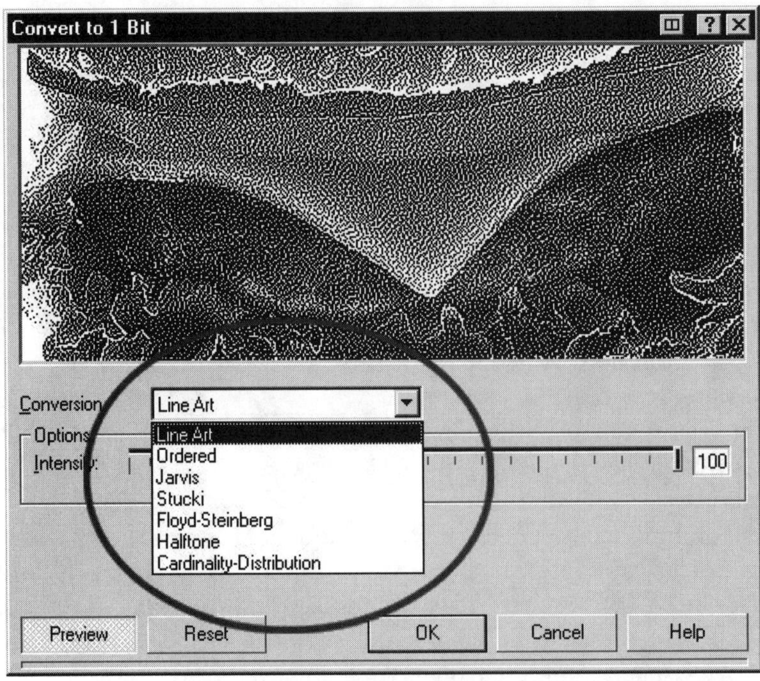

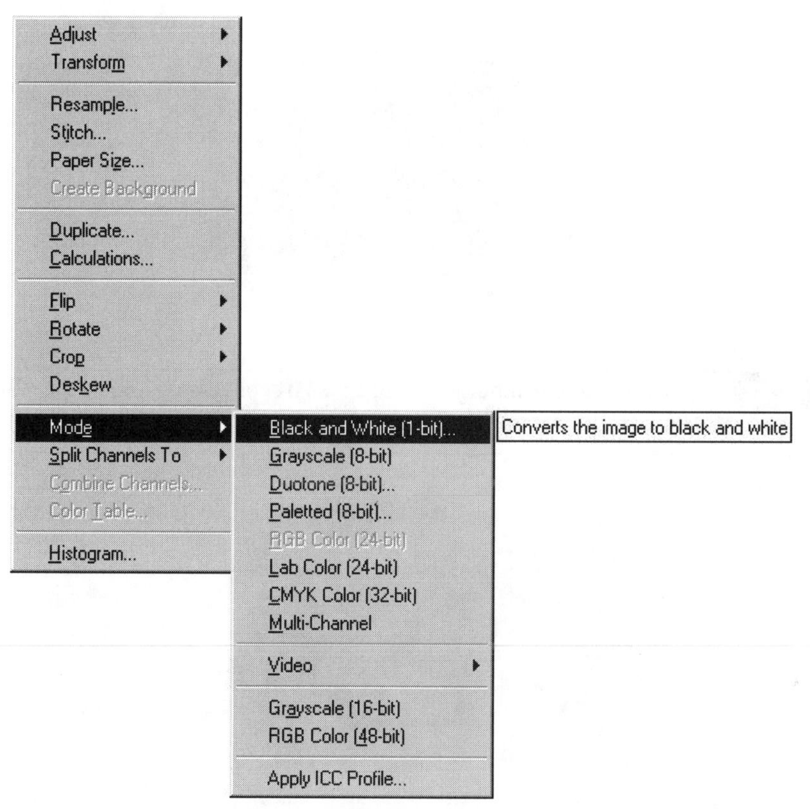

FIGURE 2-6 Selecting Mode opens a wide selection of choices for image conversion

A picture is still worth a thousand words (when adjusted for inflation). To illustrate the differences between them—and save 7,000 words—I have converted our hamburger, which is beginning to get cold, using each of the seven conversion techniques. The examples appear in Figures 2-7 through 2-12.

FIGURE 2-7 Converting the hamburger using Line Art conversion loses a lot of image detail, not to mention the bottom part of the bun

FIGURE 2-8 Using the Ordered type of error diffusion is an improvement over Line Art, but the bottom of the bun is still missing

FIGURE 2-9 The Jarvis error diffusion offers photographic quality and the bottom of the bun

FIGURE 2-10 Stucki conversion, like Jarvis, offers photorealism and the entire hamburger; it is still a 1-bit image

FIGURE 2-11 Floyd-Steinberg conversion—the name sounds like a law firm—gives arguably the best error diffusion

FIGURE 2-12 Halftone, a classic conversion, is shown with one of its six Screen Types (Fixed 4 × 4)

NOTE: *For more information about halftones than you might ever want, look in the Help files (Index) under Halftones.*

Grayscale Images

What we call black-and-white photos are, in fact, grayscale images. Photographs (color and grayscale) are *continuous-tone* images, so called because the photo is composed of continuous areas of different colors or shades. This is unlike a digital image, which is composed of square pixels. To represent a black-and-white photograph in a digital format requires dividing the image into pixels using eight bits of information for each pixel, producing 256 possible shades of gray. The shade of each pixel ranges from a value of white (0) to black (255). Grayscale is used for many other things besides "black-and-white" photos. When you learn about masks (beginning in Chapter 7), you will find out that most of the masks used in photo editing are actually grayscale images.

4-Bit and 8-Bit Color

With the explosive growth of the use of web pages on the Internet, 256-color (8-bit) images have become very popular. If you are using PHOTO-PAINT to create images for the Web, you will be using the 8-bit color depth a lot. (Four-bit color is rarely used.) Referred to as *paletted* or *256-color,* an 8-bit color image can only have one out of 256 combinations of color assigned to each pixel. This isn't as limited as you might imagine.

WHY 256 COLORS IS REALLY 216 ON THE WEB For images that will appear on web pages, you will usually want to choose from a palette that is limited to the 256 colors that most computer users can display. Users with very high-quality display monitors and adapters that provide a 24-bit variation for each pixel can view more than 16 million different colors. However, most web surfers have displays that can only handle 8-bit colors. If your images use a range of colors or a palette that is larger than the viewer's display or browser can handle, the browser will dither the colors. In other words, the browser will find colors within its palette that it can substitute for any color that is outside its palette. The result can get downright ugly.

Now for the big surprise: Mac and Windows browsers do not have identical color palettes. In the standard 256-color palette, only 216 are common to both platforms, but 40 are different and require dithering by one of the browsers. The good news is that Corel PHOTO-PAINT provides two different 216-color palettes (one for Netscape and another for Internet Explorer), so your images will always look their best.

When an image is converted to 8-bit, PHOTO-PAINT creates a *reference palette* (also called a "table") to which all the colors used in the image are assigned—hence the term "paletted."

GETTING A LITTLE TECHNICAL Here is some technical stuff that is not necessary to know but that I thought you might find interesting. Both the Netscape Navigator and Microsoft Internet Explorer palettes (in PHOTO-PAINT) are based on a simplified version of the *color cube* (the color cube is another term for the color model used by browsers). The traditional 24-bit RGB color cube is based on mixing the colors red, green, and blue in varying values from 0 to 255. So, black would be represented by 0, 0, 0—no red, no green, and no blue—while white would be represented by 255, 255, 255—100 percent red, 100 percent green, and 100 percent blue. This method results in 16,777,216 colors, which are represented by 24 bits of data: three 8-bit bytes.

The color palettes for Netscape Navigator and Microsoft Internet Explorer are based on the same idea, but using a much smaller scale. Instead of 256 values, only six values are used. These correspond to the normal color cube values of 0, 51, 102, 153, 204, and 255. Instead of resulting in the enormous 16.7 million colors, this method results in a mere 216 colors, which conveniently (and intentionally) fits within the 256 colors of an 8-bit color system.

Many people think that 8-bit color is markedly inferior to 24-bit color. That used to be true, but the process of converting the image from 16- or 24-bit to 8-bit color has been so dramatically improved that in many cases it is difficult, if not impossible, to tell the original image from the paletted one.

16-Bit Color (Thousands of Colors)

Using 16 bits to define the color depth provides approximately 65,000 colors. This is enough for almost any color image. I have seen 16- and 24-bit images side by side, and it is almost impossible to tell them apart. All things being equal, most of the photo-editing public could work with 65K color from now until the Second Coming and never notice any difference. What are the advantages of 16-bit color? Faster performance on video cards with less video RAM, because you are moving one-third fewer bits. When will you use 16-bit color? Even though PHOTO-PAINT doesn't export images in 16K color, it can open them and save them in a different color depth. You may discover that your video card is set to display in 16-bit color. This is usually the case with video cards having a limited amount of video RAM when you increase the resolution setting of your monitor. When that happens, the display adapter will change the display color depth from 24-bit to 16-bit to conserve the limited amount of video RAM.

TIP: *If your display adapter is set to display 16-bit color, it does not affect the image color depth—only the display of the image.*

24-Bit (True Color)

True-color images may use up to 16.7 million colors. They are so closely associated with the RGB color model that they are sometimes referred to as RGB 24-bit. (We will talk about color models later in this chapter.) "RGB" stands for red-green-blue. Your monitor makes all its colors by using combinations of these three colors. Your eye perceives color the same way: red, green, and blue. The three colors that make up the RGB models each have eight bits assigned to them, allowing for 256 possible shades of each color. Your monitor creates colors by painting the images with three electronic beams (called *guns*). The mixing together of three sets of 256 combinations produces a possible 16.7 million color combinations. While True Color doesn't display every possible color, it gets pretty close. It is the model of choice for the desktop computer artist.

32-Bit Color

Back in Table 2-1, did you notice anything unusual about 32-bit color? Although the color depth is increased by 25 percent over a 24-bit image, the number of colors remained the same. Why is that?

There are two answers, because there are two types of color depth that involve 32 bits: a 32-bit image and an image using 32-bit color. The first is more commonly seen on the Mac side of the world. A 32-bit image uses a 24-bit RGB model with an additional 8-bit *alpha channel.* Apple reserved the alpha channel, but it has never specified a purpose for this data. The alpha channel has come to be used by most applications to pass grayscale mask information. The second use of 32-bit color is to represent the four colors that are used in printing—cyan, magenta, yellow, and black—or as they are more commonly known, *CMYK.* (*K* is used as the designator for the color black, since the letter *B* already designates the color blue.) This will be discussed further when you learn about color theory in the next chapter.

NOTE: *Most of the graphic processors are advertising that they offer 32-bit, 64-bit, and now 128-bit graphic processor boards. This has nothing to do with color depth. It is a reference to the width of the data path. The wider the data path, the greater the amount of color data that can be moved, and therefore the faster the screens are redrawn.*

48-Bit Color

The availability of 48-bit color can be blamed on the people who market scanners. Many of the scanners today scan color depths greater than 24 bits, then extract the best information out of the scan and send it to the computer in 24-bit format. In their headlong rush to make scanners bigger and better, someone came up with the idea of making all the unprocessed digital information available to the computer. The result is huge files of questionable worth, and you still must convert to 24- or 32-bit color to print the image. You can learn about scanning in Chapter 25.

Gamma

Gamma is an important component of an image. *Gamma* can be intimidating, but really you can think of it as a brightness control with attitude. How bright or dark an image appears on a computer display depends on several factors including the software gamma setting on the computer, the physical brightness setting of the monitor, and ambient light (the light in the room).

Before we all started displaying our pictures on the Internet, life was simpler. I never thought of displaying my photographs on a Mac, just as my Mac counterpart never thought his creations would ever grace a PC screen. The Internet has changed all that. Because of different gamma settings inherent in the hardware, images prepared on a Mac will look too dark on a PC, and images prepared on a PC will look too bright on a Mac. One option is to adjust the gamma so the resulting image is somewhere in the middle. This way, images will appear just a little too bright on the Mac, and a little too dark on the PC. The common gamma setting on the Macintosh is 1.8, so a good compromise would be to set it to 2.0 when images will be displayed on the Web. PHOTO-PAINT provides a Gamma filter that allows the gamma of individual images to be adjusted.

File Compression

As the file size of images increases, so does our need for a method of compressing the image information. The file compression we use in graphics is not related to any compression that you may already be using on your disk drive. There are several compression schemes that are either built into the file formats or are offered as an option when saving the file. Before we look at the individual file format, we need to know a few things about compression and its benefits and drawbacks. Compression is generally divided into two categories: *lossless* and *lossy*.

Lossy Compression

Lossy compression offers the greatest amount of compression, but at a price. As the name implies, some of the image quality is lost in the process. Lossy compression schemes can reduce very large files from several megabytes in size to only a few kilobytes. Most of the time the loss in quality is not apparent. The image shown in Figure 2-13 was reduced from a file size of over 400K to 48K. It is degraded; can you see the difference between it and Figure 2-14 in the next section of this chapter? The most popular example of lossy compression is the JPEG format. Another compression method that is becoming popular is Wavelet compression, which also supports 24-bit color. This file format stores bitmap information at very high compression levels.

Table 2-2 compares JPEG and Wavelet compression. The Best Quality value is the one chosen by Corel PHOTO-PAINT 9 when the Suppress Filter option is enabled. The Maximum Compression category is based on the maximum compression that produced a small amount of image degradation.

FIGURE 2-13 This image was degraded using JPEG compression. Can you see the difference between it and the one in Figure 2-14?

Original File Size	Wavelet Best Quality	Wavelet Maximum Compression	JPEG Best Quality	JPEG Maximum Compression
5.02MB	202K	78K	634K	104K

TABLE 2-2 Comparison of File Compression Results

Lossless Compression

Lossless compression has been around longer than lossy compression. It generally offers a significant amount of compression without any loss of image information (quality). Most of these compression schemes offer compression ratios between 2:1 and 4:1. The file size (before compression) of the photograph shown in Figure 2-14 is 400K; it is 240K compressed. There are several popular versions of lossless compression found in Corel PHOTO-PAINT. While users have their favorites, there is little noticeable difference between them.

FIGURE 2-14 Lossless compression results in no degradation in this photograph

Image File Formats

Now that we have discussed the type of images that exist in a digital world, we need to understand some of the ways these images can be saved. A general understanding of the different formats is helpful.

There are many different file formats for saving images, each with its strong and weak points. Some formats cannot store more than 256 colors, some cannot be compressed, and others produce enormous files. Corel PHOTO-PAINT gives you a large assortment of file formats to choose from when you save a file. If you are not familiar with the choices, this blessing of a wide assortment can become confusing. In this section, we will try to take some of the mystery out of these formats with strange-sounding names.

Understanding File Formats

For some, the question will be, "What is an *image file format*?" Simply put, it defines a way of storing an image and any related information in a way that other programs can recognize and use. Each format has its own unique form, called a *file structure,* for saving the image pixels and other related file information, such as resolution and color depth.

Each format is unique and is generally identified by its three-letter file extension. For example, in the filename BUGS.CPT, the three-letter extension "CPT" identifies the file format as a Corel PHOTO-PAINT file. Images that will be used on a PC Windows platform need to have the three-character extension so the application can select the appropriate Import filter. If the wrong extension or a unique extension is used, it may be difficult, perhaps impossible, to import the image. If you know the file will be opened on a PC, be sure to add the correct extension to the filename.

When saving a file, Corel PHOTO-PAINT is aware of the color depth of the image and changes the selection of available file-format choices automatically. For example, if you have a 32-bit color image, the drop-down list will be reduced from the normal selection to the few file format choices that support 32-bit color.

Because there are dozens of file formats, it would be confusing to try to cover them all. Instead, we will look at the major ones supported by Corel PHOTO-PAINT, and discuss a few of their strengths and limitations. To take a look at the format list, choose File | Save As and click the Type arrow.

CPT (Going Native)

This is a native format of Corel PHOTO-PAINT. The term "native" means it is unique to the application. Corel PHOTO-PAINT format is the best format for your originals, because it retains all the unique PHOTO-PAINT information about the image being saved. Saving in other image formats may result in the loss of this information. Another feature of the CPT format is that it automatically compresses the image when saved (lossless) and loads faster than any other format.

PHOTO-PAINT now has three CPT formats, each one representing new features added with different releases of PHOTO-PAINT. If you save an image using PHOTO-PAINT 9's native format, you will not be able to open it with previous versions. The three versions are the original, which works with releases up through and including PHOTO-PAINT 6; the PHOTO-PAINT 7/8 version, which I hope is self-explanatory; and PHOTO-PAINT 9. It is best to save your work in the native format of the version you are currently using. Then if you need to send the work to someone who does not have that version, you can use the Export command to convert it to the desired file format.

Windows Bitmap (BMP, DIB)

BMP (Windows Bitmap) is the native image format for Microsoft Paint, which is included with every copy of Microsoft Windows and supported by nearly every Windows program. Corel PHOTO-PAINT supports BMP images up to 24-bit color (16.7 million colors). This is a popular format that decorates everyone's computer screen these days, but it may not offer compression and is generally used only for small image files (less than a few hundred kilobytes).

Graphics Interchange Format (GIF)

CompuServe created GIF (Graphics Interchange Format) long ago as a means of compressing images for use over their extensive online network. GIF has become a very popular format, especially now that everyone is jumping on the Internet. As a way to send pictures over phone lines, it can't be beat. Its single limitation is that it only supports 8-bit (256-color) images. Corel PHOTO-PAINT does not offer an option to compress images saved as GIF files because it is already a compression format. The principal advantage of GIF is the support of transparent background.

Paintbrush (PCX)

PCX is one of the original file formats, created by Z-Soft for PC Paintbrush back when Noah was working on the ark. It is one of the most popular image file formats around, mainly because PC Paintbrush is the oldest painting program for the IBM PC. Corel PHOTO-PAINT supports PCX images up to 24-bit color. The only concern with using PCX images involves importing them into older applications. Because the PCX format has been around so long, there are many versions of PCX import filters around. It is possible, even likely, that you will find an older application that imports PCX files but cannot read the file exported by Corel PHOTO-PAINT.

EPS (Supports 32-Bit)

"EPS" stands for "Encapsulated PostScript." PostScript is a page-description language used by imagesetters and laser printers. This format is a favorite of your friendly neighborhood service bureau. Many people do not think about using the EPS format when working with PHOTO-PAINT's bitmap images because of its association with vector-based drawings like CorelDRAW. Actually, EPS does work with bitmap images...for a price. By that I mean a bitmap image saved in the EPS format will be roughly three times as large as the same file saved in the TIFF format. So, why use EPS? It was once the only way to place an image into CorelDRAW without the white background. This is no longer true; CorelDRAW can import CPT files with the object/layers intact. For more information, see Chapter 5. If you must send work to a service bureau, EPS may be the only format they will accept, especially for separations.

PICT

Apple developed PICT as the primary format for Macintosh graphics. Like PostScript, it is a page-description language. While it is a default format for the Mac platform, it is a troublesome format because it is a hybrid of bitmap and vector. In a sense, it is similar to the structure of a PostScript file, except the PostScript is an accepted industry standard. Even PostScript, which works, is not the easiest file format to tangle with. If you are going to save a PHOTO-PAINT image for use in a Macintosh application, use TIFF instead.

TARGA (TGA, TVA)

This format was originally created for TARGA display boards. If you haven't seen this image format before, it is probably because it is used by a small segment of the professional market that works with high-end color and video. In Corel PHOTO-PAINT, this file format supports up to 24-bit color. TARGA does not support 32-bit color (CMYK). TARGA does support 32-bit images—24-bit color with an 8-bit alpha channel that can be used to retrieve mask information by Corel PHOTO-PAINT. Many people believe that TARGA is technically superior to any other format on the marketplace. Others feel it is only good for multimedia because it is a niche format that is not widely used. It is becoming popular with the growing 3-D market because it can process all the information that a 3-D image requires.

TIFF (Tagged Image File Format), also known as TIF

TIFF is probably the most popular full-color bitmap format around, supported by every PC and Mac paint program I have seen. TIFF is clearly the image format of choice. It is used as a default setting for every scanning program on the market.

There are many different versions of TIFF, which can conceivably cause some compatibility problems when moving images between programs. To date, the only problems we have experienced with TIFF files involved saving images as 24-bit color TIFF files and trying to read them on an application that doesn't offer 24-bit color support.

Corel PHOTO-PAINT supports all color-depth settings in TIFF format, including 32-bit color (CMYK). However, don't save your images in 32-bit color unless it is specifically requested. Because all programs that can import TIFF files do not support 32-bit color (CMYK), you may end up with a TIFF file that some older applications cannot read. Remember that 32-bit (CMYK) TIFF contains the same color information as 24-bit color TIFF.

Scitex CT Bitmap (SCT, CT)

Unless your service bureau specifically requests this file format, don't use it. High-end commercial printers use Scitex computers to generate color separations of images and other documents. Corel PHOTO-PAINT can open images digitized with Scitex scanners and save the edited images to the Scitex CT (Continuous Tone) format. Because there are several restrictions regarding the transfer of images from the PC to a Scitex drive, you will probably want to consult with the person using the Scitex printer before saving to the CT format. It is possible that a TIFF or JPEG (compression) format is preferred. Scitex is only available when the image is in 32-bit color (CMYK) or grayscale.

Photoshop (PSD)

Yes, for all these references we make to Photoshop, it is good to know PHOTO-PAINT can both read and save in PSD format. You might be surprised to know that with the exception of CPT, the native format for PHOTO-PAINT, the PSD format allows preservation of more PHOTO-PAINT internal data (channels, masks, and so on) than any other file format. This is also a very handy format to use when giving your artwork to a Mac service bureau.

Now that you understand a few terms, let's learn about resolution.

'Resolution'—A Term with Too Many Definitions

Without an understanding of resolution and its effects, you may find yourself creating beautiful images that fill the entire display screen in PHOTO-PAINT, yet appear to be smaller than postage stamps when you print them. Resolution is a very misunderstood concept in desktop publishing. The confusion is compounded because this term may have entirely different meanings depending on the device you are talking about. In this chapter, we will learn what resolution is and what it does for us in PHOTO-PAINT. The information about resolution that is discussed in this chapter applies to all image-editing applications, not just PHOTO-PAINT.

Resolution and the Size of the Image

As I said, the term "resolution" represents one of the more elusive concepts of digital imaging. In a vector-based program, we describe an image's size in the popular unit of measure for the country we live in. In the United States, we refer to the standard letter-size page as being 8½ × 11 inches. Image size in photo-editing programs is traditionally measured in pixels. The reason for using pixels is that the size of an image in pixels is fixed. So when I speak of an image being 1200 by 600 pixels, I know, from experience, approximately how big the image is. If we use a unit of measure other than pixels—say, inches—the dimensions of the printed image are dependent on the resolution of the image.

So What Is Resolution?

Resolution takes the density of pixels per inch (ppi) that make up an image and describes it in dots per inch (dpi). In other words, it is a measure of how closely each pixel in an image is positioned to the one next to it.

Let's assume we have an image that is 300 pixels wide by 300 pixels high. So how big will the image be when I import it into another application? This is a trick question. There is not enough information. Without knowing the resolution of the image, it is impossible to determine the size when it is imported into another application. If the resolution of this image is set to 300 pixels per inch, then the image dimensions are 1 × 1 inch when imported. If the resolution is *doubled* (set to 600 dpi), the image would be *half* the size, or ½ × ½ inch. If the resolution is *reduced by half* (150 dpi), the image size *doubles* to 2 × 2 inches. We can see that resolution exhibits an inverse relationship. The physical size of an image in PHOTO-PAINT is most accurately expressed as the length (in pixels) of each side. Resolution tells you how many pixels are contained in each unit of measure.

To show the effect of changing resolution, I duplicated our hamburger with PHOTO-PAINT, making three copies. Next, I changed *(resampled)* the resolution of each of the copies so that I had three photographs at three different resolutions. Even though each of the images in Figure 2-15 is a different resolution, they appear the same size in PHOTO-PAINT because PHOTO-PAINT only cares about how many pixels are in the image. When all three files were imported into CorelDRAW, the results were as shown in Figure 2-16. Why do the photos appear to be the same size in Figure 2-15, you ask? Because the physical size of the images (in pixels) remained unchanged—only the resolution changed.

Screen Resolution

No matter what resolution you are using, Corel PHOTO-PAINT displays each pixel onscreen according to the zoom ratio. That is why all the photos in Figure 2-15 appeared to be the same size even though they were at different resolutions. At a zoom ratio of 100 percent, each image pixel is mapped to a single screen pixel. This is why the size of the image remains unchanged regardless of the image resolution. The display's zoom setting has no effect on the actual image file. If you are a little fuzzy on monitors and pixels, read on. If you know them cold, skip ahead to "Resolution and Printers."

FIGURE 2-15 Although each photograph is a different resolution (size), they appear the same size displayed in PHOTO-PAINT

FIGURE 2-16 When the same photos are displayed in CorelDRAW, the image resolution causes them to be displayed at the size they would appear if printed

When you bought your monitor and/or display card, you may have been bewildered by such terms as "640 × 480," "800 × 600," and so on. These figures refer to the number of screen pixels that the monitor can display horizontally and vertically. For example, let's say you have a plain-vanilla VGA monitor. The standard resolution for this monitor is 640 pixels wide by 480 pixels high (640 × 480). If you open a file that is 900 pixels wide, the image at 100% zoom is too large to fit into the screen, as shown in Figure 2-17. With the screen resolution changed to 800 × 600 (Super VGA) the same display area now contains a width of 800 pixels by a height of 600 pixels. Since the size of the display didn't change, the pixels must be getting smaller. The image, shown in Figure 2-18, appears smaller than the photograph in the previous figure, but it is still too large to fit into the screen area. The size of the photograph hasn't changed, but the screen (or display) resolution has. To make more pixels fit into the same physical screen dimensions, the actual pixels must be smaller. With the resolution changed to 1,024 × 768 (Figure 2-19), all of the original photo can be seen on the screen. Again, the photograph remains unchanged; only the screen resolution has increased. Screen or display resolution operates under the same principle we discussed in the previous paragraph. As the screen resolution increases, the image size decreases proportionally.

NOTE: *Because the original photograph used in Figures 2-17 through 2-19 was so large, Figures 2-17 and 2-18 had to be scaled down to fit them onto the page.*

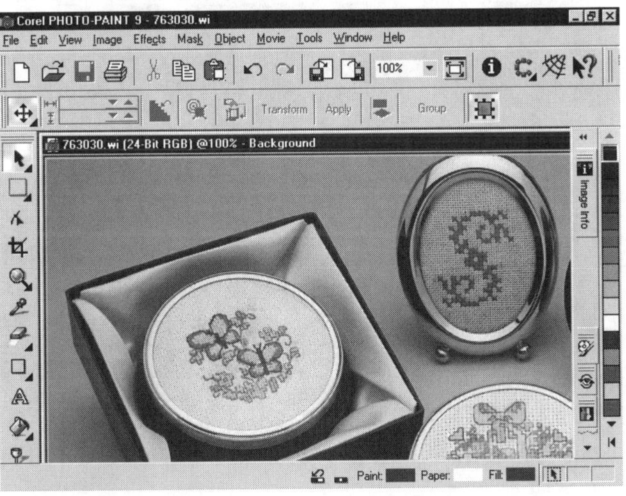

FIGURE 2-17 Displaying a photograph that is 1,400 pixels wide using a VGA (640 × 480) screen resolution

FIGURE 2-18 Increasing the resolution to Super VGA (800 × 600) makes the pixels smaller, and more of the photograph can be seen

FIGURE 2-19 Only by increasing the resolution to 1,024 × 768 can all of the image be seen

Many people have been surprised to discover that after spending a lot of money to get a high-resolution monitor and display card, their screen images appeared smaller rather than sharper. Now that you know the secret of the screen resolution game, have your friends buy you lunch and you can explain it to them, too.

Screen Setting Recommendations

With all the exciting ads for high-resolution displays and graphics adapters, it is difficult not to get caught up in the fever to upgrade. If you have a 14- or 15-inch monitor, you should be using the VGA or Super VGA screen resolution setting on your graphics card. If you go for a higher resolution on a 14- or 15-inch display, even if your monitor supports it, your friends may start calling you Blinky, because you will be squinting all the time to read the screen. Also, be cautious about recommendations from the retail clerk/computer expert at your computer superstore. Remember that last week your "expert" might have been bagging groceries and may know less about computers than you do.

With the price of 17-inch displays dropping, more people are investing in a few extra inches on their display. Just because you have a 17- or a 21-inch monitor does not mean you have a moral obligation to run it at the highest resolution that your display adapter will support. Using the wrong resolution for your monitor can sometimes damage the monitor or cause something worse, as shown next. I use a setting of 1,024 × 780 most of the time with my 21-inch monitor and it works very well. Some display adapters only support 24-bit color up to 800 × 600 without adding extra memory to the video card.

Resolution and Printers

If this were a perfect world, image resolution would be the same as printer resolution (which is also measured in dpi). Then if we were printing to a 600-dpi printer in our perfect world, we would be using a 600-dpi-resolution image, because each image pixel would occupy one printer dot. However, it is not a perfect world. First of all, pixels are square and printer dots are round. When we talk about printer resolution, we are talking about the size of the smallest dot the printer can make. If you are using a 600-dpi laser printer, the size of the dot it produces is $1/600^{th}$ of an inch in diameter. The dot it creates is either on or off—there is either a black dot on the paper or there isn't. If we are displaying a grayscale photograph, we know that each pixel can be 1 of 256 possible shades. So how does the laser printer create shades of gray from black-and-white dots? Using halftone cells. What? Read on.

Creating Halftones

If I take an area on the paper and create a box that has a width of 10 dots and a height of 10 dots, it would have a capacity to fit 100 dots in it. If I were to place printer dots at every other possible point, it would only hold 50 printer dots. The result when printed on paper would appear to the eye as gray or 50 percent black. This is the principle behind the *halftone cell.* The halftone cell created by the laser printer is equivalent to the pixel—not exactly, but close enough for the purposes of discussion. The number of halftone cells a laser printer can produce is a function of its *line frequency,* which some of us old-timers still refer to as "screen frequency." Companies that produce advertisements to sell their printers to the consumer marketplace never discuss line frequency, expressed as lpi (lines per inch). And why not? Because, in this hyper-advertised computer marketplace, bigger is better (except for price). And which sounds better—a 600-dpi printer or a 153-lpi printer? The 153-lpi printer would have a resolution of around 1,200 dpi. Names and numbers are everything in selling a product. This resolution-specification hype also confuses the scanner market as well.

So what resolution should you use? I have included the values in Table 2-3 for use as general guidelines when setting up the resolution of an image in PHOTO-PAINT.

In the next chapter we will take a look at color to understand some basics of how it works and, more importantly, how to get what comes back from the printer to look like what we see on the display.

Image Type	Final Output	Recommended Resolution
Black-and-white	Laser printer (600 dpi)	600 dpi
Black-and-white	Display screen	Convert black-and-white image to grayscale and use 72–96 dpi
Grayscale	Laser printer	150–200 dpi
Grayscale	Imagesetter	200–300 dpi
Grayscale	Display screen	72–96 dpi
Color	Color ink-jet printer	100–150 dpi
Color	Imagesetter	150–200 dpi
Color	Display screen	72–96 dpi

TABLE 2-3 Recommended Resolution Settings

Basic Color Theory

Color is everywhere. Even black and white are colors. Really. Color has the greatest and most immediate effect on the viewer of any factor in graphic design. Psychologists confirm that color has an enormous capacity for getting our attention. To use color effectively, we must have a basic understanding of it.

If you were looking for a detailed discussion on the complex mathematics of color models, you won't find it here. What you will find here is a nontechnical discussion of the basic concepts and terminology of color.

Knowing how color works in the natural world and how this "real-world" color operates in a computer will help you when dealing with the complexities of the color models. It will be simple, and I think you will find it interesting.

Why Is an Apple Red?

Without light there is no color. Pretty deep stuff. Light is radiant energy that moves in waves. Each color of light has a different *wavelength* (frequency). Here is the tricky part. As light radiates from its source and strikes an object, there are three things that can happen to the light waves. First, they can bounce off the object; that is, they are *reflected.* They can also be *absorbed* by the object. If you doubt that objects absorb light energy, place a piece of metal painted a dull black in a Dallas parking lot for a few hours on a sunny August day and try to pick it up. Hot stuff! Lastly, the light waves can go right through the object—technically speaking, they are *transmitted.* An example would be a sheet of glass. The light strikes the glass and goes through it.

Depending on the composition of the object, all the light striking it may be reflected, absorbed, or transmitted. Realistically, it will be some combination of the three. Pure, or white, light contains all the colors of the visible spectrum. When white light strikes a banana, the blue component of the light is absorbed and the red and green components are reflected. The banana appears yellow because red and green reflected light combine to create yellow. An apple absorbs the green and blue light, and we see the red component reflected—making the apple appear red as shown in the preceding illustration. If an object absorbs all the red, green, and blue components, it appears black. Conversely, if all the colors are reflected, an object appears white. Reflection, absorption, and transmission are the guiding principles behind the two basic color models that we are going to look at next.

Color Models

Color is made up of light components that, when combined in varying percentages, create separate and distinct colors. You also learned this in elementary school when the teacher had you take the blue poster paint and mix it with the yellow paint to make green. Mixing pigments on a palette is simple. Mixing colors on a computer is not. The rules that govern the mixing of computer colors change, depending on the color model being used.

There are many color models available in PHOTO-PAINT. They provide different ways to view and manipulate an image. To view different color models, you need to load the Color dialog box, which is done by double-clicking on a Paint swatch in the Status Bar and then selecting the Models tab. These color models fall into one of two basic categories: *additive color* and *subtractive color.* Additive color (also known as RGB) is the system used by color monitors, scanners, photography, and the human eye. Subtractive color (also known as CMYK) is used in four-color publishing and printing. Let's take a closer look at both.

Additive Color (RGB)

This model is said to use the additive process because colors are produced by adding one or more colors. RGB (red-green-blue) involves transmitted light as the source of color. In the additive model, color is created by adding different amounts of red, green, and blue light.

Pure white light is composed of equal amounts of red, green, and blue. For the record, red, green, and blue are referred to as the *additive primary colors,* so called because when they are added (combined) in varying amounts, they can produce all the other colors in the visible spectrum.

Subtractive Color (CMYK)

The subtractive model is so named because colors are subtracted from white light to produce other colors. This model uses the secondary colors: cyan, magenta, and yellow. We have already learned this is called the CMYK model, because equal amounts of cyan, magenta, and yellow only produce black, in theory. When printed, they produce something closer to swamp mud than black; so, to create a vivid picture, black is added to compensate for the inability of the colors CMY to make a good black. As noted earlier, K is used as the designator for the color black, since the letter *B* already designates the color blue.

CMYK is a printer's model, based on inks and dyes. It is the basis for almost all conventional color photography and commercial color printing. Cyan, magenta, and yellow dyes and inks simply transmit light better and are more chemically stable than red, green, and blue inks.

Describing Colors

If someone were to ask me to describe the color of my son's Mustang, it would be easy. It is black. The color of my wife's car is more difficult. Is it dark metallic green or deep forest green? The terms generally used to describe color are subjective. Even for simple classifications involving primary colors like red and blue, it becomes difficult to describe the exact color. Is it deep-sea blue or navy blue? In the world of color, we need a way to accurately describe the *value* of color.

When creating or picking out a color in PHOTO-PAINT, you can specify the color either by defining values for its component parts or by using a color-matching system. When using the RGB model in PHOTO-PAINT (it is the default color model), color values are expressed in shades of RGB. The maximum number of shades a color can contain is 256. For example, the value of red in an RGB model is defined as 255, 0, 0. In other words, the color contains the maximum amount (255) of the red component and a value of zero for the green and blue components. *Let me interject here that in PHOTO-PAINT, you still pick colors from color palettes that contain recognizable colors like red, green, and blue. You won't have to sit with a calculator and figure out the value of puce.*

In CMYK, the component values are traditionally expressed as a percentage, so the maximum value of any color is 100. It should be noted, however, that PHOTO-PAINT allows you to express CMYK values in both percentages and shades (0–255). The color red in the CMYK model is 0, 100, 100, 0. In other words, mixing the maximum values of magenta and yellow with no cyan and no black creates the color red.

Color Matching

While defining colors as either number of shades in the RGB model or percentage of tint in CMYK is accurate, it is not practical. Given that we cannot assign names to the millions of shades of color that are possible, we need a workable solution. The use of color-matching systems like the Pantone Spot colors provides a solution. The designer and the printer have identical books of print samples. The designer wants to use red in a two-color publication and specifies PANTONE Red 032 CV. The printer looks up the formula in the Pantone book for the percentages of magenta and yellow to mix together and prints the first sample. The output is then compared with the book of print samples, called a *swatch book.* Most corporate accounts will use one of the popular color-matching systems to specify the colors they want in their logos and ads. Color matching in the digital age is less than 10 years old. It has come a long way in its short life and is now finding its way into the design of Internet web sites. No longer restricted to four- and six-color printing, the color-matching systems are dealing with the important issues of colors looking correct on the Internet, too. Color correction on the Web is critical for companies selling products. For example, if the color of the sweater you saw on the Web isn't even close to what arrives in the box, the product will probably be returned. To accurately display colors in images has become invaluable.

RGB Versus CMYK

Each color model represents a different viewpoint. Each offers advantages and disadvantages. If you are using Corel PHOTO-PAINT to create multimedia and web pages, or just printing to ink-jet or color laser printers, knowing how to get what you need out of RGB will more than satisfy your requirements. If you must accurately translate color from the screen to the printed page, you must get more deeply involved in CMYK.

Hue, Saturation, and Brightness

The terms hue, saturation, and brightness (also called "luminosity") are used throughout PHOTO-PAINT. *Hue* describes the individual colors—for example, a blue object can be said to have a blue hue. *Saturation* is technically the purity of the color. In practical terms, it is the balance between neutral gray and the color. If an image has no saturation, it looks like a grayscale image. If the saturation is 100 percent, it may look unnatural, since the image's midtones, which the gray component emphasizes, are lost. *Brightness* is the amount of light reflecting from an object determining how dark or light the image appears.

Color Gamut

It may come as a surprise to you, but there are a lot more colors in the real world than photographic films or printing presses can re-create. The technical term for this range of colors is *gamut*. There are many gamuts—for monitors, scanners, photographic film, and printing processes. Each gamut represents the range of colors that can actually be displayed, captured, or reproduced by the appropriate device or process. The widest gamut is the human eye, which can see billions of colors. Further down on this visual hierarchy is the color computer monitor, which can display 16 million colors. Photographic film can only capture 10,000 to 15,000 colors, and a high-quality four-color printing process can reproduce from 5,000 to 6,000. We won't even discuss the limitations of color ink on newsprint.

Congratulations

If you have read through this chapter, you should have enough background to understand how the tools and commands in PHOTO-PAINT work. The good news is, there won't be a test. Now let's begin to work with PHOTO-PAINT 9. Were you thinking we weren't ever going to get to the actual program?

CHAPTER 3

Setting Up Corel PHOTO-PAINT 9

As a larger-than-average person, I've discovered that one size doesn't fit all. I also know that the same is true when it comes to the default arrangement and settings of tools of any software application—including PHOTO-PAINT. That's why Corel allows many of the features to be moved, removed, and otherwise customized.

In this chapter, you will learn how to customize your PHOTO-PAINT workspace so that it is both comfortable and productive. Corel has put a lot of features into PHOTO-PAINT that allow you, to quote a fast-food chain, to "have it your way." There are several million combinations of tool settings possible, so we are not going to look at all the configurable or customizable tools, just the commonly used ones.

You can configure existing toolbars, menus, and keyboard commands as well as create new ones. PHOTO-PAINT comes with 21 toolbars (plus 31 flavors of Property Bars), not to mention 12, count 'em, 12 Dockers. You can add, remove, and rearrange buttons on both existing and new custom toolbars. The same can be done with the commands that are available in the Menu Bar. Many of the default keyboard combinations can be altered, or new combinations can be made. While all three areas—toolbars, menus, and keyboard commands—offer unique benefits, the configurable toolbars offer some of the greatest advantages. Let's start with the toolbars.

Toolbars

Even though the Property Bar is listed in the Toolbars section of the Options dialog box, the toolbar is dedicated to a specific tool or task. The content of Property Bars changes depending on the tool. Our first step when we set up PHOTO-PAINT is to make the toolbars the right size for the display. Then we can fiddle with them.

Fitting the Toolbar to Your Monitor

Because monitors come in various sizes, Corel has made the size of the buttons, and therefore the size of the toolbars, configurable. One of the first steps in setting up PHOTO-PAINT 9 is to find the best fit for your monitor. Every button size except the smallest may cause a portion of the toolbar to drop off the end of a standard monitor. The rule for toolbar size is: The larger your display (physically), the larger the toolbar button settings can be—as long as the toolbar fits the screen. The quality of the icons on the buttons varies with size; I think the middle-sized buttons look the best. In Figure 3-1, I have placed the icons for all three sizes of toolbars side-by-side for comparison.

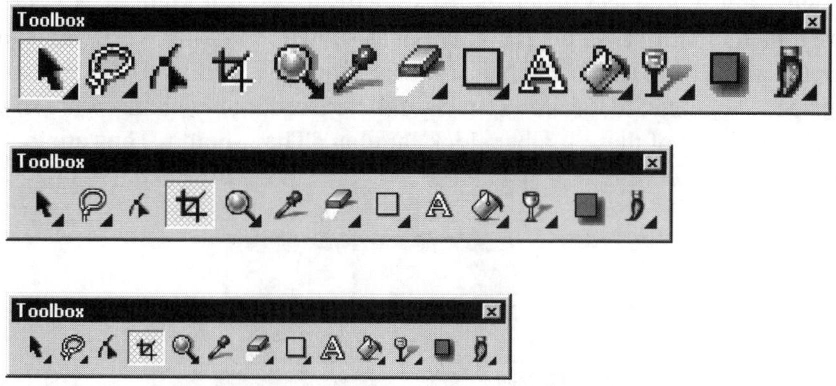

FIGURE 3-1 Toolbar buttons come in three different sizes (small, medium, and large). Sorry, no extra large

Changing the Toolbar Size and Shape

Choose Window | Toolbars. When the Options dialog box opens, it goes directly to the Customize area of the dialog box, as shown next. Move the Button slider to the desired size. Clicking the OK button in the dialog box applies the change to the toolbars. The Border slider increases or decreases the size of the border or bar that the buttons appear to sit on. Moving the slider all the way to the left means all button and no border; moving it all the way to the right means the border surrounding the buttons increases to its maximum.

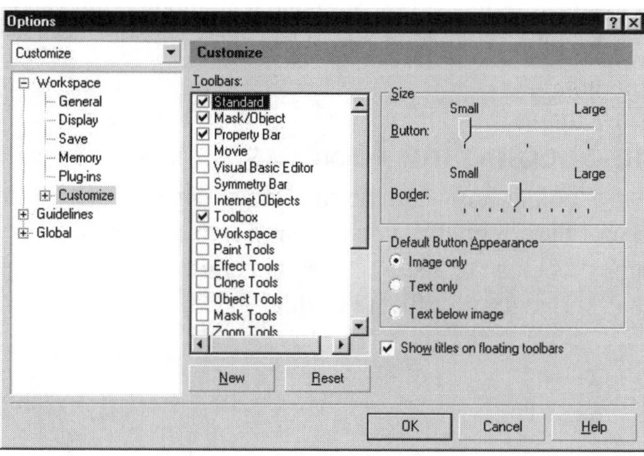

Selecting Toolbars That Are Displayed

The quickest way to select which toolbars are displayed is to right-click your mouse on a toolbar (the Status Bar counts), as shown in Figure 3-2. If you choose to display all 18 of PHOTO-PAINT's standard toolbars, you won't be able to find the image. The image that follows may seem cluttered, but even that isn't all the toolbars. Do some of these toolbars look familiar? They should. They are the flyouts from the Toolbox.

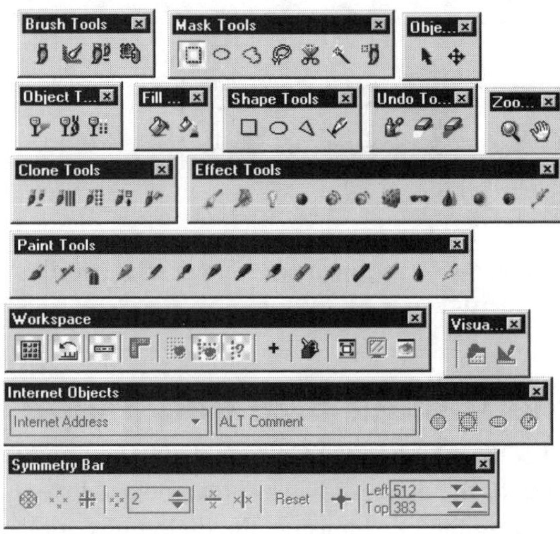

Another way to make a toolbar visible is to select Window | Toolbars and place a check by the desired toolbar, as shown in Figure 3-2. I recommend displaying five of them at all times: Standard, Mask/Object, Property Bar, Toolbox, and Status Bar. Because toolbars take up screen space and the Property Bar provides much of the functionality of the other toolbars, I recommend that you initially keep only the default toolbars selected.

Placing and Shaping the Toolbars

You can move the toolbar anywhere on the screen. By clicking on any part of the toolbar that doesn't have a button, you can drag it to any of the four sides of the window. When it gets close to a side, it will attach itself *(dock)* there. To make it a floating toolbar, move it away from the side.

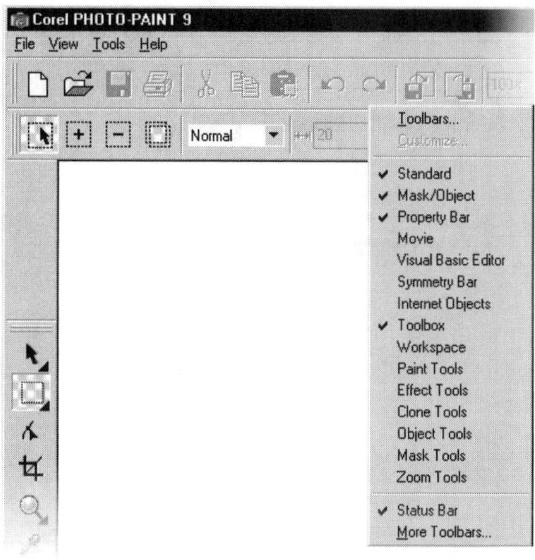

FIGURE 3-2 Right-clicking a toolbar provides a quick selection list for displaying toolbars

TIP: *Be careful when docking the toolbars. PHOTO-PAINT doesn't seem to mind if the toolbar you just docked is too long and some of the buttons go beyond the edge of the monitor, making them no longer visible.*

When toolbars are floating, you can change their shape. In Figure 3-3 I have shown just a few of the many different possible shapes for a large multibutton toolbar like Workspace. Changing the shape is as simple as putting the cursor on the edge of the toolbar until it turns into a two-headed arrow, and then clicking and dragging to the desired shape.

Customizing Toolbars

There are several ways to customize a toolbar. Here are some basic concepts about buttons and toolbars. Every command in PHOTO-PAINT has a button that can be placed on a toolbar. All these buttons can be rearranged, moved to a different toolbar, or removed from a toolbar completely. To place a copy of a button, hold

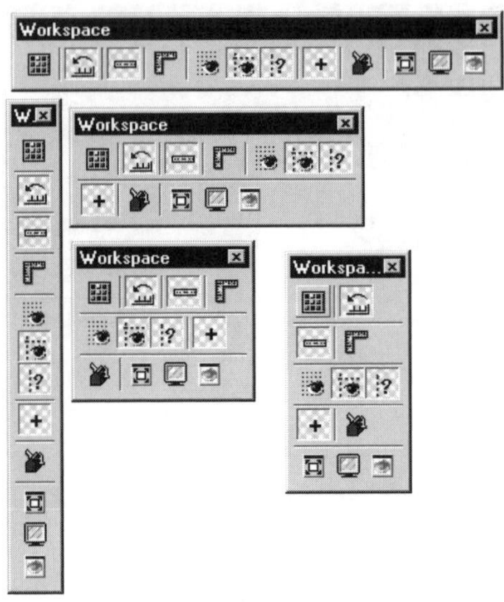

FIGURE 3-3 The toolbars can be configured to different shapes

down ALT and drag the button to its new location. If you drag a button off the toolbar, the button will be removed.

I recommend that you spend some time working with PHOTO-PAINT 9 to get a feel for what arrangement will work best for you before you begin customizing.

If you are going to be doing the projects throughout this book, here is a simple project that creates a custom toolbar to make the other projects easier to accomplish. The project also gives you practice in creating and modifying toolbars.

Building Your Own Custom Toolbar

The following procedure creates a custom toolbar. Before any customization can be done, an image must be open. I don't know why, but it must. The first step is to create or load an image:

1. Open a new file (CTRL-N), click the OK button when the dialog box opens, and minimize the image by clicking the Minus button in the upper-right corner.

2. Open the Options dialog box (CTRL-J). Open Customize and select Toolbars. The dialog box on the right, shown next, is divided into two areas: the command categories (left) and buttons (right).

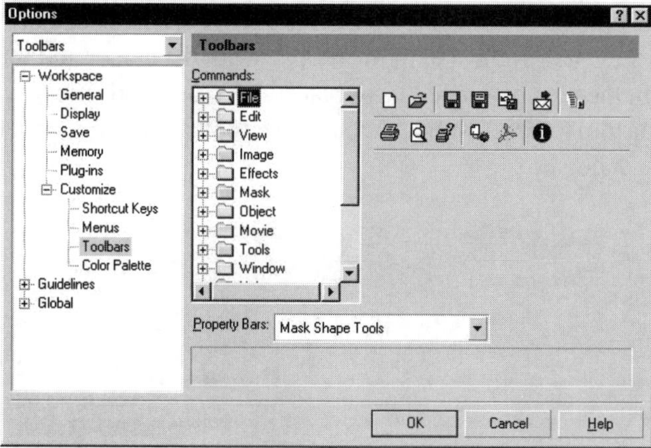

3. In the Commands list, locate Edit and click the plus sign (+) to the left of the folder icon. This action opens a list of all the Edit commands that are available in PHOTO-PAINT and displays all the icons in the buttons area. Scroll down the list until you find the Clear command, and click it once. This action surrounds the Clear icon, which looks like an "X".

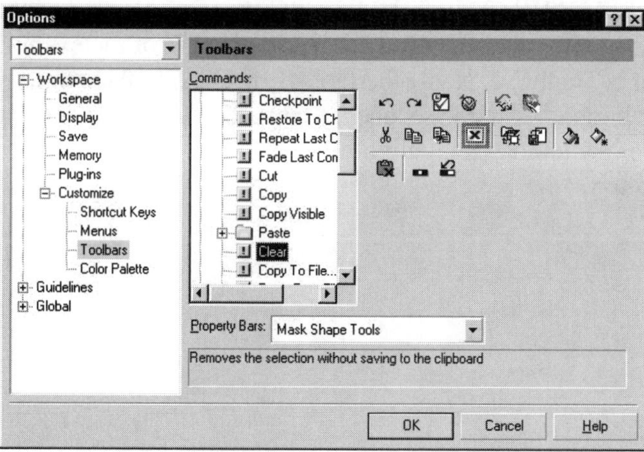

4. Click and drag the Clear button to the Desktop. When you release it, it becomes a toolbar.

5. Repeat this procedure with the Fill button. Since it's also in the Edit category, it isn't necessary to return to the Commands list to select another category. Click the button that looks like a bucket pouring paint, and drag it over to the new toolbar. When you release it, the Fill button will attach itself to the new toolbar. If the button ends up below the Clear button instead of on the side of it, grab the left or right side of the toolbar with the cursor and make the toolbar wider. In the next example I have placed six commands in the form of buttons in the custom toolbar. Notice that the new toolbar is floating on top of the Options dialog box.

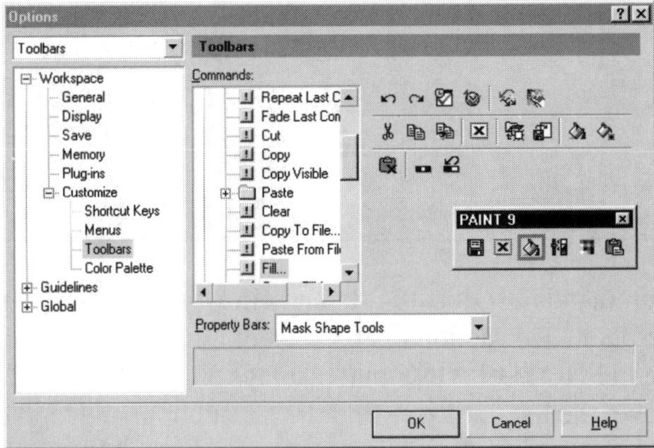

6. From the left drop-down list, choose Customize. Down near the bottom will be a toolbar named "Toolbar *n*." In the case of the example shown next, it is Toolbar 1. Name the toolbar by clicking the name with the right mouse button. From the secondary menu that opens, select Rename. The name of the toolbar is highlighted. Change the name to **Custom**. Click the OK button.

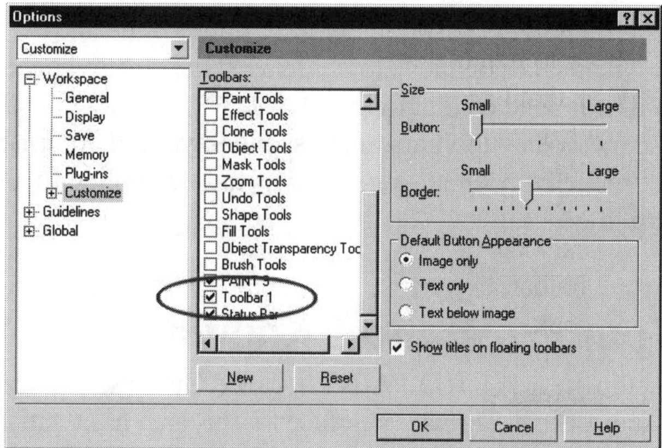

You have created your first custom toolbar. I always make a custom toolbar when I work on a project—such as this book.

To remove a toolbar that you made, or if you accidentally made an extra one or two doing the previous step-by-step procedure, use CTRL-J, select Toolbars, right-click the toolbar, and select Delete from the pop-up menu.

Menus and Keyboard Commands

You can arrange menus in a similar fashion to the toolbars. An example of rearranging the menu structure would be moving a command that is nested several levels deep to the top of the menu for easy access. Another time-saver is the ability to assign a command to a keyboard shortcut. PHOTO-PAINT comes with a large set of default keyboard combinations. Customizing a keyboard combination is self-explanatory. Assigning a keyboard combination to a command allows you to execute commands quickly without clicking a button or accessing the menu. The only disadvantage to using keyboard combinations is the need to memorize the keyboard shortcut. Also, remember that you cannot use existing reserved combinations like CTRL-S (Save). Refer to the user's manual or online help for detailed information on using either the menu or keyboard command configurations.

Each of these methods—toolbars, menus, and keyboard commands—offers you a wealth of productivity enhancements that can be applied to a specific project or to the program in general.

Making Your Preferences Known

The preference settings for PHOTO-PAINT 9, called Options, are located in the Tools menu or by pressing CTRL-J. The user interface for this area hasn't changed much since PHOTO-PAINT 8, as shown in Figure 3-4. If it looks familiar, you probably use Netscape's Communicator for your browser. PHOTO-PAINT 9 has been designed to allow multiple configurations to be saved as individual workspaces.

The three major groups of preference settings are Workspace, (Document) Guidelines, and Global (Bitmap Effects).

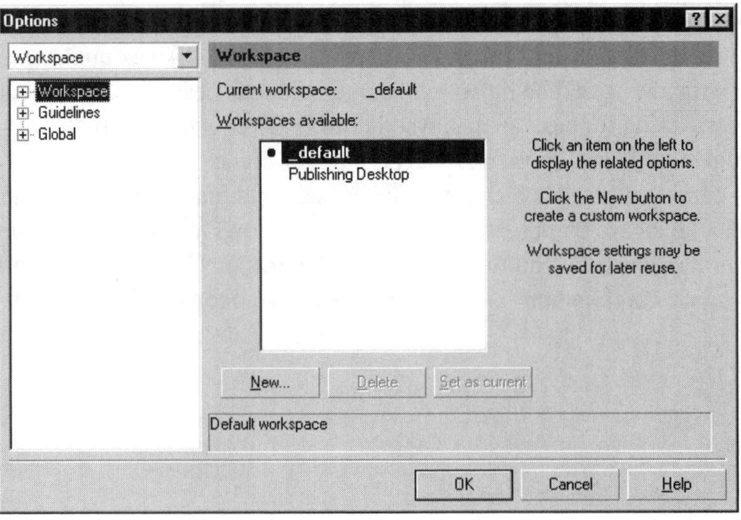

FIGURE 3-4 The Options dialog box

The Workspace Settings

This grouping includes General, Display, Save, Memory, Plug-ins, and Customize.

The General Page

The General page, shown next, contains many of the settings that determine how PHOTO-PAINT functions. The setting that determines what PHOTO-PAINT does when you launch it is found in the On Startup setting. By default, it is set to the Welcome Screen.

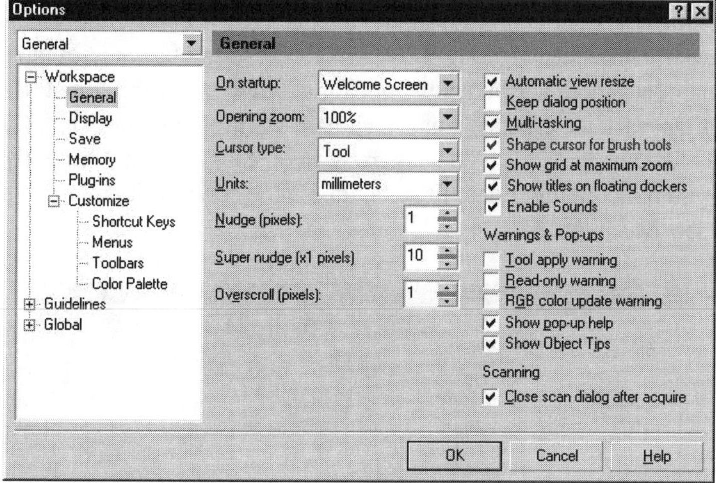

There are a few default settings in the General page that you should consider changing. I recommend keeping the Opening Zoom at 100%. If you have To Fit or some other zoom level selected, it may increase the time necessary to display an image after it is loaded on slower systems.

To the right of the Cursor Type option, an important setting is the Shape Cursor For Brush Tools check box. When enabled, this changes the cursor to the size and shape of a selected brush tool. This is important because this feature allows you to see the size of your brush tool. The only reason I know for not selecting this feature is that the cursor shape can slow down the brush tool action if you have a slow system.

At the top of the page is the Automatic View Resize option. This changes the size of the image window automatically so that it always fits the current size of the image anytime you change the zoom level. As neat as this feature is, you may want to leave it unchecked when editing an image. This option keeps the edge of the image window tight to the edge of the image, which creates a problem as the cursor approaches the edge of the image window. The program thinks you want to take action on the image window size or placement on the workspace rather than on the image, making work near the edge of the image difficult. If you will be doing the projects in this book, I recommend leaving this feature off. Having said this, I use it a lot when writing a book like this because I don't want gray edges on my screen captures.

The Display Page

This page, shown next, contains the settings to change the colors, actions, and appearance of the marquees in PHOTO-PAINT. These settings are not intended to make the marquees more aesthetically appealing, but to allow the adjustment of their colors and shapes for the types of images you are working on. For example, the Object Marquee is blue, but against a blue background you cannot see it. Generally, these settings should be left in their default state, unless the color of the image makes it difficult to see the marquees.

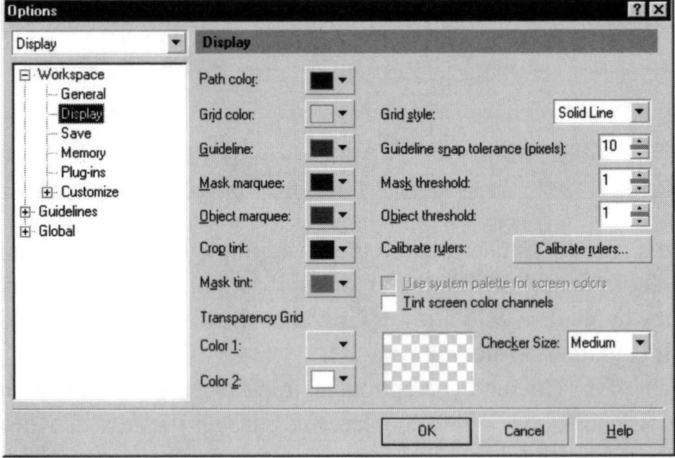

Also located on this page are some ruler and grid functions. When selected, the Calibrate Rulers button fills your screen with two sets of rulers, as shown next. The purpose of this feature is to allow you to adjust the onscreen rulers to a physical ruler (clear plastic is highly recommended). This way when you select the view 1:1, the image displayed on your screen will accurately represent the actual size of the image.

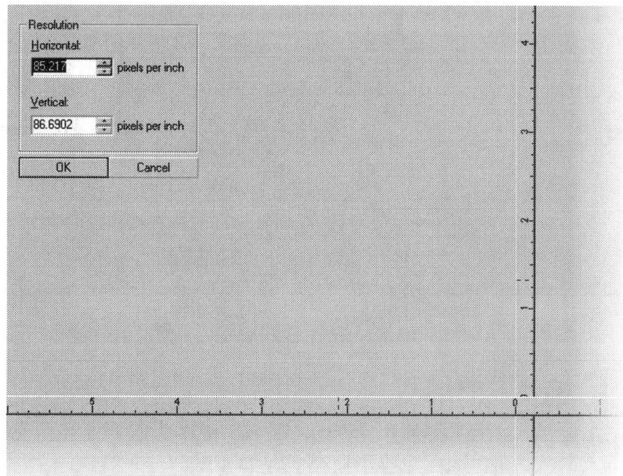

The Save Page

This is the page where you can instruct PHOTO-PAINT to automatically back up the file you are working on at specific time intervals, and enable backup copies of images to be produced when an image is saved. When the time arrives for the automatic backup of an open image, a dialog box pops up asking, "Save to file?" Then another one pops up asking, "Do you wish to turn the Auto-save feature off?" If you choose to enable this feature (it is off by default), I suggest setting it to Save To Checkpoint, as shown next. The Checkpoint command creates a temporary copy of an image. This avoids changes being made to the original file before you are ready to save them. You should leave the other settings in their default state until you become more familiar with PHOTO-PAINT.

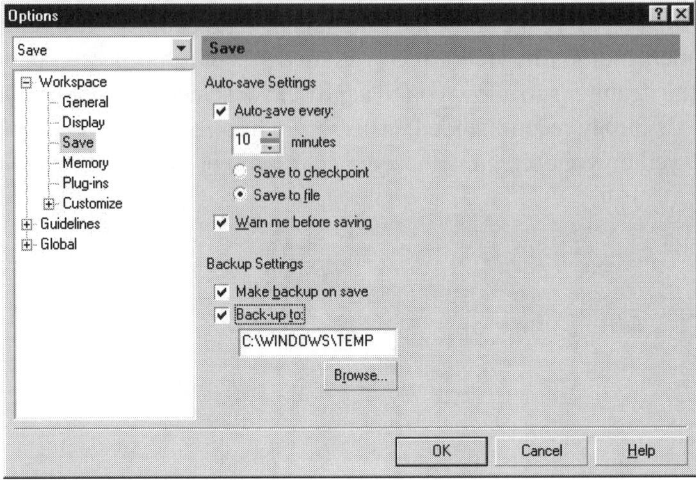

The Memory Page

The next illustration shows the Memory page, which determines which and how much hard disk space is available for PHOTO-PAINT to save temporary files, and the allocation of the system memory for image editing and Undo lists and levels. The correct settings in this page improve the performance of PHOTO-PAINT by adjusting the use of system resources to the way you work.

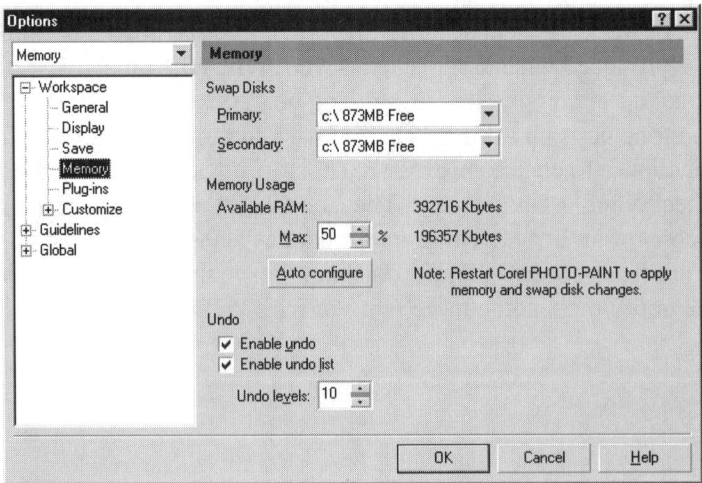

Because bitmap images require larger areas of memory than traditional Windows applications, PHOTO-PAINT uses space on your hard disk drive for temporary storage. This area is called a *swap disk.* If you have more than one hard disk drive, the program, by default, will select the first drive (alphabetically) as the primary swap disk and the second drive as the secondary swap disk, regardless of the amount of available space on the drive. Check your settings to make sure that the drive with the greatest amount of available space is set as the primary swap drive. If one of the drives is slower than the other, select the faster drive for the primary swap drive.

The Memory page has settings to enable and disable the Undo and Undo List commands. This is an important feature. The traditional problem with a photo-editing package is the lack of multiple undo levels. With PHOTO-PAINT 9, you can determine how many undo levels you have. Before you decide to set the undo level to 99, be aware that each level of undo keeps a copy of the image at that level, which uses up system resources. Setting a high Undo level can consume a lot of swap-disk space and ultimately slow down your system. I recommend keeping the undo level set at the factory default of 10/. Another feature that has been improved in PHOTO-PAINT 9 is the Undo List. Enabling this feature will allow you to undo as far back as you choose. It does this by recording each command that is applied to an image and then reapplying the commands (minus the ones that you wanted to undo) in a sequential manner. While it is slower than the normal Undo, it does not consume as many system resources as do undo levels.

You can also determine the amount of RAM assigned to temporarily store images when you open and edit them. Allotting too much RAM for the images can result in slower performance of other Windows applications. I recommend leaving this setting at its default state.

NOTE: *Any change you make to the settings in the Memory page requires the restart of PHOTO-PAINT for the changes to take effect.*

The Plug-ins Page

For detailed information on how to use the settings in this page, see Chapter 13.

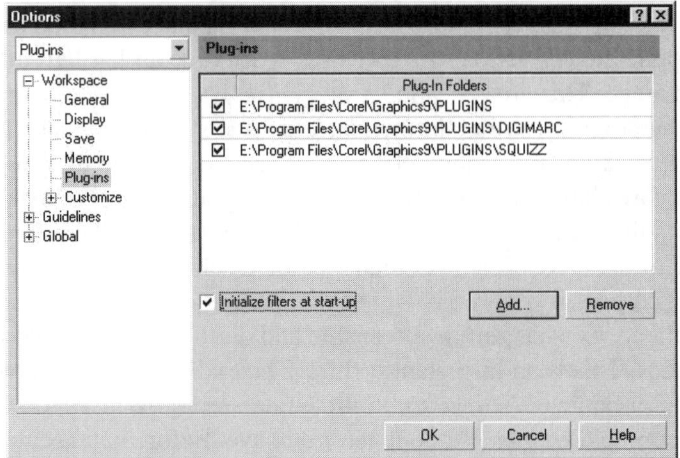

The Customize Page

This page offers selections for customizing menus, keyboard shortcuts, menus, and toolbars discussed earlier in this chapter.

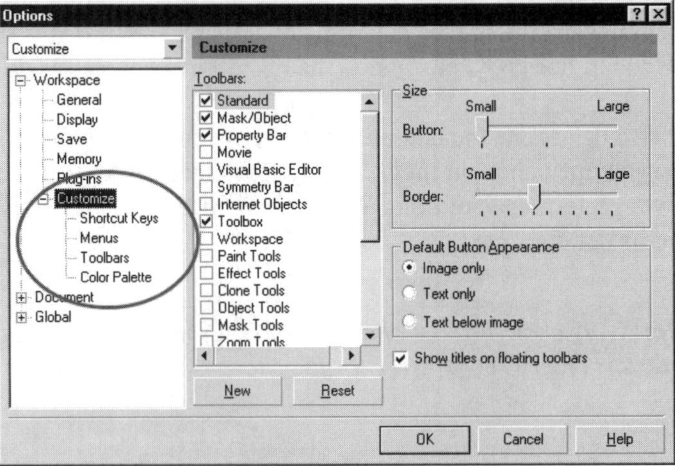

The Document - Guidelines Group

This grouping contains the settings for guidelines, grids, and rulers. The operation and configuration of rulers and guidelines is explored in Chapter 5. This group can be accessed through this dialog box or by double-clicking on a ruler. Like many other things in Windows 9*x*, there are multiple paths to the same destination.

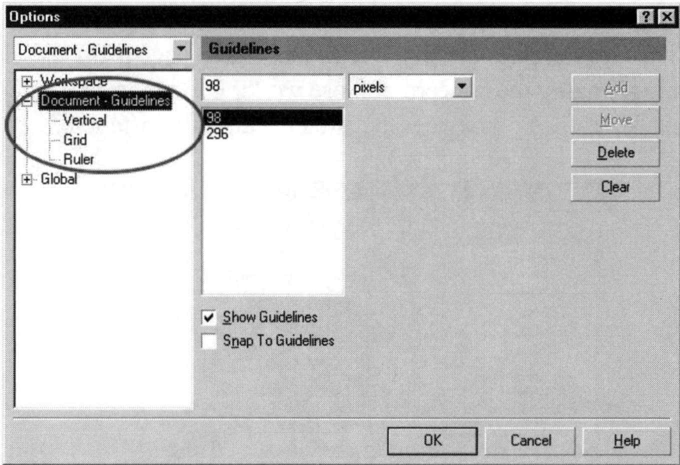

The Global - Bitmap Effects Group

The Global - Bitmap Effects Group contains three pages: Color Management, General, and Filters. From the top page you can set the initial preview mode of the filters, as shown next.

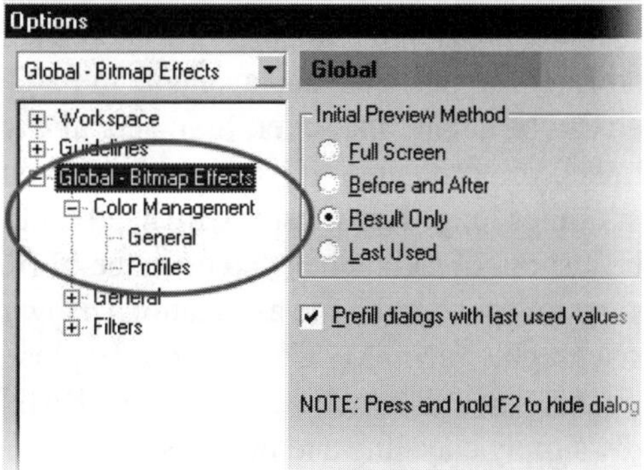

The Color Management Page

The Color Management page contains three separate pages: Color Management, General, and Profiles. Color Management, shown next, provides the controls for

3

viewing colors accurately on the display. This page contains many of the items that used to be in the Color Correction category of the View menu. While it is great to have accurate color, I recommend keeping this disabled until you get to the color-adjustment phase of your project. This feature tends to slow down the refresh of the display. The General page of the Color Management page includes selection of options that are primarily the concern of those working in prepress. The Profiles page allows you to add profiles for devices that are not currently installed.

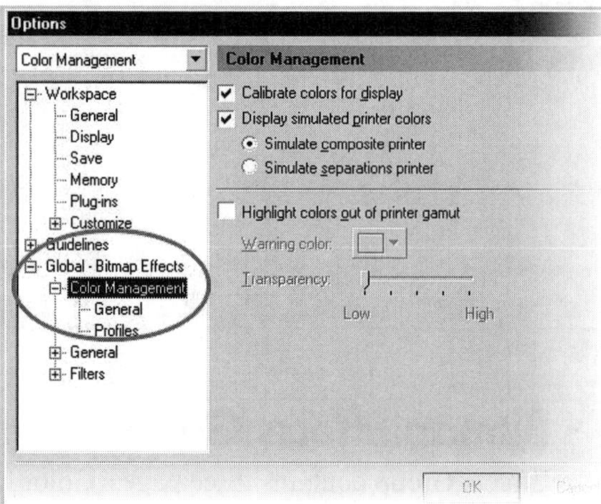

The Filters Page

This page controls two major areas of the import and export filters. First, it controls what import and export filters are installed and available in PHOTO-PAINT. This feature if properly used can be a real time-saver. If you are always working in a limited number of formats, you can "turn off" the filters that you are not using so that your list of choices isn't miles long. This is especially handy if the file format you use always seems to be just out of sight when you open the file dialog boxes. The second area controlled by this page is the file associations. How many times have you double-clicked on a graphic file in My Computer or Explorer and had the wrong application open up? In this page, shown next, you can tell PAINT which file formats are associated with it by simply checking and unchecking boxes.

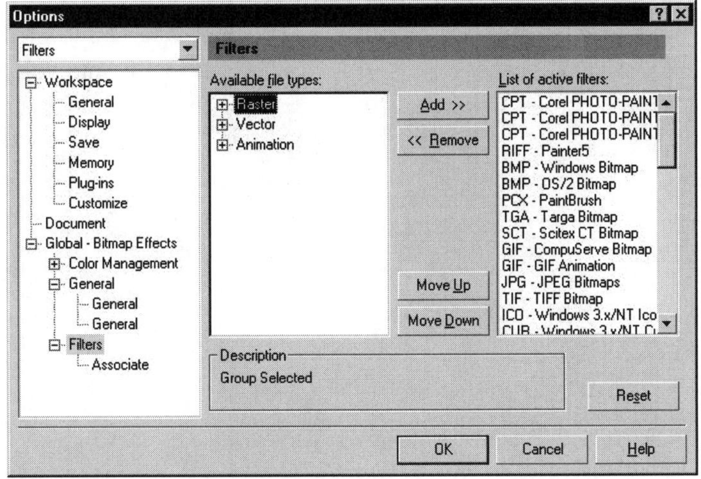

Onscreen Palette

The onscreen color palette first appears on the right side of the screen. Like the toolbars, it can be dragged and docked anywhere on the screen. You can change several of the color features by opening the Options dialog box (CTRL-J) and clicking on Workspace | Customize | Color Palette. From here you can configure the color wells and control how the right button on the mouse responds when clicking one of the color wells. I recommend keeping the default setting of Set Fill Color. It offers a quick and easy way to change fill colors.

With our system set up, we can move on to the next chapter and learn more about the Onscreen color palette and how to select that "right" color out of a palette of about a zillion.

PART II

Basic Photo-Editing Techniques

CHAPTER 4

Picking the Right Color

This chapter is a result of hundreds of e-mails I received asking about the selection of colors in PHOTO-PAINT. I wanted to put together a short chapter on how to select, create, and save colors in PHOTO-PAINT 9. Some of the material in this chapter is repeated throughout the book, but I want to make sure you get the material.

The Basic Colors—Where They Live

There are three areas in PHOTO-PAINT—*Paint, Paper,* and *Fill*—for which we are always looking for "the right color." Of the three, only Fill can be something other than a solid (uniform) color. The quickest way to tell what color each is currently set to is by use of the Status Bar, shown next. The two icons at the end are Swap Paint/Paper Colors (left) and Reset Colors (right). Reset Colors restores the Paint, Paper, and Fill colors to their default values—Black, White, and White, respectively. Swap Paint/Paper Colors swaps the current Paint and Paper colors each time it is clicked.

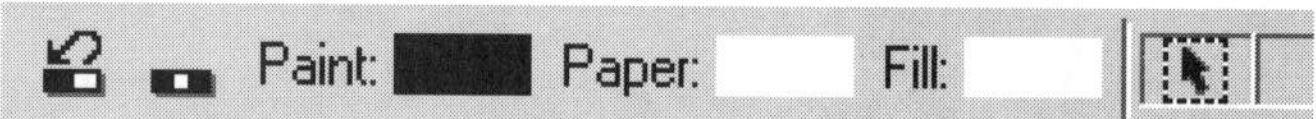

When you click the Reset Colors icon, the Paint and Fill colors become black and the Paper becomes white. Not exactly exciting stuff, but a place to start.

Once you have established what colors are in these three buckets, the next question is, how do you change them?

Changing Colors—It's Easier Than You Think

So you want to change one of the three colors? Your quickest means is the onscreen color palette. Here is a variation of it:

If you have used PHOTO-PAINT before, you may be saying, "Hey, the onscreen color palette is a long, tall thing that docks against the right side of the screen." True by default, but the onscreen color palette can also float around like I have just shown.

Picking the Paint color only requires clicking on the desired color in the onscreen palette. So far, so good.

Picking the Paper color is a little more complicated. Hold down CTRL and click the mouse button on the desired color.

The Fill color? Right-click the color.

Is that the only way? Not hardly. But for now it's good enough.

Finding a Color by Name

Often when I write articles, I want the readers to select a particular color. I could give the RGB or CMYK numbers. That's if I never wanted them to do the tutorial. Instead, I try to give them named colors that exist in the onscreen palette. To find Electric Blue, for example, place your cursor over a likely candidate and wait a moment. The name of the color appears, as shown next.

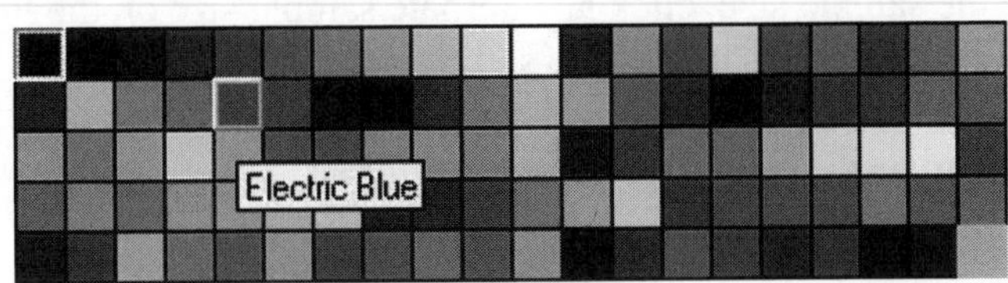

Another way to find a color by name is to use the Find Color By Name pop-up menu. To quickly access this dialog box, hold down CTRL and ALT and then click a color. Type in the desired name, choose OK, and the color is selected.

Getting the Right Color with the Eyedropper Tool

The *Eyedropper tool,* located in the Toolbox, is used to pick a specific color from an image by clicking on it. This tool has more uses than might first be apparent. Let's go through the basics of how to use the Eyedropper.

Eyedropper Tool Hot Key

To quickly select the Eyedropper tool, press the "E" key on your keyboard. This enables the Eyedropper tool. To return to the previously selected tool, press the SPACEBAR.

TIP: *The "E" key shortcut is a quick way to get a numerical color value for a spot or area. This information is very helpful when you're setting Color Tolerance values.*

Eyedropper Sample Size

The Property Bar is used to set the sample size of the Eyedropper tool. By default, the Eyedropper tool samples a 1 × 1-pixel area to determine a color value. Suppose when selecting colors for the Color Replacer tool or retouching photographs, you want an average color from an area. This is why PHOTO-PAINT gives you the ability to select different sample sizes. If you want to select a specific color, you can click the last button on the Property Bar, which opens up the Color Docker window.

To change the sample size, click an alternate sample size on the Property Bar. The Property Bar has these sample-size settings:

- **Point (1 pixel)** This is the default setting.
- **3 × 3 Area (9 pixels)**
- **5 × 5 Area (25 pixels)**
- **Selection** This enables you to click and drag the Eyedropper tool to define any size sample area.

With a click on a color, you can find the color value of the sampled color, which is very handy for retouching. With every sample size (except 1 × 1), the color selected when the mouse button is clicked represents the average of all the colors in the sample area. Obviously, with the 1 × 1 setting, it represents the color value of the single pixel under the cursor. When sampling areas of high contrast, be aware that the averaged color may be quite different from any individual color in the sampled area. The settings made in the Property Bar only affect the Eyedropper tool; they have no effect on other tools that may use an Eyedropper to define colors, such as the Color Mask tool.

Notes on Using the Eyedropper Tool

If there are multiple objects on the image, the Eyedropper tool can only read the colors on the top object whether or not the object is active or selected. A good rule of thumb is: If you can't see it, the Eyedropper can't see it.

When a large area is sampled and averaged, the result may be a color that, while representing the average color in the image, may not actually exist in the image. An example of this would be an area that had the same number of white and red pixels. The resulting color would be pink, even though there was no pink in the image.

Use the Eyedropper hot key (E) when you want to see what the color value(s) is for a part of the image to help set a tool's Tolerance values. An example of using this is when determining where a Magic Wand mask in an image is to be created. I use the "E" hot key to see what the color value is of the starting area (where I click to start the mask).

TIP: *Use the "E" hot key when retouching images. It provides a fast and easy way to pick up adjoining colors, which is critical when touching up an imperfection on a picture.*

What if you want one of those complicated colors? Then you will need to open the Uniform Color dialog box.

Selecting a Uniform Color Fill

If the color you want is not available in the onscreen palette, then from either the Edit Fill & Transparency dialog box or the Fill tool's Property Bar, select the Uniform Fill button and click the Edit or Edit Fill button. This action opens the Uniform Fill dialog box, as shown in Figure 4-1. From this dialog box you can do just about anything that you can think of with regard to solid color.

The Uniform Fill Dialog Box

The Uniform Fill dialog box is where you can pick any color in the universe. The operation of this dialog box can be intimidating. The dialog box is an essential tool for defining and correcting colors if you're doing prepress work. If you only want to make a simple modification to a color so it will look better in an image, you can do that as well.

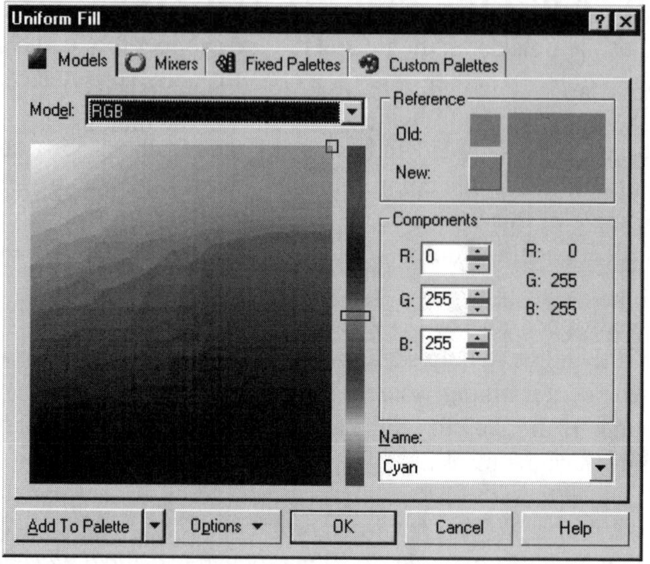

FIGURE 4-1 The Uniform Fill dialog box

Just so you know, the Uniform Fill dialog box is common throughout Corel PHOTO-PAINT as well as throughout the CorelDRAW suite of applications. Changes made to the palette in this dialog box are global. That means that they apply to the entire CorelDRAW suite of applications. The Uniform Fill dialog box allows you to choose colors from various color models and custom palettes. You can also import and select individual colors from existing image files.

How to Approach the Uniform Fill Dialog Box

There are several general approaches to using the Uniform Fill dialog box. By default the dialog box opens to the Models page. The simplest way to select the color you want is to pick the color closest to the desired color from the vertical spectrum in the middle of the dialog box. The preview window on the left will display all the colors available in that part of the spectrum. You can then pick a spot in the preview window that most closely matches the one you want. The New color is shown in the Reference area in the upper-right corner. Clicking OK returns to the Fill dialog box or to the Edit Fill & Transparency dialog box. The advantage of this approach is speed. The disadvantage of this method is that you will be using an undefined color that may be difficult, if not impossible, for someone at a different location (like a service bureau) to duplicate.

If the final image will be printed by use of an established color matching system, like Pantone, click the Fixed Palettes tab in the dialog box and choose the palette and specific color you want.

A third approach is to create one or more colors, name them, and save them on a custom palette. This way you can use the colors in another image, because the colors have been named and saved. Another site can duplicate your work, since you can send the palette along with the image. The disadvantage is that it takes longer to do. That said, let's examine this cornucopia.

Setting the Mood—Models, Palettes, or Mixers?

The operation of the Uniform Fill dialog box is controlled by whichever of the four tabs at the top of the dialog box is selected. These affect not only the operation but also the appearance of the dialog box. Your choices are as follows:

- **Models Mode** This method of choosing a color allows you to select one of nine color models from the Model drop-down list to establish the color you want. This is the mode shown in Figure 4-2. The reason for selecting a specific color model to use when choosing colors is based on the type of work you are doing. For example, if you are color correcting a photograph that will be printed using the four-color printing process (CMYK), you should choose the CMYK or CMY color model.
- **Mixers Mode** It slices, it dices, it's the Color Blender. This is a handy tool for selecting colors from RGB, CMYK, or HSB models. You select four colors and it produces a range of colors for the colors selected using gradations between four colors across a square grid. Shown in Figure 4-3 is the Color Harmonies preview, which is selected in the Options pop-up menu. Color harmonies are most useful when you're selecting several colors for a project. By using color harmonies, you are guaranteed that the colors you choose look good together. Color harmonies work by superimposing a shape, such as a rectangle or a triangle, over a color wheel. You can also manipulate the superimposed shape (the rectangle, triangle, or pentagon). As you move the black spot on the shape around the

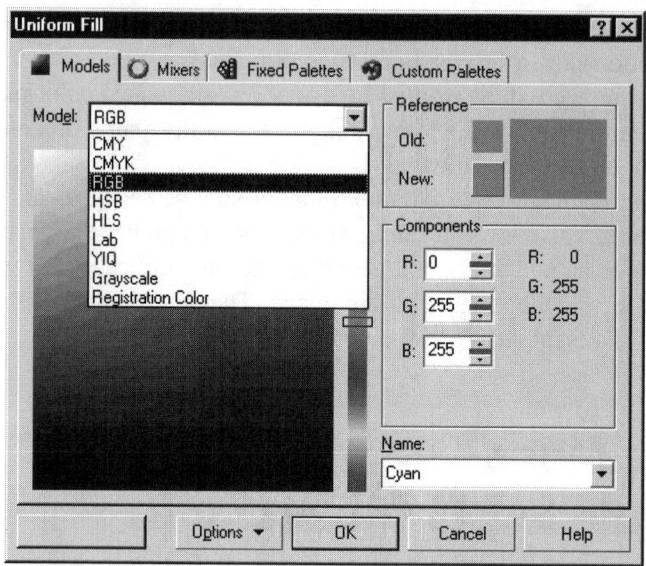

FIGURE 4-2 The Uniform Fill dialog box in Models mode

wheel, the other circles also move. The colors at each corner are always complementary, contrasting, or harmonious, depending on the shape you select. The color harmonies now allow you to select the color model you prefer to use. You can choose from several different color models, including the RGB or CMYK models.

- **Fixed Palettes Mode** Selecting this button changes the color selection to one based not on a color model but on a predefined palette, as shown in Figure 4-4. From the Palette drop-down list, pick one of 19 predefined systems, such as Pantone or Netscape Navigator. Use Fixed Palettes if you are using spot colors or working with a web site.
- **Custom Palettes Mode** This is the mode of choice, as shown in Figure 4-5, if you need to use a specific set of colors that are not part of a known palette or color matching system. Both the Corel PHOTO-PAINT and the CorelDRAW palettes are in this category.

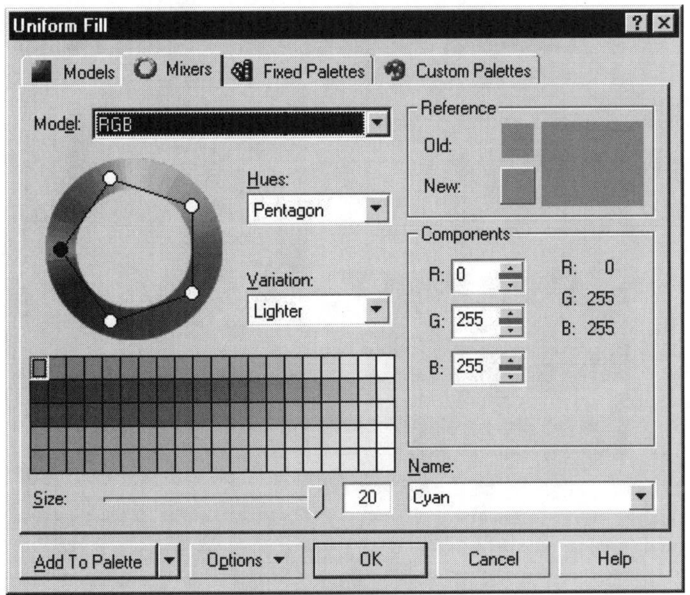

FIGURE 4-3 The Uniform Fill dialog box in Mixers mode

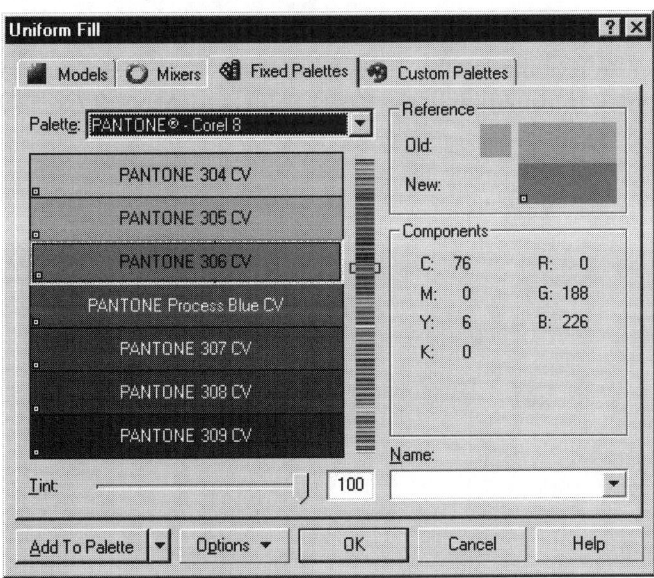

FIGURE 4-4 The Uniform Fill dialog box in Fixed Palettes mode

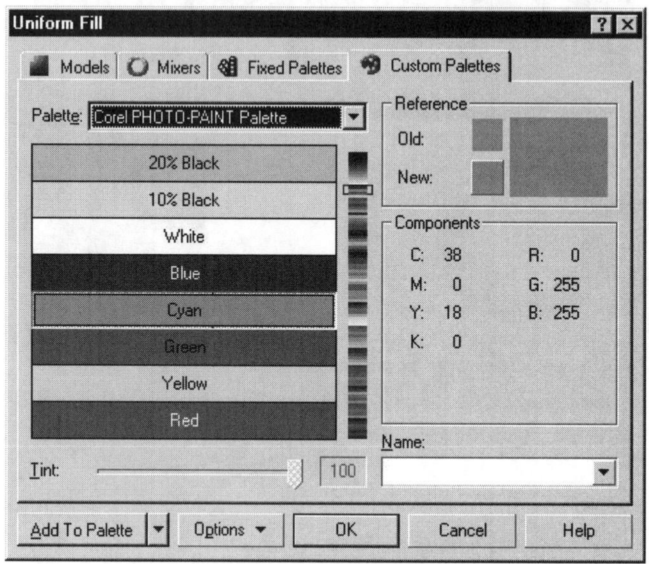

FIGURE 4-5 The Uniform Fill dialog box in Custom Palettes mode

In an effort to save trees and preserve ink, I have not included every last detail about the operation of the Uniform Fill dialog box. However, you can find excellent detailed information in the Corel PHOTO-PAINT 9 *User's Manual* and through online Help.

CHAPTER 5

Basic Tools and Procedures

Corel PHOTO-PAINT 9 provides an assortment of tools to make working on images easier. Rulers, grids, and guidelines are provided for aligning and positioning objects and masks in an image. While these alignment tools are generally associated with vector-based (CorelDRAW) or page layout (Corel Ventura) programs, they can be used for purposes other than the accurate positioning of graphic elements. In addition, there are navigation tools to help us quickly get around large images and Zoom tools that magnify areas for accurate retouching and other types of image manipulation. As powerful as these tools are, the ones we appreciate most are those that help us undo our mistakes. Fortunately, PHOTO-PAINT 9 offers a lot of ways to help us, even beyond the traditional last-action-only Undo command. We also must be able to save our images in a format that can be either archived or transported to another location. To do this we will need to be aware of some of the potential pitfalls of file compression and other image management issues.

Rulers, Guidelines, and Grids

In addition to providing one of the few visual indicators that show the physical dimensions of a PHOTO-PAINT image, rulers are also the source of guidelines. The guidelines are useful when cropping an image or aligning elements in an image to a fixed point. With the Snap To Guidelines feature, guidelines can be used like the grids, while having the added advantage of being placed where needed rather than at fixed intervals like grids. The grids, which are nonprintable, serve as both an alignment tool for placing graphic elements in an image and as a way to proportionally arrange them.

Rulers

In Chapter 2, we learned it is possible for a photograph to completely fill the screen, yet print smaller than a postage stamp. By displaying rulers on an image, you can see the dimensions of the image in inches. Here is a quick exercise for familiarizing yourself with the rulers and for visibly displaying the effects of changing the resolution of an image.

1. Select Open from the File menu (CTRL-O). From the Corel CD-ROM, select the file EXERCISE\OBJECTS\HOT AIR BALLOONS, which is shown here:

2. Select Duplicate from the Image menu and, when the dialog box opens, name the duplicate image "Copy." Reposition the two identical copies so they fill the screen as shown here:

3. With Copy active, choose Image | Resample. We will explain resampling in more detail throughout the book. For now, you only need to know that it changes the size of the image. When the Resample dialog box opens, as shown next, check the Maintain Original Size check box. In the Resolution section, double-click on the value for Horizontal, change it from 300 to 75, and click the OK button.

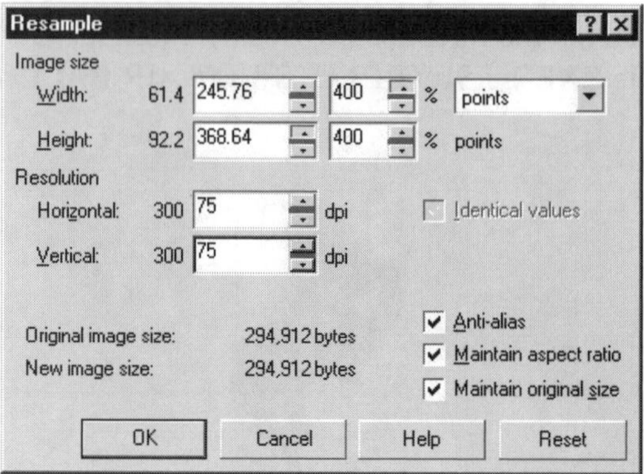

4. With Copy still active, display the rulers (CTRL-R or select Rulers from the View menu). Click on the Title bar of Hot Air Balloons and display its rulers.

5. If the rulers are displayed in pixels or some other unit of measure like do-dots (what are those anyway?), double-click the ruler to open the Options dialog box (shown next), or select Grid & Ruler Setup in the View menu. Enable the Same Units for Horizontal and Vertical Rulers check box and select inches from the Horizontal pop-up menu in the Units section.

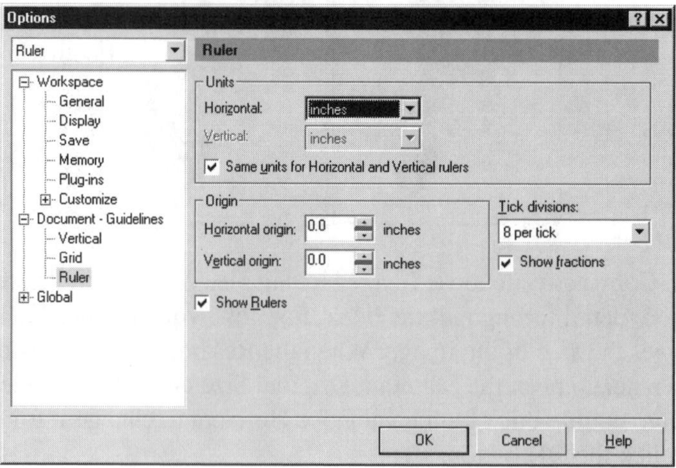

6. Click the OK button. Even though both images appear to be the same size, an examination of the rulers shows that they are not:

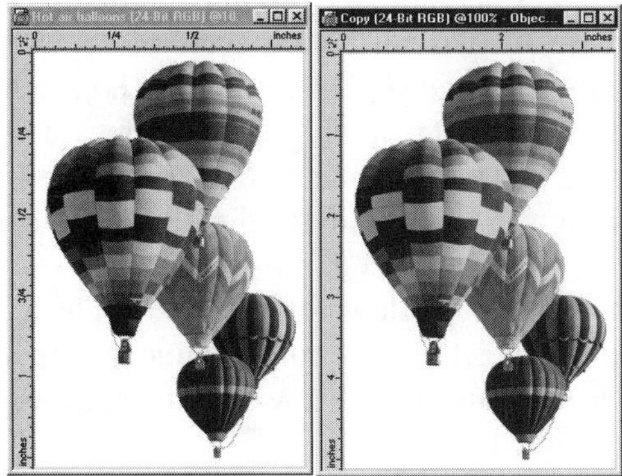

TIP: *The quickest way to open the Grid & Ruler Setup dialog box is to right-click on a ruler and select from the options in the pop-up menu.*

7. To see the images in their actual size, make sure Hot Air Balloons is still active. In the Standard toolbar, change the Zoom level from 100% to 1 to 1. Select the Copy image and change the Zoom level to 1 to 1. The following illustration shows the result of changing the resolution of both images when they are displayed using a 1 to 1 Zoom level.

Ruler Properties

The ruler normally uses the upper-left corner of the image window as its point of origin. To change this, click and drag the origin point to the new desired position. The origin point is where the two rulers intersect.

When the cursor is in the image, dashed lines on the horizontal and vertical rulers indicate the cursor position. To get a more accurate reading, increase the zoom level.

You can place a ruler anywhere on an image. There are times when placing the ruler at a different location allows you to see dimensions of a graphic element in the image more clearly.

To reposition either ruler, hold down the SHIFT key, click the ruler you want to move, and drag it to a new position. The ruler outline will appear as double-dashed lines as you move it. In the illustration below, the rulers have been repositioned and the origin point is circled.

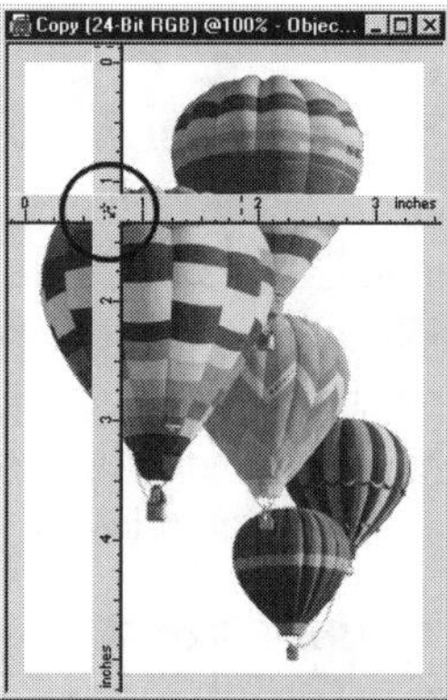

If you need to move both rulers at once, hold down the SHIFT key and drag the intersection point of the two rulers. To return both at once, hold down the SHIFT key and double-click on a ruler.

NOTE: *When you reposition and release a ruler, the image may jump a short distance (the width of the ruler—five pixels) the first time it is moved. When you click and drag the ruler and reposition it a second time, the image will not jump.*

When you change the zoom settings of the image, the scale of the ruler will change. To illustrate this, I have shown here a composite image. The numbers in the titles indicate the zoom setting of the underlying image. Notice that at a zoom setting of 1600% (max.) the ruler division markers are 1/64 of an inch.

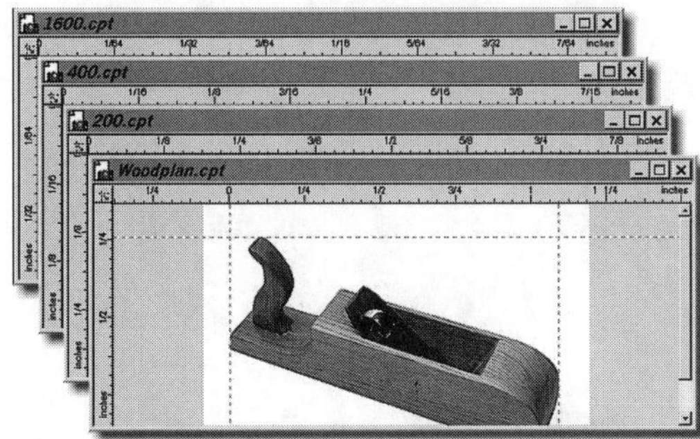

Grids

Grids are very useful for performing a variety of design functions in PHOTO-PAINT. In Figure 5-1, I have shown a simple tile pattern that was created using a grid, a mask, and The Boss filter. The actual design of the pattern would have been impossible without the grids and the Snap To Grid feature. In a step-by-step tutorial in Chapter 7, you will create the tile shown in Figure 5-2. Grids made the intricate patterns like these possible. In fact, neither of the figures could have been made without grids. When you work with objects and layers, you can align objects and masks to grids or make on-screen tracing paper.

Grid Properties

Grids are simple, so you don't need to spend a lot of time learning about them. Select Grid in the View menu to make the grid visible or invisible. Right-click on a ruler and select Grid Setup. From the Options dialog box, you can change the frequency of the grid (number of grids per unit of measure) and other grid properties. An important property of grids to keep in mind is that they are nonprintable. Even though they appear on the display, gridlines do not occupy space in the image. There may be occasions when you want to include the grid in the image, and it can be done (as shown in the following illustration). However, you can do this only by using a screen capture program, such as Corel Capture 9, and bringing the image into PHOTO-PAINT.

FIGURE 5-1 The pattern for this wood tile would have been impossible to create without grids

FIGURE 5-2 Using grids and masks, you will make this tile in Chapter 7

NOTE: *It should be noted that when a Zoom of 1600% is selected, the grid will turn on automatically.*

Guidelines

Guidelines are created by clicking on the ruler with the mouse button and dragging a guideline into the image. The guidelines can be either horizontal or vertical. For all practical purposes, you can make as many guidelines as you want. Double-clicking on a guideline with the Object Picker tool opens the Guidelines Options dialog box, shown here. While there are several different guideline settings that can be controlled in this dialog box, the one to remember is the Clear button. This setting removes all of the guidelines you created with a single action. For more details on the settings for the guidelines, refer to either the online help or the *PHOTO-PAINT 9 User's Manual.*

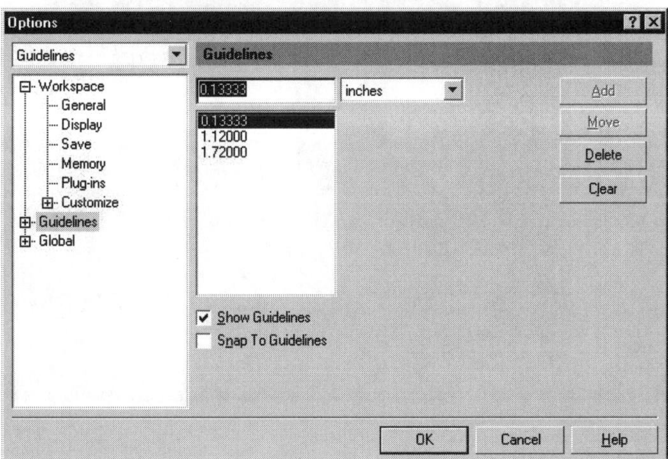

Guidelines are very handy for situations where you need to line up several objects in an image. Although you can use PHOTO-PAINT's built-in alignment commands to align both multiple objects and masks, there are times when you need a guideline to find the visual center of multiple objects in an image. In such cases, you will discover that guidelines are very useful tools indeed.

Zoom and Navigation Tools

The Zoom tools of PHOTO-PAINT 9 provide several ways of viewing and working on your image from as close up or as far away as necessary. Zoom tools magnify or decrease the size of your onscreen image without affecting the actual image size. When an image is either too large or has a zoom level too high for the image to fit on the screen, two navigational tools—the Hand tool and the Navigator Pop-up—will come in handy.

Working the Zoom Tools

You can change the zoom level in several ways in PHOTO-PAINT. You can choose a preset zoom level from the pop-up menu in the Standard toolbar, or you

Rules About Rulers, Grids, and Guidelines

Here are some little-known facts about rulers, grids, and guidelines:

- When a file is saved and later reopened, it uses its last ruler and grid settings. Guidelines remain as well.
- The grid is not always visible when a file is opened, even if the grid was visible when the image was saved.
- The Show Grid and Snap To Grid modes are turned off when an image is first opened.

can enter a value into the Zoom Level box and press ENTER. In addition to the percentile preset zoom level settings, there are seven other zoom settings:

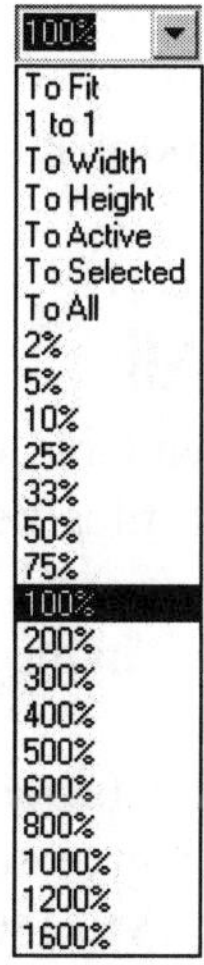

Zoom 100% Versus Zoom 1 to 1

The first time I saw these two commands, I thought they did the same thing. I was wrong. Zoom 100% matches pixels in the image with screen pixels in the display. Zoom 1 to 1 should be called "display in actual size," since it changes the zoom level to display the image at its physical size.

Zoom 100% provides the most accurate representation of the image. There are times when images in the display will appear to be degraded. This is often the result of the image being at some zoom level that is difficult for your video adapter to properly display. In the following image, a screen capture of the word "ZOOM" was made at zoom levels of 100% and 88%. The 100% zoom-level text looks smooth, with no sign of the "jaggies," those irregular edges that appear primarily on the diagonal portions of an image. The text at 88% appears to be very jagged. The insert to the left of the image is a magnification of the first letters.

TIP: *Always use Zoom 100% to see the most accurate representation of an image in PHOTO-PAINT.*

To Width/To Height

Selecting these options changes the zoom level so that either the entire width or height fits in the image window.

To Active/To Selected/To All

These three Zoom options are only available when the image contains PHOTO-PAINT objects. If you haven't learned about objects yet, don't worry: that's covered in Chapter 12. To Active and To All are always in the list when an image has objects. To Selected appears in the list when an object is selected.

TO ACTIVE This zoom setting zooms in on the object that is currently active in the Objects Docker. This setting really gets up close and personal: PHOTO-PAINT will zoom up until it fills the image screen (up to 1600%).

TO SELECTED With this setting, the zoom level is chosen by PHOTO-PAINT, so that any and all selected objects fit in the image window.

TO ALL This is just like To Selected except it applies to every object in the image. In all three of these options, the zoom setting does not include areas outside of the image. For example, if part of an object is hanging over the side of an image, and To All is selected, you will not be able to see the portion of the object that is not in the image area.

Zoom To Fit

This option changes the zoom level so that the image fits into the current window. The keyboard shortcut is F4. This is a very handy option when you want to quickly see the entire image. Remember that when you use Zoom To Fit, your zoom setting may change from 100% and you may no longer be viewing an accurate representation of the image.

The Zoom Tool (Z)

The Zoom tool, shown next and found in the Toolbox, allows you to magnify or decrease the size of your onscreen image without affecting the actual image size. To use it, click on the image to zoom in to the next preset level, right-click to zoom out to the next preset level, or click and drag a rectangle around the area you wish to zoom in on.

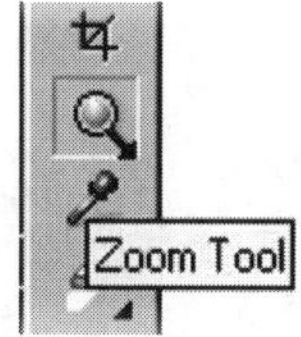

TIP: *The quickest way to activate the Zoom tool is to hold down the "Z" key while any other tool is selected. After you have finished using the Zoom tool, press the* SPACEBAR *to return to the previously selected tool.*

The Hand Tool (H)

If you zoom in enough so that the entire image is no longer visible, you can move around the image by clicking the scroll bars that appear at the side and bottom of the image window. An easier method is to use the Hand tool and drag the image. As you click and drag the image, it moves inside the window. You can select the Hand tool, which is shown below, from the Zoom tool flyout or from the Property Bar when the Zoom tool is selected.

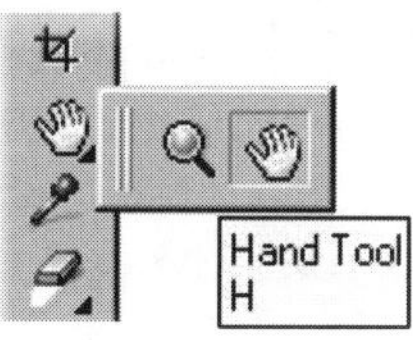

TIP: *A quick way to select the Hand tool is to press the "H" key. The Hand tool is selected as indicated by the cursor becoming a hand. Press the* SPACEBAR *to return to the previously selected tool.*

Navigator Pop-up

The Navigator pop-up is an easy-to-use image navigation tool available whenever the entire image no longer fits in its window. Placing the cursor on the icon in the lower-right corner of the image where the scroll bars meet and holding down the mouse button displays the Navigator pop-up, as shown in the following illustration. The Navigator remains open as long as the mouse button is held. The cursor moves the rectangular box in the Navigator and, as the box moves, the image moves. Releasing the mouse button closes the Navigator.

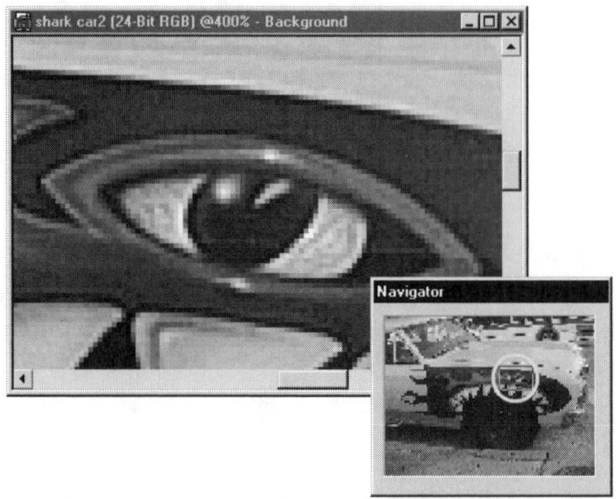

You can also activate the Navigator pop-up with the "N" key. You navigate in this window by moving the mouse, and you close the window by clicking the mouse button in the desired area.

Tools for Correcting Mistakes

Corel PHOTO-PAINT 9 has several tools that fall into two overlapping categories: those that remove previous actions and those that remove portions of the image. There are three tools in the Undo Tools flyout in the Toolbox (shown next): the Local Undo tool, the Eraser tool, and the Color Replacer tool. The Edit menu has an Undo command and the Checkpoint and Restore to Checkpoint commands. There is also the Undo/Redo Docker window, which lists the actions you have performed in sequence. Even while having as many Undo levels as your system memory resources allow, the Undo list actually works very fast. And then there is the Clone From Saved tool. Let's explore them all.

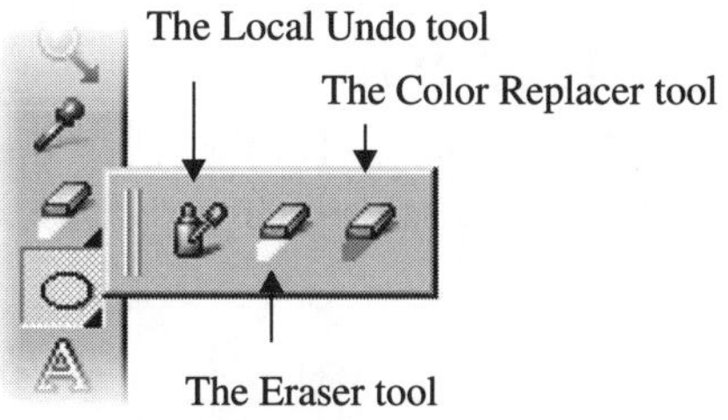

The Eraser Tool

Found on the Undo flyout in the Toolbox and on the Undo toolbar, the Eraser tool, shown here, is as simple as it gets. The Eraser tool replaces the color value of pixels in the image with the Paper (background) color as it is dragged over them. This makes it look as though that portion of the image is erased, although nothing actually is. The Eraser tool has a soft edge that makes the erased area less jagged. Don't confuse this tool with the icon to the right of the Eraser tool, showing an eraser with a gray shadow; that is the Color Replacer tool.

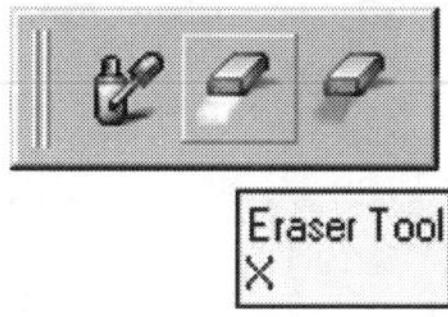

TIP: *Double-clicking on the Eraser tool button erases the selected object. Only one object can be selected and erased with this method. Notice that the object remains on the Objects Docker in name (but it is cleared). If the background is selected it completely clears the image. Think about this the next time you want to open its Property Bar by double-clicking on the button. If I had a nickel for every time I had accidentally done this . . . well, be careful.*

The Local Undo Tool (U)

Also located on the Undo Tools flyout (Toolbox) and the Undo toolbar, the Local Undo tool, shown here, allows the selective removal of the last action that was applied to the image.

Something to Try with the Local Undo Tool

While the Local Undo tool works fine for removing portions of the last applied actions, it can also be used to create some interesting effects. This demonstration will quickly show you how you can use the Local Undo tool to make a composite image from two different ones.

1. Choose File | Open and load the image EXERCISE\PHOTOS\FOREST on the Corel CD as shown in Figure 5-3.
2. Select Edit | Fill and click the Bitmap fill button and then the Edit button. Click the Load button (getting tired yet?) and when the dialog box opens, from the Corel CD-ROM, locate the file EXERCISE\PHOTOS\DENSE GREENERY. Click Open. Click OK to select the photograph we are using as a fill and OK again to apply the fill to our photograph. The imported image covers the entire image, as shown in Figure 5-4.
3. From the Eraser flyout on the Toolbox, select the Local Undo tool. In the Property Bar, change the nib size of the brush to 30 (pixels), the transparency to 0, and the soft edge to 20. Just click and drag in an area. Everywhere the brush is applied, the original image is restored. Position the brush so that it removes the portions of the image illustrated in Figure 5-5.

NOTE: *You can also use the Rectangle shape tool instead of the Edit | Fill command to place the DENSE GREENERY image over the FOREST image.*

Here are a couple of hints. First, each double-click on the Local Undo button removes the previous action in the Undo Docker. Second, try changing nib sizes to get into those hard-to-reach spots. Third, make your adjustments in the Property

FIGURE 5-3 This forest floor photograph is the start of our exercise

FIGURE 5-4 This is the photograph that replaced the original shown in the previous figure

FIGURE 5-5 A little magic with the Local Undo tool makes a great composite photograph

Bar; to find out what the controls are in the Property Bar (even I get confused), you have several options:

- Leave the cursor over the tool in question and wait for a context box to open up.
- Look at the Status Bar for a description.
- Select the Context Help tool in the Standard toolbar and then click on the control in question.
- As a last resort, you can open the Docker using CTRL-F8.

The Checkpoint Command

The Checkpoint command, located in the Edit menu as shown next, is one of the most frequently used commands in photo-editing. It lets you save a temporary copy of the current image that you can return to anytime.

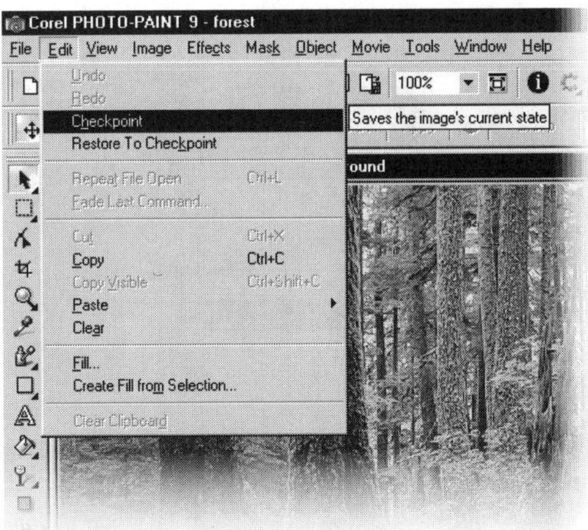

TIP: *When doing any kind of work on an image, you should get in the habit of automatically selecting the Checkpoint command each time you begin to experiment with different effects and techniques.*

The temporary file created by the Checkpoint command is closed when the image file is closed or when exiting PHOTO-PAINT (whether you planned to exit the program or it crashes). To return to the image saved by Checkpoint, select the Restore To Checkpoint command located below the Checkpoint command. This command is available only after the Checkpoint has been activated.

NOTE: *The Checkpoint command is linked to the image; you cannot save a Checkpoint file in one image and open it in another.*

The Undo/Redo Docker—Try It, You'll Like It!

The Undo/Redo Docker window, which is shown next, has been completely reworked in this release of PHOTO-PAINT. It is essentially a command recorder that frees you to experiment by providing a way to remove or restore one or more actions. If you make a change to an image that doesn't come out the way you thought it would, you can undo the change or a series of changes, and then even redo the changes you have just undone.

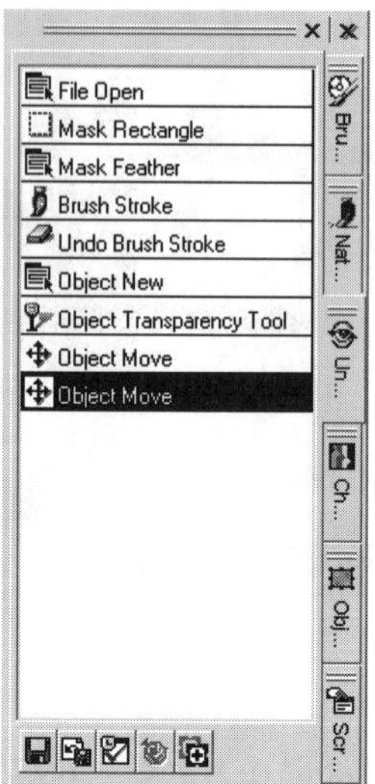

As you make changes, a list is created in sequence. By selecting an action in the list with a click of the mouse, the removed actions become grayed out. You can restore actions by clicking on them again. You cannot, however, restore or remove selected actions out of sequence.

This list continues to grow until the file is saved or the Checkpoint command is enabled. At that time, the list is cleared. The more actions that are on the list, the longer it will take your system to replay the entire list without the commands you removed, and the greater the possibility that it may not replay perfectly. Don't let that last sentence scare you. If you haven't used the Undo Docker, I strongly recommend that you try it. You will be impressed—I guarantee it.

As part of the overhaul of the Undo list, Corel has added several handy buttons at the bottom of the list, as shown in Figure 5-6.

The Save Script File As button allows you to save the Undo list as a script. The Revert to Last Saved button reverts the selected image back to what it was the last time it was saved. Checkpoint and Restore To Checkpoint were, as you remember, described in preceding paragraphs. You do remember don't you? Image Duplicate makes a duplicate of the image.

Clone From Saved—The Ultimate Undo Tool

The Cloned From Saved tool is found by selecting the Clone tool in the Paint flyout on the Toolbox and selecting the icon with the diskette in the pop-up list in the far-left corner of the Property Bar. (We will explore operation of Clone tools in

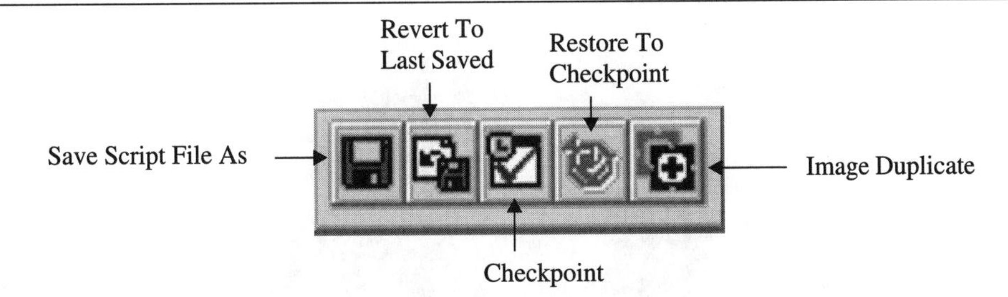

FIGURE 5-6 The bottom of the Undo/Redo Docker provides several buttons that are shortcuts to PHOTO-PAINT commands

5

greater detail in Chapter 11.) The Clone From Saved tool is actually a brush tool that uses the contents of the last saved version of an image as the source and paints it onto the same portion of the current image.

NOTE: *If you changed the size of an image since opening it, the Clone From Saved tool will not be available because the original and the current images are no longer the same size.*

Color Replacer Tool (Q)

The last tool in the Undo Tools flyout is the Color Replacer tool, shown next. On the surface, it appears not only simple but useless. It is a brush that replaces any pixels containing the Paint (foreground) color with the Paper (background) color. If only one color is replaced with another, its use would be restricted to the areas of uniform color, of which there are darned few in a color photograph.

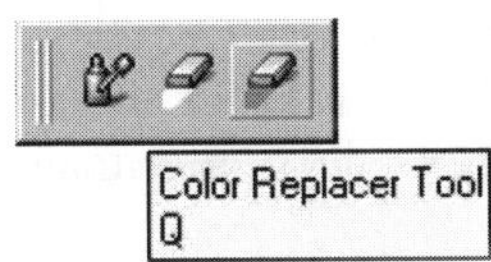

Well, the truth is, this little gem can replace a range of colors with a single color. Among other things, users can change day scenes to night or remove the matting that sometimes appears on the edge of an object. Figure 5-7(a) is a photograph of a TV remote controller (which someone at Corel categorized under computer equipment). Around the edge of the controller is the remainder of the original white background

(a) (b)

FIGURE 5-7 (a) The original photograph has a white fringe around it. (b) The Color Replacer tool is used to blend it into the background

that got included when it was made into an object. (Later in this book you will learn several different techniques to reduce or remove this fringe, formally referred to as *matting.*) By selecting the color of the fringe for the Paint color and a color similar to the background for the Paper color, the Color Replacer can instantly replace the ring around the controller, as shown in Figure 5-7(b).

To use the Color Replacer tool, use the Eyedropper tool (described next) to select the desired Paint and Paper colors and apply it either selectively with the Color Replacer brush or throughout the entire image by double-clicking it.

Getting the Right Color with the Eyedropper Tool

The secret of using the Color Replacer tool is selecting the correct color. The chances of locating the exact color you need from the onscreen palette are close to impossible, but it *is* possible with the Eyedropper tool (shown here).

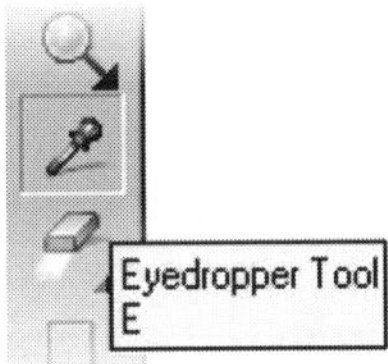

The Eyedropper tool, located in the Toolbox, is used to pick a specific color from an image by clicking on it. This tool has more uses than might first be apparent. For instance, while the Eyedropper tool is active, the color value of the pixel under the cursor is displayed in the status bar. I'll explain the usefulness of this in a moment. First, let's go through the basics of how to use the Eyedropper.

There are three color areas that can be selected using the Eyedropper tool: the Paint color, the Paper color, and the Fill color. The three color swatches on the Status Bar display the currently selected colors.

- **PAINT color** To select the Paint (foreground) color, click on the desired color with the mouse button.
- **PAPER color** To select the Paper (background) color, click on the desired color with the mouse button while holding down the CTRL key.
- **FILL color** To select the fill color, click the right mouse button.

TIP: *Holding down the CTRL and ALT keys and clicking on a color pops up the Find Color By Name dialog box. You can open the pop-up list and scroll to a specific color.*

Eyedropper Tool Hot Key

To quickly select the Eyedropper tool, press the "E" key on your keyboard. This enables the Eyedropper tool. To return to the previously selected tool, click the SPACEBAR.

TIP: *The "E" key shortcut is a quick way to get a numerical color value for a spot or area. This information is very helpful when setting Color Tolerance values.*

Eyedropper Sample Size

The Property Bar, shown in Figure 5-8, is used to set the sample size of the Eyedropper tool. By default, the Eyedropper tool samples an area one pixel wide to determine a color value. Sometimes when selecting colors for the Color Replacer tool or retouching photographs, you want an average color from an area. This is why PHOTO-PAINT gives you the ability to select different sample sizes. If you want to select a specific color, you can click the last button on the property bar, which opens up the Color Docker window. Doing this allows you to save a sampled color for other uses and is very handy for retouching.

To change the sample size, click an alternate sample size on the Property Bar. The Property Bar has a Selection setting as well as three preset sample sizes:

- **Point (1 pixel)** Default setting
- **3 × 3 Area (9 pixels)**
- **5 × 5 Area (25 pixels)**
- **Selection** Enables you to click and drag the Eyedropper tool to define any size sample area

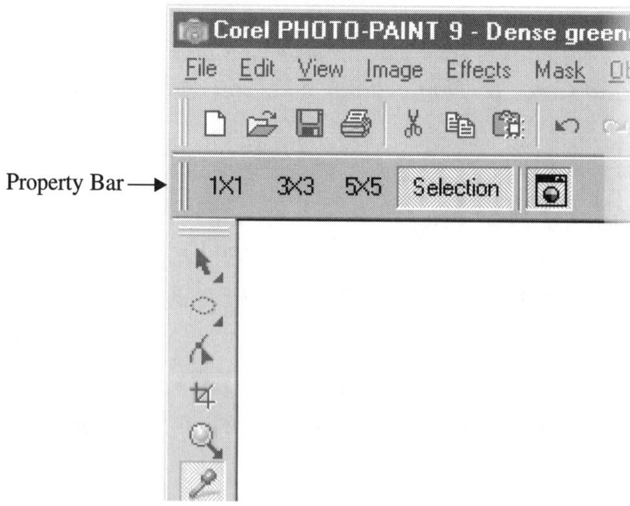

FIGURE 5-8 Setting the sample size of the Eyedropper tool is another way to determine the color that will be sampled

With every sample size (except 1 × 1), the color selected when the mouse button is clicked represents the average of all the colors in the sample area. Obviously, with the 1 × 1 setting, it represents the color value of the single pixel underneath the cursor. When sampling areas of high contrast, be aware that the averaged color may be quite different than any individual color in the sampled area. The settings made in the Property Bar affect only the Eyedropper tool; they have no effect on other tools that may use an Eyedropper to define colors, such as the Color Mask tool.

Notes on Using the Eyedropper Tool

If there are multiple objects on the image, the Eyedropper tool can read only the colors on the top object whether or not the object is active or selected. A good rule of thumb is: if you can't see it, the Eyedropper can't see it either.

When a large area is sampled and averaged, the result may be a color that, while representing the average color in the image, does not actually exist in the image. An example of this would be an area that had the same number of white and red pixels. The resulting color would be pink, even though there was no pink in the image.

Use the Eyedropper hot key ("E") when you want to see what the color value(s) is for a part of the image to help set a tool's Color Tolerance values. You would do this, for instance, when determining where a Magic Wand mask in an image is to be created. I use the "E" hot key to see what the color value is of the starting area (where I click to start the mask).

TIP: *Use the "E" hot key when retouching images. It provides a fast and easy way to pick up adjoining colors, which is critical when touching up an imperfection on a picture.*

Making the Most of Image File Management

The opening and closing of image files in PHOTO-PAINT 9 is similar in operation to most Windows applications, so I will not spend time explaining those procedures. If you need detailed information about this subject, you will find it in both the *PHOTO-PAINT 9 User's Manual* and the online help. This section covers the opening, saving, and compressing of files.

Opening a File

There are several options to make your life easier when opening a large file. You can choose the Low Res option in the File menu or choose to Resample or Crop the image before or directly after opening the large file.

Low Res

There is one feature in the File menu called Low Res that could use some explanation. It loads a low-resolution copy of a large image for you to work on. When you're finished, PHOTO-PAINT will apply the same actions to the original (larger) image. The benefit of working with smaller images is that many of the effects and other actions work noticeably faster when applied to a smaller file.

The operation of this new command is quite simple. To use, select File | Low Res | Open. Select the image you want and choose Open to open the Resample Image dialog box, shown next. Here, you determine how much smaller you want the image to be. Work on this smaller copy as you normally would and then select File | Low Res | Render. Make any adjustments in the Render Image dialog box and click OK. PHOTO-PAINT creates a new file with the applied changes on the original.

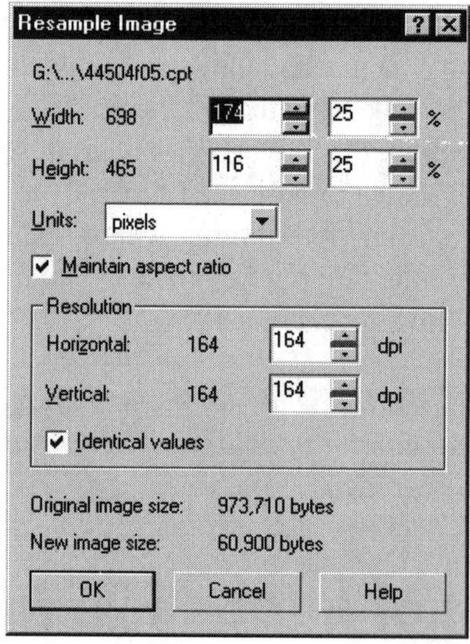

The default setting for the Low Res is 25%, meaning the final image will be reduced by 75 percent. My recommendation for selecting a size is to choose a percentage that is small enough to display at 100% on your monitor. You may find that keeping the units of measure in pixels helpful. For example, if you have an image that is 1400 pixels wide and your monitor is set for 800 × 600 pixels, you know that you are going to need to make it smaller than 800 × 600 pixels. Don't make the image so small that you have to squint to see it.

Here are a few suggestions about using Low Res. Use it when you have an exceptionally large image for your system. What constitutes a large image is determined by the amount of RAM available on your system compared to the size of the image. There's no math formula, just common sense. For example, if you are running with 32MB of RAM on your system and want to load an 80MB image, you should consider loading it using Low Res. Another thing to watch out for is applying effects that use fixed-size brushes (like Paint Alchemy). Be aware that the appearance of the Low Res version may differ slightly when the same size brush is applied to a larger image. Now on to resampling and cropping.

Resampling and Cropping

If you are opening very large images, you should consider choosing the Resample or Crop option in the Open An Image dialog box. They are found in the Full Image pop-up list. Cropping or resampling the image during the loading process saves a lot of system resources that might otherwise be tied up opening a very large image and then having to either resample or crop it. Resample on Open is the same command that is executed when you open Low Res. The difference is that this image doesn't have the Render command, which the Low Res does.

NOTE: *The Resample option available when opening files can only reduce file size—it cannot increase it.*

Saving a File

Although some of the information that follows was mentioned in Chapter 2, it bears repeating. To open the Save an Image to Disk dialog box, choose File | Save As. The Files of Type pop-up menu has several options; the native and compression formats are explained next. If you have masks and objects in your file, only the native formats will be available. If all have been combined with the background, the compression formats will also be available in the Save an Image to Disk dialog box.

Going Native—It's the Best Way

You should always save your original files in the native PHOTO-PAINT format. When an image is saved in PHOTO-PAINT format, all of the masks, objects, and layers are saved with it. The same cannot be said of other file formats.

Wonders and Dangers of Compressed Files

With your original safely saved as a CPT file, you can use the Save As command in the File menu to save the file in a different format suitable for archiving or distributing on the Internet. Compressed files have been around for some time. Corel PHOTO-PAINT offers several compression schemes for its files, including the CPT files. The types of compression fall into two general categories: *lossless* and *lossy*. These categories are also referred to as *nondestructive* and *destructive* compression, which should give you some hint about why we save an image in the CPT format before compressing it.

LOSSLESS COMPRESSION With lossless compression (for example, Packbits or LZW), the process of compressing and decompressing is not destructive to the image. The compressed image is identical to the original image. While it is nondestructive, its compression ratio is usually only 2:1. This is why lossless compression is used for graphics files that are being archived or those going to the service bureau where quality and accuracy are required. It is not a practical solution for the Internet.

LOSSY COMPRESSION During the process of compressing the graphic with lossy compression, some of the image information is forever lost. If you choose a high-quality compression, very little of the image information that can be detected by the human eye is lost; however, the greater the amount of compression, the poorer the resulting image quality will be. The most commonly used lossy compression is JPEG. Other lossy compression formats include the photo-CD (PCD) format and the Wavelet format, which is increasingly popular on the Internet as more and more Web sites are supporting it.

Compression Comparison

A picture is still worth 1,000 words (50 if it is compressed). The Wavelet Compressed Bitmap (WI) option is located in the Save an Image to Disk dialog box. Wavelet compression has a Compression range of 1 to 100, with a setting of 1 offering the best image and least compression, and a setting of 100 producing a very small but nearly unrecognizable image. With Wavelet compression, you can use settings up to 40 or 50 without any really noticeable image degradation. (The dialog box has preview options.) At a setting of 40, our 540KB file is reduced to a mere 2.7KB.

Using a JPEG setting of 2 compresses the image to 16KB. JPEG compression offers a quality factor range of 0 to 100. PHOTO-PAINT 9 offers the ability to preview the effect of your compression setting, as shown here:

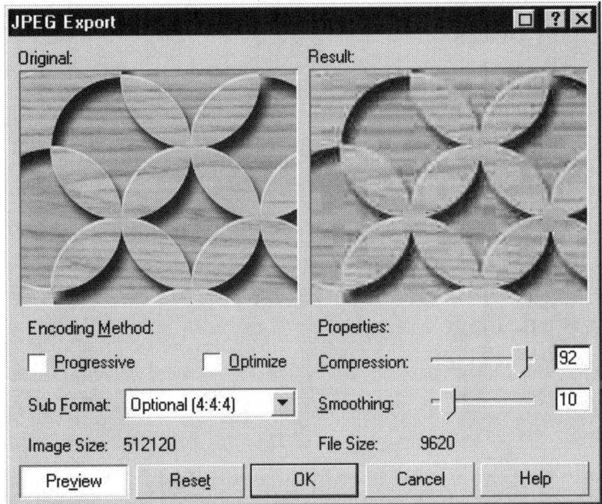

Compression Considerations

The hazard of using compression formats results from either applying too much compression when initially saving the image or continually opening, changing, and saving using a lossy compression format. We have already discussed the problems of applying too much compression. Many users do not know that every time a lossless compressed image is opened, changed, and saved, more of the image quality is lost. The best way to make changes is to open the CPT original and then save the changed file as both a CPT and a JPEG.

Closing Thoughts

We have covered a broad range of PHOTO-PAINT tools. While I realize that some of them may seem about as interesting as 40 pounds of wet fertilizer, they make the day-to-day job of working with PHOTO-PAINT easier and more productive. Now that we know how to use the tools to handle an image, in the next chapter we are going to learn how to manipulate the image itself.

CHAPTER 6

Image Size, Direction, and Format

Just as images don't always come in the desired size, they also don't always come in the desired orientation. When you are laying out a newsletter, for instance, it seems that when you get the images you want, they are inevitably facing the wrong direction. You usually want them facing inward if they are on the outside edge, and facing outward if they are on the inside edge. (I knew you knew that; I just thought I would throw it in.) Corel PHOTO-PAINT offers a collection of commands to allow the image to be reoriented quickly and easily; the majority of this chapter is committed to these commands, which are found in the Image menu.

The Duplicate Command

The Duplicate command produces a new file that is a copy of the original image. When you select Duplicate in the Image menu, a dialog box opens, as shown next. You have two decisions to make. First, you either enter a name for the duplicate file or accept the name generated by Corel PHOTO-PAINT. Second, you must decide whether to use Merge Objects with Background. If you don't know what objects are, don't be concerned; they are explored in Chapter 12. For now, objects can be thought of as bitmap images that float on top of the picture. The Merge Objects with Background option gives you the choice of making the duplicate image either with all of the objects as they are in the original or with all of the objects merged into the background. Once they are merged, they are no longer objects. The Duplicate command becomes important when you must produce copies of an image to create things like Displacement maps (which are explored in Chapter 14).

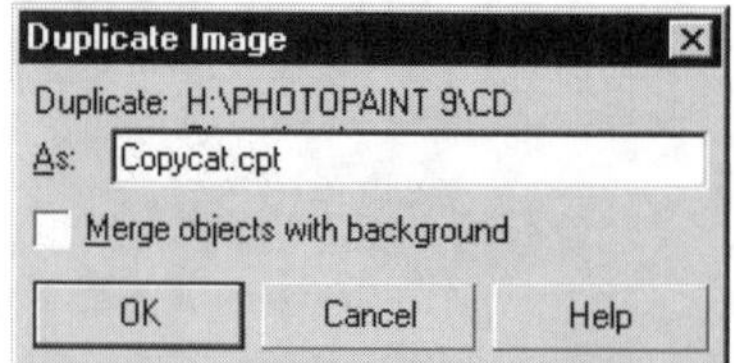

The Flip Command

This command makes either a vertical or a horizontal mirrored copy of the original image. To use the Flip command, select Image | Flip. A pop-up menu appears, as shown next, presenting the two choices: Horizontally and Vertically. Clicking on either of these executes the command, producing a copy of the image with the selected effect.

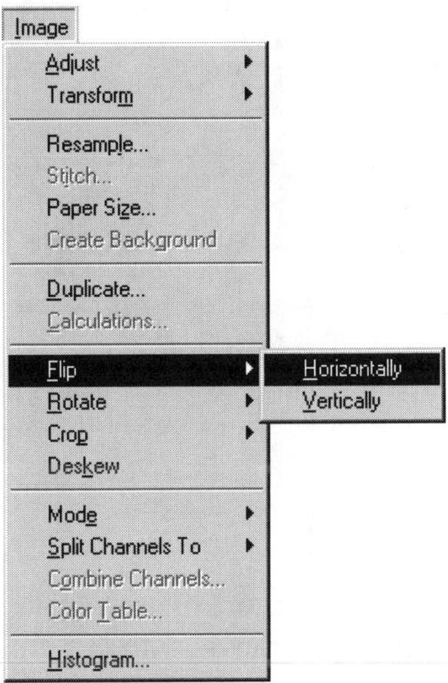

TIP: *Before using the Flip command, examine the image carefully to make sure that the image doesn't contain any text. More than once I have seen ads of nationally recognized sports figures holding footballs or basketballs on which the text was backward.*

Now, if these commands seem pointless to you, you are not using your imagination. Remember that the best tool in Corel PHOTO-PAINT is located between your ears. The AIR SHOW image in Figure 6-1 was made with PHOTO-PAINT-5. It began with a single jet. Using the Duplicate command, a second copy of the entire image was made. The Flip Horizontal command was used to make a horizontal mirror copy of the original. The Paper Size command was used to double the width of the original. The original was copied to the Clipboard and pasted as an object into the duplicate. The text and shadows were created with the Text tool.

FIGURE 6-1 This web banner was simple to create, thanks to the Duplicate command

The Rotate Command

Rotate offers the ability to rotate the entire image. Again, this may not seem like much, but there are many things you can do with this little command. Let's say you are laying out a sports magazine. You have a story about the playoffs that needs a graphic to introduce it. Everybody uses the picture of the arena packed with screaming fans and sweaty players. You want something different. You find what you want in a stock photo, as shown next. The problem is that it is a vertical photo and you wanted something to cover several columns. The problem is remedied with the Rotate command.

The original photo from the PhotoDisc library is great, but it's not wide enough to cover several columns. In the Image | Rotate dialog box, 90 degrees Clockwise was selected from the pop-up menu and produced the image shown next.

The operation took less than two minutes, you met your deadline, your editor is happy with you. Of course, if you had more time (10 minutes) and had already learned how to create and rotate objects, you could have made the graphic shown in Figure 6-2.

By using the Rotate command and a little imagination, you can create excellent banners for magazines, brochures, and so on. The first step in creating the image shown in Figure 6-2 was to make the horizontal image of the arm and hand holding the basketball into an object. The object was duplicated and rotated and its transparency was increased by 15 percent. This was repeated several times to create the image shown.

FIGURE 6-2 This is actually easier to create than you might imagine

Rotating an Image

To rotate an image, choose Image | Rotate and a pop-up menu appears with the available choices. Selecting Custom opens the Custom Rotate dialog box, shown next.

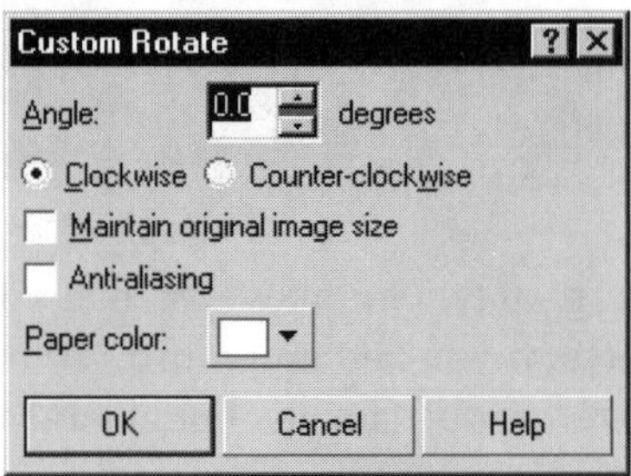

NOTE: *If the original image has objects, they will all become visible in the rotated copy. They will not be merged. This includes the hidden objects. (If you are bewildered by those last few sentences, they will become clearer when you get to Chapter 12.)*

The Custom Rotate Dialog Box

The Custom Rotate dialog box enables you to rotate the current image by a specified amount. A new image is created from the results of the rotation. The variables are as follows:

- **Degrees** Enter the amount of the rotation in whole numbers. *Warning*: The dialog box allows input of decimal numbers without giving any indication that it isn't using them.
- **Direction** Click the Clockwise or Counterclockwise radio buttons to determine the direction of rotation.
- **Maintain Original Image Size** When this check box is selected, the image height and width dimensions are fixed. The rotated image is cropped at the image boundaries. If this is left unselected, the dimensions of the image are automatically calculated (adjusted) to fit the edges of the rotated image.
- **Anti-aliasing** When enabled, this check box reduces "jaggies" on rotated images but may soften the image being rotated.
- **Paper Color** From the pop-up Color palette, you can define the color of the new background that is added when Maintain Original Size is not selected.

Nachos Supreme with the Rotate Command

Here is a quick exercise to show how you can make a placard for a cafe in no time at all. If you are reading this book from start to finish, you may not understand all of the commands—but fear not, as you read on, they will begin to make sense.

1. Choose File | Open and open the file EXERCISE\PHOTOS\NACHOS AND SALSA on the CD-ROM.

2. We are going to create a new Paper color from a color in the photograph. With the cursor over the image, press (but do not hold down) the "e" key, changing the cursor to the Eyedropper. Now hold down the ALT key and place the cursor over the image so that it is inside of the candle and on the pottery, as indicated by the arrow in the next illustration. Click the mouse once and the Paper color, as seen in the Status Bar, changes to match it. Click the SPACEBAR to return to your previous tool mode.

3. Select Image | Rotate | Custom. In the Custom Rotate dialog box, enter **15** in the Angle value box and check Clockwise and the Anti-aliasing box. Click OK. The result is shown next.

4. Change the Paint color to yellow by clicking one time on the yellow color swatch in the Color palette.

5. Click the Text button in the Toolbox (it looks like the letter *A*). In the Property Bar, change the Font to Bremen Bd BT and the Size to 96. (The font isn't critical; if you don't have Bremen installed, pick one you like.)

6. Click on the image and type **NACHOS**. Next, click on the Object Picker tool at the top of the Toolbox (the text becomes an object) and move the type so that it looks like Figure 6-3.

7. For the final step, select the Drop Shadow tool from the Toolbox. Select the settings you like and click the default setting (you may want to reduce the opacity). Click the Apply button and you are done. The result is shown in Figure 6-3.

TIP: *Anti-aliasing or not, the edge of this image has some minor "jaggies" after rotation. To correct this, I chose the Blend brush from the Effect tools (Chapter 10) and smoothed over the rough edges—so to speak.*

Resizing an Image

Resizing an image is a common practice in word processing and page layout programs. There is more to resizing than first you might imagine.

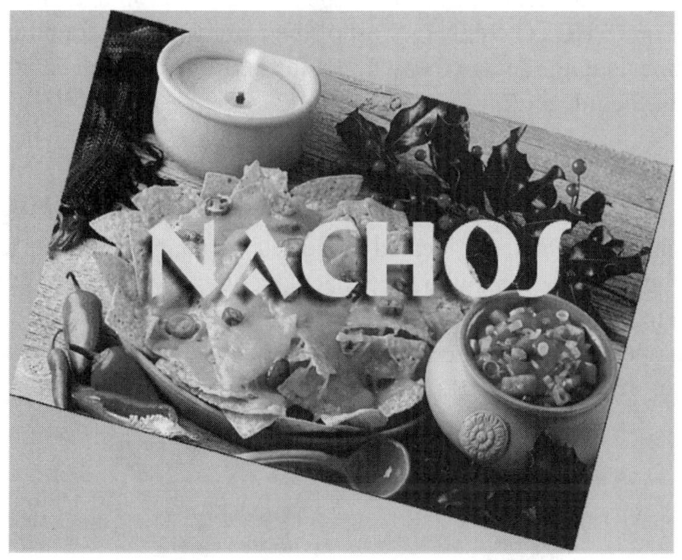

FIGURE 6-3 It only takes us a few steps and some basic tools to create this placard

Why You Shouldn't Resize or Crop an Image in Other Applications

Many page layout programs like Corel VENTURA, PageMaker, and Quark offer graphic cropping and resizing as part of the program. These features are usually fine for very minor image adjustments, but for any significant changes you should open the files in Corel PHOTO-PAINT and make the changes there. There are several reasons for doing so, as follows:

- If you crop a large image file in a word processing or page layout program, the file size remains unchanged. Even if you use only five percent of a 16MB image file, the entire file remains as part of the document file. Large document files create problems with lengthy print times and difficulty in transport to a service bureau. If you crop that same 16MB file in Corel PHOTO-PAINT, it becomes an 800K file.
- Resizing bitmap files in these applications can cause image distortion, which often shows up as unwanted moiré patterns over the entire image.

There are many different ways to change the size of an image once it has been loaded into Corel PHOTO-PAINT. Most of the commands are found in the Image menu. Commands in the Image menu affect the entire image and cannot be applied to a portion of the image.

How to Display Information About an Image

The Document Info command, located in the File menu, gives the current size and resolution of an image, along with other data, as shown next. Please note that the Document Info window is not a dialog box. Information is displayed but cannot be edited. Once opened, the Document Info window must be closed by clicking the OK button before any other actions can occur.

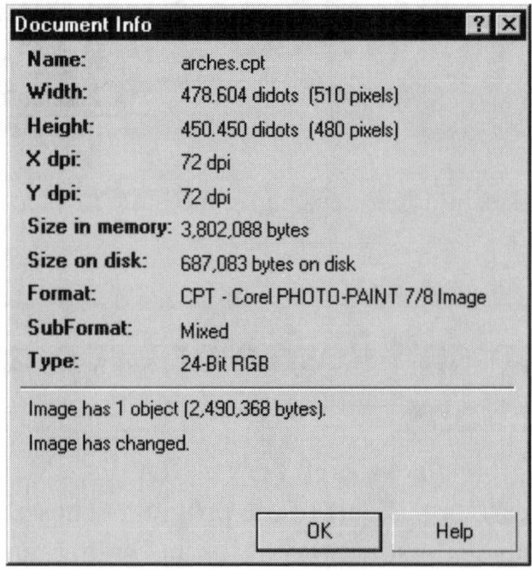

Another way to access the Document Info window is to click the Info button (the one with the lowercase "i") on the Standard toolbar. In the illustration shown next, I have circled the Document Info button on the toolbar as well as annotating the command in the File menu—in case you couldn't figure that one out. You can also click on the icon in the left corner of the image's Title Bar.

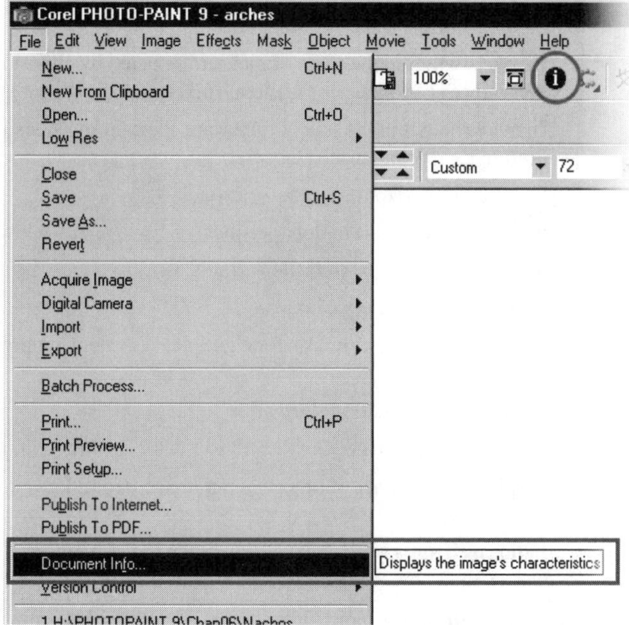

Image-File Information (Bigger Is Not Better)

Table 6-1 explains the information that is displayed in the Document Info message box just shown.

You will probably find yourself using the Info command more than you would expect. Generally, I use it most to check the dimensions (in pixels) of my image file and to verify the format of the image.

Resizing the Image Window

Although this feature is not directly related to image resizing, it is essential for working with images. To resize the Image window, move the cursor to the bottom-right corner of the Image window. Click and drag the Image window until

Name:	Filename of the selected image file
Width:	Displays width in the units of measure selected by choosing Edit | Preferences | Workspace | General (pixels always shown in parentheses)
Height:	Displays height in the units of measure selected by choosing Edit | Preferences | Workspace | General
X dpi:	Resolution (horizontal) in dots-per-inch
Y dpi:	Resolution (vertical) in dots-per-inch
Size in Memory:	Size of the uncompressed file
Original File Size:	Size of file after it is saved
Format:	Type of image file format—for example, Wavelet Compressed Bitmap (WI)
Subformat:	Displays compression information
Type:	Color Mode of Image: Grayscale, 256 color, 24-bit color, and so on
Objects:	Displays the number of objects in an image (Corel PHOTO-PAINT format only)
Status:	Indicates if any changes have been made to the image since it was opened

TABLE 6-1 The Document Info Command Provides a Wealth of Information About an Image

it is the desired size. The image size remains unchanged, and a gray border appears around the original image.

It is very helpful to increase the image area size when working on an image close to the edge. When you are working with various Corel PHOTO-PAINT tools near the edge of the image, the program reacts when the cursor touches the Image window's border. Increasing the view area prevents the cursor from changing into a double-headed arrow any time the edge is approached. Another way to prevent edge interaction is to increase the size of the non-printing border using the Overscroll settings in the dialog box, shown next, that is accessed by Tools | Options | Workspace | General. A quicker way is the CTRL-J keypress.

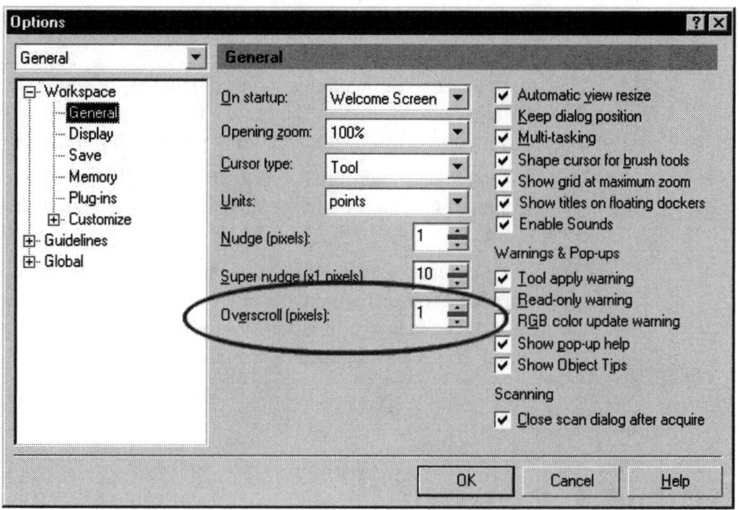

6

TIP: *For a quick resize of the image in order to see it better, grab the corner of the window and drag it until it is the size you desire, then press the Zoom To Fit (F4) key.*

Changing the Size of an Image

Images are rarely provided to you in the exact size that is required for your project. In the old days, when we needed to change the size of an image, we made a PMT (photo-mechanical transfer) of the image, which could then be reduced or enlarged. Fortunately, Corel PHOTO-PAINT provides several much simpler ways to change both the size and the surrounding working area of an image. There are several ways to change the size of an image. They include *resampling* and *cropping* and their variations.

Resizing Methods	Description
Resampling	This command makes the image larger or smaller by adding or subtracting pixels. It can also change the resolution of the image, thereby affecting the printed size without adding or subtracting pixels.
Deskew Crop Tool	This tool acts like a traditional cropping tool. It allows you to define a specific area of an image and to remove all of the area outside the defined area.
Paper Size	This handy command uses a combination of resampling and cropping. The Paper Size command increases the overall image size by increasing the size of the base image. It is as if you put a larger sheet of paper under the original. It can also be used to crop the image.

The Resample Command

The resolution and the dimensions of an image in Corel PHOTO-PAINT can be changed using the Resample command. One of the best aspects of the Resample command is that it can change the size of an image without the need for you to grab the old calculator to work out the math. Resampling should not be confused with the scaling features of CorelDRAW or other DTP programs like PageMaker and Quark. These applications stretch or compress the bitmap images, often resulting in serious distortion. Resampling actually re-creates the image, adding or subtracting pixels as required. Increasing the size of the image is called *upsampling* and is not recommended. Decreasing the image size is called *downsampling* and can be used without much concern. Figure 6-4 shows the effects of upsampling a photograph.

TIP: *Be aware that adding or subtracting pixels from an image decreases the quality of an image. Having said that, resampling remains the best way to change the size of an existing image. If you must resample, downsample (making the image smaller) and avoid upsampling (making the image larger.)*

Two Approaches to Resampling

Resampling an image with Corel PHOTO-PAINT 9 falls into two general categories: fixed resolution and variable resolution. Each method changes the image size, and each has its own advantages and disadvantages.

FIGURE 6-4 The original (shown on the left) was upsampled to 200 percent (middle) and to 800 percent (right)

Fixed Resolution Resampling

With this method, the resolution of the image remains unchanged, while the dimensions are either increased or decreased. Wait! Didn't I explain in Chapter 2 that if the dimensions are increased, the resolution had to decrease? I did. But if the resolution is fixed, Corel PHOTO-PAINT must either add or subtract pixels from the image to make it fit the new dimensions entered.

When the space between the pixels increases, Corel PHOTO-PAINT creates more pixels to keep the resolution constant. When you resample, Corel PHOTO-PAINT goes through the entire image, comparing pairs of adjacent pixels and creating pixels that represent the average tonal value. I told you that so you would know why your computer seems to take so long to resample an image.

Conversely, when the dimensions of the image decrease, as was the case with the original file of our Nachos exercise, Corel PHOTO-PAINT subtracts pixels from the image. This sounds ideal, doesn't it? Actually, you always lose some detail when you resample an image, regardless of whether you add or subtract pixels. There is no magic here. The greater the amount of resampling, the greater the amount of image degradation introduced.

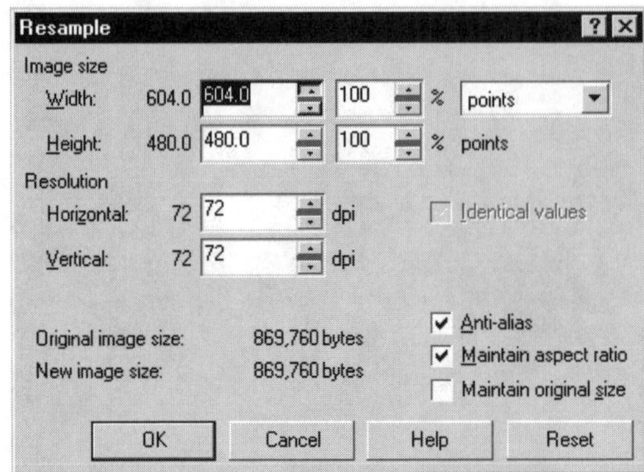

If the Maintain Aspect Ratio box in the Resample dialog box, just shown, is checked, any change made to one dimension will automatically change the other. By disabling Maintain Aspect, it is possible to change one value without causing the other to change. Whenever you change the aspect ratio of an image, you introduce distortion. The distortion will be noticeable if the values entered vary too greatly from the original aspect ratio.

Another consideration when using the fixed resolution method is the increase in file size. Table 6-2 shows how quickly file sizes increase when a photo-CD (300 dpi) file is increased in size using fixed resolution resampling.

Size Increase	File Size
100%	1.01MB
200%	4.03MB
300%	9.82MB
400%	17.23MB

TABLE 6-2 The Effects of Increasing File Size When Image Size Is Increased

Variable Resolution Resampling

The other resampling method is the one I generally use (when I must use one). Variable resolution resampling is accomplished by clicking the button labeled Maintain Original Size. By forcing PAINT to keep the file size (number of pixels) unchanged, the resolution is changed to fit the newly requested image size. You can safely allow the resolution to be reduced to 150 dpi for grayscale and 100–120 dpi for color images.

The advantages of this method are that the file size remains the same and the operation is instantaneous. The reason it happens so quickly is that the image is not physically altered. Only information in the file header is changed because that is where the resolution information is maintained.

The disadvantage to this method is the loss of image detail that results from the lower resolution. In most cases, if you keep the resolution at the recommended levels for the type of image you are working with, you should be able to resize the image without any noticeable loss of image detail. I recommend disabling Maintain Aspect when using variable resolution resampling (Maintain Original Size enabled).

TIP: *When resampling by changing resolution, you cannot see any physical change in the displayed image while in Corel PHOTO-PAINT because the program maps each pixel of the image to a pixel on the display, regardless of the resolution setting. To see the effect, you must save the image and print it.*

The Resample Dialog Box

The Resample dialog box can be opened by choosing Image | Resample. A similar dialog box, Resample Image, is opened by selecting the Resample option in the Open an Image (File | Open) dialog box, shown next. The Resample option that is available on the Open an Image dialog box is identical to the Resample command, with one exception. The Resample command can increase or decrease the image size, while the Resample option on Open an Image can be used only to decrease image size.

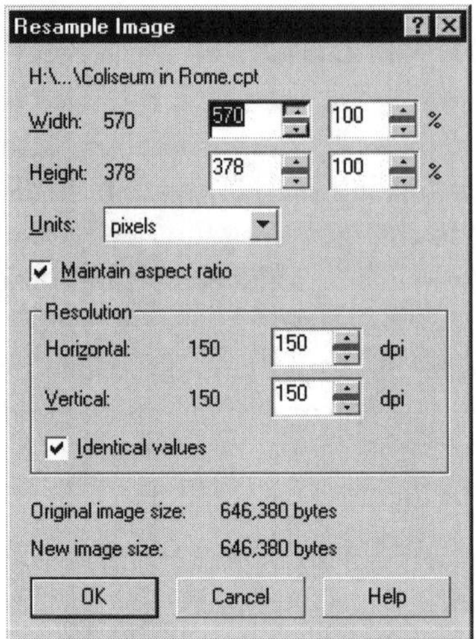

When changing resolution, remember that resolution settings that are greater than what the final output device can support will result in large image files that require extra printing time without improvement in output quality. Table 6-3 describes the Resample dialog box controls. It's not very interesting reading, but it contains handy information when you need it.

Option	Description
Units	Choose a unit of measurement from the pop-up menu.
Width/Height	Enter a number, or use the scroll arrows to choose a size (entered in units of measure), or enter a percentage in the % box. The dimensions of the image remain proportional to the original. Any value entered in one box will cause the other box to change proportionally if the Maintain Aspect check box is checked.
Horizontal/Vertical	Enter a resolution value or let PAINT select a value for you. Resolution is measured in dots-per-inch (dpi).
Maintain Aspect Ratio	If you enable Maintain Aspect Ratio, values in the Width/ Height and Resolution boxes remain proportional to the original values. For example, if you increase the height by 50 percent, the width will be increased by 50 percent. The Horizontal and Vertical resolutions also remain equal.
Maintain Original Size	When selected, this option keeps the file size the same as the original, regardless of the resolution values or Width/Height values. This option is used to resample the image by changing the resolution. Changes in resolution are not reflected on the display, only when printed.

TABLE 6-3 The Resample Dialog Box Controls

Option	Description
Original Image Size	This option displays the size of the original image.
New Image Size	This option displays the calculated size of the resampled version based on the values entered in the dialog box.
Reset	Returns all the values in the dialog box to the values of the original image when the Resample dialog box was opened.

TABLE 6-4 The Resample Dialog Box Controls *(continued)*

Cropping an Image

Cropping involves the removal of part of an image either to change its size or to enhance the composition of the subject matter. The Deskew Crop tool is in the Toolbox just under the Mask tool flyout. There is also a Crop command in the Image menu and a Crop option on the Open an Image dialog box. There are several different ways to crop an open image. To access the choices below, select the Deskew Crop tool and right-click in the image containing a mask—a pop-up menu appears:

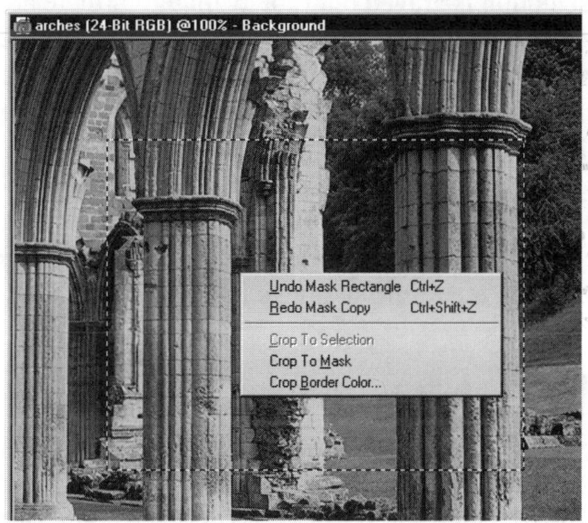

Right-clicking offers the following three choices for cropping:

- Crop to Selection
- Crop to Mask
- Crop Border Color

Crop to Selection

After you select the Deskew Crop tool, shown next, draw a rectangular bounding box that surrounds the subject and excludes the area you wish to crop. You can move the rectangle or size it using the handles that surround the box. Double-clicking the rectangle crops the image to the shape of the rectangle. Instead of double-clicking the mouse, you may right-click the mouse button and choose Crop to Selection from the pop-up menu.

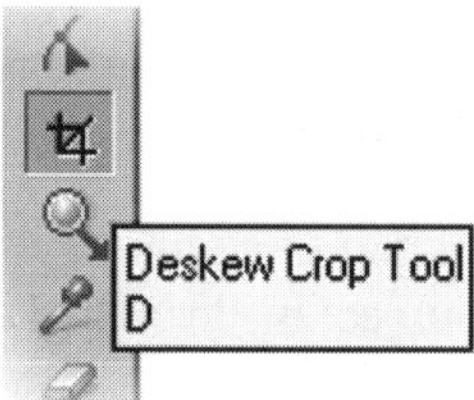

Crop to Mask

The Crop to Mask option is grayed out (not available) if there are no masks in the image. This option operates like Crop to Selection except that it crops to a mask rather than to a rectangle created by the Crop tool. To crop an area, begin by surrounding it with a mask. Select the Crop tool and right-click inside of the mask. Choose Crop to Mask.

Regardless of the type of mask you place on the image—circle, trapezoid, and so on—the Crop to Mask feature will calculate a rectangular area that will fit all of the points on the mask you have used. Figure 6-5 shows the original photograph with a circle mask on it; the resulting image is rectangular.

Crop Border Color

The Crop Border Color command removes borders of a particular color from an image. An example would be the ugly black border that seems to surround so many of the early photo-CDs. The idea is to select the color of the border and click the button, and the black border disappears. In theory, that is the way it is supposed to work. The problem is that nearly all borders are irregular and, since all crops must be rectangular, pieces of the original border do not get cropped.

(a) (b)

FIGURE 6-5 Even though this image (a) has an round mask, when we apply Crop to Mask the resulting image (b) is rectangular

The operation of the Crop Border Color option is a two-step process. After you select the Crop tool, you right-click on the image to be cropped and select Crop Border Color from the pop-up menu. This opens the Crop Border Color dialog box, as shown next.

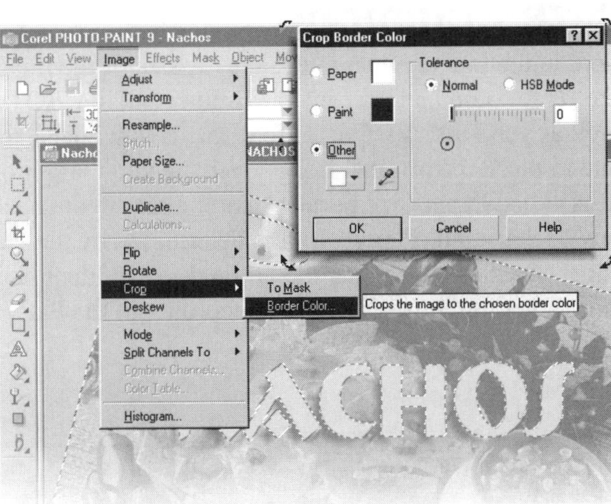

It is from the Crop Border Color dialog box that you select the color that will be used as the border color to be removed. The Crop Border Color dialog box lets you crop out the paper color, paint color, or a custom color you select from an image. The sensitivity of the cropping is controlled using the Tolerance slider associated with the two modes, Normal and HSB. These sliders control just how many shades of colors will be included in the cropping action.

A word of warning here. If the Tolerance slider is set to zero, only an exact match of the Paint color will be cropped. While the black on the border looks like the black Paint color, it may only be a close approximation. As you go through the book, you will learn about shading and numerical color values. To crop to the border color, you can increase the Tolerance (a setting between 5-10 will suffice); don't go crazy and set the Tolerance to a large value such as 200. When the Tolerance value gets large enough, it reaches a threshold that I call the "avalanche point." When it is set at such a point, almost all colors in the image are included in the border color.

For border colors that are not black or white, I recommend that you use the Eyedropper tool to select the color from the image to be cropped. Your chances of finding the right color in a standard palette are very slim. When using the Eyedropper tool to get a color match, remember that most border colors are not uniform and you will still need to increase the Tolerance if you are going to include the entire border. Of the two Tolerance modes to choose from, Normal and HSB, stay with Normal and don't worry about the HSB for the Crop Border Color command.

The Paper Size Command

Another command in the Image menu to change the size of the image area is called Paper Size. This command was changed somewhat in PHOTO-PAINT 9, but, as in its previous versions, is still used to create a new image area in the specified size and to place the original image unchanged on larger or smaller paper (background). It is called Paper Size because Corel refers to the background as "Paper." The new background (Paper) color is determined by the Paper Color setting. If the Paper Size is smaller than the original image, the image is cropped; if the paper size is larger, the image is placed according to the Placement selection made in the dialog box, shown next.

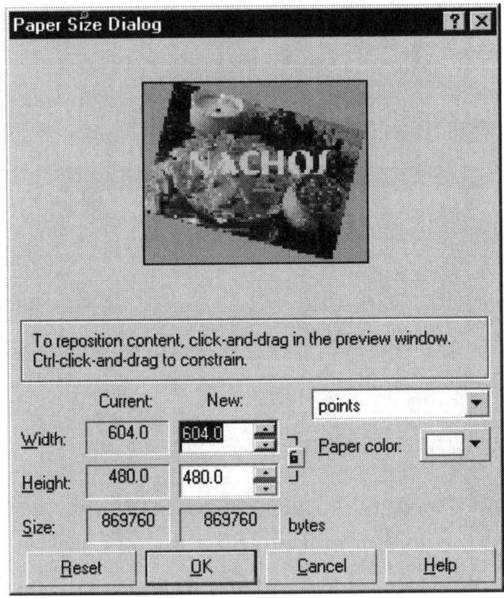

The Paper Size Dialog Box

The Width/Height values determine the new width and height of the paper according to the units of measurement. If the lock icon is enabled, the width and height values maintain their proportion to one another. The placement of the original is determined by use of the hand cursor in the Preview window to move the image to the correct location.

Making a Poster with the Paper Size and Duplicate Commands

You will find that the Paper Size command in Corel PHOTO-PAINT is very useful for a variety of projects. In this hands-on exercise, we will create the background for a poster using the Paper Size, Duplicate, and Flip commands.

1. Open the file EXERCISE\PHOTOS\LOOKING AT YOU. Click the OK button.

2. Choose Image | Duplicate and, when the dialog box opens, name the duplicate image "Righteye." Then, select Image | Flip | Horizontally.
3. Mask the entire image (CTRL-SHIFT-A) and copy it to the Clipboard (CTRL-C). Minimize the Righteye image.
4. Select the original image and choose Image | Paper Size. When the dialog box opens, make sure the lock is not enabled and then change the Units of measure to pixels and the Width value to 1280. Hold down the CTRL key and click and drag the image to the far-left side of the image window. Click the OK button. Press F4 to see the resulting image as shown in Figure 6-6.
5. Choose Edit | Paste | Paste as New Object to paste Righteye as an object in the original.
6. Select Object | Arrange | Align and Distribute (CTRL-A). When the dialog box opens, set it to Vertically: Center and Horizontally: Right, as shown next. Click the OK button. The image now fills the image window, as shown in Figure 6-7.

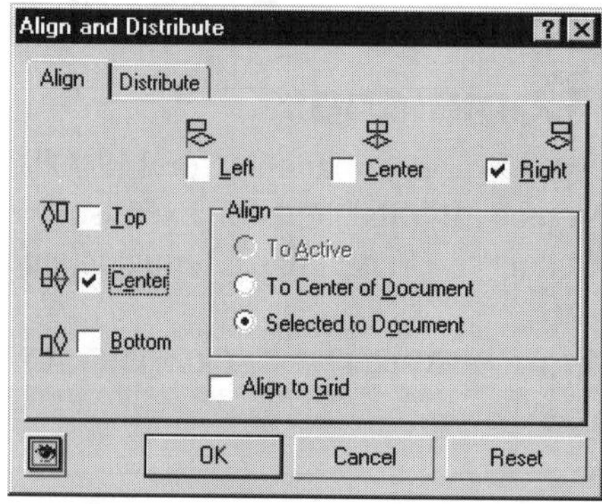

7. Select Object | Combine | Combine Objects With Background.

FIGURE 6-6 The Paper Size command expands the image background without changing the original image

8. Choose the Crop tool from the Toolbox. Place the cursor in the upper-left corner of the image, click and drag it to the lower-right corner of photograph. Do not include the white area on the right side if there is any. Double-click inside the image to complete the crop. This completes the background for the poster.
9. Save the file as WALLEYES; we will use it again in Chapter 15.

FIGURE 6-7 After putting the pieces together, the wall is beginning to develop an attitude

Tips on Changing Paper Size

The Paper Size command can be used to precisely crop an image by changing the paper size to the desired value and selecting centered placement. By moving the image with the cursor, it is possible to place the image at the exact desired position on the new paper size. Paper Size provides a method of placing an image on a larger background. You can make borders around an existing image. Try using Paper Size several times on the same image with complementary colors to make a quick border.

Image Conversion

One of the many features of PHOTO-PAINT is its ability to convert images from one graphics format to another. We discussed file formats and color depth in some detail in Chapter 2. Now we will learn about how to convert the files. The File | Save As command offers a wide variety of different formats (EPS, TIF, and so on); the File | Export command readies the file for other applications; and the Image | Mode options change the color mode of the image for work in PHOTO-PAINT.

The Mode Command—Where Most Conversions Take Place

This command used to be called Convert To, which I thought was a lot more descriptive. Think about it, do you want to change the mode of the image or convert the format? *Sigh.* The operation is quite simple. With an image selected, open Image | Mode and choose the desired format, as shown next. The formats that are unavailable are grayed out. With a Paletted (8-bit) image, for example, the Duotone option is grayed out because the image must be a grayscale to create a duotone. However, the Paletted option is still available because there are other valid choices.

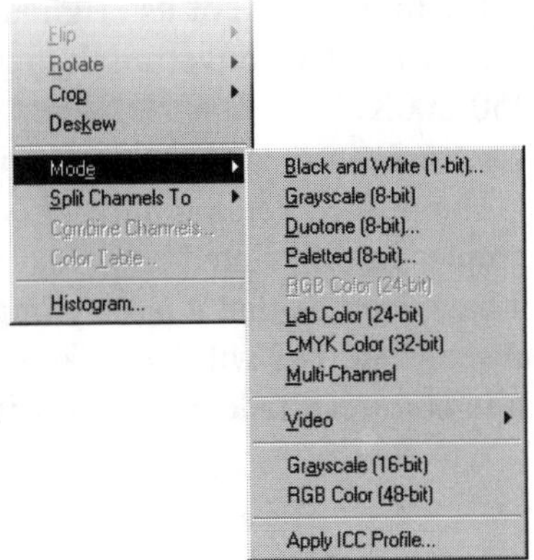

The selection of a format begins the conversion process. Remember that this process, unlike Export, does not create a copy of the image; the original will be converted. If you do not want to change the original, use the Export command to change the format or use the Save As command in the File menu to save the file under a new name before you convert it.

Why Change?

There are situations that require changing the format of an image. For example, I am a graphics illustrator at Motorola and use PHOTO-PAINT to create marketing material that must go to a color printer. No one has ever said, "Dave, just send it in any format your ol' pea-picking heart desires." No, the printers I work with, like those everywhere, have very specific size and format requirements. Most of our conversations sound like someone reading a launch preflight sequence for the space shuttle.

The advantages of converting should also be considered. Converting color images to grayscale can save enormous amounts of disk space when producing graphics that will be printed in grayscale. Converting a 24-bit color image to grayscale reduces the image file to one-third of its original size. For example, if the original 24-bit color image is 1.1MB, converting it to grayscale will result in a file size of approximately 250-300K.

Another use of the conversion feature is to view color images for pages that will be printed in grayscale. The printed version of this book is an example of that type of work. All of the examples in the printed book (except for the color insert) are printed with black ink. I have learned that it is very important to convert the images to grayscale so I can see what they will look like when they appear in the book. Colors that look great in color can fade completely in grayscale.

The Mode Options

Opening the Mode command presents you with a list of eleven different format options. At the very end of the list is an option to change the ICC profile that is associated with the image. Two of the options, Grayscale (16-bit) and RGB (48-bit), will not accept many of the Effects menu options; they are there as a result of several scanner manufacturers making unprocessed scan data available. Normally, this scan data is processed by the scanner and results in either 8-bit Grayscale or 24-bit RGB color. In short, there is no advantage to working with this data, and most filters (either Corel's or any one else's for that matter) will not work with it. Below is a short description of the options; we cover Duotones and Paletted in detail in this chapter. To convert an image, select Mode in the Image menu. A pop-up menu opens with the following choices:

Black and White (1-bit)	The image is converted to black and white (not to be confused with grayscale). This selection opens another dialog box, with the numerous choices that are explored in Chapter 2.
Grayscale (8-bit)	This converts the image to grayscale.
Duotone (8-bit)	This converts a grayscale image into a duotone image.
Paletted (8-bit)	This converts the image to 256 colors. (See additional discussion later in this chapter.)
RGB Color (24-bit)	This converts an image to 24-bit color (also called True-Color or 16.7 million color). It uses eight bits of data for each of the three channels of Red, Green, and Blue (RGB).
*L*a*b* Color (24-bit)*	This converts an image to 24-bit color using eight bits of data for each of the LAB channels.

CMYK Color (32-bit)	The 24-bit image is composed of three 8-bit channels (RGB). As discussed in Chapter 2, while theoretically it is possible to reproduce a color image with CMY (Cyan, Magenta, and Yellow), the black produced doesn't look like black. Therefore, a fourth channel—black—must be added, which is the standard separation for four-color printing. At this point, even though the image is now 32-bit (4 x 8-bit channels), the number of colors represented is still 16.7 million, the same as the original 24-bit color. It should be pointed out that image quality is lost when an image is converted from RGB to CMYK or vice versa. Just as when converting poetry from one language to another, the words are translated but the beauty is diminished.
Video	Converts an image to NTSC RGB format.
Multi-channel	This converts an image into its three basic color channels. This is different than an RGB image whose three channels can be viewed separately.
Grayscale (16-bit)	This format provides 65,000 shades of gray. Of course, you can't print anywhere near that many, but this provides them and is generally used with high-resolution scanners.
RGB Color (48-bit)	This converts an image into three channels, each containing 16 bits of information. It is generally used with high-resolution scanners.
Apply ICC Profile	This doesn't change the format of the image but rather changes the ICC profile attached to it. The format remains unchanged.

Duotones

The image shown next in the printed version of the book will look like a normal grayscale. For those looking at it in color, notice that it almost looks like a grayscale. It should be pointed out for those reading the printed edition of this book that there is an electronic version that is entirely in color. The term *duotone* is used to describe bitmap images that have *spot colors* assigned to them. Up to four spot colors can be assigned to a bitmap, creating monotones, duotones, tritones, and quadtones. A *spot color* is created by a single ink, as opposed to a process color, which is created by multiple applications of different colored inks. The original purpose of duotones was to compensate for the fact that printing inks have a limited dynamic range when printing halftone images. When inks other than black or gray are used, duotones create striking effects. Technically, a duotone refers to a two-color job, but it has come to mean any combination of spot color/bitmap assignments. In other words, when someone is telling you they want a duotone, it is a good idea to verify what they actually want.

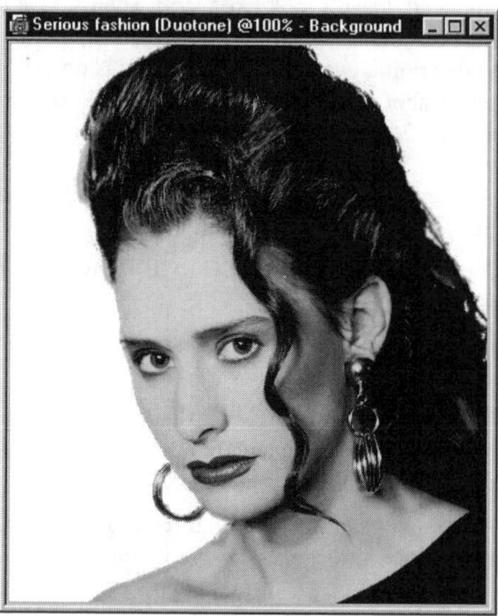

While the traditional approach has been to simply add a second color to the black image to give it a richer look, programs like PHOTO-PAINT are giving designers the tools to take a traditional technique and create some new looks.

Creating Duotones

With Corel PHOTO-PAINT the creation of duotones is simple. First, using the Image | Mode options, convert the image to a Duotone (8-bit). This opens the Duotone dialog box, shown next. If the image contains objects, you will receive a message asking you to combine all of the objects with the background before proceeding. If you wish to keep your original image with objects, you may want to use the Duplicate command from the Image menu and make a duotone from the duplicate. There are only two pages, Curves and Overprint, in the dialog box, and you probably only need to use Curves, as shown next.

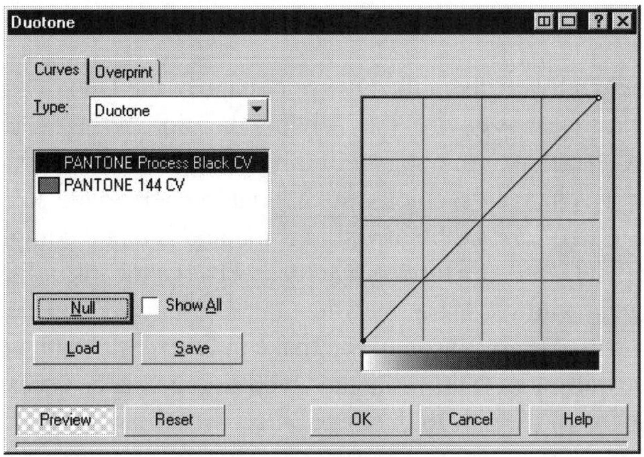

Select an option from the Type pop-up menu—monotone, duotone, tritone, or quadtone. Double-click on a color to open the Select Color dialog box and choose a color. After you have selected all the colors, you can adjust the tint by dragging in the gridbox on the right.

So Now What Do You Do with the Duotone?

If you want a commercial printer to reproduce the duotone, you must print the image to color separations. Because PHOTO-PAINT has already specified the inks to use and how much of each ink to apply, all of the work has been done for you. If you are preparing the duotone to be imported into another program, use the File | Save As command to save the image in the Encapsulated PostScript (EPS) format. The only other file format that supports duotone separations, other than native PHOTO-PAINT CPT, is the graphics standard for Quark XPress Desktop Color Separations (DCS).

After all of that talk about two-color printing, what if you want to print a duotone in a CMYK document? No problem—convert the duotone to CMYK. Not only will all of the duotone shades be preserved, but you will also have the advantage of being able to adjust colors using PHOTO-PAINT's standard color correction commands and editing tools.

Overprint

Fair is fair: I should tell you about the Overprint page of the Duotone dialog box, shown next. It allows you to control the blending of colors. When you select this tab, you are shown how each pair of colors will mix when printed. The example shows the inks for a tritone. To change the color swatch, double-click on the color and the Select Color dialog box opens. The problem with this method is that it complicates the editing process. PHOTO-PAINT doesn't actually change the ink colors or transfer functions in keeping with your new specification; it just applies the new Overprint colors. You also will lose any changes you make in Overprint when you make any adjustment of the ink colors. Yet, while the Overprint method is necessary for certain types of printing, if you are new to duotones, stick with Curves.

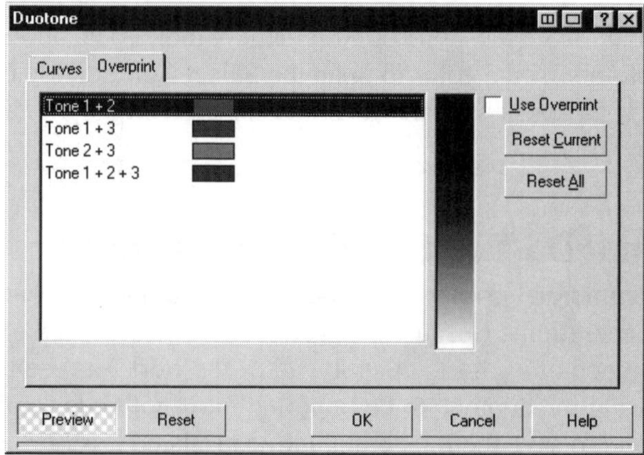

That is all we are going to do with duotones. Most of the e-mail I have received from readers indicated that they either worked in duotones all of the time or didn't want to mess with them because they were doing their work on personal color printers and not with print shops. Now let's learn a little something about reducing colors in an image.

Understanding Color Reduction

When we reduce a color image from a palette of 16.7 million colors (24-bit) to a palette of 256 possible colors, something has to give. It is much like putting 16.7

millions pounds of flour in a 256-pound sack. The conversion is accomplished by using a color table. All 256-color graphic images contain information about how color is supposed to be mapped in a feature called a *color table.* This type of file is also referred to as *indexed color file*.

In a 16.7 Million Color World, Why Convert Images to 256 Colors?

The answer is this book, the Internet, and almost any image that will be electronically displayed. In the electronic form of this book, all of the color images are 8-bit, not 24-bit, color. The explosive growth of online services demands 256 colors. If you don't do a good job converting your image from 24-bit to 256 colors, it can look terrible—yet, if I hadn't told you the images in the electronic version were 8-bit you wouldn't have known.

TIP: *Don't be too quick to dismiss the 256-color option because of previous bad experiences with a 256-color palette. Corel uses a proprietary 256-color palette that produces color that can be very close to 24-bit color but without the system overhead. (Image files in 256-color mode are two-thirds smaller than 24-bit files.)*

The Convert to Paletted (8-bit) Dialog Box

The Convert to Paletted (8-bit) dialog box shown in Figure 6-8 looks scary. Opened by the selection of Paletted (8-bit) in the Mode section of the Image menu, the dialog box is quite simple to use, despite its complicated look. The most common way of using it is to select a palette and a type of dithering and then evaluate the results in the preview window.

The dialog box shown in Figure 6-8 is divided into four tabs: Options, Range Sensitivity, Processed Palette, and Batch. The choice of the palette used to convert the image selection has the greatest influence on the output. The options are Uniform, Standard VGA, Adaptive, Optimized, Black body, Grayscale, System, Microsoft Internet Explorer, Netscape Navigator, and Custom.

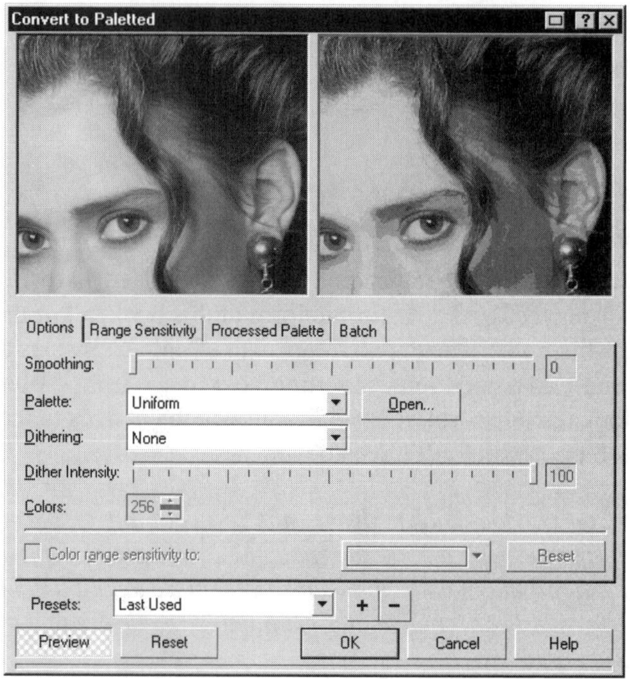

FIGURE 6-8 This dialog box is a powerful conversion tool—and a little scary too

UNIFORM PALETTE When we convert an image to a 256-color image using a Uniform palette with no dithering, the smooth transitions between different colors are lost, resulting in the posterized effect you see in the image shown here:

Using the Color Table command in the Image menu opens the color table, shown next. The Uniform palette spreads out the colors across the entire spectrum, regardless of the color content of the image. There are usually colors in the palette that don't exist in the image. For this reason, Uniform is rarely a good choice for palette selection.

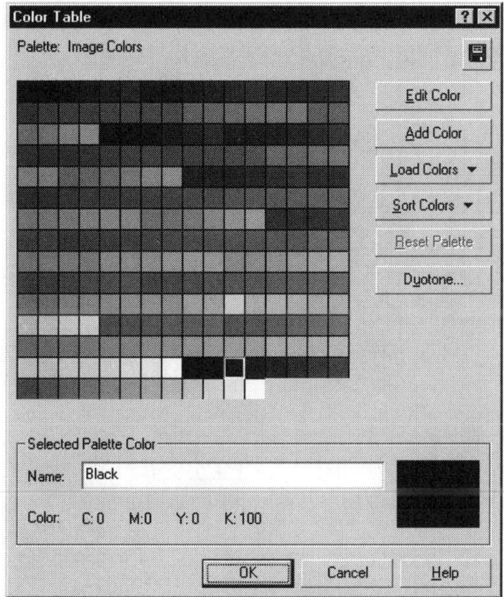

STANDARD VGA This is based on the Standard VGA color table.

ADAPTIVE PALETTE This palette is an improvement over the Uniform palette. This method takes the overall range of hues (colors) and approximates the necessary palette to accommodate the greatest range of colors in the 256-color palette.

OPTIMIZED PALETTE This is the best of all the palettes. It is a proprietary method that produces a palette that is as close to the original color as possible. The image just shown is our serious lady, which was converted using Optimized palette with no dithering. There is still some image degradation, but it is very slight and frankly I can't see it. The color table for this image is shown next. You will note that the table now contains only colors that exist in the image.

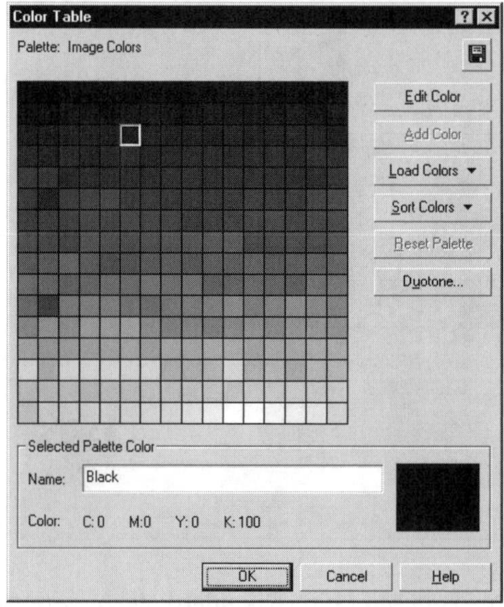

BLACK BODY This is a specialized palette for scientific work. In short, if you need this palette, you already know more about it than I do.

GRAYSCALE Selecting this palette restricts the colors to the 256 shades available in the standard grayscale palette.

SYSTEM This palette uses the current Windows system palette.

NETSCAPE AND INTERNET EXPLORER These palettes are specified by Netscape or Microsoft (Explorer). Don't agonize over which one to pick. They are nearly identical palettes; only the order of colors is different.

CUSTOM PALETTE The Custom Palette allows you to pick all of the colors in the image. I cannot think of a single reason, other than for special effects, that you would ever want to use this option. The computer can do a far better job of creating a palette than any of us ever could.

Dithering, or . . . What Do You Do with the Leftover Colors?

When we convert an image that has many thousands of colors down to 256 colors, we are sometimes forced to practice a little visual sleight of hand to make the loss of color less apparent. We do it through *dithering,* the placement of adjacent pixels in a bitmap image to create a value that the human eye sees as a color but that does not really exist. Yes, it is eye trickery, plain and simple. If the color doesn't exist, then Paint creates a combination of adjacent colors to give an approximation of the missing color.

But why do we need it? Recall that we just converted the lovely, but serious, lady without error diffusion—and she looked great. Well, the reason she did is that there were not all that many colors in her photograph, and therefore, dithering wasn't necessary. The image shown next is a close up of a part of the image we used previously (NACHOS AND SALSA). This is what the original 24-bit color looked like:

While it is shown at a zoom level of 200%, notice that there is no posterization on the candle. The image shown next was converted to 8-bit using the Optimized palette we used with our serious lady earlier. Enough said?

Three buttons determine the type of dithering performed when the image is converted. The choices are None, Ordered, and three types of error diffusion—Jarvis, Stucki, and Floyd-Steinberg. You have got to admit that together the error diffusion options sound like the name of a very large law firm.

None

The default is that no dithering is performed. This is the best choice if the image looks good without it. The colors in the image are limited to the 256 colors in the palette.

TIP: *If the image will need to be resized at a later date (on the Internet, for instance), you should definitely avoid dithering. Resizing an image with dithering produces interference in the patterns that make up the image. This patterning is called a moiré pattern.*

Ordered

With Ordered dithering, each pixel that is not in the available 256-color spectrum is evaluated, and two palette colors are applied to the two adjacent pixels to give the appearance of the missing color. For example, if the missing color is green, one pixel would be made yellow and the other blue. Together in close proximity, they would appear to be green. Of the two dithering options, this is the least desirable.

Error Diffusion

This provides the best results. It is the better of the two types of dithering. Error diffusion changes a color pixel whose value falls outside of the 256-color palette into an adjacent pixel's color. That pixel in turn replaces another pixel's color and this continues until the last pixel is determined to be close enough to one of the colors in the palette. This type of dithering produces the softest transitions between the areas of color that would normally have harsh lines of color separation.

So is there a difference between the three different error diffusions? Yes, there is, and which one you use is determined by the image's color content and type. Most of the 8-bit color images I converted for this book used the Jarvis. While the differences are slight, they do exist, so zoom in and use the preview window to find the best method for the image you need to convert.

Range Sensitivity—Picking Your Favorite Color

When you choose an Optimized palette, the computer will decide which color (or range of colors) to use to create the palette, unless you select the Color Range Sensitivity check box. The only reason you would want to do this is if the subject of the image specifically needed to have all of its colors included—at the expense of others. With this enabled, you can select the color either by using the Eyedropper tool (which is what you will do 99 percent of the time you select this method) or by clicking on the color swatch. Once the color is selected, you can go to the Range Sensitivity tab—shown next—and adjust the sliders to control the amount of the selected color you want in the palette. I know that the Range Sensitivity sliders may look complicated when you first see them, but after working with them a while they won't seem so scary—they will just be frightening. I never use them, so the only advice I can give you is to read Corel's *PHOTO-PAINT 9 User's Manual* for advice on how to adjust the suckers.

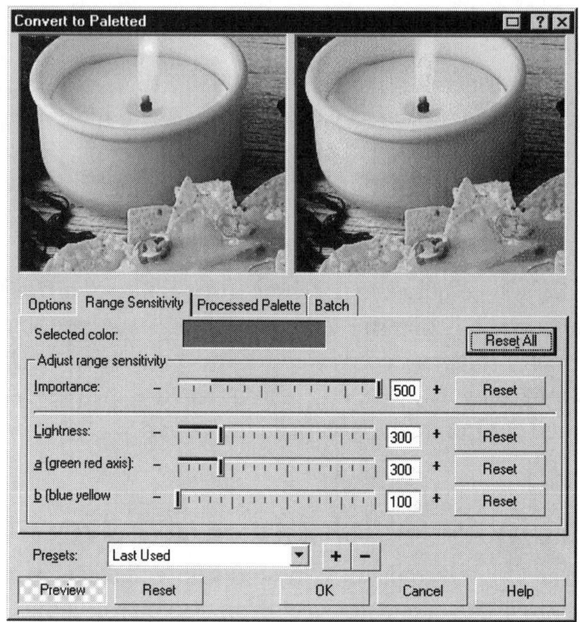

You Old Smoothie

If you select an Adaptive or Optimized palette, the Smoothing slider becomes active. As you increase the slider, PHOTO-PAINT analyzes the color differences and blends the color transitions where abrupt color changes occur. This process will have a tendency to make your image warm and fuzzy, so unless that is what you want, leave this one at its default setting.

Regardless of what you have done in this dialog box up till now, the palette (color table) shown next will be displayed by clicking on the Processed Palette tab.

Batch Conversion

So what happens when you have three different Optimized palettes on a single web page. Well, depending on which browser is being used, it will pick one of the color tables and use it for the remaining images, which actually could look worse than they would by using Uniform. The solution is to open all of the images that are going to be converted and select the Batch conversion tab, as shown next. PHOTO-PAINT will make a single Optimized palette for all of the images. This is where error diffusion really pays off.

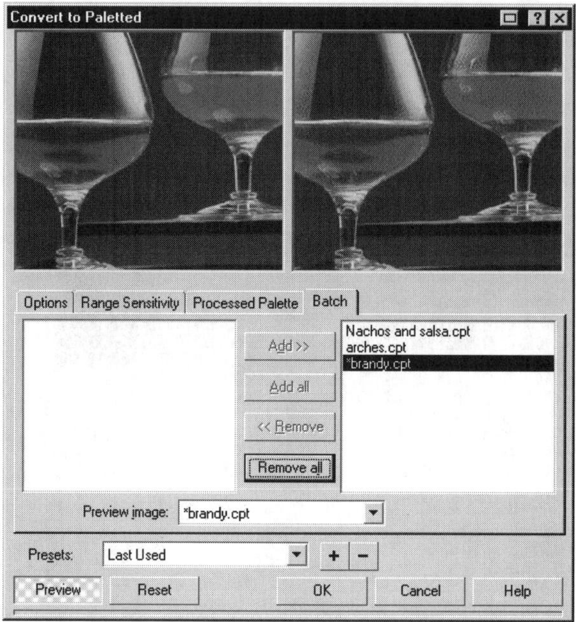

That wraps it up for Image size, Direction, and Format. We have covered a lot of information in this chapter, and it is now time to move on to masks. Masks are important. Think about it. Where would Batman and the Lone Ranger be without a mask? Where would Jim Carrey be without The Mask? Like I said, masks are important. See you in the next chapter.

PART III

Exploring PHOTO-PAINT Tools

CHAPTER 7

The School of Masks

Without masks, editing photographs on a computer would be torture. Masks make it possible to produce many special effects in photo editing that we take for granted. Apart from lasting peace in the Middle East, masks may represent the most important development in the twentieth century. Okay, maybe that last statement was a little over the top, but when you work on photos every day it seems true. Using masks is essential for you to succeed in photo editing. In this chapter, we will learn a lot about creating and controlling masks. In the following chapter we'll learn about some of the advanced features of these masks. With that said, let's begin this chapter by introducing masks.

What Is a Mask?

Put simply, a *mask* protects part of an image or the entire image, allowing us to control exactly where on the image an effect will be applied. For example, in Figure 7-1 we have a photograph of London. To change the background without affecting the foreground, we must make a mask that protects the foreground. Now

FIGURE 7-1 A perfect photograph of London except you can't see the mountains

we can change London, which is not known for its mountains, into a charming little ski resort, as shown in Figure 7-2.

The concept of a mask is simple. You used masks long before you bought PHOTO-PAINT. If you have ever painted a room in a house, you know that the objective is to get the paint on the wall but not on the windows and baseboards. You can either paint very carefully (and slowly), or put masking tape over the area you don't want painted. Masking tape protects the windows and baseboards; it acts as a mask. That's why it's called "masking tape." A mask can also be likened to a stencil. When a stencil is placed over an object, only the portion of the stencil that is cut out allows paint to be applied to the surface; the remainder of the area is masked by the stencil.

PHOTO-PAINT masks act just like the previous two examples. They protect the part of the image they cover and select the part that is uncovered. The best part is that they are much more versatile than a stencil or masking tape (and not as difficult to remove when you are done).

FIGURE 7-2 Soon we can start making travel posters for Ski London

PHOTOSHOP NOTE: *While Photoshop and PHOTO-PAINT share similar methods to select/protect image areas, they use a different naming convention for the parts. PHOTO-PAINT uses the term (mask) to describe both the selected area and the resulting mask created by the selection. In Photoshop, the part selected is called a "selection," and the image (mask) produced is called a "mask."*

Black, White, and Gray

Masks in PHOTO-PAINT are not composed of tape or stencil material. A mask is actually a separate image that covers the image you are working on. A photograph and its mask are shown in Figure 7-3. The original photograph (top) shows a leaf against a complex background. The leaf is masked as indicated by the marquee surrounding it. The image shown at the bottom of the figure is what the mask looks like. The parts of the image covered by 100% black (opaque) are protected, while any part of the image under the 100% white (transparent) is not. Simple, right? Now let's get a little more complicated.

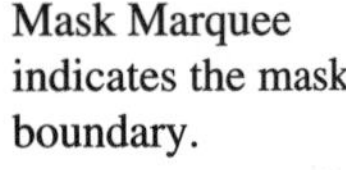
Mask Marquee
indicates the mask
boundary.

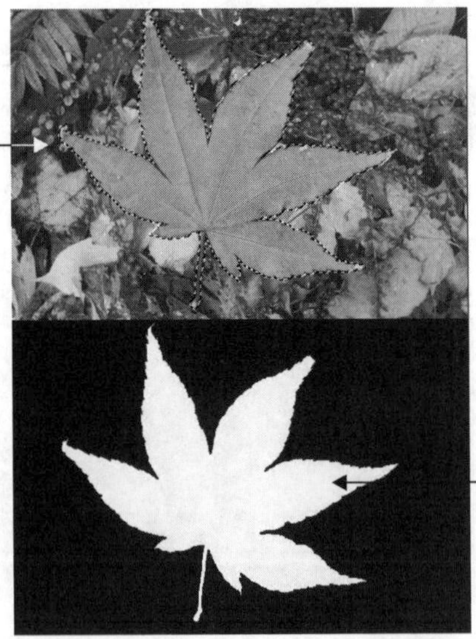
The white areas of the
mask are selected but
not protected.

FIGURE 7-3 The leaf in the photograph (top) has been selected as indicated by the marquee surrounding it. The actual mask created by the selection is the black portion (bottom)

The bottom image in Figure 7-3 looks like a black-and-white (line art) image, but it's not. In Figure 7-4, the area indicated by the circle has been zoomed at 800% to show that the mask is actually a grayscale image. If the pixels in the mask can have transparency, it means that these transparent pixels will only partially protect areas of an image. The zoomed-in area (shown in the circle) shows the mask we saw in Figure 7-3 after it has been feathered. Having the opacity of a mask gradually increase as it approaches the edge produces blurred edges of semitransparent pixels. A blurred edge allows effects to blend into the protected areas of the image. In other words, smooth transitions in an image fool the eye of the viewer.

PHOTOSHOP NOTE: *The mask tools referenced in this chapter are called "marquee tools" in Photoshop.*

Displaying Masks

Corel PHOTO-PAINT provides a large selection of both mask-creation and mask-selection tools. All these tools do basically the same thing—create masks. Although a mask lies on top of an image, it is not visible. Let's face it, invisible

FIGURE 7-4 Feathering the mask produces a blurred image that allows PHOTO-PAINT actions to blend into the image

things are difficult to work with. Therefore the thoughtful programmers at Corel put several features in the program to display them.

The Marquee de Mask

The primary way to display a mask is the marquee. When this feature is enabled, selecting an area with a mask produces a visual display of the mask boundary called a *marquee.* The marquee appears as a moving pattern of dash marks that is commonly referred to as "marching ants." Latest scientific research has determined that they are not ants at all, but rather pixels marching around the marquee carrying tiny picket signs protesting the senseless erasing of pixels in an image (sigh). Because all those moving dashes can, at times, be more of a distraction than a help, PHOTO-PAINT allows the display to be toggled on or off by use of CTRL-H, or you can go the long way through the menus: Mask | Marquee Visible. I use the Show Mask Marquee button shown next.

When you're working with a black-and-white mask, the decision of where to place the marquee is simple—on the mask boundary. But suppose the pixels that make up the mask boundary are gray—where does PHOTO-PAINT display the marquee?

Tweaking the Marquee

Many veteran PHOTO-PAINT users are unaware that the mask marquee is customizable. You can define where on a mask boundary the marquee is displayed, and the color of its marching pixels can be changed. To change the marquee settings, open Options (CTRL-J) as shown next and select Display. To change the color of the marquee, simply select a new color. A different color is often helpful in making the marquee stand out from the image. In the Threshold section we can specify the position of the marquee for feathered masks. The range of Threshold is 1 to 255, which should be a clue. If you recall, grayscale images have a tonal range of 256 shades of gray. Are you getting the idea? Choosing a threshold value of 255 places the mask marquee on the most transparent (lightest) pixels in the mask's feathered boundary, which are also the innermost pixels of that edge. A value of 1, the default setting, places the mask marquee on the most opaque (darkest) pixels of the mask edge.

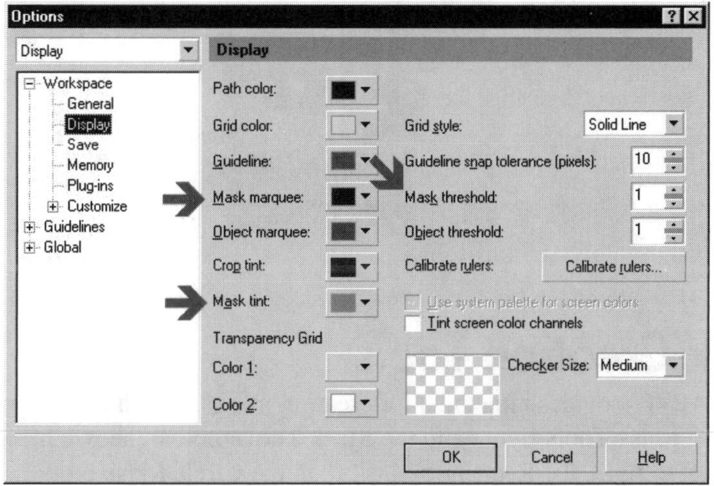

PHOTOSHOP NOTE: *The Marquee Visible command is called Hide Edges in Photoshop.*

Marquees Are Okay, but Overlay Is Where It's At

Now that I have given you the hot scoop on mask marquees, I need to confess that in over 3 zillion hours of using PHOTO-PAINT I have never had an urge to change the threshold setting. Why? Because mask overlay is better. The marquee shows where edges of the mask are. Mask Overlay places a tint over the image that shows the actual mask. The next illustration is a composite image showing the mask overlay and the marquee. In real life, enabling the Mask Overlay feature temporarily turns off the marquee. In the zoomed area, notice where the marquee says the edge of the mask is and where the actual edge is (it is the white glow surrounding the glass). Are marquees useless? Of course not. They provide a quick visual indication of the status of a mask when you're working on an effect involving extensive mask manipulation.

Mask overlay does not in any way affect the image, only the display of the image. If you don't like the default color (which looks like Barbie pink), you can change the overlay color in the same way we changed the marquee color (CTRL-J and Display).

The Mask-Creation Tools

PHOTO-PAINT provides nine tools for creating masks. Seven of the tools are found on the Mask Tools flyout and the Mask Tools toolbar, shown here. They are, from left to right, the Rectangle Mask tool, the Circle Mask tool, the Freehand Mask tool, the Lasso Mask tool, the Scissors Mask tool, the Magic Wand Mask tool, and the Mask Brush tool.

The eighth tool, The Mask Transform tool, is found on the Object Picker tool's flyout. These eight tools create masks, and the ninth one—the Path Node Edit tool—creates paths that can be converted to masks. Mask tools can be selected from the Mask Tools flyout in the Toolbox or by pressing the shortcut key. Don't be concerned about the names of mask tools for the moment. We will be examining each one of these so that you can understand their functions and the best times to use them. The mask creation tools are as follows:

Mask Tool	Shortcut Key
Rectangle Mask tool	R
Circle Mask tool	J
Freehand Mask tool	K
Lasso Mask tool	A
Scissors Mask tool	S
Magic Wand Mask tool	W
Mask Brush tool	B
Mask Transform tool	M
Path Node Edit tool	. (period)

There are two types of mask tools: those used to create regular masks and those that are referred to as the color-sensitive mask tools. The regular mask tools—Rectangle, Circle, and Freehand—create masks defined by the user. Their size, shape, and location within the image are controlled by use of the mouse or other pointing device. The boundaries of the color-sensitive masks are determined by PHOTO-PAINT based on information entered by the user in conjunction with the color values of the image. They are like an old Texas bloodhound. You tell them what color or shade you are interested in, and they will look through the entire image and create a mask based on that information. Color-sensitive mask tools are the Lasso, Scissors Mask, and Magic Wand. After a mask is made, we use the Mask Brush tool, the Mask Transform tool, and the Path Node Edit tool to edit the mask.

PHOTOSHOP NOTE: *Photoshop refers to its mask tools as "marquee tools."*

NOTE: *The default shortcut key for each tool is shown in parentheses after the tool name.*

Regular Mask Tools

These three tools create masks by clicking and dragging a cursor on the image. The Rectangle and Circle Mask tools make masks in the shape that their name implies. The Freehand Mask tool is used to create more complex shapes.

The Rectangle Mask Tool (R)

In case the name of the tool didn't give it away, the Rectangle Mask tool is used for making square and rectangle-shaped masks. To create a mask, you only need select the tool, click and hold down the mouse button, and drag until they have the size and shape you want.

MASK TOOL MODIFIERS Based on the e-mail I have received over the years, this next feature of the mask tools has confused many users. Pay close attention—there may be a quiz.

There are two keys used as mask tool modifiers: CTRL and SHIFT. That was the easy part. The action produced by pressing a modifier key depends on whether the modifier key is enabled before or after clicking the mouse button (see Table 7-1).

NOTE: *If a modifier key is held down before the mouse button is clicked, it will temporarily enable the mask mode as long as it is held. Mask modes are discussed later in this chapter. The keys only work as mask tool modifiers when held down after the mouse button is clicked.*

Key	Action
CTRL-before mouse click	Additive mask mode while held
CTRL-after mouse click	Constrains the shape of the mask to a square
SHIFT-before mouse click	Subtractive mask mode while held
SHIFT-after mouse click	Produces a mask that expands outward from the starting point
CTRL-SHIFT-before mouse click	XOR mask mode while held
CTRL-SHIFT-after mouse click	Produces a square mask that expands outward from the starting point
CTRL-ALT-SHIFT-3-J-Q-[	Produces cramps in fingers

TABLE 7-1 Mask Tool Modifier Keys

If you hold down CTRL after clicking the mouse button, the shape of the mask is constrained to a square as shown here:

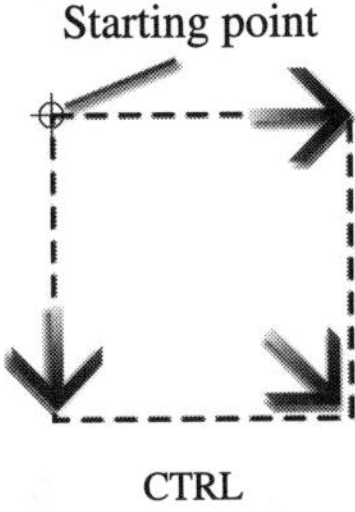

NOTE: *The modifier key can be used both as a mask mode control and as a constrain key. Hold down CTRL, click the mouse button, release CTRL, and then hold it down again. Aren't you glad you know that?*

Holding down SHIFT produces a mask that expands outward from the starting point, while holding down both CTRL and SHIFT creates a square mask that expands outward from the center, as shown next.

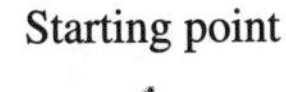

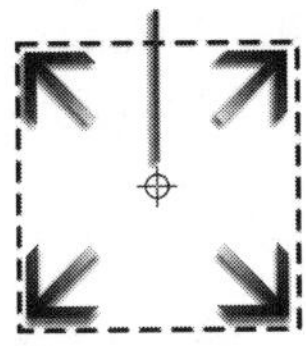

The Circle Mask Tool (J)

The Circle Mask tool, shown here, is used to create elliptical or circular masks. This Mask tool works just like the Rectangle Mask tool, except that holding down CTRL after the mouse button is clicked constrains the mask to a circle.

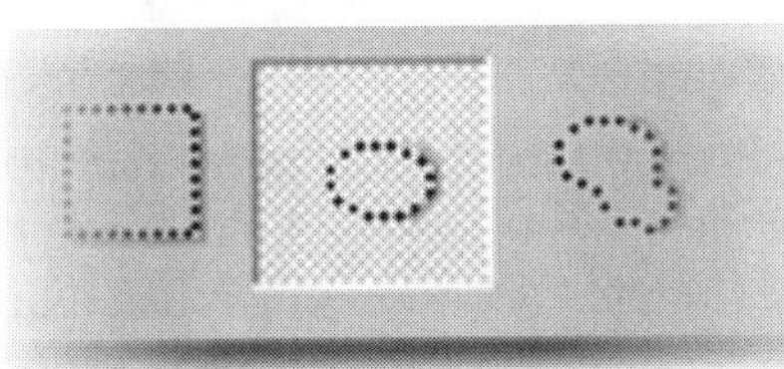

TIP: *This is one of the most useful masking tools for defining an irregular shape. Almost any curved edge can be selected by changing the mask mode to Additive mode and creating the edge of the curved edge with multiple overlapping elliptical shapes.*

The Freehand Mask Tool (K)

The Freehand Mask tool, shown next, is really two tools in one.

As long as the mouse or stylus button is held down, the mask tool is in Drawing mode and acts much as a pencil or pen would. The mask boundary is created as you draw an outline surrounding the area you want to edit. When the pointing device button is released, the Freehand Mask tool reverts to Polygon mode (what Photoshop users call a "Polygonal lasso"). In this mode, you need only click at different points in your image to define the boundaries; between each click, PHOTO-PAINT creates a straight line. When you are finished with your mask, either double-click the last point or hold down ALT and click the mouse/stylus button to complete the mask.

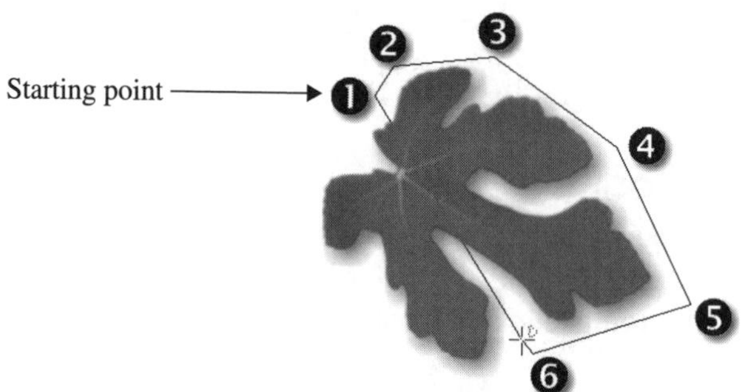

To illustrate how the Polygon mode of the Freehand tool works, look at the example just shown. The mask begins by clicking at point 1. As the cursor is moved to point 2 on the example, a continually updated display of the mask shape is shown. Each time the cursor is clicked, a new point of the mask boundary is created. Clicking DEL removes the last point. Clicking at points 3–6 produces the shape shown in the preceding illustration. The cursor still appears, because the mask has not yet been completed. A straight line is continuously displayed between the current cursor position and the starting point.

FREEHAND MASK TOOL MODIFIER KEYS Just like the other mask tools, the Freehand Mask tool has modifier keys. Holding down CTRL and the mouse button in Drawing mode constrains the mask cursor movement to horizontal or vertical strokes. To change the direction of the constraint, use CTRL-SHIFT. In Polygon mode, CTRL constrains creation of strokes to 45-degree angles. DEL is used in either mode to remove the last point on the mask. Each time DEL is pressed, another point is removed; this "undoing" of the mask can continue all the way back to the starting point.

TIP: *When clicking at multiple mask boundary points in Polygon mode, ensure you don't click the button too fast, or else PHOTO-PAINT will misinterpret it as a double-click and complete the mask. If I had a nickel for every time I did that, I'd be a rich man today.*

WHEN TWO TOOLS ARE BETTER THAN ONE Corel's dualistic approach to the Freehand Mask tool offers two advantages over the traditional freehand tool. Traditionally, a freehand-type tool is difficult to use because the mouse, being a relative motion device, does not have the control necessary to accurately trace a complex line. If you doubt this, try writing your name using a mouse. If you can write your name with a mouse, you need to date more. The other limitation of the Freehand Mask tool becomes apparent the first time you release the mouse button: Traditionally, a freehand mask is completed with a straight line back to the starting point as soon as the button is released, regardless of whether you are finished. In other words, when you begin to make a mask with a traditional freehand tool, you cannot release the button until the mask is finished.

In PHOTO-PAINT, the Freehand Mask tool simply changes mode when the mouse button is released, allowing you to rest when creating a lengthy and detailed mask. Combining the Drawing mode and the Polygon mode makes it possible to use a mouse to mask irregularly shaped objects with some degree of accuracy.

TIP: *For irregular mask creation with a mouse, I recommend using the Polygon mode of the Freehand Mask tool. If you use a stylus, the Drawing mode will allow you to quickly create a mask.*

TIP: *I strongly recommend changing the shape of the tool cursor to a Crosshair when using the Freehand tool to trace complex shapes. It is much easier to see, and thereby follow, an edge with this cursor. To change the cursor shape, open Preferences (CTRL-J), and from the General setting, set the Cursor Type to Crosshair.*

Mask Modes

If it were a perfect world, every mask you make would be perfect, never needing modification. Alas, the world is not perfect, and if you've worked in photo editing for any time at all, you've spent a lot of time adding to and subtracting from masks.

Whenever a mask tool is selected, one of four tiny icons appears in the lower-right corner of the Status Bar and is also visible in the Property Bar. These icons tell us what mask mode the mask tool is in. These tiny icons are your friends. They will save you a great deal of frustration once you train yourself to look for them.

NOTE: *The mask tools do not retain individual mask mode settings. For example, if you are using the Rectangle Mask tool and the XOR mode is selected, any other mask tool you select will also be in XOR mode.*

Normal Mask Mode

In Normal mask mode, masks are mutually exclusive. In other words, making a mask deletes any existing mask in an image. This is handy housekeeping when creating simple masks. If a mask doesn't look right, just make another one. With more complex masks, the Normal mask mode prevents modification of masks. As you may have guessed, the purpose of the other mask modes is to allow us to add to, subtract from, and otherwise modify to our heart's content any existing mask. Three of the following four mask modes are pretty much self-explanatory:

- **Normal** Every time you make a mask, any existing mask is removed.
- **Additive** Each mask tool action adds to the existing mask.
- **Subtractive** Each mask tool action subtracts from the existing mask.
- **Exclusive OR (XOR)** If the portion of the new mask being added overlaps an existing mask, the mask properties of the overlapped area are inverted. That's clear as mud, isn't it? You'll learn more about this shortly.

Selecting the Mask Modes

Mask modes can be selected from the Mask menu, through keyboard shortcuts, or through toolbar buttons. The mode of the currently selected mask tool is indicated by an icon displayed in the Status Bar and by the shape of the cursor. Figure 7-5 shows the mask mode icons that appear in the Property Bar and Status Bar when the Rectangle Mask tool is selected.

You can also select a mask mode using the following keyboard shortcuts; I never can remember them, but maybe you can.

Normal	CTRL-NUMPAD . (period)
Additive	CTRL-NUMPAD +
subtractive	CTRL-NUMPAD -
XOR	CTRL-NUMPAD *

If you recall, all the mask tool modifier keys previously described in this chapter required holding down the key after clicking the mouse button. To *temporarily* change the mask mode, click the keys just referenced *before* clicking

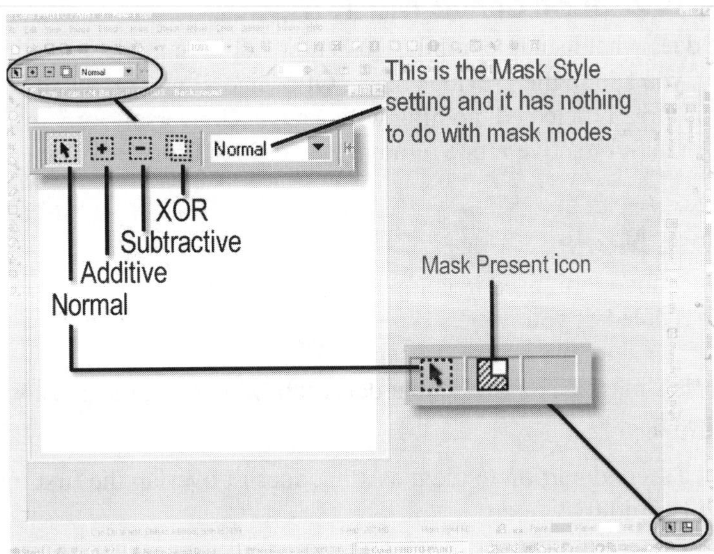

FIGURE 7-5 Corel has placed icons relating to mask modes just about everywhere

the mode. Releasing the modifier key reverts the mask to its previous mode. Here are the simple rules for using modifier keys to create masks:

- CTRL enables Additive mode.
- SHIFT enables Subtractive mode.
- CTRL-SHIFT enables XOR mode.
- Clicking the mouse key before holding down SHIFT creates a new mask that expands or contracts (depending on the direction you are dragging the mouse) from the center.

NOTE: *The preceding rules apply only to mask creation.*

TIP: *If you are unable to apply an effect to an image, check first to see if the Mask Present icon is displayed. Even if you can't see the mask, the computer will prevent you from applying any effect.*

Additive and Subtractive Mask Mode

This mode does what its name implies. When in Additive mode, each time you use a mask tool, you add to the previous mask. Of course, if you select an area of the image that is already selected, nothing will change. Conversely, any mask tool actions taken in Subtractive mode remove the portions from the selected area.

XOR Mask Mode

"XOR" stands for a term used in computer logic called "Exclusive Or." With XOR mask mode enabled, if you:

- Create a mask on an image that doesn't have a mask, the mask will act normally.
- Add a second portion to the mask that doesn't overlap the first mask, it will act like Additive mode.

- Add a second portion that falls entirely within the existing mask, it acts like Subtractive mode.
- Add a mask that overlaps a portion of an existing mask, the portion of the image already selected by a mask covered by the XOR mask will be inverted.
- Know the identity of the Lone Ranger, don't tell anyone. It's a secret.

Is the Glass Half Full or Half Empty?

This is a good time to ensure that you understand an important concept in masks. Here is a little test much like the famous glass test. Look at Figure 7-6. I have enabled the grid and used the Circle Mask tool to create the circles indicated by the mask marquee. How many masks do you see? The correct answer is one mask

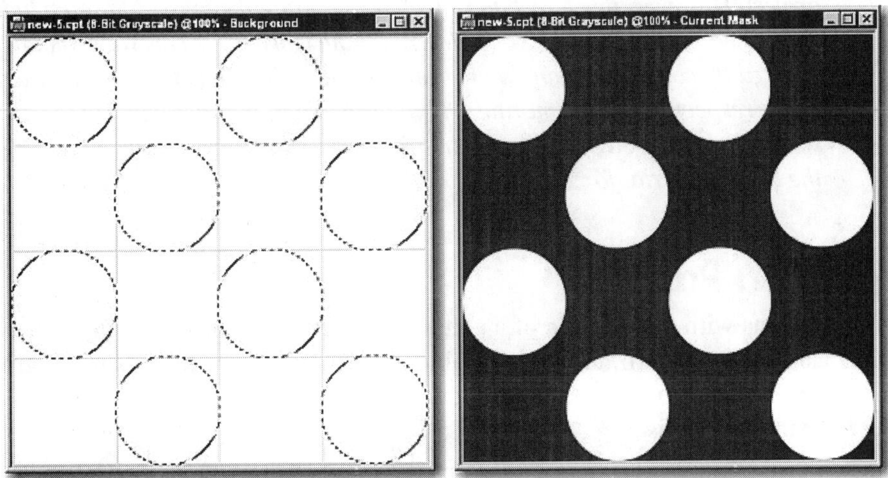

FIGURE 7-6 How many masks can you find in the image on the left? The answer may surprise you

composed of eight selected areas. The actual mask is shown at the right of the image. Now for extra credit, is the mask half full or half empty?

Making Tiles Using Masks and Mask Modes

Now we are going to put a little of what we have learned so far into practice. When I lived in the Far East, I was always fascinated by the detailed ceramic and terra cotta tiles that have been made there for centuries. In this workshop session we are going to use XOR masks to create a very intricate pattern tile similar to those I used to stare at and sketch. These tiles can be tiled (no pun intended), used for web pages, or used as the starting point for other projects. In addition, you are going to learn some of the great things that can be done with a filter called *The Boss.*

NOTE: *The image created in the following exercise will teach you a lot about working with masks, XOR masks, grids, and other kinds of cool stuff. I have timed it, and it should take you no more than 10 minutes to do the entire project. However, if you just don't feel like creating the mask, I have included the finished mask, entitled XOR MASK, on the Corel CD. This way you and your guilty conscience can do the exercise with minimum effort. Be aware, I won't respect you in the morning. If you are taking the easy way out (gee, I should be a travel agent for guilt trips), jump to the next section, "Selecting the Right Material for Your Tile."*

Making a Pattern

This tile begins with the creation of a pattern. We could use anything symmetrical as the basis for the pattern, but we are going to learn how to create one using grids and the XOR mask mode. I specifically created this mask to be used with the Tile filter later in the exercise.

1. Create a new file that is 5 × 5 inches, 100 dpi, using 24-bit color. Choose View | Grid & Ruler Setup. Change the Grid setting to Frequency. Next change the Horizontal and Vertical values to 4.0 per inch. Also check the Show Grid and Snap To Grid check boxes. Click the OK button.

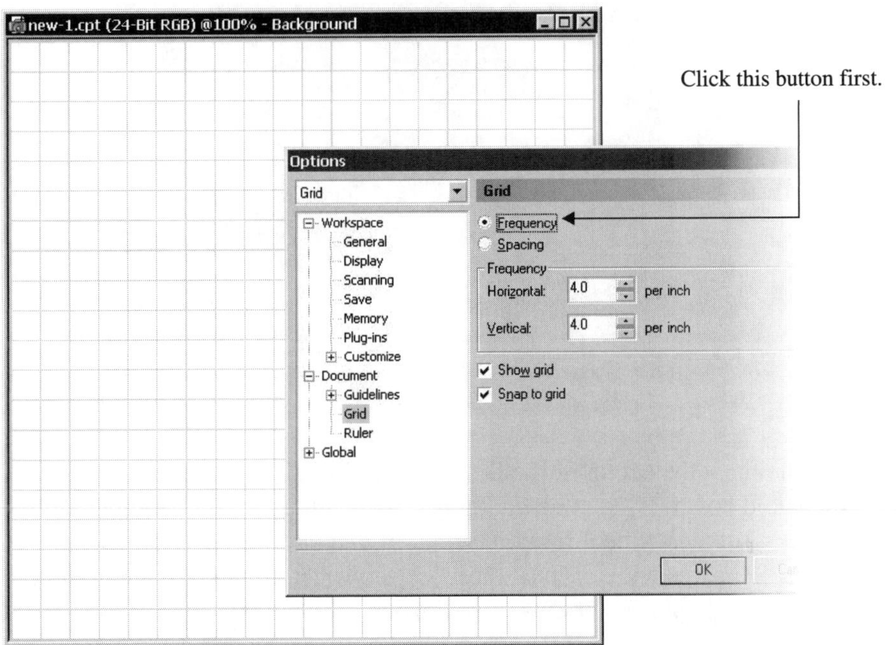

2. Make sure the entire grid is in view (F4). From the Toolbox select the Circle Mask tool from the Mask tool flyout. Choose Mask | Mode | XOR. Beginning at the intersection of the grid one square down and one square right in the upper-left corner, click the mouse button first and then hold down CTRL to drag a circle four squares wide. Click the Mask Overlay button to see the resulting circle mask more clearly.

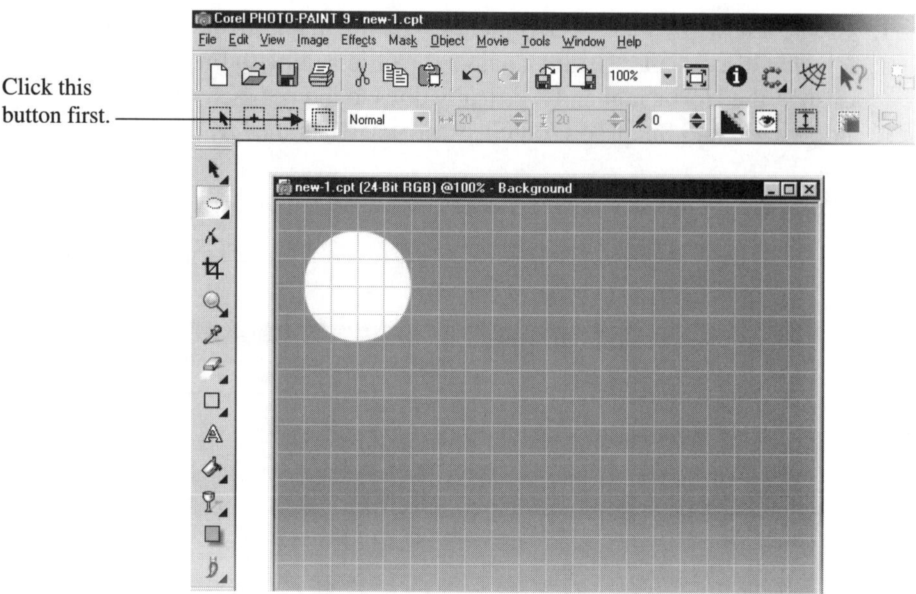

3. Beginning at the center of the first circle mask, click the mouse button and then hold down CTRL, click and drag down and to the right another circle that is 4 squares wide. From the center of that circle, click and drag a circle that is 5 squares wide. Repeat these steps on each of the remaining three corners until your result looks like the one shown next.

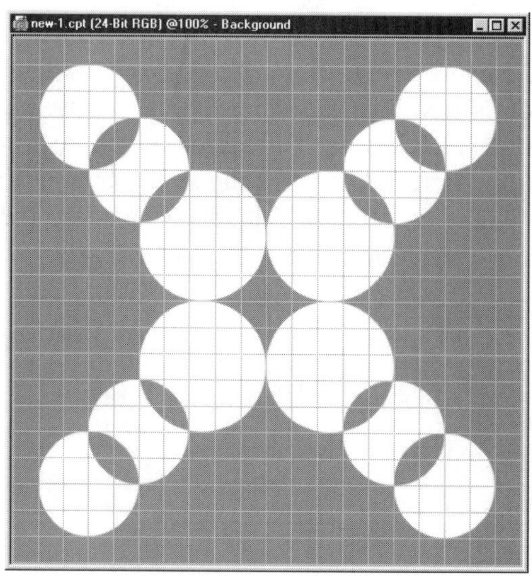

4. For the next circle begin at the intersection of the grid at a point that is 5 squares down and 5 squares to the right of the upper-left corner; click and drag a circle 10 squares wide. The second circle starts at the intersection of the grid at a point that is 8 squares down and 8 squares to the right of the upper-left corner. Click and drag a circle 4 squares wide. The result is shown next.

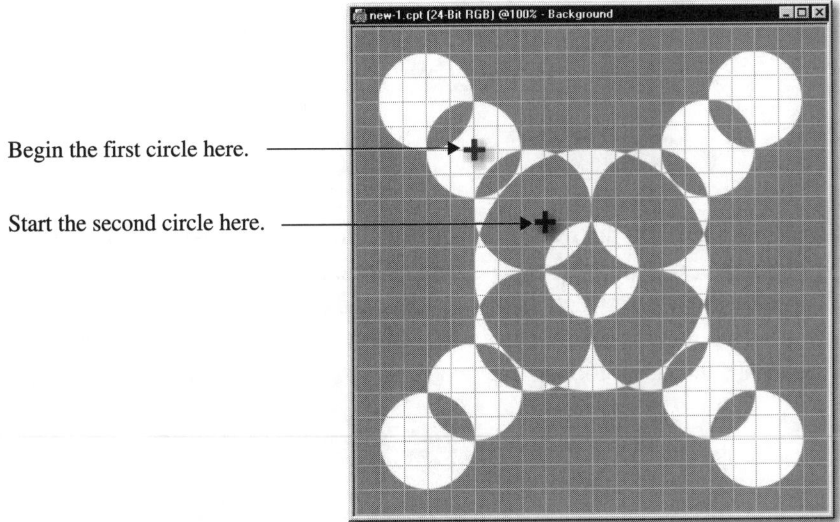
new-1.cpt (24-Bit RGB) @100% - Background
Begin the first circle here.
Start the second circle here.

5. Now that we have made the center flower, we will make smaller flowers out of the four outer circles. Click at the center of the circle in the upper-left corner, and while holding down CTRL, drag a circle up and to the left creating a circle 2 squares wide. Repeat this for the remaining three quadrants of the circle. Create a circle that is 2 squares wide in the center of the previous four. The result is shown next.

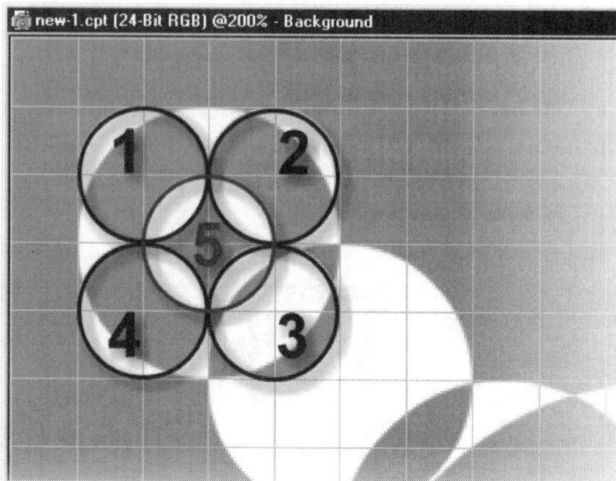

6. Repeat step 5 on the remaining three quadrants. We will now apply a similar technique to the four circles between the center and the ones we just made. The difference between the one we just did and the new one is we don't apply a circle mask in the quadrant closest to the image corner. Sound too complicated? Just look at the next image and apply to all four quadrants.

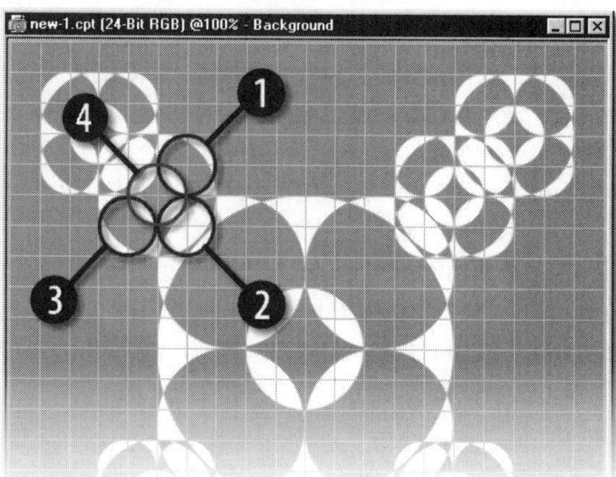

7. Place the cursor at the point indicated by the "+" on the next illustration. Click the mouse and then hold down CTRL and ALT. Drag the cursor, creating a circle that expands from the center until it is 4 squares wide. Repeat on the

remaining three sides until your mask looks like the one shown in the following image. Take heart, we are almost done.

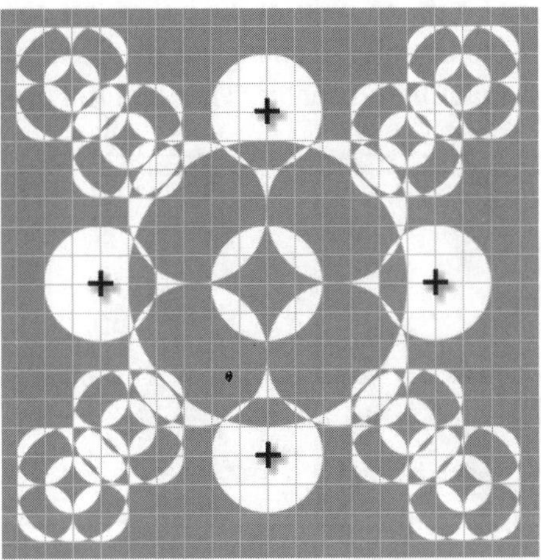

8. Repeat the technique described in step 5 to create the flowers out of the four circles we just made. The result is shown next.

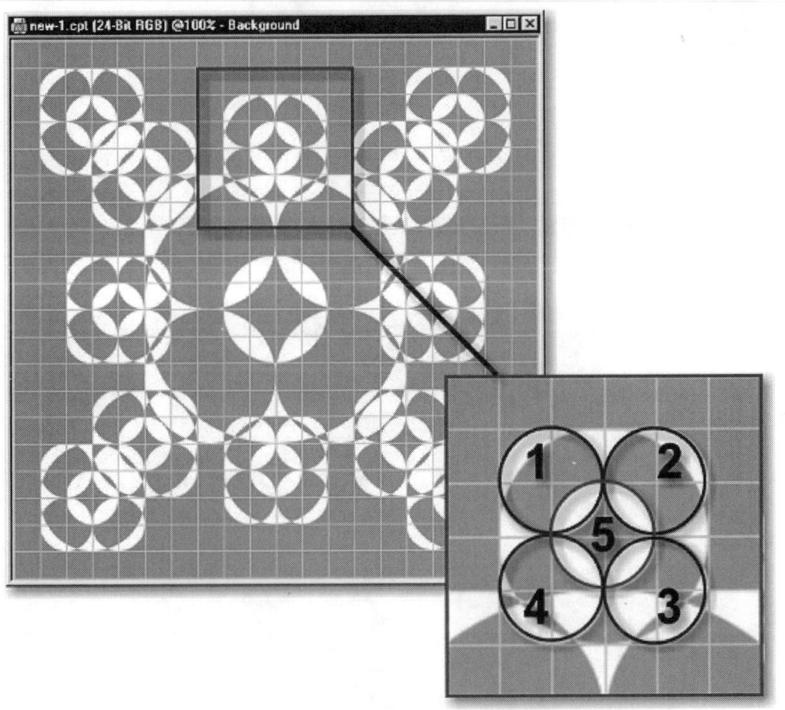

9. For the last steps, click the center of the upper-left flower, and drag a circle that is 14 squares wide to the center of the lower-right flower. At the point that is 5 down and 5 to the right of the upper-left corner, drag a 10-square-wide circle. For the last touch, change to the Square Mask tool and drag a 2-square-wide square in the center. The final mask is shown here:

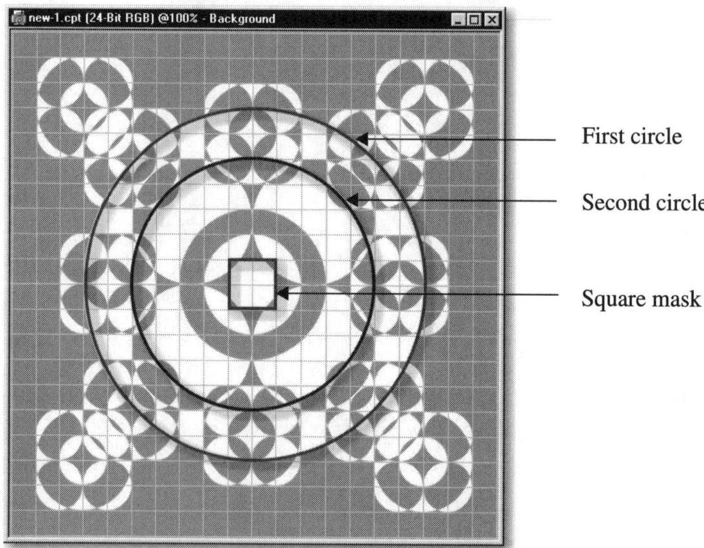

10. Turn off the grid (View | Grid), choose File | Save, and name the file XOR Mask.

Selecting the Right Material for Your Tile

You've done all the hard work (at least some of us have). The rest of the project, making the pattern, is the fun part. First, we need to choose the material we are going to use for the tile to be made of. We will use a light marble, although a dark polished wood also looks very good.

1. If you closed the previous image, choose File | Open and load the image XOR MASK. Choose Mask | Save | Save As Channel. When prompted, name the channel XOR Mask as shown here.

After tucking the mask safely away in a channel, delete the mask by clicking the Delete Mask button on the Toolbar shown next. If you didn't make the mask in the previous steps, locate EXERCISE\PHOTOS\TILE and open it.

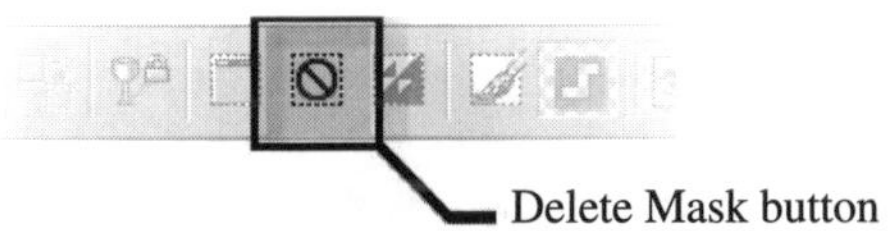

Delete Mask button

2. Choose Edit | Fill. When the Edit Fill & Transparency dialog box opens, click the Bitmap Fill button. Click the Edit button in the lower-right corner, opening the Bitmap Fill dialog box. Click the Load button and select the seamless tile TAN MARBLE in the exercise folder on the CD that shipped with PHOTO-PAINT. Click the Open button and then click OK to close the Bitmap Fill dialog box. Click OK again to apply the fill. Now we have a solid square of marble and a mask hiding in the wings (or channel, as the case may be).

3. Choose Mask | Load | XOR Mask. This loads the channel as a mask. Select Image | Adjust | Gamma. In the dialog box, shown next, select a value of 0.4 and click the OK button. This darkens the unprotected areas to enhance the effect of The Boss filter.

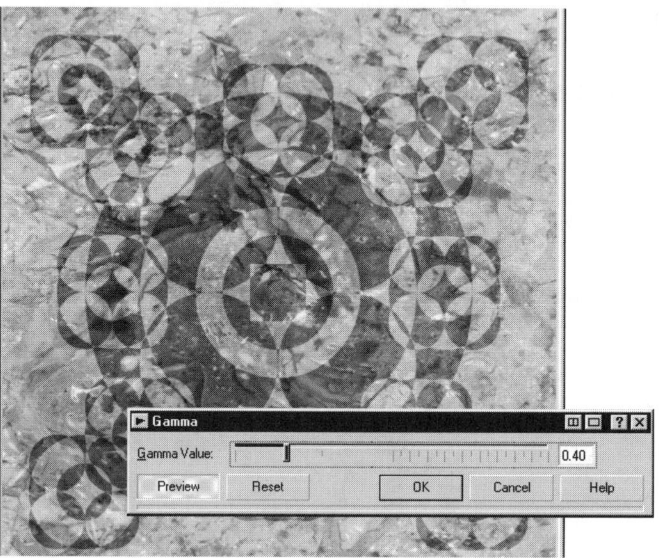

4. Choose Effects | 3D Effects | The Boss. On the Edge page ensure that the Invert box is not checked, and then change the settings of the dialog box to Width: 6, Height: 70, Smoothness: 50, and Drop Off: Flat. Now click the Lighting tab, and change the settings as follows: Brightness: 90, Sharpness: 50, Direction: 315, and Angle: 15. Click OK. The resulting image is shown next.

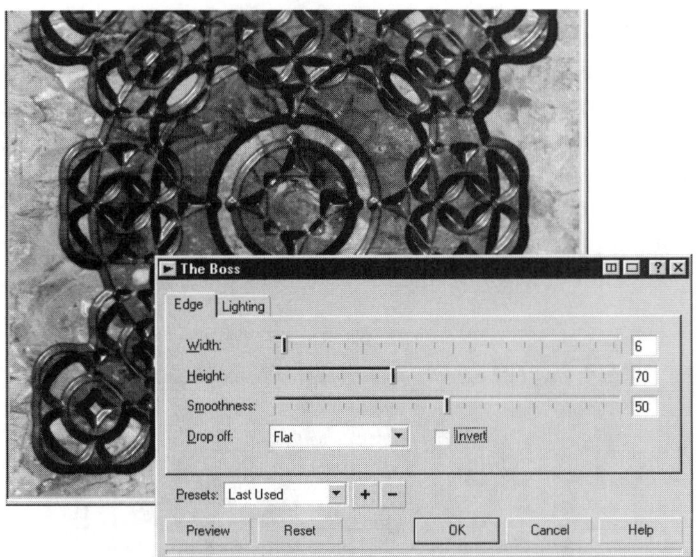

5. Now this tile is great, but I think it gets a lot better. Open The Boss again and this time select Invert and, from the Lighting tab, change the Angle to 45. As you can see in the next image, it really has a ceramic tile look.

6. Now we'll add some texture to the marble using one of the new PHOTO-PAINT 9 filters. Invert the mask and make sure the marquee is around the edge of the image file. Choose Effects | Textures | Elephant Skin. In the dialog box shown next, I have used the default Age setting of 20 and changed the Randomize value that is used to generate the texture to 157. There is nothing sacred about that number, it just happened to be the one that popped up when I clicked the Randomize button. I chose black as the paint Color. Click OK and the result is shown next.

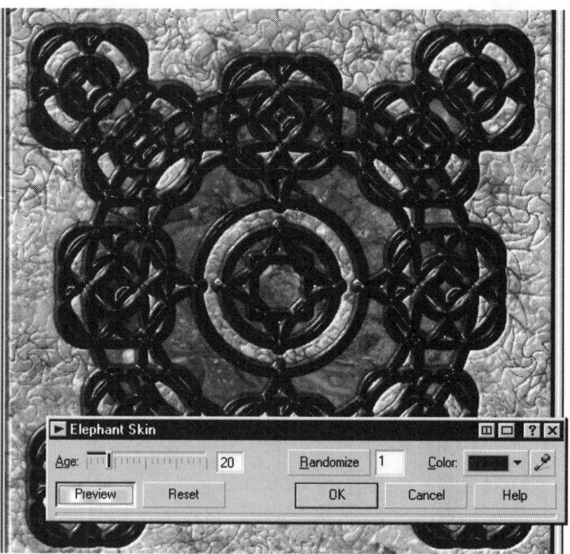

7. If we were to remove the inverted mask at this point, applying the Tile filter would just duplicate the image; however, watch what happens when we leave it in place. Select Effects | Distort | Tile. Use a value of 2 for both Horizontal and Vertical and click OK. The result is shown next. We are done with this image, so admire it a bit longer and close the file.

Now that we have learned a thing or two about regular masks, let's discover color-sensitive masks.

Color-Sensitive Masks

This category of tools allows you to create incredibly complex masks quickly—if you know how to use them. The color-sensitive mask tools are Lasso, Magic Wand, Scissors, and Color. The Color Mask tool is the only mask tool not located on the mask flyout. It is accessed through the Mask menu and explored in Chapter 8.

The success of the three color-sensitive mask tools discussed here depends on the Tolerance setting the user applies in the Tool Settings palette. The higher the value, the wider the color range that will be included in the mask. The key to finding the optimum tolerance level is experimentation. Also in the Tool Settings palette are two methods of setting tolerance: Normal and HSB. The Normal method makes its selection based on the color similarity of adjacent pixels, while the HSB method creates its selection based on the similarity of hue, saturation, and brightness levels between adjacent pixels.

The Lasso Mask Tool (A)

The Lasso Mask tool enables you to automatically create an irregular mask based on an image's color values and the Tolerance level. The lasso metaphor is perfect for this tool. I know a lot about lassoes; I've seen *City Slickers* more than ten times. On a dude ranch, a lasso surrounds an object, and when you pull on the rope, the lasso closes until it fits tightly around the object. The Lasso tool works in much the same way, but without the rope.

When you click the starting point of the mask, PHOTO-PAINT samples the composite color value of the pixels under the starting point. A mask is created in the same manner as the Freehand Mask tool. Once the mask is completed with a double-click or a right-click, the marquee shrinks until it surrounds an area with color values that fall within the limits set by the Tolerance slider in the Tool Settings palette or Property Bar.

PHOTOSHOP NOTE: *The Lasso and the Polygonal Lasso tools in Photoshop operate like the Freehand Mask tool described in the previous section. There isn't a Photoshop mask tool equivalent of the Lasso Mask tool.*

REPLACING A BACKGROUND (PROJECT) Here is a simple exercise that gives you an opportunity to try the Lasso Mask tool and get a preview of an advanced mask feature. In this session, we are going to replace the background of a photograph.

1. Choose File | Open and, from the Open An Image dialog box, select EXERCISE\PHOTOS\TAKEOFF located on the Corel CD-ROM. The image may be too large to fit on most displays (including mine), so use Zoom To Fit (F4). The image is shown next.

2. Select the Lasso Mask tool from the Mask flyout. In the Property Bar ensure Normal is chosen, and change the Color Similarity level to 10 as shown here. This tells PHOTO-PAINT to include pixels that are greater or less than 14 shades from the starting pixel value. It does this with all the pixels in the enclosed area until it is finished.

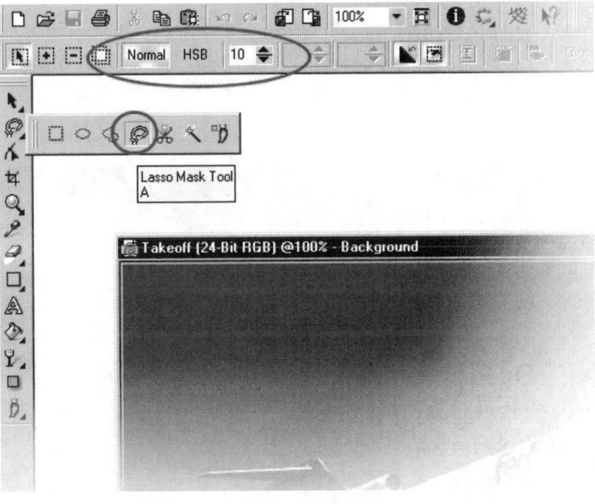

3. Click the cursor at the point marked by the *X* in the upper-left corner to establish the starting (anchor) point. The correct spot will be in the lighter blue region below the darker blue area. Now click at points around the jet. The exact placement doesn't matter, because the Lasso tool is using the value of the anchor for its calculations.

Double-click at the last point indicated to close the mask. If the marquee isn't displayed, press CTRL-H to select Mask Marquee Visible. There may be a mask fragment above and to the left of the jet caused by a piece of debris on the original negative. Ignore it. The mask should outline the jet as shown next.

4. Copy the contents of the masked area to the Clipboard (CTRL-C). Close the Takeoff image. To replace the background with something more interesting, we will require another photograph. Select File | Open From File and choose EXERCISE\PHOTOS\ENGLISH COAST.

5. To place the jet in the new photo, click the Paste As Object button in the Toolbar or use CTRL-V. Now you have a jet that is flying way too low. Of course, you can use the Object Picker to place it anywhere you want. I got it off the beach as shown next.

6. Close the file and don't save the changes. However, if you wanted to save the file, you should name it Pull up! Pull up! (just kidding—lose the file).

The Scissors Mask Tool (S)

Like a Lasso Mask tool, the Scissors Mask tool contracts around an image. Unlike the Lasso Mask, it detects edges in your image and places the mask marquee along those edges as you are outlining the mask.

The key to the operation of this mask is the *bounding box.* When you select this mask tool, a bounding box initially surrounds the Mask Tool cursor and remains centered at each successive point on the mask. This bounding box displays the area around the cursor used for color tolerance sampling. In other words, the Scissors Mask tool doesn't look at the color content of the entire image; it only looks at the area inside the bounding box.

HOW SCISSORS MASK WORKS Here is how the tool is supposed to work. With the exception of its automatic edge-detection feature, it operates like the Freehand and Lasso Mask tools. The first click establishes the sample used for Tolerance comparisons. At any time you can reset this color value by holding down SHIFT and clicking on a different point. The mask is created as you click within the bounding box. The edge will be detected (hopefully), and the boundary will be placed along the detected edge. You may find that this mask tool doesn't detect edges as well as some third-party plug-ins. One problem you may experience is when the color/shades that define the edge are too close. When this happens, either click many points close together, or click and drag the mouse like a Freehand Mask tool. For this tool to work well, the edges in the image have to be very distinct; in fact, the Lasso Mask tool can generally do the same job with less work.

PHOTOSHOP NOTE: *The Photoshop and PHOTO-PAINT Magic Wand tools, in both name and operation, are nearly identical.*

The Magic Wand Mask Tool (W)

The Magic Wand Mask tool is the converse of the Lasso Mask tool. It creates masks by *expanding* from a starting point until all the adjacent colors meeting the selection criteria are included. As with the other color-sensitive mask tools, the ability of the Magic Wand to make an accurate mask depends on the Tolerance settings in the Tool Settings palette and the actual color-value composition of the image.

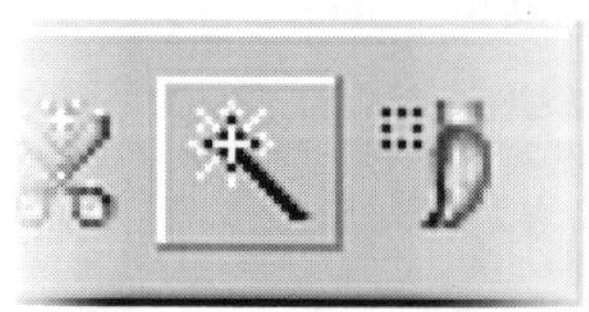

HOW THE MAGIC WAND MASK TOOL PERFORMS ITS MAGIC Two simple facts about the Magic Wand tool are (1) there is nothing magic about it, and (2) it is very simple to use once you understand the concept behind its operation. In theory, you simply click the area that needs to be masked and PHOTO-PAINT does the rest. There are actually times when this will work as intended.

PHOTOSHOP NOTE: *Tolerance settings in Photoshop use a range of shades from 0 to 255. PHOTO-PAINT uses a percentage. Therefore, a setting of 25% equals a Photoshop setting of 64.*

PHOTO-PAINT reads the color value of the starting pixel and, using the Color Sensitivity level, *expands* the mask selection pixel by pixel until it can no longer find pixels that are within the limits. For example, if the starting pixel has a value of 60 and the Color Sensitivity value has been set to 50, the mask will expand from its starting point until every adjacent pixel with a value between 10 (60 minus 50) and 110 (60 plus 50) has been included in the mask.

TIP: *When you're using the Magic Wand Mask tool, the most important decision to make is the choice of whether to mask the object or the area around the object. If the area to be protected is filled with a wide variety of colors or colors with a wide tonal range, then look at the area surrounding it. Remember that it only takes one click of the button to invert a mask.*

TAKING THE MAGIC WAND MASK TOOL FOR A TEST DRIVE Remember the photograph of London at the beginning of the chapter? In this hands-on exercise, we will use the Magic Wand tool to do a simple background replacement like we did with the Lasso Mask tool and the background.

1. Choose File | Open and select EXERCISE\PHOTOS\LONDON on the Corel CD. Click the Open button.
2. Select the Magic Wand tool from the Mask flyout in the Toolbox as shown in Figure 7-7. Ensure the Color Tolerance mode is Normal and the Sensitivity value is set to 10. Turn off Anti-aliasing to allow the mask to accurately follow the complex edges of the Parliament buildings.
3. Click anywhere on the sky in the upper part of the image, and a partial mask appears to cover part of the sky, as shown next.

Your image will look different from mine. I have performed a little PHOTO-PAINT magic on the image so the masked areas appear white. At this point we could change the mask mode to Additive and click the parts

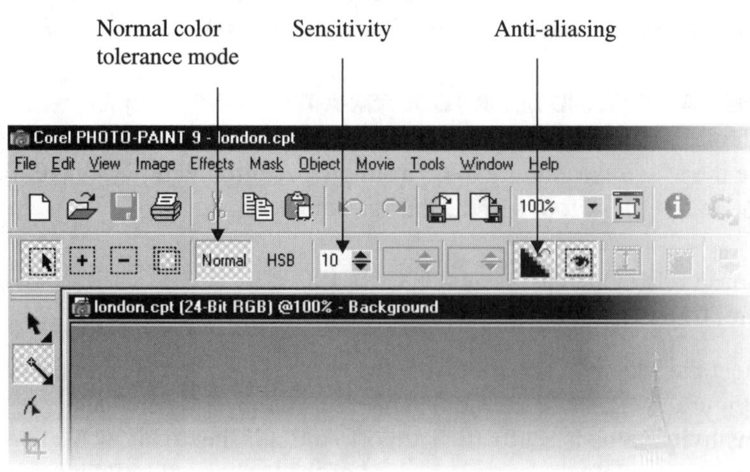

FIGURE 7-7 Property Bar settings control the operation of the Magic Wand Mask tool

of the sky that were previously out of range for the Tolerance setting. But we have another mask command we can use. Select Mask | Shape | Grow, and the mask completes the action and fills the entire background. The Grow command expands the mask created by the Magic Wand tool. The existing mask edges expand outward until they reach the limit determined by the Tolerance setting.

4. To place another photograph in the background, select File | Import. This action opens the Paste An Image From Disk dialog box, which, except for the title, is identical to the dialog box for opening an image. Select EXERCISE\PHOTOS\MOUNTAIN and click the Open button. The mountain photograph is now floating (as an object) on top of the photograph of London, and only the mask from the original photograph can still be seen.

5. Open the Align And Distribute dialog box (CTRL-A) and select Vertically Top, Horizontally Center. Click OK. The object doesn't cover the bottom completely, but that won't make any difference.

6. Choose Object | Crop To Mask. The portion of the mountain photograph that was outside the mask is removed, resulting in the image shown next. To see the image without the mask marquee, either turn off the marquee or click the Full Screen Preview (F9) key.

PHOTOSHOP NOTE: *Believe it or not, the Grow and Similar commands in Photoshop not only operate like those in PHOTO-PAINT but also have the same names. Go figure.*

The Grow and Similar Commands

In the previous exercise, we used the Grow command, so it seems an appropriate time to understand what Grow and its counterpart, Similar, actually do. These two commands increase the size of an area selected by a mask. Both commands determine the pixels to be included in the mask by evaluating a range of colors based on the current tolerance setting of the Magic Wand Mask tool.

Grow

With an existing mask on the image, choose Mask | Shape | Grow to include all pixels that neighbor the existing mask and those that fall within the range of colors included in the mask. All the pixels eligible for selection by Grow must be contiguous (adjacent to one another). The color range of pixels selected is determined by the Tolerance setting. If you need to change the Tolerance setting, it is first necessary to select the Magic Wand Mask tool.

Similar

With an existing mask on the image, choose Mask | Shape | Similar. The Similar command acts like the Grow command, except that the eligible pixels do not need to be adjacent to one another. As long as the pixel's color value falls within the color range specified by the Tolerance setting, it will be included regardless of where it is in the image.

This command is vital for isolating a complex image containing dozens, if not hundreds, of tiny areas whose colors are significantly lighter or darker than the image. Figure 7-8(a) shows a photograph of pretzels on a light-colored background. It is possible to use the Magic Wand and select all the noncontiguous areas individually, but it would take forever. To isolate the pretzels, it is necessary to place only a few masks on the background to create a sampling of all the colors and then choose Mask | Shape | Similar. All the background is selected, allowing you to replace it with a different background, as shown in Figure 7-8(b).

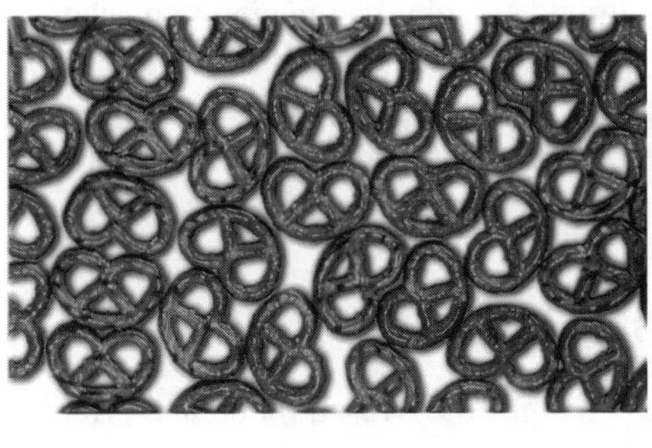

(a)

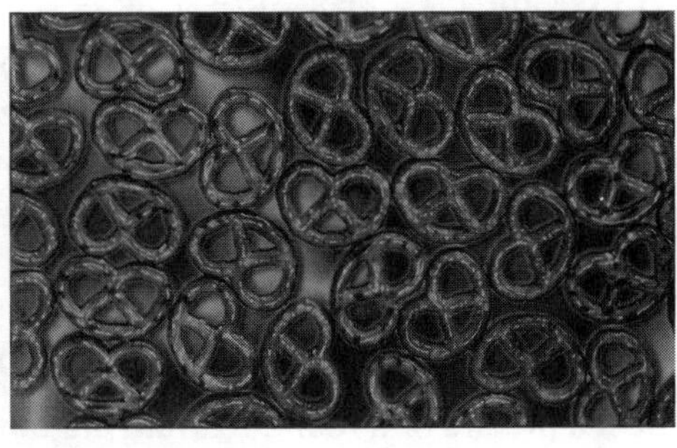

(b)

FIGURE 7-8 Pretzels anyone? (a) Masking all the individual pretzels could be a time-consuming job. (b) With the Similar command, it is a simple task to replace the background with another

Tolerance and Magic Wands

The setting of Tolerance is critical to getting satisfactory results with the Grow and Similar commands when used in conjunction with the Magic Wand. When you apply the Magic Wand using a relatively high tolerance setting (>30), applying the Grow command without changing the Tolerance value will result in a blown mask—that is, a mask that overruns most color boundaries. This happens because of the cumulative effect of applying a 30% Magic Wand Tolerance on top of a 30% Grow setting. The best way to use it is to either use low values for both selections or to use as high as necessary a Tolerance setting for the Magic Wand to do its job and then to decrease the Tolerance setting of the Grow command.

NOTE: *The figure of 30% is not some PHOTO-PAINT magic threshold figure for the color-sensitive tools. It is a relatively high threshold figure I used for an example in the previous paragraph.*

Properties of Mask and Selection

Let's review some of the properties we observed when using the mask tool in the previous tutorial. First, if you move an existing mask using a mask tool in Normal mode (except the Mask Brush or Mask Transform tool), it becomes a selection. If ALT is held down when the selection is created, the original image in the masked area remains; if not, it is replaced with the current Paper color if it is a flat image with no objects. A selection can be moved around an image, even beyond the edge of the image borders, and it will still maintain both its shape and contents. If a selection is dragged completely off the image, it becomes a new image.

Rearranging a Photograph

Be it a picture or a room, rearranging things changes the overall mood and effect. Grace, my teenage daughter, loves to rearrange her bedroom—she would do it daily if it were possible. Rearranging parts of a photograph is easier than you might imagine, and it is a whole lot easier than moving bedroom furniture.

Our goal in this exercise is to rearrange (edit) a photograph of the English coast so that it looks as it might have looked when Vikings brought terror to this island nation. To accomplish this, we must remove anything modern from the photograph. This exercise uses the Rectangle Mask tool and the Feather command. It also introduces another aspect of working with masks—the *selection.* We are going to use these tools to create and move the contents of a masked area from one part of an image to another.

1. Choose File | Open and from the Open An Image dialog box, select EXERCISE\PHOTOS\ENGLISH COAST located on the Corel CD-ROM. If the image is too large to fit on your display, use Zoom To Fit (F4). I have circled the two objects we need to remove from the photograph in Figure 7-9.
2. Select the Rectangle Mask tool (R) and then in the Property Bar change the Feather setting to 10; every mask made with the Rectangle Mask tool will have a feather that is 10 pixels wide.
3. Click and drag a rectangle mask to the left of the small building in the middle right area of the photograph, as shown in Figure 7-10(a). If the mask you made doesn't look right, there is no need to use Undo, just drag another one. The existing mask will disappear as you start another one.

FIGURE 7-9 To make this look like the English coast of the Viking era, we must remove the circled items

4. With the mask tool cursor, click inside the mask you just created. Holding down OPTION, drag the mask to the right until it covers the building as shown in Figure 7-10(b). Turn off the marquee and it becomes apparent the building is gone (see Figure 17-10(c)). You have just made a selection. If your Objects Docker was open (CTRL-F7), you saw the selection appear above the background on the palette.

5. Locate the post with the life preserver ring on it near the middle bottom of the photograph. Create a mask like the one shown in Figure 7-11(a). Drag it over the post as shown in Figure 7-11(b).

6. Figure 7-12 shows our old English coast. By using selections, we have quickly and easily removed the two items from the photograph that didn't exist in the days of Leif Eriksson. Close the file and do not save the changes.

(a)

(b)

(c)

FIGURE 7-10 (a) Creating a feather mask next to the building. (b) Dragging the selection over the building. (c) Where did the building go?

The Mask Transform Tool (M)

The Mask Transform tool is found on the flyout with the Object Picker tool. The Mask Transform tool is actually a mask modifier. All masks created with the mask

(a) (b)

FIGURE 7-11 (a) Creating a feather mask of the area adjacent to the post. (b) After dragging the selection on top of the post, it disappears

FIGURE 7-12 Our coast photo now looks the way it may have in the days of the Vikings

tools can be moved, scaled, rotated, skewed, or have perspective applied; in other words, you can do just about anything you want to with this tool.

When the Mask Transform tool is selected, eight handles appear on the existing mask. Clicking inside the mask changes the shape of the handles, indicating the transform mode. The Transform Mode also appears in the Property Bar, as shown in the preceding illustration. Figure 7-13 shows the control handles associated with the different modes and functions. There are many ways to manipulate a mask using this tool, but you will find its most commonly used function is to move a mask on an image or to change the size (scale) of a mask. The other transform functions, shown next, are mostly used when working with objects, which is explored in more detail in Chapter 12.

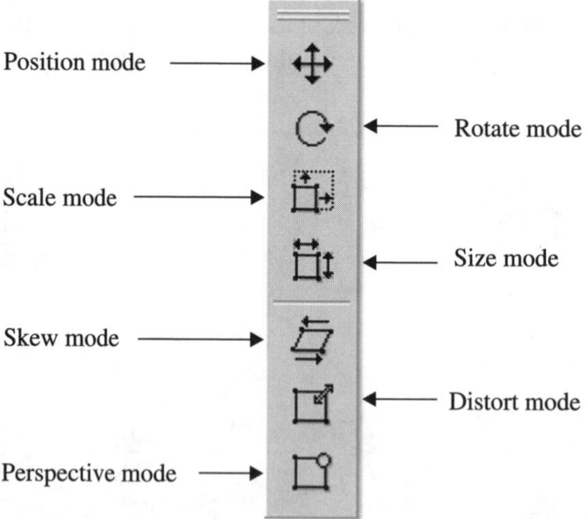

TIP: *Whenever you apply a transformation to a mask, be sure to double-click the mask to complete the transform action. Until you complete the action, most of the PHOTO-PAINT commands will be unavailable.*

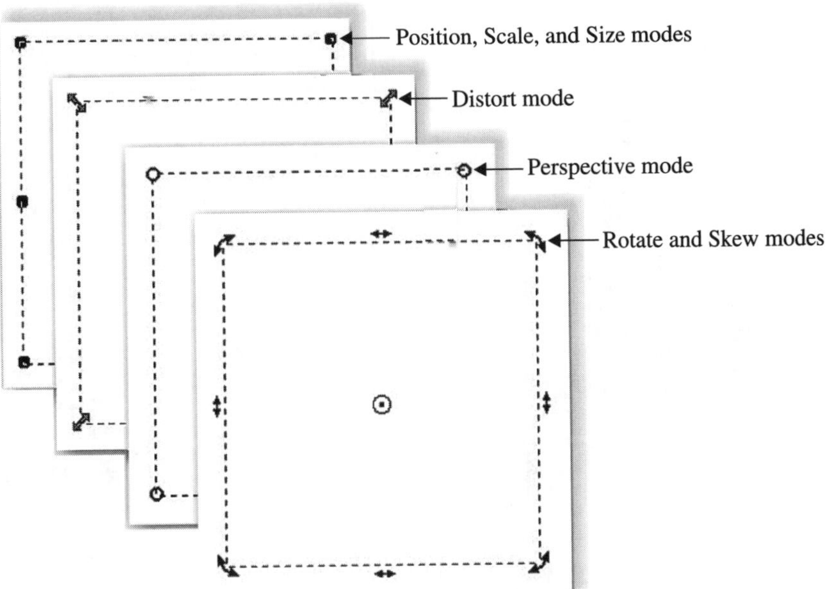

FIGURE 7-13 The handles indicate the selected mask transform mode

The Mask Brush Tool (B)

The remaining button on the Mask Tools flyout is the Mask Brush tool, which is used to modify both the regular and color-sensitive masks. This is the ultimate mask clean-up and touch-up tool. The Mask Brush tool enables you to brush or paint an area to be masked. Unlike a regular brush tool that applies color to an image, the Mask Brush tool can be used to apply or remove a portion of a mask using the Additive and Subtractive modes. The size and shape of the Mask Brush tool are set from the Property Bar.

We've covered a lot of material. If you have gone through each of the exercises, you have learned a lot about masks and how they work. In the next chapter, we will continue to learn more about these powerful tools.

CHAPTER 8

Advanced Masks

This chapter begins with the all-important topic of mask management. We will then learn about using photographs as masks, the Color Mask, and several PHOTO-PAINT mask commands buried in the Mask menu that are real gems. We will also take a brief look at the Path Node Edit tool.

NOTE: *Throughout this chapter we will be referencing the Standard toolbar (shown here). I advise that you enable it, if necessary: Window | Toolbars | Standard.*

Saving a Mask

All masks created in Corel PHOTO-PAINT can be saved and reloaded. This ability to save masks is essential because:

- Only one regular mask can be on an image at a time.
- Masks are valuable. If you spend several hours creating a mask, you'll probably want a copy for future use.
- It's a great way to copy the same size image area from several different images.

There are two ways that a mask can be saved: to disk or with an image in temporary storage called a *channel.* An image containing a regular mask that is saved in Corel PHOTO-PAINT format will have its mask saved with the image automatically. In addition to Corel PHOTO-PAINT format, masks can be saved in TARGA (.TGA) and TIFF (.TIF) formats. They are also saved as alpha channel information when an image is saved as a Photoshop (.PSD) image.

The ability to save a mask apart from the image allows a mask created in one image to be loaded and applied to other images for special effects or accurate placement of objects. How another application uses the saved mask information depends on the application. For example, Photoshop interprets the mask information in a .TIF or .TGA file as an alpha channel.

Use of the mask channel is explained later in this chapter. The following procedure is for saving a mask to disk:

1. With a mask present on the current image, choose Mask | Save. At this point, you have two choices, as shown next: Save To Disk and Save As Channel. Select Save To Disk and the Save A Mask To Disk dialog box opens.

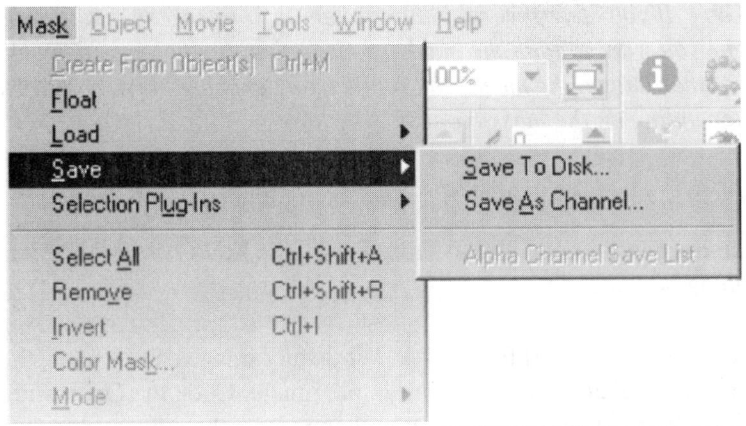

2. Choose from the Files Of Type list, name the mask, and click the Save button. The mask has been saved and can be recalled at a later time.

When naming masks, try to include "mask" as part of the name (for example, MASK FOR PROJECT 22 or TREE MASK.TIF).

TIP: *Do not use a unique extension such as MSK for the mask. The three-character extension is used by Corel PHOTO-PAINT and other applications to determine the correct import filter to use. Although the mask can be saved in any bitmap format (that is, PCX, TIF, BMP, and so on), I recommend you save masks in Corel PHOTO-PAINT's native CPT format.*

Loading a Mask

The Load Mask function allows a wide variety of image file formats to be loaded as masks. Any image file can be used for a mask. Using photographs or other

8

nonmask files may give unpredictable, although not necessarily undesirable, results. A nonmask file is any image file that was not created using the mask tools in Corel PHOTO-PAINT.

When loading a mask, it is important to be aware that Corel PHOTO-PAINT will *resize the mask to fit the image.*

Loading a mask into an image involves the following procedure:

TIP: *If you have several images open on your screen, make sure that the one you want to load the mask into is active. If you load the mask into another image, the mask may replace any existing mask in that image, depending on the mask mode.*

1. Select the image to which the mask being loaded will be applied.
2. Choose Mask | Load | Load From Disk. The Load A Mask From Disk dialog box opens.

Select the file to be used for a mask. While any image can be used, the mask will become a black-and-white or a grayscale image. Click the Open button, and a thumbnail of the mask you are loading will appear on the cursor. At this point you can click the cursor anywhere on the image, and the mask will be applied to the entire image. You can also click and drag a rectangle and the mask will be resized to the shape you dragged. While you can change the size (I don't recommend it—but you can), you cannot change the *aspect ratio* of the mask (the ratio of the height to the width).

Removing a Mask

There are several ways to remove a mask. One of the quickest is to click the Remove Mask button on the Mask toolbar shown next. A mask must exist on the active image for the mask buttons in the toolbar to be available. Other ways to remove the mask are to select Mask | Remove and to use the keyboard combination CTRL-SHIFT-R. A mask can also be removed with DEL if the mask is selected, as indicated by the control handles. (The mask is selected whenever the Mask Transform tool is selected.) If the mask is not selected, DEL will *clear the contents of the mask.* Therefore, use DEL with caution.

Inverting a Mask

One of the more useful mask functions is the Invert Mask command. When a mask is created, the area inside the mask can be modified while the area outside the mask is protected. The Invert Mask command reverses the mask so that the area that was inside the mask now becomes protected, and the area outside can be modified. The Invert Mask command can be accessed through the Mask menu on the Standard toolbar by clicking on the Invert Mask button (shown next), or with the keyboard combination CTRL-SHIFT-I.

TIP: *Some masks are so complex that it is difficult to determine what part of the image lies inside or outside the mask. A quick way to check is to select the Mask Overlay button on the Standard toolbar. Only the tinted area (red by default) is protected. The Mask Overlay is a display function and does not affect the operation of PHOTO-PAINT.*

Select All

To mask the entire image, either click the Select All button from the Standard toolbar, choose Mask | Select All, or press CTRL-SHIFT-A. You can also double-click any of the Mask selection tools in the Toolbox except the Mask Brush tool. The mask will encompass the entire image inside the image window. If the image is only partially visible because you have zoomed into an area, the entire image is still masked. In this situation, you will not be able to see the entire mask.

Mask Channel Operations

The mask channel is a temporary mask storage area. If you do any amount of work with masks, you'll love this feature. You can temporarily store masks in mask channels by using the Channels palette. When you create a mask, Corel PHOTO-PAINT makes a copy of the current mask and stores it in a channel where you can access and reuse it in the image as many times as you wish. You can also save a mask channel to a file to be opened in subsequent images.

When you save a mask and then change it, you can reflect the changes in the channel by selecting the saved channel in the Channels palette and clicking the Save To Current Channel button in the palette. There are also commands for saving a mask channel to a separate file or for opening a previously saved mask channel. The contents of the mask channel are retained when an image is closed.

The Channels Docker

The Channels Docker window can be opened several ways. I have created a little roadmap of the Channels Docker in Figure 8-1. The Channels Docker can be opened by pressing CTRL-F9, clicking on its tab in the Docker window, or by selecting the Channel button in the Property Bar (#1 in Figure 8-1) when a mask tool is selected. Clicking the button on the Docker (#2) opens a menu from which you can create and save channels, open and modify existing channels, or change the size of the thumbnails on the Channels Docker display. Selecting either Channel Properties or New Channel on the menu opens the Channel Properties dialog box (#3).

The Channels Docker provides several different command function buttons at the bottom (#4). Left to right, they are Channel To Mask, Save Mask To New Channel, and Save To Current Channel. The trashcan icon on the far right is used to delete either masks or mask channels; it cannot delete either the composite or individual color channels.

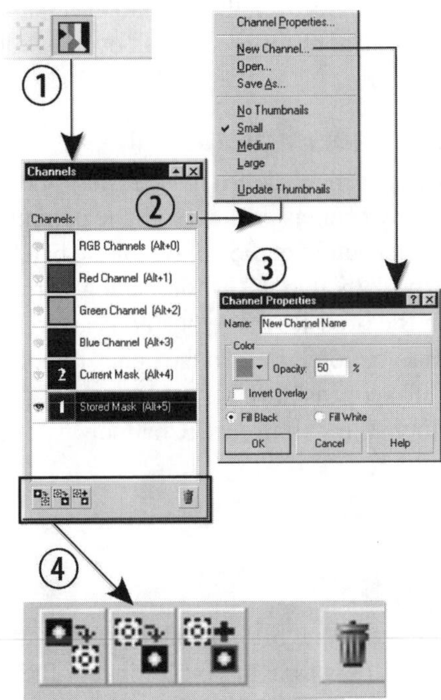

FIGURE 8-1 The Channels Docker window shown with associated menus and property boxes

Exploring Channels

The top entries in the Channel Docker are the composite (RGB in the example) and the individual channels. Whenever a mask is created, the current mask appears next to the individual channels. That's simple so far, right? Although an image can have only one mask at a time, you can store many different masks with an image in the form of channels.

Different Names and Colors

In Figure 8-1, we notice there is one channel below the current mask. If you have many mask channels, names are an easy way to keep track of them. You can assign names to channels either when you create them or by opening the Channel Properties dialog box. This dialog box provides another way to differentiate among mask channels by allowing assignment of different mask overlay colors and transparencies.

Operating the Channels Palette

You can convert a mask into a channel through the Mask menu (Mask | Save | Save As Channel) or through the Channels palette (with the current mask selected, click the Save Mask To New Channel button at the bottom of the palette). Conversely, you can convert a channel into a mask though the Mask menu or through the Channels palette. Here are a few more tidbits before we move on. You can create a new channel without a mask by clicking the little option button in the upper-right corner of the Palette and choosing New Channel. This opens the Channel Properties dialog box we saw before.

That's enough for now. We will use the Channels palette in a hands-on exercise later in this chapter.

Manipulating Masks

After a mask has been created, you often need to modify it. Corel has provided several mask-manipulation tools to help you. Probably the most often used mask-manipulation tool is the Feather Mask command.

Feather Mask

Feathered masks are the means by which you can add or subtract images or effects without the viewer being aware of it. Technically speaking, *feathering* a mask changes the transparency of the pixels located near the mask boundary. Any effect or command applied to the selection fades gradually as you get near the protected area. Feathering can be applied to a mask during or after its creation.

Feathering is particularly useful if you want to apply an effect to the masked area but not to the surrounding area. Feathering a mask makes the transition between the two areas gradual and therefore less noticeable. Figure 8-2 shows an example of an object created from a nonfeathered mask and one from a feathered mask. See if you can figure out which one was made with the feathered mask.

Whether you select Mask | Shape | Feather (#1 in Figure 8-3) or click the Feather Mask button (#2), a dialog box opens (#3) that allows you to set the direction, amount, and type of feathering to be applied to the current mask.

FIGURE 8-2 Which object was created with a feathered mask? (The answer is the one on the right)

NOTE: *New in PHOTO-PAINT 9, the Feather Mask function now has a preview button so you can preview the effect of the feather setting.*

The Width setting determines how wide a feather to apply to the mask edge. The Average Direction effectively applies a Gaussian blur to all the pixels directly inside and outside the mask; this provides the smoothest mask of the choices. Selecting any other Direction enables a choice of two different Edges: Linear and Curved.

In Figure 8-4, the Feather Mask command was applied to three identical masks using Average direction, Middle direction with Linear Edges, and Middle direction with Curved Edges settings. The masked area was filled with 100% black fill and zoomed to 300%. The Average mask (left) has the greatest amount of blurring. The Linear mask (middle) has a tendency to produce points at perpendicular intersections of a straight-sided mask. The Curved feather mask (right) doesn't spread out as much as the other two despite identical Width settings.

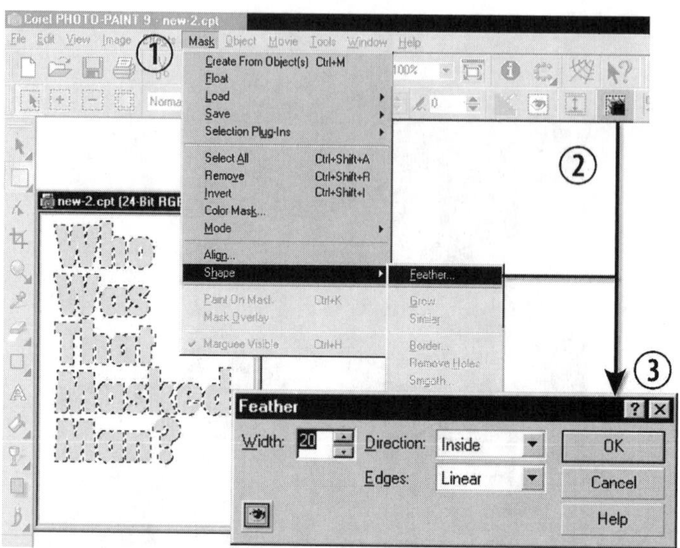

FIGURE 8-3 The Feather Mask dialog box (3) can be selected through the Mask menu (1) or by use of the Feather Mask button (2)

FIGURE 8-4 The different effects of mask's feather settings, from left to right: Average, Linear, and Curved

The Shape Category Mask Commands

Some of the other mask commands you may work with are located in the Shape category of the Mask menu, as shown next. These commands are Border, Remove Holes, Smooth, Threshold, Expand, and Reduce.

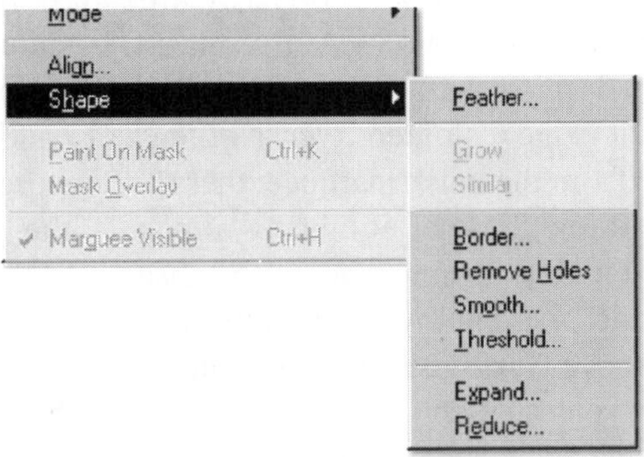

Border

The Border command removes a portion of an existing mask to a border according to the setting in the Border dialog box. It offers the option of three different Edges settings: Hard, Medium, and Soft. Borders only move outward from the mask regardless of the Mask Mode setting. Be careful when applying this command to circles; it tends to degrade the general shape of the circle. In the illustration shown next, the mask created from the ampersand character has a 20-pixel border applied, creating a diffuse glow. The preview feature of the mask is shown.

TIP: *For a creative effect, try applying the Border command to a square or rectangle mask multiple times.*

Remove Holes

Remove Holes is supposed to remove those nasty little mask fragments that tend to be left when you're using the color-sensitive masks. In Figure 8-5(a), I used the Magic Wand Mask tool to isolate the area surrounding the river. Yeah, I know it looks like a lake, but it is the Colorado river. Not *the* Colorado, but a Colorado river. As you can see from the mask marquee, there are hundreds of tiny mask fragments. Applying Remove Holes eliminates almost all the holes, as shown in Figure 8-5(b). Unfortunately, as indicated by the absence of the marquee, it also removed the river, which I did not want to remove.

Once enabled, Remove Holes goes on a merry hole hunt. As a result, there aren't many situations where you can use it, but for the few times when the conditions of the mask and image are suitable, it works great. It has no adjustable settings; it will either work or not work for what you want to use it for. Keep the old faithful Undo command (CTRL-Z) handy and give it a try.

Smooth

The Smooth command creates a more fluid mask boundary by smoothing out sharp bends (*jaggies*) in the mask that occur especially when you're creating color-sensitive

(a)

(b)

FIGURE 8-5 (a) The original mask holes; (b) after using Remove Holes masks. Some pixels that are not in the selection before smoothing will become part of the selection after smoothing; some pixels that are currently in the selection will no longer be included in it. The Smooth command can sometimes eliminate entire portions of a mask, just as the Remove Holes command can. The amount of smoothing this command does depends on the Radius setting you enter in the dialog box. Large values tend to completely change the shape of the mask. I have created a sample of a ragged mask edge in Figure 8-6(a). In Figure 8-6(b) at a setting of 10 the edges are smoother but the shape is changing. In Figures 8-6(c) and 8-6(d), the Radius setting of the Smooth command has significantly altered the shape of the mask.

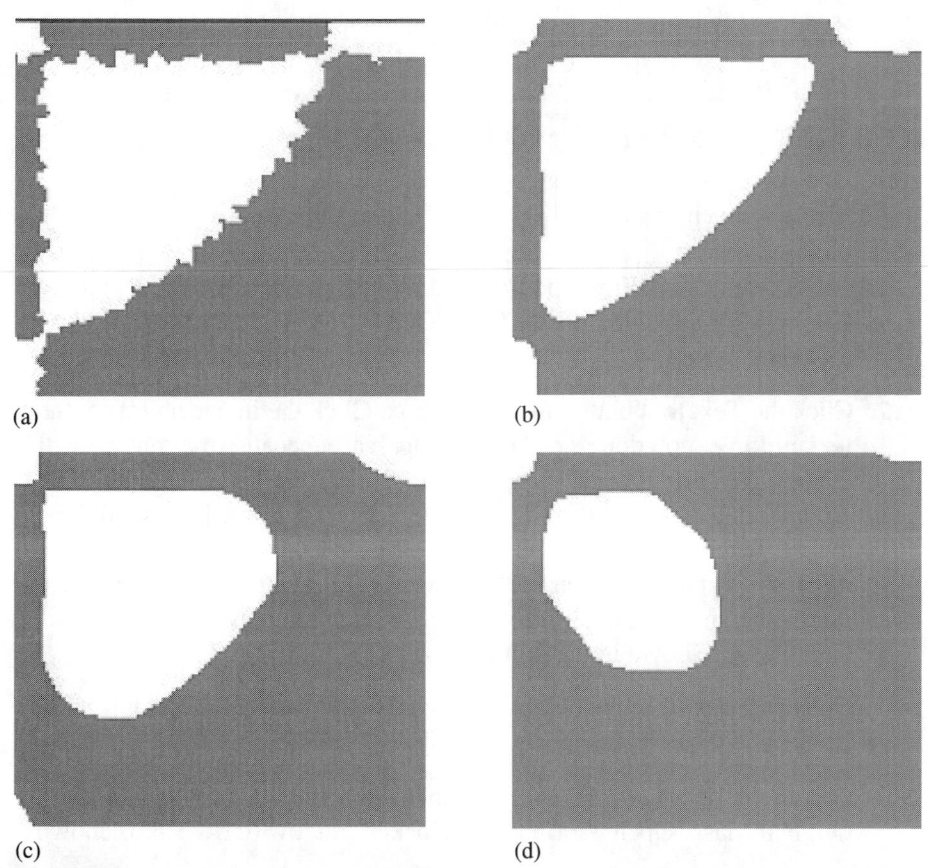

FIGURE 8-6 (a) Original mask edge; (b) Smooth applied at a setting of 10; (c) Smooth at 30; (d) Smooth at 50 (maximum)

Threshold

The Threshold command is the opposite of the Smooth command. When you have a mask with an indefinite edge, as with a feathered mask, this command makes it into a binary (black-and-white) mask by applying a Threshold function to it. If you do the hands-on exercises in Chapter 16, you will use this filter. Oddly enough, this is one of my favorite filters in the category because it allows me to make the edges of masks more distinct. The only setting, Level (1–255), determines which grayscale values in the mask become white (below the Level setting) and which become black (above the Level setting).

The Expand and Reduce commands do just what they say they do. Use them to make masks larger or smaller. Like the Border command, these commands tend to degrade shapes with large values or multiple applications.

Creating Distressed Text

In this hands-on exercise, we are going to create the illusion of text that was stenciled on a wooden crate.

1. Select File | Open. From the Import dialog box, locate the file on the CD-ROM: EXERCISE\PHOTOS\WOOD CRATE. Click the Open button to open the file.
2. Click the Text tool button in the Toolbox. Click the image and type **danger no smoking**. You don't need to use uppercase, because the font we will be using displays everything in uppercase. Change the Font to Stencil BT at a size of 72, and change the alignment to Centered. Some letters will be off the image area at this point. Click the Object Picker tool in the Toolbox. Align the text to the center of the image (CTRL-A), and it will look like the image shown in Figure 8-7. Note, your workspace may appear different from the one shown in the figure.
3. Create a mask from the object (text) by using CTRL-M. Select Object | Delete and the text disappears, leaving only the mask.
4. Choose Mask | Save | Save As Channel and name the mask channel Original Mask. Open the Channels Docker window (CTRL-F9), as shown

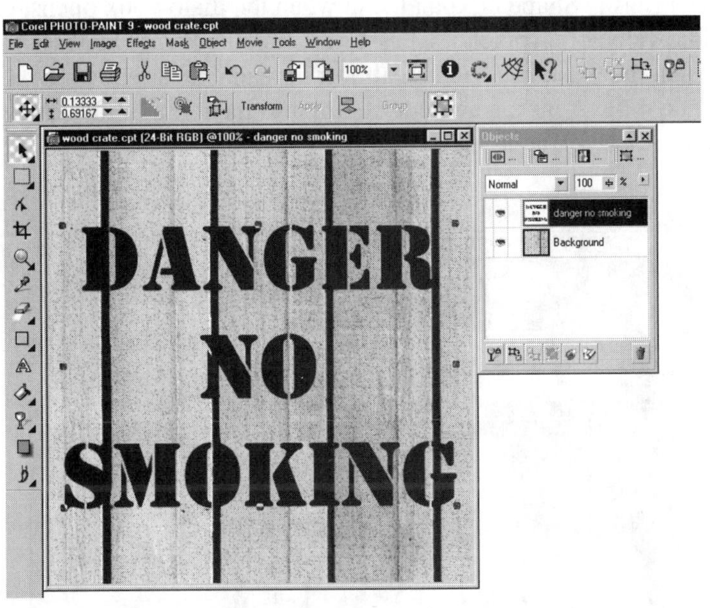

FIGURE 8-7 With the text placed and selected, we are ready to begin

next. Note that in the following image, I have enabled the Mask Overlay so that you can see the mask more clearly.

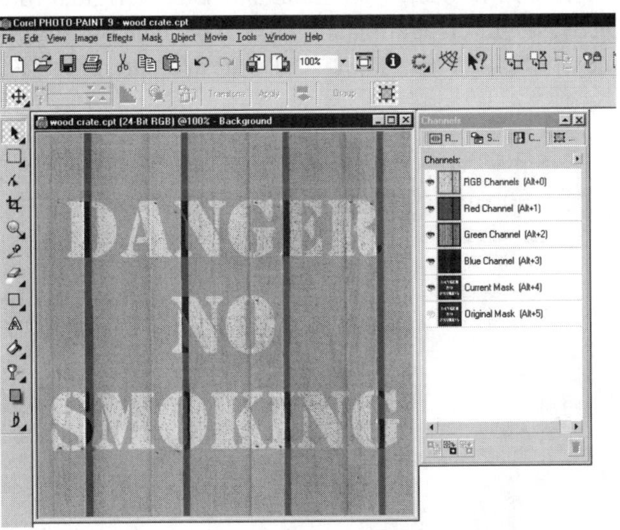

5. Select Mask | Shape | Expand, and when the dialog box opens, enter a Width value of 4 (pixels). Click OK. Click the Paint On Mask button to see that the mask has become almost unreadable, as shown next. Click the Paint On Mask button again to return it to its normal mode. Now it's time for some mask magic.

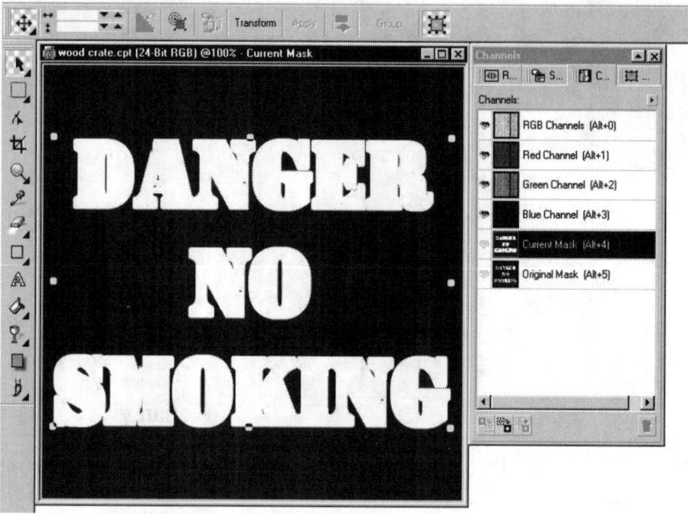

6. Choose Mask | Mode | XOR. This is the Exclusive OR mode of the mask tool that, if you were honest, you had serious doubts had any use whatsoever. Now select Mask | Load and select Original Mask. Click the Paint On Mask button again, and you will have an outline of the text, as shown next. Click the Paint On Mask button again to turn it off.

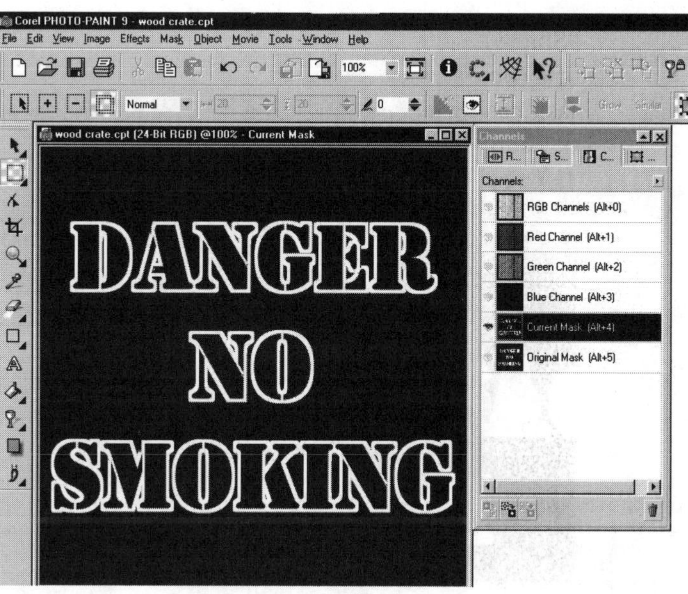

7. Click the red color swatch in the Color palette to change the Paint color to red. Select the Paint tool in the Toolbox, and open the Tool Settings Docker (CTRL-F8). In the Property Bar choose the Spray Can, and set the Brush Type to Power Sprayer. On the Docker change the Paint setting to Subtract. (Phew.) This will cause the Brush Type to change to Custom Spray Can.

8. Drag the cursor over the masked area. When you are finished, turn off the mask marquee by clicking the Show Mask Marquee button to the right of the Mask Overlay button. The Subtract Paint mode prevents the red from painting over the dark shadow areas, which would have made it look unreal. Your finished image should look like Figure 8-8. No need to save this file.

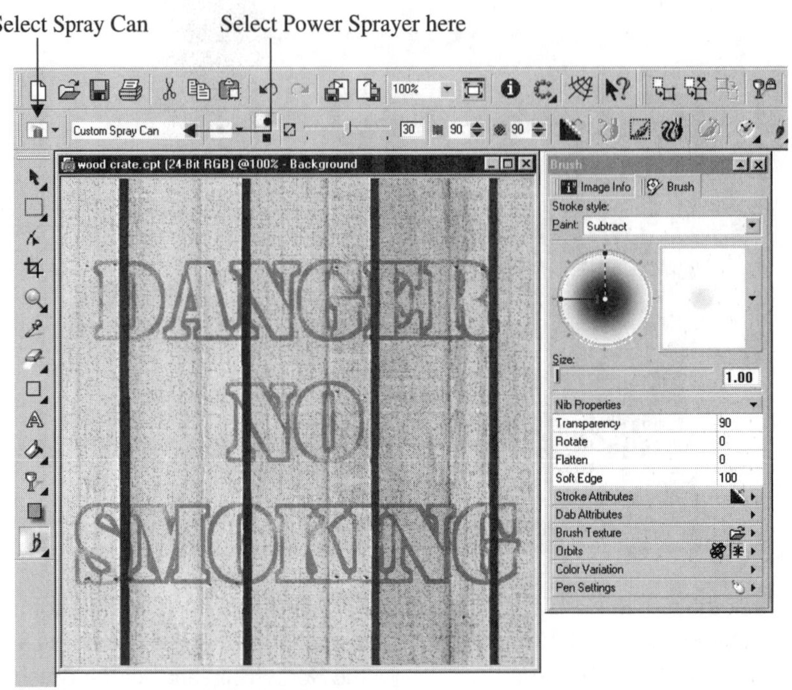

FIGURE 8-8 What's in the box? Probably all the *Godzilla* merchandise that didn't sell

The Color Mask

Most of the color-sensitive masks we have discussed until now could only include colors that were connected to the original sampled color. The Color Mask, like the Similar command discussed in Chapter 7, selects pixels based on their color content, regardless of the position of the selected pixels in relation to the original sample point.

The Color Mask

Selecting the Color Mask, located in the Mask menu, opens the dialog box shown in Figure 8-9. While it may appear a little intimidating, the dialog box is quite simple to use. Use the Eyedropper to select colors in the image that you want masked. If you don't like the result of one of the color selections, remove the check mark from its box. Use the Preview option to determine how successful the color selection process has been and click the OK button. Really simple stuff, right?

Here are some handy tips to help you get up to speed quickly:

- The Color Mask is a dialog box, so you must complete the selection of the mask and apply the mask before you can do any other operation.
- The Color Mask command does not create a color mask. It creates regular masks. When you save a color mask, you are saving the settings of the Color Mask dialog box.
- Preview of the mask made by the Color Mask tool is done on the actual image.

The best way to learn how to use this jewel is to take it for a test ride, which is what we are going to do in the next exercise.

Replacing a Background Using the Color Mask

Replacing a background in a complex image can take time, even with the Color Mask. In this case, we have a photograph of the ruins of a cathedral. The client's

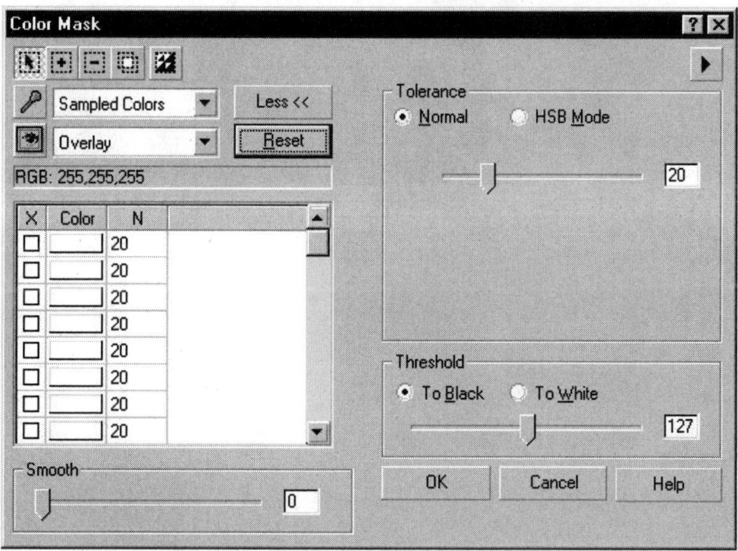

FIGURE 8-9 It looks complicated but the Color Mask dialog box is quite simple to use

art director wants the photo to have a “Gothic motif,” which, after an hour-long discussion, means you have to replace the blue-sky background with something “Gothic.” The first step is to mask the ruins. We could use the Magic Wand Mask tool if we were being paid by the hour. Unfortunately, it is a piece job, so we need to finish the job as soon possible. Let’s get started.

1. Open the image EXERCISE\PHOTOS\CHURCH IN SPAIN. Select Image | Resample, change the Width to 6 inches, and click the OK button.
2. Select Mask | Color Mask to open the dialog box. If you have the room on your display, I recommend positioning the Color Mask dialog box as shown next, so you can see the parts of the image we are masking. Click the Reset button to clear any previous settings.

3. Click the Eyedropper button, place the cursor in the image, and it will become an eyedropper. Click the image at a darker portion of the blue sky, as shown next.

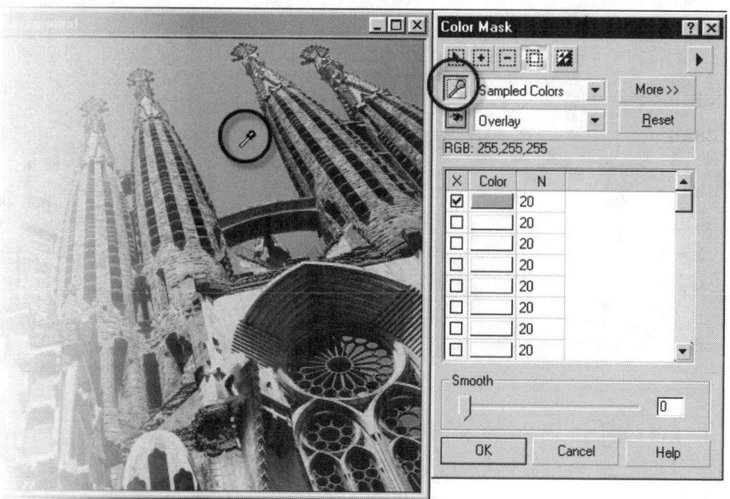

4. Click the Preview button (it looks like an eye), and the image in the Preview shows masked (protected) areas in a red tint. Click OK. Choose File | Save As and save the file as RUINS.

5. Invert the mask (CTRL-SHIFT-I). Select the Create Object From Mask button on the Objects Docker. Look at the thumbnail of the object in the Objects Docker window (CTRL-F7), as shown next. I renamed the object by right-clicking on the name of the object and choosing Properties. The bitmap image of the Ruins is now above the Background image and is an object.

6. With the Object Picker tool from the Toolbox, click the Background in the Objects palette and choose Edit | Fill. When the Edit Fill & Transparency dialog box opens, choose the Texture Fill (last button on the right) and click Edit. Choose Samples 7 from the Texture library, and choose Above The Earth from the Texture list. Click OK and then OK again to apply the fill. The result is shown next. OK, so it doesn't look "Gothic" but it soon will.

7. Select Effects | Art Strokes | Cubist, make sure the Paper Color is set to black, and click OK. The image shown next is getting more Gothic, right?

8. Choose Effects | Distort | Whirlpool and select the Super Warpo style. Click OK. The results are shown next. Close the file and save any changes.

We have a great background, but we need to change the lighting on the ruins. We will learn how to do that in Chapter 21. Until then, remember where you parked RUINS.

What the Color Mask Buttons and Controls Do

The Color Mask dialog box contains more buttons than my digital stereo. While all these controls serve a purpose, some are more useful than others are. Here is a quick (and opinionated) tour of what the controls do.

A Cook's Tour of the Color Mask

Rather than just point out all the tools, let's put them to use on a real image:

1. Open the file EXERCISES\PHOTOS\TREES. Now choose Mask | Color Mask. When the dialog box opens, click Reset (just so all our Color Masks look the same).

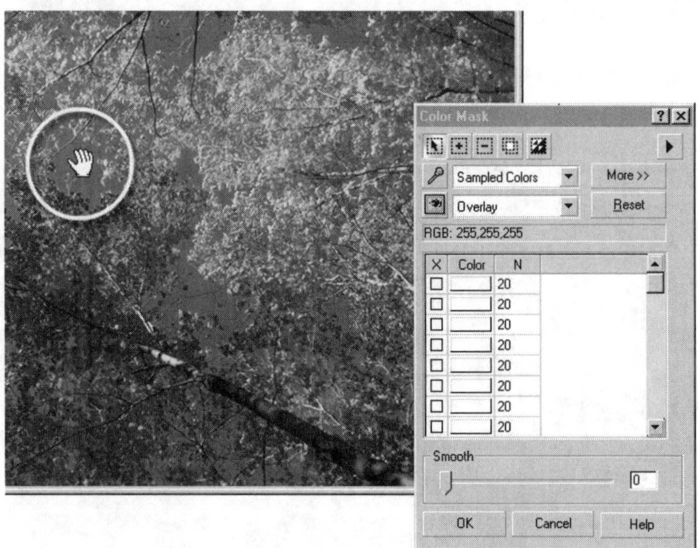

2. Your workspace should look like the one just shown. I have dragged the Color Mask dialog box so it is nearly off the image. Since I am using a 21" monitor and you may not be, you may have less room. Don't worry about it—do the best that you can. Near the left edge of the illustration I have

circled the cursor, which looks like a hand. This multipurpose cursor can zoom in if you click on the image, or zoom out if you right-click it. The current zoom factor is shown in the Title Bar. For example, in the previous image, the zoom factor is 100%. If you are zoomed in to any value equal to or greater than 100%, you can use the hand to pan the image (drag it around). The normal Zoom, Grabber, and Pop-up Navigator don't work when in Color Mask mode.

3. Zoom in on the center of the image until you reach 500%. Click the Eyedropper tool and place the cursor as indicated in the image shown next. Several things happen when you do that. The color under the cursor now appears as our reference color in the Color Mask dialog box.

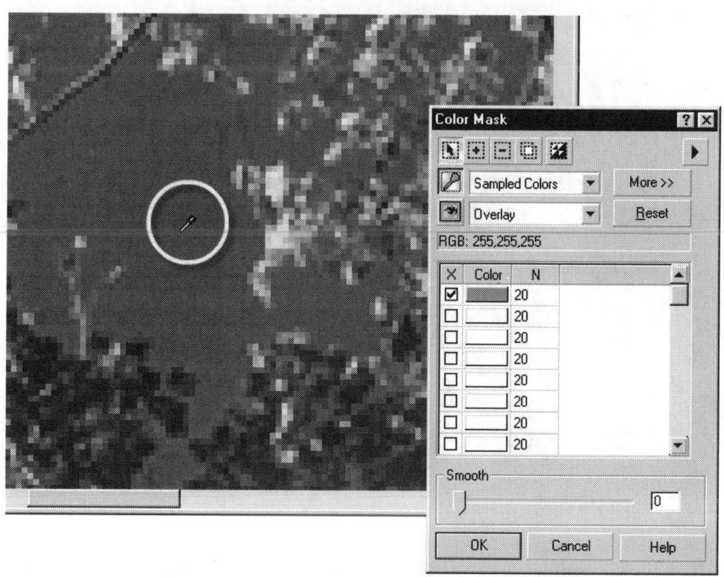

The number to the right of the reference Color swatch, 20, is the Numerical setting (N); it represents the default tolerance setting. At this setting, PHOTO-PAINT will include all shades of blue in the image that are within 20 percent of the reference color. There are several ways to change this setting. You can (1) enter a new value and press ENTER; (2) click the number, place the cursor between the up and down arrows until it becomes a two-headed cursor, and then while holding down the mouse button drag the cursor in either direction; (3) click inside the value box so the cursor is flashing, and use the up arrow or down arrow; and finally (4)

right-click the number, select Settings, and change the value in the Settings dialog box. Regardless of how you enter the numbers, it is more important to know what the numbers mean.

4. Click the Preview button shown circled in the next image. Nearly all the leaves and branches have been overlaid with a red tint (assuming you having changed the mask overlay color). This means the area not covered with red tint is selected. Now change the number to 80 and press ENTER. The Overlay tint has disappeared. Why? Because all shades of color that are within 80 percent of our reference color are now selected—which is almost every color in the image.

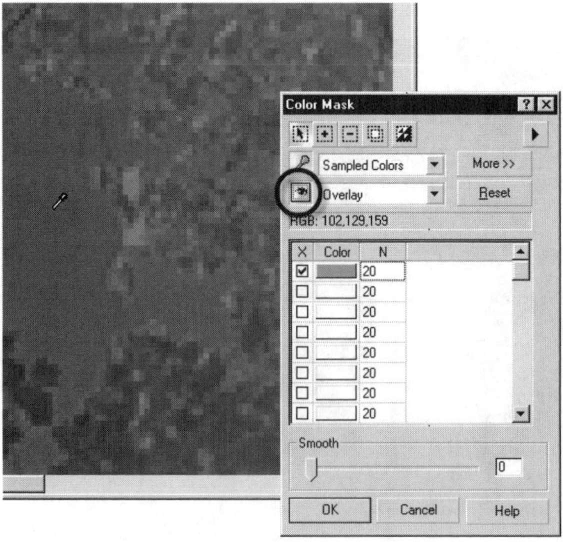

Change the tolerance value to 8 and press ENTER. Now the leaves are again protected, but the parts of the leaves that were dark around the edges are also protected. This brings up the great trade-off when using color-sensitive masks. The transition areas around the edge of objects have color components of the background. If the color tolerance is set at a high enough value, the components will be selected and therefore removed from the image. If set low enough to include them, they will not be selected. If the background color is significantly changed, these transparent edges will appear as coronas around your object. To demonstrate, with the tolerance still set on 8, click OK. The color mask has closed and returned to the photograph.

5. Make sure your Paint is set to black, choose Edit | Fill, and select Paint Color (black). In the preceding image I have changed the Zoom level to 300% and shown an area in the upper right of the photograph. You can see that many of the branches and the background were included in the selected area. Undo (CTRL-Z) and click the Remove Mask button. Open the Color Mask again.

6. Change the tolerance to 26 and click OK. Use Edit | Fill and apply the Paint Fill again. This time the tiny bluish branches are gone, as shown next, but some edge detail is lost as well. Undo (CTRL-Z) and click the Remove Mask button. Open the Color Mask again.

7. Zoom in to 300% and change the Preview to Grayscale as shown earlier. At this point you are looking at the mask just the same as if you had Paint On Mask enabled. At this zoom level the mask looks pretty awful.

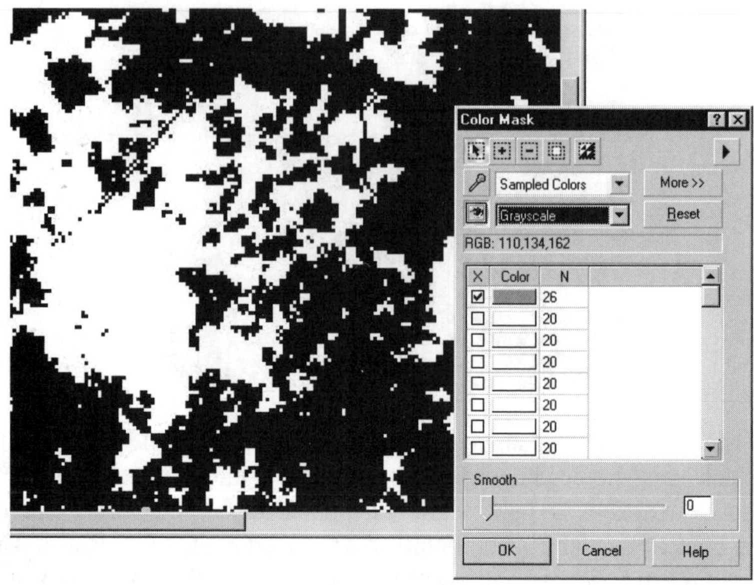

Now move the Smooth slider at the bottom to 100%. The result is shown next. If you click OK and then use Edit | Fill and apply the Paint Fill again, you will see that we have regained some of the branches that were originally lost when we increased the Tolerance to 26 without as much of the blue background.

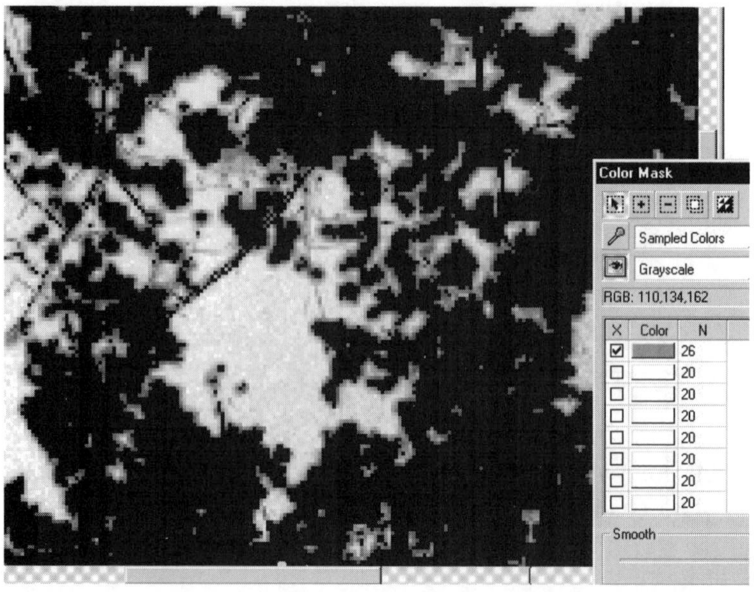

8. Undo (CTRL-Z) the Paint Fill but keep the mask. Choose Edit | Fill, select the Fountain Fill button, and click Edit. Change the Presets value to Circular - Blue 01 and the Steps to 999, as shown next. Click OK to select and OK again to apply. The finished image is shown in Figure 8-10.

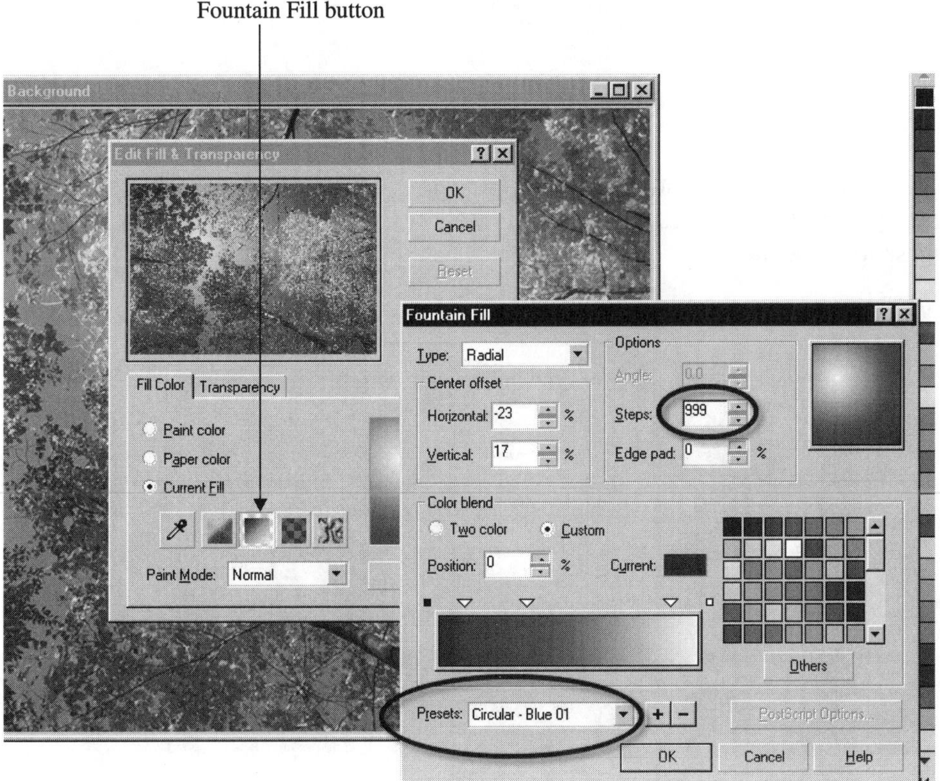

Additional Information About the Color Mask

There are other controls on the Color Mask that deserve some explanation. For example, across the top are the four Mask Mode buttons and the Invert Mask button, as shown next. The Mask Mode buttons control how the mask you make with the Color Mask tool reacts to an existing mask. The Invert Mask button is a nice feature that allows you to either protect or select the sampled colors.

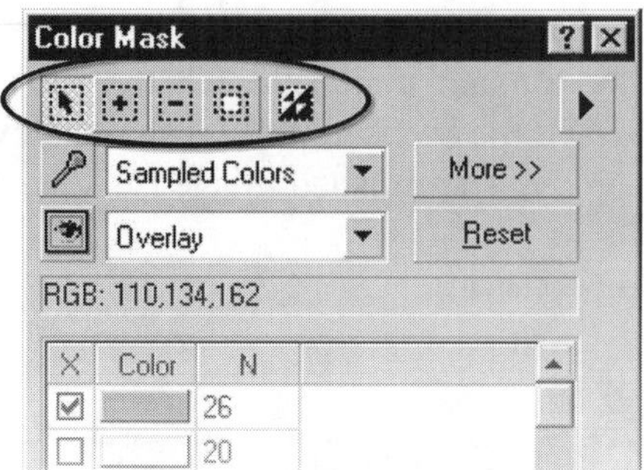

Clicking the More button on the Color Mask dialog box opens the rest of the dialog box, shown next, containing a few additional settings that modify how this mask tool operates.

FIGURE 8-10 Using the Color Mask allows us to replace the sky behind the trees

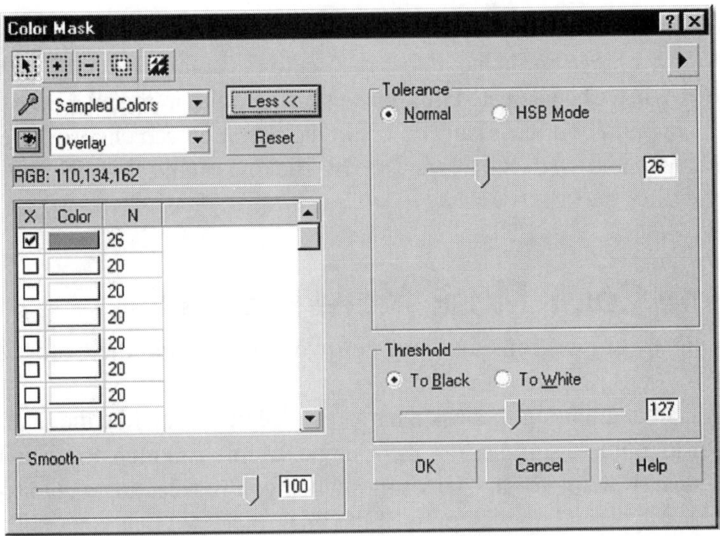

From the expanded dialog box, you can determine what criteria the Color Mask uses to select its color. You can use HSB Mode instead of Normal. For most applications, the Normal setting (default) will do the job. HSB uses a combination of hue, saturation, and brightness to select colors. You can also select to use the HSB components individually to determine which colors are selected. The Threshold settings act just like the Threshold filter. They use the value of the Threshold slider to cause the created mask to move toward either white or black.

Click the right arrow to get more options. You can save all the settings as a color mask file. This file can be opened and used at a later time. The color mask can also be saved to a mask channel through this option. Remember that the mask channel is a temporary storage area that disappears when the image is closed.

The default setting for the Color Mask tool creates a mask in Sampled Colors mode. In this mode, everything that is not selected is protected.

If you right-click one of the color selections, the Edit Color option becomes available. Choosing Edit Color opens the Color Palette dialog box from which you can specify a specific color to select. For example, if you only wanted to select every place in the image that the color PANTONE CV742 was used, this is where you would make the selection.

At the top of the Color Mask (next to the Eyedropper icon) is a large list of settings that allows you to quickly select a type or range of colors or shades. Some of the selections are not what they appear to be. For example, the setting Blues does not select everything blue in an image; rather it is set to the color Blue in the palette at a high value (50). If we had selected this as the starting point in the RUINS exercise, it would not have initially selected any colors in the sky. You can choose Blues and then change the blue that is used as the reference by clicking on the sky with the Eyedropper.

Using the Color Mask More Productively

The following are suggestions that may help you when using the Color Mask:

- If you are attempting to mask a narrow range of colors, like the blue in a sky, use multiple samples or take a single sample and increase the Numerical (tolerance) setting for it. Many times when you're selecting a color or range of colors, you end up with parts of the image selected that you didn't want selected. Rather than waste time trying to balance the Color and Numerical settings to get the "perfect" mask, use the mask tools after the mask is applied. It is always easier to remove a portion of a mask than it is to create one that has a boundary along a ragged or irregular boundary.
- When you're changing the Numerical value, the Preview window won't reflect the changes until you press ENTER or click another color.
- If you must edit photographs a lot to select and modify backgrounds, this tool will serve you well. If the background is very well-defined and noncontiguous, you may want to consider the Similar command, which is discussed in Chapter 7.

Paths

What are paths? *Paths* are vectors that are living in a world of pixels. In other words, they are line and curve segments connected by square end points called *nodes.* If you work with CorelDRAW, the paths will be familiar to you. Masks and paths share some common characteristics. A mask is created from a bitmap image. A path, on the other hand, is a vector drawing that exists on a layer above the image and is independent of the image resolution. A closed path completely encloses an area, as a mask would. An open path has start and end nodes that are not connected; this is something that a mask cannot do.

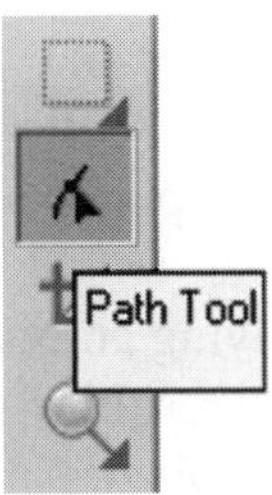

The advantage of the path over the mask is, in a word, precision. A path, being a vector image, can be precisely edited; a mask, being a bitmap image, is adjusted by adding or subtracting from it with a Brush tool or something similar. With a path, you have full Bezier level control over the points and nodes, just as you have in CorelDRAW. When you need to make accurate masks, you will want to create a path using the Path Node Edit tool.

New paths can be created by use of the Path Node Edit tool, or existing masks can be converted to paths. When the path is exactly the shape you want, you can save the path, convert it to a mask, or both. A mask can be converted to a path, edited as a path, and converted back to a mask.

If you export a mask as a part of an Encapsulated PostScript (EPS) image, the mask is converted to a path.

Corel has produced a large volume of material on paths. In the interest of saving space, I refer you to either the PHOTO-PAINT User's Manual or the extensive online help. With the online help, I recommend opening the index and entering the word "Path." You will find a lot of material on the subject.

Stroke Mask and Stroke Path Commands

These commands are used to automatically apply brushstrokes along a path defined by either a mask or a path. You can use them to apply many of the brushes. Operation is simple. Select the brush/tool you want to apply. Make any changes to the size or shape of the Nib, and then click the appropriate button in the Property Bar.

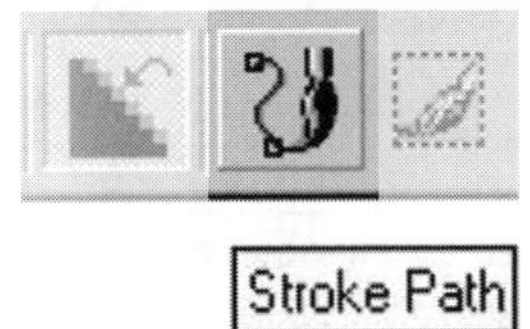

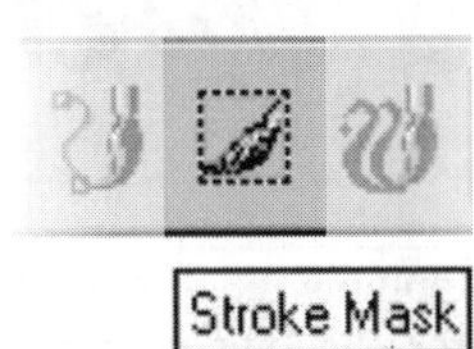

To make the Stroke Mask or Stroke Path options available, there must be a mask or path on the image and one of the following tools must be selected: the Paint tool, the Effect tool, the Color Replacer tool, the Eraser tool, or the Image Sprayer tool.

Figure 8-11 was created by applying an Image Srayer brush to a new object with the Stroke Mask command. The resulting rectangular border is an object and can, therefore, have a drop shadow applied. Another example of this technique can be found in the color insert.

TIP: *This mask has changed its address since PHOTO-PAINT 8. It is no longer found in the Edit menu. It has its own button on the Property Bar.*

This chapter and the one before it have only scratched the surface of the things you can do with masks. Now we need to move on to the daunting subject of image and color correction.

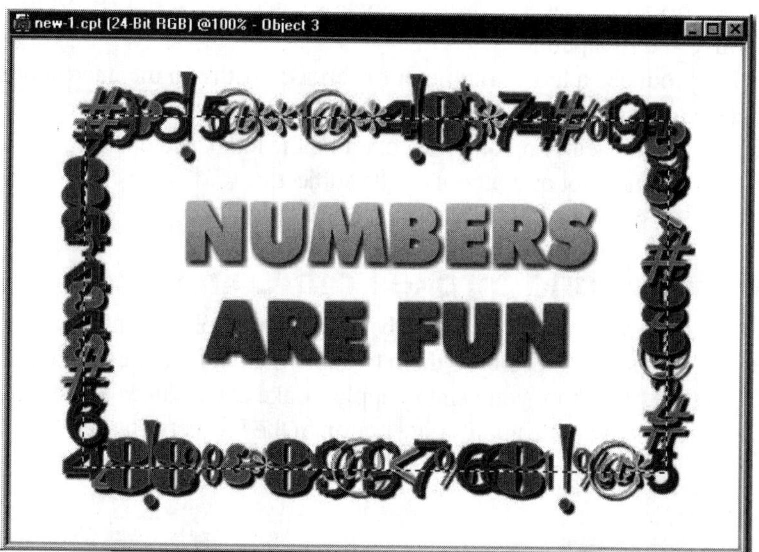

FIGURE 8-11 Applying the Stroke Mask command to a new object allows you to create drop shadows underneath

CHAPTER 9

Working with Fills and the Shape Tools

Fill tools have been around as long as bitmap paint programs. Also known as "flood tools," their sole purpose is to cover an image or a selected portion of an image with a different color, texture, or pattern. The icon for these tools is almost universally a tipping bucket, which is appropriate, since the tools act much like pouring a bucket of paint on an image. Fill tools have come a long way since the early days when programs like Microsoft Paint seemed sophisticated.

The Fill and Shape tools in PHOTO-PAINT 9 can apply an infinite number of combinations of colors, textures, and patterns in hundreds of ways. When it comes to color selection, the onscreen color palette is just the tip of the iceberg. PHOTO-PAINT offers many options concerning what to fill and what to fill it with. In this chapter, we will cover the Fill command of the Edit menu, the Fill tools in the Toolbox, and even the Shape tools, since their Property Bars have fill controls. You will learn to choose from four basic fills—Uniform, Fountain, Bitmap, and Texture—and to tweak the huge array of options available with each. You will learn everything there is to know about the subject of fills. Wow, I can hardly wait to read what I am going to say. That's it . . . I am definitely cutting back to no more than 12 cups of coffee a day.

The Fill Tools . . . So Many Choices

PHOTO-PAINT has the following four Fill tools:

- Fill command
- Fill tool
- Interactive Fill tool
- Shape tools

The Fill command, located in the Edit menu, operates on the entire image or the selected (masked) parts of it. Staying true to its computer heritage, the Fill tool uses the cursor to initiate the fill, thereby allowing application of a fill to a selected area. For example, if I have text selected, I can fill each character of a word with a different fill. The Interactive Fill tool is true to its name. It is a fill tool in which you control much of how the resulting fill is applied interactively by moving nodes on the actual image. While all these Fill tools flood an area of an image depending on a mask boundary or the image content to determine its boundaries, the Shape tools determine their own fill boundaries as they are created with the cursor. They are not a traditional fill tool, but the Shape tools are included in the fill tool arsenal because they have fill capabilities.

It could be said there is a fifth fill tool, the Edit | Create Fill From Selection command. This command creates a bitmap fill from an area of an image selected by a mask. I do not consider it a fill tool because like the Terrazzo filter it is really a tool for *creating* fills not *applying* them.

Before we can apply a fill, we have to learn how to select the type of fill we want to apply. In PHOTO-PAINT there are three ways to select and control the fill that the Fill tools apply: the Edit Fill & Transparency dialog box, the Select Fill dialog box, and Property Bars. Although all three share common parts, they essentially offer different ways to control the Fill tools.

Selecting the Right Fill

Edit | Fill opens the Edit Fill & Transparency dialog box, shown in Figure 9-1. The Edit Fill & Transparency (EFT) dialog box is the Grand Central Station for all the fills within PHOTO-PAINT. To paraphrase President Truman, "The fill starts here." While other dialog boxes and Property Bars offer some degree of selection and control, it is the EFT dialog box that offers enough controls and features to satisfy anyone. The EFT dialog box contains two pages: Fill Color and Transparency. The Fill Color page is used to set the type and color of the fill, and the Transparency page contains different transparency options that are possible with the fill.

The Select Fill dialog box, shown next, is a limited version of the EFT dialog box. It is accessed by double-clicking on the Fill swatch in the Status Bar. While it is limited in the controls and features it offers, I use it every time I write this book. Was that too subtle?

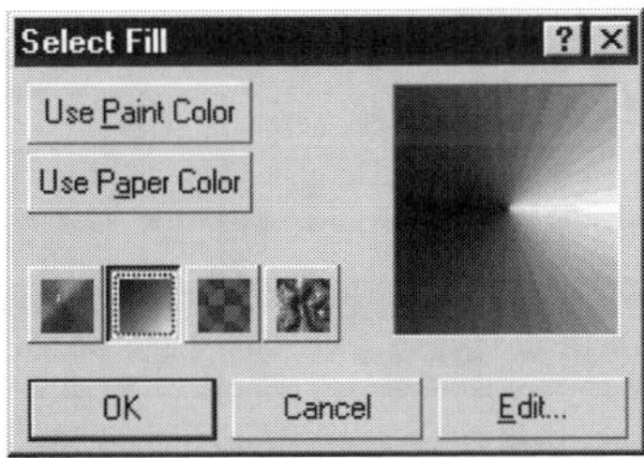

There are four Shape tools in the Toolbox flyout, each with its own Property Bar. Figure 9-2 is a dazzling display of all the Property Bars for Shape and Fill tools. Don't worry about them yet; I just wanted you to see them. We will learn about them as we go along.

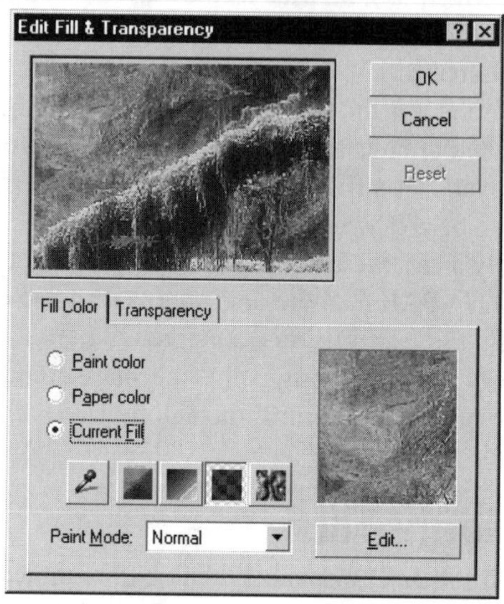

FIGURE 9-1 The Edit Fill & Transparency (EFT) dialog box is a good jumping-off point when you need to fill an entire image or a selected object

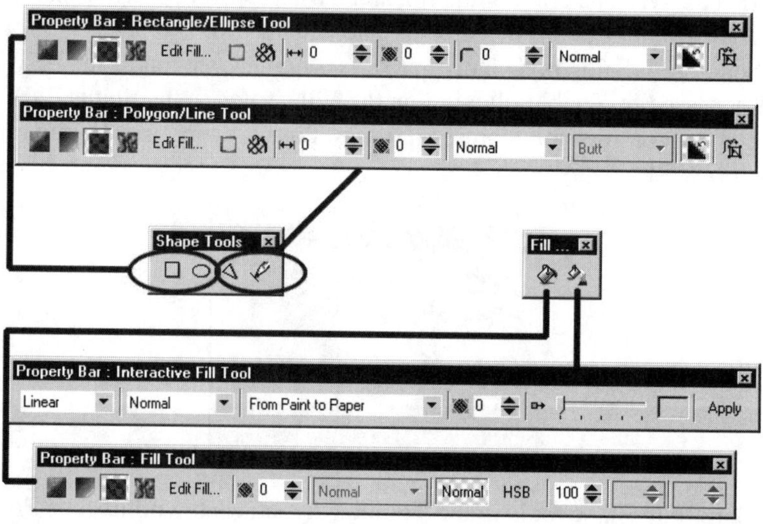

FIGURE 9-2 Here are the Property Bars for the six Fill tools that control the fills. Learn them well, as there may be an exam—a bar exam

More Fills Than You Could Have Thought Possible

Before going into detailed descriptions of the individual Fill tools, let's see what fills are available. We will learn about the different fills by using the buttons of the EFT dialog box:

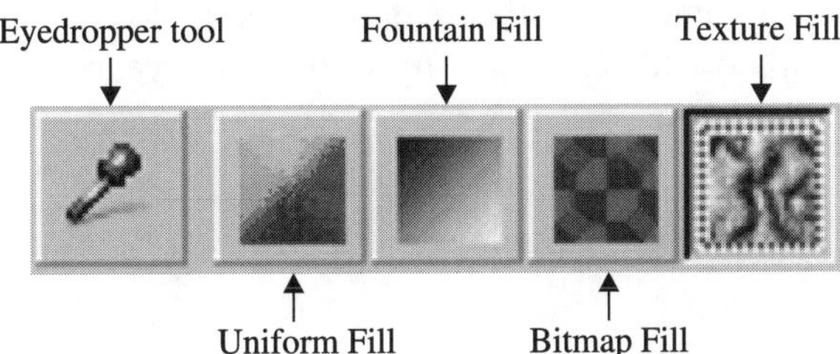

Meet the Fill Buttons

The first button—the one that looks like an eyedropper—selects the Eyedropper tool (this button is only in the EFT dialog box). Enabling this button activates the Eyedropper tool. In this mode, you place the cursor on the image and click the desired color. That color becomes the current Uniform Fill color, which happens to be the next button—Uniform Fill.

From Uniform Fill mode, you can select any solid (nongradient) color from a color palette or with the Eyedropper. Solid colors are boring, so Corel put in a Fountain Fill button (middle). Selecting this button uses the last selected fountain fill. With Fountain fills you can select a nearly endless combination of colors or shades.

Next is the Bitmap Fill button, indicated by the strange icon on the button (it used to be a checkerboard—I am not sure what it is now). The Bitmap Fill is a *tiling engine.* If that didn't make sense, try this. PHOTO-PAINT provides a collection of Bitmap fills. These are, in many cases, images that have been selected from photographs and then modified so that when they are placed side-by-side, the viewer cannot detect where one begins and the other ends. These are called *seamless tiles,* and the Bitmap Fill button uses the tile you select to fill the selected area. By the way, the Bitmap Fill will flood an area with just about any Bitmap fill, seamless or not.

The last button is the Texture Fill, the most unique in the Fill palette. This mode does not use existing tiles or patterns. Instead, it creates them at the time of use through a powerful fractal generator. You can produce some unusual and exotic textures (or patterns) with this fill.

Fill Status Line

Regardless of what fill you select, you can see the currently selected fill color/pattern (sort of) by viewing the Status Bar, shown next. Notice that there are three small rectangles located on the Status Bar. They are labeled to indicate their fill colors or fill, as shown next. The Paint color is the foreground color, the Paper color is the background color, and the Fill can be a color or pattern. Because the swatch area is small, it is sometimes difficult to accurately determine the selected type of fill. Having worked with this program for over five years, I have no complaints; it gets the job done.

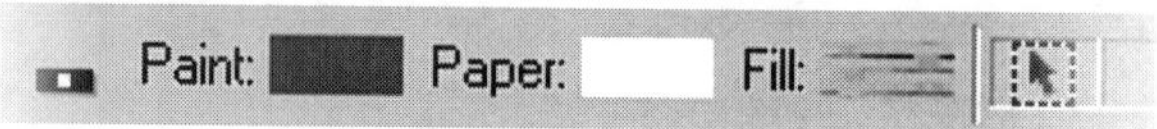

The Uniform Fill Mode

Uniform Fill is the simplest fill mode. It is used to select and apply solid (uniform) colors to an image or selected portions of it. There are several ways to select a fill color for this mode. The quickest way to select a uniform fill color is to right-click the desired color in the onscreen color palette.

If the color you want is not available in the onscreen color palette, you have a few other options. From the EFT or Select Fill dialog box, you can use either the current Paint or Paper colors. If neither has the specific color you need, then your next step is to open the Uniform Fill dialog box, as shown in Figure 9-3. There are several ways to access this color-choosing monster. The quickest way is, with a fill tool or shape tool (excluding the Line tool) selected, click Edit Fill in the Property Bar. You can also go the long way and select Edit | Fill | Uniform Fill button | Edit button. Regardless of how you get there, from the Uniform Fill dialog box, you can select or create any color. Once you enter the world of custom color selection, you may never get out.

Once you have the color you want, click OK to return to the real world. The Fill color you have selected is indicated in the Status Bar. If you have an image without a mask and choose the Edit | Fill tool, you are going to have an image of a solid color.

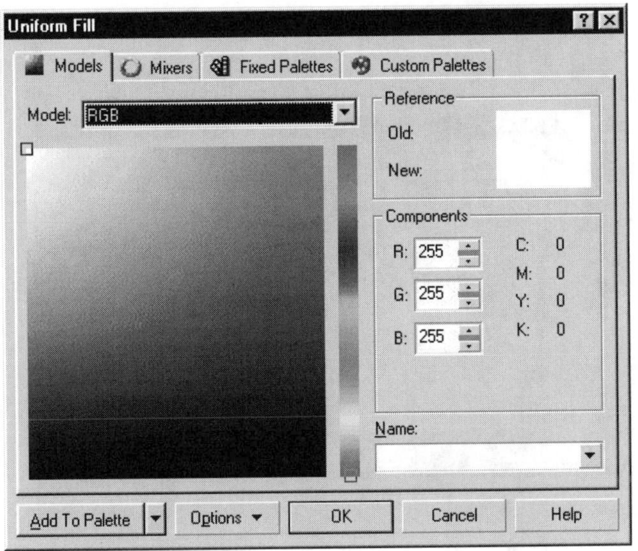

9

FIGURE 9-3 The Uniform Fill dialog box contains all the colors in this world and possibly the next

The Fountain Fill Tool

Apart from the Effect filters, the Fountain Fill tool represents the greatest tool for creating cool backgrounds and fills. A Fountain fill is a fill that changes gradually from one color to the next. This type of fill is also called a "gradient" or "graduated" fill. With the Fountain Fill button selected either in the EFT or in the Select Fill dialog box in the Property Bar, you click the Edit (fill) button, opening the Fountain Fill dialog box, shown in Figure 9-4. From here you can create a vast array of fountain fills.

Fiddling with the Fountain Fill Dialog Box

The Fountain Fill dialog box may look scary, but it's pretty simple once you figure out where the gas and brake pedals are. It is laid out in five sections: Type, Center Offset, Options, Color Blend, and Presets. The preview window gives you an idea

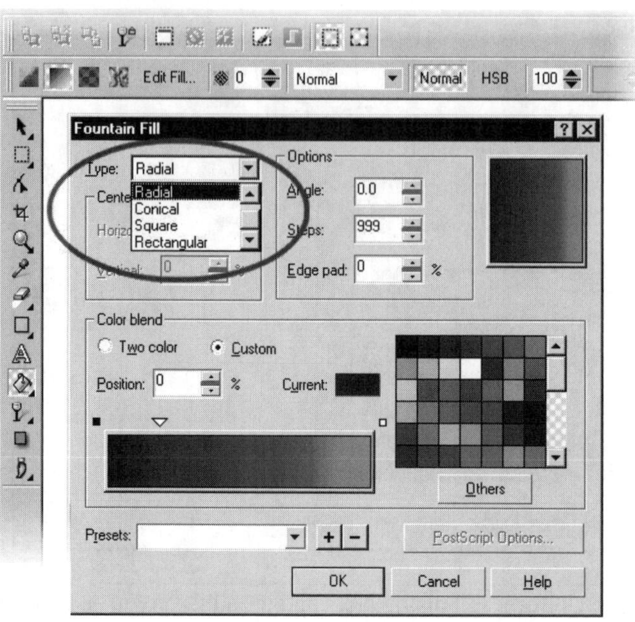

FIGURE 9-4 One of many ways to open this dialog box is to select the Fountain Fill button and click Edit

of what the finished product will look like. Let's check out each section. Refer to Figure 9-4 if necessary.

Type

Your selection of a Fountain fill will, most of the time, begin in this area. It is from here that you determine how the Fountain fill will move from one color to another. The Type section, shown circled in Figure 9-4, selects one of five types of Fountain fills. Clicking on the name of the type opens a list of the following choices:

- **Linear** This selects a Fountain fill that changes color in one direction.
- **Radial** This selects a Fountain fill that changes color in concentric circles from the center of the object outward.

- **Conical** This selects a Fountain fill that radiates from the center of the object like rays of light.
- **Square** This selects a Fountain fill that changes color in concentric squares from the center of the object outward.
- **Rectangular** This works the same as Square except it uniformly radiates to all corners of the rectangle.

Figure 9-5 displays four of the five fills. There would have been five, but when I applied the Rectangular fill to a square, it looked the same as the square—go figure.

Center Offset

The Center Offset, shown next circled, is used to reposition the center of a Radial, Conical, Square, or Rectangular Fountain fill so that it no longer coincides with the center of the object. Negative values shift the center down and to the left; positive values shift the center up and to the right. You can also click the mouse in the preview window and drag the center to the desired position.

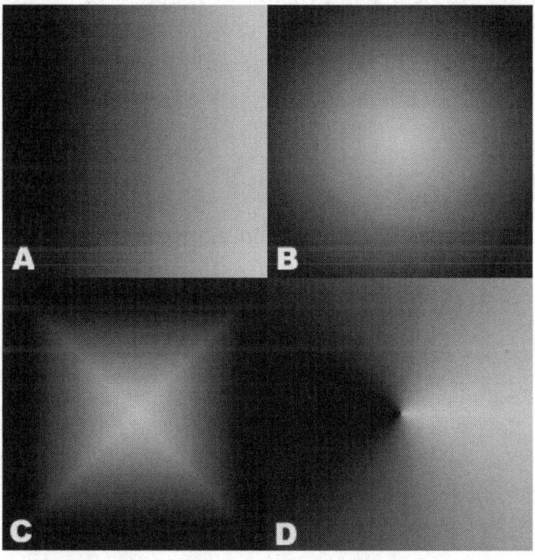

FIGURE 9-5 Four Fountain fill types: (a) Linear (b) Radial (c) Square (d) Conical

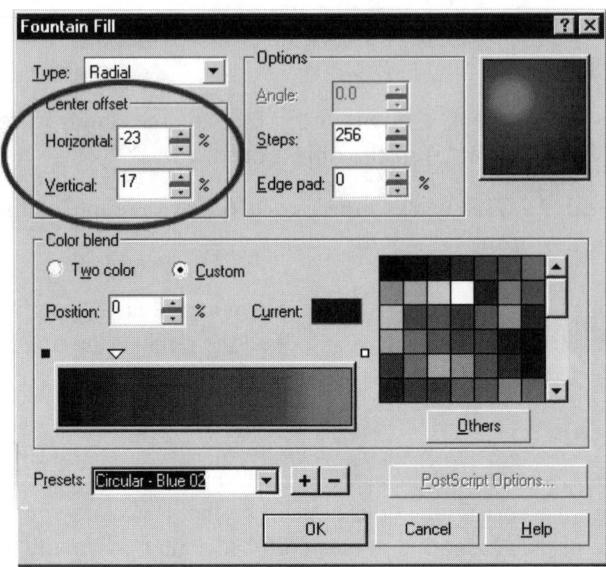

At first this seems pointless. Why would you waste time using a value system to determine where the offset is when you can move it with the cursor to the desired position in the preview window in the upper-right portion of the dialog box? (You did know that, didn't you?) However, the Center Offset is necessary when you need to make several fills with exactly the same offset values. Hey, it could happen.

The Options Section

The Options section of the Fountain Fill dialog box, shown next circled, allows you to adjust any of the settings to customize the appearance of the fountain. The choices are described in the following paragraphs.

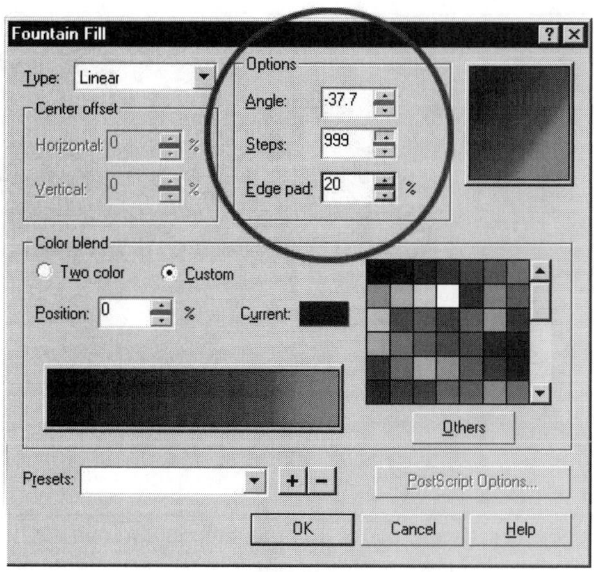

The Angle box determines the angle of either the Linear or Conical Fountain fill. You can also change the angle by dragging the line that appears when you click in the preview window with the mouse button. Holding down CTRL while dragging constrains the angle to multiples of 15 degrees.

The Steps box determines the number of bands used to display and print the fountain. Unless you have some reason to want to see some degree of banding, you should always set this to its maximum value, which is 999.

The Edge Pad (0%–49%) controls the smoothness of the transition between the start and end colors in the Fountain fill. A setting of 0% (default) creates the smoothest transition, while a maximum setting causes an abrupt change, as shown in Figure 9-6. The Edge Pad option is unavailable for Conical Fountain fills and therefore is grayed out.

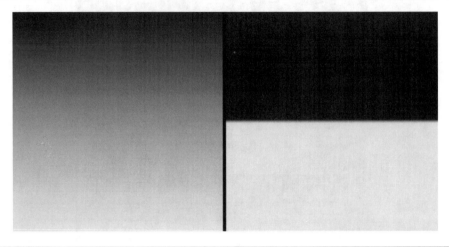

FIGURE 9-6 Edge Pad settings control the smoothness of a fountain fill's transition. The fill on the left has a setting of 0%. The fill on the right has a maximum (49%) setting

Color Blend

The Color Blend section of the Fountain Fill dialog box, shown next circled, is where you select the colors you want to use in your fill. There are two modes of operation in the Color Blend area: Two Color (default) and Custom.

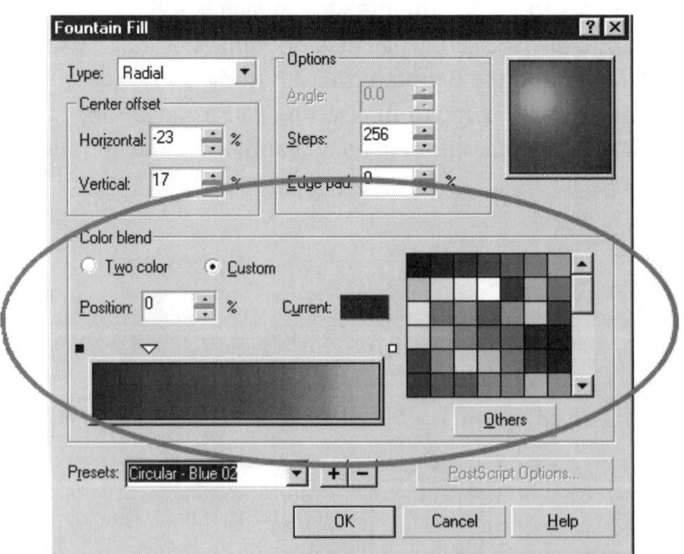

Two Color blends are fountain fills created using two colors: the From color and the To color. The operation of the Two Color blend is controlled by one of the three buttons to the right of the From and To colors. These buttons are

- **Direct** This option determines the intermediate fill colors from a straight line beginning at the From color and continuing across the color wheel to the To color. Figure 9-7 shows the button enabled (circled), and the path of the color travel is indicated in the color wheel on the right. See Figure 9-10(a) for the resulting fill. Figure 9-11 shows an example made with this type of fill.
- **Counter-Clockwise Color Path** Selecting this option causes the fill's intermediate colors to be selected by traveling counterclockwise around the color wheel between the From and To colors. Because the colors picked in the example (Red and Yellow) are very close to each other, the path shown on the color wheel in Figure 9-8 travels almost completely around the wheel. The resulting fill is shown in Figure 9-10(b).
- **Clockwise Color Path** This option, shown in Figure 9-9, determines the fill's intermediate colors by traveling clockwise around the color wheel between the From and To colors. Again, because the colors are so close together, there appears to be no difference between the Direct fill (Figure 9-10(a)) and this one (Figure 9-10(c)). Figure 9-12 shows an example made with this type of fill.

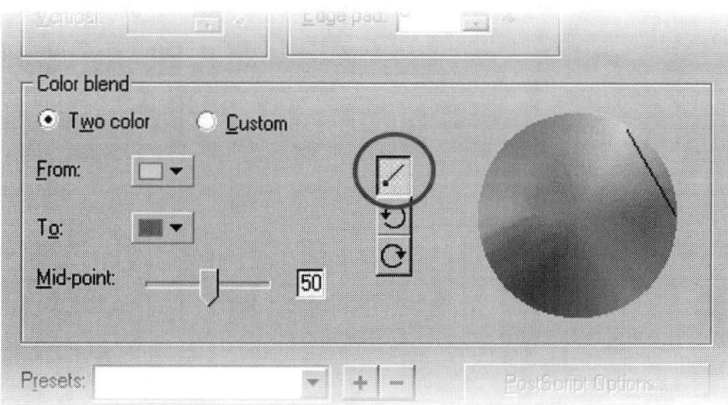

FIGURE 9-7 The Direct mode (circled button) creates fills by moving directly from one color to another

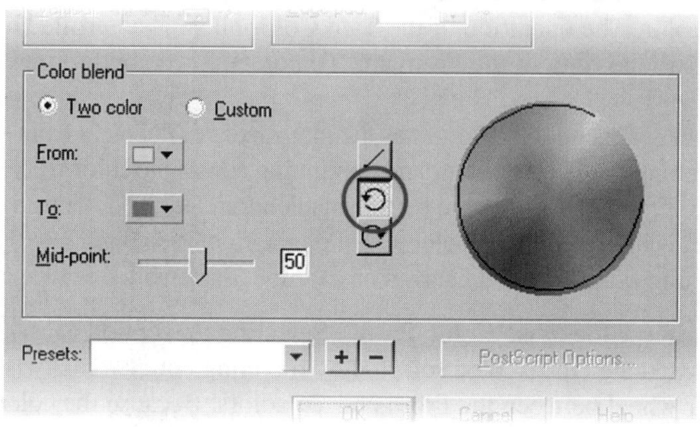

FIGURE 9-8 Counter-Clockwise creates a spectrum of colors for a fountain fill by moving through the color wheel backward

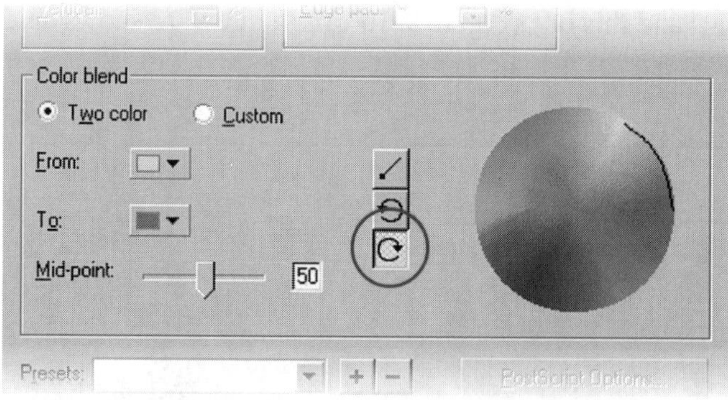

FIGURE 9-9 Clockwise creates a spectrum of colors for a fountain fill by moving through the color wheel in a forward direction

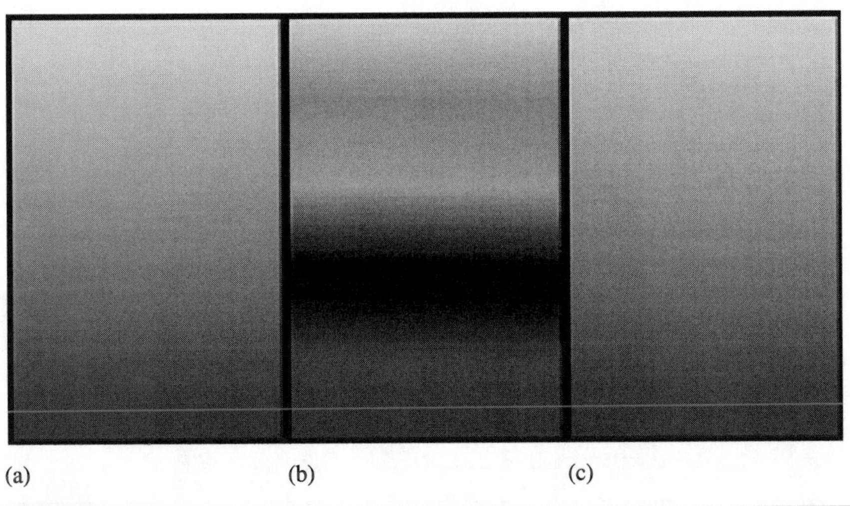

FIGURE 9-10 These three fills were made from two colors—red and yellow. (a) Direct fill (b) Counter-Clockwise fill (c) Clockwise fill

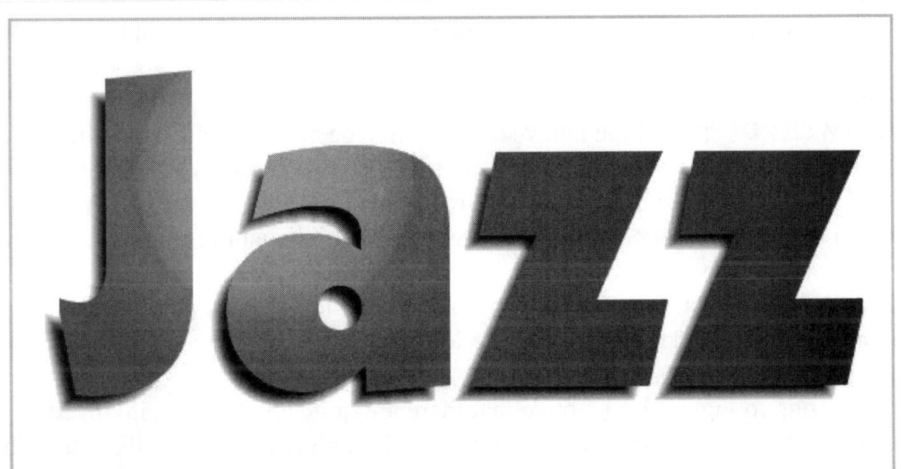

FIGURE 9-11 This image was made applying a radial two-color direct fountain fill to the text

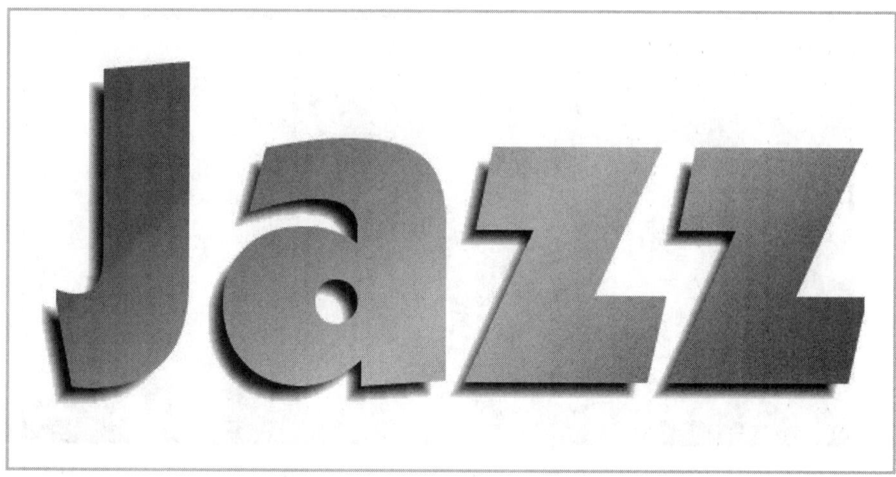

FIGURE 9-12 The same text with a linear two-color clockwise fountain fill produces a rainbow fill that, when seen in color, makes me a little homesick for the '60s

- **Mid-Point Slider** This option adjusts the midpoint between the From and To colors. The Mid-point slider allows the user to control the distribution of color/shading of the fountain fills.

CUSTOM BLEND For all the fancy stuff we have been doing with fountain fills up to this point, we have been controlling the fill with two colors. The Custom blend allows you to add more than two colors in specific locations on the fill. When the Custom button is selected, the dialog box changes as shown in Figure 9-13. Now there is a color ribbon on which you can select up to 99 intermediate colors from the palette to its right. You specify where you want the color to appear on the color ribbon by adding markers, which look a lot like the tab markers on a word-processing program.

Referring to Figure 9-13, notice that there are quite a few colors involved in making this little example I've cooked up. As with all fountain fills, there must be end colors. They are the squares at each end of the color ribbon. To add additional colors, you must add markers. There are two ways to add markers. When you double-click just above the color ribbon, a black marker will appear. Another way to add a marker is to select the To or From color square at either end of the color ribbon, specify a new value in the Position box, and then click the end color square again. (The first way works the best.)

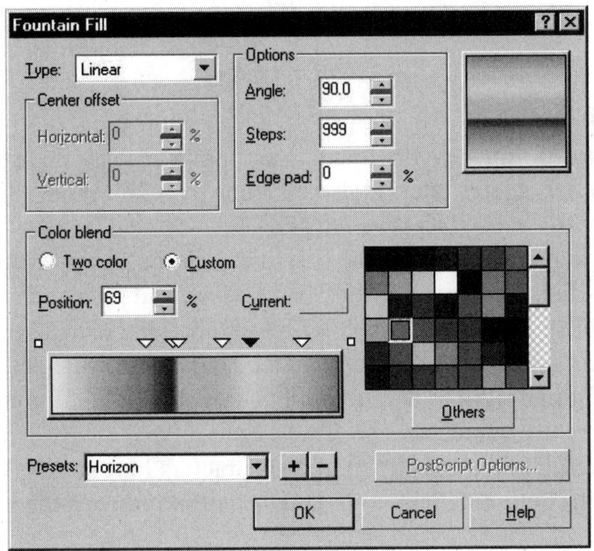

FIGURE 9-13 Custom blends allow you to create backgrounds and horizons

To change the color of either the end colors or the markers, you only need select the marker or end square by clicking it and then clicking a color from the palette to the immediate right. The color ribbon and the preview window in the upper-right corner of the Fountain Fill dialog box will reflect the change. Is the color you want not in the palette? Click the Others button to open the Select Color dialog box. Every color in the universe is in this jewel.

TIP: *Want to find the name of the color you just selected? Many times we are following directions on how to make some project and the writer will specify a color like "Electric Blue." Select the color for which you need a name, click the Others button, and when the Select Color dialog box opens, click the Custom Palettes page, and the name of the color will be highlighted (assuming it has a name).*

To reposition a color on the color ribbon, select its marker and drag it to the desired spot, or edit the value in the Position box. To delete a color, double-click the marker.

NOTE: *More than one color marker can be selected at a time by holding down SHIFT when selecting or deselecting.*

The Presets Area

The Presets area lets you save the fountain settings you specified so that you can apply them to other objects later. It also contains over 100 predesigned fills that were installed with Corel PHOTO-PAINT.

If you want to browse through the list, just click the down arrow to the right of the Presets list, click the first one you wish to view, and then each time you press DOWN ARROW or UP ARROW, the next preset will be selected and previewed. With one of the presets selected you can type in the first letter of the desired preset's name and it will jump right to it. You might enjoy doing this if your cable TV is out and you are really bored.

To save a preset, type a name (up to 20 characters long) in the Presets box, and then click the plus button. Clicking the minus button removes the selected preset from the list.

Putting Fountain Fills to Work

While it is easy to use fountain fills to fill existing text or objects, the real power of the fountain fills in PHOTO-PAINT is the ability to use the custom blend to produce backdrops for other work.

The lakeside scene in Figure 9-14 began as a fountain fill horizon similar to the one shown in Figure 9-13. By applying the clouds and trees with the Image Sprayer, I had the background I needed for a project. The water surface was created by painting darker areas with the Tint Effect tool and applying noise before hitting it with a Gaussian Blur filter.

The brass rod behind the gold lettering in Figure 9-15 is also a fountain fill. To obtain a sharp cutoff of a color, place a different color very close to it (almost on top of it).

In Figure 9-16 the entire background for the magazine cover layout is a fountain fill. The gold rods are part of the fill created by placing dark colors very close to the gold colors. Just as in the previous example, a lighter color was sandwiched in the gold/bronze colors to give the appearance of highlights. The cars were applied to the fountain fill with a clone tool using one of the unusual nibs that ship with PHOTO-PAINT.

I hope this makes you see fountain fills in a different light and begin to try your hand at a fill or two. Next on our tour of the Fill tools is the bitmap fill.

FIGURE 9-14 This lakeside image began with a fountain fill on which clouds and trees were added with the Image Sprayer tool

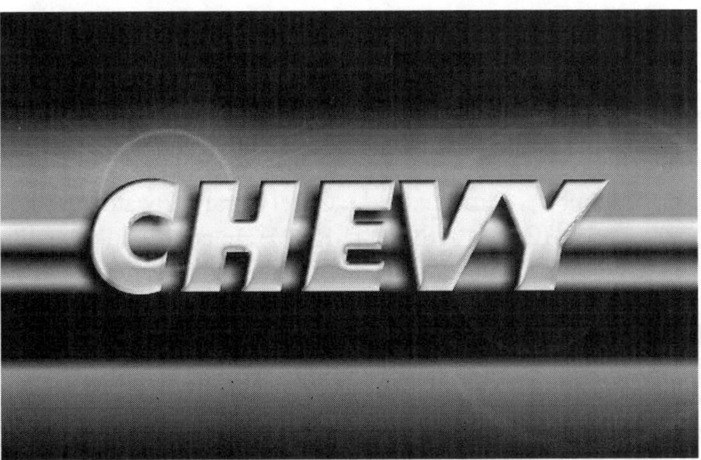

FIGURE 9-15 The brass rod against the black background is a single fountain fill

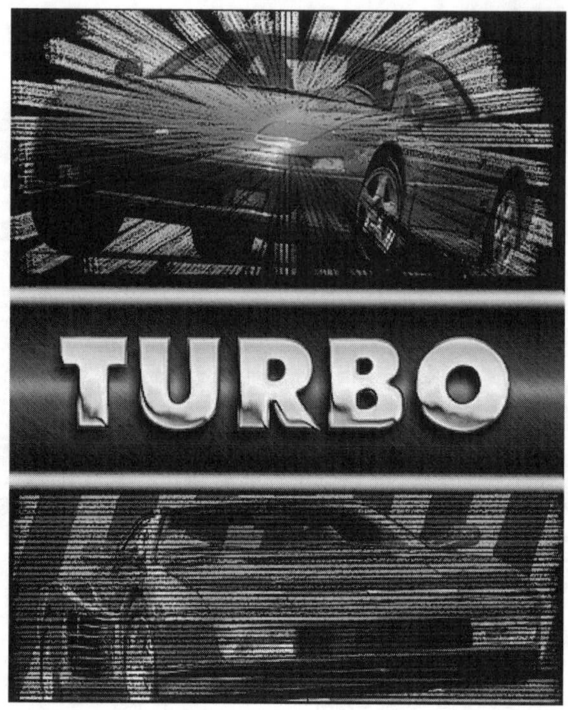

FIGURE 9-16 Fountain fills create everything but the cars and the chrome

Bitmap Fill

The Bitmap Fill dialog box allows you to fill a selected area with a bitmap image. There are a large number of images in the Corel library (located in the TILES folder on your Corel PHOTO-PAINT CD-ROM). In addition to the bitmap images provided, you can import almost any bitmap that can be read by your PC.

NOTE: *PHOTO-PAINT can import vector-based images for use as bitmap fills.*

Loading a Bitmap Image

When you invoke the Bitmap Fill, you will see the currently selected image in the preview window. To change the image, you must click the Edit button. This will open the Bitmap Fill dialog box, shown next.

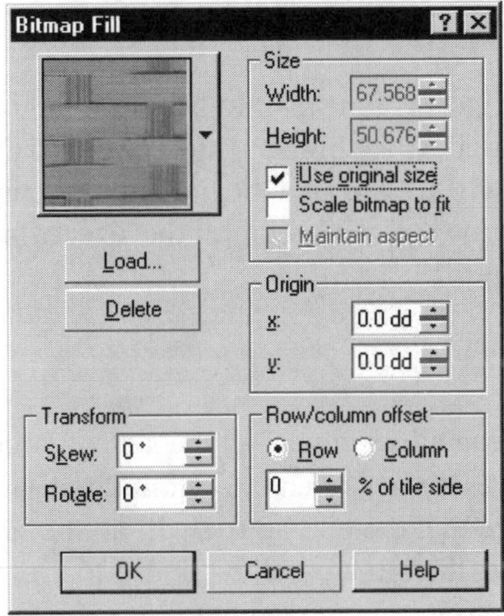

How the Bitmap Fill Operates

You have so much versatility when using bitmaps for fills that it is sometimes difficult to get a grip on all of it. Here are some pointers about using files for bitmap fills:

- Remember that if you use the Fill tool (the bucket), the fill will be calculated to the boundaries of the mask or the edges of the image. If the bitmap image is larger than the mask or the image, Corel PHOTO-PAINT will put as much as will fit, beginning with the upper-left corner of the original image.
- You can control what appears in a flood-filled area by using the origin and offset controls in the Bitmap Fill dialog box.
- The Rectangle, Ellipse, and Polygon tools, on the other hand, will fill to the perimeter of the defined area. If there is a mask, the masked area that falls within the area will be filled.

TIP: *When using Corel Photo CDs as bitmap fills, make sure to crop them in the Import dialog box to get rid of any black film border. If you don't, the results can be really ugly.*

Controlling the Size and Position of the Bitmap Tiles

If the bitmap that you import is too small to fill the area, the default settings will cause the bitmap to be tiled. If the bitmap is too large for the area being filled, only a portion of the bitmap will fill the area, beginning in the upper-left corner. By changing the default settings, you can control the size, offset, and several other parameters of the bitmap fill.

Size

The controls in this section allow you to set the size of your pattern tiles. You can choose one of the preset sizes or enter custom dimensions. By selecting Use Original Size, you ensure that the bitmap file will not be scaled to a new size. If the option is not checked, the bitmap will be scaled to the size set in the Width and Height settings. These settings are grayed out if the Use Original Size or Scale Bitmap To Fit options are enabled.

Scale Bitmap To Fit

When enabled, this option scales the tile pattern to fit entirely within the tile preview window. It also disables the entire dialog box, except the Maintain Aspect option.

Origin

Controls in this section set the offset of the first tile (and therefore the rest of the pattern) relative to the top left corner of the object. If you want the pattern to start flush with the corner, set the X and Y values to zero.

Row/Column Offset

These controls shift either the rows or columns of tiles so that the pattern is staggered rather than continuous. The % Of Tile Side setting shifts alternating rows or columns by the amount specified. This feature helps break up repeating patterns.

Transform

This section specifies the angle on which the tile is rotated and skewed. You can set the rotation value in two ways: type a value in the Rotate box, or use the scroll arrows to adjust an existing value.

Loading Bitmap Images

To the right of the preview window in the Bitmap Fill dialog box is a down arrow button. Clicking the button or anywhere in the preview window opens a color preview of the first nine bitmaps that have been imported into Corel PHOTO-PAINT. If there are more bitmaps than can be displayed, scroll bars appear on the right side of the preview window and allow you to see the remainder of the bitmap fills in Corel PHOTO-PAINT.

Choosing the Load button opens the Load Bitmap Fill dialog box, where you can import a graphic to use as your bitmap pattern. There is a large selection of existing bitmap fills available on the CD-ROM containing the TILES folder.

PHOTOSHOP NOTE: *There is no equivalent to this tool in Photoshop. Too bad, so sad.*

Putting Bitmap Fills to Work

I use bitmap fills more than any other fill. It is so much easier to make things appear photorealistic when you can make the base images from photographs. Figure 9-17 was a project for a book. Obviously, it wasn't for real life—after all, statistics show that over 99.95 percent of all chain smokers don't smoke chains. Bad jokes aside, the background is a bitmap fill. The text is also a bitmap fill that is knotted wood. It doesn't look like knotted wood because I applied Gaussian noise to it and then used an Emboss with the original color setting.

The anchor chain also began as a bitmap fill using the same fill that is in the text as shown next.

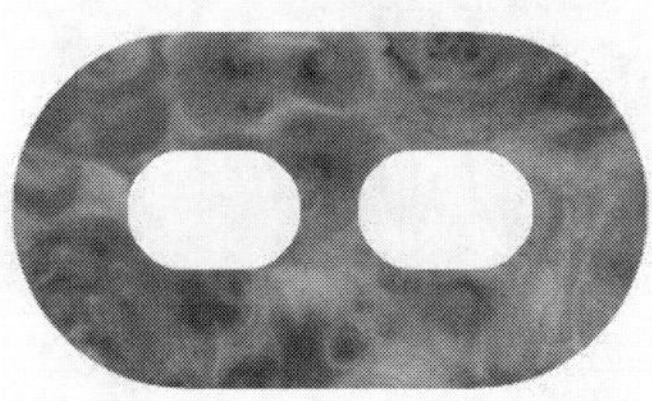

With Gaussian noise and the Emboss filter, the image, shown next, looks flat as a pancake.

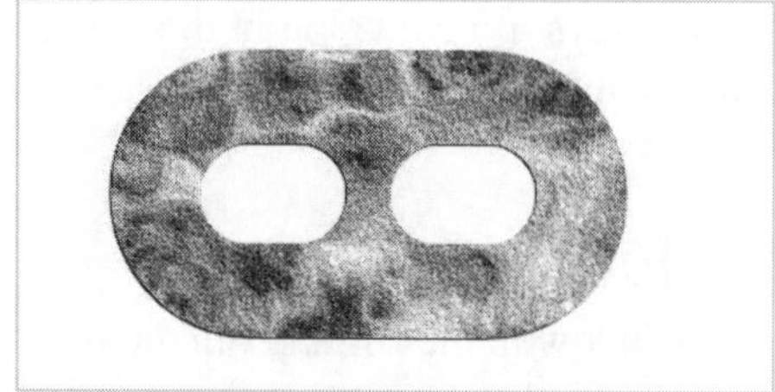

Making a mask of the shape and applying an airbrush with the Stroke Mask command, we have a depth and a nearly real link in an anchor chain.

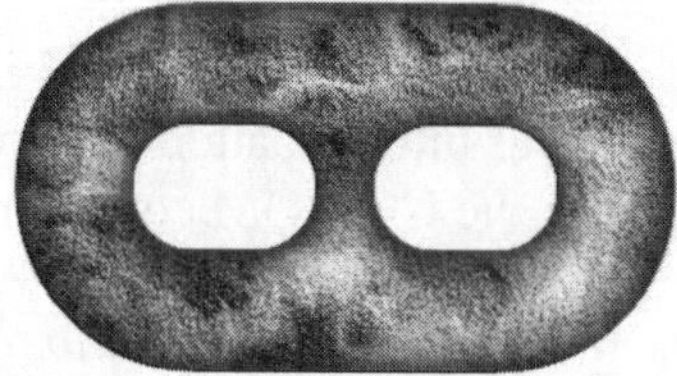

FIGURE 9-17 Three different bitmap fills were necessary to make this unnecessary sign

The Texture Fills

This is the feature that makes Corel PHOTO-PAINT unique. I don't know of another package that can do the things that can be done with texture fills. There are some tricks to using the fills effectively, but you will learn them here. The Texture Fill dialog box is used to select one of the 100+ bitmap texture fills included in Corel PHOTO-PAINT. Each texture has a unique set of parameters that you can modify to create millions of variations.

The results depend on your printer, your taste, and your willingness to experiment.

What's in a Name?

As with the filters, don't let the names of the fills confuse you. As an example, I was able to give letters the effect of a cut metal edge by applying the Rain Drops, Hard Texture fill to each character individually. This approach kept the size of the "raindrop" from getting too large. Too large? This leads to our first general rule regarding the texture fills. As in Boyle's law of expanding gases (gas expands to fit the volume of the container):

Rule of bitmap textures: A texture fill expands to fit the volume of the available area.

In the following illustration, I have created squares of various sizes and filled them with the same texture fill. As you can see, as the squares increase in area, the size of the fill increases proportionally. While this can be used to create some unusual effects, it can also catch you by surprise—especially when you apply a large image, only to find that it looks nothing like the thumbnail preview.

NOTE: *The fill size is calculated by creating a square that is determined by the greatest dimension of the mask. For example, if you made a mask that was 50 × 500 pixels, the resulting fill would be as if it were a 500 × 500 pixel square.*

Exploring the Texture Fill Dialog Box

When the Texture Bitmap mode of the Fill palette is selected, the currently selected fill is displayed in the preview window. The Edit button opens the Texture Fill dialog box, shown next. This dialog box allows you to edit and create an unlimited number of new texture fills from existing fills. You cannot import files for use as texture fills (unlike bitmap fills). The texture fills are actually fractals that are created as they are applied. This goes a long way to explain why some textures can take a long time to apply.

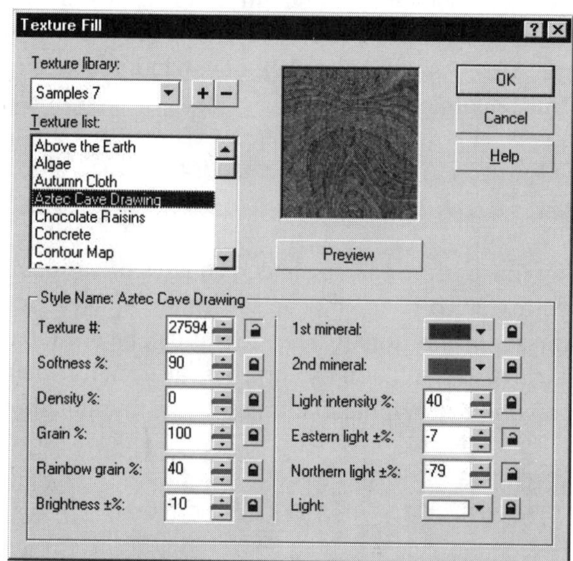

If you cannot find the exact file that you want in the 160+ preset textures that were shipped with Corel PHOTO-PAINT, you can edit the existing textures in the Texture Fill dialog box.

Texture Library

This list box displays the names of the texture libraries. Corel PHOTO-PAINT 9 ships with several libraries containing textures made with the Texture Generator. The Styles library contains samples that are the building blocks of the bitmap texture fills. It is from the textures in this library that all other samples in the other libraries are made. This library is a read-only library. If you modify a texture and want to save it, you will not be allowed to save it in this library. You must either create a new library, or save it in one of the Samples libraries. I find that I use the Night Sky and Planets textures in the Samples 5 library more than almost any other textures.

TEXTURE LIST This window lists the texture fills available in the currently selected library. Clicking on a texture in the Texture List will select it, and the default setting for the texture will display in the preview window.

TIP: *Each time a library is selected, the Texture List returns to the default texture for that library. For example, if you were in Samples 5 and had been working with Night Sky and then you switched over to look at something in Styles, when you returned to Samples 5, it would have returned to the default texture.*

Preview and Locked/Unlocked Parameters

Each time the Preview button is selected, Corel PHOTO-PAINT varies the appearance of the selected texture by randomly changing all unlocked parameters. This button does more than is apparent at first. There are over 15,000 textures, with several million possible combinations for each one. Rather than requiring you to wade through a sea of permutations, Corel PHOTO-PAINT textures have certain variables that are either locked or unlocked by default.

You can lock and unlock a parameter by clicking the Lock button next to it. You can also use the Preview button to update a texture after changing the parameters yourself.

TIP: *Until you get used to using a texture, I recommend using the default settings for the locks. They generally provide the best, quickest results.*

Save As (Plus Button)

After changing the parameters of a texture in the library (or in a new library you created), click the plus button in the upper-right corner to overwrite the original. This opens a dialog box for naming (or renaming) a texture you have created. The texture name can be up to 32 characters, including spaces. The Library Name option allows you to create a new library in which to store the textures. You can type up to 32 characters, including spaces. The Library List displays libraries where you can store the modified texture.

NOTE: *You must save any modified Style textures in a library other than the Styles library, because Styles is a read-only library.*

Delete (Minus Button)

This deletes the selected texture. Be very careful, as you can delete any textures except those in the Styles library.

Style Name and Parameter Section

This part of the Texture Fill dialog box shows the name of the selected textures. Because each texture has different value assignments, methods, colors, and lights, it would take a separate book to list even a few of the combinations provided by the parameters. The value boxes in this area list parameters for the selected texture. Changing one or more of these parameters alters the appearance of the texture. The changes are displayed in the preview box whenever the Preview button is selected. The Style Name fields list numeric parameters. All textures have a texture number, which ranges from 0 to 32,767. The names of the other parameters vary with the texture selected and have ranges from 0 to 100 or –100 to 100.

To change a numeric parameter, enter a value in the text box, or use the cursor and click either the up or down arrow.

TIP: *If you are going to ascend or descend very far on the numeric list just mentioned, you can use a speedup feature of the up and down arrows. Place the cursor between the up and down arrows. The cursor will change into a two-headed arrow cursor with a line between the two arrowheads. After the cursor changes, click and drag either up or down, and the selection list will move rapidly up or down the list (depending on which way you choose). To see the change entered, choose the Preview button.*

The right side of the Style Name section lists up to six parameters, depending on the texture selected. To change a color, click the color button and select a new color from the pop-up palette. If you desire a specific color or named color that is not on the color palette, click the Other button. The Other button opens the Select Color dialog box, which works the same as the Uniform Fill dialog box. (See "The Uniform Fill Mode" section for specific details regarding the use of this dialog box.) After you have made the desired changes, choose the Preview button to see the effect the new color has on the selected texture.

Doing Something with Texture Fills

This fill tool is almost as limitless as the Bitmap Fill tool in what you can do with it. Again, the following figures show some projects I have done with the Texture Fill tool. The purpose of these examples is to give your imagination a jump start.

Figure 9-18 shows some letters that appear to be 3-D. The fill for the letters was made using the Texture Fill tool. The shadowing on the letters was created by making a cutout from the white background, and from that placing a drop shadow on the letters. It is difficult to think of the white being cut out and the letters behind the cutout because I have placed too many visual clues—like the perspective shadow.

FIGURE 9-18 3-D letters with a fill that would have been impossible without texture fill

Did you ever wonder what happens when you apply The Boss filter to a texture fill? The answer is a pretty classy polished gemstone, as shown in Figure 9-19. Each of the letters was filled with a different texture fill.

PHOTOSHOP NOTE: *This tool acts like the Gradient tool in Photoshop.*

Interactive Fill Tool

This tool provides a way to apply a fountain fill interactively to an image without the necessity of figuring out the angles and percentages. Located on the Fill Tool flyout, the Interactive Fill tool (G) applies a graduated color blend that changes the transparency from the start color to the end color.

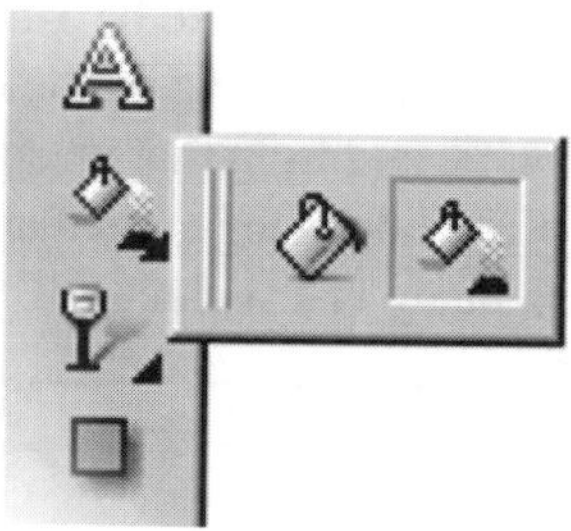

The tool properties are controlled through the Property Bar shown in Figure 9-20. There must be a zillion possible combinations—I was never very good at math. The parts of the Interactive Fill Tool Property Bar are (from left to right): Type, Paint Mode, Interactive Fill Style, Transparency, and the Node Transparency/Transparency slider.

FIGURE 9-19 Application of The Boss filter to a texture fill produces a slick polished gemstone

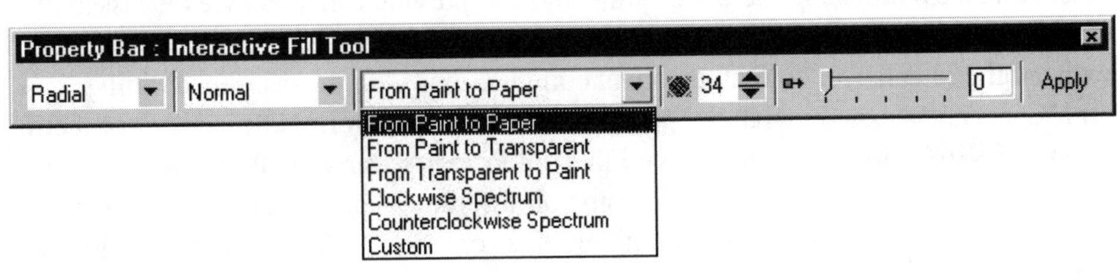

FIGURE 9-20 The Interactive Fill Tool Property Bar

Many of the Fill tools share common features with this Property Bar, so we will explore them a little more in this section.

Type

Most of the Fill tools in PHOTO-PAINT 9 offer the nine types of fill shown next. With one or two exceptions, their names describe the type of fill produced.

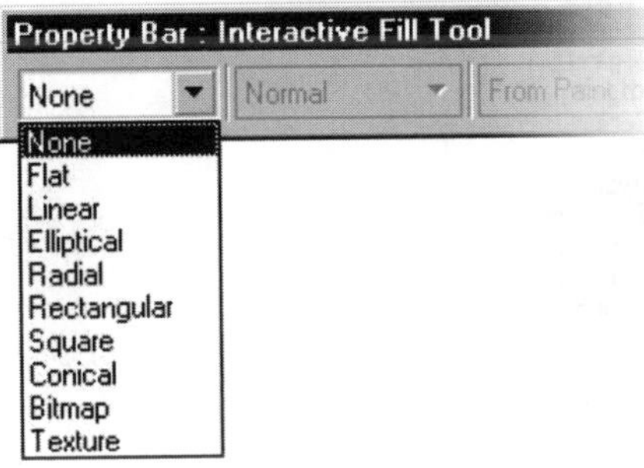

NOTE: *One of the fill types must be selected in order for the remaining parts of the Property Bar to be available. The one exception is the Node Transparency/Transparency slider, which becomes available when you click a node.*

Paint Mode

When you apply a fill in Normal paint mode, the color of each pixel in the image is changed to the color/shade of the fill. For example, if a pixel is red and I apply a blue uniform fill, its color value will be changed. As simple as that sounds, it is an important concept with PHOTO-PAINT. The color is not "flowing" on top of the other color; it is replacing the underlying color. In previous chapters we discussed that a mathematical number defines a color or shade. If I can replace one numeric value with another, I can also do mathematical computations with those color-defining numbers. That is exactly what the paint modes other than Normal do—all 27 of them. The next image shows the Interactive Fill Tool Property Bar and all the paint modes. It is nearly impossible to predict the outcome of different paint modes. That's why most of the work with the Paint Mode setting involves creating a fill and experimenting with various paint modes.

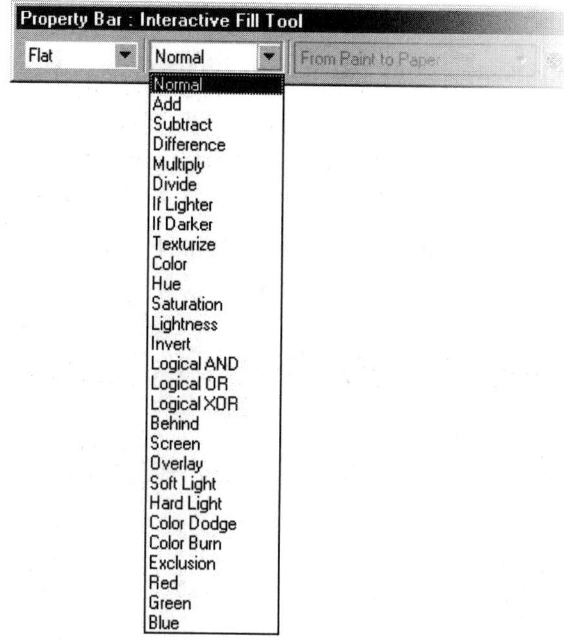

My favorite use of this tool is to create quick graduated masks in the Paint On Mask mode.

Interactive Fill Style

The Fill Style settings are unique to the Interactive Fill tool. As shown next, you have a choice of six combinations. The fill that you create will begin and end with the color you specify.

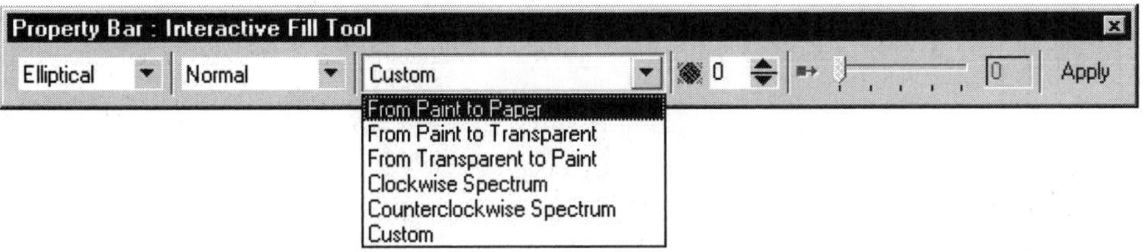

How Does It Work?

That's the best part. Just click at a point in the image and drag a line. The selected fill will be applied to the image. As you drag the cursor, the image shown next appears. This is the interactive part. For example, if the Fill Style was set to Paint-to-Paper color, the node set with the first click would be the Paint color and the end node would be the Paper color. The bar shown between the two nodes is used to slide the transparency between the nodes. You can change the colors of each node, add new colors by dragging them from the Color palette to the line, and position them as well.

The fill will be applied unless you press DEL before switching tools. Once satisfied, apply it by clicking the Apply button in the Property Bar. This tool is a great device to put a quick fill on an object or to create a graduated mask while in Paint On Mask mode.

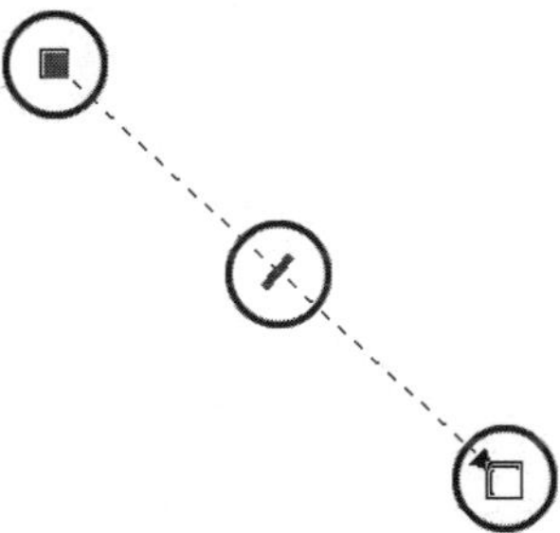

The next chapter deals with what is arguably the most important feature in PHOTO-PAINT. I am talking about objects. Did you realize that PHOTO-PAINT is the only program in which men and women can be referred to as objects and still be politically correct?

CHAPTER 10

Exploring Corel PHOTO-PAINT's Brush Tools

Brush tools are PHOTO-PAINT's tools that you apply with a brush and paint mode. The Paint, Clone, Image Sprayer, Effect, Local Undo, Mask Brush, and Object Transparency tools are all brush tools in the Toolbox. In this chapter, we will explore the Paint and Effect tools and their variations, some of which you have already seen in other chapters. The Paint tool paints an area characteristic of the type of brush selected for the current Paint color. The Paint tool's brushes replace (not cover) pixels with the currently selected Paint (foreground) color.

While the purpose of each tool differs, all of the tools can be customized using the Property Bars and Brush Settings Dockers. Before discussing individual types of brushes, we will look first at the common features.

Selecting and Configuring Brush Tools

Once you've chosen one of these tools from the flyout in the Toolbox, select a tool by clicking on its icon button from the Property Bar, as shown next. You can vary the effect of any tool by changing the brush settings and using the different paint modes found on the Property Bar. For most of the brush tools, there are seven tabs in the Brush Settings Docker dealing with different qualities of the brush. You can customize any preset brush or create an entirely new brush that specifically suits your needs.

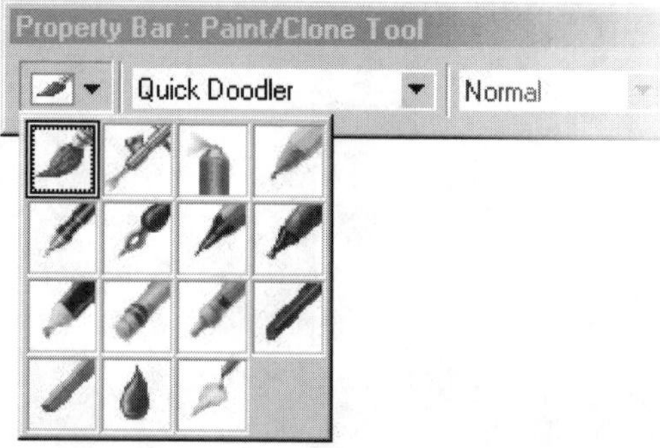

Parts of a Brush

Each brush type is a combination of different settings in the Brush Settings Docker window or Property Bar. The size and shape of the brush stroke are determined by the size and shape of the selected nib. A *nib* is the tip of the brush you use to apply effects with any of the brush tools. Brush nibs can be selected from several different locations. Clicking the Nib Shape button on the Brush Settings Docker window opens a selection displaying 16 nibs, as shown next. Sixteen preset sizes are displayed at one time, but you can access all of the nibs by using the scroll bars. You can also customize any existing nib in the Brush Settings Docker window or create one from a mask for any of the brush tools.

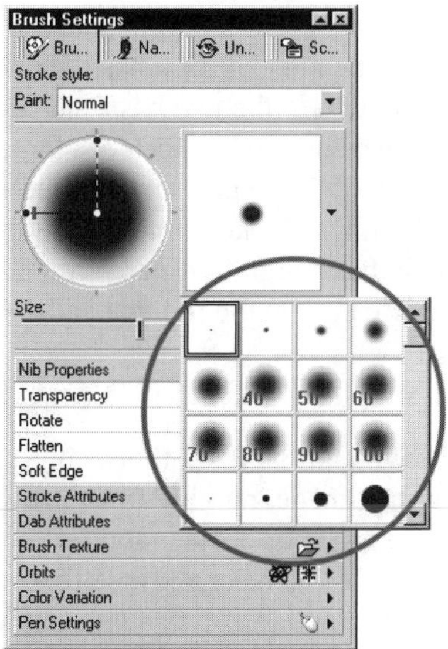

Paint Tools' Property Bar

PHOTO-PAINT allows you to customize and create your brushes using a multitude of options. Most of the options are located on the Brush Settings Docker, which is explained later in this chapter. Other options are found only on the Property Bar, and yet others, like Nib Size, are found in both. Following is an itemization of features unique to the Property Bar.

Tool Selection

To view all available tools, select the tool in the Toolbox and click the down arrow at the far left on the Property Bar to view the icons representing all of the available choices. To select a brush, click its icon. You can achieve different effects with each brush by using different types (available in the Brush Type box) or by customizing different brush settings.

Brush Type

This setting contains all of the saved brush styles for the selected tool. Many of these preset styles have names that indicate how they operate—for example, Charcoal and Soft Pastel. PHOTO-PAINT came with a lot of these presets, and you can add as many as your heart desires.

Shape Buttons

These determine the shape of the nib. The two basic shapes selectable by buttons are Round and Square. In addition to the two basic shapes, you can choose an existing Nib from the Nib Shape box, which offers a large selection of different sizes and shapes. In addition to the size and shape of the selected nib, the custom preview area in the Brush Settings Docker window shows other characteristics of the nib. For example, if a nib has a high transparency setting or a soft edge, the preview area will reflect the feature in the nib that is displayed.

Amount

The Amount, not available with all the Paint tools, controls the rate at which the effect or paint is applied to the image, ranging from 1 to 100. A higher value results in a more pronounced effect or heavier application. It controls the amount of the paint applied over time. If you have a low setting and place the tool over a spot and hold it there without moving the brush, the area will continue to have the effect applied at the rate set by this setting.

Stroke Path

When selected, this applies the currently selected brush tool to a path. The button is only available if a path is present. It provides a precise way to apply brush strokes.

Stroke Mask

This button, when selected, opens an additional dialog box that asks where to apply the brush tool. The choices are Middle of the mask, Outside, and Inside the mask. Even though the mask is present, this command uses the mask outline only as a guide. The mask does not prevent the brush tool effects from being applied in or out of the selected area.

Repeat Stroke

Officially, you can use Repeat Stroke to repeat and change the brush strokes you have applied to an image. According to Corel, this makes it easy to duplicate or adjust intricate brush strokes. Before you repeat or change brush strokes, you must save them in the Repeat Stroke dialog box. When you save brush strokes, they are saved with the list of preset brush strokes. This command and the Reverse Stroke remain mysteries as far as their practical use.

Reverse Stroke

This feature reverses the direction of the stroke applied using any of the three previously mentioned stroke commands. For example, if the stroke applied using Stroke Mask doesn't end up with the desired effect, you can click and enable the Reverse Stroke and the brush stroke will be applied in the opposite direction. If you are applying a solid color with no other brush attributes set, it won't do anything. If you have a brush tool selected that varies the attributes, it will make a difference in the final result.

Nib Options

Any nib that has been created or customized can be saved using the Nib Options button on the far right of the Property Bar.

Brush Options

Using the Brush Options button, located on the far right of the Property Bar, allows you to save and name brushes you have created or customized. Doing this saves any customization made to a brush setting. Clicking the Brush Options button and selecting Save Brush opens the Save Brush dialog box. Entering a name and clicking OK saves all of the current brush's settings in the Brush Type list for the currently selected tool. The name will appear only in the Brush Type box for the tool under which it was saved.

Brush Settings Docker

There are seven pages on the Brush Settings Docker window, shown next, which can be opened by selecting Dockers in the Windows menu and choosing Brush Settings, by pressing CTRL-F8, or by double-clicking one of the tool buttons. With the Docker open, you can select the brush preset and the type of selected brush you want from the Property Bar. It's a two-part thing. First, you pick the brush and type you want from the Property Bar as well as the major adjustments. Then, for the detailed stuff, you need to open the Brush Settings Docker.

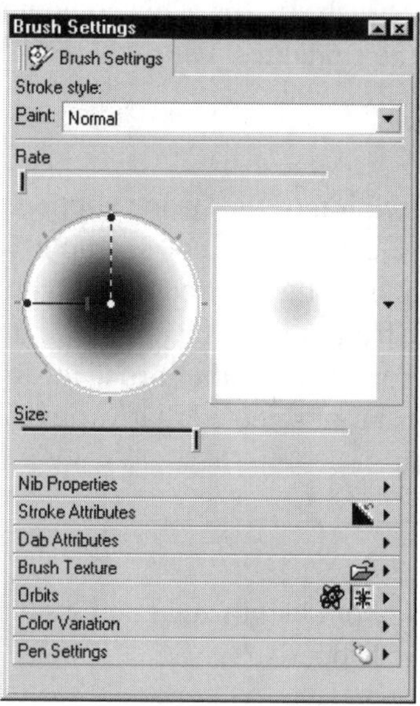

The Brush Settings Docker contains over 37 types of settings and adjustments. It is not the purpose of this book either to replace the *PHOTO-PAINT 9 User's Manual* (or online help) or to put you to sleep. I recommend that you use either the manual or the online help for information about these settings. Here, we will focus on the major features of the Brush Settings Docker and discuss their uses. At the top of the Docker are the Paint Mode and Size options, which we will discuss first.

Paint

This setting determines the way the paint pixels are applied to the image. There are up to 25 different modes, as shown next. The Paint Mode button on the Property Bar offers the same selection of Paint modes. How these modes work is discussed in detail in the *User's Manual*, and there is an excellent description in the online help.

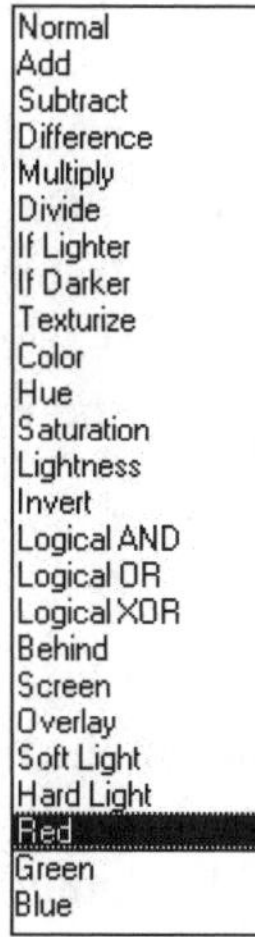

Size

You can adjust the size of the nib in many ways. You can use the slider on either the Property Bar or the Brush Settings Docker. You can also interactively change the brush size by holding down the SHIFT key and then clicking and dragging the brush either up or down on the image.

Paintbrush sizes range from 0 to 999 pixels. The size of nib selected is shown by red text in the corner of the display for nibs whose size is greater than 40 pixels. The nib size can also be adjusted by entering in a value in the Nib Size box on the Property Bar.

TIP: *You can adjust the nib size interactively on the image by holding down the SHIFT key and dragging the brush.*

NOTE: *In earlier versions of PHOTO-PAINT, the size of the Custom brush was not adjustable. Now all of the brushes can have their size changed.*

Nib Properties

There are four different settings under the Nib Properties page of the Brush Settings Docker: Transparency, Rotate, Flatten, and Soft Edge.

Transparency

This setting (range 0-99) sets the level of transparency of the brush stroke. The higher the setting, the more transparent the brush stroke. At a high setting, the color acts like a tint. A setting of 0 has no transparency, whereas a setting of 99 makes the brush stroke almost invisible, regardless of any other settings. The availability of the Transparency setting in the Property Bar is dependent upon the tool selected.

Rotate

This setting (range 0–360 degrees) rotates the nib by the amount entered. You can see the effect of the rotating in the preview window as the change is being applied. The Rotate setting is not available in the default configuration of the Property Bar for all tools.

Flatten

The Flatten setting (range 0–99 %) controls the height of the nibs. Flatten values are given as a percentage of height nib height. You can see the effect of the flattening in the preview window as the change is being applied. Using combinations of the Rotate and Flatten settings allows you to create nibs for calligraphic strokes, among other things.

Soft Edge

This determines the amount of transparency at the edges of the nib. Large settings produce soft edges, which make the brush stroke the least dense at the edges. Low settings produce hard edges, which are dense up to the edge and have little or no softening, depending on the nib size and other brush settings. The preview box displays the softness of the nib selected.

Stroke Attributes

The second page of the Brush Settings Docker, Stroke Attributes, controls the Smoothing and Fade Out features of the selected brush to make a mouse movement look as though a brush made it. The Stroke Attributes differs from the Dab Attributes in that it controls the amount of variation applied to the entire stroke rather than to individual dabs.

Anti-aliasing and Smoothing

Enabling the Anti-aliasing option, which is the weird looking triangle button circled in the image shown next, produces smooth-looking curved or diagonal edges and prevents jagged edges from appearing. In combination with the Anti-aliasing option, the Smoothing setting determines how smooth the brush stroke of the tools are. Both of these controls determine how faithfully the brush strokes follow the mouse/stylus movements. Without Anti-aliasing and Smoothing enabled, the lines made with a mouse will appear to be very jagged. Apply too much smoothness and any sharp corners in the line become smoothed out to the point where you can no longer recognize the original variations that were applied.

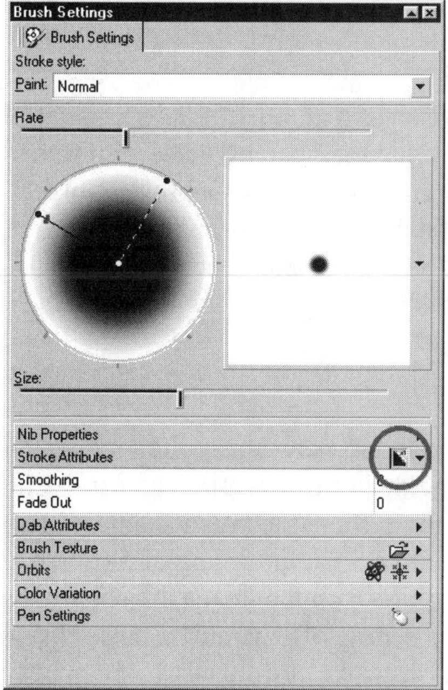

Fade Out

This setting determines the length of the brush stroke before it fades entirely by adjusting the rate at which the brush stroke disappears. This is similar to adjusting the pressure of the brush against the canvas as paint is applied. The greater the Fade Out value, the faster the fade-out of the brush stroke occurs, as shown in the next illustration. As the Fade Out value decreases, the amount of fade-out applied to the brush stroke diminishes; a value of 0 turns off the Fade Out function completely.

Fade Out works by counting the number of brush applications to determine when to begin applying the gradual fade-out function. This method is important for the following reason: since spacing controls the distance between brush applications, increasing spacing increases the distance that the brush stroke will go before Fade Out begins.

Dab Attributes

The third page is Dab Attributes. This page controls the number of dabs as well as the spacing, spread, and HSL (Hue, Saturation, and Lightness) applied when any of the brush tools are used.

Number of Dabs

A brush stroke is composed of a number of dabs as determined by the Number of Dabs setting. This value, and the Spacing value, can have a significant effect on the speed at which your computer creates a brush stroke. It is recommended that you keep the number of dabs low and the spacing as high as practical to achieve the effect you require. The Spread and Spacing controls let you specify the layout of the dabs along the brush stroke.

Spacing

This sets the distance, in pixels, between applications of the brush. To create a brush stroke, the pointing device draws a line across the image. At a frequency determined by the Spacing setting, the brush is applied to the line. For example, if a brush stroke is made with a Spacing setting of 5 (pixels), Corel PHOTO-PAINT will produce the selected brush on the image area at a spacing of every 5 pixels. While it may seem that a setting of 1 would be desired, a lower setting slows down the generation of the brush stroke considerably. It can be really slow on some systems, especially when using a large nib (>70). When a large brush is being used, the Spacing setting can be larger (and this is recommended) because of the overlap caused by the larger brush.

Spread

As the brush stroke moves along a line, this setting controls the distance between dabs along the line of the brush stroke. The setting is a measure of how many pixels each dab can be off of the stroke centerline. Higher values mean the dabs can appear at greater distances from the centerline of the brush stroke. A setting of zero means that each dab will be placed on the line of the brush stroke. For example, if a setting of 5 is used, each dab of the brush stroke will be placed within a 5 pixel radius of the brush stroke.

Constraining and Automating the Brush Tools

With a steady hand, it is theoretically possible to maintain a straight line with a brush tool, but it is very difficult. Fortunately, Corel provides some features that allow you to create straight lines with any of the brush tools. Use the CTRL key to constrain the tool to a vertical or horizontal direction. Pressing the SHIFT key changes the direction of constraint. You can automatically apply the Paint tool along a straight line between two points by clicking the brush at the beginning of a line and holding down the ALT key and clicking at the end of the line. The Paint tool will be applied between the two points automatically.

Brush Texture

The fourth tab, Brush Texture, has four parameters you can customize: Brush Texture, Edge Texture, Bleed, and Sustain Color. It also has a Load Texture button on the Title Bar. These options along with the loaded bitmap file are able to give the appearance of texture to the brush stroke. Brush Texture is the bitmap file, while Brush Edge texture is the amount the selected texture is applied to the edge. Both Bleed and Sustain Color control the amount of interaction between the brush strokes and the image on which the brush stroke is placed.

Orbits

The fifth page is Orbits. The icon on the tab may have led you to think it was the atomic tab. Orbits is an exciting new feature to PHOTO-PAINT that creates wild and crazy brush strokes. It's like an old Spirograph on steroids. Figure 10-1, which you thought was a page from a 1890 biology book, shows a few brush strokes produced by the Orbits feature.

Rather than try to explain each control in detail, here is the big picture. The most important control is the Enable Orbits icon. When it is not highlighted, the Orbits settings have no effect. Like all of the other tab settings, if you save a brush with Orbits enabled, the orbits will be enabled any time the saved brush is selected. The icon to its right is the Enable Symmetry button.

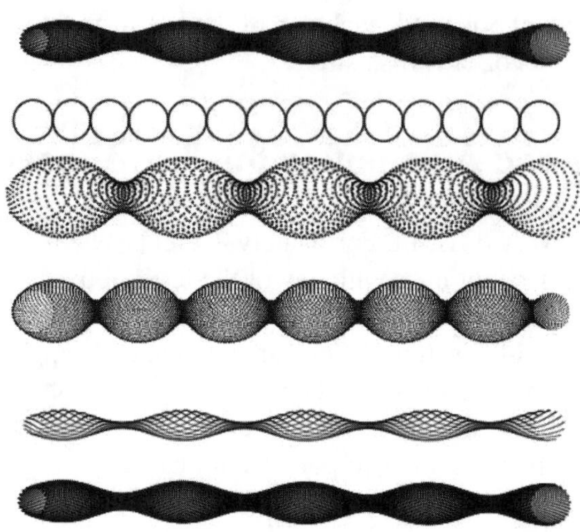

FIGURE 10-1 Orbits brush strokes produce fantastic results

Number of Orbits is similar to dabs. In the preset Rings, increasing the number of orbits makes the rings darker because they are applied to the same spot many times. The Radius isn't the size of the brush but the size of the orbits produced. *Rotation speed* can be thought of as how many times per brush stroke the orbit is going to cycle through its pattern. Grow Speed and Grow Amount control the overall amplitude and duration of the cycle. For more detailed (and accurate) descriptions of how each tool works, place your cursor on the item and click your right mouse-button. When the "What's this?" box appears, click the left mouse button and the context-sensitive description will appear.

What Can You Do with Orbits?

Let your imagination run wild. I recommend playing with the existing presets first before you begin rolling your own variations. While you are playing (sorry, *experimenting*), use the orbits in concert with other PHOTO-PAINT features.

Color Variation

The sixth tab controls the Color Variation. This determines how much the color will change throughout the Orbit cycle. Remember that black, white, and grays will remain unchanged throughout the cycle.

Pen Settings

The last tab is Pen settings. For this feature to function, it is necessary to have a pressure-sensitive pen installed. Such a pen can be used to access commands and draw your images in Corel PHOTO-PAINT. You must install the pressure-sensitive pen, along with a pressure-sensitive tablet and its corresponding Windows drivers, to use it with Corel PHOTO-PAINT.

The Attributes of the Pressure-Sensitive Pen

While the number of settings for the pressure sensitive pen might seem scary, stay with Size and Opacity and you will be safe. I have included a brief summary of what each setting is and does.

- **Size** One of the two major settings, this specifies the size (in percentage) of the brush tool. The maximum size of the tool equals the Nib size plus the percentage that you set. Use a value from –999 to 999.
- **Opacity** The other major setting, this specifies the opacity of the brush stroke. Positive or negative values have no impact if the transparency of the tool is set to 0 or is already set to the maximum. Use a value from –99 to 100.
- **Soft Edge** This setting specifies how much the softness of the edge of the brush stroke changes as a result of pressure on the pen. Use a value from –99 to 100.
- **Hue** Determines the amount of hue shift of the paint color around the Color Wheel up to the specified degree. Use a value from –360 to 360.
- **Saturation** Represents the maximum variation in the saturation of the paint color. Use a value from –100 to 100.
- **Lightness** Sets the maximum variation of lightness of the paint color. Use a value from –100 to 100.

- **Texture** This setting makes the current texture of the Paint tool more or less visible. Use a value from –100 to 100.
- **Bleed** This setting determines the variation that makes an individual brush stroke appear to run out of paint. Use a value from –100 to 100.
- **Sustain Color** Represents the maximum variation in the sustain rate of the paint color. It works in conjunction with the Bleed attribute and lets a long brush stroke that is running out of paint maintain traces of the paint color throughout the stroke. Use a value from –100 to 100.

The Paint Tools

The Paint tools offer the virtual equivalent of a fully-stocked artist's studio, but with the advantage gained by tools that work around things like the law of gravity. Choose from a wide selection of brush tools, such as water color, oil pastel, felt markers, chalk, crayons, several types of pen, pencils, spray paint, and an artistic brush with a wide variety of settings. Each of the preset paint tools has a number of variations built in, and you can customize any aspect to suit your specific needs. Many of the tools are very similar in their appearance and purpose. For example, the Airbrush and the Spray Can produce very similar brush strokes. The following section is a brief description of the Paint tools, with examples of the brush strokes they produce. For some of the Paint tools, I have included some hands-on exercises.

NOTE: *The names of some of the brushes may seem, at times, inconsistent. For example, if you select the Pastel tool, it will say Oil Pastel. That is the first of several choices. I have named each tool according to its overall description rather than the name associated with the default brush type.*

Art Brush (Paintbrush) Tool

The Paintbrush tool offers a wide selection of types. These types are also available with some of the other tools. I am not an artist, so I do very little original work with this tool. It is a great way to add texture to objects.

Airbrush Tool

The Airbrush tool is one of the most often used brush tools to create shadows and highlights on images. It produces a very soft diffuse edge.

Spray Can

The Spray Can and the Airbrush tools share the same controls, but the brush strokes produced by each are noticeably different. Where the Airbrush produces soft, diffused patterns of paint, the Spray Can creates a brush stroke that tends to appear spattered. This tool is used for creating a textured look to a surface. It is especially good when working with fonts that are associated with stencils, like the Stencil BT font.

Pencil Brush

The Pencil brush offers different types that produce a brush stroke that looks as if it was created with a pencil. If you are artistically gifted you can actually create images that appear to be pencil drawings using the pencil brush in conjunction with a stylus and digitizer pad. The recommendation for the stylus and pad is based on the well-known fact that most people on this planet cannot write, much less draw, with a mouse. If you are one of the few that can write and draw with a mouse, you are fortunate, and you need to get out more.

Making Tracing Paper

Along with the Pencil brush, the other pen-related tools require some artistic ability and a stylus to take advantage of their potential. However, there is a way to work around the lack of artistic gifting: use tracing paper. PHOTO-PAINT doesn't have any commands for tracing paper, but it is easy to create. Making excellent tracing paper can be accomplished with the help of the grid and after first ensuring that the Lock Object Transparency is not enabled, by the following steps:

1. Load the image you want to trace.
2. In the Objects Dockers window (CTRL-F7), ensure Lock Object Transparency is not enabled and click the New Object button that appears to the left of the Delete button (with the trashcan icon). You now have a

transparent layer over the original and can trace to your heart's delight without affecting the original image.

3. You may find it helpful to display the grid by selecting the Grids and Ruler Setup in the Tools menu.

TIP: *If you are used to working with pencil and charcoal, you may find yourself looking for a smudge stick. Corel provided it. It is called Light Rub and is described later in this chapter.*

Ball Point Pen Brush

This brush tool makes brush strokes that mimic a ball point pen. You may be wondering why you would use a computer costing several thousand dollars to make brush strokes that look as though they were made with a .20 disposable pen. Actually, I was wondering the same thing.

Calligraphic Pen Brush

This pen can be used to add some real "non-computer-looking" touches to images created in PHOTO-PAINT. One of the benefits of PHOTO-PAINT over a vector program like DRAW is this ability to look "real." The Calligraphy brush, like the Pencil brush, is best used with a stylus and digitizer pad. The shape of the nibs with this brush tool makes possible many of the strokes associated with calligraphy. If you are using a pressure sensitive stylus you can achieve even more "realistic" pen strokes.

The next illustration shows a treble clef that was made using the Calligraphy brush.

Felt Pen Brush

This brush tool operates like a real felt pen right down to the effect of making darker spots when you keep it in one place too long. For drawing line art and cartoons in general this one is my favorite. You really need a stylus to use this tool effectively.

Felt Marker Brush

This tool replicates the brush stroke of those felt markers we all use for making our garage sale signs. Included in the different type settings is one called Dry Tip, which drags out colors irregularly, just as a felt marker that is running out of ink does.

Hi-Liter Brush

This is a fantastic tool. It acts just like the highlighter pens you buy at office supply stores. One of the things you can do with it is to scan the text you want to highlight with a scanner. Bring in the image of the scanned paper and use the highlight tool to highlight the text, then print it out on your color printer—or you could just use a real highlighter pen that costs less than a dollar and highlight the original. All kidding aside, it is good for a quick tint or shadow.

Chalk Brush

This brush tool requires two things to look correct: the background should be a dark color and the Paint color should be light; a small nib is more effective. The large nib that is the default for the brush is too large and produces effects that end up looking like those of the Pastel brush.

Wax Crayon Brush

The Chalk, Crayon, and Pastel tools share similar properties. The Wax Crayon tool has a hard texture that makes the distinctive waxy look. For a more realistic appearance, you may want to apply it as a new object and then emboss it.

Charcoal (Light Rub) Brush

This is the tool you use with the Pencil and other pen-related tools to smear the pencil/pen strokes. It also contains the Custom Charcoal Type setting. Just as the Chalk brush needs to be on a dark background, the Charcoal brush needs to be on a light background with a dark Paint color. The viewer's mind expects charcoal to be dark.

Oil Pastel Brush

If you are working in grayscale, this will look a lot like the Charcoal. There are five choices for different pastel textures, making this a versatile brush tool.

Water Color Brush

This brush mixes all of the adjoining colors as it is dragged on the image. It can produce a brush stroke similar to watercolors and is good for making part of an image look like someone spilled water on it.

Artistic (Pointillism) Brush

I use the Pointillism brush to create neat stuff that would otherwise be impossible. For example, when I needed to add some foam to an ocean scene, I used this brush type; I changed the size to 2 pixels and the number of dabs to 30, with the spacing and spread at 400. Sounds extreme but each brush stroke applied hundreds of tiny 2-pixel white dots, making a great foam.

The Pointillism brush offers the greatest variety of settings, not in the number of settings but in how different the types are from each other.

The Effect Tools

The Effect tools discussed in this chapter are located on the brush tools flyout in PHOTO-PAINT, hence the terms *tools* and *brushes* are used interchangeably in this book. The Effect tools are accessed by clicking the Effect Tools button in the Brush Tools flyout of the Toolbox. The selection and configuration of the tools is accomplished through the Property Bar and Brush Settings Docker. The Effect tools offer a rich assortment of different effects, many of which can be found in the Effects and Image menus. Unlike their menu-based counterparts, the Effect tools can be applied selectively in small areas, sometimes without the necessity of creating a mask. Although the effects provided by many of the tools can also be achieved through various menu commands, others are unique to the Effect tools.

There are twelve different tools, shown below, that constitute the Effect tools. As with the Paint tools, the Effect tools offer multiple types for each tool. We will begin our exploration of the Effect tools with the Smear tool.

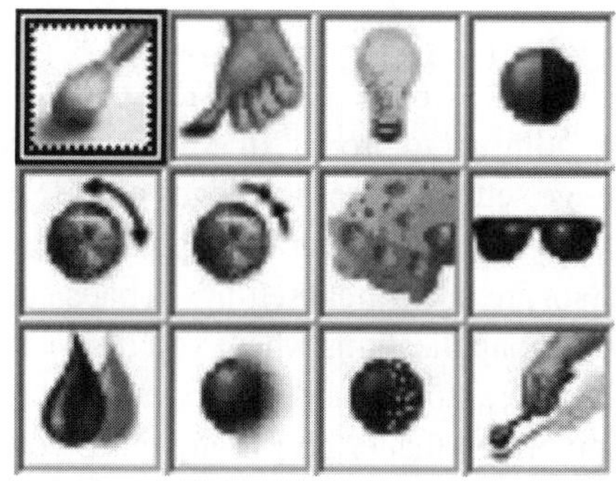

NOTE: *The names of some of the Effect tools may seem, at times, inconsistent. For example, if you select the Smear tool, it will say Pointy Smear, which is the default type setting.*

Smear Tool

The Smear tool smears colors. The same tool in Adobe Photoshop is called the Smudge tool (which can get confusing, because there is a Smudge tool in Corel PHOTO-PAINT). The Smear tool spreads colors in a picture, producing an effect similar to dragging your finger through wet oil paint. The size and shape of the Smear tool are set from either the Property Bar or the Tool Settings roll-up.

Using the Smear Tool

The purpose of this tool is to smear colors. I know I said that before, but it's worth repeating, because many first-time users of Corel PHOTO-PAINT misuse the Smear tool. That is, they use it to soften color transitions. That is the purpose of the Blur tool. Think of it this way: the results of using the Smear tool are not that much different from finger painting (except you don't have to wash your hands after you're done). Blending an area causes the distinction between colors to become less pronounced. Choosing a blending amount of 0% in the Brush Settings Docker window causes no blending to occur, although it still smears existing pixels, while an amount of 100% will give you the maximum amount of blending possible. Adjacent pixels must be different colors for the effect to work correctly.

TIP: *Make a practice of using the Checkpoint command (which makes a temporary copy of the image that can be quickly restored) before you begin application of the Smear tool or any other freehand editing tool.*

Have the Property Bar or Brush Settings Docker window open when you work with this tool. For retouching, the Soft Edge and Transparency settings in the Nib Properties page should be adjusted to produce the greatest effect without being obvious. A higher Soft Edge setting causes the edges of the Smear tool to appear more feathered, which is desirable for most Smear tool applications. Fade Out and Spacing, on the Stroke Attributes tab, are not critical settings. That said, you might want to play with the Fade Out settings for applications where you do not want the effect to end abruptly. The effect of the Smear tool is additive. Every time you apply it to the image, it will smear the pixels, no matter how many times you apply it.

For retouching, you may end up "scrubbing" the area with the tool to get the effect desired. When retouching a photo, you do not want a solid color after you are done—you need to have texture for the subject to look real.

TIP: *If you start the Smear tool well off of the image, it pulls the pixels (Paper color) onto the image. This can be used to give a brush-stroke effect on the edge.*

Creating Paper Letters with the Smear Tool

The Smear tool is not limited to retouching photographs. The following hands-on exercise shows just one example of what you can do with the Smear tool if you apply a little imagination.

1. Create a new file that is 3 × 3 inches at 96 dpi.
2. Click the Text tool and change the font to Futura XBlk BT at a size of 300. Place an **8** in the middle of the image.
3. Open the Objects Dockers window (CTRL-F7) and ensure the Lock Object Transparency is not checked.
4. Select the Effect Tool in the Toolbox and select the Smear tool from the Property Bar. Open the Brush Settings Docker (CTRL-F8). Click on the Nib preview window and scroll down the list until you find the nib that looks like the one shown next. After you have selected the nib, change the Transparency setting from 0 to 50 on the Nib Properties page.

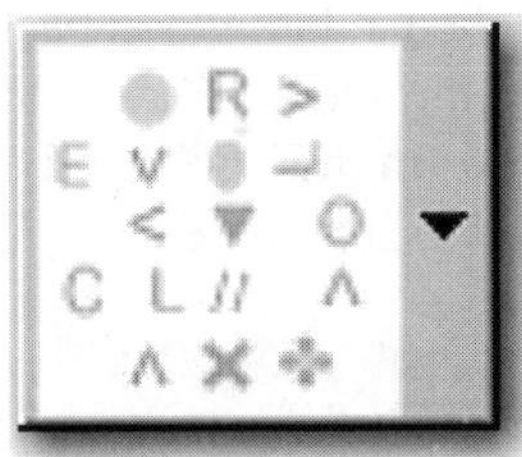

5. On the 8, click on the inside of the character and drag outward. This creates a ragged edge. Continue doing this until the 8 looks something like the illustration shown next.

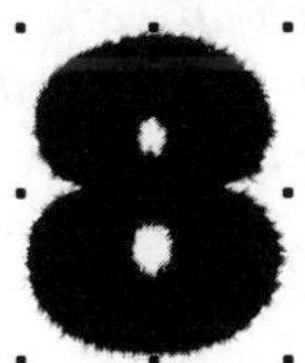

6. In the Objects Docker window, enable Lock Object Transparency. From the Edit menu select Fill. When the Edit Fill & Transparency dialog box opens, click the Bitmap Fill button and then click the Edit button. In the drop-down list in the upper-left corner, scroll down until you find the beige colored pattern that looks like canvas. Click OK to close the dialog box. Click OK again to apply the fill.
7. In the Objects Docker window, disable Lock Object Transparency. From the Effects menu, choose 3D Effects and then choose Emboss. Click the Reset button and change the color to Original color and the Depth to 4. Click OK; the result is shown next.

8. For the background, I picked a dark wood background from the Bitmap Fill drop-down list. To create the shadow, I selected the Object and then the Object Dropshadow tool from the Toolbox. I applied the Flat-BottomLeft shadow setting. The result is shown next.

TIP: *If you are doing touch-up work with the Effect tools, never count on an image being small enough to cover the sins of a sloppy touch-up job. With all of the fancy equipment in the world today, it is too easy for people to get a photo blown up to poster size, and that is when they might get real ugly about your touch-up work.*

Smudge Tool

Maybe it is just me, but the first time I began exploring the freehand editing tools, I thought Smear and Smudge sounded like they did the same thing. The Smudge tool in Corel PHOTO-PAINT is different from the tool with the same name in Adobe Photoshop. As it turns out, the Smudge tool adds texture by randomly mixing pixels in a selected area. It is like a can of spray paint that sucks up color from the area that it is currently over and then sprays it back onto the subject. Technically, it acts like a local color noise filter. I am not aware of any equivalent of this tool in Photoshop.

The Smudge Tool Settings

All of the controls are identical to those shown for the Smear tool, with one exception. The Amount setting on the Property Bar determines how fast the noise (texture) is placed on the image. A rate of flow of 1 causes the noise texture to flow very slowly; therefore, to create a noticeable change, the tool has to be held at the same location for a longer period.

Using the Smudge Tool

The Smudge tool adds texture. It is really *color noise*. The effect of the Smudge tool is additive. As long as you hold the button down, the effect is being applied, *even if the brush is not moving*.

TIP: *Always remember when working with the Smudge tool that, like with the Airbrush or Spray Can brush, you do not need to drag it across the image unless you have a high Amount setting. Just put it over the area you want and hold down the mouse button until you get the desired effect.*

Brightness Tool

Brightness is the degree of light reflected from an image or transmitted through it. The Brightness tool can be used to both lighten and darken areas of the image. This tool is similar to the Dodge-and-Burn tool in Photoshop. These tools are simulations of traditional darkroom techniques. Photographers can improve their work by using the dodge and burn technique to block out or add light from a negative in order to enhance an image. In photography, dodging is used to lighten shadow areas (the darkest portions of an image), and burning is used to darken the highlights (the brightest portions of an image). Both dodging and burning can increase the detail in a photograph. The Brighten/Darken types produce the same effect in a digital image.

Thoughts About Retouching Photographs

While the Smudge tool removes highlights very well, it must be used with caution. When the bright highlights are removed, the image appears to be "flatter" than before. This is a drawback, as we seek perfection in a photograph. Too many highlights may distract, but they also add contrast to the photograph, which deceives the human eye into thinking the image looks sharper. Another consideration is whether any removing or modifying is necessary for achieving the intended effect. Ultimately, you must make the call, but consider what you are changing before you change it. The only photographs that are digitally manipulated to perfection without regard to the original subject generally are the type that fold out of magazines.

Using the Brightness Tool

The Brightness brush brightens or darkens areas in an image. Choosing an Amount of 100 in the Property Bar causes all the black to be removed from the affected area, resulting in a much lighter color. Conversely, choosing –100 turns the affected area black.

Using the Brighten Tool

When using this tool, remember that you want the changes to be subtle. Make the changes in small increments using a Brighten tool with a round shape, unless you are working near straight lines, as in a geometric figure. The effect of the tool is applied at the set level each time the mouse is clicked.

To achieve any subtle effects in areas that have no naturally occurring visual boundaries, you must be prepared to apply the brush in several stages to reduce the sharp transition of the contrast effect.

Contrast Tool

Contrast is the difference between the lightest and the darkest parts of an image. The Contrast tool intensifies the distinction between light and dark. It operates in the same manner as the Contrast filter, except that it can be applied to small areas without the need to create masks. The Contrast Tool presets are Custom Contrast, Increase Contrast, and Decrease Contrast, plus small, medium, and large amounts of Soft Contrast and of Flat Contrast.

Using the Contrast Tool

Use the Contrast tool to bring out color in scanned photographs that appear dull or flat. Don't increase the contrast too much or the picture might appear overexposed. Some scanners have a tendency to darken the photographs when they are scanned, causing them to lose contrast. Video images that are obtained through a frame grabber also tend to be dark. Both of these applications can benefit from the selective application of contrast.

Be careful not to overuse the Contrast tool, which can result in exaggerated white and dark areas. At the maximum Amount setting for Increase Contrast, highlights and shadows are blown out. That is, the areas that are lighter become white, and almost all shades are lost. It is as if the image were converted to *bi-level* (an image composed of only black and white pixels).

The effect of the Contrast tool will be applied at the set level with each click of the mouse button.

Hue Tool

There are two hue tools, the Hue tool and the Hue Replacer tool, that at first seem to do the same thing. I found their names to be especially confusing. The Hue tool shifts the pixels of the image the number of degrees specified in the Brush Settings Docker. The Hue Replacer is used to replace the hue of pixels in the image with the hue of the selected Paint (foreground) color.

How the Hue Tool Works

The Hue tool actually changes the color of the pixels it touches by the amount of the setting. The number of degrees entered in the Amount setting relates to the color wheel. The maximum setting is halfway around the color wheel (180 degrees), which represents the complementary color of the changed pixel.

TIP: *The best way to get the most realistic color change is to experiment with the Transparency settings for the Hue tool. I have found that the default setting has insufficient transparency.*

10

Limiting the Effect of the Hue Tool

The Hue tool is like using the tint control on your color TV. The difficulty with using this tool is that it will shift every pixel you paint with the tool. To prevent unwanted hue shifts, it is best to mask the area first. By using the Color Mask, you can create a mask that is limited to the colors that you want to change. The best part about this combination of the Color Mask and Hue tool is that you need not concern yourself if the Color Mask exists in an unwanted portion of the image, since you will limit the application of the Hue shift by where you place the Hue tool.

TIP: *Use the Hue brush to create interesting shifts in color within your image.*

The effect of the Hue brush tool will be applied at the set level the first time it is applied; progressive applications after the mouse button is released will shift the hue of the pixels that much again.

Hue Replacer Tool

The Hue Replacer tool replaces the hue of pixels in the image with the hue of the selected Paint (foreground) color. By changing the hue, the color changes but the other two components (saturation and brightness) remain unchanged. The same considerations exist for the tool's masking and other settings as were mentioned in connection with the Hue tool. The Hue Replacer brush changes the colors of pixels by the value set in the Amount value box (1 to 100).

Mixing Colors and Other Confusion

The amount of the original hue that remains is determined by the Amount setting in the Brush Settings Docker window or the Property Bar. All of the traditional rules of color you learned, like yellow + blue = green, do not apply with digital color. To complicate matters further with regard to predicting the color outcome, the default color model of Corel PHOTO-PAINT is RGB. To accomplish the hue mix, Corel PHOTO-PAINT must temporarily convert the model to HSB. Pointing out these complexities is not meant to discourage you, only to help you understand that predicting the color outcome is very difficult, and the best method I am aware of is experimentation.

TIP: *Use the Hue Replacer Effect tool to replace the color of an object without removing its shading and highlights. For instance, you can change the color of a red dress to yellow, while still retaining the shading that distinguishes the folds in the skirt.*

Sponge (Saturation) Tool

The Sponge tool acts in the same manner as the Saturation filter, discussed in Chapter 10. The Sponge tool is used to increase the saturation, or intensity, of a color. When saturation is added to a color, the gray level of a color diminishes; thus making the color less neutral. The Sponge tool can also be used to desaturate or diminish the intensity of a color. When the Amount is reduced to –100 percent, the result is a grayscale image.

TIP: *Also use the Sponge brush to make colors more vibrant. For the amount, select a low negative value (–5, for example) and brush over the desired area. Nonessential colors that cause dullness are stripped away, leaving pure, vivid colors.*

Using the Sponge Tool

The Sponge tool actually removes the color of the pixels it touches by the amount of the setting. The effect of the tool is applied at the set level every time the mouse is clicked.

Tint Tool

The Tint tool tints an area in the current paint color. This may seem the same as painting with a high-transparency paintbrush, but it is not. The Tint brush is additive. That is, when the same area continues to have the brush applied to it, the paint builds up until it reaches 100 percent. The Tint tool will apply the paint color as specified by the Tint setting, regardless of how many times it is applied. The amount of tint set in the Brush Settings Docker window is the maximum level of the paint color that can be applied to the pixels in the image.

Using the Tint Tool

The first thing to remember with the Tint tool is that 100 percent tint is a solid color without any transparency. The Tint tool provides a way to highlight a selected area with a color. The same effect can also be achieved over larger areas by using the Rectangle, Ellipse, or Polygon Draw tools and controlling the Transparency setting through the Brush Settings Docker.

Another use of the Tint tool is for touching up an image. The technique is simple. When you have a discoloration to cover, pick an area of the image that is the desired color. Using the Eyedropper tool, select a large enough sample to get the average color that is needed to match the adjoining areas. Now apply the tint to the area with progressively larger settings until the discolored areas disappear into the surrounding area. If the resulting tint application looks too smooth, use the Smudge tool to add texture. You can also use the Blend tool to reduce spots where there are large differences in the shades.

Blend Tool

This is a better tool to use for some types of retouching than the Smear tool. The Blend tool enables you to blend colors in your picture. Blending is the mixing of different colors to cause less distinction among them. For example, if you have two areas of different colors and they overlap, it is possible to blend the two different colors so that the separation of the two areas is indistinct. You can use the Blend tool to soften hard edges in an image and to correct any pixelation caused by oversharpening.

TIP: *You could use this effect to blend the edges of a pasted object with the background to make it appear more natural.*

Blending an area causes the distinction between colors to become less pronounced. Choosing an Amount of 1 in the Property Bar causes no blending to occur, while an amount of 100% will give you the maximum amount of blending possible. Adjacent pixels must be different colors for the effect to work.

Using the Blend Tool

The Blend tool acts in the same way as applying water to a watercolor. The effect of the tool is additive. It will apply the effect at the set level every time it is applied.

Sharpen Tool

The Sharpen tool sharpens selected areas of the image by increasing the contrast between neighboring pixels. It operates in the same manner as the Sharpen filter, except that it can be applied without the need to create masks.

Using the Sharpen Tool

Avoid overuse of the Sharpen tool, which results in exaggerated white spots (pixelation) wherever the white component of the image approaches its maximum value. The effect of this tool is additive. It will apply the Sharpen effect at the set level every time it is applied. Progressive applications intensify the changes.

If you must be zoomed in at great magnification to do your work, keep a duplicate window open to a lower zoom value so you can see the effect in perspective.

Undither Tool

This brush, introduced in PHOTO-PAINT 7, allows you to create a smooth transition between adjacent pixels of different colors or brightness levels. It works by adding intermediate pixels whose values are between those of the adjacent pixels. Use this tool to remove dust and scratches and to smooth jagged edges. Its effect is similar to but more pronounced than that of the Smear tool.

Dodge and Burn Tool

The Dodge and Burn tool has several modes of operation, and I will do my best to describe them to you. These modes affect pixels in an image selectively, depending on where in the tonal spectrum they exist. Clear as mud? The tonal range of an image is divided into shadows, midtones, and highlights. The Dodge and Burn tool will make pixels in one of these three regions either darker or lighter. It is an excellent retouching tool because you can darken (burn) or lighten (dodge) pixels in an area without affecting pixels that are adjacent to it. For example, you can lighten an area that is close to a shadow with the midtone or highlight setting without affecting the shadow area.

Well, even though I wanted to make the chapter a bit smaller, there are so many brush and effect tools that it takes a lot of time and space to describe them.. All of the brushes up until now have painted or manipulated pixels; in the next chapter you will discover brushes that paint with pictures.

CHAPTER 11

The Picture Tools–The Clone and Image Sprayer

I call the tools described in this chapter, the Clone tool and the Image Sprayer tool, *picture tools* because, while other brush tools only paint colored pixels, these babies paint pictures. Let's begin our tour with the Clone tool.

PHOTOSHOP NOTE: *The Clone tool is called the Rubber Stamp tool in Photoshop.*

The Clone Tool

Many people assume that the primary use of the Clone tool, shown above, is to duplicate people or things in an image. The process of cloning one object over another is commonly used both in still photography and motion pictures. In the movie Forrest Gump, the actor who played Lt. Dan had special blue socks on when they shot the scenes that showed his legs below the knees. During post-production, wherever his blue socks appeared, a cloning tool was used to replace the blue with the background—one frame at a time. The result made it appear that his legs were missing. In Figure 11-1(a), I applied the same technique using PHOTO-PAINT's Clone tool to remove the man from the image, as shown in Figure 11-1(b). Other parts of the image were cloned over the area occupied by

(a)

(b)

FIGURE 11-1 (a) Breaking up may be hard to do, as the song says, (b) but not with a Clone tool on your side him until he was gone. The process is simple, but time-consuming. It took me almost 40 minutes to get rid of the guy. Of course, the easiest method would have been for her to tell him to buzz off before the photographer took the picture.

While the Clone tool can be used to replicate images or portions of them for effect, it's more often used in photo-editing for repairs and restorations. The principal role of the Clone tool is to copy (clone) a portion of an image and apply it to another part of an image. The resulting cloned area can be on the same image or even on a different one. The Clone tool is most handy when you are removing things from photos like dirt, fingerprints, or the original art your two-year-old created with a felt marker on the only picture of your favorite aunt (the one you hope will remember you in her will). Figure 11-2(a) is a part of an old photo of my brother-in-law (he is the thoughtful looking one being chauffeured in the back of the wagon). Even thought the image is small you can still see scratches and creases in it. In Figure 11-2(b), using the Clone tool we have restored the photograph and removed the stair railing by the driver's head. We will cover the subject of photographic restoration in Chapter 25.

How the Clone Tool Works

The Clone tool is composed of two basic parts, as shown in Figure 11-3. It has a part that copies (called the "origin"), which is represented by the + (plus sign) cursor. The other part is the clone brush cursor that applies what the origin copies. The Brush tool appears as either a shape cursor (represented by a circle that depicts the size of the brush) or a tool icon cursor, depending on which mode the

(a)

(b)

FIGURE 11-2 (a) When you have old damaged photographs like this, (b) the Clone tool can repair the damage

FIGURE 11-3 The two parts of the Clone tool are the origin (circle) and the brush cursor (square)

cursor is in. To toggle between the shape cursors, use the "/" key. I recommend always using the shape cursor.

When the Clone tool is first selected or reset, the two cursors are aligned with the origin cursor blinking. Clicking the mouse button anchors the origin. The clone brush cursor continues to follow your mouse or stylus movement until you click it again, at which point the clone brush begins to paint the pixels copied from the origin. As you move the Clone tool, the origin moves, operating in what is called *aligned mode,* which will be described in the next few pages.

The origin and the clone brush cursor can be on the same image or on different images. It is also possible to clone from one object to another in the same image or even in a different image.

Resetting the Clone Tool

There are three ways to reset the origin: click the right mouse button, hold down the ALT key and click the mouse button, or press the "C" key. Applying either of the first two actions resets the origin of the Clone tool to the area of the image covered by the clone brush cursor. The "C" key will reunite the two cursors without anchoring the origin. The + (plus sign) and clone brush cursors momentarily line up, and it starts all over again.

Constraining the Clone Tool

As with the other Brush tools, the "constrain" features allow the creation of straight lines. Holding down the CTRL key constrains the Clone tool to horizontal/vertical movements. The image shown next is part of a magazine cover I created, and this part was made by using one of the textured nibs on the Clone tool and using the constrain key to achieve the straight lines.

To draw a straight line in any direction with the Clone tool, click to establish a starting point, move to where you wish the line to end, hold down the ALT-SHIFT keys, and click again to create the straight brush stroke between the two points. Using this feature, I was able to clone the straight lines, as shown next, in the other part of the cover.

The size of the clone brush nib can be set numerically either in the Property Bar or interactively. With the Shape cursor selected (which it is by default) to change the size interactively onscreen, hold down the SHIFT key and click, and then drag the mouse either up or down. As you do, the size of the clone brush cursor will either expand or contract until you release the mouse button. If the shape cursor is not selected (and it should be), the change in size can be viewed in the Property Bar as the mouse is dragged.

TIP: *The quickest and best way to select the Clone tool is to press the "C" key on your keyboard.*

The Clone Tool Settings

Like the proverbial Swiss Army knife, the Clone tool contains many different tools (modes). It can operate as the world's best Undo tool, or it can let you paint patterns with a brush. You can make a pointillist painting with surprisingly good results or copy a portion of an image with the resulting cloned image looking as though it had been run over by a 16-wheeler—many times.

The Clone tool is located on the Brush Tools flyout at the bottom of the Toolbox. All of the modes of the Clone tool are accessed and controlled through the settings of either the Property Bar or the Brush Settings Docker. The Property Bar opens as soon as the Clone tool is selected. The Brush Settings Docker is shyer; to open it you must select the Clone tool and use the keyboard combination of CTRL-F8 or double-click the Clone tool button in the Toolbox.

The Clone Tool Property Bar, shown next, is identical to the Brush Settings Docker except for the clone selections. To see the entire set of clone modes, click the down arrow in the Property Bar.

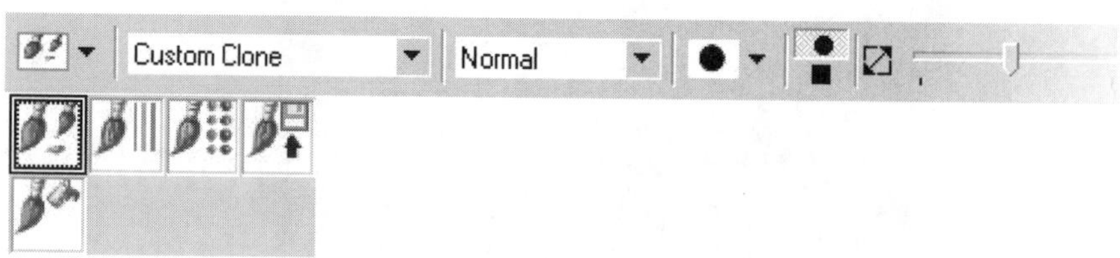

The category headings are as follows:

- Clone
- Impressionism Clone
- Pointillism Clone
- Clone From Saved
- Clone From Fill

Aligned and Non-Aligned Clone Modes

The Clone tool has two modes in which it can operate: aligned and non-aligned. Unlike in Photoshop, the Normal mode operates in aligned mode unless non-aligned mode is enabled by holding down the CTRL-ALT keys.

In aligned mode, once the origin is reset, the two cursors are locked in relation to one another. As the clone brush cursor is moved, the origin moves, and the only way to change the distance/position relationship of the two is to reset the point of origin.

While in non-aligned mode, the origin will follow the clone brush until the mouse button is released, at which time it snaps back to its starting point. This mode is great for repeatedly cloning from a single portion of an image. To enable non-aligned mode, click the cursor on a point on the image that you wish to clone. Next, while holding down the CTRL-ALT key, drag the clone brush and release the mouse button without releasing the CTRL-ALT key. When the mouse button is released, the origin point jumps back to the previous starting point. This is what non-aligned mode is all about. As long as you hold down the CTRL-ALT key, each time you release the mouse button, the origin will return to its previous (not the anchor) point. Use this mode when you want to make multiple clones of the contents of a single area.

Normal Clone

In Normal mode, shown at left, the Clone tool does not modify the pixels. As you drag the origin over an image, the pixels are copied and are simultaneously painted by the clone brush.

TIP: *To make your cloning activities less evident, use a soft edge and an increased transparency setting.*

Impressionism Clone

In this mode, the pixels from the source are modified using the Impressionist effect. This effect applies clone brush strokes to the image, causing it to look like an Impressionist painting. If you look up Impressionist paintings in an art history book, it seems they are marked by the use of unmixed primary colors and small brush strokes to simulate reflected light. You can use that definition at your next party and make people think you are an art critic.

The results that can be obtained with the Impressionism Clone fall into the "What were they thinking?" category of effects. I am still looking for a good use for this tool.

Pointillism Clone

The brush stroke made with the Pointillism Clone tool incorporates a selected number of dots in colors that are similar (for example, eight shades of red). The size, shape, and qualities of the Pointillism Clone tool are set from the Property Bar or the Dab Attributes of the Brush Settings Docker. In Pointillism mode, a dotlike appearance is added to the cloned image. Colors in the image are selected and then painted in a pointillist style. It does not reproduce areas in an image as does the Normal Clone tool—in other words, you may not recognized the image you have cloned.

Nonetheless, I have discovered it can be used to create some nice effects. The secret is to make the clone brush size very small (like 1 or 2 pixels)—any larger, and the results look pretty gruesome.

Experiment with this tool when you have lots of time on your hands and no deadlines. Use it to create special effects. Keeping the brush size very small enables the creation of a clone that looks vaguely similar to the original. Use subjects that have definite shapes, making them easily recognizable as the Pointillism tool distorts their appearance. Since the results of using this tool can be unpredictable, I recommend using the Checkpoint command before beginning your work.

Clone From Saved

This is the ultimate Undo tool, shown at left. It uses the last saved version of the image file as a source, allowing you to selectively remove any changes that had been made since the last time the file was saved. So obviously you must be working on a saved version of a file; PHOTO-PAINT will give a warning if you are working with a new file. Cloned From Saved has three presets that are unique to it, each producing a different effect:

- Light Eraser
- Eraser
- Scrambler

After you have cloned a portion of an image, you may end up with cloned material that you do not want. The Eraser and the Light Eraser allow you to restore the original pixels from the last saved version of the image. The Light Eraser allows you to control how much of the changes you want to remove, requiring multiple passes to achieve the full restoration. The Eraser removes all of the cloned pixels. The Scrambler option is a pointillism version of Clone From Saved, so it allows you to distort the current image from a saved version. (What were they thinking?)

TIP: *To restore background with the Clone From Saved feature, I recommend that you use the Eraser setting with a soft edge setting of 60-80. With this setting, the transition is gradual, and you won't need to go over the area later with a Smear or Blend tool.*

NOTE: *You must have already saved a copy of the image to use this mode. If you attempt to use it with an unsaved image, you will get a warning message.*

Rules of the Road for Clone From Saved and a Workaround

There is a strict rule regarding the use of the Clone From Saved mode: the saved original and the current image must be the same size. If you have resized the current image (using either Paper Size or Resampling), Clone From Saved will prompt an error message. A workaround for this strict rule follows:

1. Use Edit | Checkpoint to save a copy of the current image.
2. Select File | Revert to revert to the original image.

3. Select File | Document Info, make a note of the size of the original, and then click OK to close Info.
4. Choose Edit | Restore from Checkpoint.
5. Use either Image | Resample or Image | Paper Size to change the size of the current image to match that of the original.
6. Use the Clone From Saved tool.

PHOTOSHOP NOTE: *The equivalent option of Clone From Saved in Photoshop is the Rubberstamp From Option.*

Clone From Fill

The Clone From Fill tool uses the current fill as the source and applies the fill to the image with the clone brush. The advantage of the Clone From Fill is its ability to selectively apply fills with a brush tool without the necessity of a mask.

PHOTOSHOP NOTE: *The equivalent of the Clone From Fill tool is called Clone from Snapshot in Photoshop.*

To effectively use this feature, it is necessary to understand a little more about how the fill portion of PHOTO-PAINT works. Regardless of an image size, Uniform fills always look the same—I guess that's why they are called uniform. While the appearance of the other fills is affected by the image's dimensions (for example, Bitmap fills repeat and Fountain fills get stretched), it is the Texture fill that can change beyond recognition. Unlike Bitmap fills, Texture fills are actually created by PHOTO-PAINT. As a rule, the larger Texture fills become, the less they look like the original Texture fill. In Figure 11-4, I have created three samples of this effect. The top row is the original 1 × 1-inch area, and the bottom row of the figure is the same fill applied to an image that was the equivalent of 14 × 14 inches. This situation used to be a problem until I discovered a workaround using a command, the Create Fill From Selection, hidden in the Edit hierarchical menu.

Create Fill From Selection

This command creates a Bitmap fill from the selected contents of an active image. After finding a portion of an image to be used for a Bitmap fill, you only need to select it with a mask. After selecting Create Fill From Selection, you will be asked

FIGURE 11-4 Texture fills on the top row are shown in the original size, and the bottom row shows what happens to them when applied to a large image area

to name the fill you just created and to save it. This brings up the one nuisance: the file you are asked to name will be placed in the drive and folder that was last accessed. This means you must either browse and locate a folder for your custom fills or spend your free time looking for these fills. Although this command doesn't have the same restriction as the Photoshop equivalent regarding the shape of the selection, a selection that isn't square or rectangular may produce an odd-looking fill.

PHOTOSHOP NOTE: *Create Fill From Selection is called Take Snapshot in Photoshop.*

Here is the workaround I promised for applying Texture fills to large areas so the fill doesn't become too large or pixelated. This is a workaround and not an exercise.

1. Create a new image: 256 × 256 pixels at 150 dpi.
2. Select the desired Texture fill and apply it to the image.
3. Mask the entire image.

4. Select Create Fill From Selection and provide a name.

5. Apply the fill using the Clone From Fill Style in the Clone tool Property Bar.

Advanced Cloning Stuff

Most of the controls and settings for the Clone tool are common with those of the other Brush tools. There are two exceptions:

- Cumulative
- Merged Objects

Cumulative Operation

When the cumulative option is enabled, the origin copies all pixels that are on the current image, including not only the original pixels but also any cloned pixels that have been added. This process results in multiple copies, as shown in Figure 11-5. When this option is not enabled, the Clone tool makes a copy of the image contents and uses it as the origin. Any changes made to the image by the clone brush are not "seen" by the origin. This is a nice feature that prevents accidental duplications and in some ways makes cloning work easier.

Merged Objects

Until now we have considered only cloning operations using a flat image (no objects). With Merged Objects disabled (unchecked), the origin on an image that contains objects will recognize only the object that is active. When the Merged Objects option is enabled, all of the objects in the image can be cloned. The Lock Transparency option does not affect the ability of the origin to copy an object. It does limit the action of the clone brush in the same manner as any brush tool.

This discussion only scratches the surface of what you can do with the Clone tool. As you gain experience, you will begin to discover that it is one tool that can solve many photo-editing problems. While the Clone tool copies from one point on an image to another, the Image Sprayer tool, discussed next, actually paints with stored images.

FIGURE 11-5 Cumulative and non-cumulative cloning compared

11

The Image Sprayer Tool

The Image Sprayer tool, shown next, is fantastic. Instead of painting with color, the Image Sprayer paints with images—and not just with one or two images at a stroke, but with a variety of changing images. By changing the direction of the stroke, you can change the rotation of the images being applied. Multiple applications of images create "natural" effects that would be otherwise difficult and time-consuming to create. Enough of the hype, now let's learn how to use the tool. The Image Sprayer tool can be found next to the Clone tool on the Brush Tools flyout.

TIP: *Pressing the "i" key is the quickest way to select this tool. Many of the controls are common to the brush tools.*

PHOTOSHOP NOTE: *There is no equivalent of this tool in Photoshop—too bad, so sad.*

How the Image Sprayer Works

The Image Sprayer is a brush—yes, really. To use it, you must first load it with images. The images are kept in special files called *image lists*, which may contain any number of images. Usually, the images are similar and form a logical series—that is, the images progress along some order. For example, the images might rotate about a point or increase in size. While it isn't necessary that images progress in a logical series, the Image Sprayer is more effective when they do.

As you paint with the Image Sprayer, you can control the order and size of the application of images by settings in the Property Bar or the Brush Settings Docker. You can spray images sequentially, at random, or based on stroke direction. You control the images in an image file by opening the image list in PHOTO-PAINT and making changes. A normal installation of PHOTO-PAINT 9 installs a small number of image lists on your hard drive. If you want more variety in the images, locate a folder labeled "Imglists" on the CD-ROM.

A Flag-Waving International Ad

Let's take the Image Sprayer out for a test drive and see what we can do with it. In this first exercise we are going to create the background for an international company. In the process we will learn some tips about using the image sprayer, and a few other tricks as well.

1. Select File | New and create a 24-bit RGB file that is 4 × 4 inches at 100 dpi.
2. Choose View | Grid and Ruler Setup. Change the grid setting to Spacing with 1 grid dot per inch, as shown next. Check both Show Grid and Snap To Grid. Click OK.

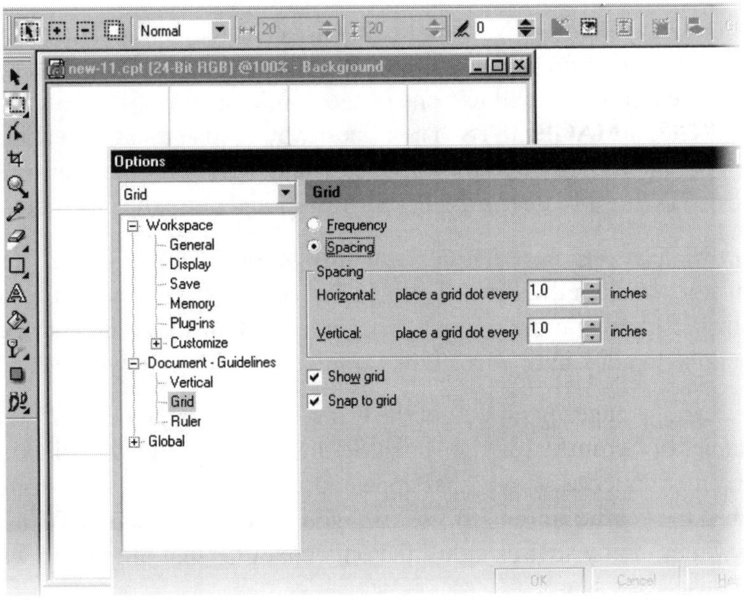

3. Select the Ellipse mask tool and drag a circle that fills the center four squares, as shown next.

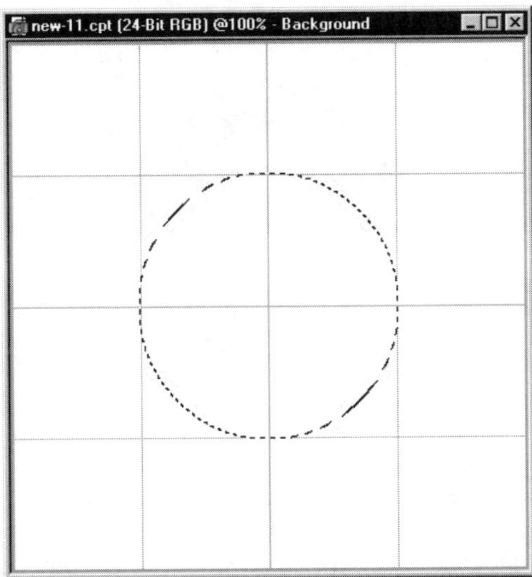

4. The grid has done its job so turn off Snap To Grid (CTRL-Y) and turn off the grid display (CTRL-').

5. Next, select the Image Sprayer brush—it is located on the Brush Tools flyout at the bottom of the Toolbox. Now we need to select an image list. For this exercise we will use one of the lists located on EXERCISE\IMAGELISTS. The easiest way to load a list is to click on the folder at the far-left end of the Property Bar. This opens a file browser. Locate EXERCISE\IMAGELISTS\FLAGS and click the Open button.

6. Now we have an image list that contains various national flags. They are too large, so open the Brush Settings Docker (CTRL-F8) and change the Size from 175 (pixels) to 120. Finally, begin to click inside of the mask circle. Continue to click until yours looks similar to the one shown next.

   Were you wondering how I got the Canadian flag in the center? I set the Number of Orbits to 1 in the Brush Settings Docker and kept clicking in the center until the Maple Leaf appeared. Now, were you wondering why I picked the Canadian flag? If you ask, you have never been in Texas during the winter months. Birds aren't the only creatures that migrate to warmer climates.

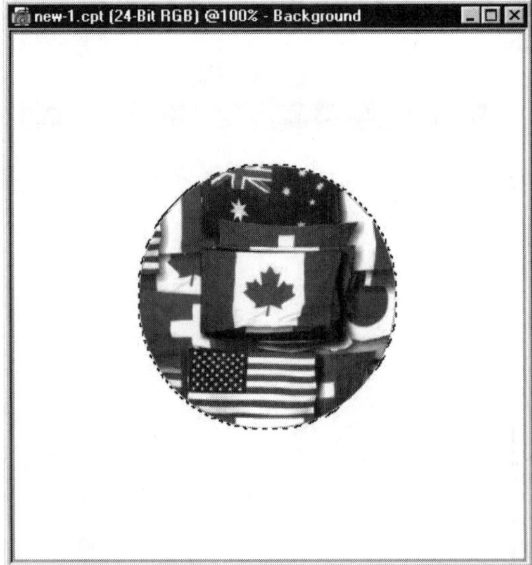

7. In the Objects Docker check the Lock Object Transparency box again to enable it. Next, select Effects | 3D Effects | Sphere (formerly known as Map to Object). Change the settings to 15%. Click OK. The result is shown next.

8. Select the Brush tool and change it to Airbrush and the Brush Type to Wide Cover. In the Property Bar make the following changes: Nib size: 85; Amount: 75; Transparency: 85. Now that's a good setting for the Airbrush. Change the Paint color to white and paint along the edges of the mask until it looks just slightly opaque, like the one next.

9. Make an object out of the masked area (CTRL-SHIFT-UP ARROW). Ensure the Lock Transparency is not enabled. Choose Object | Create | New Object. We now have a new object that is on top of the sphere we just created, as shown next.

10. Select the Image Sprayer and cover the entire image with flags, as shown next.

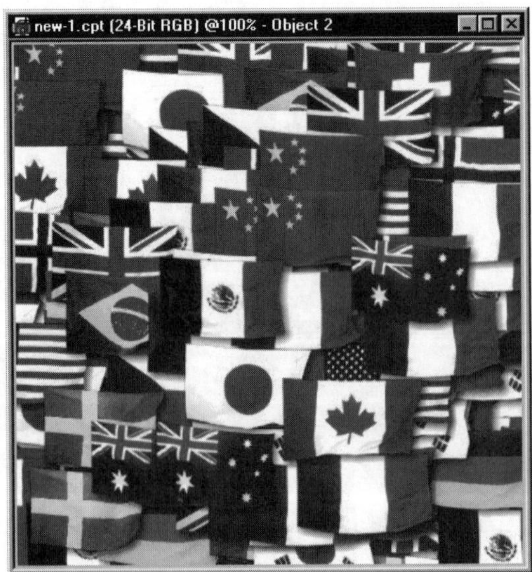

11. Now for a little magic. With the Object Picker tool, click and drag the flag layer we just created below the ball object in the Objects Docker. So we can see what we are doing, change the zoom level to 33%. Note that if you have automatic resize enabled, you will need to grab the corner of the window and return it to its original size. Click on the flag layer until circles appear at its corners (Perspective mode). Using the bottom-left or the upper-right, click and drag the handles (circles) until the polygon looks somewhat like the one shown next. Again, note in the next image that the two top circles appear at the top of the image as a result of the way the screen capture program works—yours will stay near the corners. When the flags look as though they are lying flat underneath the ball, click Apply in the Property Bar to apply the transformation. Change the zoom back to 100% (CTRL-1). The image is nearly complete, as shown in Figure 11-6.

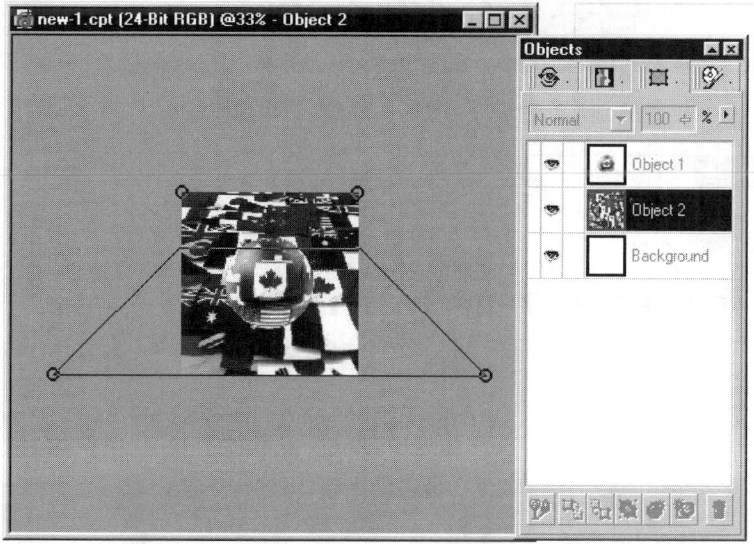

12. Let's next make some sky. Select the background in the Objects Docker and change the Paint color to navy blue and the Paper color to powder blue. Select the Interactive Fill tool and, using a Linear type with From Paint to Paper, click and drag the background, When you're happy with it, click the Apply button in the Property Bar.

13. The finishing touches are to put a drop shadow under the ball; use the Lens Flare filter to put a bright spot on the ball. The finished image is shown in Figure 11-7.

FIGURE 11-6 The flags made with the Image Sprayer are now lying flat, thanks to the perspective transformation capability of PHOTO-PAINT

How to Create Your Own Image List

If you don't like the image lists that ship with PHOTO-PAINT 9, it is quite a simple thing to make your own. You can make an image list from a single object, multiple objects in an image, or from selections (masks) on an image. The easiest image list is the one made from a single object, so let's look at that process first.

Creating an Image List from a Single Object

If you make an image list from a single object, you have the choice of using the single object or having PHOTO-PAINT create a Directional List. The Directional List is composed of a user-defined number of copies of the original object. Each copy is equally rotated. For example, if you type **4** when prompted for a Directional List,

FIGURE 11-7 All this image needs is a title in the top blue banner

PHOTO-PAINT will make three copies of the original (3 + original = 4), each rotated 90 degrees. Here is the procedure:

1. Create or select an image with one object in it. There are no size limitations (other than good sense) regarding the object used for an Image Sprayer, but the object must be selected.
2. Click the Sprayer Options button in the Property Bar and choose Save Object(s) as Image List.
3. Because there is a single object, you will be asked if you want to make a Directional List. If you select yes, you must enter the number of images and then name the new image file. Be aware that if you make the number

for a Directional List huge (>60) or if the size of the object is large, or both, the program will spend the next two weeks processing it.

4. That's it. The new image file is loaded in the Image Sprayer.

Creating an Image List from an Image Containing Multiple Objects

Creating a list from an image containing more than one object is the same as previously described with a few exceptions. All of the objects in the image that are to be included in the image list must be selected. The order or position of the objects isn't important. If the objects have drop shadows, ensure that the shadows are grouped to the object casting the shadow. If you don't do this, each shadow will appear as a separate object in the image list.

TIP: *Looking for objects with which to make an image list? There is a large collection of objects located in the folder labeled objects on the Corel PHOTO PAINT CD.*

Creating an Image List from an Image Containing No Objects

This method is a little trickier than the previous methods. Since there are no objects for PHOTO-PAINT to select, it divides the image into equal parts based on the information provided by the user. The procedure follows:

1. Select an image and click Save Document as an Image List in the Tool Settings palette.
2. You will next be prompted to input the number of images that are in each column and row. If there is only one image, leave the setting at the default of 1 and 1.
3. That's it. The new image file is loaded in the Image Sprayer.

TIP: *You can use the mask tools to select portions of the image you want to be included in the image list before creating it. This technique works best with multiple natural objects such as rocks and clouds that can overlap without looking like square blotches.*

CAUTION: *When you load a new image list, the Property Bar settings (like Spacing, Orbits, and so on) from the previous brush remain.*

Image Sprayer Presets

The Image Sprayer tool also has presets found in the Property Bar. These presets change the settings of the Brush Settings Docker and Property Bar. Of special note is the Orbits tab. This applies the powerful Orbits engine to control the application of the Image Sprayer. If the image list contains only one object, the best effects are achieved with Orbits enabled. When a list containing multiple objects is selected, the effect is diminished if not lost altogether.

Painting With the Image Sprayer and Clone Tool

Figure 11-8 shows a vertical image I created for a magazine cover. The background was created with the Image Sprayer tool. After a Fountain fill was used to create the sky, the Image Sprayer (using clouds) was used to create the

FIGURE 11-8 A magazine cover made with the Image Sprayer brush

clouds. The technique is simple. With the size of the Image Sprayer brush set to small, begin at the horizon and create several rows of clouds. Next, increase the size of the clouds and make several more applications further up the image. Lastly, use the original size of the cloud image and apply the clouds sparingly to the row nearest the top.

The Corel balls are . . . well . . . too complex to be covered in this chapter.

Conclusion

This chapter has given you some of the rules of the road for using these two power tools. While it would take over a hundred pages to thoroughly explore the basic combinations of techniques and settings for using these tools, I hope you have learned enough to want to pick up the tools and begin to explore their possibilities.

CHAPTER 12

Understanding Text and Other Objects

One of the more powerful features of PHOTO-PAINT is the ability to create and control objects. The use of objects falls into a category I call "fun stuff." There is a tabloid sold in the United States called *The Sun,* which may be one of the leading forums for unique photo-editing. You may have seen *The Sun* while standing in grocery checkout lines. One headline read "Baby Born with Three Heads." The photograph showed a woman holding an infant who fit the headline's description. Someone on *The Sun* staff had masked the face of a small child, made it into an object, duplicated several copies, and placed them on the body of the baby. Like I said, this is fun stuff. If you are an avid reader of *The Sun,* do not take what I say as criticism of the tabloid. I love *The Sun*! I stand in a lot of grocery lines, and it provides entertainment while I'm waiting for the person in front of me with 35 items in the 10-item express line.

In this chapter, we will explore objects, the Text tool, and all that can be done with them.

Pixels and Krazy Glue

Traditionally with bitmap programs like Corel PHOTO-PAINT, there is only the background. If we were to take a brush from the Toolbox and draw a wide brush stroke across an image, every pixel the brush were to touch would change to the color assigned to the brush. The brush color does not go on *top* of the original color; it replaces it. It's as if every pixel applied had super glue on it. When an action is applied to an image, it "sticks" to the image and cannot be moved. Anyone who has spent hours and hours trying to achieve an effect with these older bitmap programs will testify that the process by which bitmaps merge into the background was the major drawback of photo-editing programs. And then along came objects.

Objects Defined

What is an object? Here's one definition:

An object is an independent bitmap selection created with object tools and layered above the base image.

Let's expand that definition. In Corel PHOTO-PAINT, an *object* is a bitmap that "floats" above the background, which is also called the *base image.* Because the object is not a part of the base image, it can be moved as many times as needed without limit. Objects can also be scaled, resized, rotated, and distorted. We also have the ability to apply Perspective transformations, which greatly increase the flexibility of many of the tools. You are about to learn how to do some amazing things with objects. Most of the rules you learned in previous chapters regarding masks also apply to objects.

Expanding the Definition

Figure 12-1 appears to be a single image, and yet it is composed of a background and six separate objects. Figure 12-2 shows the background and six objects that make up the image and the Objects Docker that lists them. The misconception that the object only exists to its visible edge is reinforced by the Object marquee, which displays the "edge" of an object. In reality, an object may be composed of both opaque and transparent pixels. If Figure 12-1 were observed from the side, we would see that each object is actually the same size and dimensions as the background. It may help to think of the object as on a large sheet of clear acetate, rather than as a cutout placed on the background.

FIGURE 12-1 How many objects do you see in this picture? The answer might surprise you

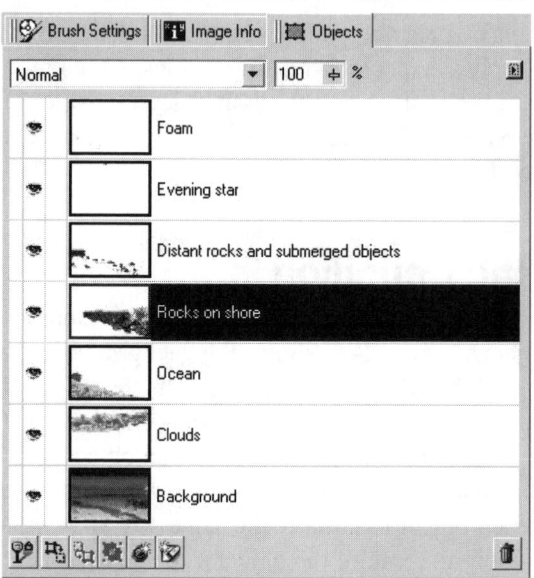

FIGURE 12-2 The Objects Docker shows not only what objects are in the image but also where they are located

The Objects Docker and Property Bar

The Objects Docker, Figure 12-3, can be opened by selecting Windows | Dockers | Objects or with the keyboard combination CTRL-F7.

The Objects Docker is the control center for all object manipulations. The following is only a partial list of the functions that can be accomplished through the Property Bar and the Objects Docker:

- Select object
- Lock or unlock object transparency
- Make objects visible or invisible
- Create objects from masks
- Create masks from objects

- Move objects between layers
- Change rate of the transparency/opacity of objects
- Apply transformations to individual objects
- Select merge modes for individual objects
- Label different objects
- Combine objects with the background
- Combine individual objects together
- Delete objects
- Get a babysitter on a Saturday night (OK, that might be pushing it)

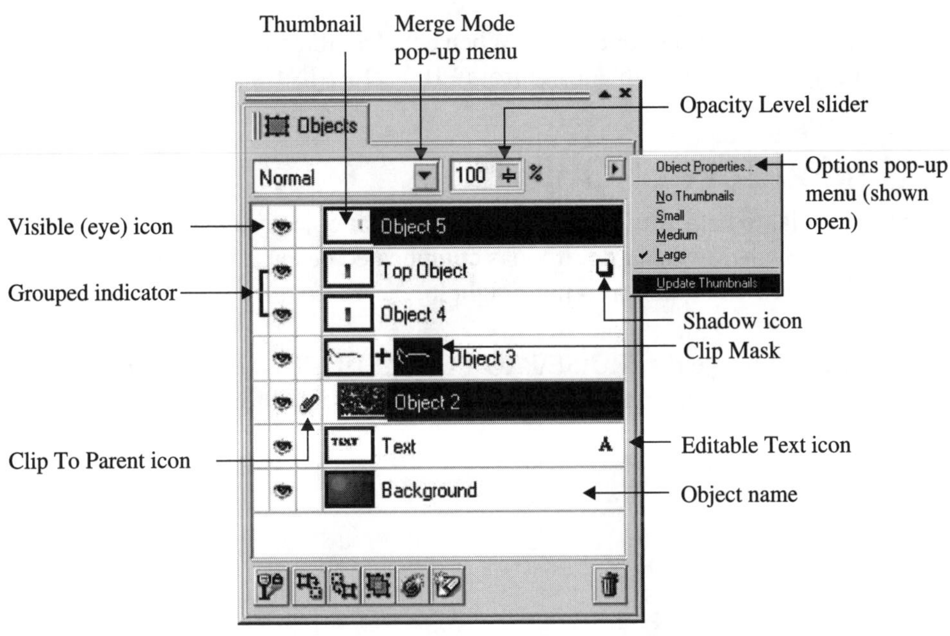

FIGURE 12-3 The Objects Docker is the control center for nearly all operations involving objects

Object Modes

How an object acts or reacts to a PHOTO-PAINT operation is determined by the mode the object is in. Here are some definitions to describe modes in the Objects Docker:

- **Selected** If an object is selected, the name is highlighted. It can be moved, grouped with other objects, or merged with the background or with other objects. An object is selected by clicking on its thumbnail or label. To select multiple contiguous objects, select the first one and SHIFT-click the last one. To select multiple noncontiguous objects, CTRL-click each object you want selected. Selected objects are not subject to PHOTO-PAINT actions (for example, sharpening, blurring, and so on) unless they are active.
- **Active** An object is active when its thumbnail has a red border. Only one object can be active at a time. An object that is active is also selected.
- **Lock Object Transparency** When enabled, this mode protects transparent areas of the object from PHOTO-PAINT actions.

A Guided Tour of Objects

This is a tutorial to help you get a better feel for what objects and all their features do and do not do—do-wacka-do. It looks complicated because there is a lot of text explaining what we are doing, so jump right in.

1. Open the image EXERCISE\PROJECTS\OBJECTS located on the Corel CD. This is a background, shown next, that I created for this exercise using a fountain fill background and Image Sprayer for the clouds, and noise for the sand.

2. Select the Text tool in the Toolbox and, on the Property Bar, change the font to Futura XBlt BT at 150. Type **COREL**. The placement of your text is not important as long as it fits within the image completely. Select the Object Picker tool. Look in the Objects Docker, and you will see that the text is now an object. Also note the letter *A* circled on the right side of the Object name. This icon tells us that the text is an editable object.

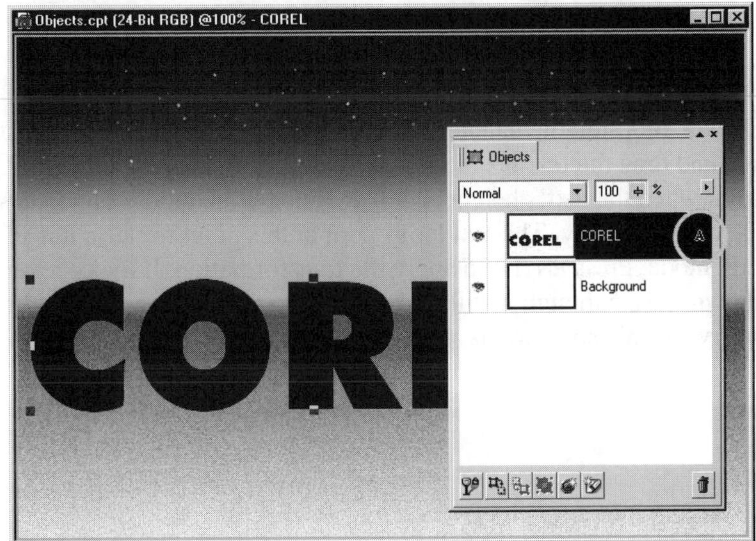

3. Select the text by clicking on it (if it is not already selected). There is a lot of information available to us at this point. Place your cursor on the object, and after a moment a box will appear, as shown next, giving details about the object underneath. It shows the object is both active and selected. It also tells us that its Opacity is at 100% and the Merge mode is Normal, and it shows us the size of the object (in pixels). In the Objects Docker, there is some of the same information. The object is labeled "COREL." Text objects use their text string as their object name. The object is highlighted (selected) and the thumbnail has a red border (indicating it is active).

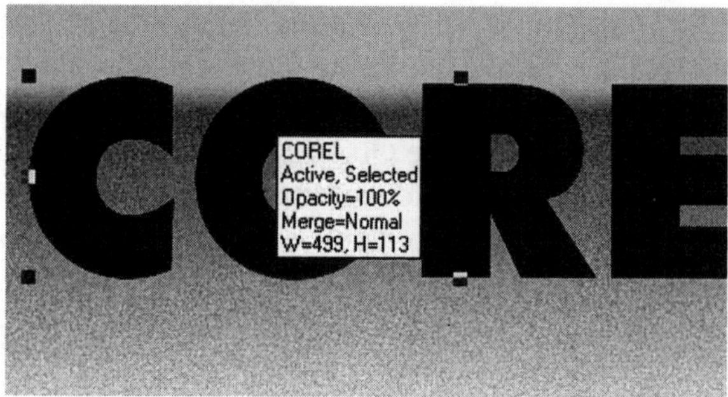

4. Click the top-middle handle of the text. Hold down the CTRL (constrain) key and drag the text up. Nothing will appear to happen until you hit a point when the text's height is 200%. Release the mouse button first and then the CTRL key. The text looks poor at this point because it is in Text Edit mode. Press ENTER to apply the transformation. It looks better, as shown next, although it still looks a little ragged on the curves—but don't worry. At this point we have Scaled the text object vertically 200%.

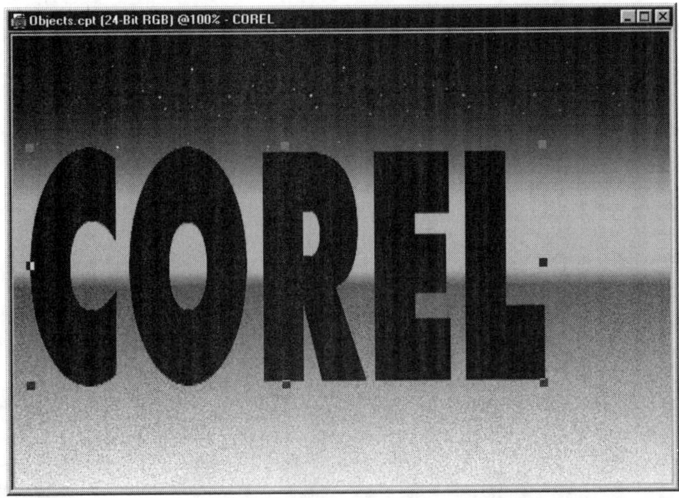

5. Select the Text tool again. Click the text. A warning box appears as shown next, warning you that if you choose OK, all the changes you have made to the text will be lost and it will revert back to its original font, fill, and size. So, remember when working with text that if you decide you want to go back and change the font, and so on, that all changes to it up to that point will be lost. Got it? Click Cancel.

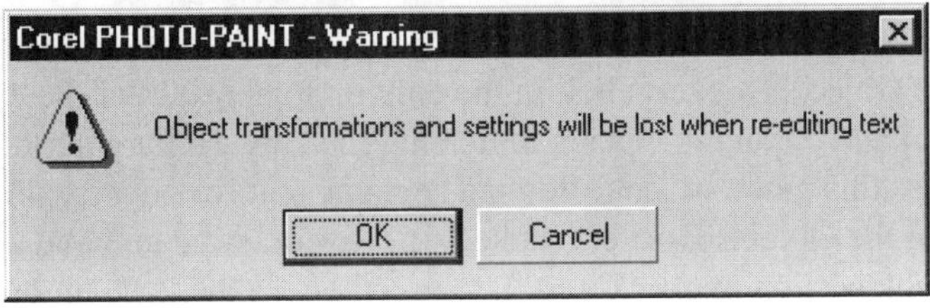

6. Choose File Import (CTRL-SHIFT-I) and when the dialog box opens, select EXERCISE\PROJECTS\CHECKERED FLAG and click Open. A thumbnail appears of the image we just selected attached to the cursor. Click anywhere in the image window, and the checkered flag we just imported covers the entire image, as shown next. Notice that in the Objects Docker, the flag is an object floating above the text and the background.

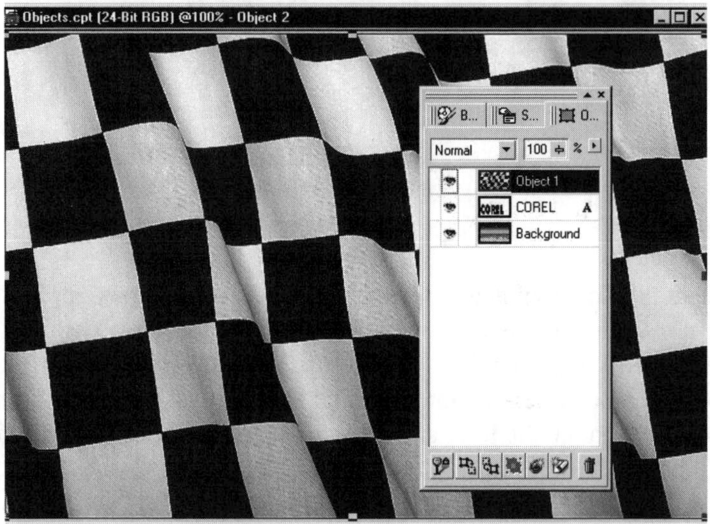

7. In the Objects Docker, click in the column to the right of the eye icon, and a paperclip icon appears indicating the Clip To Parent mode. We will discuss this mode in the following sections, but for now try this: Click the text in the Objects Docker to select it. Now drag the text and notice that only the portion of checkered flag directly over the text can be seen, as shown next. Now select the flag and move it. Again, only the portion over the object (text) is visible.

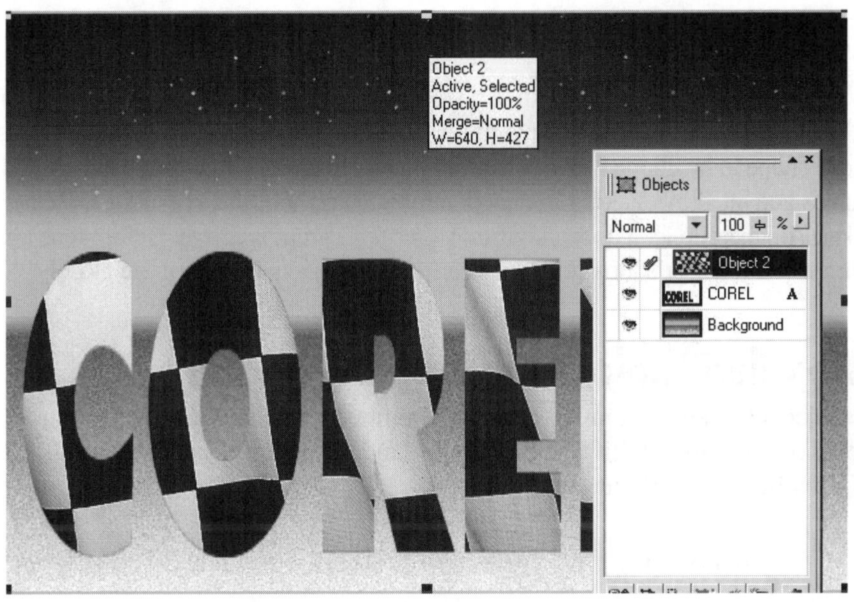

TIP: *You can select objects in an image by clicking them with the Object Picker tool. The background can only be selected in the Objects Docker.*

8. That's all for now. We are going to use this file again, so either keep it open or save the file as **Guided Tour**. Don't forget where you parked it.

PHOTOSHOP NOTE: *For purposes of clarification, the terms object and layer are used interchangeably. This is because each layer can contain only one object, and without an object there cannot be a layer. Photoshop calls them layers; PHOTO-PAINT calls them objects. A rose by any other name . . . In this chapter, we will use the term object to avoid confusion.*

Clip To Parent

So what is this Clip To Parent? Clip To Parent sounds like what happens to me when I get the phone bills my children have run up. In PHOTO-PAINT, this option causes the object's shape to be clipped to the shape of the object below it in the object list. This feature is activated by clicking in the column to the right of the eye in the Objects Docker. A paperclip icon appears to show Clip To Parent is active. Before returning to our guided tour, let's look at the controls of the Objects Docker more closely.

A Detailed Look at the Objects Docker

The Objects Docker is composed of the Thumbnail display area, the Dialog Display options, the Multifunction buttons, and the Merge/Opacity controls. Let's find out a little more about these wonders.

Thumbnail Display Area

The Thumbnail display is divided into four columns. The column on the far right shows the thumbnail and the name of the object. The bottom object is automatically named Background. It cannot be renamed or moved. Unless it is text, each time an object is created, Corel PHOTO-PAINT assigns a default name to it. The object name can be edited by double-clicking on its name, or right-clicking the name or thumbnail and selecting Properties, which opens the Object Properties dialog box, shown next. You can give the object a name of up to 39 characters.

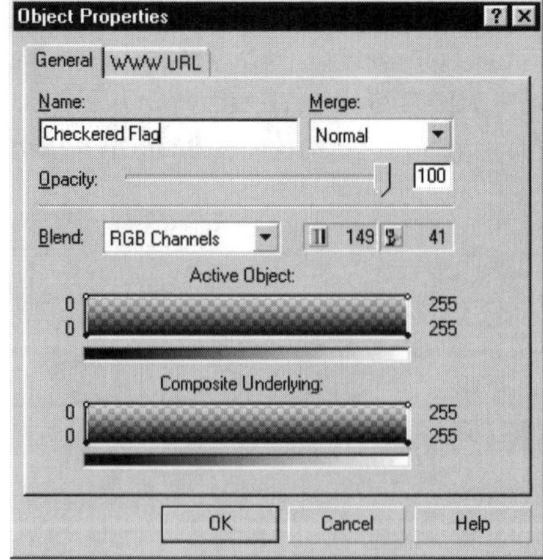

The entire bottom portion of the Object Properties dialog box contains a wide assortment of controls for blending the object with an underlying object. These controls may appear a little intimidating because they are. The following section, "Controlling the Blend of Objects," describes how this feature of the Object Properties works. It is advanced material and you may want to skip it now and refer to it later.

Controlling the Blend of Objects

You can blend objects to define how their pixels mix with the objects that lie below them in the stacking order. You can use the X-axis (slider) of the Active Object and Composite Underlying graphs to specify the grayscale values of the object pixels on a scale from 0 (black) to 255 (white). The Y-axis controls let you specify the opacity of the pixels on a scale from 0 (transparent) to 100 (opaque). Pixels in the active object that fall outside the specified range are hidden so that the pixels of the underlying object are visible. The Help files contain information on the use of this feature.

TIP: *You can also open the Objects Docker window by double-clicking the Object Picker tool.*

Left of the Thumbnail is a column that can contain the Clip To Parent icon. This icon looks like a paper clip and can only be enabled when there are two or more objects. The "eye" icon in the next column indicates the object is either visible (black) or invisible (grayed out). When an object is invisible, it is automatically protected from any PHOTO-PAINT actions. The narrow column to the far left is used to display any groupings of objects.

Objects Docker Display Options

To the right of the Opacity slider on the top of the Objects Docker is a small right-arrow button. Clicking it opens a pop-up menu that determines the size of the thumbnails displayed. The choices are Object Properties (same one we met in the previous paragraph), No Thumbnails, Small, Medium, Large, and Update Thumbnails. Why is there a No Thumbnails option, you ask? Turning off the thumbnails speeds up PHOTO-PAINT, especially on slower systems.

Multifunction Buttons

There are several buttons on the bottom of the Objects Docker. The assortment and availability of the buttons depends on the mode you are in.

- **Lock Object Transparency** With this button enabled, the shape of an object doesn't change when you edit it. When Lock Object Transparency is disabled, the shape of an object can change when you apply an effect or when you edit the object using a tool.
- **Create Mask from Object(s) and Create Object from Mask buttons** These provide a quick method to convert masks into objects and vice versa.
- **The Combine Objects Together button** This merges all selected objects with each other. Objects that are not selected are unaffected.
- **New Lens button** This button creates a new lens covering the entire image. Clicking the button opens the New Lens dialog box from which you can choose one of the 23 possible lens settings.
- **New Object button** This button creates an empty transparent object that covers the entire image. This button is not available when the Lock Transparency option is enabled. It is the same as selecting Object | Create | New Object.
- **Delete Object(s) button** If you select the objects and click this little button, the objects go screaming into the night, where they are never heard from again (unless you invoke the powers of the Undo).

Merge Mode and Opacity

The Merge box determines the way in which the colors of the object and the colors of the background image are combined when the two are merged. You can preview the result of using each merge mode directly in the image window. The Opacity slider determines the opacity or transparency of the selected object. Some people are confused by opacity and transparency. Remember that 100% opacity is zero transparency or 100% transparency is zero opacity. You can call it either opacity or transparency. It's an "Is the glass half empty or half full?" kind of question.

Clip Masks

The Clip Mask is a mask that is attached to an individual object. As you may recall from Chapter 7, there can only be one mask on an image. Through the use of Clip Masks, you can apply a Clip Mask to every object. One of the primary uses of the Clip Mask is to provide a nonpermanent transparency. Later in this chapter, we will learn about the Transparency tools that achieve the same effect as the Clip Mask. The advantage of the Clip Mask, however, is that the transparency action can modify the object at any time and becomes permanent only when you combine the Clip Mask with the object. Let's return to our guided tour, and it will make more sense.

1. Open the file we made previously called GUIDED TOUR.
2. With the Object Picker tool select the text object in the Objects Docker. Create a mask of the text (CTRL-M). Save the mask to a channel (Mask | Save | Save As Channel), and when prompted, name the mask channel **Text**. I have included one for you named Corel text just in case.
3. Before doing our Clip Mask thing, we are taking a very brief side trip. You will like the effect, and it will make your system work a little faster. Select the Brush tool and, in the Property Bar, choose the Airbrush and the Wide Cover Brush type. Make the following changes: Nib size: 40 and Transparency: 90. The Brush Type now reads "Custom Airbrush."
4. Ensure the Paint color is black. In the Objects Docker select the checkered flag object. This is because we want to apply the airbrush strokes to the flag texture. Choose the Stroke Mask button on the Property Bar, shown next, and when a dialog box opens, choose Middle Of The Mask Border and OK. To enhance this 3-D effect, select the Object Picker tool and while holding down SHIFT, press RIGHT ARROW. This is called a *super nudge,* and it moves the checkered flag object 10 pixels to the right. Repeat this action except use the DOWN ARROW key . The result is shown in Figure 12-4.

12

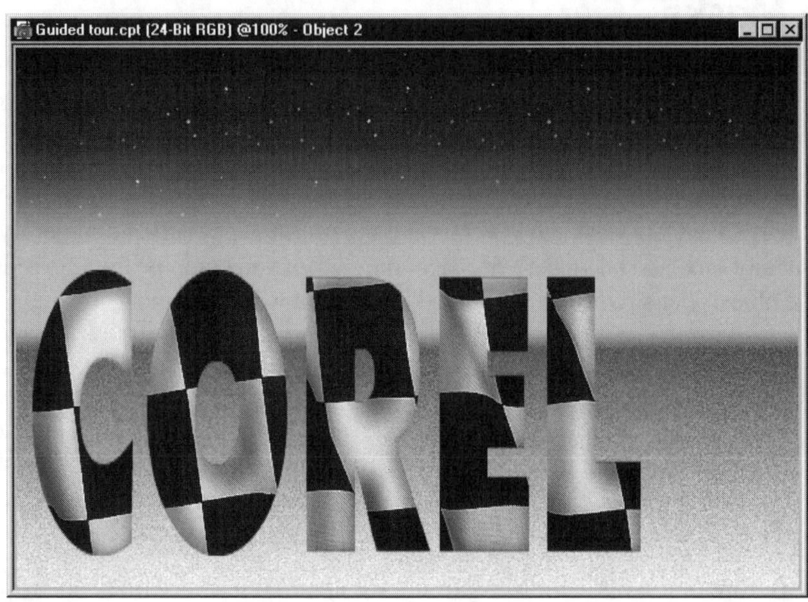

FIGURE 12-4 Stroke Mask gives our text a 3-D quality

5. At this point there is no advantage to keeping the text and the checkered flag object in the Clip To Parent relationship. Hold down SHIFT and select the text. Both should be selected at this point. Click the Combine Objects Together button at the bottom of the Objects Docker. The text and the

object have become a single object. Also note that the name changed to "Object" and that the "A" icon is no longer there. When we combined the objects, the text could no longer be edited as text.

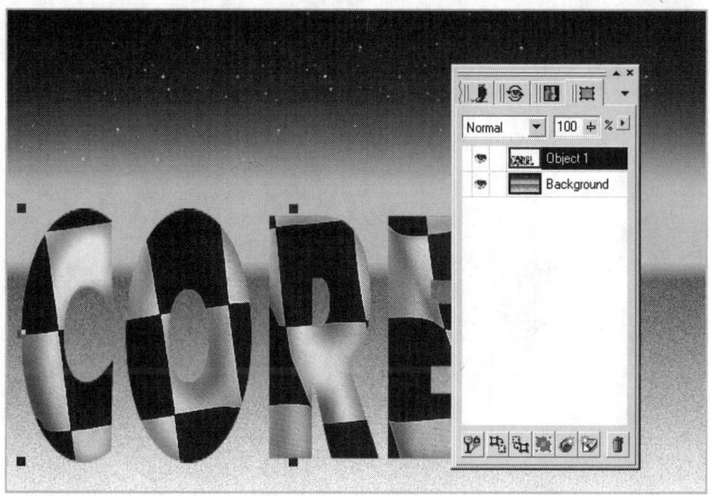

6. If there is a mask on your image, remove it. At the bottom of the Objects Docker click the New Object button. From the Brush Tools flyout select the Image Sprayer tool. In the Property Bar choose Brown Rope. Click and drag a rope roughly the shape of the one shown next. The Objects Docker, like all dockers, can be grouped or can change shape. During the course of this guided tour you will see several different combinations in the illustrations.

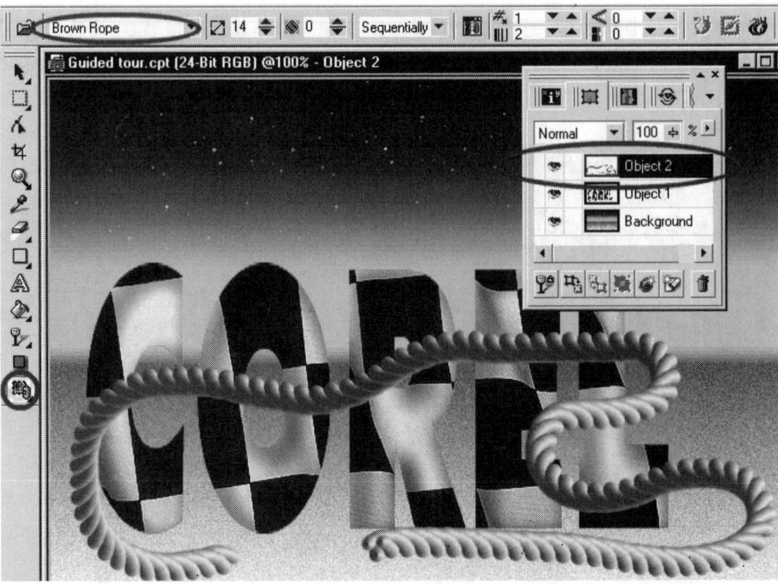

7. Now we are going to use Clip Mask and have some fun while we are at it. With the Object Picker tool ensure the top object (the rope) is selected. Create a mask of this object (CTRL-M). Now we are going to make this mask into a Clip Mask. Choose Object | Clip Mask | Create | From Mask (whew). Notice the change in the Objects Docker window, shown next. Another thumbnail representing the Clip Mask has appeared and is active, as indicated by the red rectangle around it. This means that any action we take on the image now is applied only to the Clip Mask.

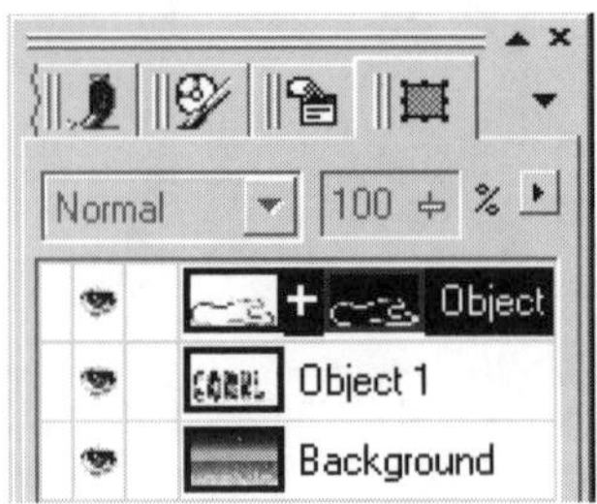

8. We are about to thread the rope through the letters. Before we can do this, we need some protection, so we only remove the part of the rope that coincides with the text. Load the mask we saved in the channel. Choose Mask | Load | Text. The Clip Mask and a regular mask can exist on the same image at the same time. If your mask marquee is on, you can see that mask, but there is not a visual indication on the image of the Clip Mask.

9. We are almost ready. Select the Brush tools and change the brush from the Airbrush to the Art Brush; the style should be Quick Doodler. With the Paint color still black, paint on the rope that crosses the letter *C*. Note that you are actually painting black on the mask. Everywhere on the mask you paint black, the rope becomes transparent. The text mask we loaded keeps the transparency from going beyond the boundaries of the text. The result is shown next.

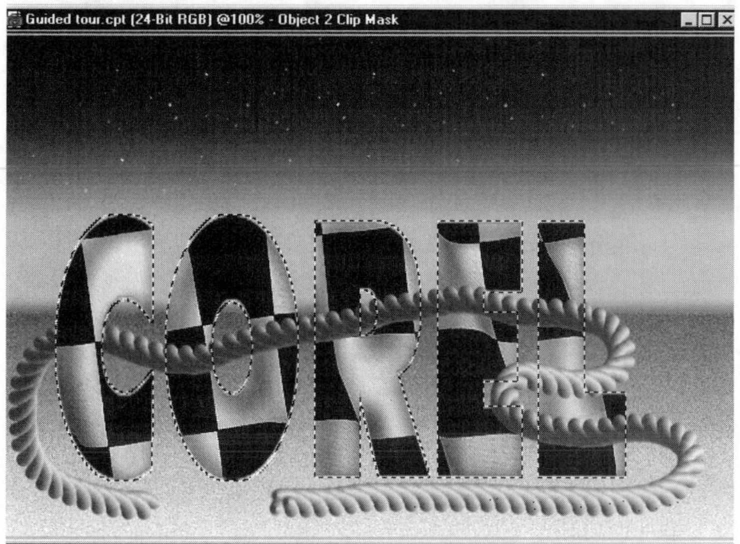

10. Continue to paint on the rope where you want it to be transparent. If you change your mind, you can change the rope's transparency by setting the Paint to white and brushing on the Clip Mask. My completed Clip Mask rope is shown next; yours probably will look different.

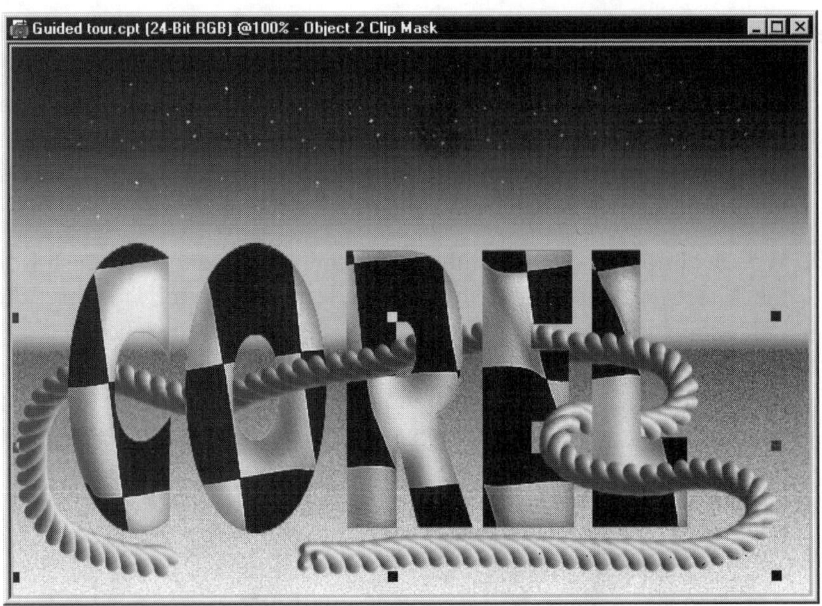

11. Okay, we've done a lot. Close the file and don't save the changes.

Figure 12-5 is an example of both Clip To Parent (photo in the text) and Clip Mask (rope through the letters).

More Stuff About Clip Masks

Everything we did to the rope in the previous exercise, we could have done with the Object Transparency tools. The big difference is that the changes made with Object Transparency tools are permanent, while the changes made with the Clip Mask are only there until you remove or change the mask. To make the changes permanent, select Combine (which is now available as a choice from the Clip Mask part of the Object menu), or right-click the Clip Mask in the Objects Docker and a pop-up menu will appear, as shown next. Choosing Disable Clip Mask will turn off the effects of the Clip Mask, but the mask will still be there. Combine Clip Mask will permanently apply the mask effects to the object. If Remove Clip Mask

FIGURE 12-5 This image was easy to construct using the PHOTO-PAINT's advanced features

is selected, the mask is discarded and the object returns to its pre–Clip Mask appearance.

Select All
Disable Clip Mask
Combine Clip Mask
Remove Clip Mask
Properties...

Editing Clip Masks

Remember that the Clip Mask is an extra mask that applies only to the object to which it is attached. Clip Masks have nothing to do with regular masks, although you can view and edit them like regular masks with some effort. In fact, I couldn't figure it out and had to ask the PHOTO-PAINT (Windows) Product manager, Doug Chomyn, and he provided the following procedure to view and edit Clip Masks:

- Select the Channels Docker (CTRL -F9).
- Click the eye icon beside the channel identified as "Object ## Clip Mask" while any of the color channels are visible; this produces a Mask Overlay view.
- If you hide all the color channels by clicking each one while the Clip Mask is selected in the Channels Docker, the Paint On Mask (grayscale) view will appear, as shown next. In this mode, you can modify the mask just as if you were in Paint On Mask mode. In the example next, I have modified the Clip Mask with the Smear Effect tool.

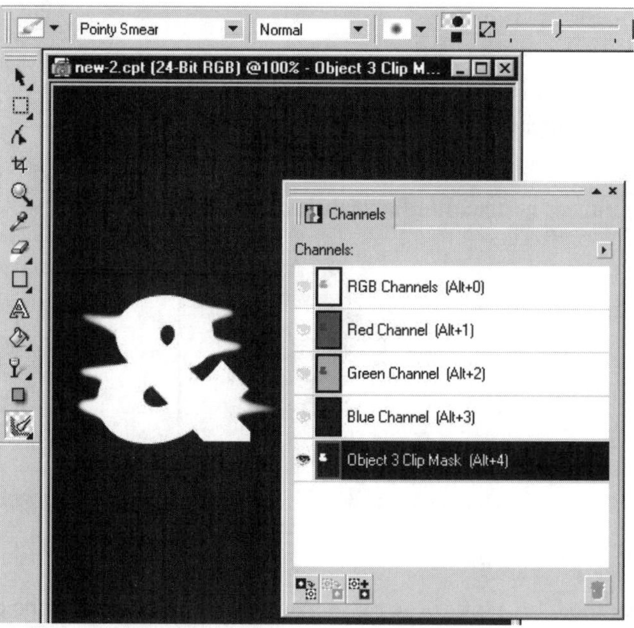

Object Transparency Tools

You can change the transparency of an entire object, or you can change the transparency of part of an object. When you change the transparency of an object, you change the grayscale value of its individual pixels. Grayscale values range from black, which has a value of 0 (transparent), to white, which has a value of 255 (opaque).

Up until now, we have learned about changing the transparency of an object evenly throughout the entire object, revealing the image elements that lie beneath the object. You can change the transparency of parts of an object by using the three Object Transparency tools in the Toolbox. The Object Transparency Brush tool lets you change the transparency of an object by applying brush strokes. You can use the Object Transparency tool to apply a transparency gradient to an object, or you can use the Transparent Color Selection tool to make specific colors (or ranges of colors) transparent. To change the transparency of an object in relation to underlying image elements, you can use the Blend controls in the Object Properties dialog box to specify which pixels are visible.

There are three Object Transparency tools located on a flyout in the Toolbox, as shown here (along with each tool's keyboard shortcut):

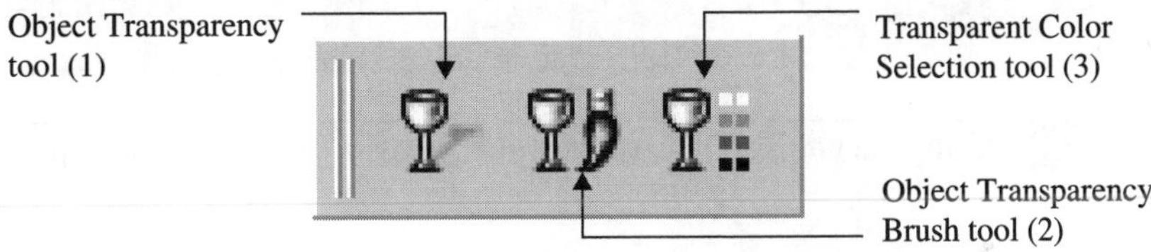

The image in Figure 12-6 was made by use of the original photograph of the steps on the bottom and another photograph of a different set of stairs on top of it. The Transparency tool was used to gradually blend the two together.

Operation of the Transparency tool is identical to the Gradient Fill tool. You click to place a starting point and then drag the point out to an ending. I have created a little work session to demonstrate the tool.

12

The Object Dropshadow Tool

The Object Dropshadow tool in the Toolbox creates objects that look like shadows.

The Object Dropshadow's Property Bar has two modes: Flat and Perspective. While the choices appear complicated, they are not hard to use. They are accessed by toggling the Dropshadow Mode button.

FIGURE 12-6 Using the Object Transparency tool, you can seamlessly blend photos together

Flat Shadow Mode

The Orientation portion shows the direction of the shadow. You can change the direction by dragging the arrow dial indicator to the desired position, entering a numerical value, or changing the direction interactively on the image. You can also change the distance of the shadow interactively as well. Check boxes allow restricting changes to 45-degree increments and displaying the distance as a percentage.

Opacity is one of the two most important settings; the other is feathering. The Opacity controls how soft the shadow appears. The larger the Feather width (in pixels), the more diffused the shadow appears.

TIP: *The Opacity of the shadow can be adjusted in the Objects Docker after the shadow has been created. The same is not true of feathering.*

What do you want to do today? The following color pages give just a hint of what you can create with Corel PHOTO-PAINT 9.

Using Clip To Parent and Clip Mask, explored in Chapter 12, you can make an image like this in a few minutes.

You can use the Clone tool, Chapter 11, on a photograph (right) to remove defects as well as old boyfriends (below).

By using shadows, you can create the illusion of engraving (above).

Apply the Image Sprayer tool to a rectangular mask to produce a decorative border (below).

In Chapter 7 you will learn how to make this intricate tile.

While it looks difficult, in Chapter 15 you will learn to create both the text effect and the background shown on the right in only a few steps.

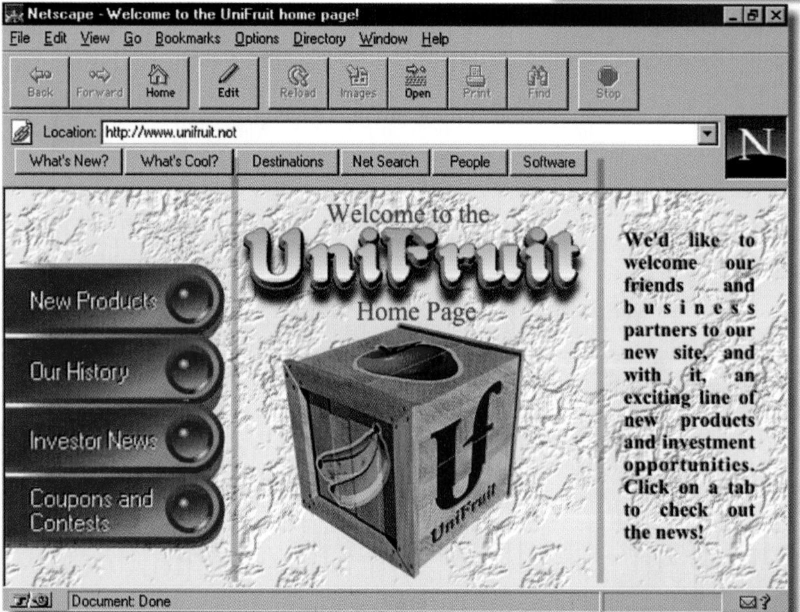

Creating a web page? In Chapter 24 you will learn how to put together this web page and others like it.

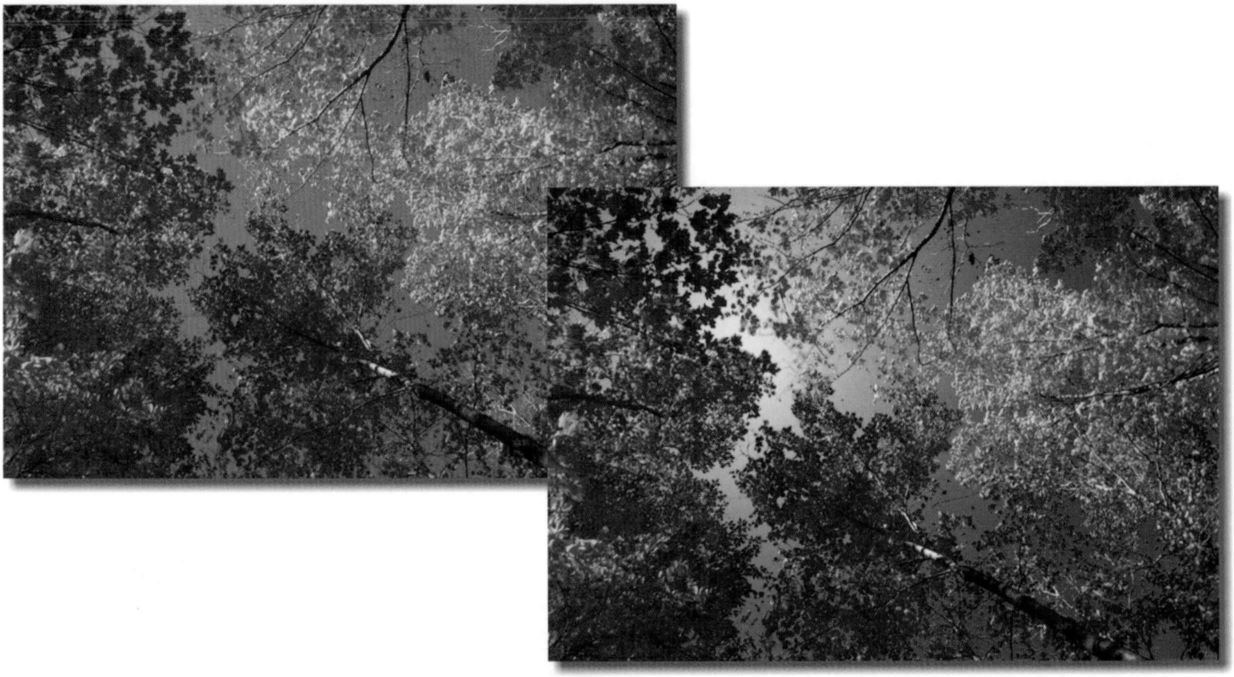

You can use background replacement to enhance a photograph or a subject in a photograph, or to completely change a photo. In Chapter 8 you will learn how to replace the background in the trees as shown above. In Chapter 7 you'll find out how to change the dull sky behind the jet (below) into a dramatic backdrop. The polar bear at the left is my favorite example of background replacement, dating back to PHOTO-PAINT 5 Plus.

In Chapter 15 you'll discover how easy it is to convert this photograph of graffiti on a wall into a 3-D object as shown at right.

In Chapter 14 you'll learn how the Offset filter can change a photograph of a nautilus shell (above left) into the background shown above on the right.

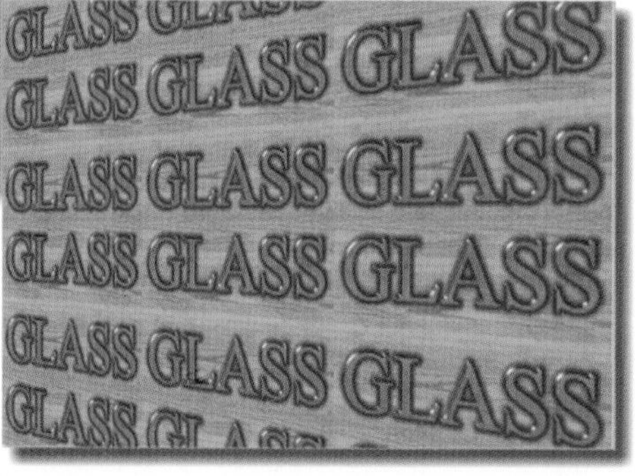

The Glass filter tutorial in Chapter 15 will teach you not only how to make a great glass effect, but also how to apply the perspective shown on right.

The Mesh Warp filter does some pretty amazing things. The beer shown on the right was made Texas size, and the eyes on the wall shown below can be made to look either really mad or very sad.

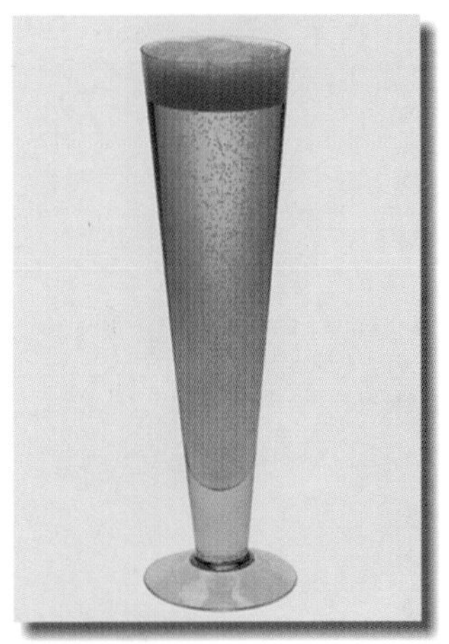

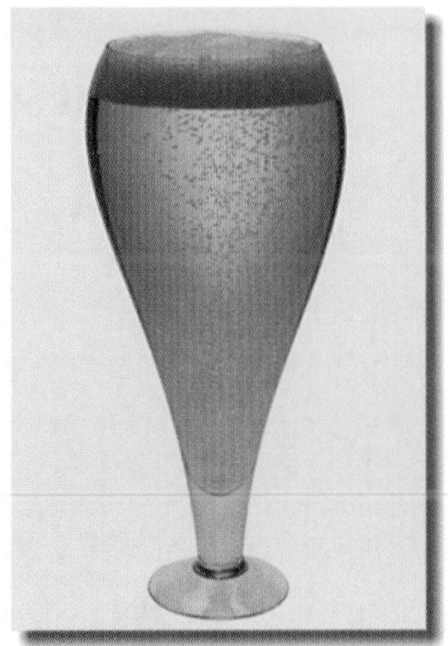

When filters are applied to humans, the results can be entertaining and possibly libelous. The model shown below (far left) is having an Elvis hair day (left) as created with the Mesh Warp filter. The "nose job" on the middle photograph was done with the Punch filter. The photograph on the right, where the model looks like she pumps iron, was created with the Pinch filter.

In Chapter 11 you will create the glass ball of flags, shown above, using the Image Sprayer tool.

Transforming flowers in a photograph into a glass sphere is quite simple to do. In Chapter 15 you will learn by creating the image shown below.

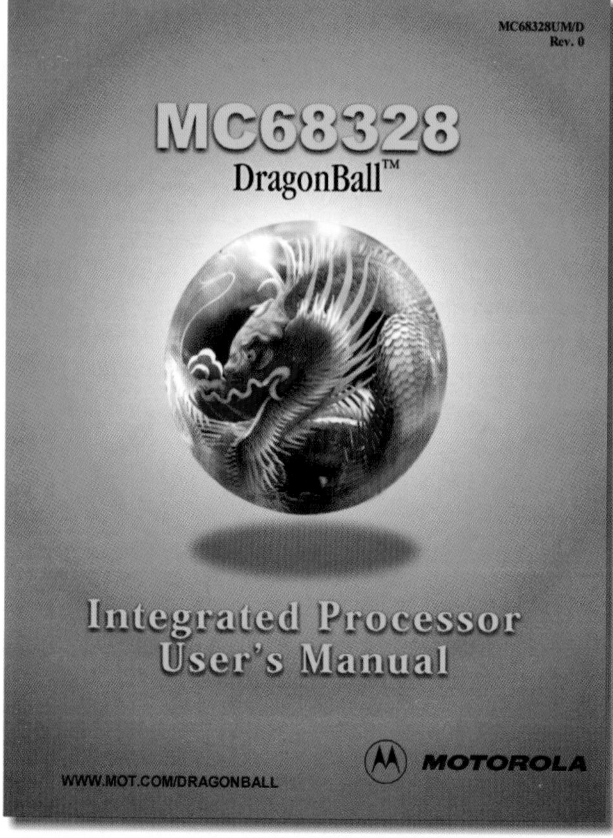

The design applications of the glass sphere are limitless. I used the sphere to create the DragonBall™ logo for Motorola®, shown at left.

The image above was created for the background of a brochure for a wildlife-awareness group.

In Chapter 25 you'll discover recoverable information in the background of a photo (below) as you go step-by-step to learn the recovery process.

Even stock photography like the photograph of the lovely late Lady Di, shown above left, needs correction. In Chapter 25 you will learn how to correct the colors in this photograph.

A common problem with pictures taken with a digital camera (above) is a greenish color cast, which is easily corrected (below) in PHOTO-PAINT 9.

Sometimes repairs are simple, like removing the scratches on the original black-and-white photo below left. The finished photo, below right, has the scratches removed. Did you notice what else was removed?

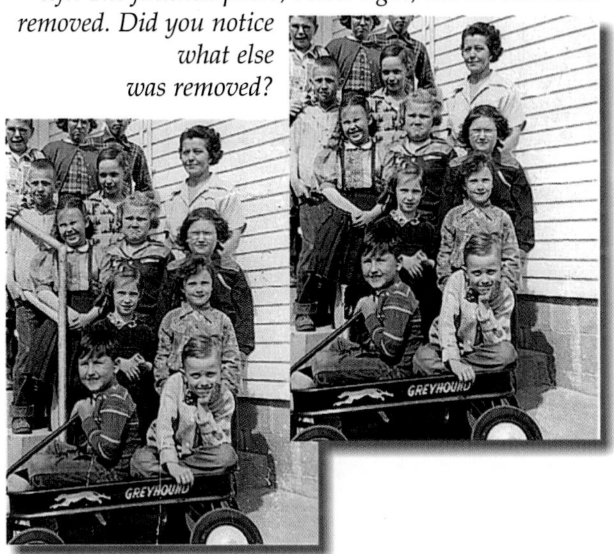

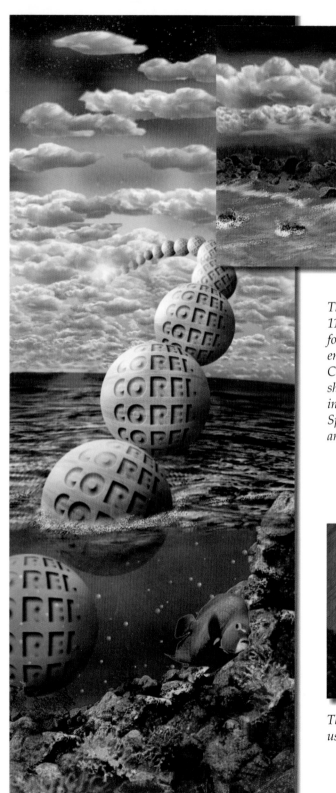

The Image Sprayer, explored in Chapter 11, is an incredible tool. The background for the image on the left was created entirely with the images that come with Corel PHOTO-PAINT. The image shown above was created at a trade show in less than three hours. The Image Sprayer tool isn't limited to landscapes and still-life images (see below).

The image shown above was made more realistic using the Image Sprayer to add the plants.

Metallic effects are always popular for design work. In Chapter 16 you will learn how to make the hammered-metal effect shown at right in a step-by-step tutorial.

In Chapter 26 you will create the twisted and worn metal shown above. To the right and below are variations of that same technique.

In Chapter 14 you will discover how to make metallic effects that look rusty and deteriorated.

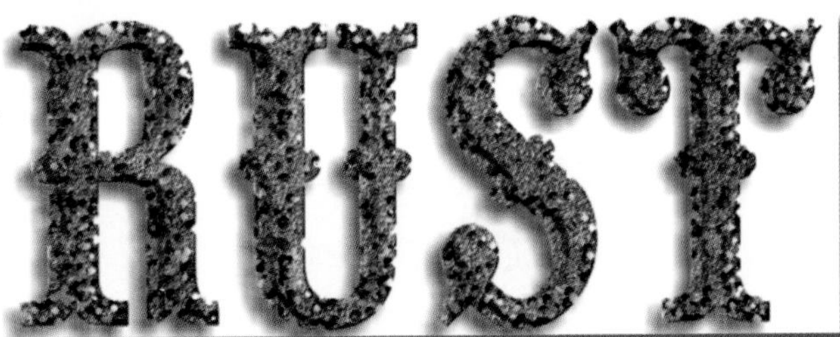

The image shown above is the one you will create in the tutorial. The image on the left is a variation of the same technique.

On the opposite page (top) is a display of the effect created by several of the new PHOTO-PAINT 9 filters. The original image is in the center. The top two images were created using the Conté Crayon filter. The bottom-left image is the result of applying the Watercolor filter; the bottom-right one received an early snowfall from the Weather filter—I added the snow on the ground using a brush tool.

The jigsaw puzzle effect that was applied to the beer (left) is one of the many presets found in the new Bump Map filter, which is explored in Chapter 18.

The photograph of a crab (left) is converted to a watercolor (below) by use of the Watercolor filter, one of many new Art Strokes filters.

The new Mosaic filter changes existing photographs so that they appear to have been created from individual mosaic tiles.

This page debuts as a readers' gallery, containing digital images sent in by users of previous versions of PHOTO-PAINT. For this edition of the book, it seemed appropriate to use images from Alex Link, who has created effects with PHOTO-PAINT that are both realistic and quite stunning. If you've created an image or effect with PHOTO-PAINT, send me a copy at www.davehuss@austin.rr.com. Who knows, you may see your images in the PHOTO-PAINT 10 color pages.

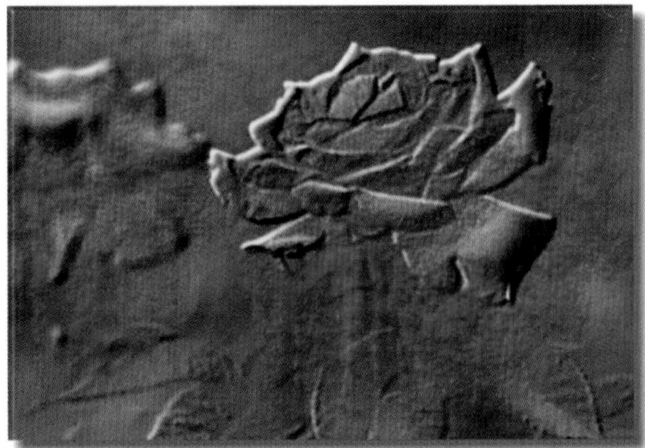

Both metallic roses on the right began as a photograph of a rose. Look carefully to see the faint reflection of the same rose in the sphere below.

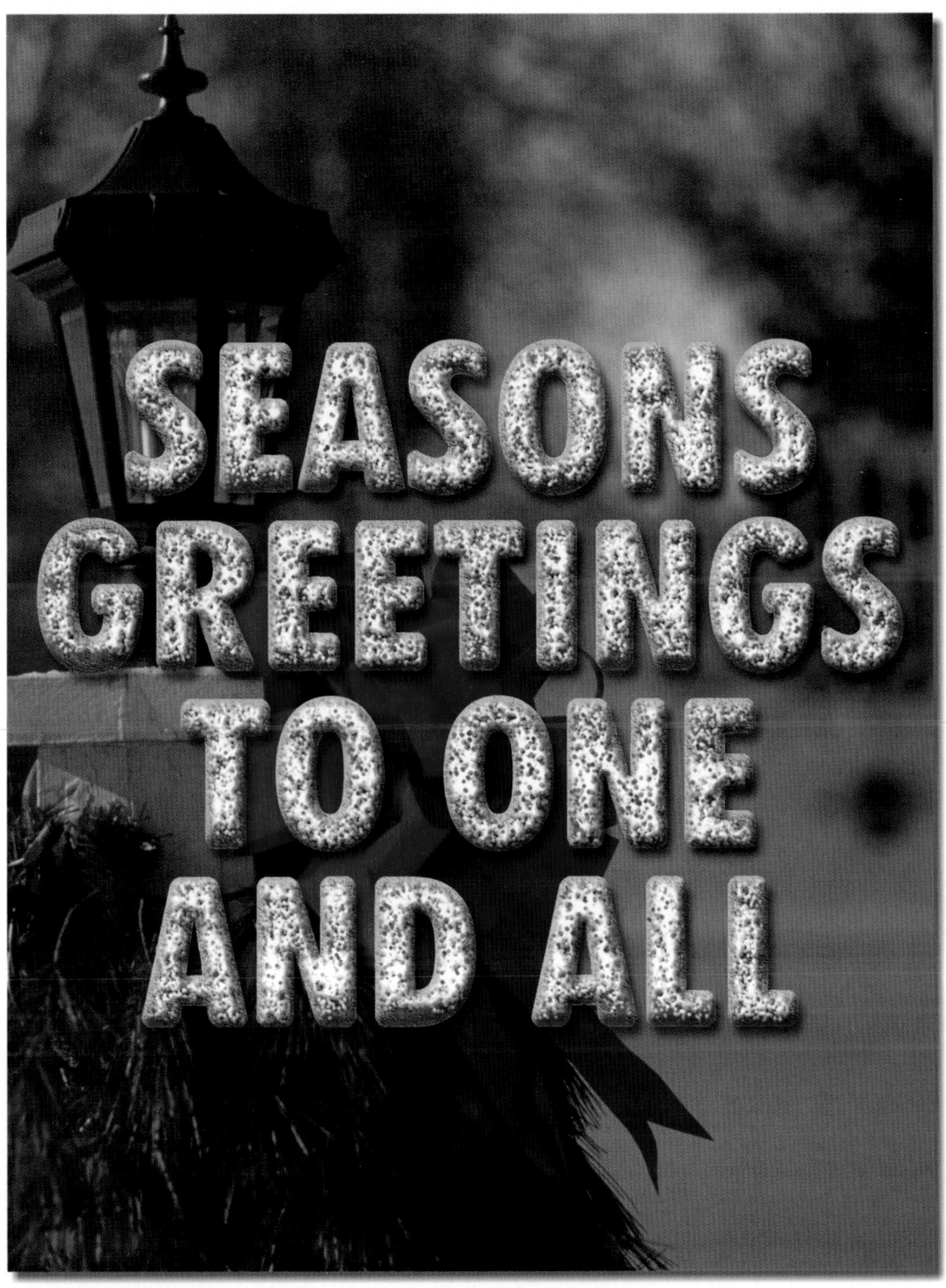

This is the cover art I created for the December cover of Corel User Magazine (UK). The cookie treatment of the text is a technique that I am quite proud of, except for the fact that I discovered it while trying to create Egyptian hieroglyphics . . . sigh.

In the future, I will be adding to the techniques described in this book. This page and the one that follows show techniques that will be posted for downloading every month beginning in June 1999. Each new technique (PDF format) will be available for downloading from http://www.osborne.com or http://www.i-us.com.

The above Jazz logo was created using multiple drop shadows to produce the 3-D shading.

The weathered wood in the image to the right was created by use of a combination of Distort and 3D Effect filters.

The image on the left was created for the CorelDRAW Journal and represents a challenging technique to produce clear plastic/glass letters.

The image on the right is a fun project. Everything in this image was made from scratch, including wires and screws.

London
London
London
London

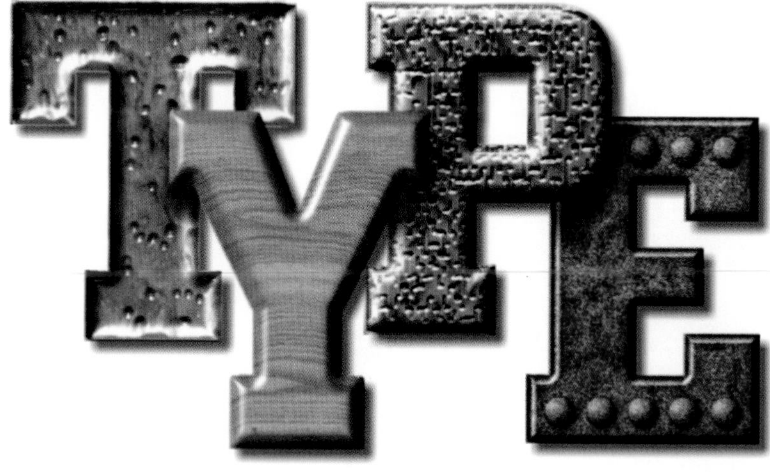

Whether it involves tying a knot or making text appear submerged (yes, the text below says "underwater" in German), PHOTO-PAINT is capable of creating any effect your design job requires. All these effects as well as those shown on the previous two pages (including the cookie text) will eventually be available for downloading—one per month.

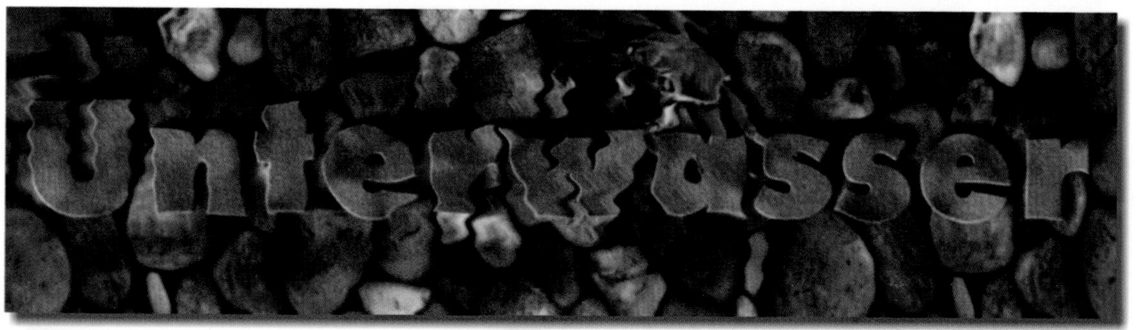

The step-by-step tutorial in Chapter 16 shows how to use a gradient mask to gradually increase the blur of the background photograph to give the illusion of depth as well as to provide a softened area in which to place the text (left).

When creating this little piece of fluff (above) in Chapter 21, we discover the power of the often-overlooked Julia Set Explorer. I figured this was the perfect name to use to demonstrate a filter that although powerful, most users haven't seen recently.

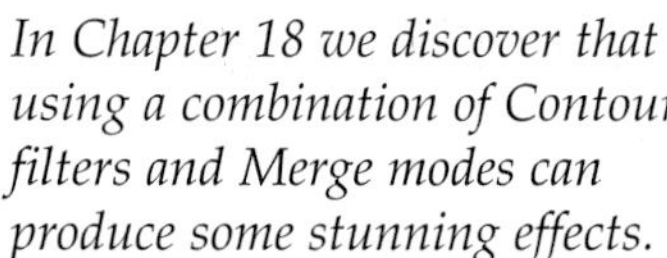

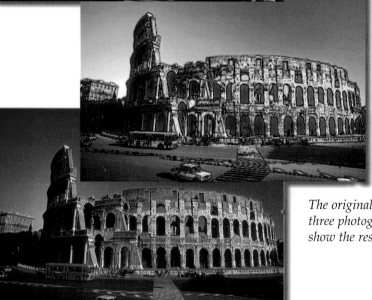

In Chapter 18 we discover that using a combination of Contour filters and Merge modes can produce some stunning effects. The original image appears at the top of the three photographs. The two images below it show the results of the step-by-step tutorial.

The Property Bar offers several controls concerning the feathering of the shadow: The Feather value determines the width (in pixels) of feathering applied to the shadow. This setting of how blurry the shadow is makes the difference between a shadow that looks fake and one that looks real. The Direction pop-up gives you four choices: Average, Middle, Inside, and Outside. Inside places the feathered portion inside the shadow's edges. Outside adds pixels just outside the shadow's edges. Middle places approximately as many feathered pixels inside the edge as outside. Average samples all pixels in the defined width and assigns a color value to each one individually. This results in some pixels being inside and some being outside, and creates a more gradual transition in color between the shadow object and the background, much like a gradient.

The Edge pop-up allows you to select Curved or Linear.

The Presets pop-up on the far left of the Property Bar contains some preset shadow settings the Corel artists have created. This is a wonderful feature for someone who wants to reapply several settings. Operation is simple. Get the settings the way you like them, click the Plus button, and name the setting.

Dave's Shadowy Rules

When working with shadows, here are some basic rules that may help you:

- If the object is to appear far away from the background, the shadow should be larger, very transparent, and blurred.
- If the object is to appear close to the background, the shadow should be much darker (less transparent), very close to the size of the object, and have only a small amount of blurring.
- To make some glow, set the Distance to zero, and increase the Feather width. The Opacity setting will determine how much go you put into your glow.
- Never forget that the shadow is to fool the eye. It is not and never should be central. If you apply a shadow, and someone viewing the picture makes a comment on how lovely the shadows are, you did something wrong.

Perspective Shadow Mode

With the Dropshadow Mode button enabled, the Perspective mode is active. This operates very similarly to the Flat shadow, with a few exceptions. An angle of 90 degrees creates the longest shadows, while a setting of zero degrees creates the shortest. The Fade option adds a real touch of realism in making the shadow fade away as it gets further from the object. An example of both the Flat and Perspective shadows is shown in Figure 12-7.

When you click OK, a shadow object is created and appears as part of the Object in the Objects Docker. The new shadow object is a part the original object. If you want to make any adjustments to the shadow, you must first separate it from the original object by right-clicking on the object in the Objects Docker window. You will see three choices: Delete Shadow, Combine Shadow, and Separate Shadow.

Now let's move on to the Object Transform modes. It's boring reading, but great reference stuff when you get stuck and are wondering why something doesn't work.

Transform Modes

There are seven Transform modes that provide all the control that you could ever dream of when it comes to manipulating and transforming objects. With the Object

FIGURE 12-7 Making shadows is much easier with the Object Dropshadow tool

Picker tool selected, all these modes are available either through the Property Bar or by clicking on the object to cycle through the modes.

The Property Bar for objects provides a powerful and easy way to precisely manipulate objects. There are seven selections from the pop-up menu that control the following:

- Position mode
- Rotate mode
- Scale mode
- Size mode
- Skew mode
- Distort mode
- Perspective mode

The Transform modes are explained in painful detail in the Corel user's manual and the Online Help file.

The Object Picker tool's Property Bar has the following common functions:

- **Apply To Duplicate button** This button creates a copy of the selected object with the effects applied, while leaving the original object unchanged. For example, with the Rotate mode selected, a value of 15 degrees was entered. Clicking the Apply To Duplicate button would create a copy of the object that was rotated 15 degrees while leaving the original unchanged.
- **Transform button** Clicking this button displays a preview of the transformation of the selected object in the image window. This is a preview only. You can either press ESC or double-click outside the object or marquee in the image window to cancel the transformation and return to the original state.
- **Apply button** After clicking the Transform button, click Apply in the Property Bar, press ENTER, or double-click inside the object to apply the transformation permanently. This control is available for both the Object Picker tool and the Mask Transform tool.

Additional Tips for Working with Objects

- Transform Options will be unavailable when anything other than the Object Picker tool is selected from the Toolbox.
- Objects do not have to be the same size as the image. You can paste or drag and drop an object into an image that is larger than the page size and not have the area outside the image boundaries clipped.

It is the ability to create, modify, and position objects that makes Corel PHOTO-PAINT 9 such a powerful photo-editing program. We have only covered the basics to this point.

How to Group Objects

To group objects, you must have two or more objects selected. There are several ways to select objects for grouping in an image:

- Using the Object Picker tool, you can drag a rectangle over (marquee-select) the objects you want grouped together.
- From the Objects Docker, you can select objects by clicking them.
- If you want to select all the objects in the image, you can choose Object | Select All.
- You can select the first object, and then, holding down SHIFT, select more objects. Each time you select an object, it is added to the number of objects selected. The action is a toggle, so if you select an object you do not want, click it again to deselect it.

After you have selected the objects, press CTRL-G. All the selected objects will become grouped together. How will you know the objects are grouped together? Looking at the Objects Docker gives a visual clue of what objects are grouped. When objects are grouped, they are joined together with a black bar in the left column of the Objects Docker. To ungroup the objects, select the group and press CTRL-U, or choose Object | Arrange | Ungroup. You may also toggle the Group button in the Property Bar.

The Text Tool

The text capabilities of Corel PHOTO-PAINT 9 have changed somewhat since PHOTO-PAINT 8. Not only can we see the text displayed on the screen as we enter it, but we also can return to the text and change the fonts, size, or other attributes at any time. Only when the text is combined with the background does it cease to be editable. When the Text tool is used in combination with the fill capabilities and layers/objects, stunning effects can be produced quickly. The major change in the way fonts work is that you can now have multiple fonts in different colors and sizes on the same line. You know what I mean—the stuff they tell you never to do in most page layout books, we can now do in PHOTO-PAINT.

Paragraph Text and Corel PHOTO-PAINT

As great as Corel PHOTO-PAINT's text capabilities are, if you are planning to add paragraph style text to a Corel PHOTO-PAINT image, it is best to use another program like CorelDRAW. It is a simple procedure. Just finish whatever enhancements to the image are needed, and save it as a PHOTO-PAINT file. Next, import the file into CorelDRAW or a similar graphics program, and add the text at that time. While I have mentioned this before, it bears repeating. When text is created in Corel PHOTO-PAINT, it is a bitmap image that is resolution dependent. Text in a program like DRAW is resolution independent. This means that text placed in Corel PHOTO-PAINT will be the resolution of the image. If it is 300 dpi (dots per inch), then the text will be a bitmap image that is 300 dpi, regardless if it is printed to a 300 dpi laser printer or a 2,450 dpi imagesetter. If the same text is placed in DRAW, it remains text. If it is output to a 2,450 dpi imagesetter, then the resolution of the text will be 2,450 dpi. The result is sharper text.

Basics of the Text Tool

Text is by default an object that floats above the image background. Text properties—the font, style, size, kerning, leading, and other effects—are determined through the Property Bar. You can manipulate, edit, format, and transform the text object while it is still an object. Once you've combined the text object with the background, you can no longer edit it as text. The Render Text To

Mask button on the Text tool's Property Bar, when selected, converts the text automatically to a mask. It is a real time-saver.

If you have worked with recent versions of word processors in Windows, everything on the Property Bar should be familiar to you. The first box shows all the available fonts that are installed. The second box displays the selected font sizes in points (72 points = 1 inch). While the font size pop-up list shows a long list of available sizes, you can select any size you need by typing the desired font size (in points) in the Font Size box. Any change you make in the Text toolbar is instantly reflected in the text displayed in the image area. You can also move the rectangle containing the text by clicking on its edge and dragging it with the mouse.

There are no system default settings for the Text tool's font selection. The typeface is always the first element of the list of installed fonts. Since lists are maintained alphabetically, the typeface whose name is first alphabetically (that is, Aardvark) will always appear as the default. The last settings of the text toolbar remain until changed again or until Corel PHOTO-PAINT is shut down.

Here are the facts about the Corel PHOTO-PAINT Text tool:

- The color of the text is determined by the setting of the Paint (foreground) color. It is easy to change the color of the text in Corel PHOTO-PAINT. To color each letter individually, change the Paint color before typing the letter. To change it all at once, double-click with the text tool and click a color.
- When you select existing text with the Text tool, all transformations that have been applied to that text will be lost.
- To correct a text entry, use BACKSPACE or DEL.
- To check the spelling of text, use a dictionary. Sorry, no spell checker.
- There is no automatic line wrap (soft carriage returns) of text. This is because Corel PHOTO-PAINT has no idea where to wrap the line.
- Text always looks ragged until it becomes an object.

TIP: *When you go into Text Edit mode, the text will look pretty ugly (lots of jaggies). Don't worry. It will look fine once you exit Text Edit mode by selecting a different tool.*

There are other hands-on exercises involving text throughout the book. Check the Table of Contents or the Index for their location.

PART IV

PHOTO-PAINT Filters

CHAPTER 13

Introducing Filters

Filters are the magic stuff of photo-editing programs like PHOTO-PAINT. Whether you need to create images like those from Andromeda Software shown below or to automatically mask an image or enhance a photograph, there is probably a filter that does it. In this chapter, we will explore how to enable the filters that are included in PHOTO-PAINT 9 and how to install filters from other vendors. Along the way, there will also be some tips about the use of filters in general.

Understanding Plug-in Filters

The concept of plug-in filters is simple. A company, like Corel, provides an access to its software, like PHOTO-PAINT, that allows specific-purpose programs to control parts of the application. The programs created by outside vendors are generally referred to as third-party plug-ins. In addition to third-party plug-ins, there are internal plug-ins created by Corel that use the same method to access PHOTO-PAINT as do the third-party plug-ins. The plug-in concept first appeared in Adobe Photoshop many moons ago and is now being used in a variety of applications, including page-layout and vector-drawing programs. In this chapter we will learn about the filter dialog boxes that control plug-ins. It is important to have a clear understanding of how these dialog boxes operate so that you can more effectively use the filters. Well, not really. The truth is, it is important that you learn how to use the filter dialog boxes in this chapter so that I don't have to repeat the same information in all of the other filter chapters. We will also talk about some of the cool plug-ins available out in the marketplace today. In the chapters that follow, we'll explore the filters that were provided with PHOTO-PAINT and find out some of the many things we can do with them.

Different Jobs, Different Filters

Just as there are many different tasks in photo-editing, there are also many different types of plug-in filters. For purposes of discussion, filters can be loosely classified as either *utility* or *artistic*. An example of a utility filter would be one that provides automatic masking functions (a real time saver). Those that provide artistic or painterly effects represent an *artistic* type of filter. An example of an artistic filter would be the Kai's Power Tools from Metacreation Corp. (one of the more popular plug-ins). Some of the filters do a little bit of both. Regardless of the type of filter, they must first be installed.

Installation of Filters

When you initially open the Effects hierarchical menu, the list of filters appears, as shown next. The filters in PHOTO-PAINT are either internal or installed. Installed filters are built into PHOTO-PAINT, making them faster and inaccessible to other programs. Installed filters—including the ones shipped with PHOTO-PAINT 9—are connected to PHOTO-PAINT in the same way as third-party plug-ins. Installed filters appear either below the line of the Effects menu or in one of several categories in the File menu, such as Import.

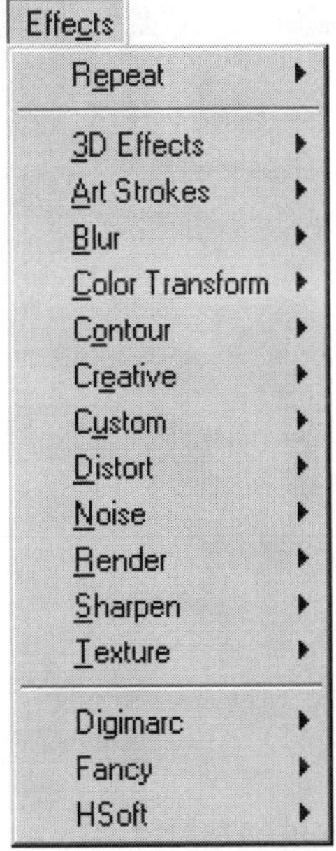

NOTE: *Some plug-ins also appear in the Import Plug-ins and Export Plug-ins sections of the File menu. There are also Mask Plug-ins that appear in the Mask menu under Selection Plug-ins.*

The procedure for installing plug-in filters is a breeze. First, follow the manufacturer's directions to install the filter. To make plug-ins appear in the list in the Effects menu press CTRL-J to open the Options dialog, shown in Figure 13-1. Under Workspace, click on Plug-ins to select it. If all it says in the left column is Workspace, click on the Plus (+) symbol to open it up.

Once selected, the area on the right side of the dialog box displays the filters that are already installed in PHOTO-PAINT.

TIP: *You may find that some of the plug-ins allow automatic installation of the filters for Corel PHOTO-PAINT. If this is the case, make note of the location where the program will install them. They may be loaded in an unexpected area.*

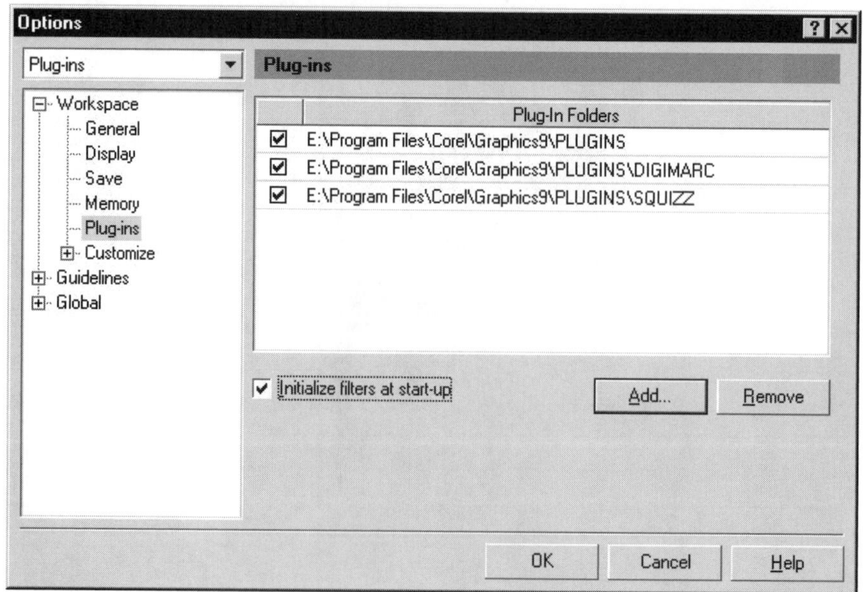

FIGURE 13-1 This is where your PHOTO-PAINT and third-party filters are managed

Managing Your Plug-ins

The Plug-ins area of the Options menu provides a nice place for managing your plug-ins. Note the close-up of the three installed filters shown next. Each line is composed of two parts. On the left there is a check box, and on the right side there is a path describing the location of the filter. By either checking or unchecking the check box, you can turn filters on or off without the need to restart PHOTO-PAINT. This feature provides that, with a large number of filters installed, you can go through Options | Plug-ins to select the ones you want to make active.

	Plug-In Folders
☑	E:\Program Files\Corel\Graphics9\PLUGINS
☑	E:\Program Files\Corel\Graphics9\PLUGINS\DIGIMARC
☑	E:\Program Files\Corel\Graphics9\PLUGINS\SQUIZZ

To add an installed filter to the set of filters, you must first tell PHOTO-PAINT where the filter has been installed. Do this by clicking the Add button opening the dialog box shown next. Select the location of the plug-in and click OK. The path will appear in Options | Plug-ins, and, when you close the Options dialog box, PHOTO-PAINT will verify that the filters are there and add them to either the Effects list or wherever they are to be displayed.

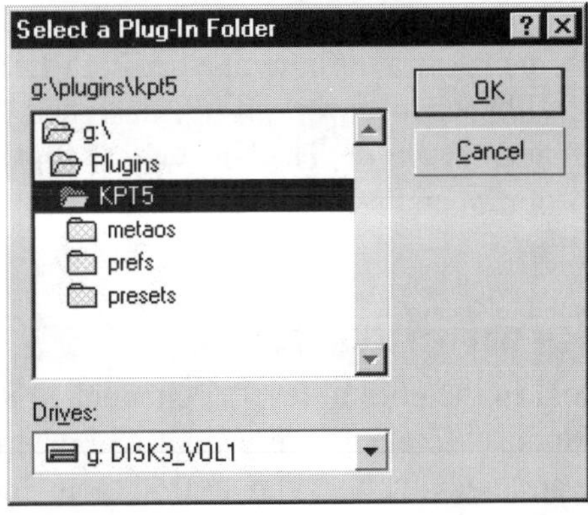

To remove a filter, highlight it and click the Remove button. No thoughtful message box will appear asking you if you are sure you want to banish the filter. It is gone and there is no Undo. It isn't a big deal because you haven't removed the file from your system; you've only removed its link from the Plug-in manager.

You can click the Add button and add it right back again or you can click Cancel on the Options dialog box. When you open the dialog box again, any changes you made from the time you opened Options last will not be there.

There is one other little check box, which affects the initialization of filters at start up (of PHOTO-PAINT). If this box is checked, PHOTO-PAINT will take a little longer to start up when it is launched. If it is not checked, the first time you select Effects, PHOTO-PAINT will quickly initialize all of the filters. Reminds me of that oil commercial that was popular a few years back: "you can pay me now or pay me later." Regardless of when the filters are initialized, they have to be initialized. To me when you do it, is immaterial.

So that's the built-in Plug-in manager. Isn't it sweet? My favorite part about it is that, unlike other photo-editing programs (which shall remain nameless), you don't have to have all of your filters in the same location.

Not All Filters Are Created Equal

All filters appearing on the market today are designed to work in a 32-bit environment, like PHOTO-PAINT. These 32-bit versions offer the advantage of greater processing speed and functional capabilities. There are older, 16-bit filters still available in the marketplace. Corel PHOTO-PAINT 9 allows the use of these filters in most cases, but I strongly recommend that you stick with the 32-bit versions.

Question: Will plug-in filters designed for Adobe Photoshop work in PHOTO-PAINT 9? The answer is a definite maybe. If a filter is written as a general plug-in filter, it will probably work; if it is designed to control specific and unique Photoshop commands, it won't. The best way to find out is to call the vendor who wrote the program and ask.

Finding Additional Plug-ins

Most plug-ins are not sold in the normal reseller channel. With few exceptions, the companies that make these filters are very small. So where do you find out about them? In this day and age, the best way to find them and find out more about them is through the Internet. A good location to begin your search is http://www.ius.com. The I-us.com web site has several sites dedicated just to plug-ins.

As long as we are discussing the downloading of filters, I should point out that PHOTO-PAINT works with nearly all of the Filter Factory filters available on the

Internet. The Filter Factory is a user-definable type of filter that many people have used to create unique effects. After downloading the filter files and reading a lot of text files, you can use the filters they have made or roll your own.

A Philosophy to Plug Into

When I first began to work with PHOTO-PAINT, I wanted to get as many plug-ins as I could. I assumed the more plug-ins I had, the more I could accomplish. After working in photo-editing over the past seven years, I have found that most effects produced by third-party plug-ins can be achieved or surpassed using the native tools and filters found in PHOTO-PAINT. Please keep in mind that as an established photo-editing author, I can have any plug-in for free! Am I a purist? No, in fact there are a few third-party plug-ins that I wouldn't be without—probably 3 out of the 46 available in the marketplace. I want to discourage the headlong pursuit of these jewels and recommend that you seriously consider your needs before shelling out your hard-earned bucks. Thank you, I will get off of my soapbox now.

Introducing the Filter Dialog Box

The dialog box in PHOTO-PAINT continues to improve with each release and this release is no exception. Since a majority of the controls for the filters share a common dialog box, we are going to take a quick look at one and see what options it offers. Although the portion of the dialog box containing the sliders, check boxes, and number boxes changes to accommodate the different filter controls, the view options remain generally the same.

Preview Options

Back in the early days (right after they discovered electricity) filters did not have a preview. We were thrilled when microscopic little thumbnail called preview windows appeared. You really couldn't tell much but we didn't care—it was a preview. Next came onscreen preview, and now in PHOTO-PAINT 9 we preview the effect of our filters any way we want. Let's see what is available in different preview modes. The following image shows a dialog box for Edge Detect—a pretty basic filter. There are four buttons in the upper-right corner; our concern is with the two shown circled. The button on the left determines if the preview is onscreen or a preview window in the dialog box is used. The dialog is currently in onscreen preview—hence no preview windows. The button on the right determines whether the preview is a large single window or a split window in a traditional before-and-after format.

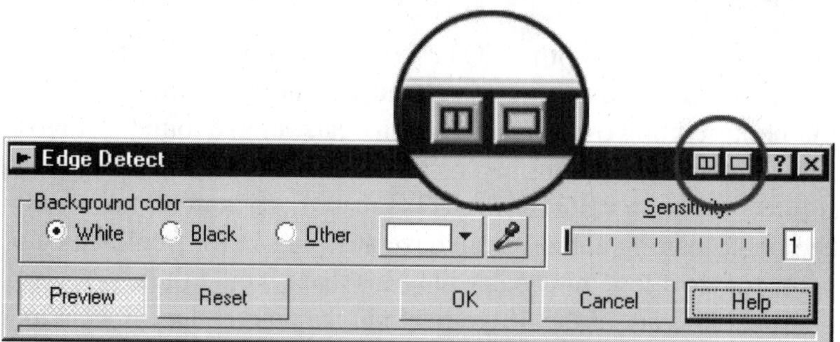

A different filter dialog box is shown below in split window preview mode. Notice that icon on the left button has changed. Split screens show preview thumbnails of the original image as well as what the image will look like after application of the filter. The advantage of this approach is that you can see and compare the result against the original. The disadvantage is that the preview windows are smaller than the single screen preview.

Panning and Zooming

You will notice in the following image a hand I have circled in the left preview screen. This is a combination zoom and grabber tool. Whenever the cursor is placed over the left preview, it becomes a hand, which is very handy (groan). Left-clicking on the preview zooms in and right-clicking zooms out. If you click and drag in the left preview you will drag the image—called *panning*. The results of this panning and zooming happen in real time in the left preview; in the right preview the results occur after the filter has processed the image and generated the preview.

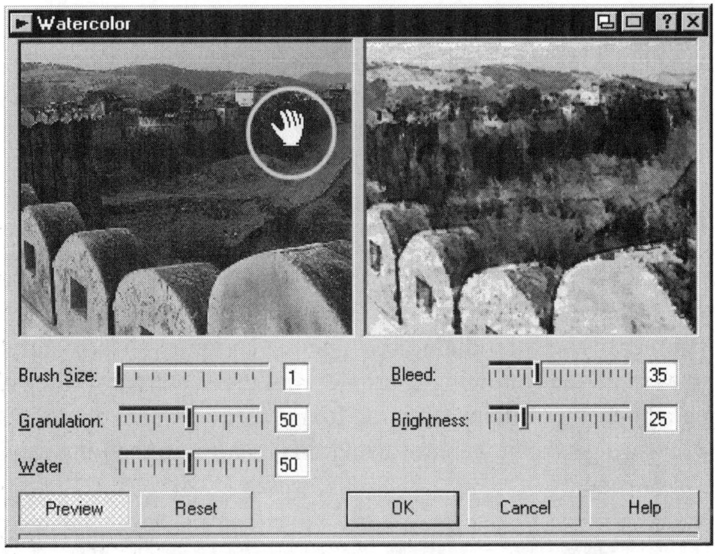

In the single pane preview, shown next, the pan and zoom hand works in the entire preview window. If the filter is complex, like the Watercolor filter that is shown, there will be a delay as the computer tries as quickly as possible to update the display. You would be best advised to turn off the preview (button in lower-left corner) while fine-tuning the zoom and position of your preview window.

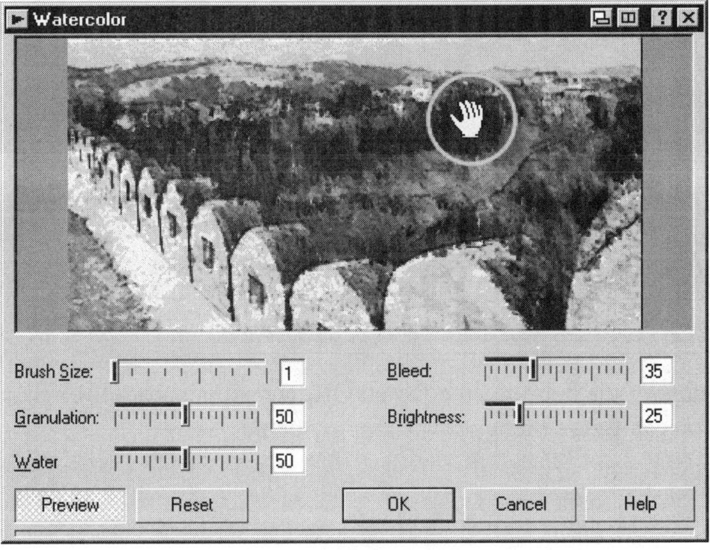

Onscreen preview, some will say, is the best way to preview filter actions. Using the actual image to preview the effects gives the most accurate possible form of preview. For what is it worth, I use PHOTO-PAINT about 6 to 8 hours a day and I find I use all three preview modes.

Other Effects

Corel has provided a shortcut to other effects that avoids having to cancel the current filter and go back through the Effects menu. A button located in the upper-right corner of the filter dialog box opens a combined list of both the Effects and Image menus. In the following example from the Watercolor filter dialog box, I have opened the menu of items from the Image menu and am about to select Tone Curve. Please get in the habit of using this feature. In the long run it will save you a lot of time.

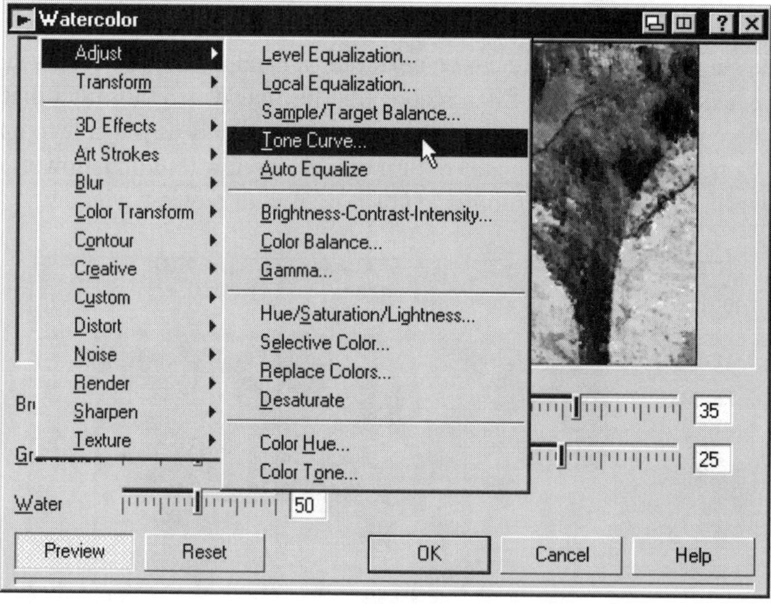

The remainder of the buttons, like Reset, OK, and so on, are self-explanatory, and I believe you can figure them out without my help.

Repeat and Fade Last Commands

There will be times when you want to reapply a filter's effect one or more times. You could reopen the filter dialog box and apply the effect again, but there's a better way. PHOTO-PAINT has several commands that allow you to repeat a command or reapply the last command at a reduced level. These commands are not limited to filters.

Repeat Effect and Command

You can repeat an Effect by choosing Effects | Repeat | Repeat *effect name* as shown next. The last effect will be applied just as the last time it was applied. A shortcut for repeat last effect is CTRL-F. You could also repeat the effect or any other command with Repeat command in the Edit menu or CTRL-L. The name of the Repeat command varies according to the last operation you performed. For example, if you want to repeat a brush stroke that you just applied to an image using the Paint tool, the Repeat command is called Repeat Tool Stroke.

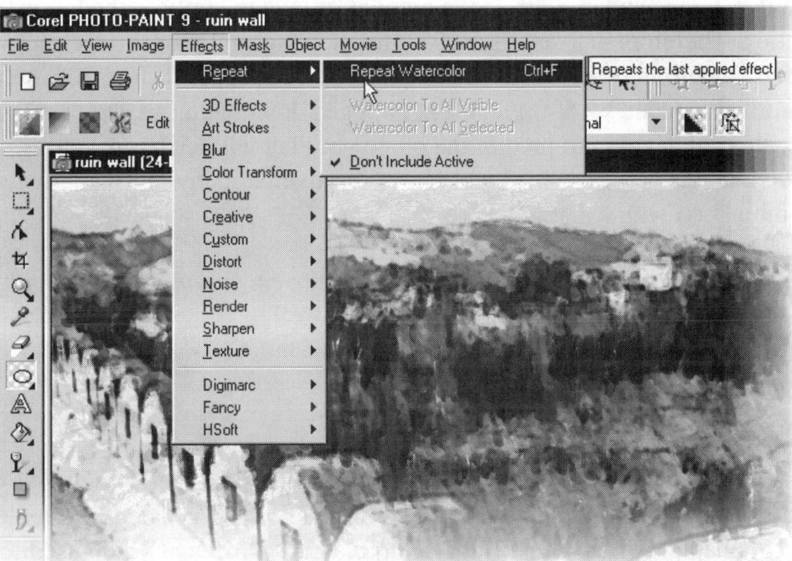

Fade Last Command

While the Fade command can be used with other effects, it adds a special dimension to filter applications. With the Fade Last Command, you can reapply a filter using one of the Merge Modes. When filters are initially applied using their regular filter dialog box, it is done in Normal merge mode; there are no options to use the different merge modes. When the Fade Last Command is used, however, the last effect is undone and reapplied using the percentage and merge mode selected in the dialog box shown below. The onscreen preview can be turned on and off by clicking the eye icon in the upper-left corner:

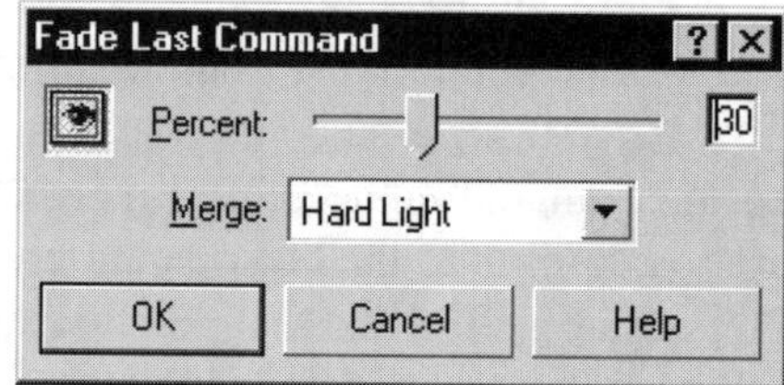

The Percentage slider controls the amount of fade to apply to the last effect application. Therefore, if I set it for 99% (max) in Normal mode, the effect will be completely faded. In other words, the last effect is not applied. At a 50% setting the last effect is faded by 50%. Don't get bogged down with this; you can't sit down with a calculator and predict the outcome. Play with different settings. Fade Last Command is very powerful and I have discovered many unusual effects using it in combination with existing filters

NOTE: *Onscreen preview is the only preview option available with the Fade Last Command filter.*

Into Undiscovered Country

Now that we know the principles of operation for the filters, let's begin to explore the vast array of filters included in PHOTO-PAINT. Our filter odyssey continues in the next chapter, where we will look into the Distort filters (which used to be called 2D filters).

CHAPTER 14

The Distort Filters

This group of 12 filters, shown next, comprises some of the most unusual and complex filters in Corel PHOTO-PAINT. In case you thought you had just come upon a whole new set of filters in PHOTO-PAINT 9, I need to inform you that the Distort filters were called 2D filters in the previous versions of PHOTO-PAINT. On top of that, several of the filters have had name changes as well.

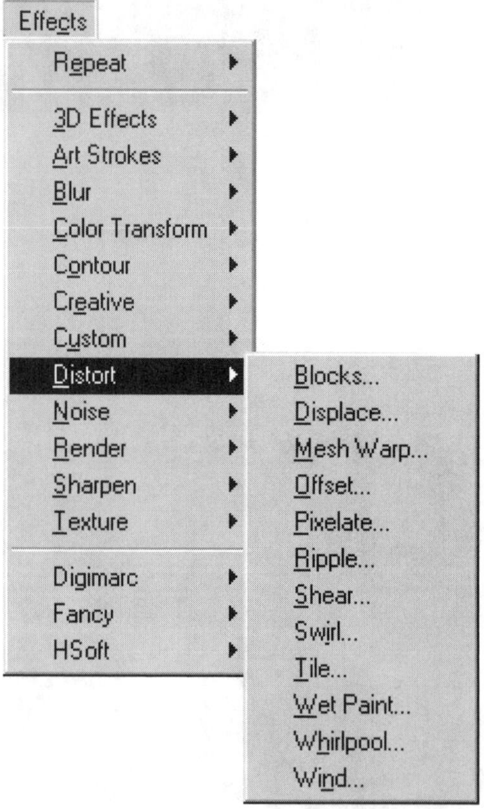

Many of the Distort filters are not needed for day-to-day photo-editing work, but they can be genuine lifesavers in some situations. The listing of the filters in this chapter is in the order of their appearance in the pop-up menu. For general operation of the filter dialog boxes, refer to Chapter 13.

The Blocks Filter (Formerly Known As the Puzzle Filter)

The Blocks filter lets you break down an image into small blocks—which I admit doesn't sound very interesting, but let's see exactly what that means. The filter is pretty simple to use. In the filter dialog box, shown next, the Block width and Block height sliders (1–100) control the width and height of the blocks created by the filter. If the lock icon at the other end of the dialog box is enabled, these two controls will have identical values.

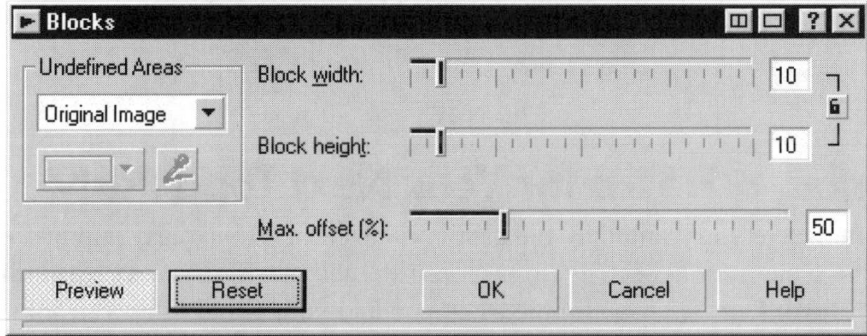

The Max offset (%) slider controls the offsetting, or shifting, of blocks. It is important to note that the offset is a percentage of the Block size. For example, if the Block size is set to a width of 50 pixels and the Max offset % slider is set to 10, the offset will have a maximum shift of 5 pixels (10 percent of 50). Therefore, increasing or decreasing block size changes the effect the maximum amount of offset has, even though the numbers don't change.

When applying the filter to an object, the Undefined Areas section is not available. When applying the Block filter to a mask or background, something must take its place. The Undefined Areas section offers five options:

- **Original image** Uses the colors from the original image as a background
- **Inverse image** Inverts the image adjacent to the shifted blocks and applies it as the background
- **Black** Fills the offset area with a black background

- **White** Fills the offset area with a white background
- **Other** Fills the offset area with either a color selected from the palette or, using the Eyedropper, a color from the image.

The obvious thing to do with this filter is shown next. Use the Block filter to break apart an object like a text block and then apply the Emboss filter to the pieces and place shadows underneath them. Here are a few other thoughts for what you can do with this baby.

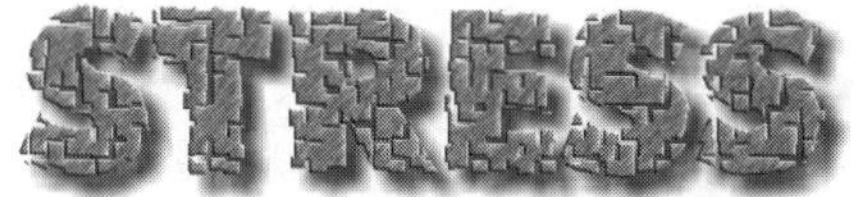

Creating a Fresco for Your Next Toga Party

How often have you wanted to make an invitation for a toga party and just didn't have the right fresco (not to be confused with a soft drink with a similar name)? Never fear—in four simple steps you and your Block filter can solve this thorny issue.

1. Open the photograph named ARCHES located in the EXERCISE\PHOTOS folder on the Corel CD.

2. Choose Effects | Distort | Blocks. Change the settings to 10 pixels (width and height), the Max offset to 50, and the Undefined Areas to Original Image, as shown next.

3. At this point it looks pretty ugly, so choose Edit | Fade Last Command. Change the Merge mode to Divide (it may possibly be the only time you will use Divide in your lifetime so enjoy it). Change Percent to 75. If you cannot see the effect being previewed on your image, click the Preview button (the eyeball). The result of these changes along with the Fade Last Command dialog are shown next.

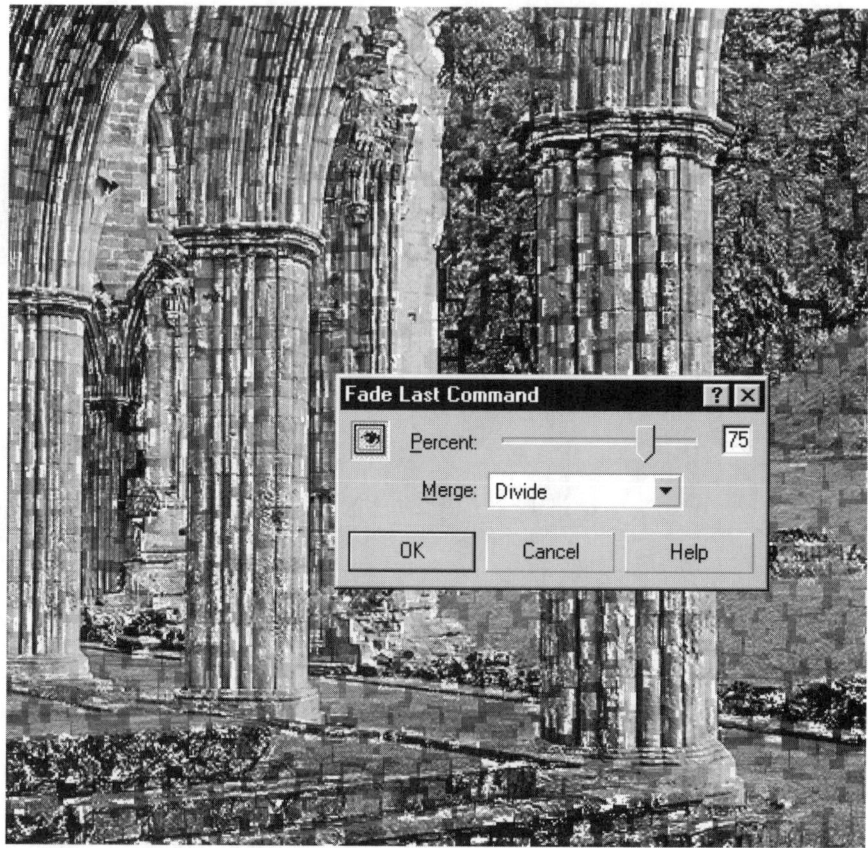

4. This last step isn't necessary, but I had to add it anyway. Choose Effects | Texture | Brick Wall. Click the Reset button and apply the filter by clicking OK. The finished objet d'art is shown in Figure 14-1.

The Displace Filter

The Displace filter (formerly named . . . the Displace filter—one of the few filters in this category that wasn't renamed) distorts an image by moving individual pixels and not moving others. The direction and distance that the chosen pixels move are determined by a separate image that is called a *displacement map.* What happens is that the Displace filter reads the color value of every pixel in the image and every pixel in the displacement map—hey! Those speed-reading courses really do help. After all of that reading the filter then shifts the image pixels on the basis

FIGURE 14-1 Using the Block filter and one of the new Textures, we have a great fresco—now we only need a toga

of the values of the corresponding pixels in the displacement map. Clear as mud, right? A visual demonstration may help.

Figure 14-2 is an illustration of how a displacement map works (the Grid has been added to help show the effect). While the Displace filter uses both color value and brightness to determine displacement, we need only be concerned about brightness. The top of the figure shows a displacement map going from 70 percent Black to 30 percent Black in 12 steps. The map was applied to the original image (middle), and the result appears at the bottom. Notice that the 70 percent Black end on the left was pushed (offset) down, the 30 percent Black end on the right was pushed upward, and the 50 percent gray point in the middle is unaffected. Sound boring? Wait until you see what we can do with this little jewel.

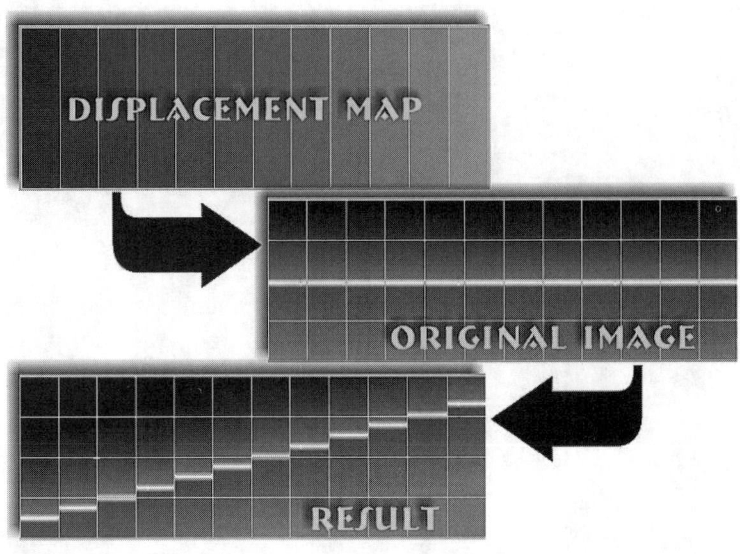

FIGURE 14-2 The graduated scale in the displacement map causes the original image to be displaced accordingly

More Technical Information about Displacement Maps

Were you wondering what PHOTO-PAINT was reading when I told you it read each pixel? It reads the brightness values of the pixels in the displacement map. Their values tell PHOTO-PAINT which pixels to move and how far to move them. It is important to remember that Brightness values apply to grayscale and color images. The three determining brightness values are:

- **Black** Areas in the displacement map that contain black will move the corresponding pixels in an image being affected to the right and/or down by the maximum amount defined by the Scale settings in the Displace dialog box. Values between black and 50 percent gray move pixels a shorter distance.
- **White** Areas in the displacement map that contain white will move the corresponding pixels to the left and/or up by the maximum amount defined by the Scale settings in the Displace dialog box. Values between white and 50 percent gray move pixels a shorter distance.

- **Middle gray** Areas in the displacement map that are composed of gray with a brightness of 50 percent cause the pixels to remain unmoved.

Before we take leave of this very versatile filter, I have included an exercise named Deteriorated metal that makes use of this filter.

Creating Deteriorated Metal

Water and metal don't mix—period. When water, especially salt water, comes in contact with metal for prolonged periods of time a chemical reaction occurs that we call just plain rust. After time, the edges begin to perforate as tiny holes develop in the metal as it is slowly dissolved. The Deteriorated Metal technique, which works with most typefaces, may seem complicated, but I believe the finished product is worth the effort. In addition, you will see it has several variations.

1. Create a 24-bit RGB image. The sample shown in the exercise is 4 inches wide, 1.5 inches high, and 150 dpi.
2. Set your Paint to Black and select the Text tool in the Toolbox. In the Property Bar, select URWWOODTypD at a size of 150. If you don't have this font installed, you can install it using Fonts in the Control Panel. Be aware it is in the "W" folder, not the "U" folder. Once you have that sorted out, click inside the image and type in the word **RUST**. Select the Object Picker tool, converting the text into an object. You may need to use the Zoom To Fit command (f4) to allow the entire image to fit into your display. Just remember that the appearance of the text suffers at any zoom setting other than 100% (CTRL-1). This is only a function of the display drivers and does not affect the actual image.

3. In the Objects Docker window, ensure the Lock Object Transparency button is depressed (indicated by the circle in the image below). Center text in the Image Window with the Align command (CTRL-A). Choose Edit | Fill

14

and choose Bitmap fill. Click the Edit button and then click the Load button. Choose WOOD08L from the EXERCISE\TILES folder on the Corel CD. Click Open to select the fill and click OK again to apply the fill.

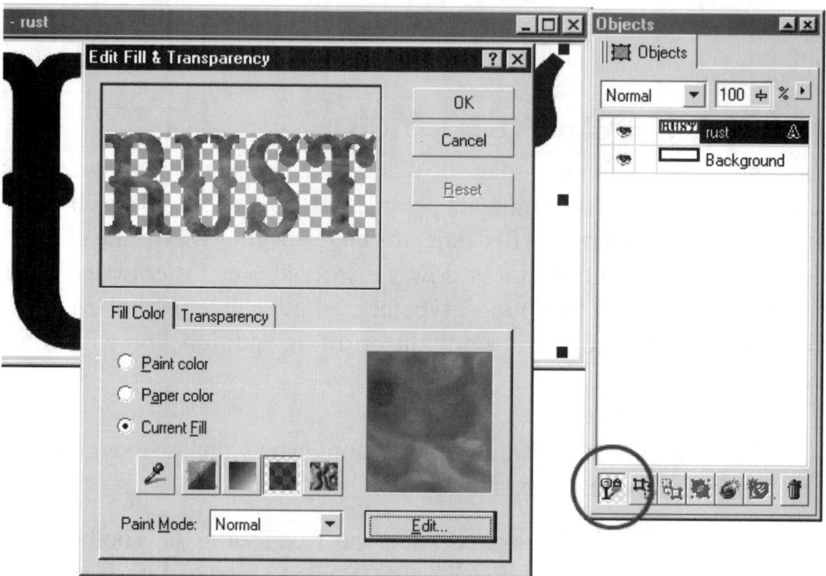

4. Select Effects | Noise | Add Noise. Select Gaussian and change the Level to 30 and the Density to 50. Click OK.

5. Choose Effects | 3D Effects | Emboss. Change the settings as follows: Emboss Color: Original color; Depth: 1; Level: 200; Direction: 135. Click OK. Congratulations, you have made rust.

6. With the object selected (handles appear on the corners), create a Mask from the text object (CTRL-M). Enable Paint on Mask (POM) (CTRL-K). While in POM we modify the mask created from the text. Choose Effects | Distort | Displace. Finally, we get to the Displace filter. Click the Reset button. In PHOTO-PAINT 9 this loads the displacement map *Rusty* and restores the default settings. Leave the Scale mode and Undefined Areas settings unchanged. The Scale slider settings are the only settings that control the effect we want for this technique. Change both sliders to 60, as shown next. Click OK.

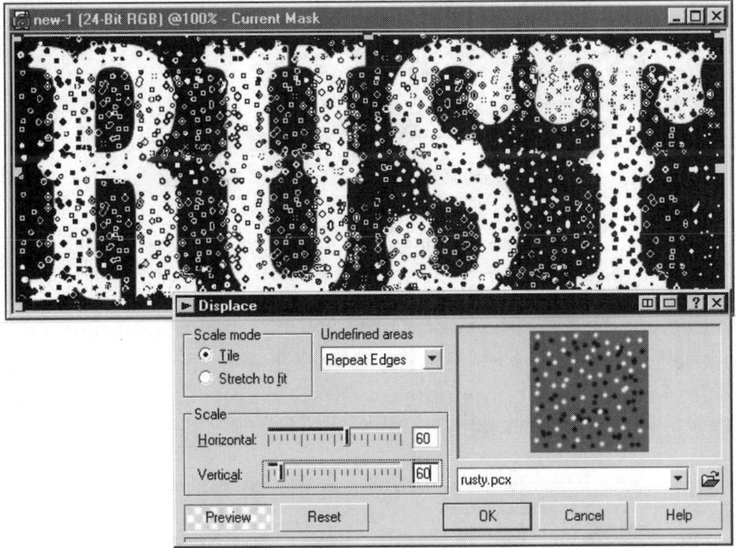

What Is POM?

We have used this technique in other applications. Basically, you view and can work on the mask you just made. POM (Paint on Mask) is a mode that temporarily replaces the image with a grayscale representation of the mask. In POM mode, the protected areas of your image are black, while the fully editable areas are white. Pixels included in the selection that are partially protected are displayed in varying degrees of gray.

7. The previous step created random holes, but there are so many fragments that we need to consolidate them a little in order to use the The Boss filter effectively. Choose Effects | Noise | Median. Use a Radius setting of 1, as shown next. Click OK.

8. Either click the POM button or use CTRL-K again to return to normal mode. Choose Effects | 3D Effects | The Boss. Change the settings as follows: Width: 3; Height: 50; Smoothness: 20; Drop off: Gaussian; Brightness: 100; Sharpness: 20; Direction: 315; Angle: 45. Click OK.

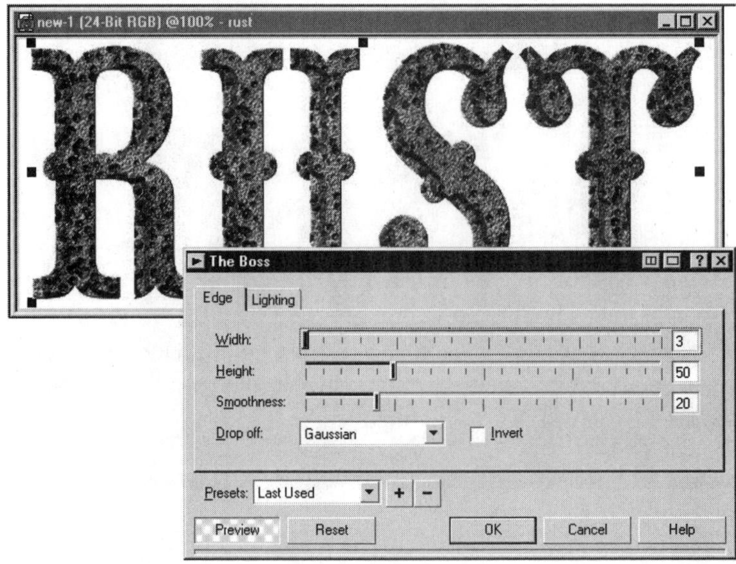

9. This looks pretty worn, but we are not finished. Select Object | Crop To Mask. This produces holes the viewer can see through in the text.

With so many holes we need a shadow to restore some of the appearance of original text. Select the Object Drop Shadow tool in the Toolbox. Change the settings as shown next or as follows: Shadow Direction: 225; Shadow Offset: 12; Shadow Opacity: 60; Shadow Feather: 10; Direction: Average.

10. That's it for that one. Close the file and discard any changes.

Variations on a Theme

Several factors control both the size and shapes of holes. The physical size of the holes in the displacement map is fixed, so the only way to make the holes larger or smaller is to increase or decrease the size of the image. Figure 14-3 shows a sample of three different The Boss filter settings. The resolution of the image is 300 dpi, which makes the number of pixels in the image twice as large as the exercise we just finished. Since the spots (holes) in the displacement map are a fixed size, the holes in the image appear smaller.

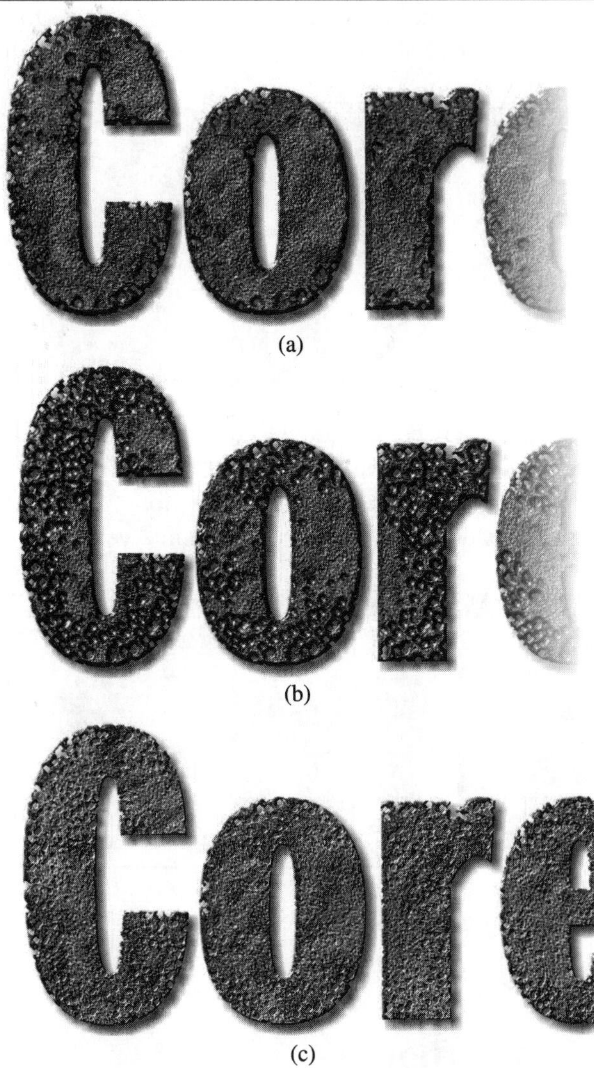

FIGURE 14-3 Variation caused by different settings: (a) maximum smoothness setting, (b) same setting as exercise, and (c) height setting of filter reduced to 30 pixels

The shape of the holes is determined by the Smoothness setting. The greater the setting, the fewer the holes that appear. The image at the top had a Smoothness of 100 (maximum), while the one in the middle had the same setting as the one in our exercise. The bottom of the three samples had the same Smoothness setting, but the height was reduced to only 30 pixels.

Using the technique we've just employed, in Figure 14-4. I created a rivet and applied it (as objects) to the type. I then used a photograph of some old wood for the background. My only regret is that the metal effects and the color of the wood are too close to each other.

The Titanic letters sinking back into the deep blue in Figure 14-5 use the deteriorated metal effect. To make them look like they are partially underwater, I applied the Object Transparency tool, which makes the letters fade as though they were under water. The ripple in the metal is accomplished by applying the Ripple filter to the bottom portion and preserving the background and upper-portion of the text with a mask.

Suggestions for Creating Displacement Maps

This filter is a virtual storehouse of effects, and I speak from experience when I tell you that it is possible to waste many hours working (playing) with it. Here are some practical suggestions for creating displacement maps to work with the Displace filter.

Remember that 50 percent gray is the neutral color that keeps the pixels from moving; therefore, it is a good background color when creating a displacement map. Next, when making displacement maps, keep the image area small. Some of the most effective displacement maps that Corel provides are smaller than 20 × 20

FIGURE 14-4 It is fun to make objects that look older than me

FIGURE 14-5 Here is a portion of a Titanic project on which I was working

pixels. Keep the Horizontal and Vertical displacement settings small for the best effects. Also, you will find that some of the more effective displacement maps are those that contain smooth transitions between the bright and dark components. Resolution and file formats are not critical factors.

The Mesh Warp Filter (New Neighborhood)

The Mesh Warp filter (which kept its name but had to move from its old neighborhood—3D effects) distorts an image based on positioning of grids in the dialog box. The user, through the dialog box, determines the number of gridlines positioned over the Grid using the No. gridlines slider bar. Technically, the greater the number of nodes selected, the smoother the Mesh Warp distortion. In actual use I find that fewer nodes allow you to control larger areas more smoothly. Each node can be moved by clicking on it with a mouse and dragging it to a new position. Each node moves independently and can be positioned anywhere in the Preview window. There is no way to group-select and move the nodes. I wish there were.

The Mesh Warp effect can be a little tricky to use at first, but once you get the hang of it, it's … still tricky, but fun. Use the Preview button to view the effects of a Mesh Warp transformation to ensure that it is acceptable before applying it to your entire image.

The Mesh Warp Filter Dialog Box

When the Mesh Warp dialog box opens, shown next, click and drag the No. gridlines slider to determine the number of gridlines that will appear on the image. The first horizontal gridline lies along the top, and the first vertical gridline is on the left. Be aware that they can be hard to see, depending on your display. At each point where a horizontal and a vertical gridline intersect, a node is positioned. To move the node, click on it and drag it. The gridlines in the preview window will twist and bend accordingly and after a few moments the image will change to preview the distortion. While it doesn't offer onscreen preview, the preview window is large enough so you can see a good-sized representation of the finished result.

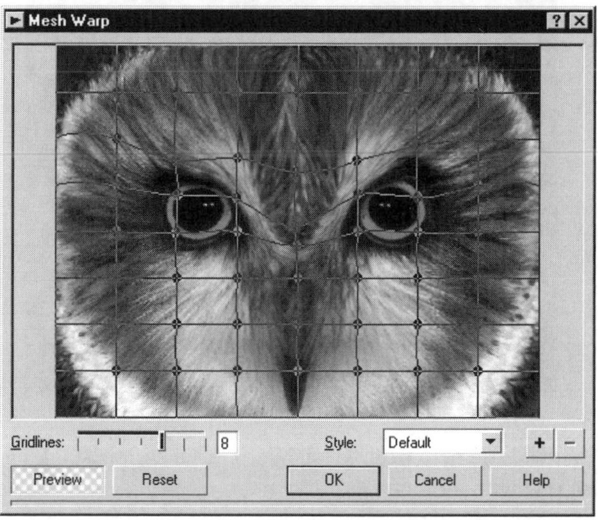

So . . . What Can You Do with It?

From a practical day-to-day standpoint, not very much. You can use the selective distortion capability to distort people and places. While this can be cute, it isn't particularly useful. It does allow you to distort or "morph" images or photos with some interesting results. Figure 14-6(a) shows the original photograph of an owl, looking curious. After the application of the Warp Mesh filter (Figure 14-6(b)), he looks mad enough to start a fight.

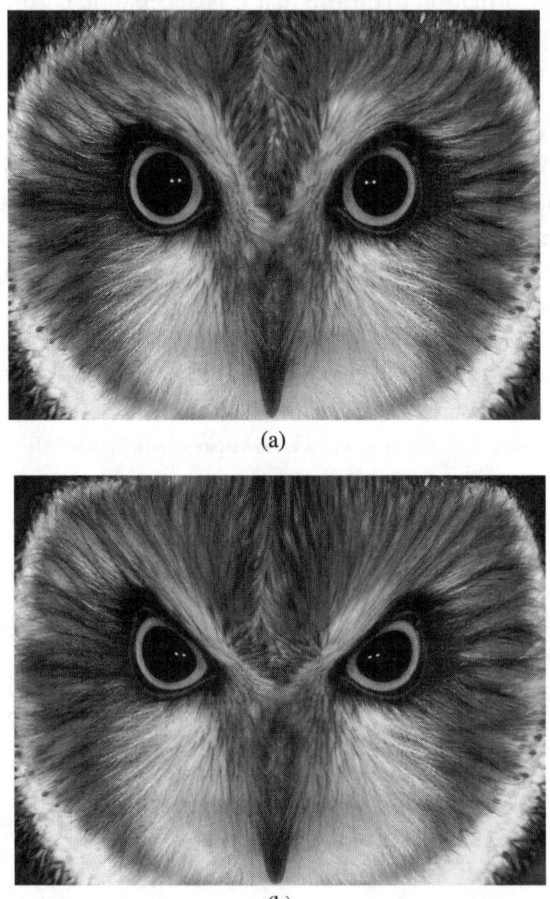

(a)

(b)

FIGURE 14-6 With a little help from Mesh Warp, (a) a curious-looking owl becomes (b) an owl with attitude

It is surprising what you can do to people with this filter. Remember our serious model? In Figure 14-7 we have refashioned her hair. There was a little trick in getting this effect. To get a smooth sweep to her hair without spending several hours, I used the minimum number of nodes. The result was great hair but the face was distorted. So how come her face looks OK now? Because I used the Local Undo tool to remove the distortion that naturally (or unnaturally, as the case may be) was applied to her face. Now the only question that remains is "How is Elvis and have you seen him lately?"

FIGURE 14-7 After applying the Warp Mesh filter, you can almost see a curl in her lips and hear the words "pretty mama"

People and owls aren't the only things to which you can apply the Mesh Warp filter. In Figure 14-8(a) I took what is arguably the second most popular drink in Texas (iced tea is first) and used the Mesh Warp filter to improve the shape and size.

Giving a Wall Some Attitude

If you completed the exercise in Chapter 6, you have a file called WALLEYES. If you didn't, you still have a file called WALLEYES that I made for you. While the eyes on the wall looked interesting, in this session we are going to find out how simple it is to give the wall some serious attitude.

1. Open the file WALLEYES. This can be the one created back in Chapter 6 or the one in the EXERCISE\PHOTOS folder of the Corel CD-ROM. It is shown in Figure 14-9.

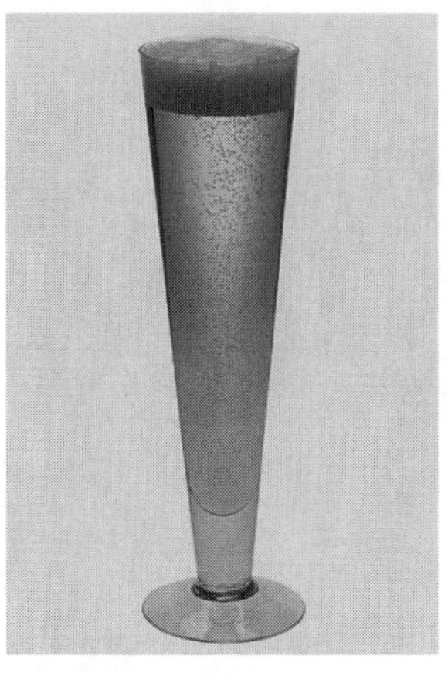

(a)

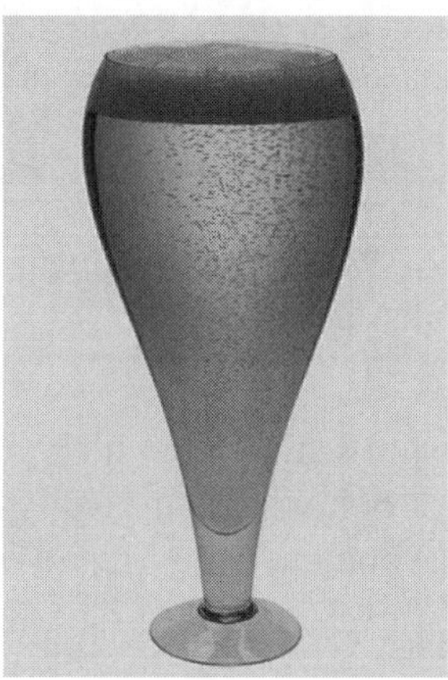

(b)

FIGURE 14-8 (a) A beer is good, but (b) Mesh Warp can really improve a glass of beer

FIGURE 14-9 Here's looking at you kid

2. Anyone who has ever drawn cartoons (I confess I have done it) knows that to make a character appear mad, you need to arch the eyebrows. Choose Effects | Distort | Mesh Warp. When the dialog box opens ensure that the number of gridlines is set to 4. Click and drag the top-center control node straight down until it is on top of the middle node. Click OK. The resulting image is shown in Figure 14-10.

3. As an alternative, You can move the top-right and top-left nodes straight down so that they coincide with the center of the eye. The result is a sleepy wall, like the one shown in Figure 14-11.

Notes About Using the Mesh Warp Filter

I need to reemphasize one point before we move on. As I said before, the greater the number of nodes, the smoother the transitions on the image. Because each node is independent, each must be individually moved. There is a trade-off between the smoothness of the transition and the time required to move all of the nodes. Since there are no constrain keys to keep the gridlines on the horizontal or vertical plane, use the gridlines themselves as your guide. As long as the line in the preview window appears straight, the line is still in line with its respective plane.

FIGURE 14-10 It's never a good idea to get a wall mad at you

FIGURE 14-11 Using the Mesh Warp filter gives a whole new meaning to the word Walleye

The Mesh Grid value represents the number of nodes on each line of the Grid. (The two end nodes on each gridline are out of view and not adjustable.)

NOTE: *There is no Zoom or Pan function in the preview window of the dialog box. There is also no Onscreen preview or Original/Results preview.*

In versions of PHOTO-PAINT prior to PHOTO-PAINT 8, applying the Mesh Warp filter to objects was not recommended, as the results could be unpredictable. In the current version such application is not only possible but it is recommended. In the illustration shown next, I applied the Mesh Warp to some text that I had filled with a wood bitmap fill. The shadow was created using the Drop Shadow command.

The next filter is not in the Distort category but its operation and effect are so close to the Mesh Warp filter that I decided this was the best place for it.

The SQUIZZ Filter

The SQUIZZ 1.5 filter made it first appearance in the PHOTO-PAINT 7 Plus package. Located in the plug-in portion of the Effects menu under HSOFT, this filter opens with the splash screen shown next.

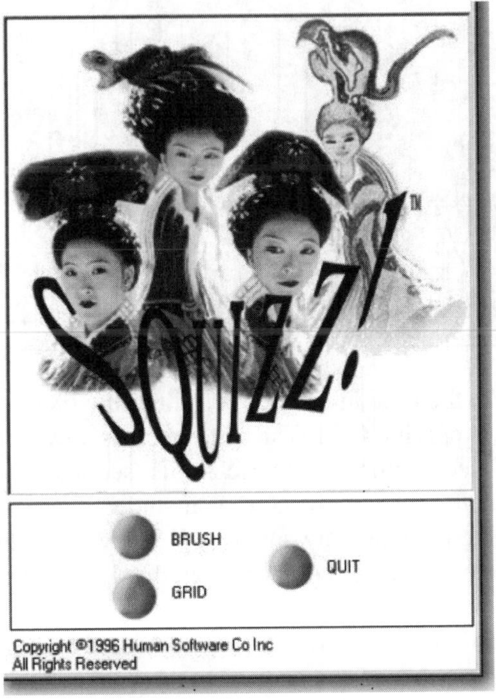

What can you do with this filter? Well . . . you could use it to distort images much as we demonstrated with the Mesh Warp filter. I like to think of this filter as Super Mesh Warp. When the SQUIZZ splash screen opens, you are presented with two possible options: Brush and Grid.

Grid Warping

Selecting Grid opens the Grid Warping screen shown next.

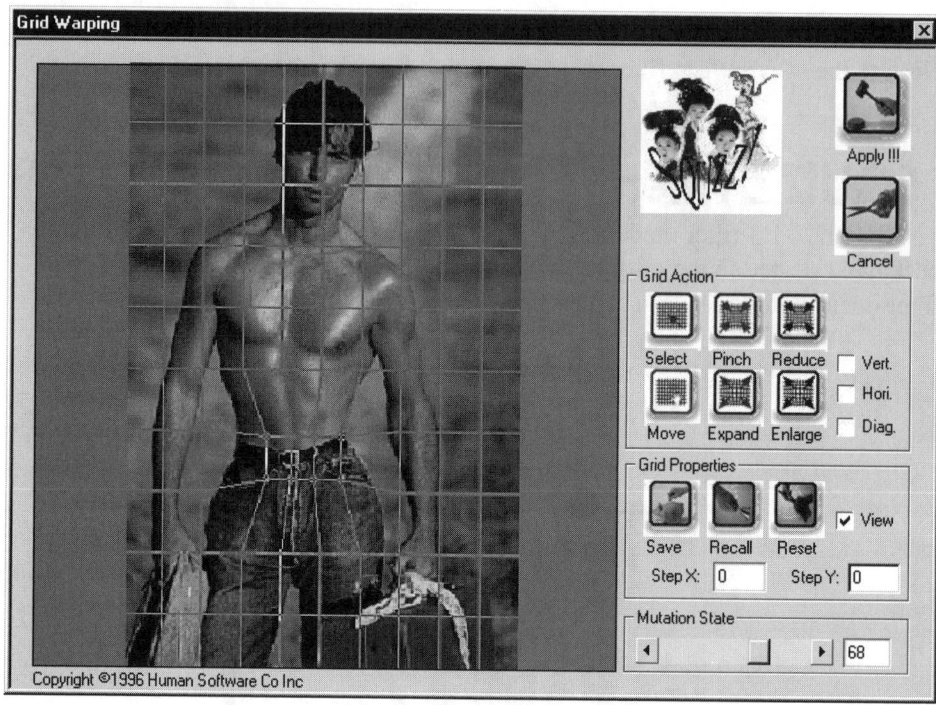

Although it looks like the Grid in Mesh Warp filter, the operation of this filter is somewhat different. Applying Grid Warping effects is a two-step process. The first step is to click the Select button in the Grid Action section. In the preview screen, marquee-select the nodes that you want to be included. Once the nodes are selected, choose the action that you want to apply. If you use the Move action, click inside the selected nodes and drag them in the desired direction. For the other actions, click inside of the selected area and drag. Each time you click the mouse, all of the selected nodes move in the direction indicated by the selected action. Multiple effects can be selected and applied to the image, but there is no preview. Click the Apply button to apply the SQUIZZ effect to the image.

Brush Warping

Choosing the Brush opens the Brush Warping screen shown next. This mode applies the distortion using a brush stoke. As with Grid Warping, you can create multiple effects on the image before clicking the Apply button. One of the unique settings is the Undo mode, which acts like the Local Undo command and is used to remove an action that was applied before the Apply button is clicked. The PHOTO-PAINT Undo command does not work while working in the SQUIZZ filter.

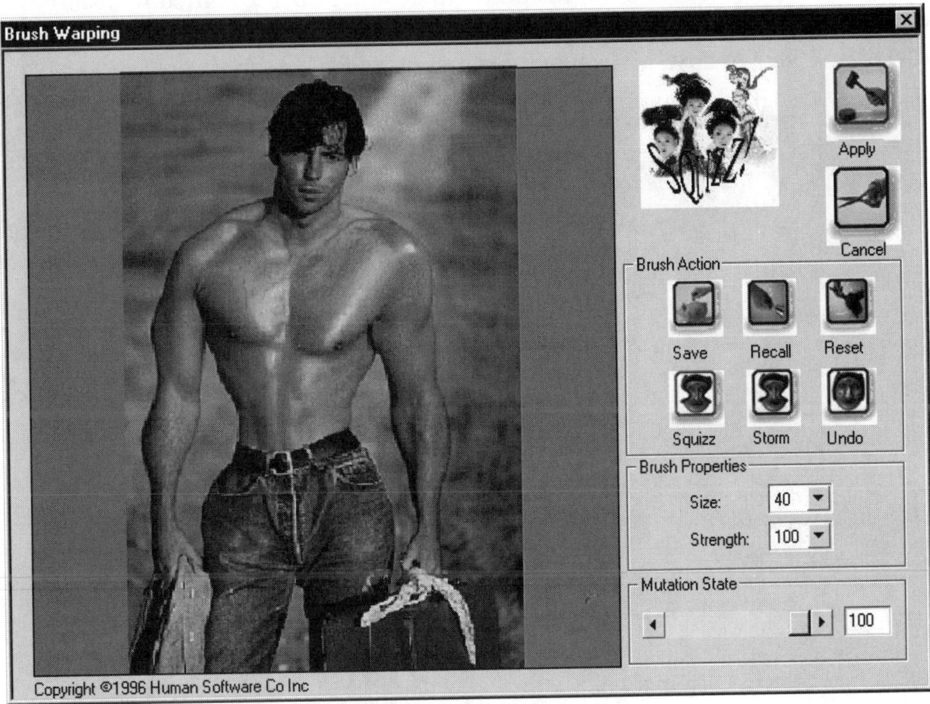

What Can You Do with SQUIZZ?

While surrealistic distortions are OK, I love using it to mess with images so that the viewer is not immediately aware that the image has been distorted. The advantage of the SQUIZZ filter is the ability to apply effects in localized areas using a brush style tool. There is also a Grid format tool that acts very much like the Mesh Warp filter. The interface for the filter is mildly intuitive, but you are advised to use the Envoy viewer provided with PHOTO-PAINT to look at the user's manual located on the CD-ROM disk.

The Offset Filter

The Offset filter is a pixel mover. Much like those hand games you play when you must move little tiles around to form a word, the Offset filter moves pixels in an image according to either a specified number of pixels or as a percentage of image size. The filter will shift the entire image unless there is an area enclosed by a mask. If a mask exists, none of the pixels in the image being shifted will shift outside of the mask. When there is a shift, an empty area is created. The Offset dialog box, shown next, gives you three options to fill the empty area.

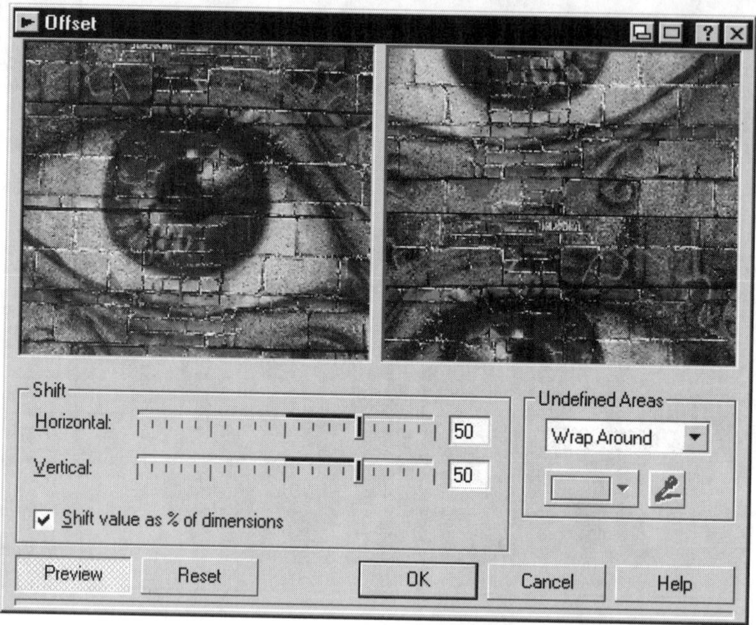

NOTE: *The Offset filter is a favorite of those Photoshop users who were heavily involved in channel operations (called CHOPS). This filter remains critical to many techniques described in many Photoshop books. Most of the techniques involving the Offset filter were developed before the advent of objects and layers. It allowed you to create an image, save it to a channel, and offset the duplicate to create highlights and shadows. Today it is easier to do that by creating objects and positioning the objects.*

Controlling the Offset

The Offset filter dialog box controls are divided into two areas: the Shift controls and the Undefined Areas options. Horizontal and Vertical Shift sliders determine the amount of shift in the horizontal and vertical. The values in the boxes to the right of the sliders represent either the number of pixels shifted or the percentage, depending on whether the Shift Value box is checked. When the Shift Value as % of Dimensions checkbox is enabled, it causes the coordinates of the horizontal and vertical shift values to be calculated as a percentage of the size of the image. Enabling this check box with the Vertical Shift set to 50 and the Horizontal Shift set to zero causes the image to shift along the vertical plane by a distance corresponding to exactly one-half the size of the image. The keys to the operation of this filter are determined by the Undefined Areas options:

- **Wrap Around** Wraps another part of the image around the edges of the window when shifted.
- **Repeat Edges** Fills the space vacated by the shifted image with the color(s) currently appearing along the edge of the image.
- **Color** Fills the space vacated by the shifted image with a color chosen from the image with the Eyedropper tool or from the Color pop-up palette.

If a mask is present, all of the effects will happen inside the mask. If the object being masked is a solid color and Wrap Around is chosen as the option, it will appear as though nothing had happened.

Creating a Backdrop Using the Offset Filter

This is a hands-on exercise using the Offset filter to create a graphic for a coming shell exhibit at the museum. It seems our little shell exhibit has done so well we need to design a cover for it.

NOTE: *The fonts used in this exercise are not automatically installed by PHOTO-PAINT; it may be necessary to install them.*

1. Find the file EXERCISE\PHOTOS\NAUTILUS SHELL. Click the OK button and the original image appears, as shown next.

2. Select Effects | Distort | Offset. Click the button to enable Repeat Edges in the Undefined Areas section. In the Shift section, set the Horizontal to 30 and the Vertical to 25. Ensure the Shift Value as % of Dimensions box is checked. The result of the offset is shown next.

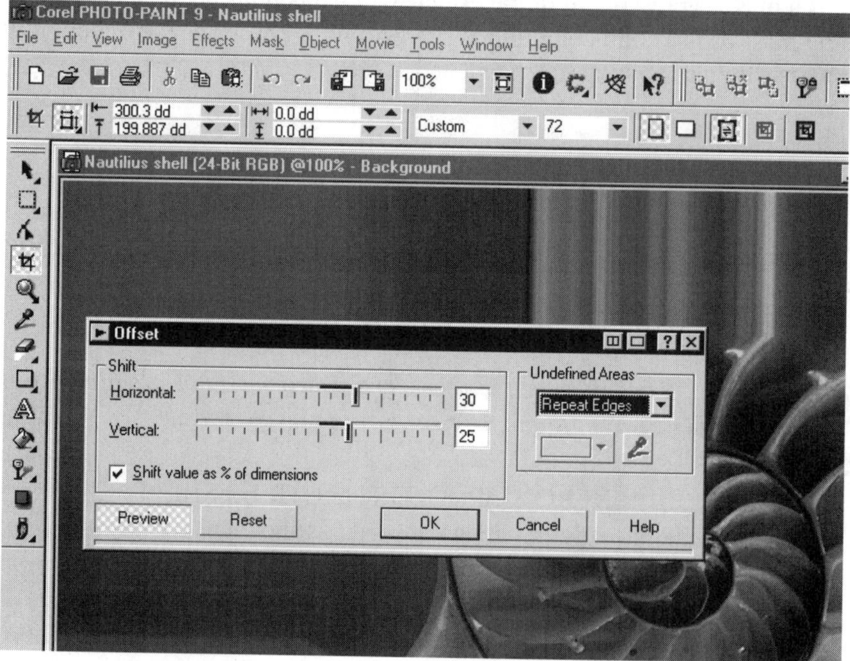

3. To accomplish the next piece of magic we are going to use another filter in the Distort family: the Tile filter. When you open the Tile filter, change both settings to 2, as shown next, and click OK.

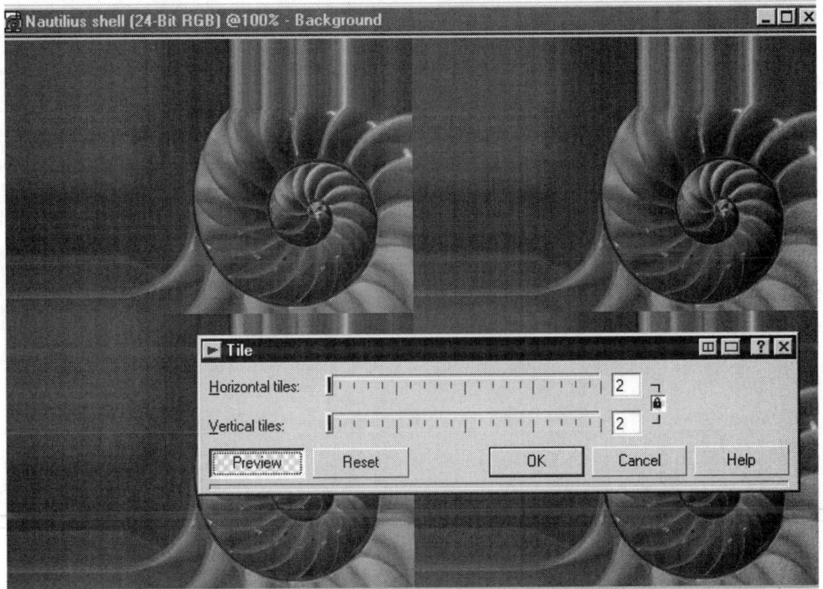

4. The next stage requires a little accuracy, so we must enlist the help of the Grid. From the View menu choose Grid and Ruler Setup. First of all, change the Units of measure to pixels by clicking on Ruler on the left side of the dialog box and then return to the Grid. We need to divide the image into four equal quadrants. Since the image is 640 x 420 pixels (you can find that out from the Document Info button), we need only divide each value by 2. Fear not, this is as complicated as the math gets. So, set the horizontal to 320 and the vertical to 210. Check View Grid and Snap To Grid, as shown next.

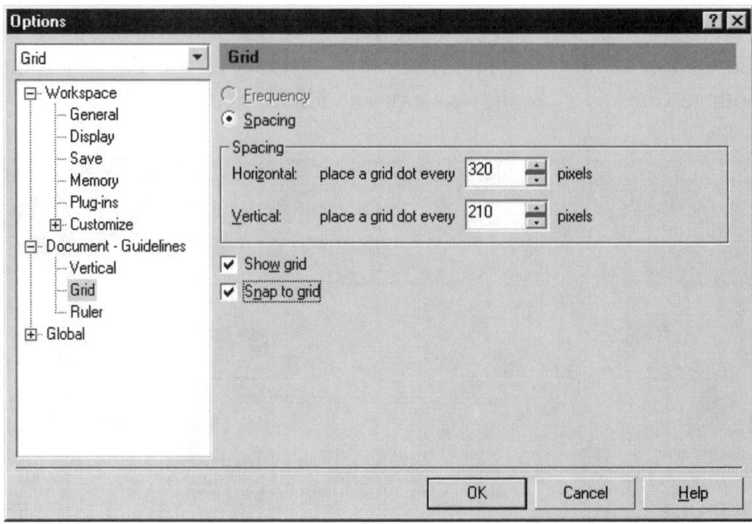

5. Select the Rectangle Mask tool (R) in the Toolbox. Click and drag a mask in the upper-right portion of the image. The mask will snap in place thanks to the Grid. Make an object of the mask area (CTRL-UP ARROW). Choose Object | Flip | Vertically. The result is shown next.

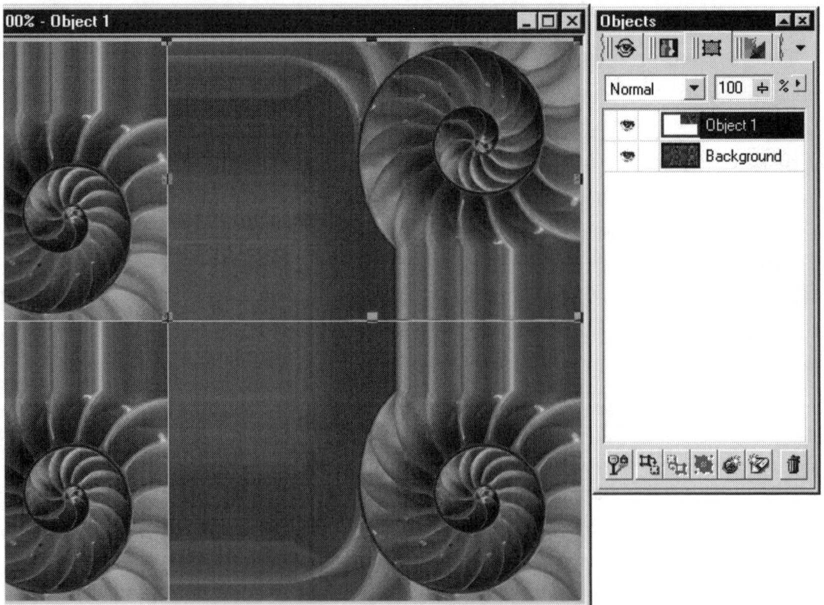

6. Duplicate the object (CTRL-D). Click and drag the duplicate to the upper-left quadrant. Again, the Snap To Grid feature will snap the object into place when you let go of it. Flip this one horizontally. Duplicate this object and drag it down to the bottom-left. Flip it vertically.

7. To tidy up, we must first open the View menu and turn off Snap To Grid and the Grid by clicking on them in the menu. You will need to open the View menu twice since PHOTO-PAINT rudely closes the menu when you click on one of those options. With the Grid off, you may now notice a fine line between the quadrants. Select one of the three objects (remember the one in the lower-right corner is not an object but the background) and use the arrow keys to adjust the placement. *Hint*: Use the TAB key to move the selection between objects. The adjusted image is shown next.

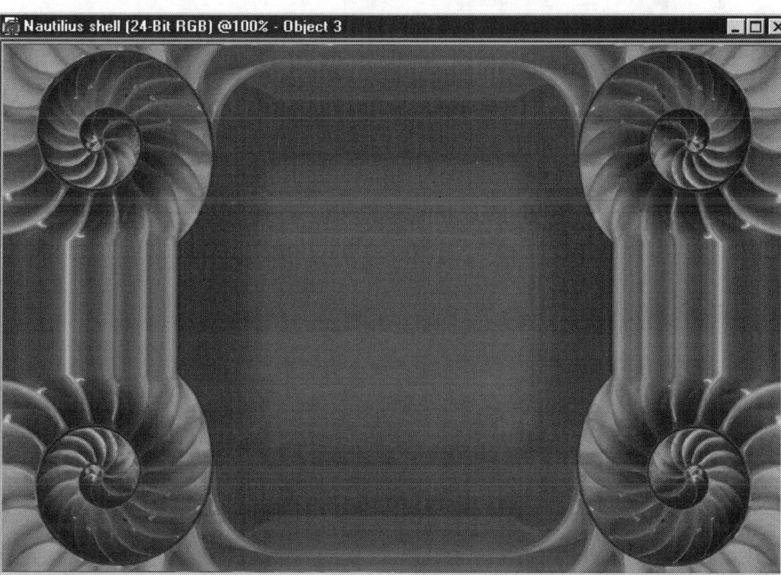

The Pixelate Filter

The Pixelate filter gives a block-like appearance to the entire image, the area enclosed by a mask, or the selected object. You have seen the effect many times before on newscasts, where certain persons had their features pixelated to prevent viewers from seeing the face of the person talking. Because the pixelation was done on a frame-by-frame basis, the boundaries of the pixelation varied from frame to frame, which produced an apparent movement around the edges.

You can control the pixelate effect by selecting either Rectangular or Circular mode and changing the size and opacity of the blocks. This filter can be used to create backgrounds that have the appearance of mosaic tiles.

Width and Height values (1–100 pixels) for the size of the pixel blocks can be entered independently. The effects of pixel block size are dependent on the image size. A value of 10 in a small image will create large pixel blocks. A value of 10 in a very large image will produce small pixel blocks. Use the Opacity % slider (range is 1–100) to control the transparency of the pixel blocks. Lower values are more transparent. The shape of the blocks of pixels is controlled with the Pixelate mode buttons. Square and Rectangular modes arrange the pixel blocks on horizontal lines. The Circular mode bends the blocks of pixels and arranges them on concentric circles beginning at the center of the image or the masked area.

Using the Pixelate Filter

Since Corel PHOTO-PAINT 9 can import and work on video files (if you have a video capture board), the most obvious use for the Pixelate filter is to pixelate the faces of key witnesses to gangland murders for the local news station. If that opportunity is not readily available, the Pixelate filter is very handy for creating unusual backdrops or converting background into something akin to mosaic tile. When working with backgrounds, remember that the best effects occur when there are contrasts in the image that is being pixelated. In the sample image shown next, the Pixelate filter was applied to our serious model but the white area was unaffected.

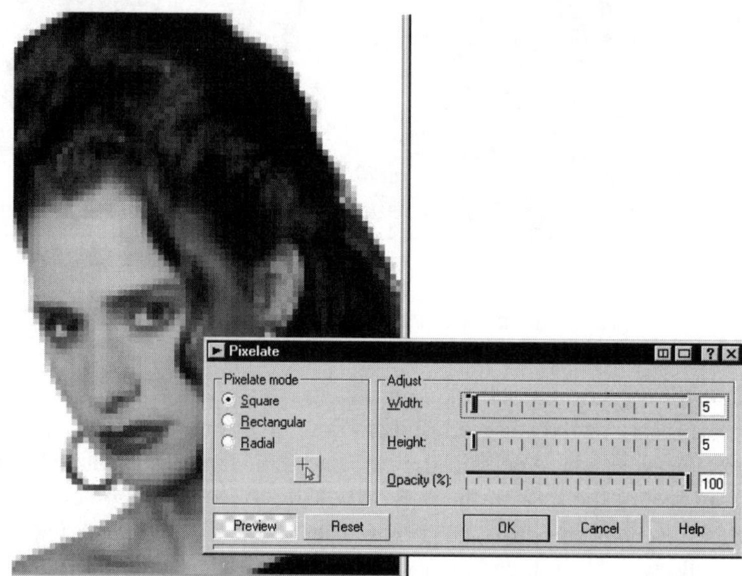

The Ripple Filter

The Ripple filter is one of the "fun" filters. There is just *so* much you can do with it. While it is of little use in the day-to-day work of photo-editing, when it comes to photo-composition tasks, it is a very powerful tool. The Ripple filter creates vertical and/or horizontal rippled wavelengths through the image.

Controlling the Ripple Filter

The Ripple dialog box provides control over the amount and direction of the ripple effect. The Primary wave (by default running horizontally in the diagram to the right) has two controls, Period and Amplitude. The Period slider (1–100) controls the distance in between each cycle of waves. A value of 100 creates the greatest distance between each wave, resulting in the fewest number of waves. The Period setting works on a percentage basis of image size—the larger the image, the larger the number of waves created. The Amplitude slider (1–100) determines how big the ripples (amount of distortion) are. In the diagram, the straight vertical line is the Perpendicular wave. Checking this option on the left allows you to change its Amplitude.

The Angle value (0–180) determines the angle of the ripple effect. Enabling the Distort Ripple option causes the ripple produced by the filter to be distorted by placing a ripple in both directions.

A Simple Ripple Exercise

I don't know, maybe it's because I was raised in California, maybe it was the '60s, but just thinking about Ripple gives me a headache. Back to work. So what can you do with this filter? Like I told you before, have fun. This is a technique that is so simple it is criminal in several countries. Even though it is simple, it has a nice 3-dimensional quality. While it works best with long words, it also works on short words, as we are about to demonstrate.

1. Create a new image. Change the Units of measure to pixels and choose 640 × 480 from the Size pop-up list. Click the landscape button, change the resolution to 150, and click OK.

2. Select the Text tool and choose font Swiss911XCm BT at a size of 150. Change the character spacing to –2. Type **WAVE**. Select the Object Picker tool and center the text in the document (CTRL-A).

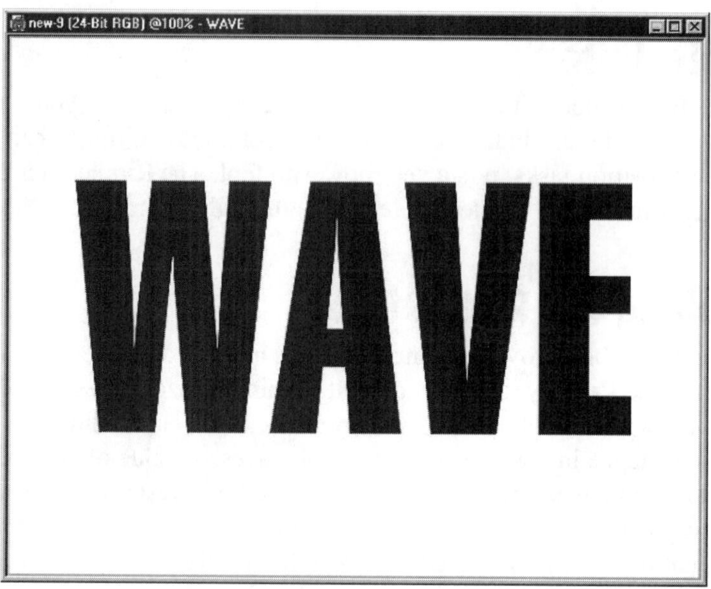

3. In the Objects Docker window, click the Lock Object Transparency button. Choose Edit | Fill. Click the Bitmap Fill button. Click Edit and then click on the Preview window, opening a selection of bitmap fills. Choose the large basket weave bitmap fill. Click OK to select the fill and OK again to apply the fill.

4. Uncheck Lock Object Transparency. Choose Effects | Distort | Ripple. Click the Reset button and then change the settings to Period: 60; Amplitude: 15; Angle: 90, as shown next.

5. Click on the object with the Object Picker tool until the handles become small circles. The object is now in Perspective mode. Click and drag the upper-right and the lower-left handles until the object looks like the illustration shown next. If you are not familiar with Perspective mode, you can make all of the changes you need and the changes are not applied until you either double-click the object or press the ENTER key. To undo unwanted changes, use the ESC key before pressing the ENTER key, or use Undo (CTRL-Z) after you have applied the changes.

6. To give the object an appearance of thickness, duplicate the object (CTRL-D). In the Object Docker window, enable Lock Transparency and select the original object. It is the one that is labeled WAVE. Choose Edit | Fill and click the Paint button—this is assuming your Paint color is Black. This makes the middle image black, as shown next.

7. Select the top object and use the arrow keys to move the image so it looks like the one shown next. Choose Object | Feather and choose a value of 2.

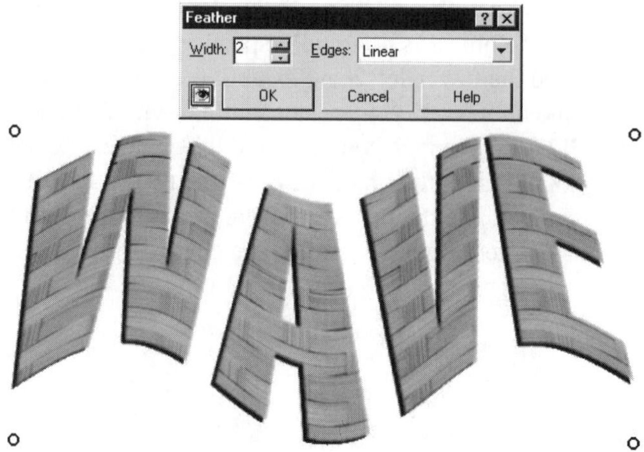

8. In the Objects Docker, shift-select both objects and click the Combine Objects Together icon at the bottom of the Docker. Now, select the Object Drop Shadow tool, click the Shadow Mode button on the Property Bar, and change the settings to match those shown in the next image. Click Apply in the Property Bar.

9. Select the background. Choose Effects | Creative | Vignette. Change the settings to Black; Ellipse; Offset:117; Fade: 43. Click OK.

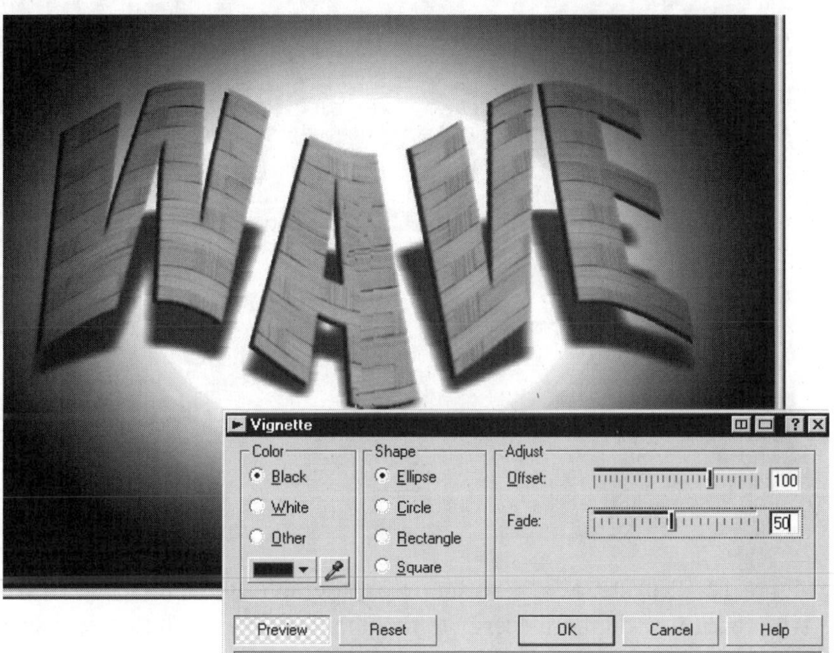

The Shear Filter

Here is another distortion filter that is lots of fun—a real time waster. The Shear filter distorts an image, or the masked portion of it, along a path known as a Shear map. You can load and save maps with the options in the Shear dialog box and edit the Shear Map preview by dragging points with your mouse. The Undefined Areas options are the same as with the Offset filter. In a nutshell, the Shear filter twists the image to the shape defined by the Shear map path, as shown next. The actual amount of displacement caused by this filter is set with the Scale slider. As the amount of Scale increases, the amount of displacement increases.

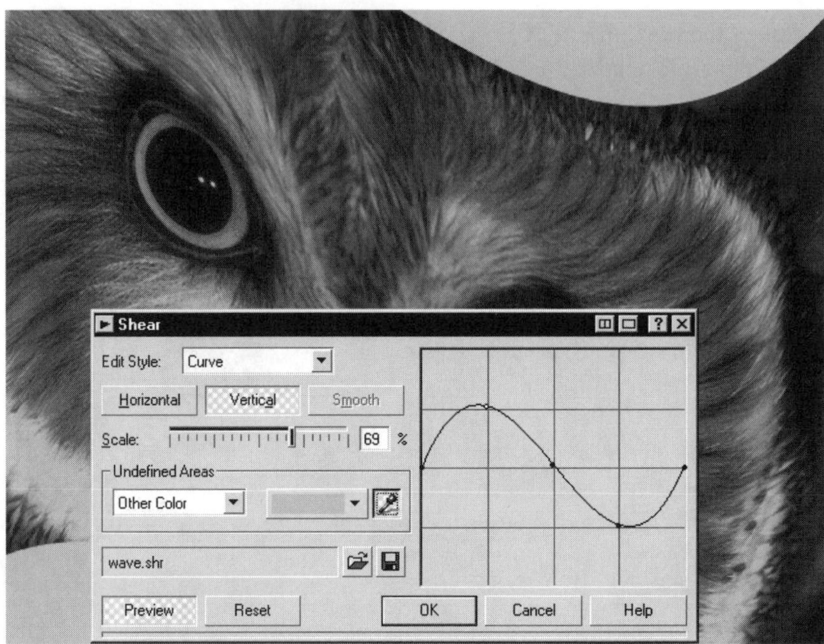

Figure 14-12(a) shows a good action photograph. By using the Shear filter with the Tilt preset, we add more energy to the photograph as well as create space to add a short banner under the motorcycle, if desired. The results are shown in Figure 14-12(b).

As I said, this is a fun filter and easy to use. There are more things you can do with it, so I suggest that you experiment with it to see what the limits are. Try applying it to objects; the result might surprise you.

The Swirl Filter

The Swirl filter is the original no-brainer. It rotates the center of the image or masked area while leaving the sides fixed. The direction of the movement is determined by Clockwise or Counter-Clockwise options. The angle is set with the Whole Rotations slider (0-10) and the Additional Degrees slider (0-359). Multiple applications produce a more pronounced effect. The dialog box, in all of its simplicity, is shown next with the effect it has on a brew. Clearly this filter is

(a)

(b)

FIGURE 14-12 (a) The original photograph already has some action. (b) The Shear filter gives the rider a lift and gives a sense of action to the photograph

also a time saver, as it would take someone an entire evening to get to the point where the glass looked like that, and the Swirl filter can to it in seconds. Isn't science amazing?

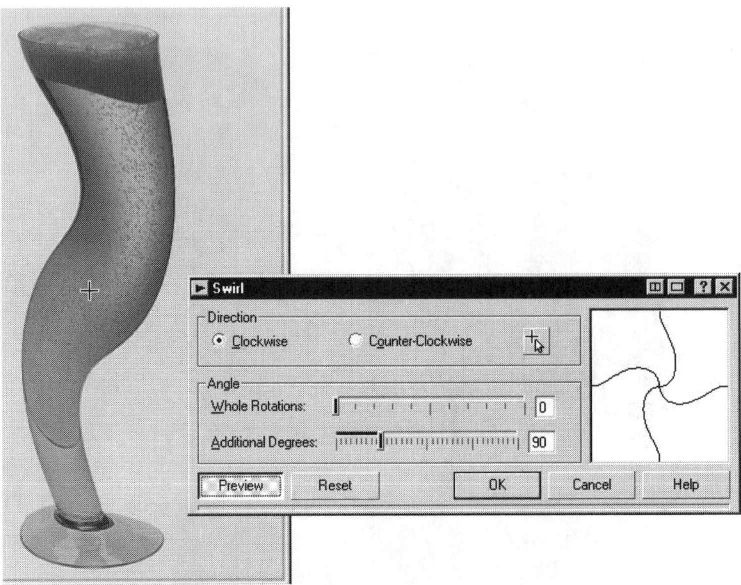

Here is some food for thought when using this filter. In the next illustration, I created a 200 x 200 file and filled it with a simple conical fill. Next, I applied the Swirl filter set to 360. Using the CTRL-F keyboard shortcut, I applied the Swirl filter twice more. The next image shows the application a total of four times. By using the Swirl filter, you can make excellent ornaments and effects for your desktop publishing projects.

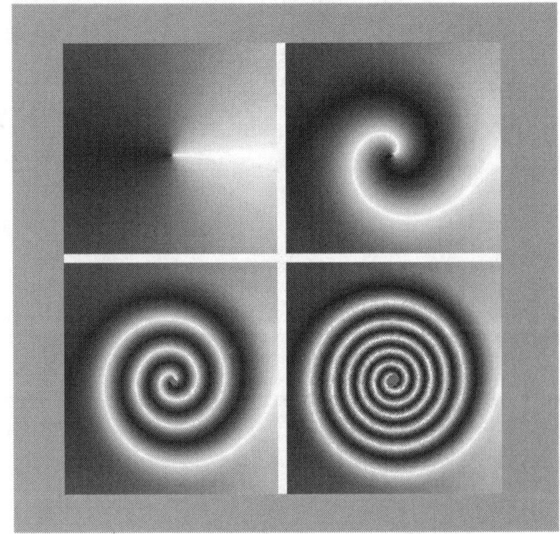

The Tile Filter

If you have been doing the exercises in this chapter you have already used the Tile filter. This is a very simple and quite useful filter. The Tile filter creates blocks of a selected image in a grid. You can adjust the width and height of the tiles using the Horizontal and Vertical Tiles sliders in the dialog box. The values entered represent the number of images duplicated on each axis. So what can you do with it? The Tile effect can be used in combination with flood fills to create backgrounds as well as make wallpaper for Windows. Just remember that the Tile filter does not produce seamless tiles. The best effects are achieved when the number of tiles in relation to the original image is small. If you have a large number, then the original subject becomes so small as to be unrecognizable. The background shown in the next image was created using the Tile filter.

The Wet Paint Filter

This filter can quickly create some neat effects. It isn't necessary for you to think of images that need wet paint. In the image below, it makes the brandy glasses look like someone left them outside too long. The two controls for the Wet Paint filter are Percent and Wetness. Percent refers to the depth to which the wet paint look is applied; in other words, it determines the length of the drip. For example, if you set low percentages, the amount of wetness appears to affect only the surface of the image.

The Wetness values determine which colors drip, as shown in the next illustration. Negative (–) wetness values cause the dark colors to drip. Positive (+) wetness values cause light colors to drip. The magnitude of the wetness values determines the range of colors that will drip. Maximum values are +/–50 percent.

The Whirlpool Filter

I have referred to the Whirlpool filter as a "Smear tool on Steroids" to describe the blender operation it performs on poor unsuspecting pixels in an image. Jeff Butterworth of Alien Skin Software, the original creator of the filter, states, "We just couldn't resist throwing in something fun, which is why we developed it. Whirlpool uses state-of-the-art scientific visualization techniques for examining complex fluid simulations. This technique smears the image along artificial fluid streamlines." This also may be one of the most CPU-intensive filters in the bunch. Be prepared for this filter to take a little time to complete its action. By selecting Effects | Distort | Whirlpool, you open the Whirlpool filter dialog box. This filter, unlike it cousins, The Boss and Glass, does not require a mask to operate.

The Whirlpool Filter Dialog Box

The Whirlpool filter has several options that are unique to this type of filter. These controls are described next.

SPACING SLIDER All you really need to understand about spacing (of Whirlpool) is that it randomly places whirlpools in the selection and then smears the selected area with them. The Spacing slider controls approximately how far apart these whirlpools are from one another. A large spacing setting creates more of a "painterly" effect. Smaller settings make the whirlpools close together and create effects that are reminiscent of 1960s design.

SMEAR LENGTH SLIDER Smear Length controls how much the underlying image (background) is blurred. Low values create noisy results, while large settings create smoother results. This is the one setting that has the greatest effect on how long the filter will take to process the image. A longer (higher) Smear Length setting results in longer processing time.

TWIST SLIDER The Twist slider controls whether the flows go *around* or *out* of the whirlpools. Twist angles near degree 0 make the whirlpools act more like fountains, because the fluid flows outward in a starlike pattern. Twist angles approaching 90 degrees flow around in rings.

STREAK DETAIL SLIDER Whirlpool is a form of blurring, so it can remove detail from your image or make your image altogether unrecognizable. To recover some of the image detail, increase the setting of Streak Detail.

WARP When the Warp check box is checked, the simulated fluid stretches the image "downstream" along the stream lines. Warping makes the whirlpool effect more striking, but it may not be desirable if you want the original image to remain recognizable. Turning Warp off causes smearing without moving the underlying image.

STYLE The Style drop-down list box lists several whirlpool effect presets. When you choose a preset, dialog box values change to reflect its settings.

Here is something to try with the Whirlpool: What would happen if you applied the Whirlpool filter to a mask in Paint On Mask mode and then used the resulting mask with The Boss filter? You would have an effect like the one shown next.

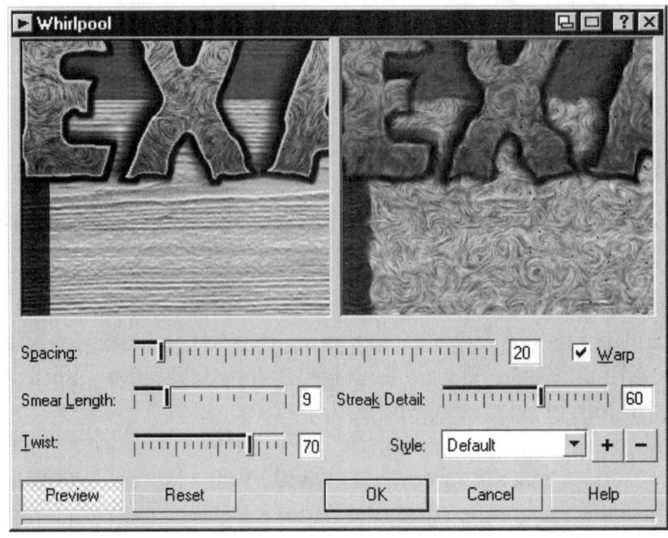

The Wind Filter

The Wind filter is described as creating the effect of wind blowing on the objects in the image. Most PHOTO-PAINT users don't use this filter because they rarely desire to put wind into their image. But the Wind filter does more than create wind; it can be used to create some artistic effects with objects and masks.

The Wind filter smears pixels as a function of their brightness. The brighter the pixel, the more it gets smeared. Click and drag the Opacity slider (1–100) to determine the visibility of the wind effect. Higher values make the effect more visible, while lower values make the effect more subtle. The Strength slider (0–100) controls the amount of distortion. The direction of the smearing can be entered numerically or by clicking on the direction compass in the dialog box.

There are a few things to know about the operation of this filter when working with objects. It needs to have a source for the pixels it is "blowing" across the image. If you apply the Wind filter to an object, it will not work unless the background is unlocked or there is some unlocked object behind it.

I hope this chapter stirs your imagination a little. Always remember not to let the name of a filter dictate what you use that filter for. I know the original designer of the Wind filter didn't think, "Boy, this would be great for making textures and other stuff." Now that we understand the 2-D side of the world, let's prepare to move to the world of 3-D filters, which should be called pseudo-3D. Why, you ask? Read on and find out.

CHAPTER 15

3D Effect Filters

Corel PHOTO-PAINT has a rich collection of ten filters that can be loosely grouped under the 3-D category. Some of the filters that used to reside in this group have moved on to other categories. Some of the filters have changed their names. Most give effects that appear to be 3-D, but none are true 3-D filters. All ten filters, shown next, are available with grayscale, duotone, 24-bit, and 32-bit color images. You can use 3D Rotate, Sphere, Cylinder, Perspective, Pinch/Punch, and Zig Zag filters with Paletted (256 color) images. I put this stuff about what filters work with what at the beginning, so every section that describes a filter doesn't begin with "This filter works with blah, blah, blah." The bottom line is, this category contains filters I can't imagine working without and others that I can't imagine what useful purpose they serve. We will be looking at filters in their order of appearance, so leading off the lineup is 3D Rotate.

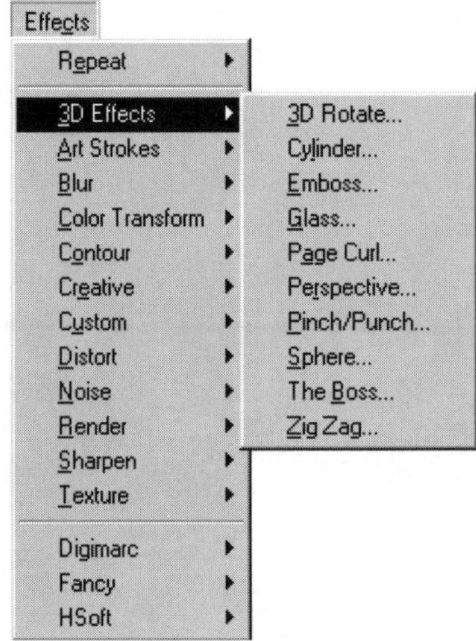

3D Rotate Filter

The 3D Rotate filter rotates the image according to the horizontal and vertical limits set in the 3D Rotate dialog box. The rotation is applied as if the image were one side of a 3-D box.

The 3D Rotate Dialog Box

The dialog box is shown next. The operation of the sliders is pretty obvious. The preview (either preview window or onscreen) shows the perspective of the image with the current slider settings. The plane of the little box in the preview window that is shaded represents the image. By moving the Vertical and Horizontal sliders, you can orient the preview box into the correct position. If the Best Fit check box is checked, the resulting effect will be made large enough to fit inside the image window borders. If it is not checked, it will be smaller as the program tries to calculate a size of the proper scale for the rotation selected.

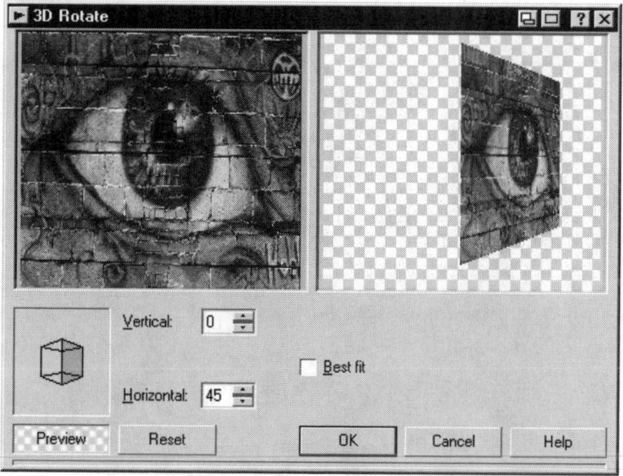

Using the 3D Rotate Filter

The 3D Rotate filter may be applied to the background or to objects, although the Lock Transparency option should not be enabled, as the results may be unpredictable. The basic problem is that while the rotation of the image occurs within the object, the object retains the same shape.

There are a few limitations to this filter. Although you can apply rotation to both the horizontal and vertical axes simultaneously, it is not recommended. The resulting image loses varying degrees of perspective. Also note that the preview doesn't always display the 3-D perspective correctly.

Now that I have told you the bad news, let's play with it and make something cool.

Eye in the Sky

In this hands-on exercise, we are going to create a box with eyes. The exercise is so simple you have no excuse for not doing it.

1. Open the file EXERCISE\PHOTOS\LOOKING AT YOU. Click the OK button. To create this box, we need this image to be a square. We could crop it, but we will try something a little out of the ordinary. Choose Image | Resample and when the dialog box opens, uncheck Maintain Aspect Ratio. Change the Units Of Measure to Pixels (it makes it easier), and then change the Width so it is the same as the Height (427). Click OK and the resulting image is squished, as shown here, but it still looks good.

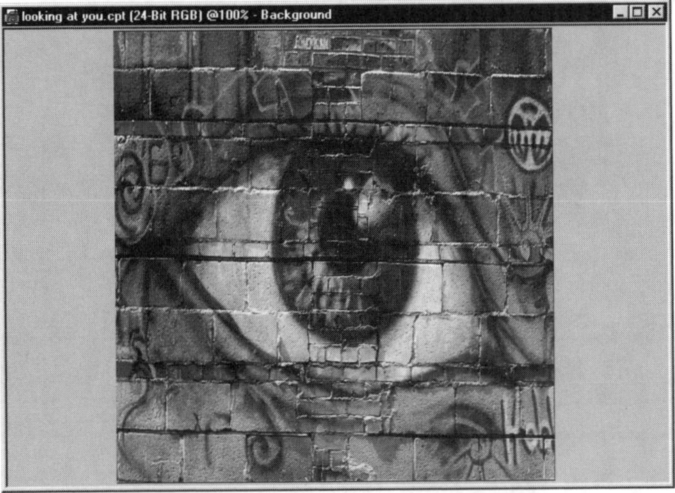

2. Mask the entire image (CTRL-SHIFT-A), and then change the masked image into an object (CTRL-SHIFT-UP ARROW). Select the Object Picker tool in the Toolbox. Open the Objects Docker window (CTRL-F7), and ensure that Lock Object Transparency is not enabled.

3. Choose Effects | 3D Effects | 3D Rotate. When the dialog box opens, enter a value of **45** next to the horizontal slider. Uncheck the Best Fit box. Click OK. The resulting image is shown in Figure 15-1.

4. Duplicate the object (CTRL-D). Choose Object | Flip | Horizontally. Use the Object Picker tool to move the objects so they look like the ones shown here. Use the arrow keys to make minor adjustments to the position of either object.

TIP: *A good method for aligning the objects is to marquee-select them both and use the Align command (CTRL-A) to align them vertically—not horizontally.*

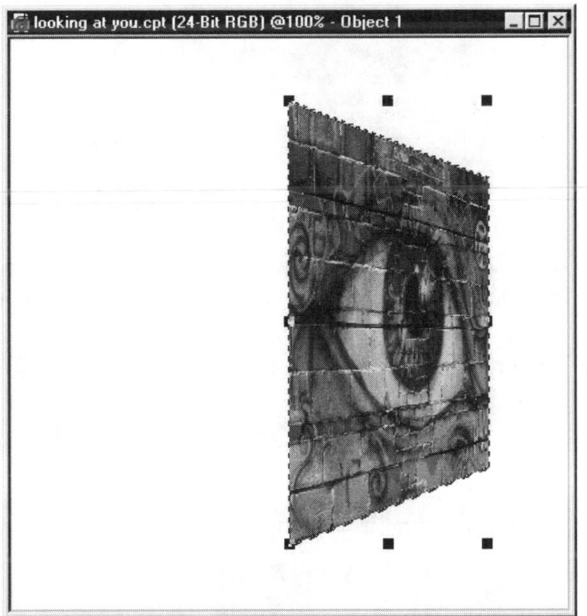

FIGURE 15-1 The beginnings of a perfectly square and wondrous box

5. It looks more like a 3-D box now, but not quite. There are no shadows to fool the eyes. Let's fix that. Select the left side of the box with the Object Picker tool. Choose Effects | Creative | Smoked Glass—not Stained Glass. Click Reset, make sure the Color is set to black, and then click OK. The results are shown here:

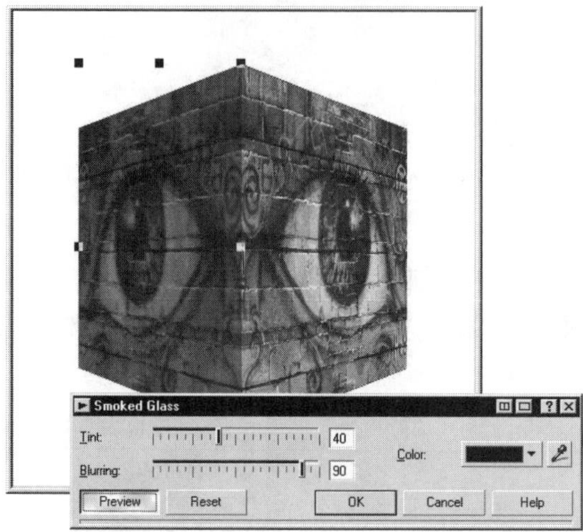

6. We need a background. In the Objects Docker click the background to select it. Choose Edit | Fill. Select the Texture Fill button and click the Edit button. Choose Samples from the Texture Library list and Clouds, Midday from the Texture List, as shown here:

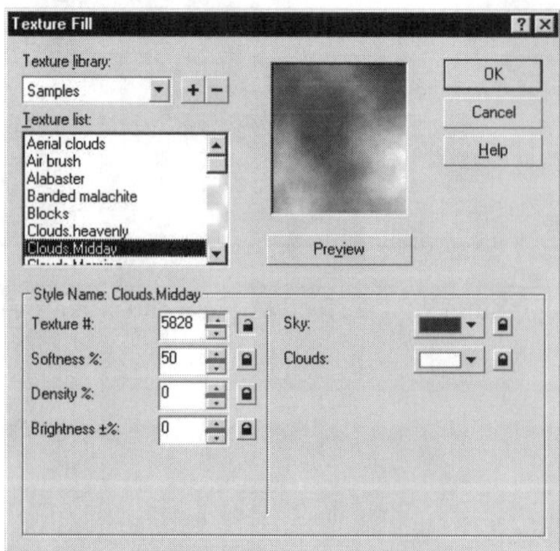

7. Click OK to select the fill and OK again to apply it. The resulting image is shown in Figure 15-2. We will not be using this file again.

The Cylinder Filter

This filter used to be one of the variations of the Sphere filter. Now it is out on its own. The purpose of the filter is to distort an image along either a horizontal or vertical plane to give the appearance of a cylinder. It provides a good start for making a cylinder, but I find shading and highlights much more effective to create the effect.

The Emboss Filter

Embossing creates a 3-D relief effect. Directional arrows point to the location of the light source and determine the angle of the highlights and shadows. The Emboss filter has its most dramatic effect on medium- to high-contrast images. Several filters can be used in combination with the Emboss filter to produce photorealistic effects.

FIGURE 15-2 A cool floating box that takes less than three minutes to create

The Emboss Dialog Box

The Emboss dialog box, shown next, provides all the controls necessary to produce a wide variety of embossing effects.

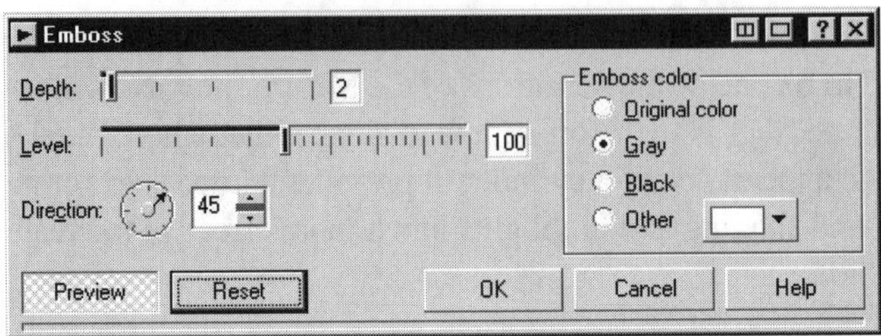

The Emboss Color section determines the color of the embossed image. When Original Color is selected, the Emboss filter uses the colors of the image to simulate the relief effect. When Black or Gray is selected, the entire image fills with that color. Oddly enough, Gray is the default color and the one all the PHOTO-PAINT wannabe programs display when showing their emboss filters. Maybe I spent too many years in the canoe club (Navy), but I have never had a desire to see something embossed in battleship gray. Now that I have said that, Gray is the preferred color to see the effect of the embossing before switching to Original Color. To select another solid color except black or gray, you must click the Other button and choose from the Color palette.

The Depth slider sets the intensity of the embossing effect. Take care not to use an excessive value (greater than 5), since it can cause enough image displacement to make you think you need to schedule an eye appointment. The Level slider controls the radius of the effect. The effect on the image is that the white offset appears to be whiter. You can use a larger amount of Depth without distorting the image. Direction specifies the location of the light source. Light direction is important because it determines if the image has a raised or a sunken surface. The best way to use these two sliders is when one is at a high value, make the other low. Follow that rule and you'll stay out of trouble.

Making Jade with the Emboss Filter and Friends

The Emboss filter is used in several of the hands-on exercises throughout this book. There are few tricks to using it effectively. One of the standard uses of the Emboss filter is to produce textures. Here is a quick session to demonstrate the creation of a smooth and worn jade texture.

1. Open the file EXERCISE\OBJECTS\CELTIC. This little time-saver was created for this exercise. It is a text object filled with a bitmap fill.

2. Choose Effects | 3D Effects | Emboss. Change the settings to Depth: 2, Level: 240, Emboss Color: Original Color, and Direction: 45, as shown here:

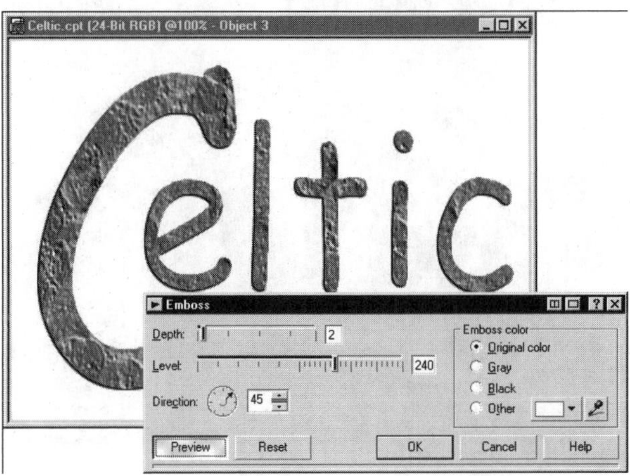

3. At this point it looks like a metal, but we will change all that. Choose Effects | Texture | Plastic. Change the settings to Highlight: 90, Depth: 52, Smoothness: 75, and change the Light Color to mint green. The image is shown here:

4. Use the Object Shadow tool and add a Flat-BottomRight Shadow. In the Objects Docker, select the Background. Choose Effects | Fancy | Julia Set Explorer 2.0. In the Presets section choose Earth Tone Frame and click OK. The result is shown here:

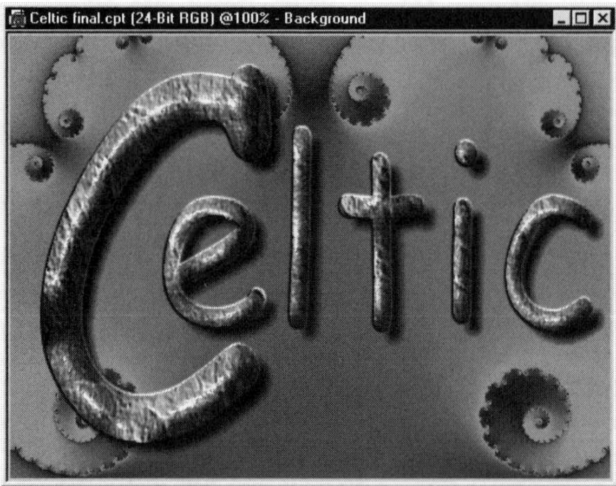

5. Now choose Effects | Texture | Elephant Skin. Click Reset in the dialog box and click OK. The texture fills the image, as shown in Figure 15-3. We will not be using this file again.

The Glass Filter

The Glass filter creates the effect of a layer of glass on top of the image. Keep in mind that the sheet of glass is the 3-D part, while the image remains flat. By adjusting the combination of light filtering, refraction, and highlights, you can achieve some striking effects with this filter.

The Glass filter requires a mask to do its job. The shape of the mask controls the shape of the glass sheet. The top edge of the glass bevel occurs along the mask. Feathering the mask has no effect on this filter's operation.

The Glass Dialog Box

The Glass dialog box, shown next, is a little complicated, just like organic chemistry is a little complicated. I'm just kidding, organic chemistry is much easier. In fairness, the dialog box has a certain logic to it, and it works pretty well

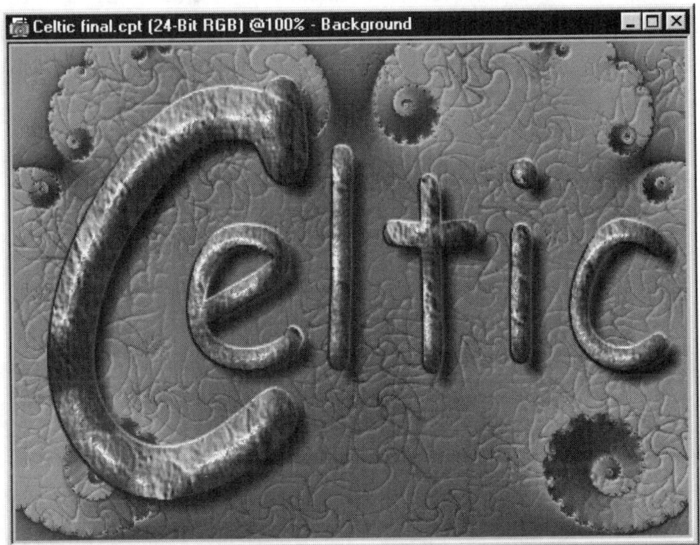

FIGURE 15-3 Fantastic effects in only five steps with the Emboss and other filters

even if you don't read what I have written next. But if you really want to get the most out of this filter, you should at least skim over the material.

Glass
Lens | Lighting
Bevel width: 20
Smoothness: 70
Refraction: 80
Opacity: 100
Drop off: Mesa
Style: Wet + −
Preview | Reset | OK | Cancel | Help

The dialog box is divided into two pages: Lens and Lighting. Clicking on its respective tab accesses each page. The Style portion of the dialog box, circled next, is common to both pages. It contains a drop-down list of presets that are provided with the Glass filter. Choosing any of them changes the controls in the dialog box for the selected presets. Custom settings are also saved in the Style area by changing the controls to the desired settings and clicking the plus (+) button to the right of the style name. Another dialog box opens that allows you to name the new style. The minus (–) button is used to remove a saved style.

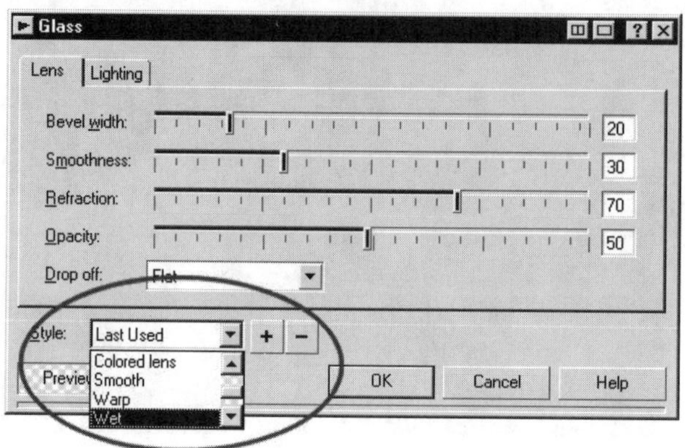

The Lens Tab

This page contains all the controls for determining the width, breadth, and depth of the effect as well as the type of effect that is applied.

THE BEVEL WIDTH SLIDER The Bevel Width slider is used to set the width of the bevel. In most cases getting the bevel width to a small value produces the most dramatic effect. The *bevel* is the area around a masked object that is slanted to produce that glassy 3-D look.

THE SMOOTHNESS SLIDER The Smoothness slider is used to set the sharpness of the edges of the bevel. A low-level smoothness produces sharper edges, but may also display the steps used to create the embossed look. A higher smoothness level removes the jagged edges and makes for rounded edges.

THE REFRACTION SLIDER The most striking 3-D effect of the Glass filter is *refraction,* which occurs when the direction of light rays is changed (bent) as a result of passing through a material such as glass or water. Since we are looking directly at the glass sheet, refraction only occurs at the beveled edges. The Refraction slider sets the angle at which the light is to be bent at the bevel.

TIP: *To make the refraction effect more noticeable, try using a wider bevel. This will increase the area of glass that does not directly face the viewer.*

THE OPACITY SLIDER Colored glass affects light, and it affects it more where the material (the glass) is thicker. The Opacity slider is used to set the transparency level of the glass sheet. The more opaque you make the glass, the stronger the underlying image will be tinted to look like the glass color.

DROP-OFF TYPE The *drop-off* is the area adjacent to the bevel effect and is selected from a list. The following choices are available:

- **Gaussian** Use the Gaussian drop-off when you want a very subtle effect. On a complex image, it gives a wet appearance to the masked area edge. The Gaussian drop-off has an "S" shape; it starts and ends with a round and gradual slope that becomes steep in between. It results in a smooth and less noticeable transition between the bevel and the rest of the image.
- **Flat** Because the Flat drop-off produces a sharp drop-off bevel, the areas around the edges are sharp. The effect on text with dark colors may not even be noticeable. This effect works best with objects that have smooth, rounded edges. The Flat drop-off is a straight diagonal line starting at the bevel area and ending on the image. The transition is not as smooth as a rounded bevel, but the slope of the bevel is less steep.
- **Mesa** This drop-off style probably gives the best overall glass effect of the three. The Mesa drop-off is a curve that begins abruptly (almost a 90-degree angle) and ends with a rounded gradual slope.

The Lighting Tab

The controls on this page, as shown next, control the highlights and reflections of the effect as well as the angle and direction of the light source and the color of the glass.

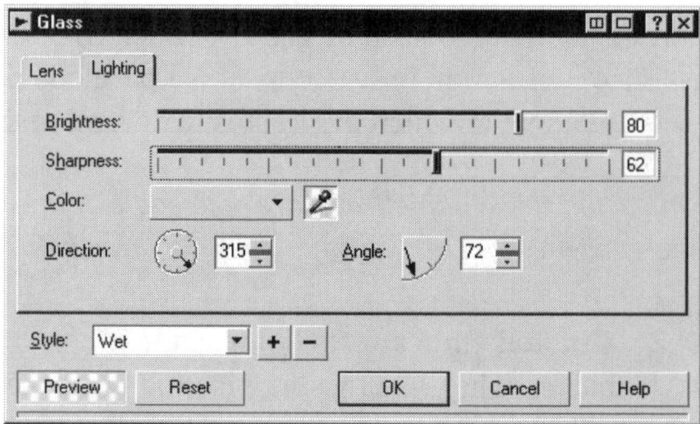

THE BRIGHTNESS SLIDER The Brightness slider in the Adjust Lighting section controls the intensity of the highlights in the glass. A higher setting produces more highlights on the glass.

THE SHARPNESS SLIDER Theoretically, the Sharpness slider controls the sharpness of the light striking the edges of the bevel. That is, this setting controls the amount of reflections off the bevel. Here's the best part. The lower the setting, the greater the amount of reflections.

COLOR The glass can be any color you choose. You can click the color swatch, opening a color palette, or use the Eyedropper button to select the color from the image. Dark glass will color the underlying image more strongly than light glass, so if you are experiencing difficulty in getting a noticeable glass effect, try darkening the glass color.

DIRECTION AND ANGLE CONTROLS You can control the direction that the light comes by using the Direction and Angle controls. High light-angle values illuminate the selection from directly above the surface, which tends to cause lighting that is bright and even. Low light-angle values tend to make shadows stronger, accentuating the 3-D effect. The angles are referenced to the horizon. High angle (90°) is similar to the sun being directly overhead, whereas low angle (0°) is like the sun sitting on the horizon.

- **Direction Dial and Value Box** The Direction dial controls the direction of the light striking the bevel. The bevel is the area around a masked object that is slanted to produce the 3-D look. You can drag the dial to point toward the light source, or you can enter a value directly in the value box.

- **Angle Dial and Value Box** The Angle dial controls the angle at which the light is to be bent at the bevel. This distorts the image at the bevel location, which is the most striking effect of the Glass filter.

TIP: *You get better effects with the Glass filter if you have a textured or high-contrast background to accentuate the glass effect.*

Glass Raised Text Using the Glass Filter

The Glass filter is an excellent filter, but it takes some practice to get the hang of how and where to apply it. The following hands-on exercise will give you some experience using the Glass filter, and you will learn some of the tricks to make it work better for you. We are going to make text that looks like it is composed of raised glass.

1. Create a new 24-bit RGB image. From the dialog box, select Inches for Units Of Measure. From the Size pop-up menu, select the Photo 5 × 7 option, and then click the Landscape button. The resolution should be 72-dpi. Click the OK button.
2. The glass effect looks better when there is high-contrast content in the background. Select Edit | Fill. From the Edit Fill & Transparency dialog box, click the Bitmap Fill button and click Edit, opening the Bitmap Fill dialog box. Open the preview palette of fills in the upper-left corner. Scroll down until you find a light-colored wood near the bottom. Click it to select it and then click OK. Click OK again to apply the fill. The resulting image is shown here:

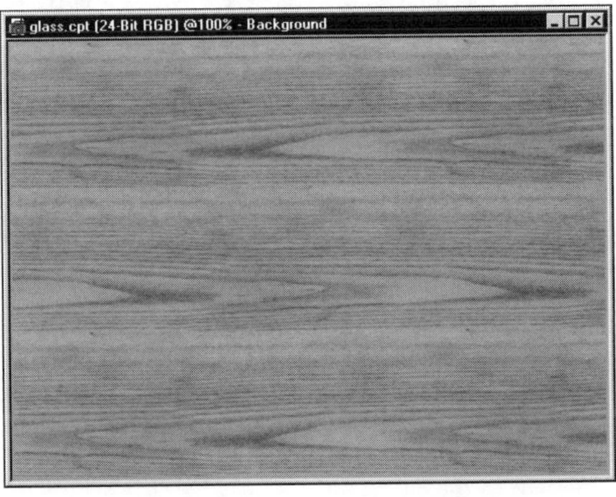

15

3. Click the Text button on the Toolbox. Change the Font to Times New Roman at a size of 150. Click in the image and then select Bold. Ensure the intercharacter spacing is at zero. Click inside the image and type **GLASS**. Press ENTER and type **GLASS** again. Click the Object Picker tool. Open the Align dialog box (CTRL-A), and select To Center Of Document. Click OK.

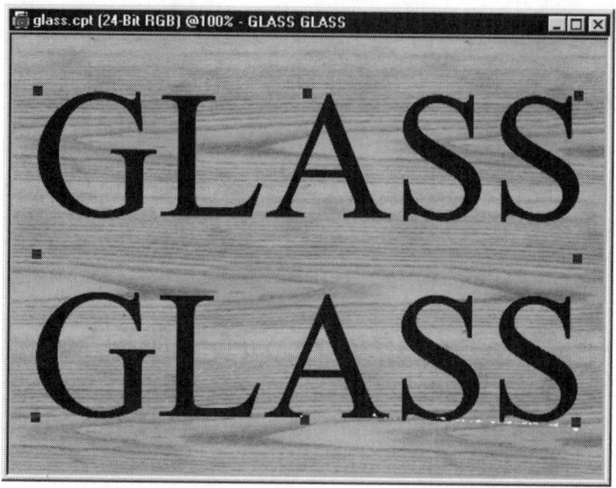

4. Click the Create Mask button on the Toolbar (CTRL-M). Open the Objects Docker window (CTRL-F7), and select the background by clicking it. Select Effects | 3D Effects | Glass. When the Glass dialog box opens, select Wet from the Style pop-up menu. Click the OK button.

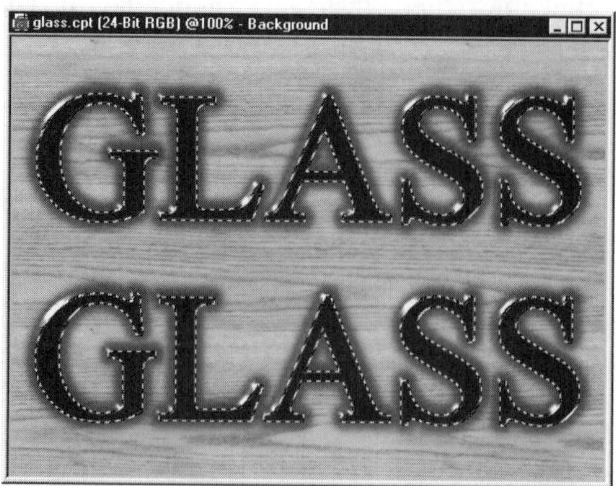

5. For the final touch, use the Object Picker and select the text object. Choose Edit | Fill and apply the wood fill used to flood the background. Change the Merge mode at the top of the Objects Docker window to Exclusion. This lets the highlights created on the background text by the Glass filter appear through the text. The result is shown in Figure 15-4. Choose File | Save and save the file as GLASS. We will use it again in this chapter.

The important issue to remember when working with this filter is that it tends to make the image darker. We worked around that in the previous exercise by placing a copy of the original object on top of the background.

Page Curl

This is a really superior filter. Its only drawback is that when it first came out, it was overused. I've seen a lot of flyers that have used the Page Curl filter, but its popularity has begun to wane. (I'm just warning you in case your clients seem less

FIGURE 15-4 The Glass filter makes the text looks like it is on embossed glass

than enthusiastic when you show them something with the Page Curl filter.) Page Curl simulates the effect of a page being peeled back, with a highlight running along the center of the curl and a shadow being thrown from beneath the image (if your image is light enough to contrast with a shadow). The area behind the image, revealed by the page curl, is filled with the current paper color. An example is shown next.

The Page Curl Dialog Box

The Page Curl dialog box is shown next with a curled edge that I added to the image we just created with the Glass filter. The curl effect begins in one corner of your selection and follows a diagonal line to the opposite corner. You also may notice a slight transparency to the curl if there is any pattern or texture in the selected portion of your image.

The origination point of the curl is controlled by use of the four keys in the Page Curl dialog box. The Vertical button creates a vertically oriented page curl, which curls the page across the image (from left to right or right to left). Experiment with this setting to achieve the effect you want. The buttons are mutually exclusive; that is, selecting one deselects the other. The Horizontal button creates a horizontally oriented page curl, which curls the page upward or downward through the image (from top to bottom or bottom to top). The Width % slider controls the vertical component of the page curl, regardless of whether it is a vertical or horizontal page curl. The Height % slider controls the horizontal component of the page curl regardless of whether it is a vertical or horizontal curl.

The Opaque and Transparent options for Paper determine if the underside of the curled page is opaque or transparent. Choose the Opaque option if you want the curl to be filled with a blend of gray and white to simulate a highlight. Choose the Transparent option if you want the underlying image to be displayed through the curled paper.

TIP: *To apply the effect to a portion of the image, select an area using a mask before you choose the effect. The page will only curl inside the masked area.*

The Perspective Filter

This filter has been around for a long time and fell into disuse when the Perspective transformation feature became available back in PHOTO-PAINT 7. Still, there are a few things we can do with it, and you should be aware of this filter.

The Perspective filter gives the impression of 3-D perspective to an image. In the dialog box, shown next, there are two types in the Perspective filter: Perspective and Shear. Perspective applies the look of 3-D perspective to the image according to the movement of the four nodes in the preview box. The nodes are moved by clicking on them with the mouse and dragging them to the desired location. Shear also applies perspective, but it holds the original size and shape, similar to skewing.

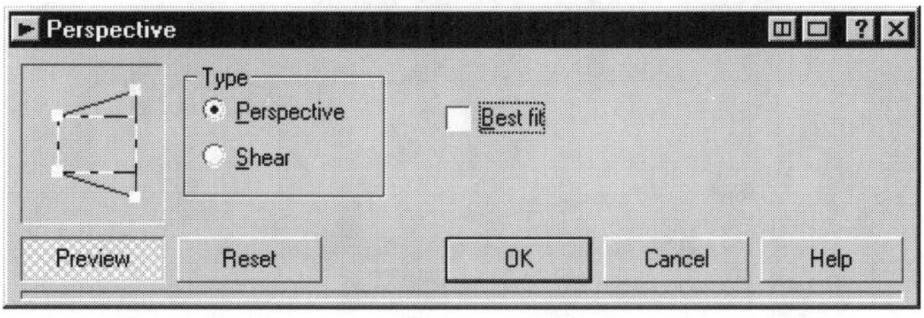

An Exercise in Perspective

Here is something easy to do to show off this filter. It requires the GLASS file we made previously. If you didn't make it, I want you to write on the board 100 times . . . . Actually, I made one for you, and it can be found in EXERCISE\OBJECTS. You're welcome.

1. Open the file GLASS. Choose Effects | Distort | Tile. Change both settings to 3 and click OK. The Result is shown next.

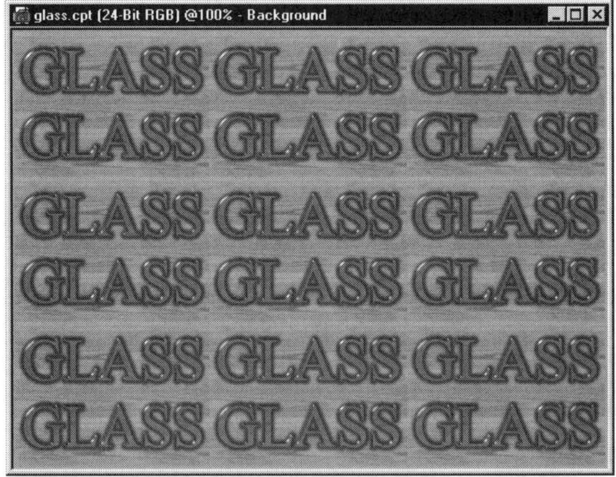

2. Choose Effects | 3D Effects | Perspective. When the dialog box opens, enable Perspective and uncheck the Best Fit box. Now grab one of the right handles in the control box, and drag it until it looks like the one shown next. Click OK. The resulting image is shown in Figure 15-5.

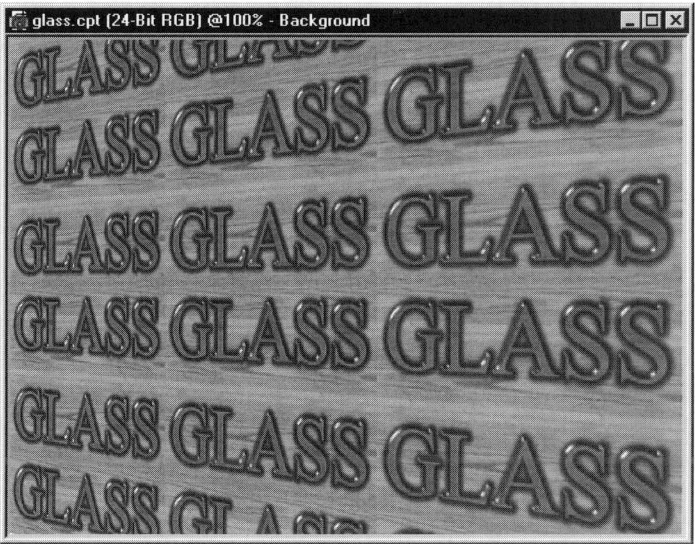

FIGURE 15-5 A nice wall text effect is achieved quite easily with the Perspective filter

TIP: *After applying the Perspective filter, you may consider applying the Adaptive Unsharp filter. I applied it to Figure 15-5 at 100%.*

The Pinch/Punch Filter

The Pinch/Punch filter either squeezes the image so that the center appears to come forward (*pinch*) or depresses the image so that the center appears to be sunken (*punch*). The results make the image look as if it has been either pulled out or pushed in from the center. The primary use for this filter is distorting people's faces so that they will consider suing you.

15

The Pinch/Punch Dialog Box

This filter reminds me of the house of mirrors in the amusement park near where I grew up. They had mirrors that distorted your features. This filter does the same thing. The Pinch/Punch dialog box, shown next, lets you set the distortion effect attribute. In the dialog box, moving the slider in a positive (+) direction applies a Pinch effect, and moving it in a negative direction (–) produces a Punch effect.

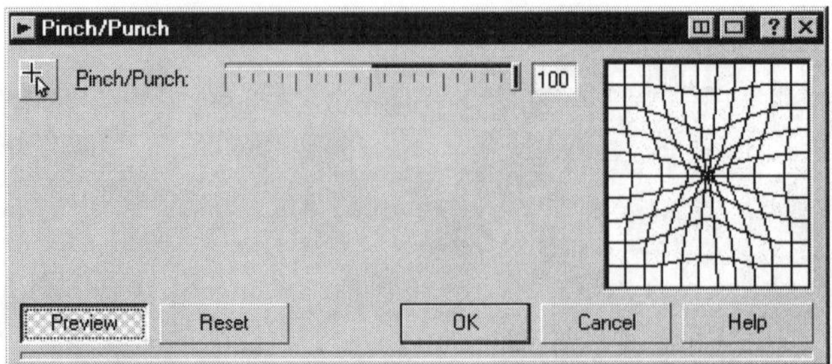

When using this filter, you can apply the filter to the entire image, as I have done to our poor model in Figure 15-6, or you can restrict the application to a small area defined by a mask—like her nose (see Figure 15-7). The effect is more pronounced and effective if the object has horizontal and vertical lines. The most important thing with this filter is to check the image and make sure the person you are profoundly distorting isn't a lawyer.

FIGURE 15-6 The Pinch effect when applied to the entire image has an interesting effect

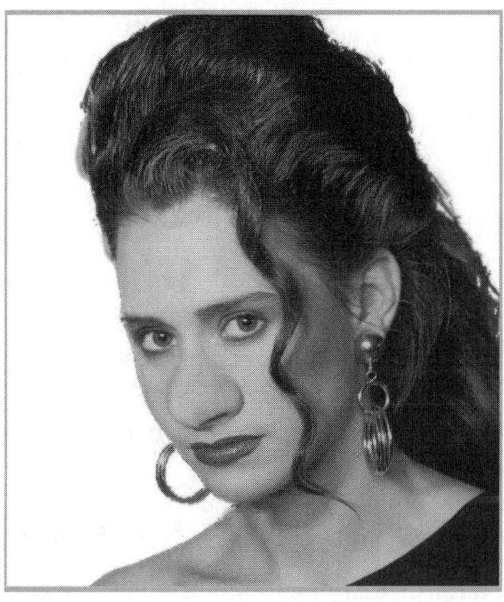

FIGURE 15-7 The Punch effect when restricted to a small area with a mask can result in an inexpensive nose job

The Sphere Filter (Formerly known as Map To Object)

The funny part about the name change is that in PHOTO-PAINT 5 the name of this filter was Map To Sphere. The Sphere filter creates the impression that the image has been wrapped around a sphere. The sphere is easy to work with.

The Sphere Dialog Box

The Sphere dialog box, shown next, is as simple as it gets. There is a button that allows you to choose the center of the effect and a slider to determine how much of an effect to apply. While there is a cute mesh model to show you the strength of the effect, the actual preview is still the best.

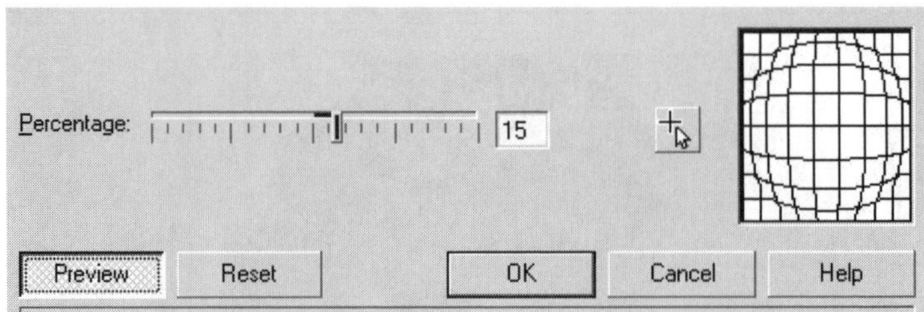

The filter can be applied to the entire image, but some of the most dramatic effects are achieved by applying it to a smaller area of the image that has been defined by a circle mask. The effect is more pronounced and successful if the object has horizontal and vertical lines. Almost all uses of the Sphere filter will require the application of highlights and shadows with an airbrush to enhance their appearance.

Making Glass Spheres with the Sphere Filter

This is one of those exercises that have little or no practical use but make up for it in fun.

1. Load the image EXERCISE\PHOTOS\DAISIES and open it.
2. Select the Circle Mask tool, and drag a circle in the middle of the image. Remember to use the Constrain tool; you must click the mouse button and then hold down CTRL. The result is shown next.

3. Choose Effects | 3D Effects | Sphere. Click the Reset button and then click OK. The glass ball we created is shown here:

4. Even though we applied the Sphere filter, for some reason it doesn't look much like a glass ball—yet. This is the fun part. Select the Paint tool (F5) and from the Property Bar, choose the Airbrush. Change the Brush Type to Wide Cover. Make sure the Paint color is white. Change the Transparency to 70.

5. The effect we are attempting to create is that of opacity. As the glass gets thicker at the edges, it becomes lightly opaque. Using the edge of the Airbrush tool, apply a small amount of color around the edges. The resulting image is shown here:

6. For a final touch, with the mask still in place, choose Effects | Render and select the Lens Flare. Use the 105 mm Prime setting at 100%. The result is shown in Figure 15-8.

In Figure 15-9 I have placed a glass sphere of sunflowers I made on top of a piece of lace made with the Symmetry tool which is lying on top of a table made with a Bitmap fill and the Perspective filter.

The Boss (Emboss) Filter

The only thing I don't like about this filter is its name. After all, if I use correct grammar (and who does these days?) we would call this filter the The Boss filter. Corel PHOTO-PAINT has two emboss filters: Emboss and The Boss. The Boss filter makes the selected area look as if it is pushed out of the image. The big difference between these two filters is that The Boss can be used to create some exciting 3-D effects. The Boss filter effect is achieved by putting what appears to be a slanted bevel around the selected area. It is called The Boss to avoid confusion with the original Emboss filter.

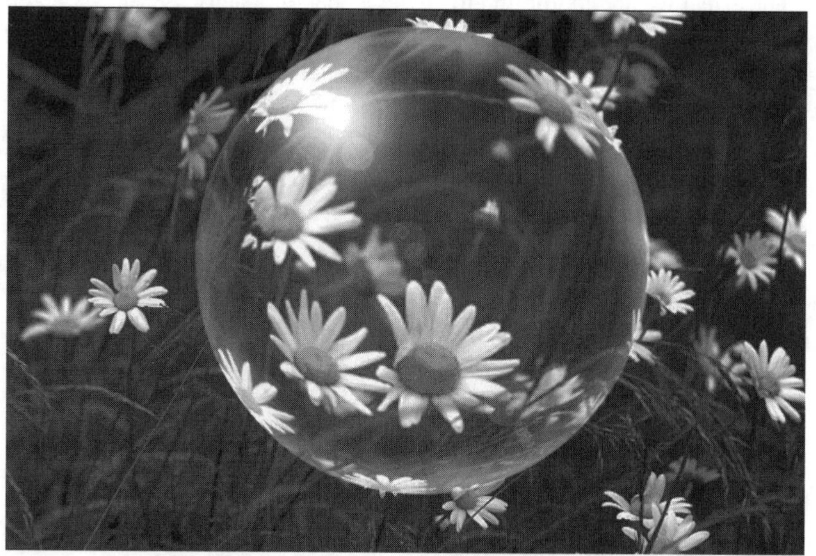

FIGURE 15-8 The Sphere filter and a little airbrushing make a nice glass sphere

FIGURE 15-9 The glass ball made with the Sphere is only one of many things in this image made with PHOTO-PAINT

The Boss Dialog Box

The Boss filter and the Glass filter operate similarly. This is because they use the same filter engine (program) internally. This is not an uncommon practice. I only mention it because if you have already read about the Glass filter, you may experience a feeling of déjà vu. The controls will be covered in order of use, not appearance.

The dialog box, shown next, contains two pages—Edge and Lighting—and a common Presets section.

The Edge Tab

The Edge controls of The Boss dialog box affect the shape of the bevel around the selection.

The Width slider controls how much of the image is taken up by the bevel. This is the primary way to control the amount of the 3-D effect, and in most of the exercises it is the Width that will determine what effect is achieved with this filter. Be aware that the bevel grows around the area selected by the mask. Therefore, if it gets too wide or the objects selected are too close together, they will begin to merge into one another. Thin bevels appear steeper than wide ones, so the Width also controls the strength of the 3-D effect.

The Height slider controls how far the selection pushes out of the screen toward the viewer.

The trade-off with the Smoothness setting is between too many "jaggies" and no sharp lines. Instead of deciding how much The Boss filter would "melt" the bevel, Corel added a Smoothness slider, so you can make the decision yourself. When Smoothness is set low, the edges will be sharper, but little steps in the bevel will be more noticeable. When Smoothness is high, the edges will be more rounded, and it will look like your objects are floating on marshmallows.

Lastly, Drop Off controls the general shape of the bevel.

The Lighting Tab

Part of the realism of 3-D is in how reflections of light are displayed. These controls determine the source point and brightness of the light source.

Brightness is the bright reflection of the light off the 3-D surface. The Brightness slider can make the highlight disappear at the lower settings, or it can wash out part of the image at the higher settings. The Sharpness slider lets you control how small and crisp the highlight is. Sharper highlights tend to make the surface look shinier or even wet. Dull highlights are more spread out and make the surface look chalky.

The shape of the bevel interacts with the highlights. Sharper bevel corners (low width, high height, low smoothing) will make sharper highlights, so you will have to experiment to see how all these parameters combine to make the final 3-D effect.

You can control the direction that the sun or light source comes from using the Direction and Angle controls. High light angles light the selection from directly above the surface, which tends to cause bright and even lighting. Low light angles tend to make shadows stronger, thus accentuating the 3-D effect.

The Zig Zag Filter Dialog Box

The dialog box for the Zig Zag filter, shown here, has three controls that give you many options in using the filter's effects.

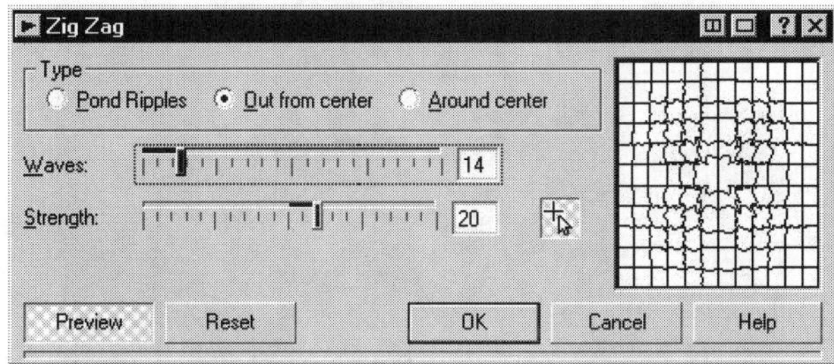

The Type settings control the direction and overall effect of the distortion. The Waves slider controls the distance between each cycle in the wave. Using larger values creates greater distances between each wave, resulting in a minimal number of waves. Smaller values create so many waves that it almost looks like a Fresnel lens. The Strength slider is used to control the intensity of the zigzag distortion. Keeping this value low helps most when you're trying to imitate the effect of ripples in the water. With the Around Center option, an additional Adjust option, Damping, becomes available.

To create Figure 15-10, I applied the Stone Bitmap fill to an empty image. Next the Zig Zag filter with Pond Ripples was applied. The clock is an object (which Corel calls a "watch") that was placed in the center by use of the Paste From File command.

In Figure 15-11, some blurry shadows were added to the text before the Zig Zag filter was applied. I made this image for a German magazine, so that is why "underwater" is spelled that way. Still, I do want a spelling checker for PHOTO-PAINT.

We have seen that while the 3D Effect filters are not true 3-D, the variety of effects give the viewer the impression that they are. In the next chapter we will discover a filter that can turn photographs into paintings.

FIGURE 15-10 *Ripples in Time* was easy to create with the Zig Zag filter

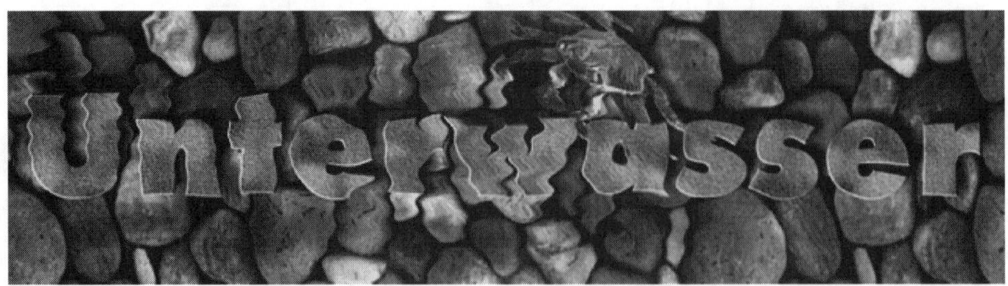

FIGURE 15-11 The Zig Zag filter and some shadows make objects appear under water or *Unterwasser,* as the case may be

CHAPTER 16

Blur Filters

The blur filters represent a fundamental category of filters that is essential to photo-editing. Blur filters accomplish what their name implies: they make selected portions of an image blurred—in other words, out of focus. They accomplish this magic by softening the transitions between adjacent pixels. If you are new to photo-editing, it may seem that blurring an image is the last thing you would want to do. In fact, there are many reasons to blur an image, ranging from creating the illusion of depth of field to creating special effects.

Here is some factual information about blur filters that is about as interesting as cold coffee. The Blur category in the Effects menu contains a collection of nine filters that produce a wide variety of blur effects. There is also a Tune Blur filter, which allows you to apply four of the Blur filters from one dialog box. The type of blur filter you select is chiefly determined by the type of image you are working with and by the effect you want to obtain. None of the blur filters will work with Paletted (8-bit) or line art (images composed of only black-and-white pixels). When working with Grayscale 16-bit or RGB Color (48-bit), Jaggy Despeckle is the only blur filter available. To access all of the blur filters, the image must be either grayscale or color (24-bit, CMYK, or Multichannel). Of all of filters in this bunch, the Gaussian Blur filter is undoubtedly the most used, so we will begin there.

The Gaussian Blur Filter

This filter, although deceptively simple, is used every day to make shadows, produce glows, diffuse backgrounds, and aid in many of the special effects created with PHOTO-PAINT. At its lower settings, the Gaussian Blur filter can give an image a slightly out-of-focus look, while at higher settings it can make the image into fog. I have heard it said that this filter can be used to improve the quality of images containing jaggies, with some loss of detail. In practice, I have found that once there is enough blur to make jaggies acceptable, the picture looks as though it were shot in London on a very foggy morning.

The Gaussian Blur Filter Dialog Box

Selecting Blur in the Effects menu and selecting Gaussian Blur opens the dialog box shown below. This dialog box has a Radius slider and a corresponding Pixels number box.

The Radius slider has a range of values between 0.1 and 250 pixels. With a setting of 5, for example, the blur will be averaged over a radius of five pixels around each pixel in the image. The greater the Radius slider setting, the greater the amount of blurring of the image. High percentage values (more than 30) can turn almost any image into fog. Although it would seem that any setting above 50 pixels is pointless, that is not so. If the blur is applied to a large image, say 6,000 pixels in width, the same settings wouldn't have the same effect as in a smaller image. Because the slider setting is in pixels (and not a percentage) the number of pixels affected appears smaller when there are more pixels in the image. For example, a setting of 30 pixels would turn a standard screen shot of 640 × 480 pixels into fog. The same setting applied to a photograph that is 6400 × 4800 pixels would make a nice blur.

PHOTOSHOP NOTE: *Adobe Photoshop users prior to Photoshop 5 were accustomed to seeing three separate controls for Gaussian Blur. Corel PHOTO-PAINT combines the functionality of three controls so that a single percentage setting will allow you to determine the filter's effect. While it can be argued that three separate control settings give the user a greater degree of control, I have found the single slider to be more than sufficient to produce the necessary blur. Obviously Adobe agrees, since it now uses a single control, just as does PHOTO-PAINT.*

Subtle Emphasis by Creating a Depth of Field

Creation of a pseudo depth of field by slightly blurring an area of the image is a good way to subtly emphasize a subject without making a big show of it. While it

All Things Gaussian

In digital photo-editing, you often hear the term *Gaussian.* I am sometimes asked why Gaussian is capitalized and who is this person with a blur filter named after him. The term *Gaussian* comes from Dr. Carl Friedrich Gauss, a German mathematician who was born in 1777. Dr. Gauss did not invent the Gaussian Blur filter, but he did discover the mathematical principles that the programmers use to create it.

Dr. Gauss demonstrated the mathematical principle of normal distribution, which is the distribution of values described by what is called a *normal curve.* The few of you who actually stayed awake in at least part of Statistics 101 recognize normal distribution as one of the first things you were shown just before you dozed off. Because the shape resembles that of a bell, the curve is also known as a *bell-shaped curve* or *bell curve.*

When I was going to school (way back when) and everyone in the class was doing poorly, the teacher often graded "on the curve," meaning that all of the grades would have been distributed uniformly above and below the average of all the test scores. The result would have been a few A's, more B's, mostly C's, some D's, and a few F's. That is because the score necessary to get a grade of "C" would be the center of the curve (the average of all the scores), rather than an absolute, like 70 percent. This principle of Gaussian distribution is the basis for the Gaussian Blur filter and many other tools in Corel PHOTO-PAINT work.

In photo-editing, the Gaussian Blur filter distributes the blur effect based on a bell-shaped curve. This curve is generated by mapping the color values of the pixels in the selected area and then distributing the blurring around the center value. So what's so hot about Gaussian blurring? Good question. It provides a true blurring, not a smearing, of the pixels, resulting in the blurred area appearing to be out of focus. End of history and math lessons.

is easy to define edges of buildings and other straight-line objects, in day-to-day photo-editing work, you have edges that require a more subtle approach. In this session, you will learn how to define the edges of the subject using a path.

1. Open the image EXERCISE\PHOTOS\BRANDY on the CD-ROM.
2. Select the Freehand Mask tool in the Toolbox and click in the image at the points around the glass, as shown in Figure 16-1. Don't spend a lot of time

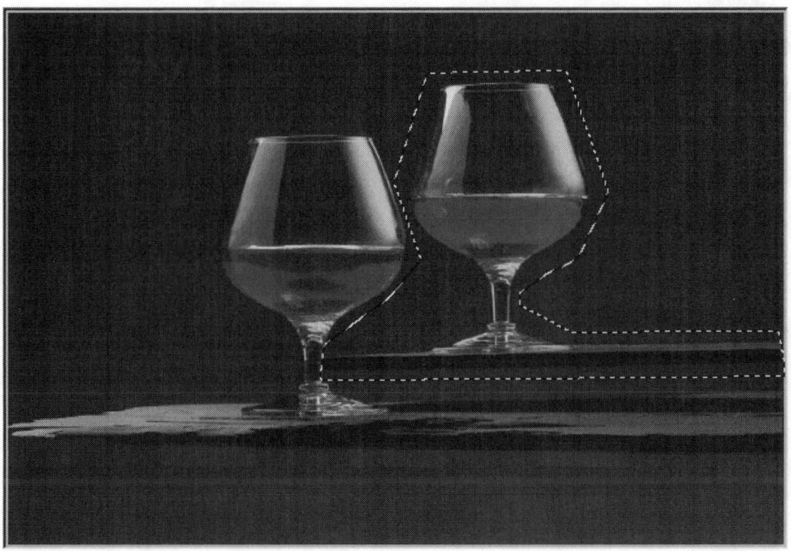

FIGURE 16-1 The Freehand Mask tool is used to select the subject to be blurred

trying to get the exact position of the mask—just get close. Complete the path by double-clicking near the point of origin.

TIP: *When creating a mask to isolate a part of the image for blurring, you should consider feathering the mask so the transition isn't apparent to the viewer. In this exercise it isn't necessary because the background is uniform.*

Select Effects | Blur | Gaussian Blur. In the dialog box, use a setting of 2 and click the OK button. The result is shown in Figure 16-2.

3. Close the file when you're finished.

The glass on the right in Figure 16-2 now appears to be some distance away from the glass on the left. This exercise was easy because the area between the two of them consisted of a diffuse uniform color. This type of background prevents the rough edges of the crude mask we constructed from becoming obvious in the transition areas between the blurred and nonblurred areas. In the next exercise it won't be as easy. Hey, if it was easy, anyone could do it.

FIGURE 16-2 The second snifter either appears more distant or illustrates what it looks like after you have had a few too many

Depth of Field

When working on photographs (digital or film) it is important to become acquainted with some of the terms. Any serious photographer knows about the phenomenon named *depth of field*. If you're not familiar with the term, read on to find out more.

Unlike the brain, which has two "lenses" (the eyes) to produce three dimensions, most cameras have only one lens, which produces two dimensions on the film plane. Unlike the eyes, however, a camera lens records a scene in a split moment of time. We humans believe we see sharply over large areas, but this is an illusion. The reason everything within our vision appears sharp (assuming I am wearing my glasses) is that our eyes are constantly refocusing on whatever has our attention. Most of these refocusing movements are so tiny that we aren't even aware of them. The camera lens cannot re-create what our stereoscopic and constantly refocusing eyes view naturally. Instead, it focuses on one object. The amount of the picture in front of and behind the object that is also in focus is determined by the size of the lens opening (aperture), called the *f-stop setting*. The smaller the f-stop, the wider the plane of focus (or depth of field) and the more the image is in focus. The wider the f-stop, the shallower the depth of field and the less the image is in focus.

The viewer who doesn't know anything about depth of field still unconsciously makes use of its principles. When shown the image in Figure 16-3, a viewer knows that all of the globes are grouped together. When shown the image in Figure 16-4, the viewer assumes the two globes that are slightly out of focus are much further behind the three globes in the foreground.

Background De-emphasis by Blurring

In the photograph in the following exercise, the background is cluttered and needs to be slightly blurred for the title page for the flora section of a gardening book we will create. We want to emphasize the beautiful flowers in the foreground but need to de-emphasize the flowers in the background, over which we will be placing the text. If we made a path/mask as in the previous exercise, there would be a very obvious line separating the blurred from the non-blurred areas. The blurring must occur gradually beginning near the front (bottom) of the image and moving back (up).

FIGURE 16-3 With all the globes in focus, it appears they are all grouped closely together

FIGURE 16-4 Blurring two of the globes causes them to appear more distant from the others

1. Open the file EXERCISE\PHOTOS\FLORA, shown here. Now we need to make a graduated mask. Select Paint on Mask (CTRL-K) and make sure the Paint is set to Black and the Paper is set to White.

2. Select the Interactive Fill tool from its flyout in the Toolbox as shown here:

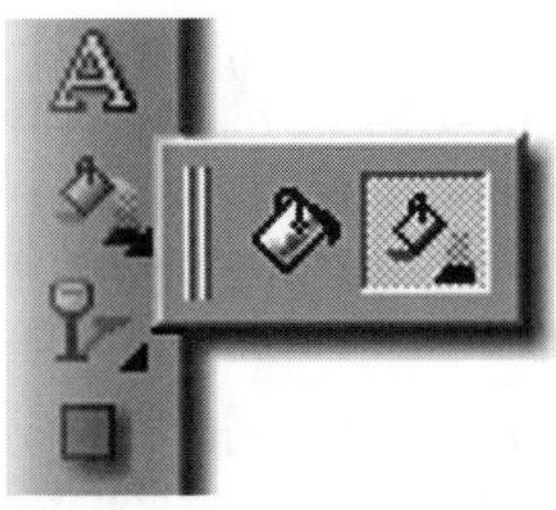

Change the settings of the Property Bar to Type: Linear; Paint Mode: Normal; Interactive Fill Style: From Paint to Paper; Transparency: 0, as shown in Figure 16-5. Click inside the image near the center and, while holding down the mouse button, drag upward until it looks similar to the image shown next. You can adjust the position of the starting and termination points by placing the cursor inside the squares and dragging it to the new location. The position of the mask is not critical; just get close. When you feel you have it where you want it, make sure Node Transparency/Transparency is set to 0 and click the Apply button on the Property Bar.

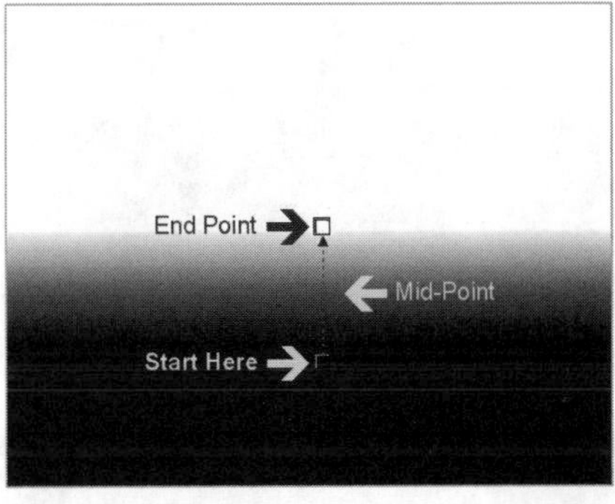

FIGURE 16-5 The Interactive Fill Property Bar

3. Exit Paint on Mask mode (CTRL-K). You now have a mask that controls any effect you apply to the image. Because the top of the mask is almost transparent, the blur effect on the image will be maximum. Likewise, the bottom of the mask is almost 100% black, and, therefore, the blur effect will be minimal. Most importantly, the transitions between the maximum and minimum will be gradual, so the viewer is not alerted to the fact we have been messing with the photo.

4. Select Effects | Blur | Gaussian Blur and change the Radius setting to 2. Click OK. To make the difference more apparent, invert the mask (CTRL-SHIFT-I) and choose Effects | Sharpen | Directional Sharpen. Use a setting of 40. Click OK, and the result shown in Figure 16-6 is produced.

5. To complete the session we need to add the title. Change the Paint color to Chalk or Pale Yellow by clicking the mouse button on the desired color in the onscreen color palette. Select the Text tool in the Toolbox. Change the font to GoudyOlSt BT at a size of 96 and Bold. Click inside the image and type **FLORA**. Select the Object Drop Shadow tool from the Toolbox and create a shadow using the Flat-BottomLeft preset. The result is shown next. Close the file and don't save the changes.

FIGURE 16-6 The mask restricts application of the Gaussian Blur to the upper portion

When applying blurring to a background, you must remember how the human eye sees things. Objects near the viewer are usually slightly out of focus, and those further away are even more so. Effects that go against what the mind expects to see look fake or artificial, even though the viewer in most cases cannot tell you why.

Removal of Banding Using the Gaussian Blur Filter

The Gaussian Blur filter can also be used to diminish the effect of banding in a fountain fill. The text shown in Figure 16-7(a) contains a six-step fountain fill to make the banding apparent. After the application of the Gaussian Blur filter, there is no evidence of the original banding (Figure 16-7(b)). Be careful not to set the amount of Gaussian Blur too high. At very high settings, you will turn the entire image into fog.

FIGURE 16-7 (a) The original text has serious banding problems. (b) The Gaussian Blur filter removes the banding

The Motion Blur Filter

The Motion Blur filter is designed to create the impression of movement in an image. It achieves this effect by determining the edges of the image for the direction selected and smearing them back and forth across the adjacent pixels. There are several issues to consider before using the Motion Blur filter. First, the ideal subject is something—people, events, or things—associated with speed. After all, it looks wrong to see a photograph of two chess players in Central Park with speed blurs coming off of them. Not only does the subject need to be associated with movement, but the direction the subject is facing is also important. For instance, the photograph of a racing car shown in Figure 16-8 is a good choice because it appears to be traveling across the field of view. If it were coming directly at or away from the viewer, it would be more difficult to achieve the effect.

High-speed films can freeze the action so that the subject in the photograph appears to be standing still. In fact, there isn't any indication in this photo that there is movement. It looks look the vehicle is parked on the raceway. When using a photograph like this in an ad or brochure, you want to convey a sense of action to the viewer. You can achieve apparent motion using the Motion Blur filter.

FIGURE 16-8 The photograph, taken with high-speed film, makes the car look parked

There are two ways to approach the application of motion. You can blur the subject or blur the background. Blurring the subject makes it appear to be moving fast but has the drawback of making the subject blurred. A popular technique used in car advertisements these days is to blur the background. This approach is most effective since it conveys the sense of speed and keeps the product (car) in focus.

A mask is necessary to limit the areas being blurred. If you apply the Motion Blur filter to the entire image, it will just appear to be an out-of-focus picture. To limit the effect to just the background, a mask was placed around the car and then inverted. A mask with hard edges will produce areas of transition where the blur begins and ends abruptly, which looks very strange. To eliminate this, the mask must be feathered.

In Figure 16-9, the background had a large amount (70 pixels) of Motion Blur applied. This amount made the background unrecognizable, but, since the subject is the car, it heightens the effect of apparent motion. The Motion Blur filter created a faint halo around some of the car edges because the mask had been feathered. Doing this also helps convey the sense of motion to the viewer and is more the result of perceptions we humans have regarding things in motion than of laws of physics.

FIGURE 16-9 Blurring the background while leaving the car in focus is one way to give the impression of speed

Figure 16-10 shows the result of applying the Motion Blur filter directly to the subject and then using the Local Undo tool to remove the effect on the front, top, and sides of the cars. Not wishing to remove all of the effect, I set the Transparency value of the Local Undo tool (in the Tools Setting palette) to a moderate-to-high value. Remember that when the Local Undo tool is selected, you must use CONTROL-F8 to open the Tool Settings palette. Double-clicking the Local Undo tool removes the entire application of the effect. I did this more than once myself, so learn from my mistakes.

TIP: *You can undo a Local Undo action only once. If you try it a second time, you will get the error message, "This tool requires an Undo Buffer."*

Creating Hammered Metal Effect

The Motion Blur filter can be applied to masks (in Paint on Mask mode) to create some exciting textures. The following session demonstrates just such a technique, and you will also learn how to create text that is not on a straight baseline. It is

FIGURE 16-10 A more subtle way to show speed is to blur the subject

important to remember that many of the settings in this session will need to be modified when used with objects that are smaller or larger.

1. Create a new RGB 24-bit image with a white background that is 5 × 7 inches at 72 dpi. Ensure that the Landscape button is enabled and click OK.

   In this step we need to create a word with text composed of characters of different sizes. Set the Paint to Black and select the Text tool from the Toolbox. In the Property Bar change the font to Garamond at a size of 400. Click the Bold button in the Property Bar. We want the characters to be independent of one another, so click inside the Image window and type an uppercase ***C***. Click at some other area of the Image window, beginning a new object. Change the font size to 300 and type an ***o***. Repeat, creating the *r*. Place the remaining characters, *e* and *l*, in this manner but at a size of 400 points.

2. Each character is now a separate object. Position the characters so they look like the ones in the image below. Only the *l* requires resizing. Select the *l* with the Object Picker tool and click on it until the handles

surrounding it are squares. Then click and drag the top-center handle up until it looks like the image shown below. To verify that the letters are all separate objects, select CONTROL-F7 to open the Objects Docker window.

3. In the Object menu, choose Select All. Next combine all of the objects into a single object (CTRL-ALT-DOWN ARROW). Create a mask of the new object (CTRL-M) and then save the mask as a channel (Mask | Save | Save As A Channel) and, when asked, name it **Original**. At this point we are finished with the text so you can delete it (DEL).
4. Enter Paint On Mask mode (CTRL-K). Choose Effects | Blur | Motion Blur. Leave the Direction setting at zero and change the Distance to 60. Click OK and the resulting image will appear as the one shown here:

5. Exit Paint On Mask mode (CTRL-K) and select the Rectangle Shape tool (F6). In the Property Bar click the Bitmap Fill button and ensure the Render to Object/Selection button is not enabled. Next, click the Edit Fill button and, from the dialog box, click on the swatch to open the pop-up menu as shown in Figure 16-11. Scroll down until you find the gold, click on it, and then click OK.

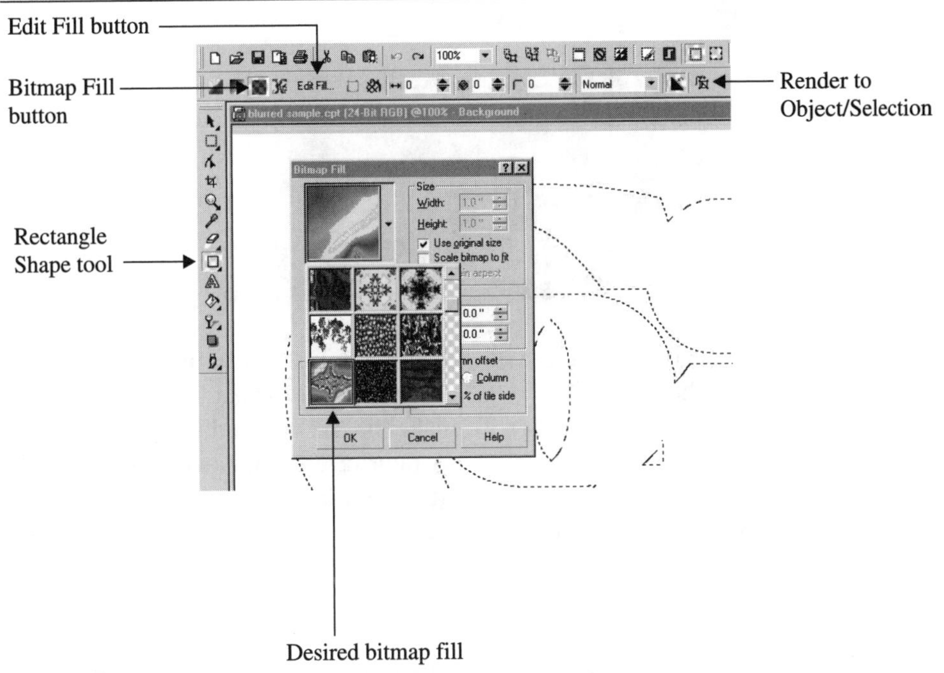

FIGURE 16-11 Gold is where you find it…especially in the Bitmap Fill dialog box

NOTE: *There is even a better way to go for the gold than through the Bitmap Fill dialog box; however, it is a little more complicated to get to. Here is the map: Select Effects | Fancy | Julia Set Explorer 2.0. From the Presets at the bottom choose Molten Titanium. Click on the color bar in Color Outside. Drag down the list until you get to Metallic and then choose Gentle Gold (phew!). Click OK (bottom-right).*

6. Place the cursor at a position in the upper-left corner of the image so that it is just outside of the mask. Click and drag the mouse until the rectangle that appears just covers the entire mask and then release the button. The result is similar to the one shown here:

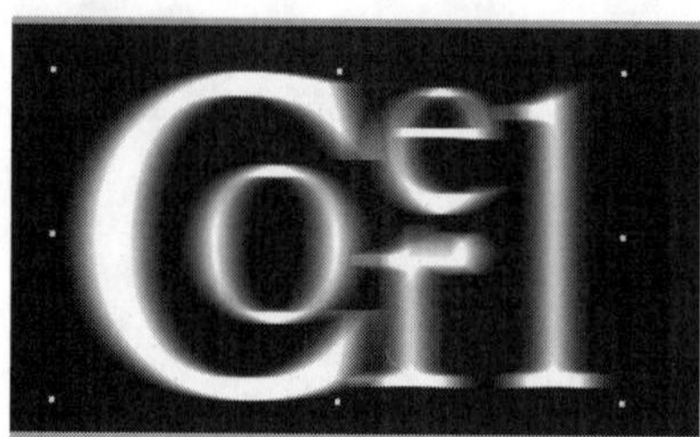

7. Choose Effects | 3D Effects | Glass. Select the Default setting and click OK. Remove the mask (CTRL-SHIFT-R) and select Mask | Load | Original. Invert the mask (CTRL-SHIFT-I). To make the background white, ensure Paper is set to White and double-click the Eraser tool. Now we need to add the hammered metal texture, so invert the mask again and choose Effects | Texture | Stone. Click the Reset button and then OK. The resulting image is shown here:

8. Apply the Texture filter again, except this time choose Plastic instead of Stone. Click the Reset button and change the Depth to 4. Click OK. At this point we have completed the hammered metal effect as shown here. The next few steps are strictly window dressing and are therefore optional.

9. To make the gold look like copper, select Image | Adjust | Hue/Saturation/Lightness and change the settings as follows: Hue: -22; Saturation: -10; Lightness: 0. Convert the masked area into an object (CTRL-SHIFT-UP ARROW).

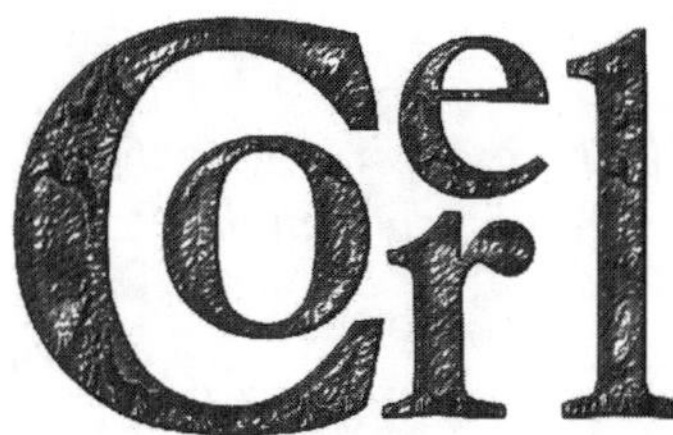

10. In the Objects Docker window, select the background. Ensure that the mask has been deleted. Select the Fill tool (F), the Bitmap fill button, and then the Edit Fill button. Next, click the Load button and choose EXERCISE\PHOTOS\WOOD background from the Corel CD. The image we are using for the background comes from the Corel Professional Photo CD named "Textures," by James Dawson. Click Open and then OK and then click the cursor anywhere on the background—we have now created a wooden backdrop. Select the Object Drop Shadow tool to create an appropriate flat shadow. I used Direction: 315; Shadow Offset: 3; Shadow Opacity: 90; Shadow Feather: 6. The final image is shown here:

The Jaggy Despeckle Filter

The Jaggy Despeckle filter scatters colors in an image to create a soft, blurred effect with very little distortion. It also smoothes out jagged edges (*jaggies*) on images. There are a few techniques that benefit from the Jaggy Despeckle filter. When applied to a photograph, it has a tendency to blur the image slightly. Jaggy Despeckle operates by performing edge detection on the image. After the filter thinks it knows where all the hard edges are, it applies anti-aliasing to the edges to give a smoother appearance.

PHOTOSHOP NOTE: *Photoshop refers to this filter by its last name—Despeckle—and it is found in the Noise rather than Blur category.*

Using the Jaggy Despeckle Filter

My favorite use of this filter is for descreening a scanned image. When halftone images are scanned, the halftone patterns have this nasty tendency to make their presence known. Here is my recipe for remove halftone screens from scanned images.

1. Scan the image at 200% of the size of the desired finished image. For example, if the final image is going to be 3 × 4 inches, scan the image in at a size of 6 × 8 inches.
2. Apply the Jaggy Despeckle filter at a low setting. This will break up the halftone pattern.
3. Resample the image to its desired size and apply the Unsharp mask filter to restore the image sharpness.

Another application of the Jaggy Despeckle filter is to correct an individual color channel that has a lot of noise or areas that are exhibiting jaggies. This happens a lot with the images you get from digital cameras and occurs mainly with the blue channel. If you use this approach to reduce noise in an image, check each channel in the image to see which one exhibits the greatest amount of noise (it's always blue, trust me). Next, with a mask tool, select the area of the channel image needing the Jaggy Despeckle filter. Be aware that applying a large setting to an individual channel or applying the filter to the entire image may cause multicolored artifacts to appear when the channels are viewed together.

The Radial Blur Filter

The Radial Blur filter changed with PHOTO-PAINT 9. For reasons that are not exactly clear (after all, it is a blur filter, right?), Corel chose to separate the Spin and Zoom options of the old filter by placing them in the Radial Blur filter and the Zoom filter, respectively. The Radial Blur filter creates a blurring effect by rotating the image outward from a central point. The area immediately surrounding the center point is relatively unaffected, while the degree of the effect increases as it moves away from the center point. The crosshair button is used to set the center point of this effect. Setting the Center Point involves clicking the button and then clicking on the image, either on the screen or in the preview window, to place the center point of the effect.

Like most of the filters, the key to using the Radial Blur filter effectively is either to use it with images whose subject matter has a symmetry that naturally flows with the flow of the filter or to control affected areas with masks.

The first session demonstrates the use of the filter with a photograph that has the subject in or very near the center to achieve an unusual effect.

1. Open the image EXERCISE\PHOTOS\SURF'S UP from the Corel CD.

2. Choose Effects | Blur | Radial Blur and, when the dialog box opens, place the center point on the surfer's face (he won't mind). Click OK. Be advised that this filter is one of the most mathematically intensive, so that it may take longer than you expect to produce the effect. After the blur has been applied, use the Local Undo tool to remove the parts of our surfer that got blurred. Now the photo really emphasizes the surfer. That's it—close the file and we will move on to the next session.

16

Zoom Filter

This filter acts in the same way as the previously discussed Radial filter, except the Zoom filter smears pixels outward from the center point. It is meant to duplicate the effect a photographer gets when moving a zoom lens in or out while taking a picture. This is a great filter for creating dynamic attention-getting effects with sports and action photos. One of the limitations of this filter is the lack of a slider control that adjusts the amount of offset about the center point. No problem—there are two easy workarounds.

Making an Action Photo

In this session we are going to learn two different techniques for applying the Zoom filter to a sports photo. The easiest technique is the one we will do first.

1. Choose File | Open and select the image EXERCISE\PHOTOS\SKI BOAT.

2. Select Effects | Blur | Zoom filter. Change the Amount setting to 20 and place the center point on the rider's body just under his forearm and click OK.

3. The filter did its job and now you have a lot of action but small details, like the rider, are lost. To correct this, select the Local Undo tool in the Toolbox and in the Property Bar change the Nib size to 50, Soft Edge setting to 100, and Transparency to 40. These settings allow you to remove portions of the just-applied effect without creating transition areas that attract attention. Remove the Zoom effect from this head and shoulders as shown here:

4. To try your hand at the second technique, select File | Revert. Select the Freehand Mask tool and place a loose mask around the rider's upper body. It is important that the mask not be too close to the body or it will produce a halo effect. Invert the mask (CTRL-SHIFT-I) and repeat step 2.

The Directional Smooth Filter

The Directional Smooth filter analyzes values of pixels of similar color shades to determine in which direction to apply the greatest amount of smoothing. You adjust the Percentage. Sounds great, right? Remember, this is a blur filter. The Directional Smooth is nearly identical in operation to the Smooth and Soften filters, although the results obtained are slightly different.

The Smooth Filter

The Smooth filter tones down differences in adjacent pixels, resulting in only a slight loss of detail while smoothing the image of the selected area. The differences between the effect of the Smooth and Soften filters are subtle and may only be apparent on a high-resolution display, and sometimes not even then.

The Soften Filter

The Soften filter smoothes and tones down harshness without losing detail. The differences between the effect of the Smooth and Soften filters are subtle and may only be apparent on a high-resolution display or in the mind of the person who programmed this filter.

Getting It All Together—the Tune Blur

This feature, which used to be called "Control," was of limited value in previous releases because you could only see the effects on a small preview window. In

PHOTO-PAINT 9, it is possible to view the results onscreen. Choosing Effects | Blur | Tune opens the dialog box called Tune Blur, shown in the following illustration. Four blur filters—Gaussian, Smooth, Directional Smooth, and Soften—can be applied to the current image. When you adjust the number of Steps, the thumbnail of each filter reflects the changes. Clicking the thumbnail of the desired filter applies the filter to the image in the Result window. To Undo the last filter application, you can click the Undo button. Repeatedly clicking this button lets you step back through a group of effects applied. To return to ground zero, hit the Reset button. Different filters can be applied multiple times using the Tune Blur dialog box.

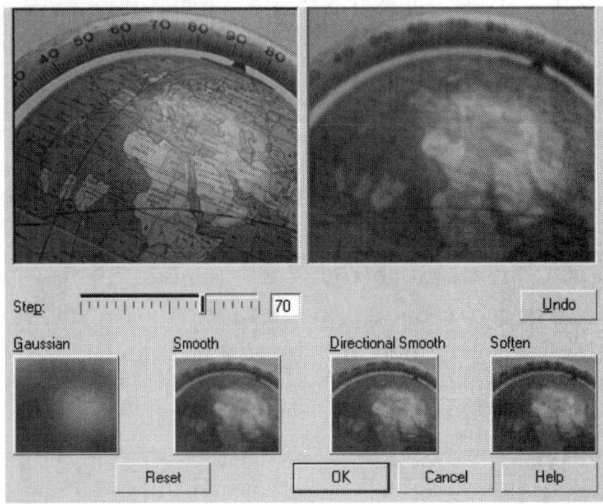

The Low Pass Filter

The Low Pass filter is not a traditional blur filter. What makes this filter unique is that it selectively blurs. It does this by detecting and removing high-frequency (highlight) portions of the photograph, leaving shadows and low-frequency detail. The dialog box contains two Slider bars, one for Percentage (0–100) and the other for Radius (1–20). The Percentage value controls the intensity of the effect, and Radius controls the range of pixels that are affected. At higher settings, the Low Pass filter creates a blurring effect, which is why it is in the blur filter section. This action erases much of the image's detail. If you need only to de-emphasize (smooth) highlights, use a lower percentage setting.

Congratulations, you have made it through yet another chapter of filters. The next chapter introduces you to the exciting world of noise. Noise—not the kind that comes from a boom box—is a fact of life in digital imagery and these filters help create, remove, and control it.

CHAPTER 17

The Transform Filters

This is a collection of eight filters that run the gamut of usefulness from essential to goofy. The first four filters listed below are located in the Color Transform category of the Effects menu. The remaining four are in the Transform category in the Image menu. Except for the Invert filter, none are available for use with black-and-white files. Other exceptions are noted in the descriptions of the individual filters.

- Bit Planes
- Halftone
- Psychedelic
- Solarize
- Deinterlace
- Invert
- Posterize
- Threshold

The Bit Planes Filter

This filter, available with all images but black-and-white, applies a posterization-style effect to each channel individually. One Corel document describes the Bit Planes filter as "a powerful tool for analyzing gradients in images." So, we should find some images with gradients to analyze, right? I have a better idea—let's find something creative to do with this little wonder. First of all, what does it actually do? The filter reduces the image to basic RGB color components (even if it is a CMYK image) and emphasizes the tonal changes.

The Bit Planes dialog box is accessed through the Color Transform category of the Effects hierarchical menu. The color plane sliders—Red, Green, and Blue—control the sensitivity of the effect. Higher settings display fewer tone changes and gradient steps. At the highest setting, the image contains a large amount of black-and-white areas, since the effect is displaying only extreme tone changes. Lower color plane settings display more tone changes and gradations. At the lowest setting, a photographic image will appear like color noise, as subtle changes are virtually random.

The color sliders can be used separately to see the tone changes in a specific component color, or together to see all tone changes. The Bit Planes filter is used to apply unusual color effects to an image—as you will soon see.

Creating Special Effects with the Bit Planes Filter

In this hands-on exercise, you will learn to use the power of the Bit Planes filter to make a mock cover for a fashion magazine. In the following steps, it is assumed that you already know how to use most of the PHOTO-PAINT tools, so the descriptions may seem somewhat brief.

1. Open the file EXERCISE\PHOTOS\RUNWAY FASHION. Click the OK button.
2. Next we need to remove the background. Load the mask I made for you by selecting Mask | Load | Model. If your mask marquee is enabled, your photo should look like the one here.

3. Make the model into an object (SHIFT-CTRL-UP ARROW) and, with the Object Picker tool, select the Background in the Objects Docker window. Choose Edit | Clear. The result is shown next.

17

4. Select the object and duplicate it (CTRL-D). Choose Effects | Color Transform | Bit Planes, which opens the filter's dialog box. Move all three sliders to 7 and click the OK button. The result follows.

5. From the Objects Docker window, select the original object. Open the Bit Planes filter again, but uncheck the Apply To All Planes option and drag the Blue slider to 5. Click the OK button. Use the Object Picker tool to position the two objects as shown next.

6. Click on the Background in the Objects Docker to select it. Choose Edit | Fill, click the Texture Fill button, and then click the Edit button. From the Samples 7 Texture Library, choose Neon Spandex. (Don't look at me—I don't make up these names.) Click the Preview button until you find a background you like, or you can enter **8357** for the Texture # setting. Click OK to return, and click OK again to apply the fill.
7. For the finishing touch, click the Text button in the Toolbox and click inside the image. Change the Paint color to Yellow by clicking on the color

swatch in the Color palette. Type **FASHION** and then change the font to Futura XBlk BT and the size to 30. With the text selected, choose the Object Drop Shadow tool and apply a shadow pointing down from the text with a Feather of 14. That's it. The result is shown in Figure 17-1.

Here are a couple of pointers about using the Bit Planes that I learned while spending way too much time on this chapter. For reasons I cannot explain, the best effects seem to occur when the filter's sliders are at their maximum, with only one of the channels (usually blue) reduced. The best images tend to be subjects filled with solid colors placed on a solid, preferably white, background color. Now, on to halftones.

The Halftone Filter

The Color Halftone filter can make a perfectly good image look as though it were printed in the Sunday comics. Available with all images except black-and-white, Paletted, L*a*b* files, Grayscale (16-bit), and RGB (48-bit), the Halftone filter simulates the effect of using an enlarged halftone screen on each channel of the

FIGURE 17-1 Call it art or pop, the Bit Planes filter allows you to create a modern style of image quickly

image. The technical description of the filters says: "For each channel, the filter divides the image into rectangles and replaces each rectangle with a circle. The circle size is proportional to the brightness of the rectangle." Aren't you glad you know that?

What *is* important to know is the Halftone filter converts color images into color halftone images. Use the Max Dot Radius slider to control the maximum radius of a halftone dot, and the Cyan, Magenta, and Yellow slider bars to control the channel angle in order to determine the color mixture and to produce a wider range of colors.

NOTE: *The Black slider is available only if the image format has a separate black channel, such as CMYK.*

So what can you do with the Halftone filter? It's great for taking existing nonphotographic clip art and making it look like the Sunday comics. Don't laugh; Roy Liechtenstein made a fortune doing the same thing. Although there is nothing to prevent you from using this filter on photographs, you'll get the best results using it on images with solid fills. Figure 17-2(a) shows a clip-art image with the Halftone filter applied at the default setting.

This technique is not limited to clip art, however. In Figure 17-2(b) I have placed a photograph over a clip-art background before applying the Halftone filter.

(a)

(b)

FIGURE 17-2 (a) Using clip art as a starting point makes the best comics. (b) The halftone effect also works on photographs

Using the Color Halftone Filter

To open the Color Halftone dialog box, select Color Transform from the Effects hierarchical menu and choose Halftone from the pop-up menu. In the Color Halftone dialog box, shown below, the Max Dot Radius slider sets the radius of a halftone dot between 2 and 10. When using this filter on small images, the minimum size of the halftone dot (2) will be more than the image can handle. I have had the greatest success with this filter when I used a 300 dpi setting for the rasterization of the image, making a big image, applying the Color Halftone filter, and resampling the image back to the desired size. The one note of caution is that the halftone effect can disappear when applied to some halftone screens used by printers.

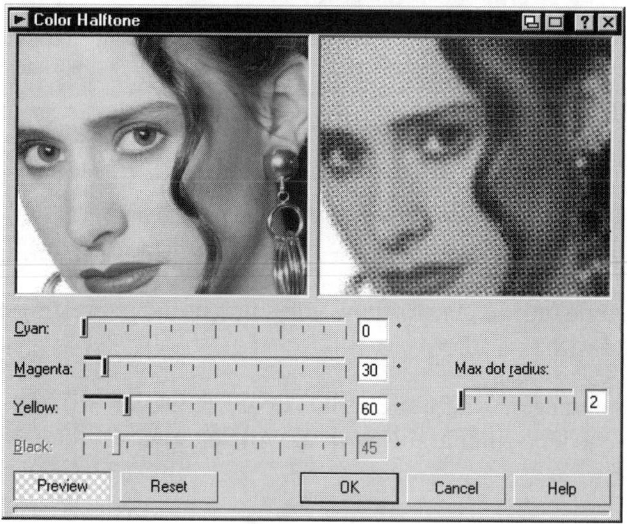

From the dialog box, you can also enter a screen-angle value for each channel, indicating the angle of the dot from true horizontal. You will see little or no difference regardless of the settings, so I recommend leaving it at the default setting. Click Reset to return all the screen angles to their default values.

The Psychedelic Filter

If it isn't bad enough that the 60's are showing up in the fashion world, we've got a 60's style filter in Corel PHOTO-PAINT. (It has been said that if you clearly remember the 60's, you weren't really there. Perhaps this filter will bring back those years.) This filter is available with all images except black-and-white, Paletted (256-color), 24-bit L*a*b*, Grayscale (16-bit), and RGB (48-bit) images. It changes the colors in selected areas or images to bright electric orange, hot pink, banana yellow, cyan, lime green, and so on. The Psychedelic dialog box, shown here, is accessed through the Color Transform category of the Effects hierarchical menu. The Level slider in the dialog box spans a range of 256 shades (0–255). Used in large doses, it can induce flashbacks.

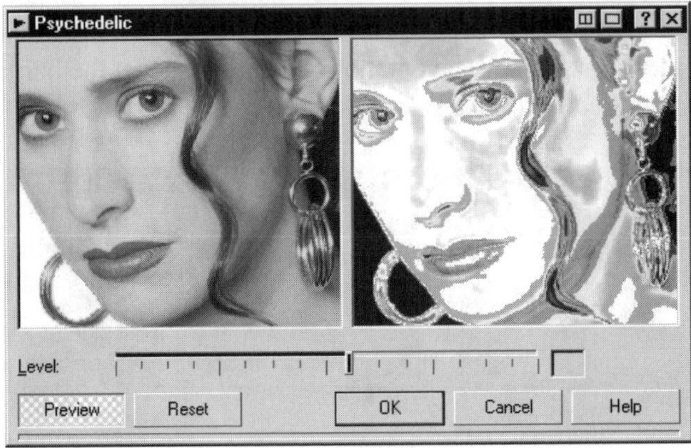

Here is a hands-on exercise to show you some of the interesting effects that can be achieved with this filter.

1. Open the image EXERCISE\PHOTOS\SERIOUS FASHION. If we apply the Psychedelic filter at this point it will be ugly.

2. Choose Effects | Sharpen | High Pass. Set Percentage to 100 and Radius to 15. Click OK, and now you can see why people don't like the High Pass filter. Although it doesn't look promising, let's see what it does to help us.

3. Select Effects | Color Transform | Psychedelic and click the onscreen preview mode so you can view the effects of the different settings. There are three different settings I want you to try. First, set the Level to 11, then move it to 33, and finally try 99. The results of the three different settings are shown in Figure 17-3.

(a) (b) (c)

FIGURE 17-3 (a) a setting of 11 gives us a blue lady; (b) a setting of 33 completely shifts many of the colors; (c) at a setting of 99, the colors are really moving toward white, giving a look like an old linoleum cut

The Solarize Filter

The Solarize filter, available with all images except black-and-white, gives the effect of a photographic negative. This effect will be more pronounced when used with color images. When applied using the maximum of 255 shades, the Solarize filter produces a negative or inverted image. It simulates an old photographic technique that required the photographic plate to be briefly exposed to sunlight outside of the camera. This resulted in the darkest areas being washed out—just how washed out was determined by how long the plate was exposed. (The emulsions they had in the old days were very, very slow.)

The Solarize filter operates in a similar fashion, except that instead of regulating the time the image is in the sun, it controls the shades of color that will be affected by the filter. The Solarize dialog box is accessed through the Color Transform category of the Effects menu. A setting of zero in the dialog box, shown next, makes the image very dark. As the setting increases, the overall image becomes brighter, emphasizing the affected parts. Not all colors are affected. In the preview image shown below, the greens of the image are the least affected.

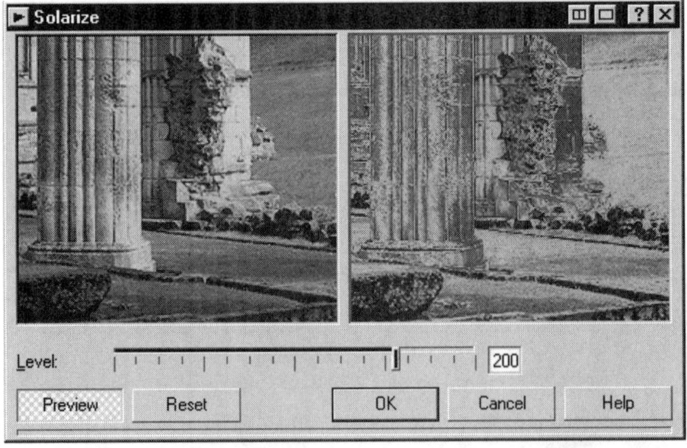

Like the Invert filter, the Solarize filter transforms colors to appear like those of a negative photographic image. Unlike with the Invert filter (which produces an absolute effect where the image colors are completely inverted), you control the intensity of the application to achieve different results.

There are a number of special effects that require the Solarize filter. One is the creation of the chrome effect that everyone seems to want these days. While the procedure to create chrome is too complex to cover in this chapter, at least now you know there really are things you can do with the filter.

The Deinterlace Filter

The next four filters are found in the Transform category in the Image menu but can also be accessed from the Effects pop-up menu found on the dialog boxes. The Deinterlace filter, available with all images except black-and-white, Paletted, 24-bit L*a*b*, Grayscale (16-bit), and RGB (48-bit), removes even or odd horizontal lines from scanned or interlaced video images. You can fill the spaces left by the discarded lines using either of two methods available on the dialog box: Duplication fills in the spaces with copies of the adjacent lines of pixels, and Interpolation fills them with colors created by averaging the surrounding pixels.

The Invert Filter

This filter, available with all images, is both the simplest and the most essential filter. The Invert filter changes the colors in an image so that they appear as a photographic negative. The Invert filter can also be used to reverse a portion of the image and to change colors.

The procedure used to make Figure 17-4 is simple. To make the image, I first masked the left half of the drawing using the Rectangle Mask. I then applied the Invert filter, after which the mask was removed and the Blend Effect tool was used to blur the line between the inverted and non-inverted areas. The text was made slightly transparent and the water drops were applied to the text using a Bitmap fill.

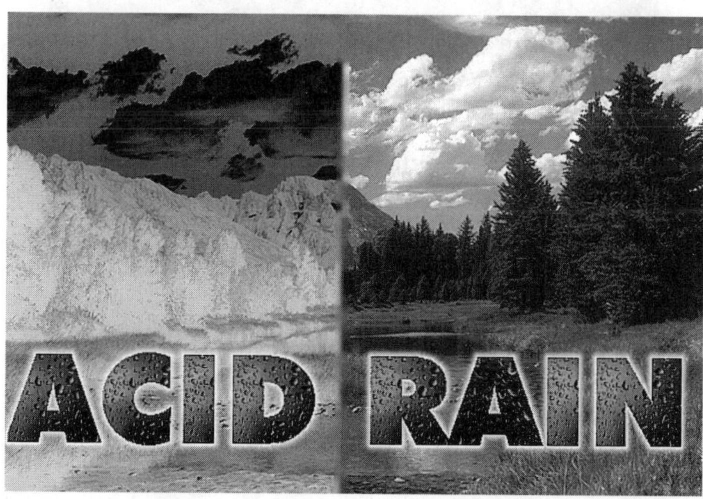

FIGURE 17-4 The Invert filter can provide a strong negative visual impact

The filter does not have a dialog box. To apply the filter, select Invert from the Transform category of the Image menu.

Making Day out of Night with the Invert Filter

Many times you will have an image that will not reproduce well in either grayscale or photocopying. While the following procedure won't work with many images, on occasion it might help you out of a bind and will make everyone think you're an artistic genius.

1. Locate the image EXERCISE\PHOTOS\COLUMNS IN ATHENS. Load the image. The original image is shown here:

2. Select Image | Transform | Invert. The result is shown in Figure 17-5.
3. Close the file and don't save the changes.

Using the Invert Filter to Change Colors

The last exercise for the Invert filter demonstrates its power to change colors. Just because you apply this filter doesn't mean the image will look like a negative. In fact, there are times when it is easier to invert the opposite of a desired color than to create it. I know that sounds dumb, but when it comes to creating gold and bronze colors, I do much better finding a rich blue and inverting it.

1. Open the image EXERCISE\PHOTOS\PATIENT CARE. The photograph is shown here:

2. Choose Image | Transform and then Invert. The result is shown next. Quite a change, isn't it? Close the file and don't save any changes.

FIGURE 17-5 An inverted image can sometimes be very effective

The Posterize Filter

This is a type of filter used throughout photo-editing. The term used to describe the breaking down of smooth color transitions in an image is called *posterization.* The Posterize filter, available for all but black-and-white images, removes gradations, creating areas of solid colors or gray shades. This function is useful when you need to simplify a complex color image without converting it to 256- or 16-color mode.

The Posterize dialog box, shown next, is accessed through the Transform category of the Image menu. Another way to use this filter is to apply the Posterize effect selectively to individual channels through the Channels Docker. Please note that individual color channels display grayscale images. Posterizing an image with a setting of three and four shades, which is a standard use of this filter, removes gradations, creating areas of solid colors or gray shades. Doing this is useful when you need to simplify a complex color or grayscale image for use as a background. The Level slider specifies the number of gray or color channels. The lower the value, the more pronounced the poster effect will be. Figure 17-6 shows a typical

FIGURE 17-6 The original photo is a well-composed color image

outdoor sailing picture, while Figure 17-7 shows the effect of applying the Posterize filter at a setting of 3.

FIGURE 17-7 The Posterize filter reduces the number of shades for a modernistic effect

The Threshold Filter

One of the many uses of the Threshold filter, available with all images except black-and-white and L*a*b*, is to convert grayscale or color images into high-contrast, line-art images. As an alternative to scanning images at high-resolution black-and-white (not grayscale), it is sometimes advantageous to scan images in as grayscale and then use the Threshold filter to remove the light gray background. Another use is to convert specific colors in an image to black, white, or both, through multiple applications.

The Threshold dialog box, shown next, is accessed through the Transform category of the Image menu. The ideal candidates for this filter are high-contrast images that do not contain large shadow areas. The photograph of London in Figure 17-8 is such an image. Figure 17-9 shows the application of the filter using the Bi-level setting. This setting converts the image into black-and-white, almost as if you were using the Convert To command in the Image hierarchical menu. The benefit to using the Threshold filter is that you can control what is converted to white and what is converted to black.

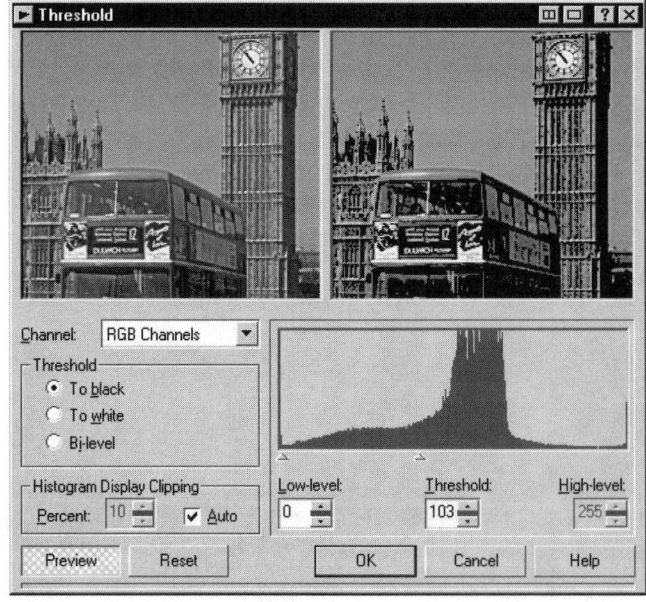

FIGURE 17-8 Original photograph of London

FIGURE 17-9 The Threshold filter reduces the image to its basic parts

Making the Filter Work Better

In the previous illustration of the Threshold dialog box, notice the triangle above the Threshold value box, in the lower right corner. Sliding the arrow back and forth helps define the image the way you want, but we can improve the results of the Threshold filter by first applying the High Pass filter (from the Sharpen group) to the image. Figure 17-10 shows the result of first applying the High Pass filter at a maximum setting. The Bi-level setting of the Threshold filter was then selected. Notice how much more detail is visible because the High Pass reduced the parts of the image that are not important when applying the Threshold filter. Figure 17-11 used the same (High Pass) image as Figure 17-10, except that the To White option in the Threshold dialog box was enabled. (A note of confession here: the skies in Figures 17-10 and 17-11 had some resulting ugly spots that I removed with the Eraser tool. I bring this up because it leads into how to operate the filter.)

FIGURE 17-10 The use of the Highpass filter prepares the image for the Threshold filter

The Threshold filter can do some dramatic things to color images that are not bound for Pleasantville (grayscale). Remember our serious model that we subjected to psychedelic torture? If we apply the filter to her at the default setting (To Black) and then go back with the Local Undo tool we get the unusual treatment shown in Figure 17-12.

If we are not content to leave well enough alone, we can take the original image and apply the To White setting to get the effect shown in Figure 17-13.

Making a Woodcut with the Threshold Filter

Woodcuts date back to the 1600s and fall in and out of popularity. The image rules discussed earlier for the Threshold filter (high contrast, no large shadow areas) still

FIGURE 17-11 The To White option in the Threshold dialog box produced this result

FIGURE 17-12 The Threshold filter adds dramatic impact to a studio photo

FIGURE 17-13 Using the To White setting gives a completely different effect

apply. So in this exercise, we are going to turn a photograph of a butterfly into a woodcut . . . of a caterpillar (just kidding).

1. Locate and open the image EXERCISE\PHOTOS\BUTTERFLY. The original photograph is shown here:

2. Just so you can see the difference the High Pass filter makes, Choose Image | Transform | Threshold. By default, the dialog box has the To Black option enabled and the Threshold set to midpoint. Ensure that you are in onscreen preview and move the Threshold slider in each direction to see if you can get a good image. Fat chance. Click the Cancel button.
3. Choose Effects | Sharpen | High Pass. Set the Percentage to 100% and the Radius to 10. Click OK. Yes, the photograph, shown here, now looks as though it were shot in Los Angeles on a smoggy day.

4. Now choose the Image | Transform | Threshold filter. Big difference, right? Now click the To White option and you should have the woodcut I promised you. Move the Threshold slider to the left and right. Notice that as the detail increases, the background become solid. You should also click the Bi-level and the To Black settings. Click OK to apply the filter. To complete the image, choose Image | Adjust | Auto Equalize. The result is shown here:

5. Close the file and don't save any changes.

TIP: *Use the Threshold filter to remove slightly gray backgrounds from grayscale images. This trick is especially good for scanning tiny black-and-white logos from slightly off-white business cards.*

Well, that wraps up our little family of color transformation filters. While these filters are not often used, when they are required, you will be very glad Corel included them.

CHAPTER 18

The Contour and Custom Filters

The Effects menu in PHOTO-PAINT 9 has two new categories, Contour and Custom, which together contain seven filters. All but one are PHOTO-PAINT veterans returning for another season; the Bump Map filter is the flashy newcomer to the PHOTO-PAINT family. You may find some of its effects irresistible. Even though most of the filters were here before, I think you will discover some really clever things you can do with them. In addition to learning about the seven filters, we will also be delving into the Paint modes to gain some understanding about not only how they work, but also what we can do with them. Our first stop will be the Contour category.

The Contour Filters

The three filters contained in this category are Edge Detect, Find Edges, and Trace Contour, as shown next. All three filters in one fashion or another detect and accentuate the edges of objects, items, and selections in your image. These filters had been located in other categories in previous releases of PHOTO-PAINT.

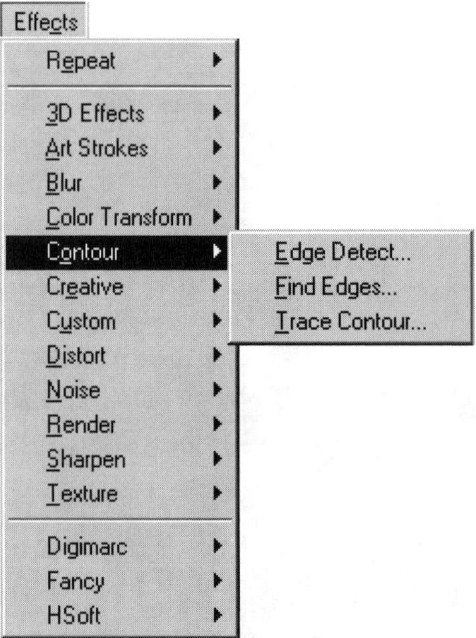

The Contour filters are equipped with controls that let you adjust the level of edge detection, the type of edges that are selected, as well as the color of the edges that you define.

The contour filters are

- **Edge Detect** This detects the edges of items in your image and converts them to lines on a single-color background.
- **Find Edges** Like Edge Detect, this determines the edges in your image and lets you convert these edges to soft or solid lines.
- **Trace Contour** This is very similar to Edge Detect, except it uses a 16-color palette rather than a single-color background.

The Edge Detect Filter

The operation of the Edge Detect filter is extremely simple. The Edge Detect filter dialog box, shown next, has only two areas in which to make a choice. One allows you to choose the Background Color. This color will replace every part of the image that doesn't have a line in it. The other is the Sensitivity slider (1-10), which determines the intensity of edge detection. As you move the slider to the right, more of the original area surrounding the edges is included. A large sensitivity value can create the appearance of noise in the finished image. When this happens, use the Eraser tool to remove the noise from the image.

I used to recommend using this filter to convert photographs for reproduction on a photocopier. With all of the improvements in PHOTO-PAINT's Mode error diffusion, discussed in Chapter 2, this filter is no longer the best choice for that.

The Edge Detect filter can work with both color and grayscale images. When used on a color image, it will generally produce lightly multicolored lines. To make all of the lines black, convert the image to a grayscale. Be aware that some images, especially low-contrast photographs, really look ugly after having this filter applied. If that happens, another alternative is to use the Band Pass filter, discussed later in this chapter, and then the Threshold filter.

TIP: *An application of contrast or equalization before applying the Edge Detect filter improves the resulting effect in most photographs.*

The image shown in Figure 18-1(a) is a good candidate for the Edge Detect filter. There is a lot of dark area, which uses lots of ink and which printers hate (because of the extra time necessary for drying). In Figure 18-1(b), I have applied the Edge Detect and, instead of using white, I chose a color (chalk) from the palette in the dialog box. I finished it by applying the Canvas texture at its default setting. While it looks only so-so in grayscale, it is much more appealing in color.

Find Edges

I love this filter; it kind of makes a colored pencil drawing. Find Edges is unlike any other filter in this chapter. Even though it is not a general image-enhancement tool, it allows you to obtain some effects that would not otherwise be possible. What is really great about this filter is something I only learned about last year from one of our PHOTO-PAINT family of readers. First, though, let's talk a little about the basics of the filter.

(a)

(b)

FIGURE 18-1 (a) The original has lots of dark, which take lots of ink. (b) The Edge Detect filter and an application of the Canvas texture give it a different (improved) look

Find Edges Dialog Box

The Find Edges dialog box contains a Level slider that controls the threshold that triggers the Find Edges filter. As the value increases, the threshold decreases, allowing the filter to include more of the edge. As the slider value decreases, less of the edge component is included, making the edges thinner and therefore lighter. You adjust the Level slider to set the sensitivity value. The higher the number, the more the edges become big, thick, ugly blobs. The Edge Type options determine the type of outline produced. For dark bold lines, choose Solid. For lighter, more diffused outlines, choose Soft.

So What Can You Do with Find Edges?

The Find Edges filter can create an outline effect. Our first example is the placement of some text over a photograph of leaves, as shown in the top of Figure 18-2. The Find Edges filter determines the edges on everything in the image and removes everything that is not an edge, including the black fill of the letters. The Level

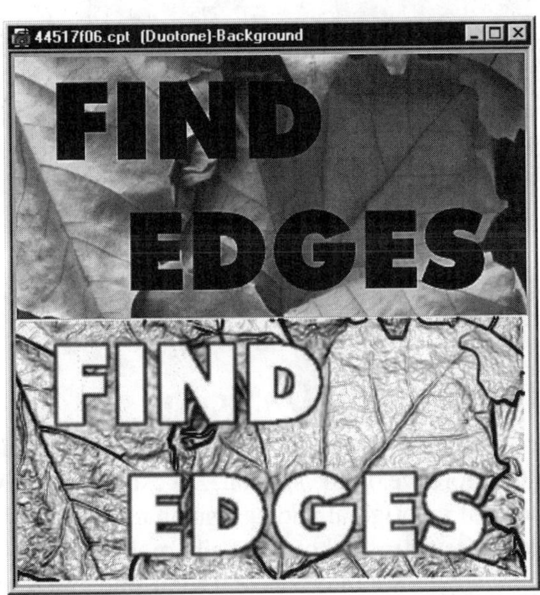

FIGURE 18-2 One use of the Edge Detect is shown when, after it is applied to a photograph (top), only an outline remains (bottom)

setting for the image shown at the bottom of Figure 18-2 was 80, which produced darker lines.

Another use is to create art. To explain this technique requires explaining Paint modes, so let's get through the last filter in the Contour menu, and then I'll show you how to become a great impressionist artist.

The Trace Contour Filter

With the Trace Contour filter you can highlight the edges of the objects in an image just like the first two filters in this category. What makes this filter different from the previous two is that you can specify which pixels are highlighted by setting a Threshold Level, as can be seen in the dialog box shown next. You can then choose an Edge Type. If you choose the Lower Edge Type, pixels with a brightness value below the threshold level are highlighted. If you choose the Upper Edge Type, pixels with a brightness value above the threshold are highlighted. The Trace Contour filter supports all color modes except 48-bit RGB, 16-bit grayscale, paletted, and black-and-white.

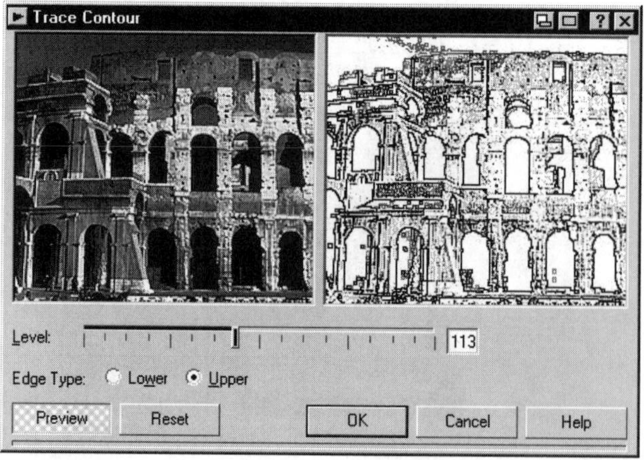

Making Art with Edge Detection

I hope you like this as much as I do. It is very simple to create and the possibilities are literally endless. Before we do the session, I'll explain what we are doing. In short, we place a copy of an original photograph on top as an object. Next, apply the Find Edges filter to it and then choose a Paint mode to combine the two. Doesn't sound like much, does it? Let's take it for a spin and find out.

1. Open the file EXERCISE\PHOTOS\COLISEUM again on the Corel CD-ROM.

2. Select the entire image with a mask (CTRL-SHIFT-A) and make an object from a copy of the masked image (CTRL-UP ARROW).

3. Choose Effects | Contour | Find Edges. Choose Soft at a Level of 70, as shown next.

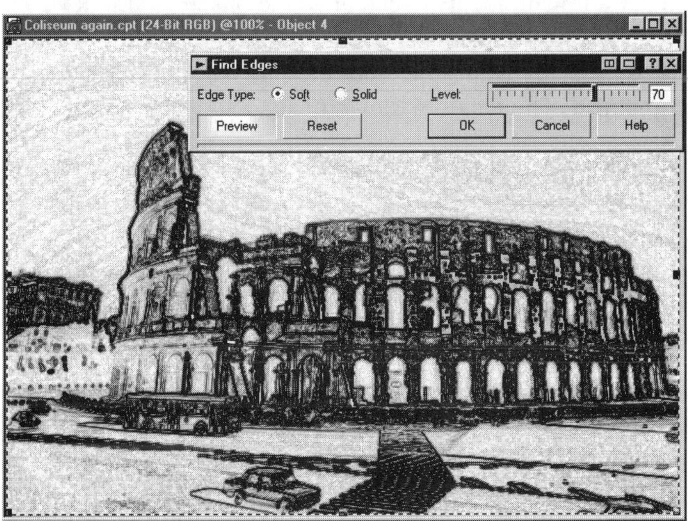

4. We picked up a lot of pixel garbage in the sky when applying the Find Edges filter. To clear out the debris, open the Level Equalization filter (CTRL-E) and change the White Input Value Clipping value (upper-right corner) from 255 to 190. Click OK.

5. From the Objects Docker, change the Paint mode from Normal to Overlay. The resulting picture, shown next, looks a lot like a pen and watercolor painting. But this is only one of 28 Paint modes available for an RGB image.

6. Change the Paint mode (also called Merge Mode) to Hue. It will take your computer a few moments to calculate the onscreen preview. The color in the top object to which we applied the Find Edge filter is showing through, so choose Image | Adjust | Desaturate. This turns off the display of color in the top object. The result is shown next.

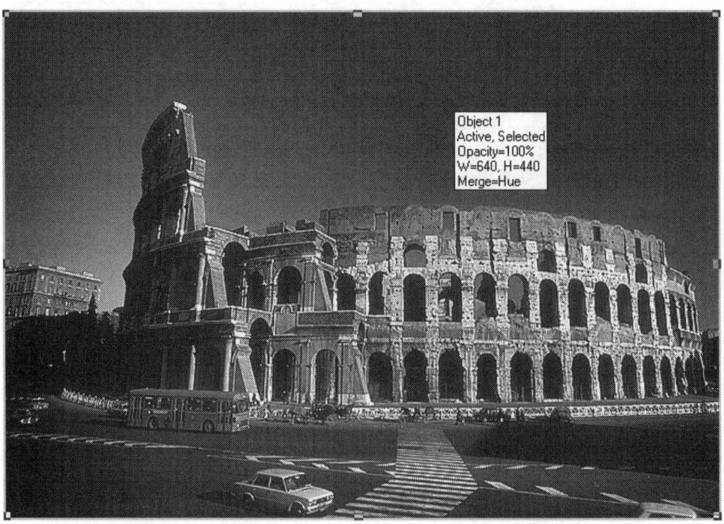

7. A last variation is to open Level Equalization again (CTRL-E), except this time change the Black Input Value Clipping (on the left) from 0 to about

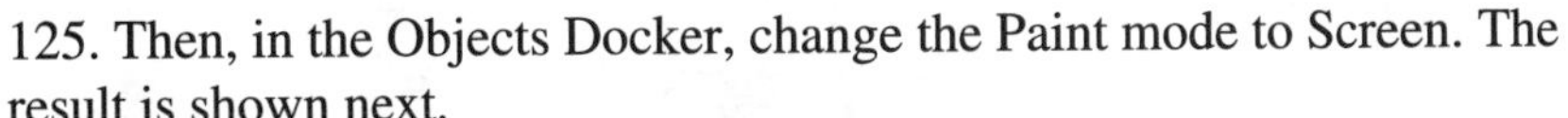

125. Then, in the Objects Docker, change the Paint mode to Screen. The result is shown next.

Here are some samples of this technique using the Find Edges filter. All of the images were photographs. In Figure 18-3, I used the same technique we applied to the Coliseum, with the only difference being that I applied the Maximum filter (under Noise) to the top layer, and then, when it was finished, I applied the Canvas texture.

The photograph of the lighthouse shown next is unique in that I used the Object Transparency tool and reduced the transparency of the upper-right corner of the top object, allowing you to see through to the original and giving the appearance of shafts of light breaking through the mist.

FIGURE 18-3 This photograph was changed into a watercolor using the Edge Detect filter

Merge Modes or Paint Modes—A Rose by Any Other Name . . .

So, what are these modes and what is their magic? Quite simply, it is a numbers game. In Normal mode the value of the pixel on top replaces the value of the pixel underneath it. That is the way things normally work in photo-editing. Since the content of the pixels is nothing more than numbers, some programmer who was working way too long at this began to wonder, what if…? For example, what if I took the value of the underlying pixel (base pixel) and added it to the value of the pixel on top (merging pixels)? The resulting value would be the sum of the two values. Give the process a descriptive name (Add), and you have a mode you can always count on to produce results that are very bright; as we already know, the higher the number the brighter the color.

Now, depending on the color depth of the image, there can be as many as 18 different modes with strange sounding names. I was going to tell you what each mode did—I really was. But the truth is, it is close to impossible to predict the results of a Merge mode, so that is why I use the onscreen preview and move down the list of modes using the up and down arrow keys (as does everyone else).

For detailed information on all of the different modes, go to Help and type in **Paint Mode**; when you see it, select it and click Display. You will have a second choice. Select Overview: Choosing a Merge Mode. It will take you to an excellent verbal and visual explanation of the Merge modes.

TIP: *Some previews of the modes take longer to display, so wait for them or you may pass them by.*

Now let's move on to the other category of filters, the Custom filters.

The Custom Filters

As I said earlier in the chapter, all of the filters in this category, shown next, are old veterans, except for the Bump Map filter. Let's look first at the three old timers: Alchemy, Band Pass, and User Defined; and then we'll look at the new kid on the block. All Custom filters are available with Grayscale and 24-bit RGB image files.

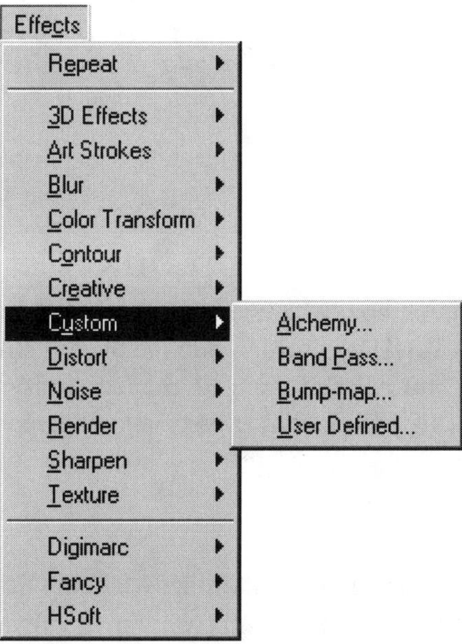

18

Alchemy Effects

The Alchemy Effects filter applies brush strokes to selected areas of your image in a precisely controlled manner. As with all filters, you can use masks to apply Alchemy Effects to part or all of an image. You can use one of the many brushes provided with the filter or create your own brushes. It's not hard to create effects with Alchemy Effects; the key to using and enjoying it is experimentation.

TIP: *As you learn how to make changes to the Alchemy Effects filter styles, I recommend limiting your changes to one at a time so that you can keep track of the effects.*

Starting Alchemy Effects

Before this release of PHOTO-PAINT, the Alchemy filter was located with the other installed filters, and it had its own unique UI. Now, it is an integrated filter, and the filter dialog box is like all of the other Corel filters, just a little more complicated. Choosing Effects | Custom | Alchemy opens the Alchemy Effects dialog box.

NOTE: *Alchemy Effects is only available with Grayscale and 24-bit color images.*

The Alchemy Effects Dialog Box

The Alchemy Effects dialog box, which is shown in Figure 18-4, is divided into two sections: control tabs and style controls. While the overall shape of the dialog box and the location of the controls have changed, the functions of the controls haven't changed since the Alchemy Effects dialog box first appeared in PHOTO-PAINT 5.

The Control Tabs

The controls on the five tabs let you customize Alchemy Effects. Only one tab can be visible at a time, but the controls on all five tabs are always active. To switch between tabs, click on the tab labels at the top.

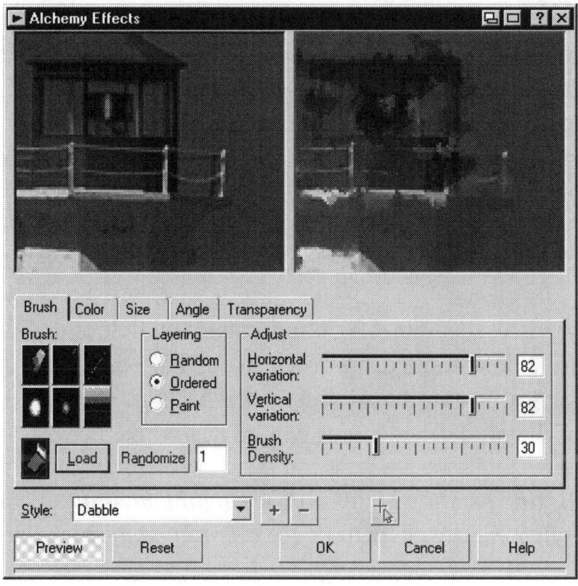

FIGURE 18-4 The Alchemy Effects dialog box

The Style Controls

The style controls, shown next, let you select one of the 75 preset styles included with Alchemy Effects, modify an existing style so that it can be saved as a new style, or remove an old style. Before you begin modifying the preset styles, I encourage you to work with them to get a feel for what they do. If you do change a style and like the results, you can save these settings as a style.

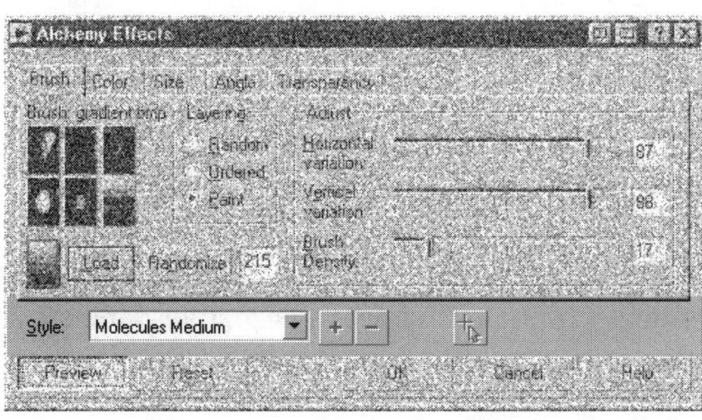

Using Styles

You can use Alchemy Effects to create an enormous variety of effects. With 30 parameters to change and the ability to use custom brushes in addition to those provided, the number of possibilities is virtually limitless. To allow you to keep track of your favorite settings, Alchemy Effects offers the ability to save all of the filter settings as styles.

Each style is a complete record of the settings of all the controls. By loading a style, you can reproduce exactly that incredible filter effect that so wowed your client.

Loading a style is very simple. You only need to click on the down arrow to the right of the Style box, and a drop-down list of 75 predefined styles appears. You can use the styles that Corel provides with Alchemy Effects, or you can create your own. Any of the predefined styles can be customized.

TIP: *Altering existing styles and saving the new settings under a new name is often the best way to begin creating your own styles.*

Creating a Custom Style

Alchemy Effects, like many paint-oriented filters, can take a long time to apply to an image. When you begin experimentation in search of the custom look that is going to win the Corel Design contest for you, consider selecting a small area of the total image by using a mask. Smaller image areas can be processed much faster. When you find the style you want, you can then apply it to a larger image to make sure all of the settings work before you save it as a style.

The following steps, only a guideline, are nonetheless a recommended procedure for creating new styles.

1. Find an existing style that is closest to the style you want to create. Use the settings from that style as your starting point.
2. Reduce the number of brush strokes (the Density) on the Brush tab until you can see what the individual brushes are doing. Using the Zoom feature of the preview window, zoom in on individual brush strokes and make necessary adjustments to appropriate parameters (size, transparency, and so on).

3. Change the attributes on the Color control tab until you can see how the controls change each brush stroke. Once you are comfortable with the color controls, adjust your colors.
4. Increase the Brush Density (number of brush strokes) on the Brush tab until the angle of application becomes clear. Now you can adjust the brush stroke angle on the Angle tab.
5. To save a new custom style, click the Plus button. You are asked to enter a name for the new file (it may be a name of seemingly endless length, but you can only see the first 40 characters in the Style box). The current settings are saved with the name you provide, and the new style is added to the Style box list in alphabetical order.

Changing a Custom Style

To change a custom style, do the following:

1. Select the style to be changed.
2. Make the changes desired.
3. Click the Plus button.

Saving a custom style will substitute the current style settings for those of the Alchemy Effects style with the same name.

TIP: *A quick way to return to the default setting for any style is to click on the style name. Use either the up or down arrow key to move to an adjacent style and then, using the opposite arrow key, return to the original setting.*

Removing a Custom Style

To delete a custom style, you need only select it and click the Minus button. A warning box (I like to call them "second-chance" boxes) asks you if you are sure you want to delete the style. If you click OK, it's all over.

The Brush Tab

The Brush tab is the tab you see when Alchemy Effects is first opened. This tab is the heart of Alchemy Effects. The description in the Xaos Tools' Paint Alchemy manual can't be beat: "The simplest description of what Paint Alchemy does is this: It applies a whole bunch of brush strokes to your image. As a result, the shape of the brush has a profound effect on the look that is produced."

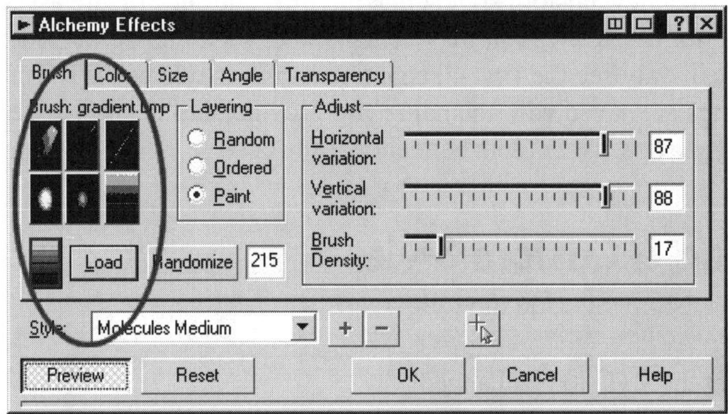

The Brush tab displays seven of the standard brushes, as just shown. When I first began working with this program, I thought the best brush for the application was displayed along with what were also likely candidates for the effects. Wow, was I wrong! The seven standard brushes that are displayed never change, regardless of the current brush that is loaded. The currently selected brush has a highlighted border around it. (On my system, it's red.)

Loading a Custom Brush

There are 30 custom brushes included with Alchemy Effects. They are located in the GRAPHICS9\CUSTOM\BRUSHES directory . Click on the Load button and the Load Brush dialog box opens, as shown next.

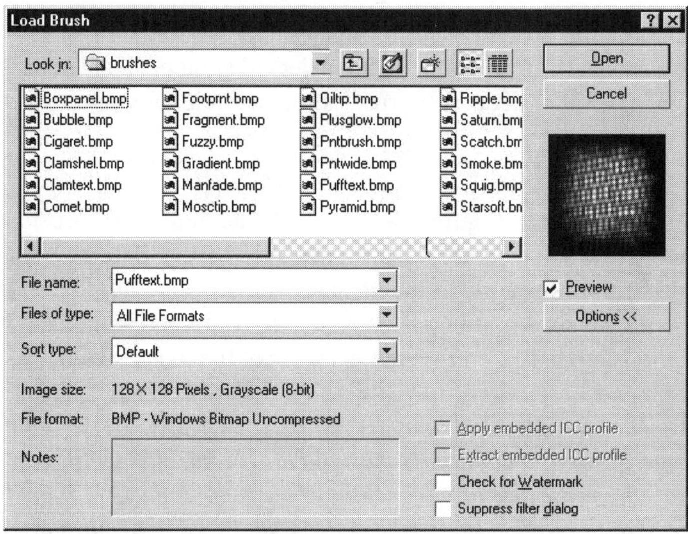

From here, you can select any BMP file as a custom brush. Here are the general rules regarding brushes.

You can load any BMP file as a brush as long as it meets the following parameters: 128 × 128 pixels (or 64 × 64, or 32 × 32), grayscale (8-bit), and 300 dpi. If any one of these parameters is different, the custom brush won't work. The exception is that the resolution can be 100 dpi. The brush icon will appear, but the resulting brush may be distorted.

Using the default settings, brushes are completely opaque where white, and transparent where black. Gray areas are semitransparent; the darker they are, the more transparent they are. Black portions of your brush will not change your image, while the white portions define the area in which your selected effect is applied.

TIP: *When making brushes in Corel PHOTO-PAINT, it is not necessary to paint white-on-black. Do all of your work in black-on-white, then use the Invert filter.*

Styles that are built around custom brushes depend on the brushes remaining in the PLGBRUSH folder. If the brush that a selected style needs is not available when the style is selected, a default brush is loaded in its place.

Density

The Density slider (refer to Figure 18-4) controls the number of brush strokes that will be applied to the selected area. Density is used to calculate how many brush strokes should be used for a given image size. The absolute number of strokes that will be used with the current image size is displayed to the right of the slider. All of the calculations are based on the image size, not the mask size.

TIP: *The time required to apply the effect depends directly on the number of brush strokes: the more strokes, the longer the effect will take. The other factor here is the size of the image or the size of the mask. If the image is large and the mask is small, the processing will still occur more quickly because the effect is only calculated for and applied to the masked area.*

Horizontal and Vertical Variation Sliders

These sliders are far from self-explanatory. They add randomness to the position of the brush strokes. When the Horizontal and Vertical Variation sliders are both set at 0, the strokes are placed on a regular grid. The Horizontal Variation slider controls side-to-side brush stroke deviation. The Vertical Variation slider controls the up-and-down motion of the brush stroke deviation. With most of the styles applying multiple brush strokes one on top of another, there are many styles that seemed to be changed very little by the positioning controls.

Layering Methods

There are three choices for layering methods in the Brush tab: Random, Ordered, and Paint.

RANDOM LAYERING The brush strokes are applied so that they randomly overlap.

ORDERED LAYERING The brush strokes are applied so that strokes that are above and to the left always overlap those that are below and to the right. With a square brush, this can look like roofing shingles. With a round brush, it can look like fish scales.

PAINT LAYERING With Paint layering, the brightest portions of each brush stroke take priority in the layering. The effect it produces is highly dependent on the shape and coloring of the brush. You will need to experiment with Paint layering to find out what it can do. It can also cause brush shape to be lost when brushes overlap too much. The overlapping brush problem is resolved by lowering the Density setting or reducing the brush size (on the Size tab) to reveal more of the brush.

NOTE: *The Paint method of layering can cause aliasing (the dreaded "jaggies") when a brush that has hard black-and-white (or bright) edges is used.*

Randomize

Before you read this, click the Randomize button and see if you can figure out what it does. For those of you who understand techno-babble, it is a *random-seed generator.* For those who do not speak the language, it is the Randomize setting, which lets you set the initial value used in the random-number generation, a value that is called the *seed number.*

Clicking the Randomize button will randomly change the seed. You can also type a number directly into the box that is adjacent to the button. As a rule, forget the button. The fine folks at Xaos Tools, however, give two examples where you might actually want to use this function, as follows.

CHANGING THE SEED TO SUBTLY CHANGE THE EFFECT You may want to change the seed if you like the general effect that Alchemy Effects is producing but not the way some brushes work. Changing the seed puts the brush strokes in slightly different random positions, and this may produce that final correction you were looking for.

MAINTAINING THE SEED TO ENSURE REPEATABILITY Using the same seed number guarantees that the exact same series of random numbers will be used for Alchemy Effects' internal calculations, and thus all of the effects will be identical. This application, however, sounds a little fishy to me. How can it be a true random-number generator if identical results occur every time you use it?

BONUS: PICKING THE NUMBERS FOR YOUR STATE LOTTERY This is my idea. The numbers that you get each time you click the Random button are indeed random, so you can use this function to pick lottery numbers in much the same way that they are picked by the state, untainted by the sentimental and unscientific "favorite numbers" technique. The only hitch is that most big-money lotteries are based on two-digit numbers. No problem. Just use the last two digits of the random number for the lottery. By the way, if you win using this method, it is only fair for you to split the winnings with me and the editors who let this piece of nonsense get into print.

Creating Your Own Brushes

Creating brushes is one of the slicker things you can do with Alchemy Effects. It is easy to make a brush, but it is a little more difficult to make one that looks great when it is used in Alchemy Effects. Here is a summary of brush-making tips from Xaos Tools and from my own experience working with Corel PHOTO-PAINT and Paint Alchemy.

You can open the existing brush files in Corel PHOTO-PAINT. (The brushes are BMP files located in the Brushes folder.) You can then use Corel PHOTO-PAINT to alter the appearance of the brushes. If you change one of the original brushes that came with the program, make sure you save it only under a new name. All of the styles in Alchemy Effects were designed to use one of these brushes. If you change the brush, you will need to reinstall PAINT to restore the original brushes. If you want to save changes you made, use Save As.

When you create a new brush from scratch, use an image size of 128 × 128 (or 64 × 64, or 32 × 32) pixels with a resolution of 300 dpi. Also, remember to make the image a grayscale. If the brush you create is too large, it will not load into Alchemy Effects.

TIP: *To change the brush that is used by a style, select the style before you select the brush. Every style has a brush associated with it. If you load the brush and then the style, the style will load its own brush, forcing you to reload your brush.*

The Color Tab

You can use the Color tab, shown in Figure 18-5, to create effects such as pastel-like colors or even improved black-and-white styles.

TIP: *To create pastel-like colors using the Color tab, set the Brush Color to From Image and the Background to Solid Color (white). Then set your brush strokes to be partially transparent.*

Brush Color

Each brush stroke is a single, solid color. To determine the color of your brush strokes, use the Color tab. You can set the colors of your brush strokes by using the colors of the image you are working on or by selecting a specific color using the Brush Color controls.

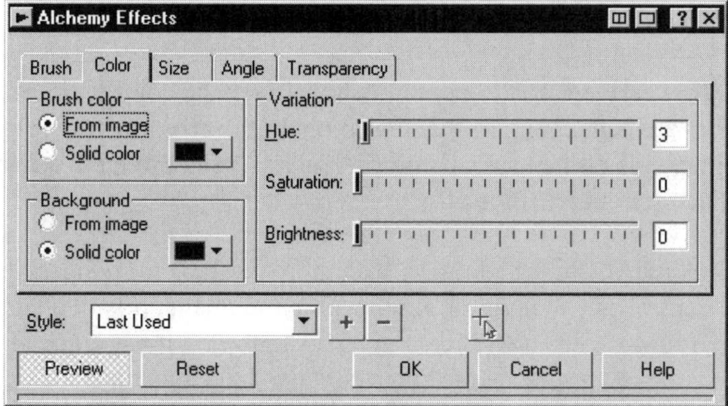

FIGURE 18-5 The Color Tab portion of the Alchemy Effects dialog box

FROM IMAGE The color of each brush stroke is based on the color of the image at the center of each brush stroke or on the color selected from the color swatch.

SOLID COLOR The color of all brush strokes is based on the color that you select. To select the color, click on the color preview window to the right of the Solid Color button to open up the standard color-selection palette.

Background

You can choose to apply Alchemy Effects brush strokes with a Paper (background) of solid color using the Background controls.

FROM IMAGE The brush strokes are applied to your image on the basis of the color of each brush stroke.

SOLID COLOR The brush strokes are applied to a Paper (background) of a solid color. To select the color, click on the color preview window to the right of the Solid Color button to open up the standard color-selection palette.

The Hue, Saturation, and Brightness Variation Controls

These controls operate in a similar manner to the Impressionism or Pointillism brush tools. They allow you to vary from the initial Brush Color settings. The amount of variation can be controlled independently for the hue, saturation, and brightness of the brush color. These controls affect the brush stroke of both the From Image and the Solid Color settings.

HUE VARIATION Hue Variation controls how much the color varies from the starting color. A small setting causes the colors in the brush to vary just a few shades to either side of the original color. A large setting produces a rainbow of colors, producing a confetti-like effect.

SATURATION VARIATION Saturation Variation has the least noticeable effect of the three. It controls the amount of gray level in the image. It isn't a simple relationship; for example, 100 percent gives lots of gray. It has a greater effect in images where the color scheme of things contains large quantities of gray. Play with this control, but expect subtle rather than great changes in the image.

BRIGHTNESS VARIATION Brightness Variation has the effect of controlling contrast. Officially, it controls the amount of variance in brightness between the starting color and the additional colors that are created by Alchemy Effects.

Image Enhancement

As with many of the other filters, you can increase the effectiveness of the Color tab by using the other controls and filters in Corel PHOTO-PAINT to modify the image before working on it with the Alchemy Effects filter. If you have a low-contrast image, you should consider applying the Equalization filter to stretch the dynamic range of the image or increase the contrast of the image to produce more dramatic results.

The Size Tab

The Size tab, shown in Figure 18-6, does just what it says: It enables you to vary the size of the brush strokes that are applied. There are several controls on this tab that are evident when you open it. The Adjust controls vary according to the Vary Brush Size selection on the right side of the dialog box. When I first opened the Vary Brush Size drop-down list, I was greeted by a lengthy list of, shall we say, interesting names. However, once you understand the thinking behind the designers at Xaos, these names might make a little more sense.

The Vary Brush Size Control

Clicking on the arrow button to the right of the name box produces a list of eight sets of brush variations. The names of the presets are the same as on the Size,

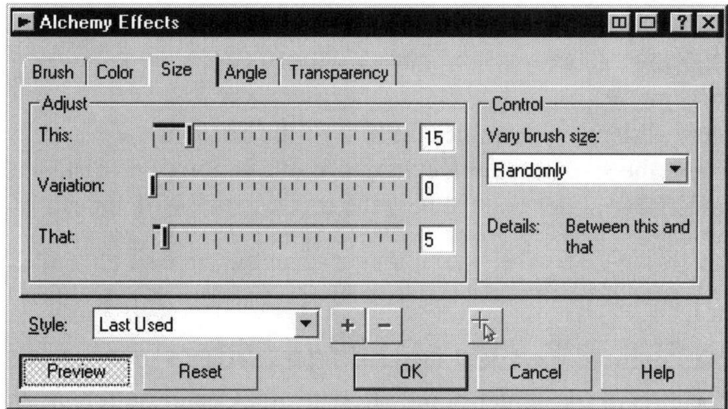

FIGURE 18-6 The Size tab of the Alchemy Effects dialog box

Angle, and Transparency tabs. What follows is a description of the action of each of these variation sets.

NO VARIATION Here's the only set that is self-explanatory. Well, sort of. When this option is selected, all of the brush strokes will be the same size. The size of the brush is set using the Size slider. The size is scaled from the actual size of the brush image selected. In practice, it is a percentage of the size of the original. For example, if the BMP file that makes up the brush is 128 × 128 pixels, a size value of 128 would produce brush strokes of the same size. If the value were set for 50 (50 percent), the brush strokes would be 64 × 64 pixels in size. Now for the weirdness.

What does a Variation slider in the Adjust section do in a No Variation setting? It overrides the No Variation option in the Control section, of course. Thus, larger numbers cause larger variations in brush size in the No Variation setting. Is that clear? I think I'm getting a headache. By the way, the preceding explanation applies to all of the Variation sliders. The Transparency slider controls the opacity of the brush stroke, providing various degrees of transparency to the brush strokes.

RANDOMLY When this option is selected, the brush strokes vary in size randomly. I love the two settings for this one: This and That. You use This and That to set the minimum and maximum size allowed. It doesn't matter which is which. The larger setting will be the Maximum and the smaller will be the Minimum. And then there is the Variation slider! This one does the same thing as the Variation slider in No Variation: It overrides the This and That slider settings.

BY RADIAL DISTANCE With this option, the brush strokes will change smoothly in size, in a circular manner. The brush strokes start out at one size in the center and gradually change to another size at the edge of the circle.

- **Center slider** Determines the size of the brush at the center of the circle. Because the size of the brush varies as a function of its distance, this slider and the Edge slider control how the brush stroke will appear.
- **Edge slider** Sets the size of the brush at the edge of the circle.

Variation Slider: Center and Edge Sliders

To set the location of the center point, click the Set Center button, as shown circled next. By clicking on the image or the preview on the place that you want to be the center of the circle, you place a small crosshair on the image at the point where you clicked.

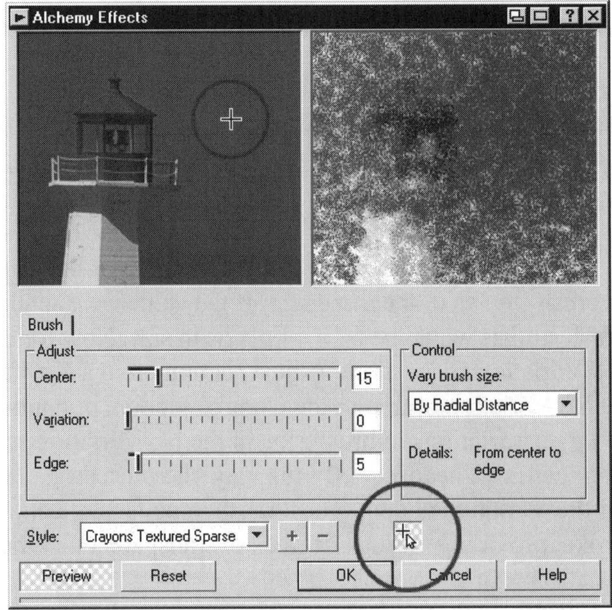

NOTE: *The Set Center point determines the center of the circle used by the Size, Angle, and Transparency tabs. It is available on the Size, Angle, and Transparency tabs when By Radial Distance is selected on each.*

BY VERTICAL POSITION With this option, the brush strokes change smoothly in size from the top to the bottom of the image. You set the sizes using the Top and Bottom sliders.

BY HORIZONTAL POSITION With this option, the brush strokes change smoothly in size from the left to the right of the image. The sizes of the brushes are set using the Left and Right sliders.

BY HUE With this option, each brush stroke is scaled according to the hue of the image at the location of each brush stroke. You set the minimum and maximum sizes using the Warm and Cool sliders. For example, the default By Hue setting for the Spatula style is Warm 5, Cool 30. The warmer colors will be limited to variations of up to 5 percent of the brush size, while the cool colors will be allowed to become up to 30 percent of brush size. So what do we mean by *cool* and *warm*? On a color wheel, the dividing line between cool and warm runs through red. Therefore, by using the By Hue option for determining brush size, brush strokes that are applied to areas of the image that contain colors on the yellow side of red are given the Warm size values. Those colors that fall on the magenta side of red are given the Cool size values. (This detailed explanation is so that you know how it works. I have yet to sit down with a color wheel that can calculate this stuff. Experiment on small images or the preview window.)

BY SATURATION With this selection, each brush stroke is scaled according to the saturation of the image color at the location of the brush stroke. You set the minimum and maximum sizes using the Unsaturated and Saturated sliders. If you are very health conscious, you can use these settings to make images that are high in unsaturates (just kidding). Setting the values for Saturated to be larger than the values for Unsaturated results in brush strokes over richly colored areas that will be larger than the brush strokes over black, white, or gray areas.

TIP: *While working with this larger/smaller brush stroke thing, remember that smaller brush strokes retain more detail of the original image and may be more desirable than larger brush strokes.*

BY BRIGHTNESS With this option, each brush stroke is scaled according to the brightness of the image color at the location of the brush stroke. You set the minimum and maximum sizes using the Dark and Bright sliders. Setting the values for Bright to be larger than the values for Dark results in brush strokes over bright areas of the image that will be larger than brush strokes over dark areas.

The Angle Tab

You use the Angle tab, shown in Figure 18-7, to set the angle of your brush stroke and to change the brush angle on the basis of its position in your image. The Adjust options vary according to the Control option chosen. You can also control the brush angle by the color content of your image, or you can change brush angle randomly. This tab is similar in operation to the Size tab.

Vary Brush Angle

The Vary Brush Angle drop-down list lets you specify what should control the orientation (the amount of rotation) of your brush strokes. You can apply all of the brush strokes at the same angle, or you can have them vary randomly, according to information in the image or by their position. The following are descriptions of what each option does.

NO VARIATION When this option is selected, all of the brush strokes will be rotated by the same angular amount. The amount of rotation (–180 to +180) is set using the Transparency slider. If Transparency is set to 0, the brush strokes will not be rotated at all; they will have the same orientation as the picture of the brush that is displayed on the Brush tab. If the Transparency slider is set to 180 degrees, the brush will be upside-down.

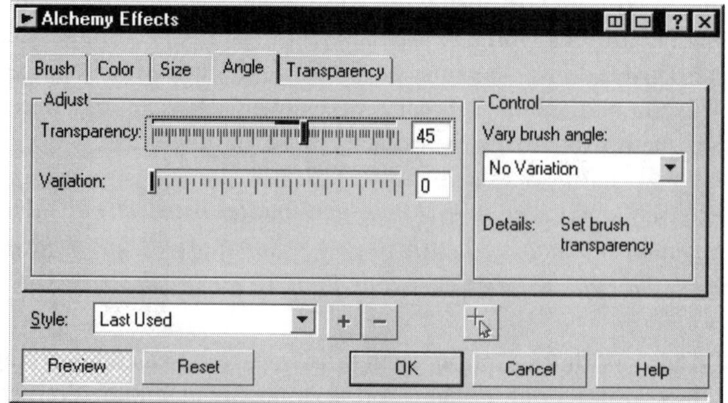

FIGURE 18-7 The Angle Tab portion of the Alchemy Effects dialog box

RANDOMLY With this option, the brush stroke angle varies randomly. You use This and That to set the minimum and maximum angles. It doesn't matter which is which. The larger setting will be the Maximum and the smaller setting will be the Minimum.

BY RADIAL DISTANCE With this option, the brush strokes will change their orientation smoothly in a circular manner, starting at one angle in the center and gradually changing to another angle at the edge of the circle. The operation of these controls is described in the By Radial Distance section on the Size tab.

BY VERTICAL POSITION Using this selection, the brush strokes change their angle smoothly from the top to the bottom of the image. You set the angles using the Top and Bottom sliders.

BY HORIZONTAL POSITION With this option, the brush strokes change their angle smoothly from the left to the right of the image. You set the angles of the brushes using the Left and Right sliders.

BY HUE With By Hue selected, each brush stroke is rotated according to the hue of the image at the location of each brush stroke. You set the minimum and maximum angles using the Warm and Cool sliders. Therefore, when using By Hue for determining brush stroke angles, areas of the image that contain colors on the yellow side of red are given the Warm size values. Those colors that fall on the magenta side of the red are given the Cool size values. If you set the angle for Cool to be larger than the angle for Warm, brush strokes over the blue areas of the image will be rotated more than brush strokes over yellow areas. (You are encouraged to experiment on small images or the preview window.)

BY SATURATION With this option, each brush stroke is rotated according to the saturation of the image color at the location of the brush stroke. You set the minimum and maximum angles using the Unsaturated and Saturated sliders. Setting the values for Saturated to be larger than those for Unsaturated results in brush strokes over richly colored areas that will be rotated more than brush strokes over black, white, or gray areas.

BY BRIGHTNESS With this option, each brush stroke is rotated according to the brightness of the image color at the location of the brush stroke. You set the minimum and maximum angles using the Dark and Bright sliders. Setting the values for Bright to be larger than the values for Dark results in brush strokes over bright areas of the image that will be larger than brush strokes over dark areas.

Angle Variation

The Variation slider in the Adjust section lets you add randomness to the stroke angles. The higher this value, the more your strokes will vary from their set angles.

The variation is calculated as degrees of offset from the brush angle. Thus, if you set Vary Brush Angle to No Variation, the Transparency slider to 90, and the Variation to 10, you will get brush strokes with an angular range of from 80 to 100 degrees.

The Transparency Tab

The Transparency tab, shown in Figure 18-8, is used to control brush stroke transparency and to change the transparency on the basis of the brush position in your image. The Adjust options vary according to the Control option chosen. You can also control transparency on the basis of the color content of your image, or you can control it randomly. This tab is similar in operation to the Size tab.

The Vary Brush Transparency Controls

See the previous section on the Size Tab for information on using these controls.

Well, I hope that wasn't too painful. If Alchemy has a problem it is that it is too powerful; you could spend half a lifetime learning to control its power. Now let's move on to the Band Pass filter.

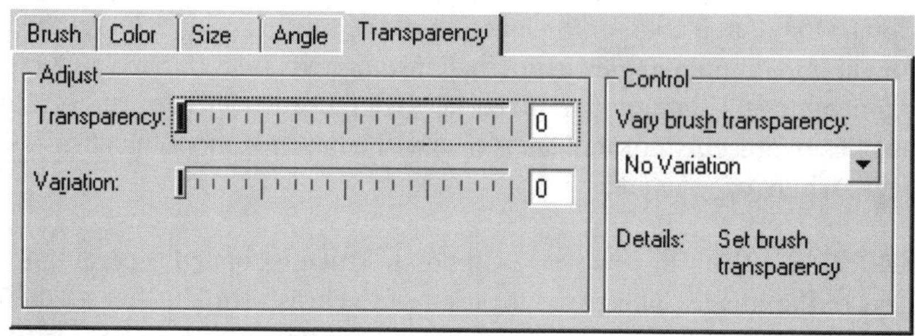

FIGURE 18-8 The Transparency tab portion of the Alchemy Effects dialog box

The Band Pass Filter

While the operation of this filter is a little difficult to comprehend, it does have some uses—I think. The Band Pass filter, which is shown next, lets you adjust the balance of sharp and smooth areas in an image. Sharp areas are areas where abrupt changes take place (for example, color changes, edges, noise). Smooth areas are areas were gradual changes take place. Smooth areas of the frequency plot represent low frequencies, while sharp areas represent high frequencies. The Frequency slider sets the frequency levels that determine the threshold. The Bandwidth slider sets the bandwidth or, in other words, the width of the frequency that components are going to pass. The filter in PHOTO-PAINT 9 works faster than any previous implementation of this filter. The previous ones were so slow it took minutes to see a preview. So, maybe between now and PHOTO-PAINT 10 I can figure out a use for this filter.

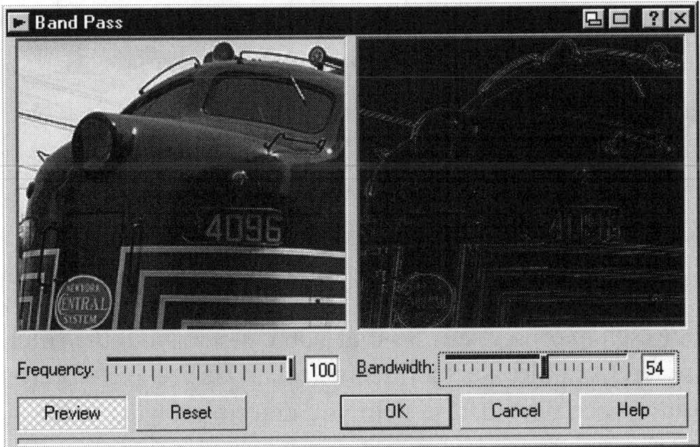

The User Defined Filter

The User Defined effect lets you "roll your own." Yes, you can make your own filters. The User Defined filter enables you to design your own *convolution kernel,* which is a type of filter in which adjacent pixels get mixed together. The filter that you make can be a variation on sharpening, embossing, blurring, or almost any other effect you can name.

The dialog box, shown in the next illustration, displays a matrix that represents a single pixel of the image at the center and 24 of its adjacent pixels. The values you enter into the matrix determine the type of effect you create. You can enter positive or negative values. The range of the effect is determined by the number of values you enter into the matrix. The more boxes you give values to, the more pixels are affected.

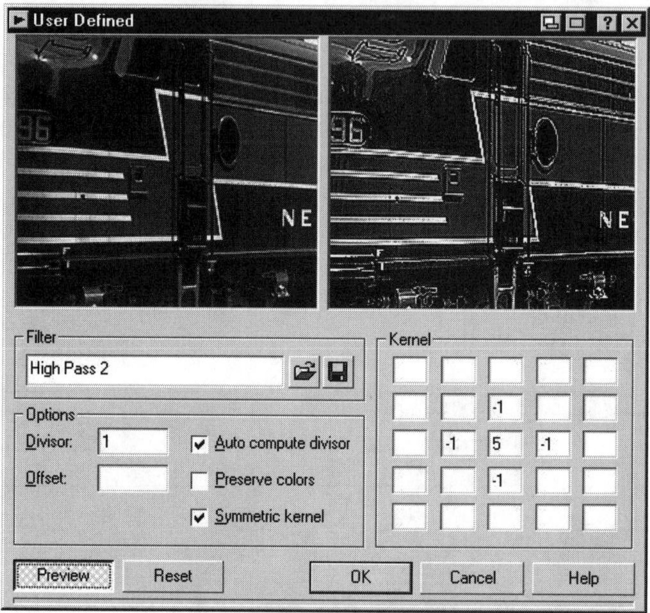

This filter is not for the faint of heart. To understand the operation of this filter would take a chapter in itself. So that you can see what the filter does, Corel has provided several sample user-defined effects. Use the Load button for this. These effects have been provided to help you determine what values to enter into the matrix.

For more information about User Defined filters, in PHOTO-PAINT depress the F1 function key, select the Index tab, type in **User**, and select User Defined Filters, Using. Finally, click the Display button.

Bump Map

The folks that make up the Corel PHOTO-PAINT development team were really excited about this jewel. Here is a filter you can get lost in. I am still trying to find all of the things that are possible with this filter, but I will share with you what I have already learned.

The Quick and Simple way to use this filter is to open the dialog box, shown next, pick a preset in the Style pop-up menu, and click OK.

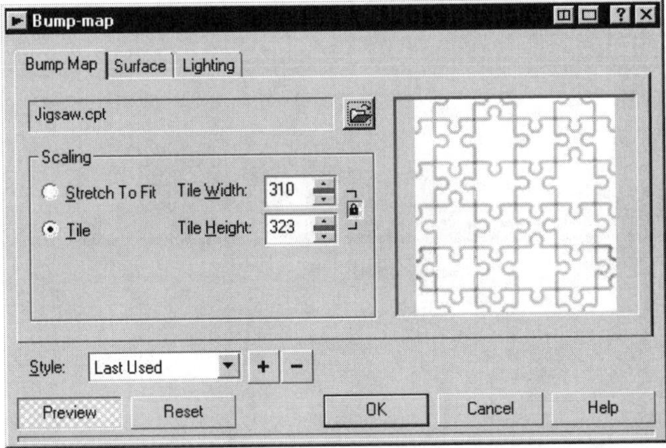

The principle underlying the operation is there is something similar to a displacement map called a bump map. It is called a bump map because it bumps or displaces pixels on the basis of the values of the pixels in the bump map. The size of the bump map on the image is controlled by the Tile Height and Width values. Figure 18-9 shows the default setting for the Jigsaw puzzle bump map.

Applying the bump map in Figure 18-9 with the Bump Map filter at its default settings results in the image shown next.

Changing the Tile Width (I reduced the Width from 474 to 149 pixels) reduces the size of the jigsaw puzzle effect as shown next.

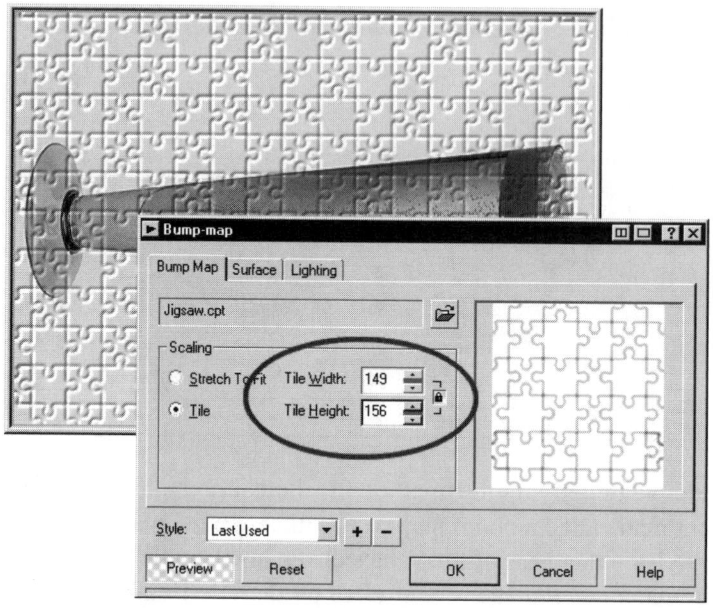

FIGURE 18-9 This simple image is a bump map image

The key to using this filter is either to select one of the predefined styles near the bottom of the dialog box or to select one of the Bump maps and create your own effects. Once you have created something exciting, you can save it as a style.

Well, that wraps up yet another chapter. I hope you're awake because the next chapter is dedicated to the one thing that America's youth loves—Noise.

CHAPTER 19

Noise Filters

N*oise,* those random pixels that appear in your digital images, is unavoidable. However, you can control it, get rid of it, and even add it to your images. It can be used to add an apparent sharpness to a soft image or "grit" to an otherwise smooth surface. Yet naturally occurring noise, which can result from poorly scanned images or from the film grain of certain film types, can be distracting. Whether noise needs to be removed or added, Corel PHOTO-PAINT provides the necessary filters. The Noise subgroup in the Effects menu has the following eight filters: Add Noise, Diffuse, Dust & Scratch, Maximum, Median, Minimum, Remove Moiré, and Remove Noise. The Tune Noise dialog box has a group of nine filters: More Spike, More Gaussian, More Uniform, Diffuse, Minimum, Median, Maximum, Jaggy Despeckle, and Remove Noise.

Noise in digital images is normally a bad thing, akin to visual static. Like an uninvited guest at a party, noise seems to show up in the worst possible places in an image. For example, during scanning, it is difficult for the scanner elements to pick out detail in the darker (shadow) regions of a photograph. As a result, these areas will contain more than their fair share of noise. All those ugly little specks on the faxes you receive are caused by noise. Because of the physical composition of noise, it tends to stand out and make itself known in a photograph, especially when you sharpen an image. In this chapter, you will learn how to minimize noise, but first let's see how useful noise can be when added to digital images.

The Add Noise Filter

Why would you want to add noise? Actually, adding noise has more uses than you might first imagine. Noise can give the effect of grit and texture to a picture. With images containing fountain fills or uniform colors, the addition of noise can make them appear more realistic. Adding noise can be helpful in softening the look of stark image areas. When you are retouching photographs that have unwanted film-grain texture, it can be helpful to add noise so the blending is less apparent.

The Add Noise filter creates a granular effect that adds texture to a flat or overly blended image. There are several neat tricks that can be done with this filter. Let's begin with a description of how it operates.

PHOTOSHOP NOTE: *If you are an old hand with Photoshop, you probably know much of this already.*

The Add Noise Filter Dialog Box

Like many of the dialog boxes, the Add Noise dialog box was redesigned in PHOTO-PAINT 9 and greatly improved. As with the other filter dialog boxes, there are three possible preview modes for this filter: Onscreen, Original/Result, and Single Result preview. The application of noise is determined by the level, density, and type of noise.

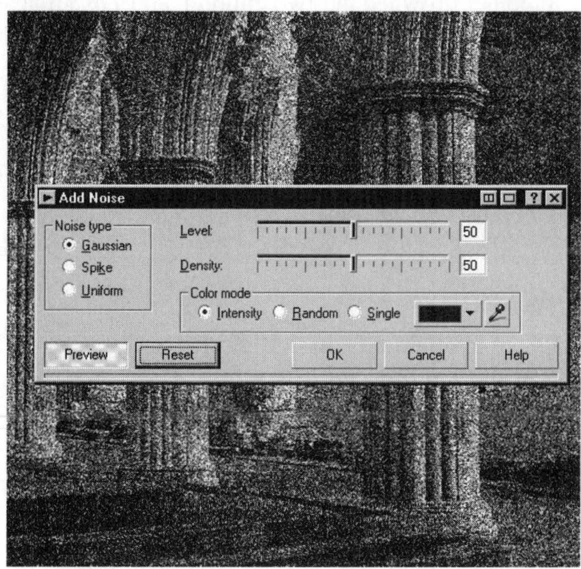

Two different settings, the Level and the Density sliders, determine the amount of noise applied to an image. The Level slider, just shown in the Single Result preview mode, controls the intensity of the noise pixels. In other words, the white component of the noise becomes much more apparent. The slider operates on a percentage scale of 0–100. A lower setting makes the noise barely visible; a higher setting moves right into dandruff. The default setting of 50 for this slider is much too high for most applications. A Level setting of 6 is recommended as a starting point.

The Density slider, operating on a percentage scale of 0–100, controls the number of noise pixels added to the image. A lower setting adds very few noise pixels; a higher setting produces something so dense you can't see the original without squinting.

This dialog box also has the Color Mode options. Intensity produces black specks, Random produces multicolored specks, Single allows you to choose a color from the pop-up color swatch, and the Eyedropper allows you to choose a color from the image. Color noise looks like someone put a rainbow into a blender and then hit the frappe button. I think selecting a specific color is a neat idea, but at this point, I haven't made much use of it. This doesn't mean there isn't one, it's just I haven't thought of one yet.

Color noise is a horse of a different color. Applying color noise to a color photograph is a great way to give a negative or distressed feeling to a photograph. A few years back, a mother drowned her two children and *Time* magazine put her on the cover. The only photograph they had was less than their usual high quality. The solution was simple—they applied color noise. Defects in the photograph were no longer apparent, and the color-speckled graininess added a strong emotional impact to an already grievous crime. Regardless of the color you pick, you must also choose what type of noise. Corel offers three choices: Heavy Metal, Grunge Rock, and Yodeling. Just kidding—no e-mails, please.

Types of Noise

Three types of noise are available: Gaussian, Spike, and Uniform. The difference between the Gaussian and Uniform noise is slight. The Spike noise appears as tiny speckles on the image.

- **Gaussian** This is the noise of choice. The other two noise options are included only because Corel is an equal opportunity employer. Technically, the filter prioritizes shades or colors (if color noise is selected) of the image pixels along a Gaussian distribution curve. (See the blur chapter, Chapter 16, for a detailed explanation of Gaussian curves.) What makes Gaussian such an excellent choice is that the distribution of the noise is visually more random and thereby more natural. The next photograph shows the application of Gaussian noise at its default setting of 50/50. You could also use 20/20, but that setting would result in blurring, as many a college student could testify.

- **Spike** This filter uses shades or colors, if color noise is selected, that are distributed around a narrow curve (spike). A thinner, lighter-colored grain that looks like black-and-white specks is produced. In fact, it is almost impossible to see, unless you use a very high setting. In the illustration shown next, I have the filter set to its maximum setting, 100/100, just so you can see it.

- **Uniform** This filter provides an overall grainy appearance that is not evenly dispersed like the Gaussian noise. In the illustration shown next, it has been set to the default setting. Use this option to apply noise in an absolutely random fashion. You will discover that this is a good choice when combined with the Emboss filter to create rough textures.

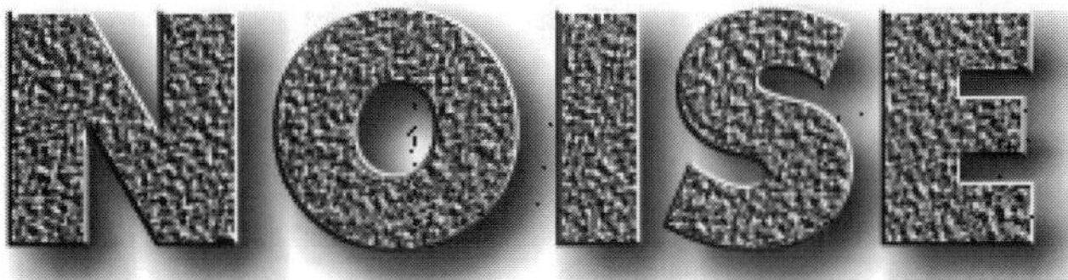

Noise Filter Effects

The noise filters are used to create a wide variety of effects, from creating textures to adding dramatic touches to an image.

Removing Banding from a Radial Fill

Many times, if a radial fill (or any gradient fill, for that matter) is applied to a large area, some banding occurs. *Banding* is the phenomenon wherein the changes of color or shades appear as bands in the image. This effect is more pronounced in low-resolution than in higher-resolution output. It is also more apparent in grayscale or 256-color fills than in 24-bit color. In Chapter 20, you will learn that while a Gaussian Blur filter could reduce or remove banding, it also blurs the subject matter. In some cases, it is better to remove the effect of banding with noise. In Figure 19-1, an eight-step fountain fill was applied to some text to simulate banding (top). Next, a Gaussian noise with a Level setting of 29 and a Density setting of 100 was applied to disguise it (bottom).

Making Metallic Effects

The noise filter not only can remove banding from fountain fills, but also can create unusual textures. In the following hands-on exercise, you will apply several different filters to some applied noise to create gold metallic characters.

1. Create a new image that is 24-bit RGB with a white background, select Photo - 5 × 7, and click the Landscape button, leaving the resolution at 72 dpi.
2. Click the Text tool button in the Toolbox. The font used is Futura XBlk BT at a size of 96. The line spacing is set to 80, so the two lines aren't too far apart, and the Center justification option is enabled. Locate the gold color

FIGURE 19-1 A little noise can hide banding in fills

in the Color Docker, click it to set the Paint color, and type **BRUSHED METAL.** Click the Object Picker button in the Toolbox.

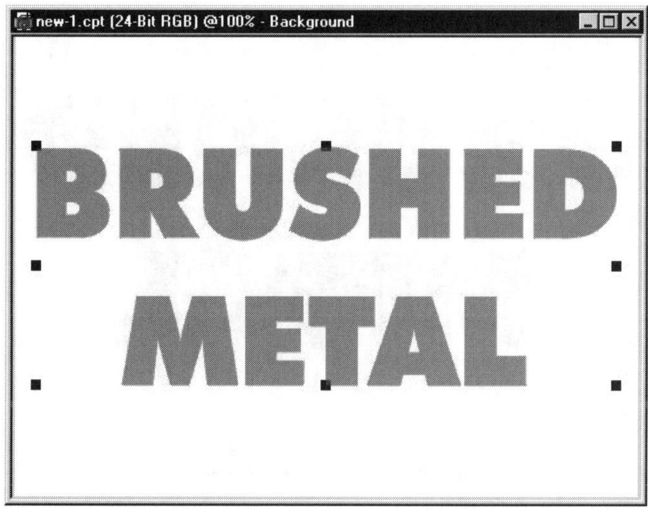

3. Open the Objects Docker window (CTRL-F7) and, with the text selected, enable the Lock Transparency by clicking its button at the bottom of the Docker window (far left).
4. Choose Effects | Noise | Add Noise. Click the Reset button and then OK. The result is shown in Figure 19-2.
5. Choose Effects | Blur | Motion Blur. In the dialog box, change the settings to Distance: 10, Direction: 120, and Off-Image Sampling: Ignore Pixels Outside Image. Click the OK button. The pixels are blurred up and to the left as shown in Figure 19-3.
6. Select Effects | 3D Effects | Emboss, and change the settings in the dialog box as follows: Emboss Color: Original Color, Depth: 9, Level: 25, and Direction: 45. Click OK. The text now has a three-dimensional quality, as shown in Figure 19-4.
7. The texture of the text now looks smooth—too smooth—so to roughen it up (without getting arrested), use the Sharpen filter as shown next. Select Effects | Sharpen | Sharpen, and change the dialog box settings to Edge Level (%): 27 and Threshold: 53. Click the OK button.

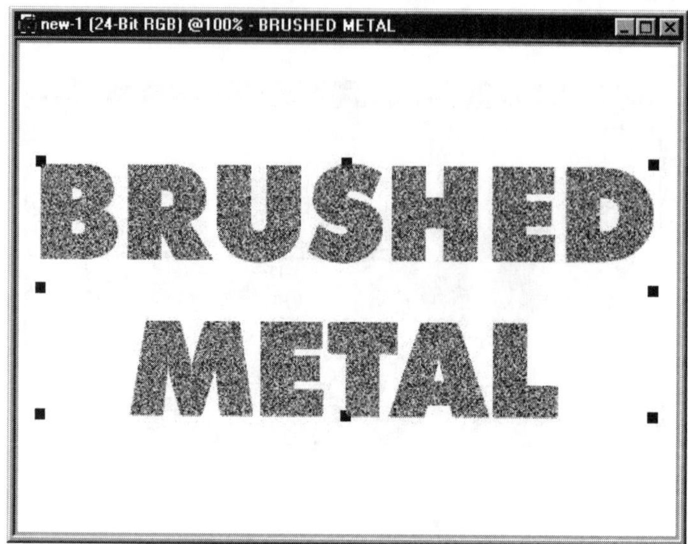

FIGURE 19-2 Addition of Gaussian noise to text adds grit to an otherwise smooth fill

FIGURE 19-3 The Motion Blur filter streaks the noise

8. Select the Drop Shadow tool in the Toolbox to add a drop shadow, as shown in Figure 19-5. Choose the Flat-BottomLeft Shadow preset in the Property Bar. Close the file and don't save it.

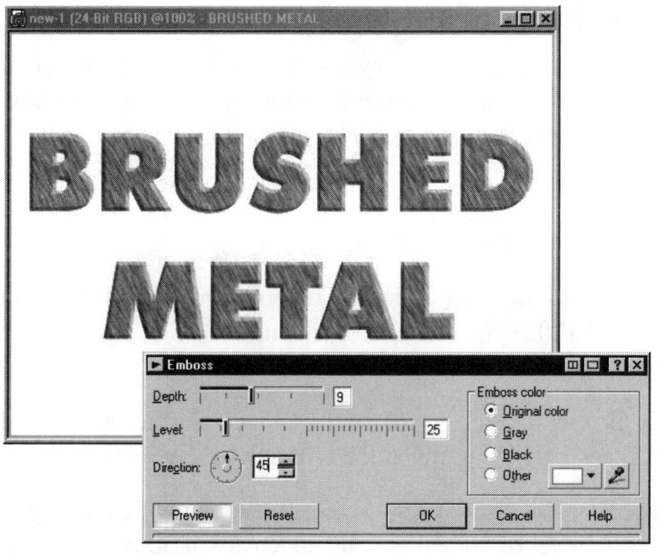

FIGURE 19-4 Embossing adds a 3-D quality

FIGURE 19-5 Sharpening and shadows increase the realism

Noise and Embossing

Noise serves as the foundation for many textures and effects. Using a combination of noise and embossing to make a stucco-like texture is a favorite technique of mine.

Try this little hands-on exercise:

1. Create a new image that is 24-bit RGB with a white background, 6 × 2 inches, at a resolution of 72 dpi.
2. Click the Text tool button in the Toolbox. The font used is Futura XBlk BT at a size of 120. Type **NOISE**. The Paint color is not important. Mine happened to be set to Sand.
3. Select the Object Picker tool. In the Objects Docker window, click the Lock Transparency button at the bottom of the window.
4. Choose Effects | Noise | Add Noise. In the dialog box, apply a Gaussian noise at a Level of 50 percent and a Density of 50 percent. Leave Intensity as the Color Mode, as shown next.

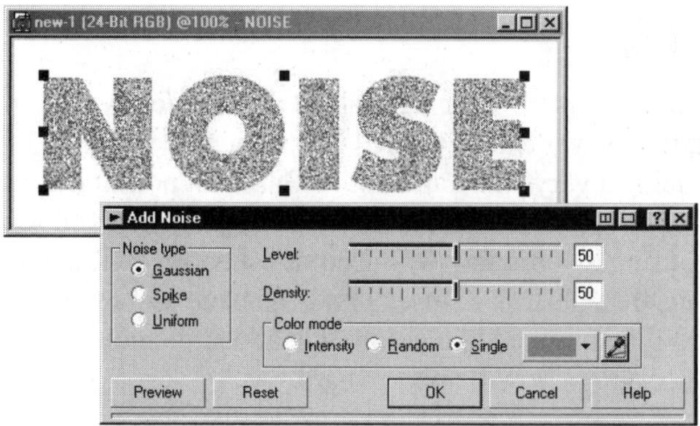

5. Select Effects | 3D Effects | Emboss, and click the Reset button. Then choose Other as the Emboss Color. Click the drop-down button and select Olive Drab or some other medium-intensity color, as shown next. If you pick a very light or dark color, you will not see the effect.

6. Click OK and then add a Drop Shadow using the Flat-BottomLeft setting. The resulting image is shown here.

Noise and Focus

Because the human eye believes images are in sharper focus when it sees areas of higher contrast, the viewer can be tricked into seeing an image as being in sharper focus by introducing a very small amount of Gaussian noise onto a soft image. This process is often referred to as *dusting* the image. When you see the results, you may think at first that nothing was accomplished. In fact, to the operator, the image appears noisier. That's because (1) it does have more noise, and (2) you know what the original looked like before you added the noise. To a first-time viewer of the photograph, it will appear sharp.

Removing Noise Without Buying Earplugs

Up until now we have been adding noise. The remaining filters in this chapter are dedicated to removing noise. While names like Diffuse, Maximum, and Minimum don't sound like the names of filters that remove noise, you will learn that removing noise is what they were designed to do. I'm not saying that all these filters actually remove noise, just that removal of noise is what they were *designed* to do.

The Diffuse Filter

The Diffuse filter scatters pixels in an image or a selected area, creating a smooth appearance. Like the Gaussian Blur, the Diffuse filter scatters the pixels, producing a blurred effect. So why is the filter listed in the Noise section of Effects? Because its operation is to reduce noise, which is correct. When an image is blurry, you can't see the noise very well, or anything else for that matter.

This filter is a no-brainer. The Level slider in the Diffuse Filter dialog box controls the amount of diffusion in the image. The Level slider in the dialog box can be set to a value between 0 and 100. The important question is what to do with the Diffuse filter. In the illustration shown next, the character in the middle is the original. One of the characters had the Diffuse filter applied three times at 100%, and the other had a Gaussian Blur applied once at a setting of three pixels. Can you see the difference? Neither can I. OK, just to save the e-mails, the one on the right had the Diffuse filter applied, or . . . was it the other one?

&&&

The Dust & Scratch Filter

The Dust & Scratch filter does a fantastic job of removing noise. It removes or reduces image noise at areas of high contrast, softening the appearance. The Dust & Scratch filter is not a magic cure-all, but it is quite effective in removing garbage from an image that would take too long to manually remove with a brush. To clean up problem areas without affecting the rest of the image, you may wish to mask the dirty area before applying the filter. Make sure you feather the edge of the mask before applying the filter so there are no visual indications that you have been playing with the image.

Most of your adjustment to this filter should be done with the Threshold slider (0–255). By setting Threshold low, you are telling the filter that all levels of contrast above the Threshold setting are considered noise. The Radius slider (1–20) determines the number of pixels surrounding the noise that will be included in the removal process. Be advised that increasing the Radius setting dramatically increases the area affected. In almost all cases you should be using settings at or near 1.

Using the Dust and Scratch Filter

Figure 19-6 is a dirty picture (no, not that kind of dirty picture). The best way to remove the dust and debris is to take the photograph (or negative, in this case), clean it, and rescan it. This option is usually not available, so the second-best solution is to use the Dust & Scratch filter. With an image this dirty, I recommend a two-stage approach. First, use the Mask Brush tool (in Additive mode) to select all the worst areas. (See Chapter 8 for tips on using the Mask Brush tool.)

The resulting image, shown in Figure 19-7, looks like someone has been putting calamine lotion on it. With these bad boys isolated, you can apply an extreme setting of the Dust & Scratch filter that would, if applied to the entire image, be excessive. In this case, the Threshold is set to 0, meaning the filter will affect every pixel selected by the mask. The Radius is set to 2; anything greater causes parts of the image to break down. The resulting image is shown in Figure 19-8.

FIGURE 19-6 This photograph has a lot of dirt and debris

FIGURE 19-7 The Mask Brush tool is used to isolate areas

FIGURE 19-8 The worst areas are improved—it's a start

To clean up the general noise, remove the mask and apply a milder setting of the Dust & Scratch filter. The easiest way to determine the optimum setting is to set the filter to operate in Onscreen Preview mode and adjust the Threshold slider until the image looks right. The best setting will be a compromise between noise reduction and loss of image detail. The image shown in Figure 19-9 is the result of using the Dust & Scratch filter on the entire image. To correct for the loss of image detail, you can either apply a small amount of the Effects | Sharpen | Unsharp Mask filter, or use the Contrast Effect tool in the Brush Tools flyout and apply the contrast only in areas that require it. (See Chapter 10 on using this Effect tool.) I did a little of both as well as using Image | Image Tone to adjust the saturation, brightness, and contrast. The finished image is shown in Figure 19-10.

Messing with Masks

The next three filters—Maximum, Minimum, and Median—are in the Noise category because they theoretically remove noise. Just because I've never seen the noise removal concept actually work using these filters, doesn't mean they don't remove

FIGURE 19-9 Applying the Dust & Scratch filter to the image reduces overall image detail

FIGURE 19-10 Applying the Contrast Effect tool locally helps recover image detail

noise. They just don't remove noise for me. So are they useless? Not in the least. They are the principal tools for a category of techniques that involved extensive operations with the individual channels in Photoshop. They were known as *channel ops,* or CHOPs for short. Before Photoshop got sophisticated, most of the effects we take for granted were created using CHOPs. Now that we have fancy filters, the need for CHOPs has diminished, but the Maximum, Median, and Minimum filters still have an important role to play in the area of mask manipulation. To give you some idea what these filters can do, the illustration shown next will serve as a reference image. This mask, which was made from text that was then deleted, is shown in Paint On Mask mode. As we discuss these three filters, we will see just what the filters can, and cannot, do.

Maximum Filter

The Maximum filter makes the lighter pixels larger and shrinks the darker ones. With the Percentage slider (0–100 percent), you can control the amount of filtering applied to the affected pixels. The greater the value, the darker the affected pixels become. The Radius slider (1–20 pixels) determines the number of pixels that are successively selected and affected. In the next image, the Radius was set to 10 pixels and the Percentage set to 50%. The result visually demonstrates the filter action. The white area expands by 10 pixels in all directions, while the black area shrinks. However, the percentage setting dictates that the 10-pixel expansion be only 50% affected, so the expanded area is 50 percent gray. Now, what is the difference between applying the Maximum filter to a mask and using Mask | Shape | Expand? Other than the ability to control the percentage, the results are identical.

The Minimum Filter

Quite simply, the Minimum filter is the evil twin of the Maximum filter. It makes the lighter pixels smaller and the darker ones larger. When applied to a mask in Paint On Mask mode, the white portion of the mask shrinks. Applying the Minimum filter to a mask is equivalent to choosing Mask | Shape | Reduce, except for the ability to modify the percentage of effect. In the illustration shown next, we have applied the Minimum filter to the original mask at a Percentage of 50% and a Radius of 10 pixels. Notice that with both filters, the expansion or reduction of the mask does not follow the shape of the original very well. That is because the greater the increase, the greater the amount of distortion that is introduced into the resulting shape.

TIP: *The best way to expand or contract the mask of a single object or single character of text is to use the Mask Transform tool and drag the corner handles. This technique will not work on a string of text because the kerning (spacing between the characters) goes out the window.*

What can you do with an expanded or reduced mask? Here is a suggestion for something you can experiment with. Type some text (use a thick sans-serif text, because on thin text the effect is lost). Create a mask from the text. Next select Paint On Mask mode and apply the Minimum filter with a percentage of 50% and a Radius of 15. You now have a nice border surrounding your text. While still in Paint On Mask mode, select Edit | Fill and choose a different fill. Invert the mask and apply The Boss filter to the edge. The result is shown here:

The Median Filter

This filter simplifies the colors or shades in an image by reading the brightness of adjacent pixels of noise and averaging out the differences. Its ability to remove noise is dependent on the type of noise (sharp and high-contrast or blurred and low-contrast) in the image. One use is to smooth the rough areas in scanned images that have a grainy appearance. It does remove noise, but at the expense of making the image much softer (which sounds better than "blurry"). In Figure 19-11 the original image (left) has the Median filter applied at a radius of 5. As you can see, the noise, along with about everything else, has been removed.

This filter uses a Radius slider to set the percentage of noise removal that is applied. The filter looks for pixels that are isolated and, based on the Radius setting in the dialog box, removes them. The Median filter tends to blur the image if it is set too high. What's too high? It has been my experience that if you are working on an image smaller than a billboard, you don't want to use a setting higher than 2.

FIGURE 19-11 The original on the left and the image after the application of the Median filter

Unleashing the Real Power of Median

Based on what we have learned so far, the Median filter appears to be about as useful as a screen door in a submarine. The secret is to use it with the Paint On Mask mode. Here is a quick session that will prove my point.

1. Create a new image that is 4.2 × 2 inches at 150 dpi. Make sure the Paint is set to black, select the Text tool, and change the font to GoudyOlSt BT at a size of 72. Select Bold. Type **Antique**. Select the Object Picker tool, and center the text on the image (CTRL-A).

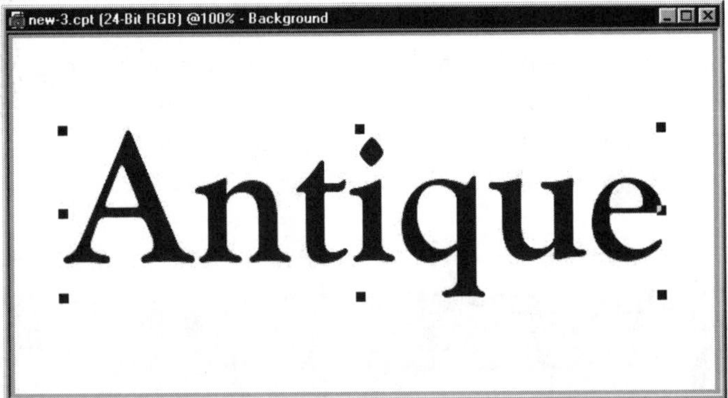

2. Create a mask (CTRL-M) and select Paint On Mask (CTRL-K). Choose Effects | Distort | Displace. The displacement map should be Rusty.PCX. Change the Horizontal and Vertical settings to 20. Click OK.

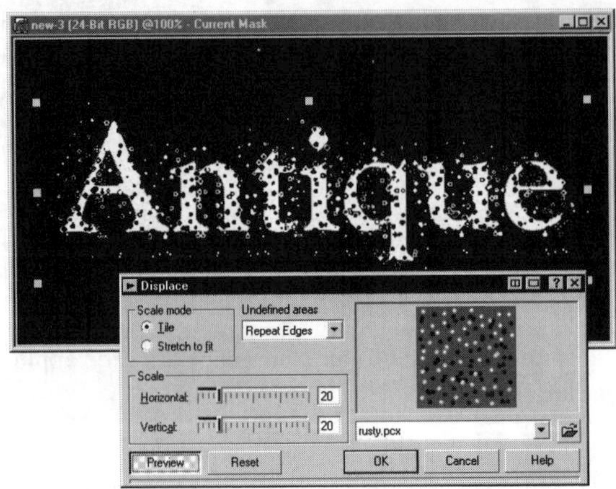

3. Choose Effects | Noise | Median. Change the Radius setting to 4 and click OK. The amount of Radius used depends on the size of the object. When I originally created this tutorial, I used a font size of 150, and the resulting Radius setting needed to be 6.

4. Exit Paint On Mask (CTRL-K) and choose Object | Crop To Mask.

That's all there is to it. Didn't I tell you this filter was useful? I also use this filter to create corroded and perforated metal effects. Here are some additional ideas. You can use the Fill tool to add a background that looks a little like parchment or old paper. The bitmap fill tile that looks like parchment in PHOTO-PAINT was too orange, so I reduced its saturation using Image | Adjust | Hue, Saturation & Brightness. For the finishing touch I applied a small amount of Noise | Spike (yep, there is a use for it) to give the paper grit. The finished image is shown in Figure 19-12.

FIGURE 19-12 The Median filter is the key to creating old weathered text like this

The Remove Moiré Filter

Moiré patterns are nasty patterns that sometimes appear when you scan halftone or screened images. You rarely see the moiré patterns in PHOTO-PAINT, because the images are resampled when you change the size of an image. These unsightly patterns can also originate when you're resizing a dithered image. As the pixels in the image are moved around, their proximity to other pixels causes patterns to develop. Removal of these patterns is also called *descreening*.

Internally, the Remove Moiré filter uses a two-stage process to break up the patterns that cause the moiré effect. First, the equivalent of a Jaggy Despeckle filter is applied to soften the entire image. Second, the filter applies some sharpening to reduce the softening produced by the first step.

PHOTOSHOP NOTE: *This filter is also known as a "descreening" filter in other scanning or photo-editing applications.*

The Remove Moiré filter provides an Amount slider, ranging from 0 to 10, to determine the amount of offset applied to the image. As the Level is increased, the shift applied to the pixels is increased. Larger amounts produce greater softness and loss of detail. The Better and Faster Quality buttons allow you to experiment if you have a really slow machine or a very large photograph (billboard). The output resolution of the filter provides the option of decreasing the resolution (downsampling). If you select to downsample the final output, it will make the image smaller and increase its apparent sharpness. It's a Yin-Yang thing; one softens, the other sharpens.

TIP: *OK, before we leave this exciting topic, let me give you my easy recipe for descreening a scanned image. Scan the original at 200% of what will be the final size. If the image has a lot of flat colors, apply the Jaggy Despeckle filter. If not, skip to the next step. Resample at 50%. Resampling the image applies anti-aliasing, which almost always breaks up any patterns in an image. Finally, apply Effects | Sharpen | Directional Sharpen at 50%. That's it.*

The Remove Noise Filter

This filter acts as if you had combined the Jaggy Despeckle filter with the Median filter. The Remove Noise filter softens edges and reduces the speckled effect created by the scanning process or from line noise in faxes. Each pixel is compared with surrounding pixels, and an average value is computed. The pixels that exceed the value of the Threshold setting in the dialog box are removed. This operates in the same manner as the Jaggy Despeckle does on objects (reducing jaggies by softening edges), but, unlike Jaggy Despeckle, it also removes random pixels (noise) in the image.

The operation of this filter is similar to the Remove Dust & Scratch filter described earlier. The most important setting on this dialog box is the Auto check box. Use it! The Auto check box, when enabled, automatically analyzes the image and determines the best Threshold setting for it. The Threshold setting cannot be changed when Auto is selected. The Threshold slider controls the amount of threshold (0–255) the program uses to differentiate between noise and non-noise. Use the preview window to see the effects of different slider settings. While this slider can be set manually, I don't recommend it.

TIP: *You can improve the performance of this filter on really trashy scans by masking the worst areas and applying the Remove Noise filter to them first. This speeds up the operation (because the area is smaller) and also keeps the filter from modifying areas that do not need to have any noise removed.*

Moiré Patterns

Moiré patterns are one of most annoying things that happen when you're working with scanned bitmap images. You see them every now and then, especially when you scan printed originals—you know the ones I'm talking about—those copyrighted pages that we aren't supposed to scan.

The physical nature of moiré lies in the interference of two or more regular structures with different halftone frequencies. You can see this effect in real life if you watch a video of a computer display. The video is recording the image of the display that is slightly different from the one used by the computer display. It is the difference between the scan frequency of the recording camera and the scan frequency of the display that produces a third frequency, called a *beat* frequency, as illustrated in the next image. Please note that the moiré pattern has been greatly enhanced to make it visible in this book. Have you figured out what it is a photograph of yet?
The bottom of a beer glass.

When an image is converted to a halftone (screened) to be printed, the two linear patterns of the screen have different frequencies, and being superimposed, they will show a frequency pattern as can be easily seen on the illustration.

Want to get more technical? When you scan an image, a line of *CCD* (photosensitive elements) digitizes it. The optical resolution of the scanner and the size of an image determine the number of elements. For example, if you scan with the 600-dpi scanner and the image is 3 inches wide, then 1,800 CCDs will take part in digitizing the image. Each CCD is a discrete unit.

When the image has a pattern (such as plaid), it is superimposed with the scanner grid (the line of CCDs) that may cause interference and result in moiré patterns. This is especially true if you scan printed originals, because usually a photograph (continuous-tone image) is printed with halftone screens. The screen frequency and a scanner resolution may mismatch, producing those dreaded moiré patterns. A misaligned or rotated original produces them, too.

Obviously the best way to remove the moiré patterns is to avoid scanning printed originals. Always choose the photographs and slides when possible.

Tuning Up the Noise

As with many of the filters in PHOTO-PAINT 9, there is a Tune function that allows you to apply and combine many different types of noise in a single spot (see Figure 19-13). It's kind of one-stop shopping for noise. Using this jewel is

FIGURE 19-13 The Tune Noise dialog box allows previewing combinations of noise—and yet it is silent

pretty straightforward. For detailed instruction on how the Tune dialog box functions, check out Chapter 13.

This concludes the noisiest chapter in the book. Of all the features in a photo-editing program, I use the filters in this category as much as the blur filters. The next chapter, on the sharpening filters, covers some of the most valuable but generally misused filters in the lot. After reading the chapter, you'll know how to carefully handle these very sharp tools.

CHAPTER 20

Sharpen Filters

Back in Chapter 16 we learned about blur filters. Now we will learn about their counterparts: the sharpen filters. The blur filters, as you recall, reduced differences between adjacent pixels, thereby softening the image. Sharpen filters do the opposite: they increase the differences, giving an apparent sharpness to the image. No matter how crisp your original photograph and how great your scanner, you will always lose some sharpness when any image is digitized. An image also loses sharpness when it is sent to an output device or when it is compressed. As a result, most images will appear "soft" when printed unless some degree of sharpening is applied. Corel PHOTO-PAINT contains several sharpening filers that can help make your images as sharp as possible. The Sharpen category of the Effects menu contains six filters that provide a wide range of sharpening effects that can be used to both improve image quality and create special effects.

The Sharpen Filters

The Sharpen subgroup of the Effects menu has the following filters:

- Tune
- Adaptive Unsharp
- Directional Sharpen
- High Pass
- Sharpen
- Unsharp Mask

Three of these filters—Adaptive Unsharp, Unsharp Mask, and Directional Sharpen—act in roughly the same manner, introducing small amounts of distortion to the image to reduce noise enhancement. The Sharpen filter is a true sharpen filter that sharpens both the image and its noise equally. The High Pass filter removes low-frequency detail and shading, while emphasizing highlights and lighter areas of an image. The Tune filter allows you to apply all but the High Pass filter to an image from the same dialog box.

NOTE: *If you have used previous versions of PHOTO-PAINT, you may have noticed that Find Edges is no longer in the Sharpen category. It seems that the filter got tired of being odd-man-out among all of the other sharpen filters, and it moved into a new category, Contour, along with Edge Detect and Trace Contour.*

Please notice that in the group of filters called the sharpen filters there is an individual filter called the Sharpen filter. As a point of clarification, when I talk about the Sharpen filter, I am referring to the specific filter and not to a general type of filter. If you find that confusing, wait until you learn that the best sharpening filter is called the Unsharp filter. Before we learn more about the individual filters, let's look at what happens when we sharpen an image.

What Is Sharpening?

Edges are what sharpening is all about. The human eye is influenced by the presence of edges in an image. Without edges, an image appears dull. By increasing the difference (contrast) between neighboring pixels, PHOTO-PAINT can enhance the edges, thus making the image appear to be sharper to the viewer, whether it is or not. While sharpening filters help compensate for images or image elements that are out of focus, don't expect sharpening to bring a blurred photograph into sharp focus. Figure 20-1 shows a photograph before sharpening was applied; Figure 20-2 shows the result of selective application using one of the filters in the sharpen group. In this example, a mask protected the background and the sharpening was applied to the architecture.

When to Apply Sharpening

Some argue that the best time to apply sharpening is when an image is scanned. I have seen several comparisons between images that were sharpened during scanning and those done with sharpen filters after the scan; believe me, the sharpening on the scanned images was visibly sharper. In fairness, the scanner was a $500,000 drum scanner and the operator was an experienced professional. Once the image is in electronic form, the decision to apply sharpening during the scanning process has already been made for you. If your image didn't have sharpening applied during the scan, then to sharpen it, you will need to use one of the filters included with Corel PHOTO-PAINT.

TIP: *Sharpening is one of the last effects you should apply. Apply it after tonal and color correction, as it will affect the results of both.*

How Sharpening Affects Noise

In Chapter 19 we learned that all computer images include noise. Noise consists of pixels that may produce a grainy pattern or the odd dark or light spot. Images from

FIGURE 20-1 The original photograph lacks detail

FIGURE 20-2 Application of sharpening brings out detail in the ancient building

photographs will always have noise. Actually, any image, including those captured with digital cameras, will have noise of some sort. The most pristine photo in your stock photo collection that was scanned on a ten-zillion dollar drum scanner will exhibit some noise. The only exception to this concept of universal noise is the Uniform color fill, which has no noise—or detail.

What does noise have to do with the sharpen filters? When we sharpen an image, we "sharpen" the noise as well. In fact, the noise generally sharpens up much better and faster than the rest of the image because noise pixels (like the tiny white specks in a black background) contain the one component that sharpening filters look for, namely, the differences between adjoining pixels. Since the act of sharpening seeks out the differences (edges) and increases the contrast, the edges of the noise are enhanced and enlarged more than the rest of the pixels in the image.

A Noisy Demonstration

To illustrate how noise rears its ugly head, I have scanned and cropped a photograph of Sandy, a good friend of mine who has always wanted to have her picture in a nationally published book (not the kind with fold-out pages). Figure 20-3(a) shows a normal scan with no sharpening applied. It is one of those "glamour shots"—always (intentionally) a little out of focus—so popular these days at the shopping malls.

After I applied an excessive amount of the Sharpen filter to the masked area, as shown in Figure 20-3(b), it looks as though she had dandruff and it got on the black curtain. The white specks in the background are the enhanced noise. The noise in the background was always there; the application of the Sharpen filter made it visible.

Specular Highlights and Dark Areas

The Sharpen filter increases the difference between adjoining pixels, eventually reaching the limits of the tonal spectrum. The white can have a maximum value of 256, and the black can't be any lower than zero. The extreme values resulting in Figure 20-3(b) caused the shades that were nearly white to be pushed to the maximum, creating the white specks we see in the background and in Sandy's hair. Light shades that have been all pushed to the same value are known by several different names: *blowouts, specular highlights,* and *tiny-white-blotches.* The effect is the same whether it is noise, dust specks on the original negative, or the small bright reflections you get from glass or highly polished metal. When the same effect happens on the dark side of the tonal spectrum (you thought I was going to say "Force," didn't you?), the result is loss of detail in the shadow region as the darker shades all become the same shade of black. This effect is often referred to as plugging up the shadows.

(a)

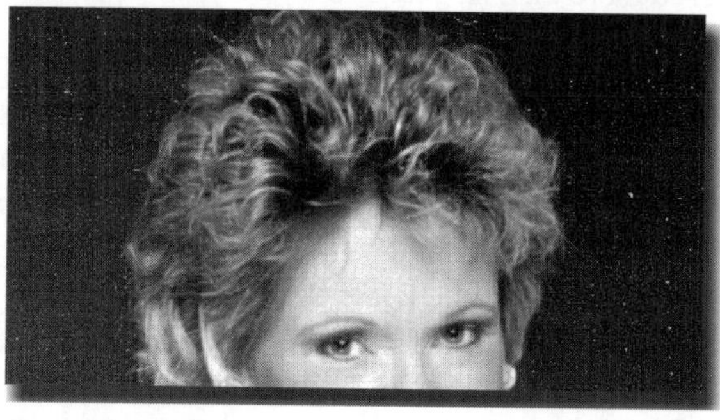

(b)

FIGURE 20-3 (a) This photograph of Sandy looks normal. (b) When sharpening (excessive) is applied, she looks like she is in a snowstorm

The Sharpen filter can very easily create these unwanted bright and dark areas. It is not the filter of preference for sharpening an image. Does this mean you shouldn't use the Sharpen filter? Not at all. It is useful for creating effects, just not for general sharpening. So, if the Sharpen filter is not recommended for sharpening an image, what filter is? The Unsharp Mask filter, of course.

Unsharp Masking Filters (USM)

In the trade, there is a group of filters generically referred to as *unsharp masking filters* (USM). The word *unsharping* is confusing to first-time users of photo-editing programs. Unsharping is named after a traditional film compositing technique that highlights the edges in an image by combining a blurred film negative with the original film positive, which results in a sharper image without enhancing the noise. In PHOTO-PAINT, the Adaptive Unsharp, Directional Sharpen, and Unsharp Mask filters fall into this category.

The Unsharp Mask filter can minimize the effect of the noise by distorting the image. Don't panic—when I say *distorting,* I am referring to the effect of toning down the sharp borders of noise while providing general sharpening of the other pixels in the image. The result is an overall sharpening of the image without enhancing the noise.

The Adaptive Unsharp and Directional Sharpen filters produce more subtle effects than the Unsharp Mask filter because the Radius setting of these filters is fixed. It is not uncommon to make several applications of these filters, even at a setting of 100 percent. It can be difficult to evaluate the effect of these filters using only the Original/Results window of the Filter dialog box; I recommend using the onscreen preview mode. Apply a relatively large setting, evaluate the effect of this setting, and then reduce the setting until the effect looks right. By now you will have forgotten what the original looked like, so apply the filter and then use Undo (CONTROL-Z) and Redo (CONTROL-SHIFT-Z) to see the "before and after" setting. At this point you can use the filter setting or just Undo and then apply the filter again. When applying any filter that sharpens the image, you must always be looking at the light or bright area of the image for blowouts (which are usually the first symptom of excessive sharpening).

The Unsharp Mask Filter

The Unsharp Mask filter, like the Sharpen filter, compares each pixel in the image to its neighboring pixels. It then looks for amounts of contrast between adjacent pixels. PHOTO-PAINT assumes that a certain amount of contrast between adjoining pixels represents an edge. After it has found pixels that appear to be an edge, it creates a light corona around those pixels. USM can also produce an undesired effect by creating halos around detected edges when applied in excessive amounts. The Unsharp Mask filter (and any other filter in the Sharpen group) is best used selectively.

The Unsharp Mask filter dialog box offers three control sliders: Radius, Percentage, and Threshold. Radius is the first control you should consider adjusting. It controls the width of the halo that is produced around each pixel. Start with an exaggerated amount and reduce it until you get the desired sharpening. The Percentage slider controls the amount or the intensity of the halo created. Increasing the Percentage value creates big tonal shifts that push the shades that make up the edge into the black and white. Threshold determines how much contrast must exist between adjoining pixels before the effect is applied. As the Threshold value (0–255) increases, the number of pixels affected decreases. In other words, the Threshold slider controls which pixels in an image will be included in the effect.

PHOTOSHOP NOTE: *If you are familiar with Photoshop's USM filter, Corel PHOTO-PAINT's Percentage slider corresponds to Photoshop's Amount control.*

The Adaptive Unsharp Filter

With the Adaptive Unsharp filter, you have local control over the sharpening process around each pixel, rather than a global sharpening amount applied to the image in general. Adaptive Unsharp uses a process that evaluates statistical differences (Adaptive) between adjacent pixels to determine the sharpening amount for each pixel. The effect of the Adaptive Unsharp filter is very similar to the other two Unsharp filters, Directional Sharpen and Unsharp Mask. Testing done while writing the book has shown some subtle differences, mainly that Adaptive Unsharp appears to produce slightly less contrast than the other two.

The Directional Sharpen Filter

This is another sharpening filter with local sharpening control. With this filter, sharpening amounts for each pixel are computed for several compass directions, and the greatest amount of these will be used as the final sharpening amount for that pixel. In other words, the Directional Sharpen filter analyzes values of pixels of similar color shades to determine the direction in which to apply the greatest amount of sharpening. I have found that the Directional Sharpen filter usually increases the contrast of the image more than the Unsharp Mask filter does. The Directional Sharpen filter also produces good sharpening but with higher contrast than either the Unsharp Mask or Adaptive Unsharp filter. I prefer to use the Directional Sharpening for any image that contains lots of strong diagonals.

The Sharpen Filter

The most important thing to remember about sharpening an image is that the Sharpen filter is rarely the best filter to use. Use one of the three USM filters discussed in the previous paragraphs. Why? Because the Sharpen filter doesn't care about noise; it just sharpens everything in the photograph. It is a powerful filter that will blow the socks off of your image if you are not careful. The Sharpen filter sharpens the appearance of the image or a masked area by intensifying the contrast of neighboring pixels. There are times when this filter may be preferred over any of the previously described filters, but they are rare.

The Sharpen filter dialog box contains three controls. The Edge Level (%) slider controls the amount of sharpening applied to the image. Use this filter at higher settings with some degree of caution. Higher values usually produce blowouts. The Threshold slider determines the level of contrast between adjoining pixels that is necessary for the filter action to occur. For example, if the Threshold value is set high, more pixels meet the minimum requirement and the sharpening effect will be applied to more of the image. If the Threshold is set low, only the high-contrast elements of the image will be affected. The Preserve Color checkbox, when enabled, prevents dramatic shifts in hue when applying a sharpening effect.

TIP: *The Sharpen filter has a much greater effect at 5 percent than the USM filters do at the 100 percent level.*

Let's Sharpen Our Sharpen Skills

After all this talk about the pros and cons of different Sharpen filters, wouldn't you like to see how they really work? I thought so. In this simple exercise, we are going to take a "soft" image and see just what the Sharpen filters can really do.

1. Open the image EXERCISE\PHOTOS\COLISEUM IN ROME. It is a photograph of the Roman Coliseum, as shown in Figure 20-4. (Did you know it had a basement?)

   Our first and most important step in this process is to see what the image needs. It is soft (meaning low contrast), but it is not out of focus. It has some areas of white (rectangular stones in the middle, the group of tourists waving at you near the back of the Coliseum), so we must watch these areas closely after we apply the sharpening. Don't make a big thing out of this. You are not looking for hidden mystical symbols in the image, just the presence of bright/light and dark/shadow areas. If there are large areas of either, we will be limited in the amount of sharpening we can apply. The other thing you should be in the habit of looking for is image detail. If this image had been out of focus, there wouldn't be any. How can you tell if there is any detail to recover with sharpening? The next step shows you how.

FIGURE 20-4 The original scan of the photograph is soft and needs to be sharpened

2. Use the Zoom tool and zoom in on one of the tunnel-looking things in the Coliseum basement. At times like this, the pop-up navigator in the lower-right corner really comes in handy. Try 600% or until the pixels look like bricks. If the pixels look like different-colored bricks like those shown below, then there is image detail that can be recovered in most cases. If the original image had been out of focus, all of the pixels would have been nearly the same color and would barely be distinguishable from one another. Of course, we've got bricks in this image; that's why I picked it. Return to 100% Zoom (CTRL-1).

3. Select Effects | Sharpen | Directional Sharpen and set the Percentage to 80. Click the OK button. The image shows marked improvement, as shown below. Look carefully at the highlight and shadows to see if there are any blowouts or large dark areas. In fact, there are not. As described earlier, Directional Sharpen has a tendency to increase the contrast slightly more than does Unsharp Mask, making it a good choice for a secondary application of sharpening. Applying sharpening twice is rarely recommended, but this image can benefit from it.

From the Effects menu, choose Sharpen and then Unsharp Mask. Set the Percentage to 20. The resulting change is subtle as shown in Figure 20-5. If you use a greater percentage, the whites in our friendly tourist's shirts will blow out (lose their shading detail and become pure white pixels). Click OK

The High Pass Filter

I placed this filter last because it is unique. Officially, the High Pass filter removes low-frequency detail and shading, while emphasizing highlights and luminous areas of an image. This filter enables you to isolate high-contrast image areas from their low-contrast counterparts. The action of the filter makes a high-contrast image into a murky gray one. Now you may rightly wonder why you would ever want a filter to do something like that. The answer is that this filter is best used in preparation for other filter actions.

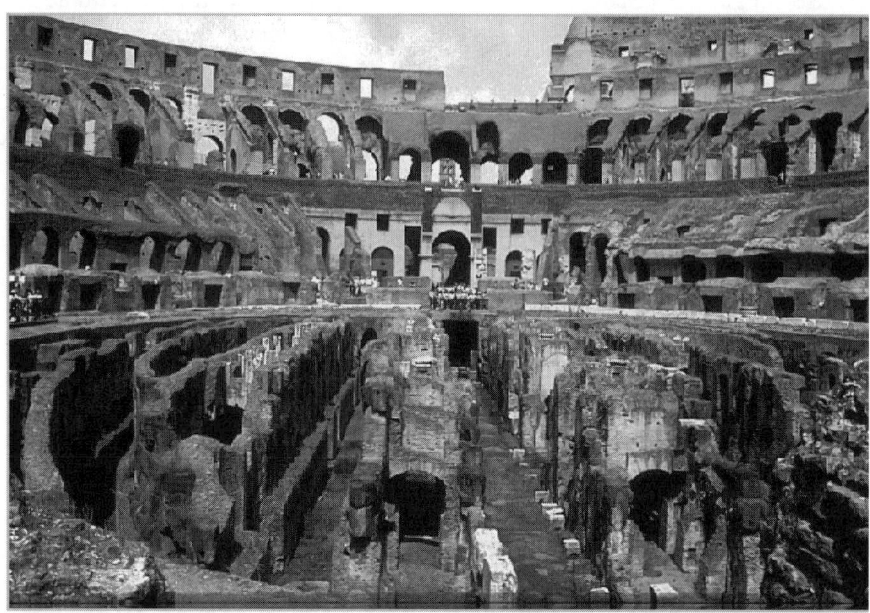

FIGURE 20-5 A little bit of sharpening makes a big difference

In the High Pass dialog box, the Percentage value controls the intensity of the effect. The default setting is 100 percent, which is far too high for many applications. Low Percentage values distinguish areas of high and low contrast only slightly. Large values change all high-contrast areas to dark gray and low-contrast areas to a slightly lighter shade of gray. At higher settings, the High Pass effect removes most of the image detail, leaving only the edge details clearly visible. If you only want to emphasize highlights, use lower percentage settings. The Radius slider determines how many pixels near the edge (areas of high contrast) are included in the effect, meaning the higher the setting, the more contrast is preserved.

Using the High Pass Filter

The High Pass filter is especially useful as a precursor to the application of the Threshold filter. By first applying different levels of High Pass to an image, you can produce a wider variety of effects with the Threshold filter. (The Threshold filter is found in the Image menu in the Transform hierarchical menu and is discussed in Chapter 17.) You can also use it to help differentiate objects in an image when creating a mask. This effect is possible because the High Pass filter sees an image in terms of contrast levels, which is one of the ways your eyes perceive images in real life. Using the High Pass filter as the first step helps in the creation of a mask of an image element that is visually unique but difficult to isolate with a mask. By applying the High Pass filter with a Percentage level of 50 percent and a Radius of 20, you can often create an outline around the object you want to isolate. After the mask is created, save it and use the Revert command to restore the image to its last saved state. Then reload the mask.

The Tune Sharpness Filter

Now that you know what all of the Sharpen filters do, you can see them all (except High Pass) at once with Tune Sharpness. While having the filters grouped together facilitates multiple application of different filters, there is a loss of control. The Edge Level (%), Preserve Colors, and Threshold controls found on the Sharpen Filter dialog box are missing in the Tune Sharpen filter as are the Radius and Threshold controls of the Unsharp Mask filter.

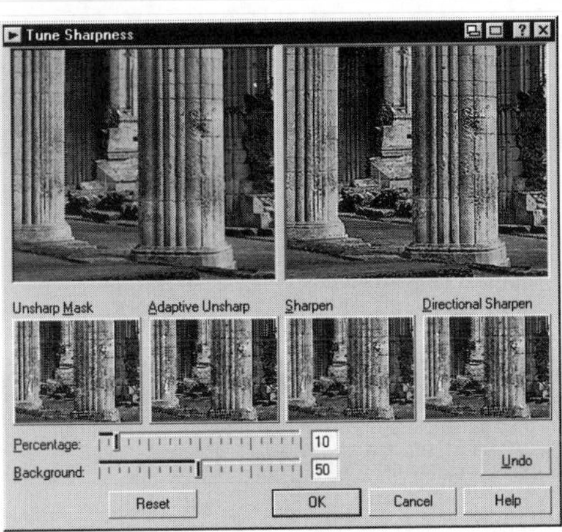

The Tune Sharpness dialog box, just shown, provides a quick way to compare the results of different filters side by side. The operation of this dialog box is explored in detail in Chapter 13.

Now you know a lot more about the sharpen filters. Please, if you remember nothing else from this chapter, remember that excessive sharpening brings out noise, lots of noise.

CHAPTER 21

The Render and Fancy Filters

The Render and Fancy filters have been in PHOTO-PAINT a long time. While the Render filters, including 3D Stereo Noise, Lens Flare, and Lighting Effects, haven't changed names or locations, the number of filters included in the Fancy category continues to diminish each release. This is because the Fancy filters are not integrated into PHOTO-PAINT, but instead they are plug-ins. As the filters in this category become integrated into PAINT, they move to other locations in PHOTO-PAINT. Back on the subject, let's look at the Render filters.

The Render Filters

Render filters are used to produce special effects, backgrounds, and novelty images. All three are available with 24-bit RGB images. Other exceptions are noted as each filter is discussed. The Render category of the Effects menu contains three filters:

- 3D Stereo Noise
- Lens Flare
- Lighting Effects

3D Stereo Noise

This filter (originally from the Kai Power Tools 2.0 collection) is my least favorite because it has become such a fad. The 3D Stereo Noise filter takes a perfectly good image and converts it to something akin to a printer failure all over your paper. By staring at the paper, you can see the original image with depth effect, similar to those stereogram posters that have gained such popularity at suburban shopping malls in recent seasons. (It's rumored that if you can stare at it for over an hour, just before the onset of a migraine, you can see Elvis.)

3D Stereo Noise was discovered a long time ago at Bell Laboratories. The researchers observed that when certain points on an image were shifted, it gave the appearance of depth. As used here, the term "stereo" should not be confused with music. Human beings were designed with stereoscopic sight—two eyes that render a single image from two slightly different angles, thus producing depth perception.

The 3D Stereo Noise effect produces the best results on images that use gray levels, are slightly blurred, and do not have extreme contrast. Don't waste precious system resources by using 24-bit color; the result will be grayscale. The 3D Stereo Noise filter generates a pixelated noise pattern that has horizontal frequencies corresponding to the gray levels of the initial image. This means that white will map to the highest frequency and appear closest to the viewer, and black will map to the lowest frequency and appear furthest away.

Preparing an Image

First, create a grayscale image that uses text and simple objects. Although you can apply the filter in all modes, the best images initially use gray levels. The smaller and more detailed the image you choose, the harder it will be to focus the stereo image. Apply a standard Gaussian Blur filter to the objects. This will soften the edges of the image for easier viewing.

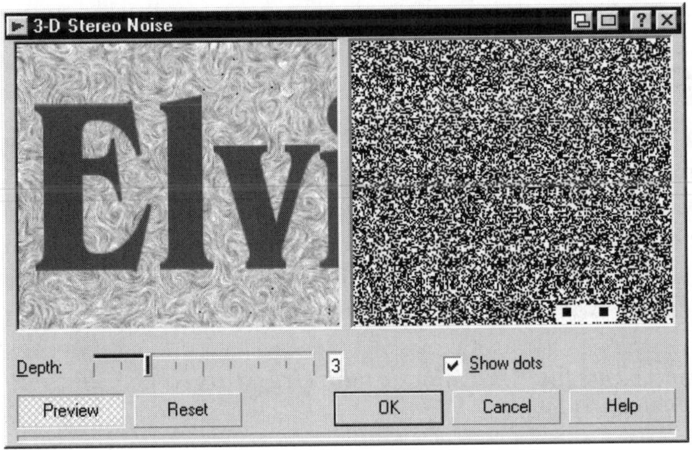

Make sure there are no masks and all objects are combined with the background. Then open the Effects menu, click in the Render category, and click on 3D Stereo Noise. There are only two options in this dialog box (which was shown just previously): a Depth slider with a relative depth range of 1–9 and a Show Dots check box, which enables the creation of two dots in a box near the bottom of the image to help the user focus on the 3-D image. The two dots that appear in the Result window are used to guide you in focusing correctly on the image; adjust your focus so that the dots fuse into one and a 3-D effect is achieved. Apply the filter to the entire image. The result will appear to be a random array of black-and-white noise.

Viewing 3D Stereo Noise Pictures

After you have created a stereo noise picture, it is time to focus your eyes and energies to see the image. I was never able to perceive the depth onscreen. Maybe you can do better here than I did. Don't feel bad if you don't see the image right away; it may take a few tries. In fact, there are some people who just cannot see it at all. There are several ways to view the image in-depth. Try enabling the Show Dots check box to produce black dots about a half-inch apart at the bottom of the image. Unfocus your eyes and gaze through the image as if you were looking into the distance. The dots you placed at the bottom will separate into four. If you focus so that the middle two dots fuse, depth should pop in or out. Another way is to try crossing your eyes to fuse the four dots into three. You may also try holding the edge of a thin object such as a floppy disk or your hand between your eyes in order to separate each eye's vision.

Lighting Effects Filter

The Lighting Effects filter lets you add one or more light sources to your image. Choose from a list of presets or create your own customized lights using the controls in the dialog box shown in Figure 21-1. You can add multiple lights and individually control the attributes of each. This is a rather intimidating dialog box. Using it is not quite intuitive. After opening the filter, the Preview window displays what the lighting effect will look like with the default or the last used setting.

NOTE: *This filter is available with Grayscale (8-bit), 24-bit RGB, and Multichannel images.*

Setting Up the Lighting Effects Filter

The first step in using this filter is to choose one of the two Type settings: Spotlight or Directional, as shown in Figures 21-2 and 21-3. The Spotlight gives the appearance of a beam light source (like a spotlight?) with clearly defined edges and a hot spot. In Figure 21-2, I have shown the dialog box using the default setting (except that I repositioned the light). Note that the text is an object and the background is unaffected by the filter. The other choice, Directional, uses a light source that is very close to being omnidirectional. It provides even lighting—unlike our spotlight. In the image shown in Figure 21-3, the Style setting in the dialog box has been set to the Texturize. You can also add and remove your

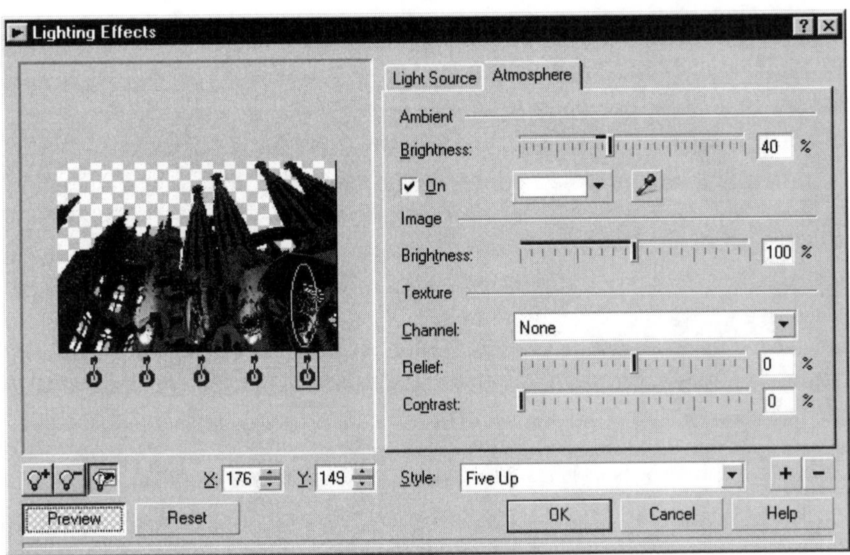

FIGURE 21-1 The Lighting Effects dialog box

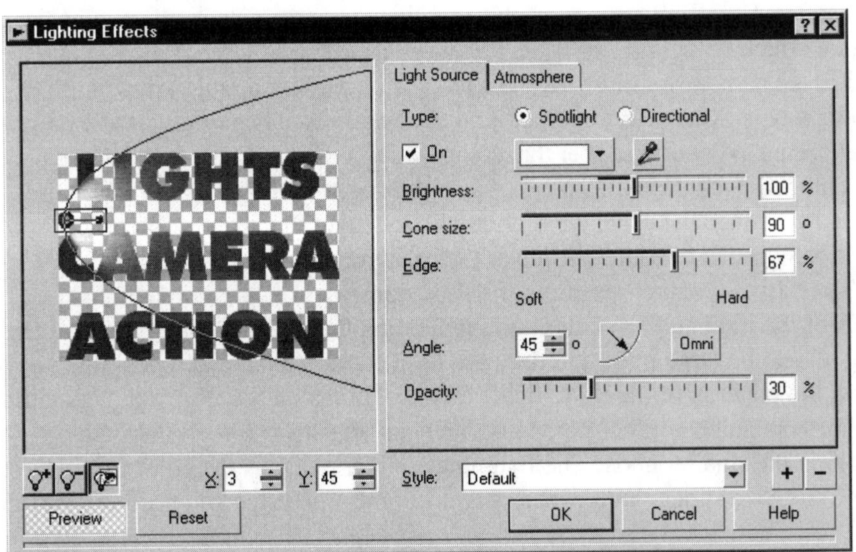

FIGURE 21-2 The Spotlight has definite edges and a hot spot—just like the real thing

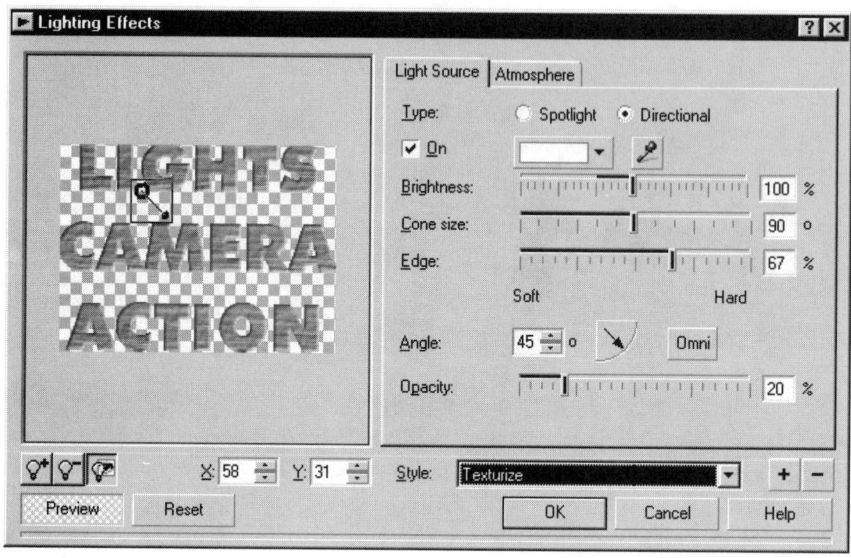

FIGURE 21-3 The Directional light is close to ambient light

own styles. Each light source has been assigned appropriate settings to achieve a unique effect.

For the purposes of illustrating the use of the various controls, we will use the Spotlight type. After selecting Spotlight, choose a color for the light; white provides a good starting point. Remember that colors add a color cast to an image. For example, I recently changed the background of a brightly-lit photograph to that of a sunset. I applied an orange tint using the Lighting Effects filter to make the foreground look like it belonged in the same picture as the background.

The barbell icon representing the light consists of a large node indicating the focus of the light and a smaller node indicating the direction and height of the light. Click the large node and drag the light source to a desired position. As you adjust the position of the light, the X and Y settings on the Position page indicate the horizontal and vertical positions. You can adjust the direction of the light by dragging the smaller node. The Brightness slider changes the color of the light. The Cone Size slider changes the range of light. The Edge slider determines how to spread the light in relation to the cone—that is, a 100 percent setting spreads the light all the way to the cone.

This filter allows you to add up to 18 additional lights. Of course, with 19 lights, the rendering time will drastically increase. Clicking the Plus button below the Preview window adds another light; clicking the Minus button removes the currently selected light.

The texture controls of the filter are located on the Atmosphere page, as shown next. You can create pseudo-shadows on surfaces that enhance the effect of the filter in some cases.

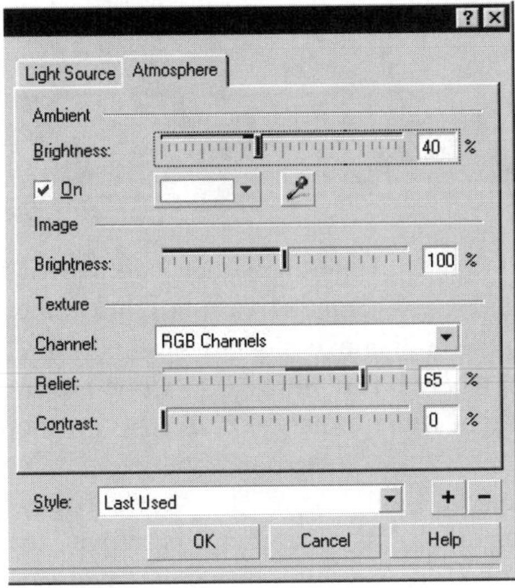

Lighting Up the Ruins

If you did the exercise in Chapter 8, you have a file that contains ruins of a cathedral with a great Gothic-looking background. If you didn't (did your dog eat your homework?), I left a copy for you on the Corel CD-ROM. The problem with the image is that the original photograph was taken in bright daylight. It isn't a problem to correct this with the Lighting Effects filter.

1. Load the file you made in Chapter 8, RUINS, and, in the Objects Docker, select the object (which should be the ruins), as shown next.

2. Select Effects | Render | Lighting Effects and, when the dialog box opens, select the Style: 5 Up. This puts five spotlights in the image pointing up. Click and drag the big node to move the lights. Click and move the smaller node to control where it is pointing. The Cone Size makes the light coming out of the spotlight wider or narrower. Add a few more lights by clicking on the lightbulb button with the plus sign (+) on it. You can position the lights anywhere you want. Figure 21-4 shows where I placed mine. Click OK to apply the effect. The final image is shown next. After you have finished, close the file. We won't be using it again.

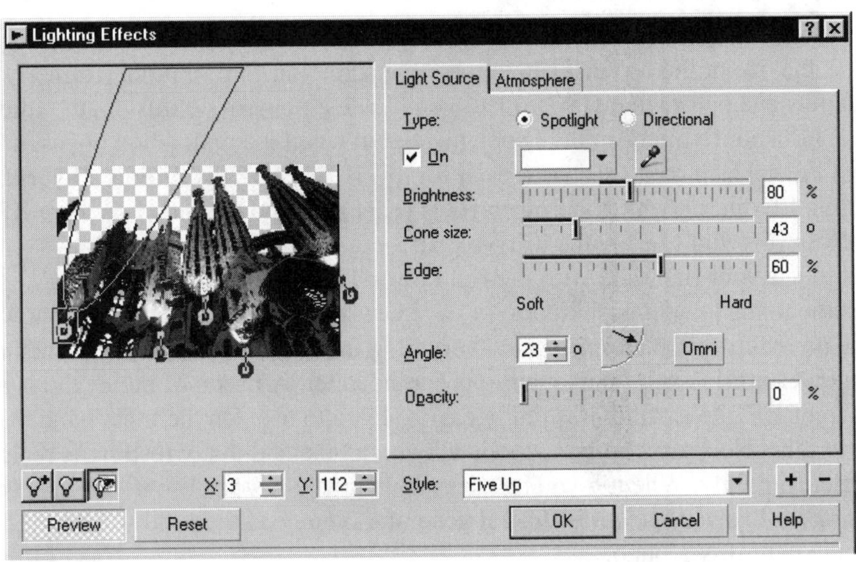

FIGURE 21-4 "Out, Damned Spot!"—Do you think Shakespeare was thinking about the spots in the Lighting Effects filter when he wrote that?

This is only a sampling of some of the many things that you can do with the Render filters. As you work with their different features, you will discover more and more things that can be done with these filters.

The Fancy Filters

The Fancy Filter neighborhood got a little lonely when PHOTO-PAINT 8 came out and the Glass and The Boss filters moved to the 3D Effects category. Now in PHOTO-PAINT 9, Paint Alchemy has moved on to the Custom category of the Effects menu. The two remaining filters, Julia Set Explorer 2.0 and Terrazzo, are two popular third-party plug-in filters in their own right. They are available with Grayscale, 24-bit RGB, CMYK, and Multichannel images.

TIP: *Are you looking for the Paint Alchemy filter? It's moved to the Custom category.*

Julia Set Explorer 2.0

This is the one of the original filters from Metacreation Corporation, (formerly Metatools and before that HSC). Just to eliminate a point of confusion, the filter is called Julia Set Explorer in the Fancy menu, but when the dialog box opens, it is called Fractal Explorer 2.0. The reason for this is simple. This filter is a hybrid of the Julia I Explorer from Kai Power Tools (KPT) 1.0 and the interface from KPT 2.0. Now you won't lie awake worrying about it.

If this is your first time with the Kai Power Tools (KPT) user interface, welcome to the jungle! Just kidding. I have heard this user interface (UI), shown in the next illustration, described as everything from the best UI on the planet to a Klingon Control Panel. I personally opt for the latter. A friend of mine who is a big fan of KPT insists that it is really easy to learn to use. On the other hand, he believes that Neil Armstrong's moonwalk was a fake and that wrestling is real, so judge accordingly. Whether you hate it or love it, you have to use it. So, to get the most out of this very powerful fractal generator, you need to spend some time learning your way around.

Fractal Explorer Basics

As you may have already noticed, the Fractal Explorer UI (shown in Figure 21-5) doesn't look like your average Windows dialog box.

TIP: *The Fractal Explorer UI requires the monitor to be in 16.7 million (24-bit) color to display properly. If your UI looks horrible (by that I mean the graphics look muddled), make sure your display is in the proper mode.*

To make the UI less confusing, many of the options, like Help, remain dimmed until you place the cursor over them. The dialog box can be moved around the screen by clicking on the Title Bar and dragging the dialog box anywhere on the screen. The UI always restarts in the center of the screen.

Temporary Resizing

Placing the cursor over the button in the upper-left corner with the Kai circular logo on it brings up the program credits for Kai Power Tools. Double-clicking this button reduces (that is, minimizes) the Fractal Explorer to its preview window. Clicking once repetitively on the preview window magnifies the image increasingly. Double-click on the preview window, and the Explorer is returned to its original happy self.

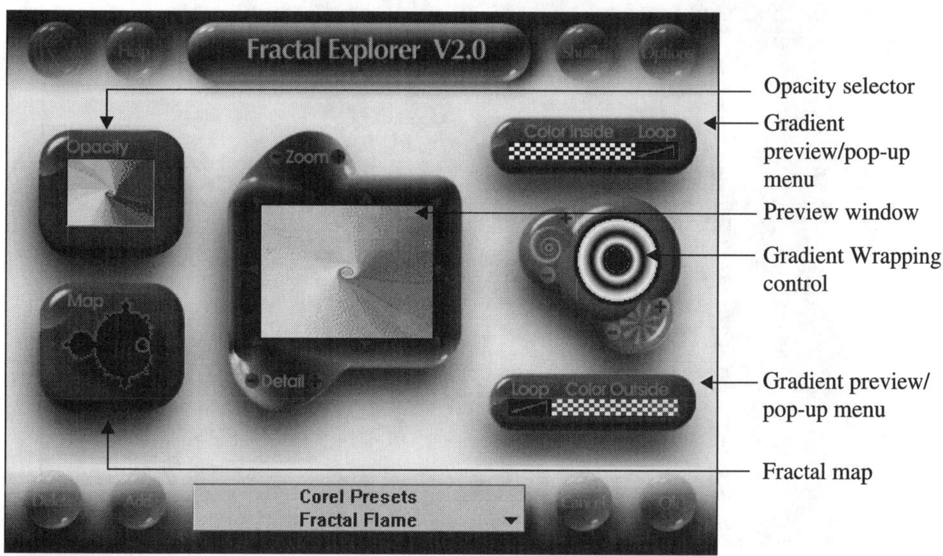

FIGURE 21-5 The Fractal Explorer UI

Help

Clicking on the Help button (to the immediate left of the Title Bar) brings up the Help menu for Fractal Explorer Kai Power Tools 2.0. Be sure to take the Guided Tour of the product, which is one of your choices from the Help menu. You can also get help by pressing the F1 key, which turns the cursor into a question mark. Clicking on any part of the UI brings up context-insensitive help. No matter what you click, you are going to get the opening Help screen.

TIP: *Once you launch the F1 context sensitive Help, you may be wondering how to turn it off. Use the ESC key.*

Options Menu

In the upper-right corner is the Options button. Clicking on this button brings up menu choices, as shown next, that deal with Apply modes, which are discussed in detail later in this chapter.

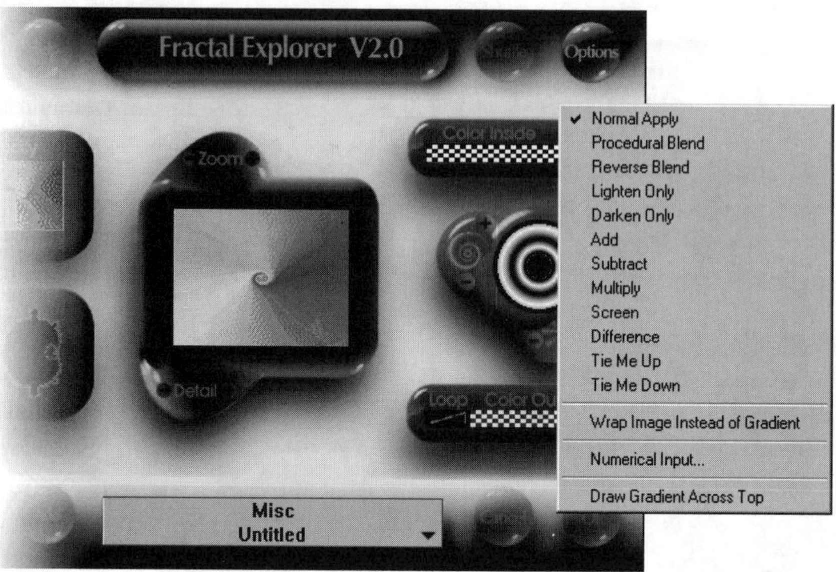

Fractal Explorer Controls

Here is an explanation of the controls on the Fractal Explorer dialog box (refer to Figure 21-5). Most of these controls have their own title on them. (Finally! After how many releases?)

Preview Window

The real-time preview window in the center shows the fractal while it interacts with the underlying image. The initial preview window displays a rough version of the fractal very quickly, followed by increasingly refined views. Repeat clicks preempt the preview computation, allowing fast exploration of the fractal space. Color choices are instantly mapped onto the set.

Opacity Selector

The opacity selector on the UI controls the underlying image view. It is useful when there is a special Apply mode or transparency in the gradient that is part of the fractal. Click on it to sample one of eight preset test images or to view the current selection or the contents of the Clipboard.

Fractal Map

The fractal map is represented by the shape of a traditional Mandelbrot set. When the cursor is over the fractal map, it changes to a small hand. Click and drag the small circle around the fractal space inside of the fractal map (or simply click), and the circle moves to the spot you've clicked to. The real-time preview window displays the changes immediately, without requiring the manual input of any numbers. As you move around the fractal map, you may stop to zoom in or out, using the controls on the preview window, at any time.

Zoom Controls

Zooming within the Fractal Explorer is accomplished in a number of different ways. The easiest method is to simply place the cursor in the real-time preview window and click to zoom in and ALT-click to zoom out. The zoom controls on the top of the preview window frame allow centered zooming, and clicking on the preview window enables direct zooming. Whenever the cursor is over the preview window, the arrow changes to a magnifying glass with a plus (+) sign. Click on the spot you wish to magnify inside the preview window, and it zooms in to that spot and makes it the new center of the preview. Holding down the ALT key changes the magnifying cursor to "magnify-minus." Clicking with the ALT key held down zooms out from that point.

CENTERED ZOOMING For centered zooming, use the two controls on the upper left of the preview window frame. The plus sign (+) zooms in, the minus sign (-) zooms out, and the center of the window stays constant. If you click on the word "Zoom" on the interface, a pop-up slider will appear. Drag the slider in either direction to zoom in large steps. This is a fast way to zoom all the way in or all the way out.

Panning Control

The Panning control allows 360 degrees of continuous panning of the fractal through the preview window.

HOW TO PAN On the outside edge of the preview window are eight small arrows. Click on any of the arrows to move the main preview window in that direction. Clicking anywhere on the frame surrounding the preview (in between the arrows) moves the fractal in that direction.

DRAG PANNING Holding down the CTRL key turns the cursor into a hand, which can be used to drag the fractal around the preview window for precise positioning. Limitations don't end at the preview window boundaries. Drag as far away as the screen allows.

Detail Settings

Increasing the detail settings on any fractal set adds new elements to it. Repeated zooms on a fractal set seem to eventually zoom "through" the fractal to nothing. Increasing the detail settings fills the space by increasing the viewer's ability to discern small changes, particularly inside the fractal's interior. The higher the detail is set, however, the more computational time is required for rendering. Use the two controls on the lower left of the preview window frame to control the detail in the fractal image. The plus sign (+) increases detail; the minus sign (–) decreases detail. Clicking on the word "Detail" shows a slider for more precise detail settings.

Gradient Preview/Pop-Up Menu

On the right-hand side of the Fractal Explorer dialog box are two gradient preview/pop-up menu dialogs. The top one governs the interior of the set, and the bottom one governs the exterior of the set (which is most often the dominant area). The pop-up menu for gradients is the same menu that is used by the Gradient Designer, complete with hierarchical categorization of gradient presets. The Triangle/Sawtooth icon shows the looping control and further affects the way that the gradient is mapped to the fractal set.

Gradient Wrapping Control

Also on the right side, between the Gradient Preview controls, is the Gradient Wrapping control. The fractal set may be colored with any gradient you choose. You can obtain more interesting renderings with the same gradient by controlling the repetition of the gradient as it applies to the set in two different directions. There are two controls for mapping the gradient frequency to the fractal set.

The Spiral setting, on the upper left, controls how fast the color cycles as it moves from one potential line to the next. The lines are expressing the potential of any point in four-dimensional space to fall toward the attractors, roughly analogous to space around an electric charge with equal attraction to the electrostatic center. Within a ring, the electrostatic pull is the same and there can be many such rings moving toward the center of the charge. You can make changes by clicking on the "+" or "–" sign or on the spiral itself.

The Spoke setting, on the lower right of the Wrapping control, determines how often the gradient will be repeated over the entire 360-degree circle around the set. Next to the Spoke setting is the Radial control. These two settings interact with each other. Variations in the Spiral setting will result in widely divergent effects. You can make changes by clicking on the plus (+) or minus (–) sign or on the spoke itself. You can also make changes by dragging within the black-and-white diagram.

The Preset Menu

The Preset Menu, located in the bottom center, is where all of the named or saved fractals are stored. When you press the letter A or click on Add, a dialog box will prompt you to save your fractals.

Shuffle Button

The Shuffle button, located in the upper-left corner, allows the selection of different Fractal Explorer parameters to randomize. If you hold the mouse button down, a list of parameters appears. You may check All or None or select from the list. Each time the Shuffle button is clicked, the selected parameters are shuffled. The parameters that can be shuffled are the following:

- Exterior Colors
- Interior Colors
- Exterior Looping
- Interior Looping
- Apply Mode
- Test Image
- Equipotential Speed
- Radial Speed

Options Button

Clicking on the Options button displays a menu with the Apply Mode list and three other options. Those options are as follows.

WRAP IMAGE INSTEAD OF GRADIENT This option allows the user to grab color data from an Opacity preview mode, which can be the underlying image, the Windows Clipboard, or a Selection. The Fractal Explorer takes the color data, contained in the selection, image, or Clipboard and wraps it around the gradient.

NUMERICAL INPUT Numerical Input enables the "expert fractalists" to find previously explored spaces or to explore new fractal spaces by "hard-coding" the algorithm variables.

DRAW GRADIENT ACROSS TOP This feature creates a bar across the top of the fractal image you create to indicate the gradient that was used. It is not active in all modes.

TIP: *If a bar appears across the top of your image after applying the effect and you are wondering where it came from, it is there because the Draw Gradient Across Top option is set.*

A Quick and Slick Exercise

Let's take a quick trip with this filter and see just a tiny bit of what it can do. The directions will be sparse because I figure if you are this far into the book you must know where most of the major buttons are located.

1. Create a new 24-bit RGB image that is 8 × 3 inches at 72 dpi.
2. Select the Text tool and change the Font to FuturaBlack BT. Change the size to 200. Click inside the image and type **ELVIS**. After doing that, select the Object Picker tool and use CTRL-A to align the text to the center of the document, as shown next.

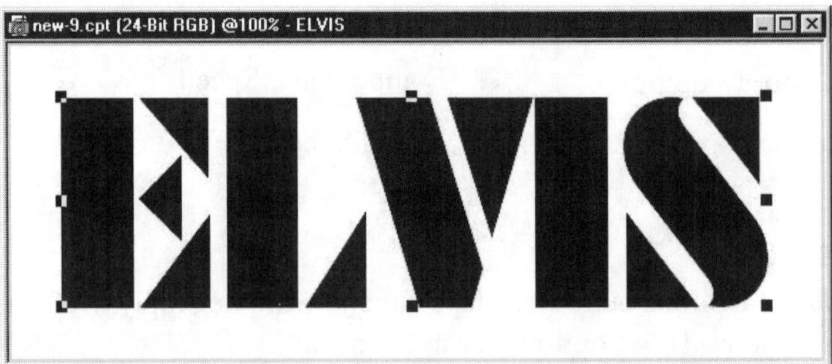

3. In the Objects Property Bar, click the Lock Object Transparency button to enable it. Choose Effects | Fancy | Julia Set Explorer 2.0. At the bottom of the dialog box click and hold "Corel Presets" and then drag down the list until you

find Totally Tubular (don't blame me, I don't make up the names). Once it is selected, click the OK button. The result is shown next.

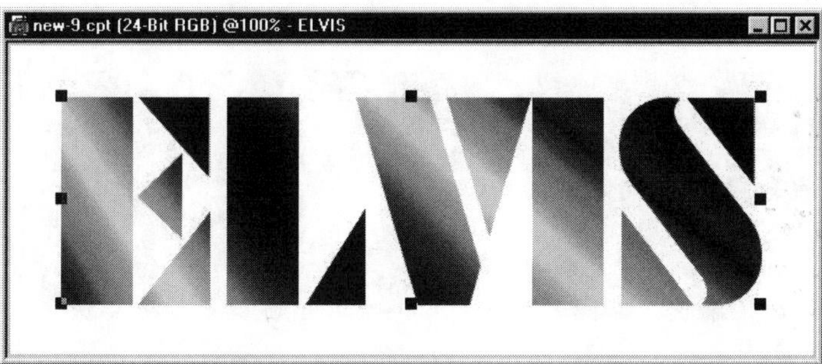

4. Open the Explorer again and this time, under Presets, choose Morning Frost. Click OK. Ugly, right? Trust me.

5. Choose Image | Transform | Invert.

6. Choose Effects | 3D Effects | Emboss. Change the settings to Depth: 1, Level: 400, and Direction 135. Click OK. Select the Object Dropshadow

tool and choose the Flat-Bottomleft setting. There you have it. We won't need this file again.

Considering all of the techniques we have learned so far, it is high time to put them into use. In the next chapter we'll discover how to use the creations made in PHOTO-PAINT in other Corel applications as well as in non-Corel applications.

PART V

Extending the Power of PHOTO-PAINT

CHAPTER 22

The Ins and Outs of PHOTO-PAINT

Unless you are doing all of your original work on the computer, you will have to find some way to get the source images that you need into the computer. Corel provides many ways to bring images into and out of PHOTO-PAINT. The scanner used to be the primary way we got photographic images into PHOTO-PAINT. New in PHOTO-PAINT 9 is a Digital Camera input that allows you to input images directly from your digital camera into PHOTO-PAINT. There is also CorelCAPTURE and Photo-CDs. Once you get an image in, you need to be able to get it out, and for that Corel has a wide variety of import and export functions that allow you to move images between PAINT and other Windows applications. In this chapter, we will look at the myriad ways to get stuff in and out of PHOTO-PAINT.

Scanners and Scanning

The most commonly used device to input photos, line art, or hand-drawn pictures into a computer is a scanner, like the one shown in Figure 22-1. You need to use a scanner, either yours or one at a service bureau, to bring existing photos and artwork into PHOTO-PAINT.

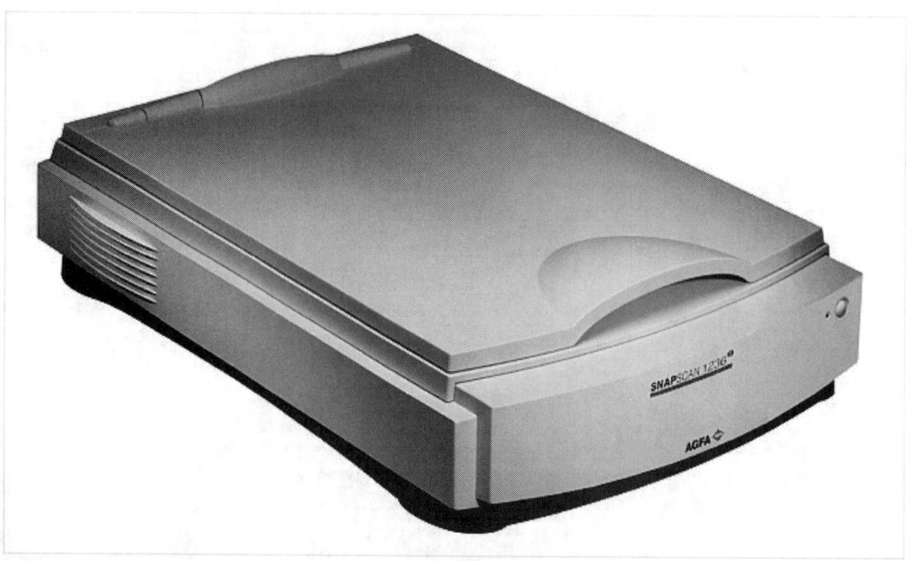

FIGURE 22-1 A flatbed scanner, like this SnapScan 1236S from Agfa, is one of the most frequently used ways to get photos into PHOTO-PAINT

Some Basics About Scanners

A *scanner* is a device that captures an image and converts it into a digital pixel map for computer processing. Think of it as a camera and a photocopier combined and connected to a computer. Like a camera, most scanners capture an image with depth (grayscale or color), whereas a copier records only black and white. As with a copier, the object being scanned is usually placed on a glass plate (the *copyboard*), where it is scanned. The image, however, is not captured on film or reproduced on paper, but rather is stored in a computer file where it can be opened with Corel PHOTO-PAINT and manipulated to the limits of one's imagination and work schedule.

Bringing Digital Images into PHOTO-PAINT 9

There are several paths by which a digital image can get into PHOTO-PAINT. Digital cameras, photo CDs, and scanners are the most popular methods in the market today. Of these three, scanning probably accounts for about 95 percent of all images getting sucked into computers. Most scanners provide a TWAIN interface that allows programs like PHOTO-PAINT and others to interface directly with the scanner. Another method that is gaining popularity is to use an import plug-in. With either method, PHOTO-PAINT opens the software (called the user interface or UI for short), and it is this software that controls the scanner and is used by you to achieve the best possible scan.

Selecting Your Scanning Source

The TWAIN method is pretty straightforward. It involves two steps: select the TWAIN source and acquire the image. Figure 22-2 shows a typical selection process. Simply choose File | Select and the dialog box appears from which you can select your TWAIN source. The Select Source dialog box in Figure 22-2 appears to have a lot of choices, but in truth only two of those scanners are installed; I just installed the software for many of the scanners shown in Figure 22-2 so it would look good in the figure. Gasp! The work I go through to make this book look interesting.

Once you select a TWAIN source, PHOTO-PAINT remembers your selection. In fact, the only time you need to use select again is when you change sources. If you have only one TWAIN source, you don't even need to select it—it is selected already. After you have selected your TWAIN source, you can begin your scan by Choosing File | Acquire Image | Acquire. You can also begin a scan with your selected TWAIN device from the Welcome screen—yeah, like that ever happens.

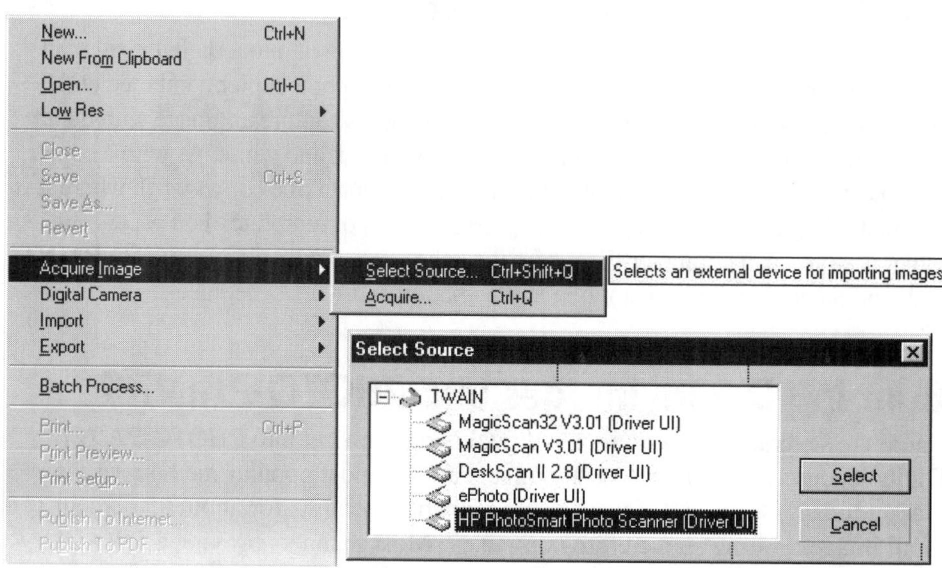

FIGURE 22-2 Selecting a scanner is easy, knowing which one to pick is trickier

TIP: *Are you scanning a lot of images? Use the keyboard shortcut (CTRL-Q) to begin your scan with the selected TWAIN device. You can also leave Acquire (scanning software) OPEN meaning that it will NOT automatically close after a scan. Simply go into your Options and remove the check mark for "Close scan dialogue after acquire."*

Figure 22-3 shows an example of a TWAIN interface provided by the manufacturer, in this example it is the Deskscan Software for an HP flatbed scanner. Look at the figure again and you will notice my daughter Grace in the preview window—OK, back to business. TWAIN interfaces provided by scanner manufacturers range in functionality from the bare essentials to very sophisticated interfaces, which provide many presets and automatic scanning functions. If you want more information on TWAIN, see the story about it in the upcoming box.

With all of this TWAIN talk we need to be aware that Import plug-ins are another way to input and control a scanner. Import plug-ins are installed just like other third party plug-ins (discussed in detail in Chapter 13). The difference is that they do not appear in the Effects menu; instead they appear in the Import menu, as

FIGURE 22-3 This UI provides all of the necessary controls to achieve a good scan

is shown next. This is an Import plug-in for SilverFast, which is an automated scanning UI that was shipped with an Epson scanner. This particular scanner did not know where to install its plug-in filter since the only photo-editing package its installation program recognized was Photoshop. This will happen on occasion. The solution is to tell PHOTO-PAINT where the scanner installation program put its import plug-in.

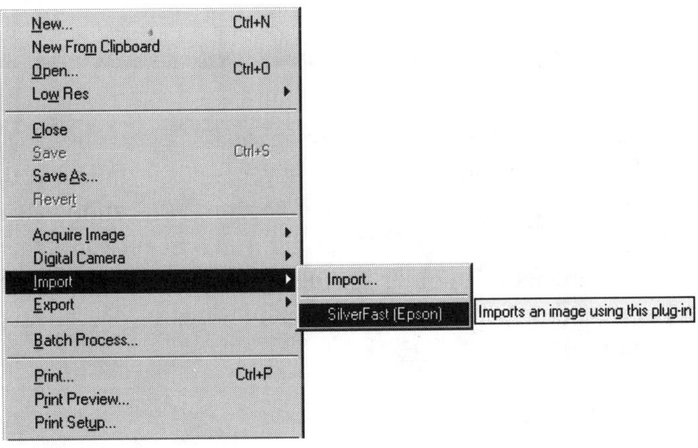

The Story of TWAIN (Not Mark)

Not so long ago, it was the responsibility of every company that wrote paint (bitmap) programs to provide the software programs necessary to communicate with the scanner. However, every scanner spoke its own language, so to speak, and the result was that unless you owned one of the more popular scanners, you could not access the scanner from within your paint or drawing program. Most of the time, it was necessary to run a separate scanning program (provided with your scanner) to scan in an image. After the image was scanned, you could load it into your favorite paint or OCR program. That may seem like a lot of work, and let me assure you, it was.

Then one day all of the scanner people got together and said, "Let us all make our scanners speak one language" (sort of a Tower of Babel in reverse). So, they came up with an interface specification called TWAIN.

Why is the interface specification called TWAIN? This is one of those mysteries that might puzzle computer historians for decades to come. I have never received a straight answer to the question, only intriguing possibilities. My favorite explanation is credited to Aldus (now Adobe) Corporation. They say TWAIN means "SpecificaTion Without An Interesting Name." Logitech, one of the driving forces behind the specification, gives a different answer: "It was a unique interface that brings together two entities, application and input devices, in a meeting of the 'twain'."

Whatever the origin of the name, the TWAIN interface allows Corel PHOTO-PAINT (or any other program that supports TWAIN) to talk to the scanner directly through a common interface, and for that we should all be thankful.

All of the installed TWAIN drivers in Windows 9*x* appear on the TWAIN list. If your scanner does not appear, its TWAIN driver is not installed. If there are no TWAIN drivers installed, then a message will appear. You cannot use any scanner until one is installed. To install a TWAIN driver, run the software that came with your scanner. If you are using an older scanner, you must use a TWAIN driver written for Windows 95 or Windows 98. If you do not have one, then contact the manufacturer of your scanner.

NOTE: *Some older or discontinued scanners do not have WIN95 TWAIN support and cannot be used to scan directly into PHOTO-PAINT, or into anything else for that matter.*

Some Basics About Scanning

Scanning is not difficult—we aren't talking brain surgery here. It is simply knowing a little and working a little to extract the most out of a printed image. Over the last few years, the price of desktop scanners has dropped while the performance has increased dramatically, resulting in more and more people owning and using them. Sadly, many users, including graphics professionals, do not understand some of the basics necessary to get the best-quality image from a scanner into Corel PHOTO-PAINT and out to a printer.

A Trick Question

During a recent 51-city Corel WordPerfect roadshow, I had the opportunity to ask literally hundreds of attendees the following question: *"If you are going to print a photograph on a 600 dots per inch (dpi) laser printer, at what resolution should you scan the image for the best output?"* More than half answered they would use a resolution of 600. Was that your answer? If so, read on. If you answered with any resolution from 100 to 150 dpi, you are correct. Take two compliments out of petty cash. For some of you, this may be review, but even if you knew the correct answer, I hope that in reading this part of the chapter, you either learn something new or remember something you once knew.

Scanning and Resolution . . . Making It Work for You

It seems logical that the resolution of a scan should be the same, or nearly the same, as that of the printer. The problem is that when we talk about the resolution of the scanner in dots per inch (dpi), we are not talking about the same dots per inch used when describing printer resolution. In Chapter 2, we learned about pixels. Scanners scan pixels, which are square, and printers makes dots, which are round. The resolution of the scanner is measured in dots per inch, which is inappropriate because its resolution is more accurately described in samples per inch. Each sample represents a pixel.

The resolution of the printer dot is measured in dots per inch. The resolution of the printer determines the size of the dot it makes. For example, each dot made by a 600-dpi printer is 1/600 of an inch in diameter. These printer dots only come in two flavors: black and white. To produce the 256 shades of gray that exist between black and white on a printer, these tiny dots are grouped together to form halftone cells. For example, let's assume for the sake of illustration that each halftone cell made by our printer is 10 × 10 dots in size. Each halftone cell can hold a maximum of 100 dots. To print the shade 50 percent gray, the printer turns half of the dots on in each halftone cell and leaves half off. This gives the appearance to the eye of being 50 percent gray.

Here is an example of this principle. In Figure 22-4(a), I have created four squares—two are white and two black. In Figure 22-4(b), the tile filter was applied making those 4 squares into 400 tiny squares. In Figure 22-4(c), the filter was applied again, and the result is 50 percent gray.

When we talk about scanner resolution, we are actually talking about samples per inch. Each sample of a scan at 600 dpi is 1/600 of an inch square (remember that pixels are square). Unlike the printer's dot, which can have only two possible values, each scanner pixel can have one of 256 possible values (for simplicity, we are assuming grayscale). The relationship between scanner pixels and printer dots is shown in the photograph taken during a conversation between the two of them:

At this point, we can see that a scanned pixel is much more like a printer halftone cell than the original printer dot. So how do you determine how many halftone cells per inch your printer is capable of producing? If you look in the back of your printer manual, you won't find a setting for halftone cells per inch, but you may (I emphasize the *may* part) find a setting for either screen or line frequency.

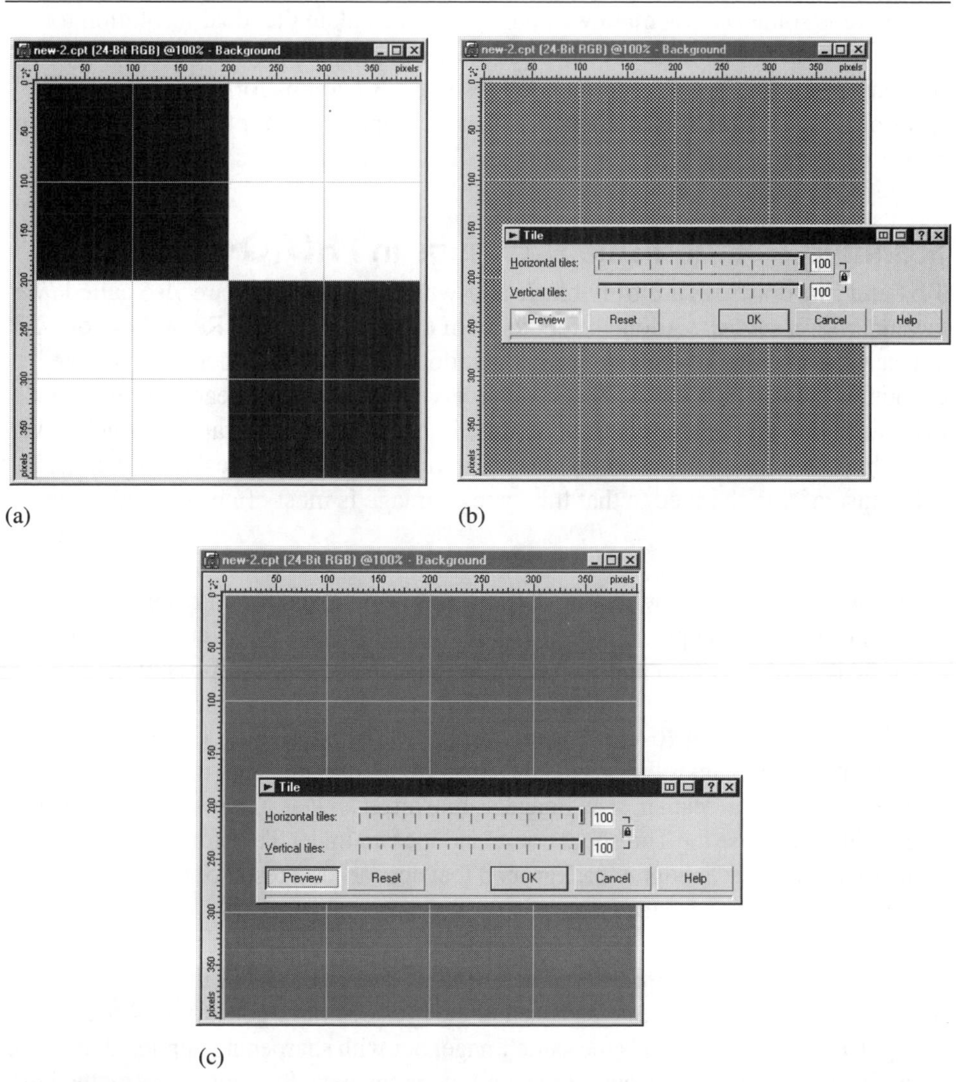

(a)

(b)

(c)

FIGURE 22-4 Making gray from black and white: (a) simple black-and-white squares; (b) after applying the Tile filter at a setting of 100; (c) after applying the Tile filter again

Line frequency is measured in lines per inch (lpi). An old rule of thumb for scanning used to be: scan at twice the line frequency of the final output device. This rule has become pretty outdated. You should scan at roughly 1.5 times the line frequency of your final output device.

There is some serious math we could use to calculate the ideal resolution to match the scan to the output device, but there is a simpler way. The following sections give some basic recommended resolutions and tips for scanning different types of images. These recommendations are compiled from information provided by various scanner manufacturers and service bureau operators.

Scanning Text and Line Drawings in PHOTO-PAINT 9

Text and line drawings are truly black-and-white images. They are also called *line art* and *bilevel images*; Adobe refers to them as *bitmap images*. Regardless of what you call them, either a white dot or a black dot is scanned and then printed. We encounter these all the time. When you receive a logo or letterhead to scan, it is invariably line art. Unlike continuous-tone images (like photographs), which have smooth transitions, changes in line art are abrupt, which produces a sharp edge. It is because of this sharp edge that this type of image is most often scanned using the following rule:

> Scan line art and text with a resolution equal to the maximum resolution (in dpi) of the final output device, up to but not more than the scanner's maximum optical resolution, and apply sharpening with the scanner (if possible).

There is another way to scan line art into PHOTO-PAINT that deserves consideration. Sometimes the original has many fine lines that tend to plug up when scanned. Rather than scanning the image as line art, scan it as a grayscale image with sharpening. Then use the Threshold command located under Transform in the Image menu to remove any light gray background that appears as a result of the color of the paper the original was printed on.

Figure 22-5(a) shows an old woodcut printed on a poor grade of paper that was scanned as line art at 635 dpi without sharpening. There are a lot of fine lines in the feathers in the lower-left corner and around the eyes that have gone to solid black, thus losing detail. Figure 22-5(b) is the same image, but with sharpening applied during the scan. The sharpening brings out more detail in the feathers. In Figure 22-5(c), the bird is scanned as a grayscale image with sharpening. In this scan, we have much more of the image detail, but the paper the original was printed on creates a background that is a light shade of gray. The way to remove the background is to apply the Threshold filter to convert everything below a specified threshold to white. After applying Threshold, we have an image that looks like a black-and-white image, Figure 22-5(d), but with more image detail. The operation of the Threshold filter is discussed in Chapter 17.

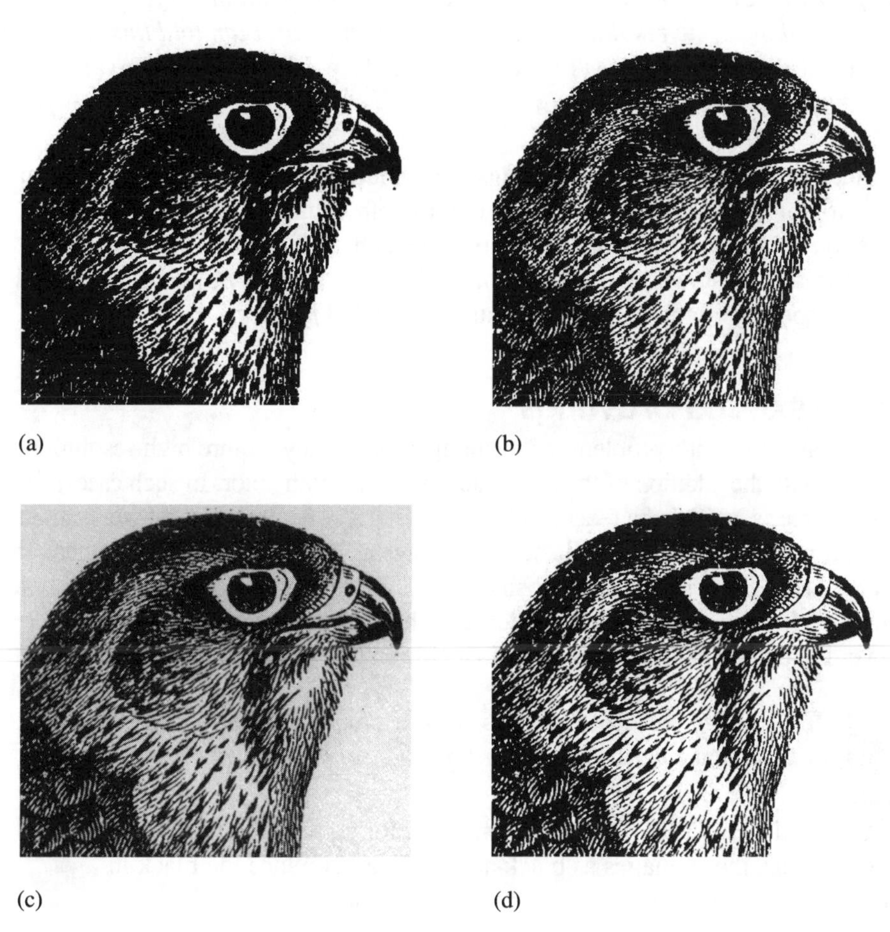

FIGURE 22-5 An image scanned (a) as line art at 635 dpi and (b) at 635 dpi with sharpening; and (c) as grayscale at 200 dpi with sharpening and (d) with light gray background removed using Threshold filter

A word of caution if you scan at the maximum resolution of your scanner: You may find it causes problems with the RIP (raster image processors) when you are outputting to an imagesetter. RIPs seem much more sensitive to the high resolution of these images than they are to the image size. It is not uncommon for the RIP to output a 20MB grayscale image with a resolution of 200 dpi with no problems and have it throw a hairball when it gets a 1000-dpi image, even if it is a small one.

TIP: *Black-and-white bitmap images seem to print much faster if the art is at the same resolution as the imagesetter itself. I am told this is because the imagesetter doesn't have to rescale the work, so the image gets sent right through.*

Line art and text are the only things that should be scanned at the maximum resolution of the scanner. Because the color depth value of each pixel is binary (either on or off), the file sizes do not become extremely large. If you scan this type of image at a lower resolution, you will discover that it produces jagged edges that are especially apparent on diagonal lines (called *jaggies*).

Color Text and Drawings

These images present a problem for scanning because they require high-resolution scanning with the addition of the overhead associated with color. In such cases, file sizes become as large as the federal debt in a big hurry. There are several work-arounds to this. If your scanner supports it, scan the image at 256 colors. If your scanner can only do 24-bit color, scan the image into PHOTO-PAINT and convert it to 256 colors using the Mode command and the Paletted (8-bit) option in the Image menu. Converting the file to 256 colors reduces its file size by 66 percent.

TIP: *When converting to 256 colors, choose the Optimized palette and not the Uniform palette. Keep dithering set to None.*

You could use CorelTRACE to convert color text and drawing to a vector image, or scan these images as black and white and replace the black in PHOTO-PAINT with colors similar to the original.

Photographs

Continuous-tone images (such as photographs) can be color or black and white. This type of image is less detailed and requires lower resolution than line art. The rule for this is simple: *Scan photographs at 100–200 dpi.*

Some variations to this rule are as follows:

- For 300-dpi laser printers, scanning at 100 dpi is usually sufficient.
- For 600-dpi lasers, scan at 150 dpi.
- For imagesetters (including high-resolution lasers that produce camera-ready art), scan at 200 dpi.

Why You Shouldn't Scan at Excessively High Resolutions

Even after going through all of the explanations about the best settings to get a good scan, some still believe that scanning at a higher than necessary resolution somehow gives their image extra detail or makes it look sharper. In fact, doing this rarely improves image quality and produces very large file sizes. Remember that each time resolution is doubled, the file size quadruples. Large image files take a long time to process, and time is money at your local neighborhood service bureau. Also, scanning at a resolution higher than the output device can reproduce tends to cause detail in the shadow area to be lost, and if the resolution is high enough and the image small enough, the final result may actually be a blurry picture. Let's move on to some other scanning-related commands and issues.

The Deskew Command

After scanning an image, if you notice it is crooked, lift the lid on the scanner, straighten the image, and scan it again. Sounds simple, right? You would be amazed at how many users will accept a crooked scan and not do that simple step. Don't be one of them. If you receive a scan with a crooked image, you can straighten it in PHOTO-PAINT using the Deskew command located in the Image menu. The Deskew command places imperfectly positioned images squarely in the image area, but the image being deskewed needs to appear against a light background that PHOTO-PAINT can recognize. The deskewing action works well and causes little to no distortion of the original image. Located in the Image menu, this filter has no user-definable settings.

In the following image, I have deliberately misaligned a photograph of Grace (you've already met):

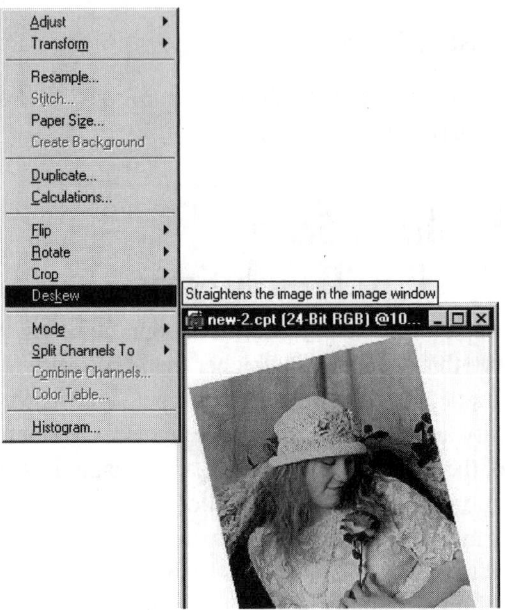

The image resulting from use of the Deskew command is shown here. A failure? Not really, I am trying to visually make a point. The image I scanned was scaled down 50 percent to around 200 pixels.

Next, look at the results when the same command is applied to the same image when it has some size to work with. In the following illustration, I had to apply the Deskew command twice but the resulting image is very close to vertical. Again I cannot emphasize enough that the Deskew command in not a substitute for straightening out the photo on the scanner.

Tips for Using Deskew

Don't be concerned if the image is cropped closely, as the Deskew command will increase the size of the final image to fit the deskewed image. I want to qualify my next suggestion by saying that all of my testing done with this version of Deskew has been accomplished using a late beta version, so check this theory out for yourself. I have found that scans that are very dark overall don't seem to deskew as well as lighter ones. I tested several scans and found that lightening the scanned image (including the background) with some Gamma (Image | Adjust) many times improved the accuracy of the scan. By accuracy I am referring to how straight up and down the final image is.

Removing Dust, Scratches, and Other Debris

When you apply sharpening to an image, all of the dust and other small artifacts in the image make themselves known. They have always been there—they just blend into the image until sharpening is applied. I want to warn you not to fall into the trap of spending hours removing specks of dust and debris from a scanned image with

PHOTO-PAINT that could have been prevented in the first place by either dusting the original photograph with a fine-hair brush or a can of compressed air, cleaning the glass on the scanner with some glass cleaner before scanning, or both. If you feel the glass on your flatbed scanner is clean and doesn't need this attention, try this test. Lift the lid and start a scan. Look at the glass from the side as the light moves. Surprised?

If the dust and debris are part of the image you have scanned, you may need to use the Dust & Scratch filter, which is discussed in Chapter 19.

So much for scanning. There are times when we need to get our image directly from the computer screen. This type of application is found mostly in technical documentation, including this book. For this purpose, Corel included CorelCAPTURE 9. For information on using CorelCAPTURE, see Chapter 23.

Photo-CDs

Developed by Kodak as a consumer file format, the photo-CD was initially a failure. Later, it become popular as a method of distributing photographic images, and for a time it became a common form of exchange for such images. Now the popularity of this format is beginning to wane. Corel Corporation is the world's largest supplier of images on photo-CDs, although there are none in the CorelDRAW 9 release. Ironic, isn't it? Corel PHOTO-PAINT 9 provides several adjustments and options for use with photo-CDs, which we will look at briefly in this section.

Picking the Right Size When Opening a Photo-CD

When a photo-CD is initially opened, the dialog box appears as shown in Figure 22-6. If color adjustment is not desired, the only choices that must be made are the size of the image and the color selection. The size choices and their size in pixels are found in the Resolution pop-up list: Thumbnail (96 × 64), Wallet (192 × 128), Snapshot (384 × 256), Standard (768 × 512), Large (1,536 × 1,024), and Poster (3,072 × 2,048). The available color selections found in the Type pop-up list are 16.7 million (24-bit), 256 Color Paletted (8-bit), and 256 Grayscale (8-bit).

TIP: *Larger file sizes require large amounts of system memory, take longer to load and to apply effects, and require more disk space for storage. Therefore, always try to pick a size and color depths that are sufficient for your application.*

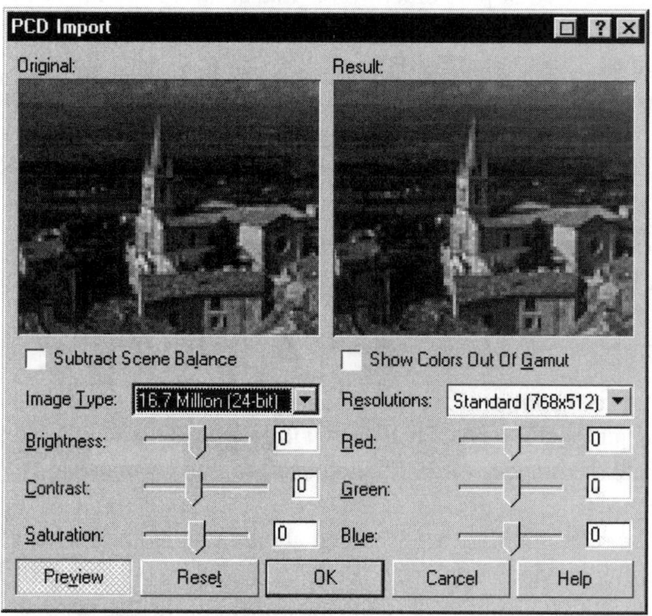

FIGURE 22-6 The photo-CD dialog box

Applying Color Correction When Opening Photo-CDs

If you want to apply color-adjust, you can make some of the not-so-great Photo-CDs on the market look a little better. All of the adjustments are pretty much self-explanatory except for Subtract Scene Balance. Enabling this button on the PCD Import dialog box removes the scene balance adjustment, which is made by the photo-finisher at the time the original image was scanned and preserved on the photo-CD disc. We could fill two pages with the math behind this jewel, but instead I will tell you the secret to using it. Ready? Check it and click Preview. Does the Preview look better? Then leave it checked. If not, uncheck it.

The other button that may have you intrigued is Show Colors Out Of Gamut. If the adjustments you've made are too extreme, the preview will display out-of-gamut pixels as pure red or pure blue. Colors that are out of gamut cannot be printed accurately, and it is important for critical prepress work for all colors to be within gamut boundaries.

Color correction takes time. If you have images that have not been color corrected, it is worth the time spent trying to apply correction at this stage rather than in Corel PHOTO-PAINT. Another source for images is CorelDRAW and other Windows applications. In the following section, we will look at some of the different ways we can move an image between these programs.

Moving Images Between Applications

Just because this is a book on PHOTO-PAINT doesn't mean that I think everything should be done in PHOTO-PAINT. In fact, I think you should always explore other options. Get into the practice of deciding which program(s) to use to create a project *before* you begin.

Many of the rules you may have learned about moving images between applications using previous versions of PHOTO-PAINT have changed. This is good news, since PHOTO-PAINT 9 makes the movement of images between applications very simple. In this section, we will cover the basics of moving images between both Corel and non-Corel applications. This section of the chapter is like a cookbook—full of recipes for different ways to get from here to there and back again. If you are reading this book from front to back, you will encounter tools and terms that have not previously been introduced. I have included some brief explanations, exercises, and cross-references so that you won't get too confused.

PAINT to DRAW and Back Again

Since most people ask how to move images between PHOTO-PAINT and DRAW, we will cover this process first. In previous releases, doing this was a little complicated, but now there are so many ways to move images between the programs that it is difficult to sort them out. Talk about an embarrassment of riches!

From PAINT to DRAW (Save Method)

This is the simple one. In PHOTO-PAINT, save the image in PAINT (*.CPT) format. In DRAW, select Import from the File menu. Locate the CPT file and click Import. The cursor changes to the filename, allowing you to click and drag to the size you want.

- The size of the image in DRAW is controlled by the resolution of the image in PAINT. The higher the resolution, the smaller the image. Use the Resample command in PAINT to change the size.
- If the PHOTO-PAINT image contains more than one object (bitmaps that float above the image), the objects will appear grouped as objects in DRAW.
- If the PHOTO-PAINT image contains a mask, only the area surrounded by the mask will appear on the image in DRAW.
- One of the objects will be a rectangle, which is the background. To remove the background, you must ungroup the objects, select the background, and delete it.

The following session takes you through the procedure of bringing a PHOTO-PAINT image that contains an object into DRAW.

Importing PHOTO-PAINT Images into CorelDRAW (Tutorial)

This is an easy exercise for importing a PHOTO-PAINT 9 image into DRAW.

1. In PHOTO-PAINT, create a new image. Make the image 5 × 5 inches and 24-bit color at 72 dpi.
2. Select Fill from the Edit menu. When the Edit Fill & Transparency box opens, click the Fountain Fill Tool button and then click the Edit button. When the Fountain Fill dialog box opens, click the down-pointing arrow at

the right of the Presets value box and select Circular - Blue 02. Change the number of steps to 999. Click the OK button to select the setting and click the next OK button to apply the fill. The resulting image appears next. (This image can be seen in color on the CD version of this book that comes with the application.)

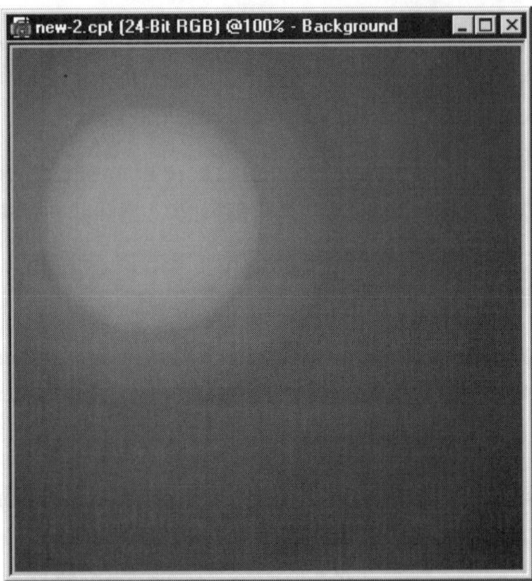

3. From the Effects menu, choose Custom and then Alchemy. In the Alchemy Effects dialog box, choose Bubbles Pastel from the Style drop-down list. Click OK. Now the blue image looks as if it lost a fight with Lawrence Welk. Save the file as BLUE and close it.

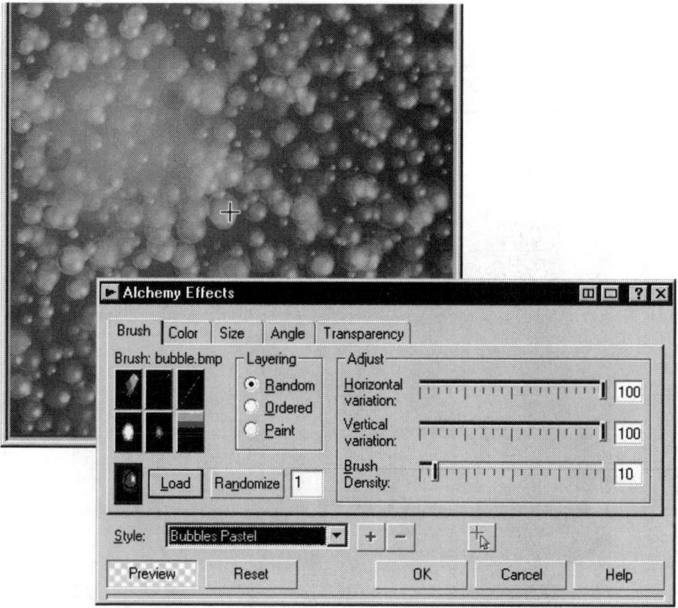

4. In DRAW, choose New from the File menu. Select the Object Picker tool (called the Pick tool in Draw) at the top of the Toolbox and, from the File menu, choose Import (CTRL-SHIFT-I). When the Import dialog box opens, locate the file BLUE and click Import. When the cursor changes, click on the page.

5. Next, import FISH02 in the EXERCISE\OBJECTS folder of the Corel CD-ROM. Click and drag this image on top of the blue image. The result appears in Figure 22-7.

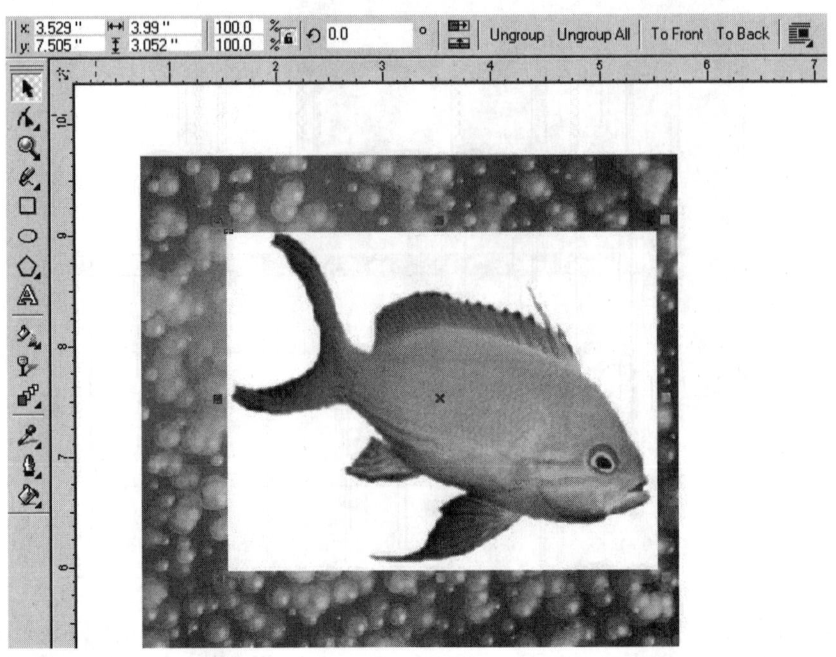

FIGURE 22-7 The fish imported with a white background

6. To remove the white rectangle, you must first ungroup the fish from it. With the fish object still selected, click the Ungroup button in the Property Bar.

7. Click somewhere outside the images to deselect the two objects, then click on the fish again. This time, only the top object is selected. Press the TAB key to change the object selected to the white background and press the DEL key. Now we have the fish without the background, as shown next. There is a better way. Leave DRAW and PAINT open while I explain.

A Recap of What We Just Did

In the previous hands-on session, we imported a PHOTO-PAINT image that contained an object and a background. An *object* is a bitmap image that floats above the background. A background is . . . well, you know, a background. The image actually contained two objects: the background and the fish. CorelDRAW treats the objects in PHOTO-PAINT files just like regular objects in DRAW, even though it is a bitmap and not a vector drawing. If the image has no objects, CorelDRAW imports the entire image as a bitmap image.

PAINT (with Masks) into DRAW

Some of the rules in this area have changed with the release of the DRAW 9 suite, so if you are an experienced PHOTO-PAINT user, I recommend spending a few moments reading through this section.

It isn't necessary to have objects in a PHOTO-PAINT image for the subject to be clipped to the boundary of the image. In PHOTO-PAINT, the subject of the image that you want to bring into DRAW can be defined by a mask. A *mask* is a layer over the entire image that is used to define areas in the image. For more information on masks, see Chapter 7. In previous releases, it was necessary to mask the desired portion of the image and save it as an Encapsulated PostScript file (EPS) for the mask to define the edges of the image with what is called a *clipping boundary*.

While this method is still necessary with other non-Corel applications, the DRAW 9 Import command now recognizes and defines the image clipping boundary based on the mask that is in the image. Say what? Let me show you this visually. A picture is still worth more than a thousand words, even accounting for inflation. Figure 22-8 is my favorite Corel Professional Photos of a child. The circle around his face is a mask. Saving this image as a CPT file with the mask and then importing it into CorelDRAW 9 produces the image shown in Figure 22-9. While the visible portion of the image is constrained to the mask, the imported image is the size of the CPT image in full; it's just got a transparent background. Notice in Figure 22-9 that the edge is not sharp and distinct. This is because I feathered the mask in PAINT. Don't be concerned if you

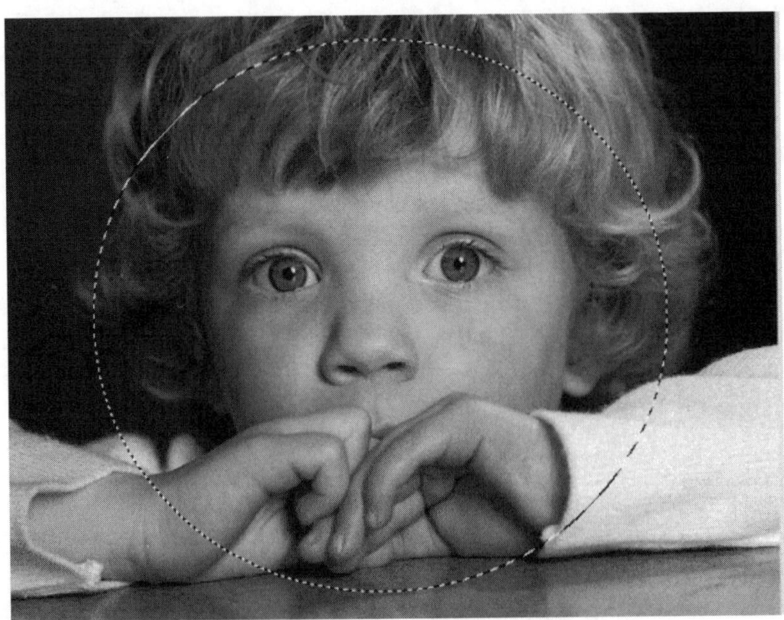

FIGURE 22-8 The mask marquee shown in PHOTO-PAINT 9

FIGURE 22-9 The mask defines the image boundary when imported into DRAW 9

don't know what feathering is at this moment; just remember that DRAW recognizes and applies mask attributes. Here are a few more rules about masks when importing into DRAW.

On importing, DRAW does not:

- Recognize or apply lenses
- Apply masks to objects—only the background

Getting From PAINT to Both Corel and Non-Corel Applications

To save an image so the subject will be clipped to the masked area, select Export in the File menu in PHOTO-PAINT and save the image as an Encapsulated PostScript (EPS) file. When the EPS Export dialog box opens, as shown in Figure 22-10, check

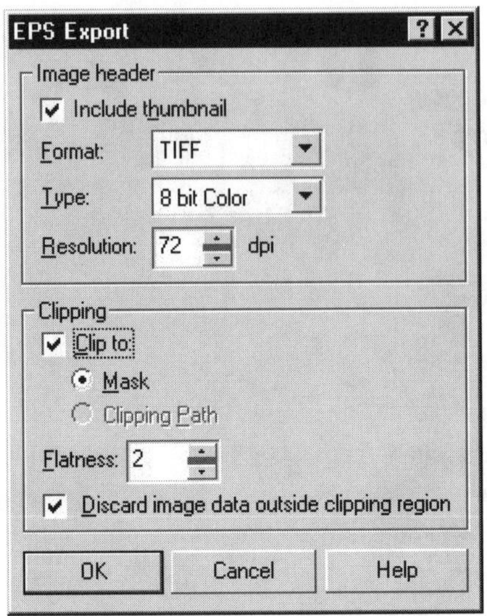

FIGURE 22-10 The EPS Export dialog box

Include Thumbnail and then in the Clipping section, select Clip and enable Mask. Finally, select the Discard Image Data Outside Clipping Region option.

After the image is saved, you can, in DRAW, select Import from the File menu and only the masked area appears. If you are going to be sending the work out to a service bureau, I would strongly recommend exporting as an EPS file. I say this because the service bureau or printer is used to working with, and understands, EPS files. When you import the EPS image, it may not display properly on the screen, meaning the white rectangle may remain but will not be printed as long as you print it on a PostScript output device.

TIP: *In previous releases of PHOTO-PAINT, you could use the Save As command to create an EPS file. Now, you must use the Export command.*

Getting Images from DRAW into PAINT

Getting an image from DRAW into PAINT involves a process called *rasterization* (see the following sidebar). The Corel image, or the portion of the image, that you

EPS Export Dialog Box

The Image Header section allows you define what the bitmap file of the file looks like. This header file is used for placement of the image in another application. This is why an EPS image may sometimes look very poor—because you are not actually looking at the image but at the low-resolution header file.

The Clipping section is available if either a mask or path is present in the image. When the Clip To feature is enabled, it saves the contents of the mask marquee on the image in the EPS file. The program converts the mask to a path before saving, so the process may take some time, depending on how complicated the mask is. The sections of the image that are outside the mask marquee are still in the image but will not be visible nor will they print when you use the EPS file in another application. You can still see those sections if you open the image in Corel PHOTO-PAINT.

To delete the sections that are outside the mask marquee, enable the Discard Image Data Outside Clipping Region option at the bottom of this dialog box.

want to bring into PAINT is saved as a Corel CDR (vector) file. The CDR file can be brought into PAINT using PAINT's Open or Import command in the File menu. If you're using the Open command, selecting the CDR file (or any vector file) opens the Import Into Bitmap dialog box, which is described in the next section. Select the settings and it will take a few moments to rasterize the image. The image will load as a new CPT file with one Object and No Background; it will be necessary to mask the area of the image you want and convert to an object. If you use the Import command, there is no dialog box; you must click and drag the cursor in the image file to place it as an object on the current background.

Import Into Bitmap Dialog Box

Use the Import Into Bitmap dialog box, shown in Figure 22-11, to specify how you want to rasterize the CDR or other vector-based image. Many users are intimidated by all the choices that are available to them in this dialog box. Never fear; after you read this section, they will begin to make sense.

Rasterization and Dithering

When we go from CorelDRAW to PHOTO-PAINT (or any other bitmap application), it is necessary to convert the vector (or line) format into bitmap (or paint) format. This process is called *rasterization.* How the rasterization is accomplished determines how faithfully the image we import into Corel PHOTO-PAINT is reproduced.

When a color in the original image cannot be produced precisely (either because of display or color mode limitations), the computer does its best to make an approximation of the color through a process called *dithering.* With dithering, the computer changes the colors of adjacent pixels so that, to the viewer, they approximate the desired color. Dithering is accomplished by mathematically averaging the color values of adjacent pixels. The use of dithering can also affect the process of getting an image from CorelDRAW to PHOTO-PAINT.

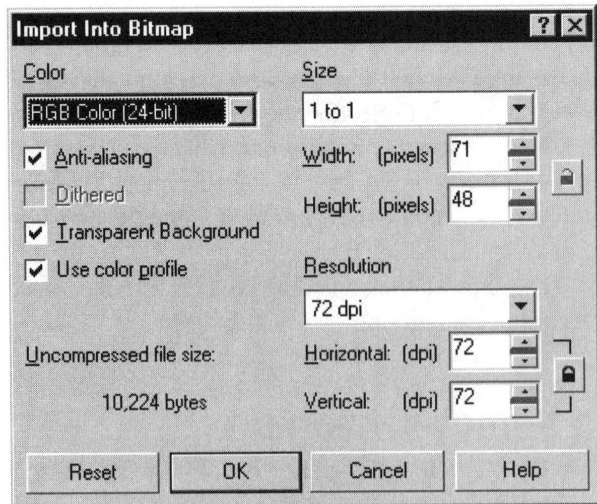

FIGURE 22-11 The Import Into Bitmap dialog box

Color

This directs PHOTO-PAINT to rasterize the CorelDRAW file either as a black-and-white image, as shades of gray, or as color. The greater the number of colors, the larger the exported file, and the better the image will appear.

Use Color Profile

This uses the color profile assigned to the internal RGB profile.

Transparent Background

The transparent background is for use with images that will be placed on the Web.

Dithered

This dithers the colors of the DRAW file. Dithering is only available when you have selected a Color setting of 256 shades or less of color or the Black and White option (it is disabled in grayscale). If the image contains fountain fills or color blends, dithering can cause obvious banding in the exported bitmap. Here are some guidelines to help you decide whether to dither the bitmap:

- If you are importing an image with 16 or 256 colors or black and white, use dithering.
- If you intend to scale this bitmap in PHOTO-PAINT, dithering is not recommended.

Size

This is the setting that ultimately determines the size of the image in PHOTO-PAINT. The Size setting specifies the dimensions of the resulting rasterized bitmap. If you choose 1 to 1, the image will be the same size as it was in CorelDRAW. You may also choose one of the preset sizes from the list box (not recommended) or choose Custom and enter the dimensions in the Width and Height boxes.

By default, the size of the image in CorelDRAW is used, which is why I recommend the default setting of 1 to 1. Smaller bitmaps (with lower resolution) or larger bitmaps (with higher resolution) can be created by scaling the image up or down in CorelDRAW prior to exporting. When Custom is selected, make sure the Maintain Aspect Ratio Lock icon is enabled.

NOTE: *If you choose one of the preset sizes from the list box, the dimensions you choose may not be proportional to the bitmap's original aspect ratio. The exported bitmap will distort unless you place an empty border around your bitmap with the same ratio as the preset. For example, in DRAW, create a rectangle around your image—6.4 × 4.8 inches if you are exporting at 640 × 480. Then assign No Fill and No Outline to the rectangle. Now the aspect ratio of the image will be maintained when you export.*

Resolution

This setting specifies the resolution (in dots per inch) for bitmaps. The Resolution choices in dpi are 72, 96, 150, 200, 300, and Custom. The Custom choice is handy for making the image larger or smaller. Enter the resolution in the DPI box.

NOTE: *As resolution increases, so does the size of the export file and the time required to print the image.*

Anti-aliasing

There are three choices for anti-aliasing. Anti-aliasing produces smoother bitmap rasterization. By default, it is set to Normal. Super-sampling is a method that takes longer but produces superior results. You can also choose None.

The Express Route from DRAW to PAINT

This is so easy it's almost criminal. Use the Windows Clipboard as follows:

- In DRAW, select the object or objects you want to place in your PAINT image, then copy to the Clipboard (CTRL-C).
- In PAINT, with the image open, click the Paste As Object button on the toolbar and the DRAW objects will be rasterized to the resolution of the open image—no questions asked.

This next method, drag and drop, used to produce badly dithered results—but not any longer.

The Drag and Drop Method

Another way to move an image from one application to another is *drag and drop.* When dragging from DRAW to PAINT, this method will create a file at 72 dpi if there isn't an existing image open in PHOTO-PAINT 9. Otherwise, the object will be rasterized at the Resolution of the image.

Using Drag and Drop

If you decide to use drag and drop, you should follow these guidelines. They hold true for going either way, but they are explained as if you are going from DRAW to PAINT:

- Both applications must be open**.** This means that neither one can be reduced to a little icon in the taskbar.
- To drag an image from CorelDRAW, you must click on it and drag it into the PAINT application. When the cursor is over the PAINT application, the icon will turn into an arrow-rectangle icon.
- PHOTO-PAINT does not need to have an image area open. If an existing image is not open, a new image will be created with the resolution restricted to 72 dpi. If there is an existing image, it is rasterized at the resolution of the image.
- If you are dragging a DRAW object into an existing PAINT image, you can use the right mouse button to drag it over, and you will have the choice of copying (original remains in DRAW) or moving the object (original in DRAW is gone).

TIP: *When dragging an image into PAINT, be patient. It sometimes takes longer than you might expect for the cursor to change into the arrow-rectangle icon. As Radar would say in M.A.S.H: "Wait for it."*

TIP: *Another way to prevent an object from being deleted in CorelDRAW when it is dragged into another application is to hold down the* CTRL *key AFTER you have begun to click and drag, and a copy of the object will be dragged into the other application.*

- To restore the image that was dragged kicking and screaming out of CorelDRAW, just click anywhere in the CorelDRAW window (which makes it active again) and select Undo Delete from the Edit menu or press the CTRL-Z key.

When to Use PAINT and When to Use DRAW

You may want to use PHOTO-PAINT to enhance bitmap images and then bring them back into DRAW for adding text. An exception to this rule occurs if you need to apply special effects to the text. The reason for placing text in DRAW is that the resulting output text will be much sharper. When text is created in PAINT, the text is a bitmap image that is resolution-dependent. In other words, the text is no longer text but a bitmap picture of the text. It is fixed to the resolution of the image it is placed in. This means that text placed in PAINT will be the resolution of the image. If it is 300 dpi, then the text will be a bitmap image that is 300 dpi, regardless of whether it is printed to a 300-dpi laser printer or a 2,450-dpi imagesetter. Text in a program like DRAW is resolution-independent. Any text that is placed in DRAW remains as text. At printing time, DRAW sends the font information to the output device, allowing it to be printed at the maximum resolution of the device. If it is output to a 2,450-dpi imagesetter, then the resolution of the text will be 2,450 dpi. The result is sharper text.

Using OLE

It is a widely advertised fact that the entire Corel line of products, beginning with DRAW 4, supports OLE 2.0 (Object Linking and Embedding). Corel PHOTO-PAINT 9 and CorelDRAW 9 now both support in-place editing. OLE is a powerful interapplication program that is routinely demonstrated by dragging an image from one application and dropping it into another. OLE is given a lot of hype by Microsoft and the press. On paper, OLE looks great; in practice, it carries a lot of overhead.

In-place editing means that when you place a PHOTO-PAINT image into a word processing application like Microsoft Word, you can actually open PHOTO-PAINT inside of Word by right-clicking on the image. By copying the image to the Clipboard and then using the Paste Special command in the Edit menu of Word (or other OLE-compliant applications), you can right-click the image and PHOTO-PAINT will open up within Word. For the average PHOTO-PAINT user, this isn't a big issue. Because of the resources needed for photo-editing in PHOTO-PAINT, I cannot recommend using OLE's in-place editing unless you have a really powerful system with lots of memory. Even then, I am not sure what the great advantage would be. I guess this means I will get a lump of coal in my stocking from Santa Bill Gates this Christmas. Enough said about OLE.

We have covered a lot of material in this chapter, which I hope will help you use both Corel and non-Corel applications together to make some incredible projects.

CHAPTER 23

Corel Graphic Utilities

In this chapter we will look at a few of the essential graphic utilities included with PHOTO-PAINT that are indispensable for production work. These include Corel CAPTURE 9, Batch Process, the Recorder Docker, and Scripts. We will begin with Corel CAPTURE.

Corel CAPTURE: PHOTO-PAINT's Swiss Army Knife

Probably there is no more useful utility in PHOTO-PAINT than Corel CAPTURE. If you think that a screen capture utility is only for authors who need to include screen shots or to display images in their books, you need to read a little more. There are several "shy" features in PHOTO-PAINT that require a screen capture program to either print them or post them on the Web. By "shy" I am referring to nonprintable features like grids and duotones. Figure 23-1 shows a grid that is part of the image. Grids in PHOTO-PAINT are nonprintable and therefore can only be preserved by use of Corel CAPTURE. Duotones, grayscale images colored with two inks—in most cases, the first ink is black and the second is colored—have been around for some time. This feature of PHOTO-PAINT allows us to quickly give a vintage look to a photograph, which is becoming quite the popular look. While you can print a duotone, you cannot convert it into a format that can be seen on the Web or in the electronic version of this book without using a screen capture program. These are a few of the advantages of a screen capture program like Corel CAPTURE 9. Now that I have convinced you of this program's worth, let's learn how it works.

TIP: *Corel CAPTURE is not limited to screen captures in Corel applications; it works with all Windows applications.*

Exploring CAPTURE 9

Corel CAPTURE seems to change shape in nearly every release of PHOTO-PAINT. As one who uses the program all the time, I wish they would quit changing it. The latest incarnation, CAPTURE 9, is the result of recommendations from users. All I know is, I didn't ask for the changes. Have I complained enough yet?

FIGURE 23-1 The grids in this image could not be seen in print without a screen capture program

Corel CAPTURE is a stand-alone application. You can launch it from the Application Launcher inside Corel PHOTO-PAINT 9, as shown next, or from the PROGRAMS folder in Windows.

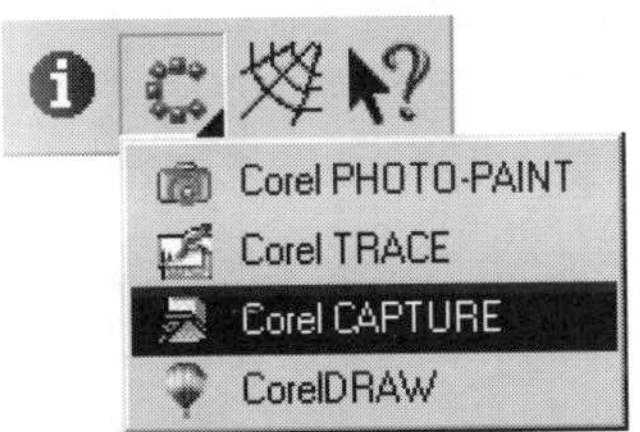

However you launch it, the Corel CAPTURE dialog box, shown in Figure 23-2, opens. It is from this dialog box that you will select the how, what, and when of CAPTURE's operation. There are three buttons at the bottom. The Help button is obvious (I hope). The Close button exits the program. The CAPTURE button sets the trap—so to speak. By default, once CAPTURE is enabled, the only indication you have that it is working is the tiny icon in the Windows system tray shown next. The icon is green when it is waiting to capture and red when in the process of capturing an image. While this may seem silly, since in most cases it means it is red for less than a second, we will discover that CAPTURE has a delay feature that allows you to see if you have started a capture sequence.

The dialog box contains four tabs: Source, Destination, Activation, and Image. We will look at each one of them separately.

Selecting the Source

You can specify which part of the image you want to capture on the Source page, shown in Figure 23-2. Most of the available selections are self-explanatory, and if they aren't, the preview window on the left changes to show what part of the window is being captured.

Here are some tips I learned while working with this page. In previous releases of Corel CAPTURE, if you needed to capture a mask or other software marquee, it was necessary to use the Full Screen option. If you used anything less, only part of

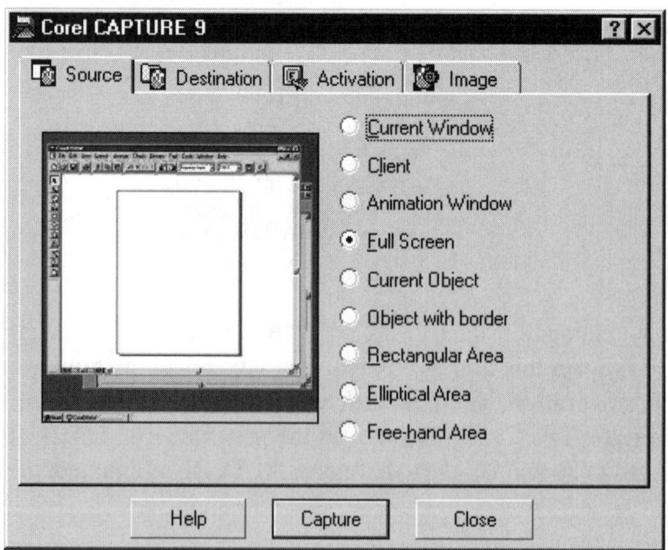

FIGURE 23-2 This is the dialog box that controls all of Corel CAPTURE's operations

the marquee was captured. In Corel CAPTURE 9 the program captures mask and other marquees without the necessity of using Full Screen. This saves a lot of image cropping later on.

The best way to capture an image window, dialog box, and so on, is to use the Current Object setting. If the Object With Border option is selected, the Title Bar on the image window will be included. The Elliptical Area and Rectangular Area features do not have a constrain key, so you must create your circle and square capture areas by using a steady hand on the mouse and your calibrated eyeball. If you use any setting that captures an area that is nonrectangular, the resulting capture will be in a rectangular image area.

Selecting the Destination

The Destination page, shown next, allows you to choose where to send the screen capture you create. There are several choices—File, Clipboard, Printer, or OLE Automated Application—the last of which has a pop-up menu. Since I must make a lot of screen captures for books and articles, I often save the image to the Clipboard and then use File | New From Clipboard in PHOTO-PAINT to make it into an image. The only caveat is to remember that the Clipboard can only hold one object at a time. More than once, I have saved a screen capture in the Clipboard and then, before unloading it in PHOTO-PAINT, proceeded to copy some text to the Clipboard while in another application, thus wiping out my screen shot. Other than this small consideration, the Clipboard works best for me.

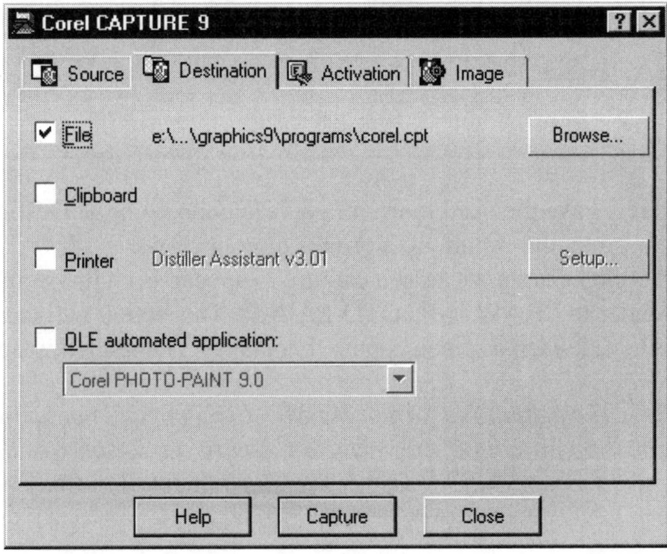

Selecting the File option creates a file containing the capture each time the hot key is selected. When you click the Browse button, you can choose the type of file it creates from the Capture As dialog box, shown next. In this dialog box, you specify the name, type, and location of the file. If you are recording a sequence of events, the Use Automatic Naming feature is handy. With each capture it will create another file with a sequentially numbered name beginning with the first number you place in the Start Naming At setting. If you don't use automatic naming, the CAPTURE program will overwrite the same file each time you press the hot key, just like the Clipboard. The Save In pop-up menu is important because it determines where your files will be placed when they are created. The default location is an obscure area deep within the CorelDRAW program files.

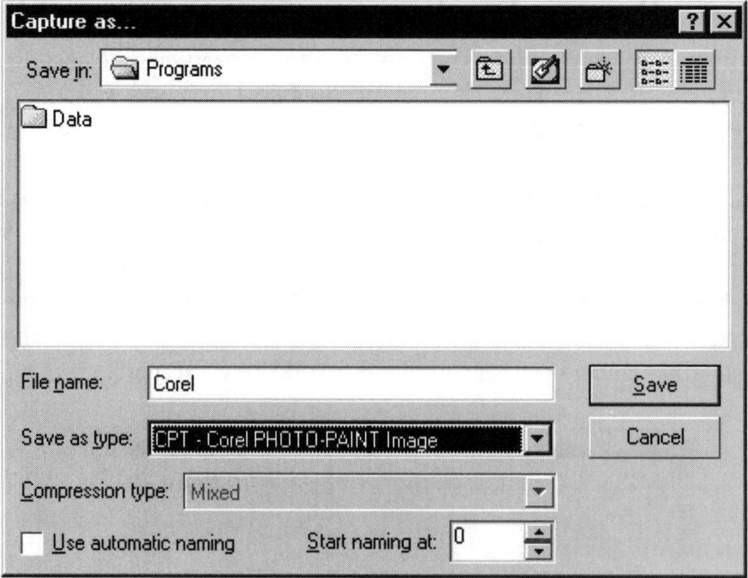

While I rarely have the need to use it, you can choose on the Destination page an option for sending the capture to a printer of your choice.

The OLE option causes the screen capture to appear as an image in an OLE application (either to DRAW or PHOTO-PAINT). This action will launch the application selected when a screen capture occurs if it is not already open.

NOTE: *The default file format is BMP. I recommend not using any lossy compression format (JPEG, Wavelett, and so on) for images that you may later want to modify, for reasons explained in detail in Chapter 2.*

Activation

From the Activation page, shown next, you can pick the hot key you want to use for activation of the program as well as hot keys for many other operations.

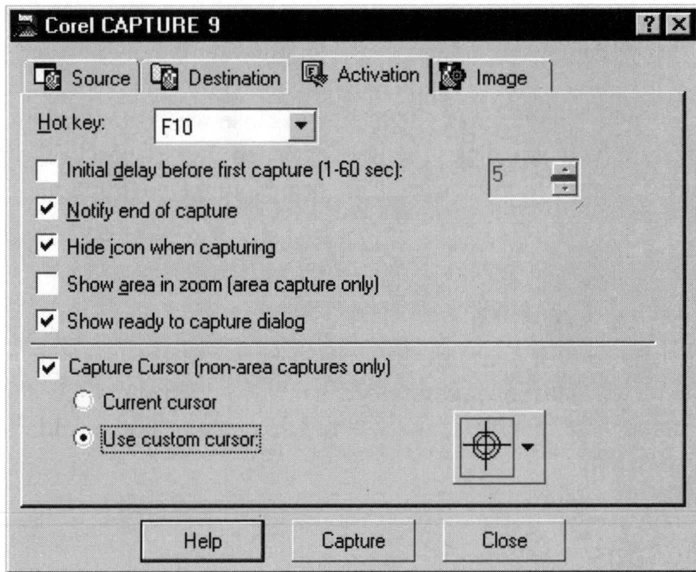

By default, the Hot Key is set to the function key F7. If the User Defined option is chosen in the pop-up menu, another dialog box opens, as shown next. From here you can enter the hot-key combination you desire. This is a very useful feature when you're working with a program that already has defined the hot key you normally use.

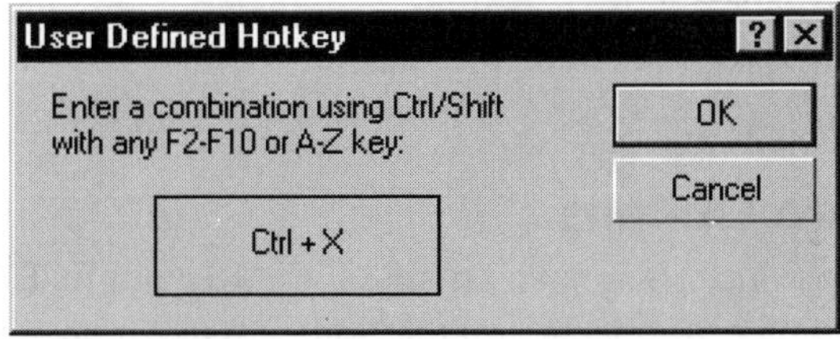

Here are some opinions about the rest of the options on this page.

Initial Delay (Not the Post Office)

This is like the timer on your camera that allows you, the photographer, enough time to run around and get into the group picture—assuming you don't trip over the cat. Initial Delay Before First Capture is enabled by default and set to 5 seconds, which is just enough time to make a new user wonder if the darn thing is working or not. The delay feature sets a delay between pressing the hot key and initiating the capture. This allows you to capture shy elements on the screen, such as flyouts and menu lists, which have a nasty tendency to close when you push the hot key. Using this feature, you can click your hot key, open the shy part of the program, and wait for the capture to take place. That brings up the next option—Notify End Of Capture.

Notify End of Capture

Always enable this one. It pops up a little message box that tells you that the capture has been completed. This is necessary because full screen shots saved to a file may take a few moments to complete, and without this feature you wouldn't know when they were done.

Other Options

The other options are interesting. The Hide Icon When Capturing option is the secret-agent setting that causes the program icon to "hide" when making the capture. While I can't believe it makes any difference to anyone, it's nice to have it—just in case. The Show Area In Zoom option lets you view the capture area in detail. This option can be used only for the Rectangular, Elliptical, and Free-hand Area captures. The next option is Show Ready To Capture Dialog. This puts an annoying message box on your screen like an overeager-to-please puppy dog telling you CAPTURE is ready to capture. If you enable this one, you may find a lump of coal in your stocking next Christmas.

Cursor Capture Options

This one is pretty obvious. It is not available if the Rectangle, Elliptical, or Free-hand Area options are selected on the Source page. You can capture the current cursor; not capture any cursor (if nothing in this section of the dialog box is checked); choose a custom cursor from the pop-up menu; or select a program (via the Other button in the pop-up menu) containing the program that contains the cursor you want to display in the screen capture. While I generally use the No

Cursor option, I have used all these successfully during the course of making this book. Before I got into computers, the only cursors I knew about were senior bos'n mates aboard my ship—boy, those sailors knew how to curse.

The Image Page

It is from this page, shown next, that you select the color depth of your capture as well as the size. From here you can determine the resolution and scaling as well. A few comments may help clear up some confusion. The Resolution setting doesn't change anything except the resolution setting of the captured image. This can be changed at any time with the Resample command. For example, if a full screen capture at 96 dpi is 1,024 pixels wide, at 300 dpi it will still be 1,024 pixels wide. The Scale feature *does* change the size. Figure 23-3 shows two screen captures of the Mask Tool flyout. The top one was captured at 100 percent and the bottom at 200 percent. The top image is 244 pixels wide, while the bottom one is 488 pixels wide. Many of the toolbar and dialog box images captured in this book used the Scale feature.

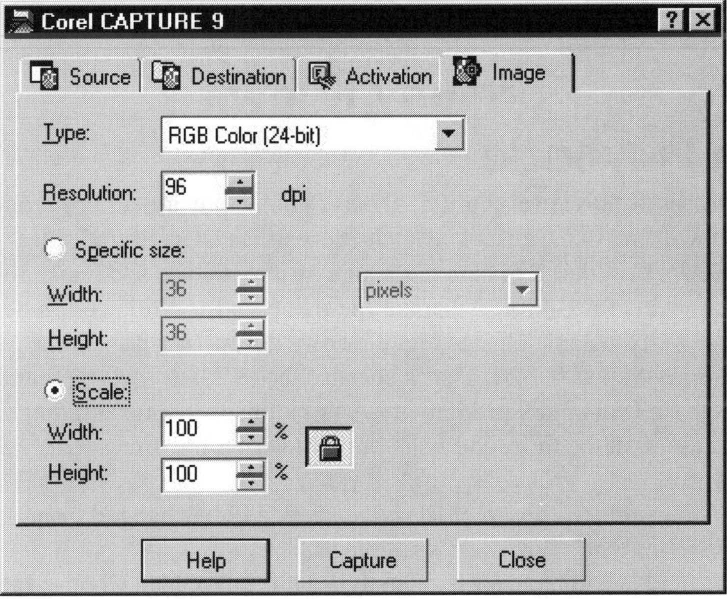

NOTE: *When using the Scale feature, be aware it is resampling the capture without anti-aliasing. For most screen captures, that's a good thing.*

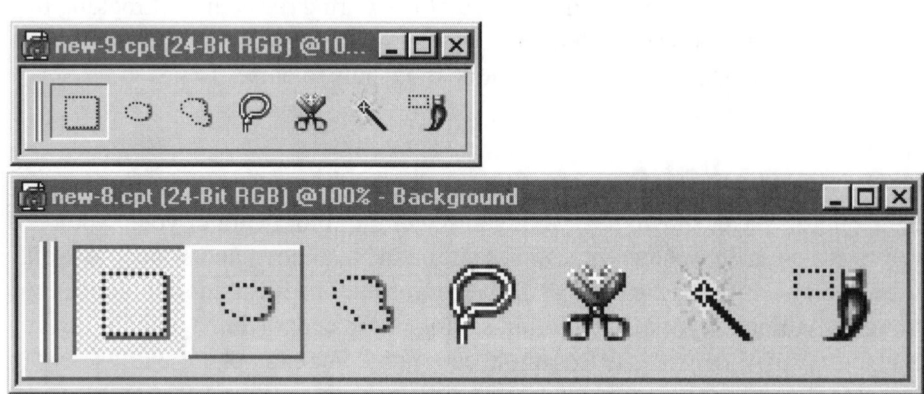

FIGURE 23-3 The Scale option increases the size of the capture. The top image was captured at 100% scale and the bottom one was grabbed at 200%

That pretty well wraps up Corel CAPTURE 9. Let's take a quick look at the Batch Process command.

Batch Process (Formerly Known as Batch Playback)

This is another of those useful utilities that if you do any amount of production work, you will find indispensable. Batch Process has been around since PHOTO-PAINT 6. It used to be located in a different place and had a different name. That was before the let's-change-the-name-and-location committee found it. Regardless of the name change and the new address (it's now in the File menu), it works just as well as before. That's because the let's-improve-the-command committee hasn't found it yet. Many users think this is just for running scripts. Not true. I use it all the time, and I can only think of a few times that I have used it with a script.

Have you ever had a group of files that needed to be changed from one format to another? With Batch Process it's simple as pie.

You do not have to have a file open to use this command. Choose File | Batch Process, opening the dialog box shown in Figure 23-4.

Add the files you want to process by clicking the Add Files button. Unlike with certain Internet browsers, you can use SHIFT-select to select all the contiguous files between two points, or use CTRL with the mouse to individually select multiple files.

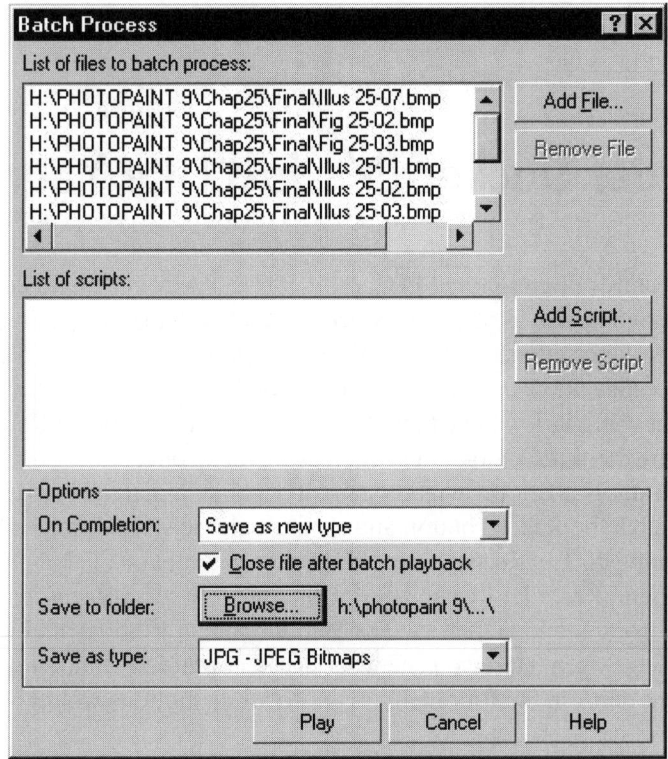

FIGURE 23-4 The Batch Process dialog box is simple to use but still powerful

After you have all the files you want, you can add scripts—it's your choice. These scripts can be something simple, like "add 10 percent contrast to every image." We will discuss scripts a little when we talk about the Recorder Docker in the next section.

With the files selected and scripts optionally selected, we need to select what we want the Batch Process to do with the files after the scripts (or no scripts) are run. The On Completion pop-up menu contains the following choices: Don't Save, Save Over Original, Save To New Folder, Save As New Type.

All the choices are self-explanatory except Don't Save. It would allow you to apply a script to multiple images (both open and not) and keep them open. I would be careful about having too many image files open, which leads to the next option: Close Files After Batch Playback. If you are processing a lot of files, you want to make sure this is enabled. If it isn't and too many files are open, your system may throw a hairball.

So the next time you have a large number of files on which to do something repetitive, remember how easy Batch Process is to use. The Recorder is also pretty easy to use and it's next.

The Recorder Docker (It's Just Like Your VCR, Sort Of)

One of the features often ignored in Corel PHOTO-PAINT is the Recorder. It is a powerful tool that allows you to produce some effects that might otherwise be considered too labor intensive. If you haven't used the Recorder before, it may have been because the documentation borders on being vague. I had a different reason for not using it. I believed that the gains made by using the Recorder were outweighed by the time it took to use it. Was I ever wrong.

The Recorder is a Docker window, and it acts like a macro recorder (think VCR). You click the Record button and go through the steps of the task that you want to accomplish. The Recorder records each step until you click the Stop button.

You open the Recorder by choosing Window | Dockers | Recorder, or by using the keyboard combination CTRL-F3. The Window menu is not available unless there is an image open. Here you see what the Recorder looks like. I have already recorded some steps in the following image so all the buttons would be available.

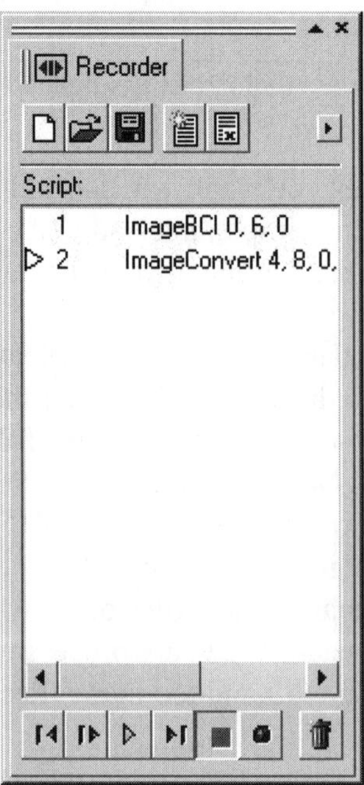

The buttons at the top of the Recorder Docker window (shown next) from left to right are standard Windows buttons: New will erase the current recording and start a new one; Open will open the Load Script dialog box; and Save Recording will open the Save Recording dialog box. The next two buttons are for editing the command contents of the script. Insert New Command inserts newly recorded commands in a recording or script or overwrites the existing commands. Newly recorded commands are inserted when the button appears pressed. The other button has, I think, the longest name in PHOTO-PAINT. It is the Enable/Disable Selected Command(s) button. As its name says, it enables or disables selected commands in the command list so that only enabled commands are played. When a command is disabled, it appears grayed out in the list. It is a toggle operation, meaning that the same button that disables the command can be used to enable it.

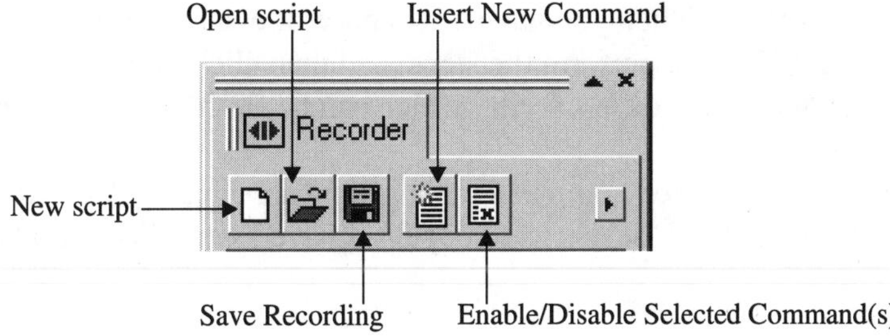

The button on the far right opens an Option Popup menu, as shown next.

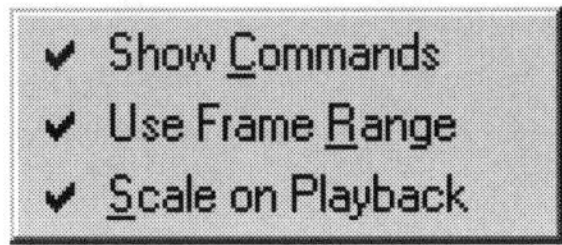

Show Commands/Use Frame Range

Show Commands toggles the display of the commands in the Docker on and off. Use Frame Range, when enabled, allows the Recorder actions to be restricted to a range of frames in a movie. If you're not working with animation or video, the setting doesn't affect anything.

Scale on Playback

When this is enabled, the commands that are applied to images are scaled as a function of the image size. For example, using the Resample command with Scale On Playback enabled will produce the same final image size each time it is played, regardless of the original image size. I discovered this when making all the illustrations for the buttons in this book. I created a script with the Recorder that would resample the screen shot to a size of 0.75 inch. Yet because many of the buttons are different sizes, running the script without enabling the Scale On Playback feature produced buttons of varying sizes. Therefore, if the button was a smaller size than the one I used for the original script, it would produce a button smaller than 0.75 inch. This feature is important because there are many operations that require the user to ensure the image to which the script is applied is the same size as the original when the action was recorded.

The VCR-style buttons at the bottom of the Recorder Docker provide the following functions (from left to right): Rewind, which returns the marker to the first command; Step Forward, which plays one command at a time; Play; Fast Forward, which advances to the last command; Stop; and Record. The Docker operates like a VCR. When you have a sequence of events you want to record, you click the Record button, perform the steps, and then click the Stop button. The resulting list of commands is a script, which can be saved, reloaded, and replayed at a later date.

To save your recorded commands as a script file, click the Save Recording button at the top of the Docker, which opens a Save Recording dialog box, shown here:

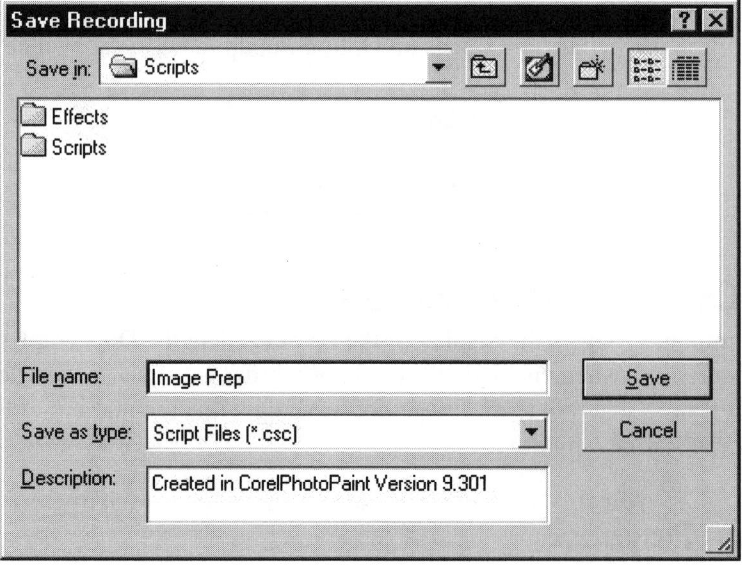

The commands are saved as Corel Scripts. The Script file (CSC) is the native format. If you made scripts with Corel PHOTO-PAINT before this release, you may need to rerecord them. When you save the file, you can open it in the Corel Script editor and add all kinds of functionality to it. It becomes a real programming type of task at that point. The CSC file can be run from the Recorder or from the Scripts Docker, where all the other scripts hang out.

What got me working with this Recorder to begin with was a need to apply a tonal adjustment to over 100 screen captures. With a script and the Batch Process feature, this was a snap. Now, follow along and we will enter the world of PHOTO-PAINT automation.

NOTE: *While Photoshop Actions resemble Corel Scripts, the two are completely different and not interchangeable.*

Creating a Script

This is a simple text effect in which the automation is helpful when it is necessary to evaluate the effect on many different fills. Don't begin recording until instructed.

1. Create a new image that is 24-bit RGB color, 6 × 2 inches at 100 dpi. Open the Recorder Docker (CTRL-F3).
2. Select the Text tool from the Toolbox, and change the Font to Lithograph at a size of 96. Click inside the image window, enable the Bold option, and type **SCRIPTS**. Select the Object Picker tool, and align the text to the center of the document (CTRL-A), as shown next.

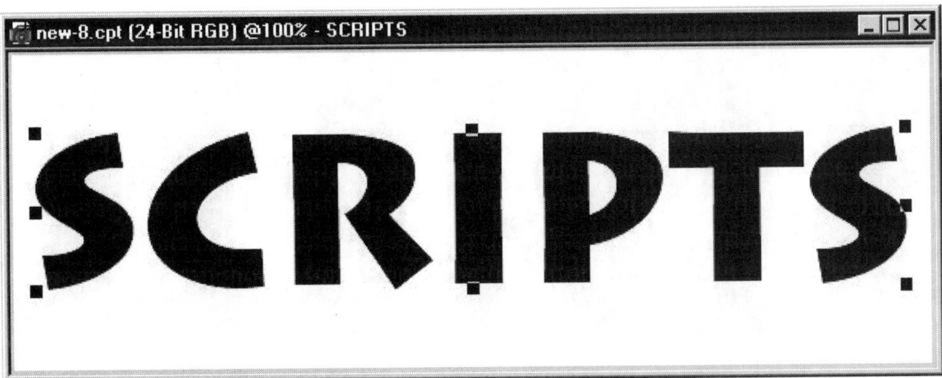

3. Ensure that Lock Object Transparency is enabled, and apply a fill to the text. For the example, I chose Edit | Fill | Bitmap Fill and selected a light-colored wood, as shown next.

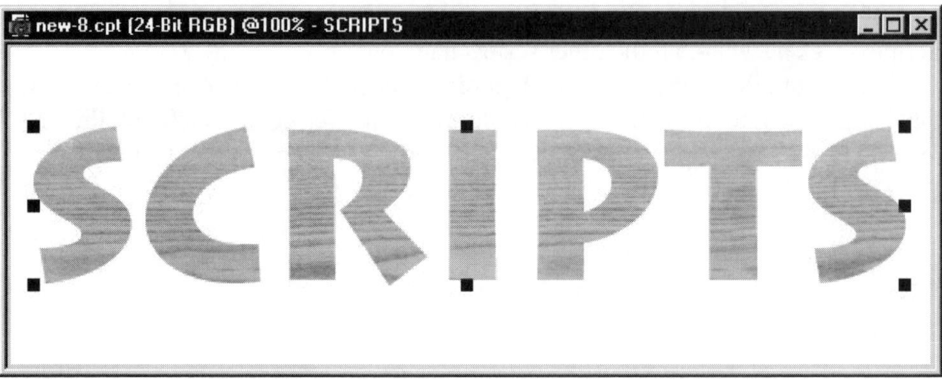

4. Now we begin to record by clicking the little red button at the bottom of the Recorder Docker.
5. Create a mask (CTRL-M).
6. Choose Effects | 3D Effects | The Boss, and change the settings as follows: Width: 3, Height: 200, Smoothness: 60, Drop Off: Mesa, Invert check box: enabled, Brightness: 100, Sharpness: 3, Direction:135, Angle: 64, and click OK.
7. Remove the mask (CTRL-SHIFT-R) and click the Stop button (to the left of the Record button). The result is shown next.

8. Now comes the fun part. Click the Rewind button on the Recorder Docker. The Current Position indicator moves to the top of the list of commands. Next apply a different fill to the text. You can use anything. My only recommendation is not to make the fill too dark. I used a weave fill from the \TILES\TEXTURE folder of the Corel CD. Click the Play button and the result is shown next.

9. The script we created is shown in Figure 23-5. Once a file works, you can save it as a script by clicking the Save Recording button at the top of the Recorder Docker. I saved mine as Boss Edges. Default scripts are saved in either the EFFECTS or the SCRIPTS folder. They can be saved anywhere your little old heart desires, but those two folders are where the Scripts Docker is expecting to find them. Before we conclude this chapter, let's take a brief look at the Scripts Docker.

Scripts Docker

The Scripts Docker (CTRL-F6) is where scripts are selected and launched. Shown next, it is only necessary to double-click the script to launch it. The first time you open the Scripts Docker, you should see two choices for folders: SCRIPTS and EFFECTS. The EFFECTS folder contains scripts that are applications of the

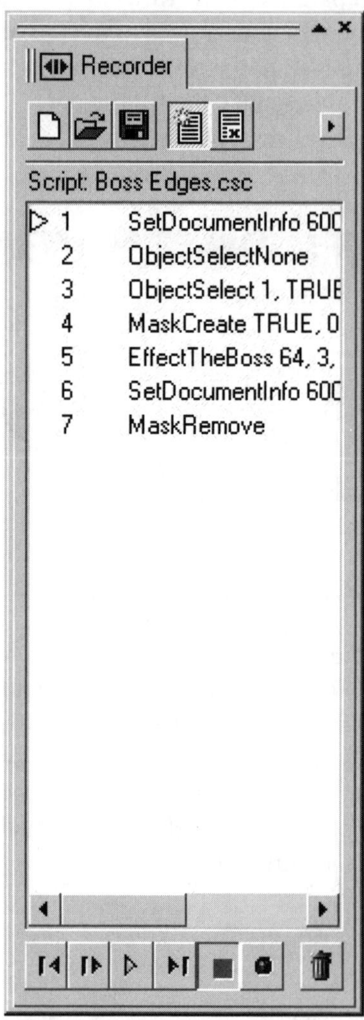

FIGURE 23-5 The script is simple, but it saves a lot of time when you're comparing effects on different fills

filters; the SCRIPTS folder tends to contain more complex sequences. Corel has preloaded a lot of scripts, and it is well worth your time to check them out.

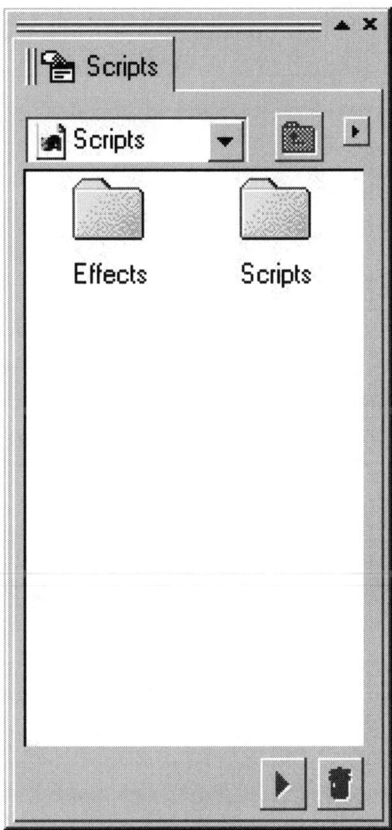

Now it's time for learning about the Internet from one of my favorite authors. Yep, you guessed it—I didn't write the next chapter. While I know something about the Internet, the best-selling author who graciously agreed to write the chapter is an expert. Enjoy.

CHAPTER 24

Creating Elements for the Web

Let's face it: no one gets into computer graphics because they think it's a "practical career," like postal inspector or insurance agent. Nope, we all got into it for two reasons:

1. We have a talent that needs expressing to the world and an ego to feed.
2. We aren't athletic enough to become sports stars and have our name on a $200 pair of sneakers. And our parents won't let us become rap singers.

But, believe it or not, the computer graphics field, more than 20 years old, is a mature, stable, and fully populated market. The really cool stuff is *not* in designing granola boxes and furniture ads with your computer. All the action today is on the Web—for business (Michael Dell of Dell Computers does millions of dollars in sales a day on the Web); for entertainment, leisure, and events (you can even get married on the Web); and, most importantly, for the "content creators"—in short, *us*!

But we designers have to move fast, because the World Wide Web (WWW, the "Web") waits for no one. It's more than three years old and travels at the speed of light. You already have competition out there from others with similar skills, but not to worry. With PHOTO-PAINT and this chapter as your guide, you'll not only get up and running, but you'll also learn how to beat your competition by using a piece of information here and a scrap of HTML code there.

As with any new medium of creativity, to best use the tools, you have to understand the rules. So let's begin our supersonic expedition to web design with a brief history and some details about web use, and work our way up from there.

Understanding the Web

The underlying purpose of the World Wide Web is to add graphics capabilities to Internet connections. The Internet dates back to the 1960s, when scientists and academic folks used computers networked across vast distances to share information. But it was not until Marc Andresson came up with the idea in college to construct a *subroute* of communications on the Internet, and to make it graphically interesting (the Internet is actually text only), that—boing!—we had the World Wide Web. From a designer's point of view, the Web can be divided into two components:

- **Media** This is where text, images, animations, page layout, and sometimes sound and video are required. This is usually considered the fun part of web graphics design.

- **Hypertext Markup Language (HTML)** This is the delivery system for the Web, the "binder" that holds all the media together. HTML consists of commands and tags in a script-style language that determine how a web site appears when visitors to a site peer at your work through their browser (which is usually Microsoft Internet Explorer or Netscape Navigator/Communicator).

So, necessarily, if you're to become a smash hit with your PHOTO-PAINT web creations, you'll need to learn a little about HTML. But don't worry—the focus of this chapter is on art for the Web. We'll discuss only the relevant HTML tags that will help you to complete your designs.

The Concept Dictates the Art

The best way to start learning about web creation is to break the important components of a web page into their basic parts and then to understand how to create these parts. The first thing on your web creativity list should be a *concept.* There are far too many web sites on the Internet today that are all sizzle and no steak. Think of your audience, think of what you're trying to communicate to them, and then let this target play a role in the colors, shapes, and layout of the web site.

Let's suppose, for example, that your client is the (fictitious) UniFruit Company, importers of a wide range of seedless and other fruits. UniFruit is seeking global name-brand recognition. The company wants the world to notice its seal on a piece of fruit and remember it on every shopping trip. Therefore, your concept for a web site is a fairly easy one: the company logo will appear frequently on the site, and the mood for the site will be graphically attractive and appealing.

The Most Important Rule of the Web

As we progress through this chapter, always keep in mind that the finished art for a web site has to be, in a word, *small.* "Small," as measured on the Web, means the file size of each element including graphics needs to be as tiny as possible without compromising the artistic merit of the element. "Small," as you will see, can be achieved in three ways: if an image contains very few colors, it can be saved as a small file. Similarly, if the overall dimensions of a graphic are small (as measured in *pixels,* the official unit of measurement for this chapter <grin>), it, too, will download quickly to the visitor's browser. Long download times mean losing your audience's interest. Finally—and this applies to a specific piece of web media—the best animated GIFs contain few colors, small dimensions, *and* a minimal number of frames. "Small" doesn't need to cramp your style if you get inventive within the confines of the web as a gallery.

The Four Visual Elements

We're going to cover four specific types of visuals for a web page that require nothing special of the visitor's browser, so virtually everyone who hits this site will see it as you envisioned it. The four elements you'll see how to create are the following:

- **The background to the site** It can be a solid color (yawn), a texture saved to GIF or JPEG format, or it can be an animated GIF, which can sometimes be a mindblower for your audience, and if done incorrectly becomes a headache.
- **A headline or logo** This can be a specific piece of 2-D, or more interestingly, 3-D, artwork that visitors focus on first (always plan where you want attention directed on web pages).
- **Buttons** Navigation and link buttons are the two types of buttons most commonly found on sites. *Navigation* buttons should be on the top page of a site as "directory assistance" for exploring the rest of the site. *Link* buttons (although all buttons you create can serve any purpose) tend to be smaller than navigation buttons, and lead the visitor to a specific area that might or might not be on the host site. You'll learn how PHOTO-PAINT creates an *image map*—a single piece of code that links to numerous places on the Web—while using only a single graphic.
- **Animated GIFs** It's really easy to build an eyesore instead of an attention-getting mini-movie with this file type. You'll see how to build an animated GIF in this chapter, but also see how to make it subtle and attractive instead of producing the flashing, blinking nonsense seen too often on the Web.

The first two things you need to do before actually applying paint to your virtual canvas are to determine what color model you'll use for elements, and to determine how large a single web page should be.

Let's put all this theory into practice now. If you'd like to follow along, building the UniFruit site using the steps listed, all the elements you'll need are in the WEBTOOTS\EXAMPLES folder. The finished site can also be played from the CD in your web browser by loading the INDEX.HTML file in the WEBTOOTS\DONE folder.

Measuring Color and Pixels

By default, PHOTO-PAINT displays "print legal" colors on the color palette. *Print legal* means that the colors onscreen are fairly accurate renditions of how colors will look when printed to color separations. Color separations, usually, are single color printing plates to which cyan, magenta, yellow, and black inks are applied. Then, progressively, the inked plates are pressed onto paper, until all four inks in concert represent the original design. The colors by default shown onscreen in PHOTO-PAINT are, therefore, called *CMYK legal* colors—none of the colors fall outside of the CMYK color space.

However, the Web doesn't *know* about these CMYK "legal" colors—the color space of the Web is the same as your monitor—it's measured in amounts of red, green, and blue.

If you open PHOTO-PAINT right now, we'll walk through how to change screen colors.

You need to get to the Color Management area of the Options palette in PHOTO-PAINT. When an image is loaded, you can go directly to the Color Management option by choosing Tools | Color Management. Without an opened image, press CTRL-J to open the Options palette, click Global to expand the menu tree, and click Color Management, as shown in Figure 24-1.

Next uncheck the Display Simulated Printer Colors check box and click OK. Now watch the color swatches on your screen. Obviously, you cannot see the color palette change in this screen figure, but if you do this in your copy of PHOTO-PAINT, all the colors on the palette will brighten, reflecting the true combination of red, green, and blue primary colors.

It's a good idea for novices to create a layout of what a web page should be, to the exact dimensions as the page will be seen. This is confusing, because everyone on Earth (and beyond) uses different monitor resolution, different color modes, and a different web browser on their computers. Which should you pick?

My suggestion: as they say in theater, "Play to the cheap seats"; that is, seek the lowest common denominator for your page dimensions to assure that even the most meager of systems can see your site the way you intend it to be seen. Okay, we don't go lower than 640 × 480 pixels in screen dimensions, and probably the oldest browser that folks still use is Navigator 3, so we should account for the

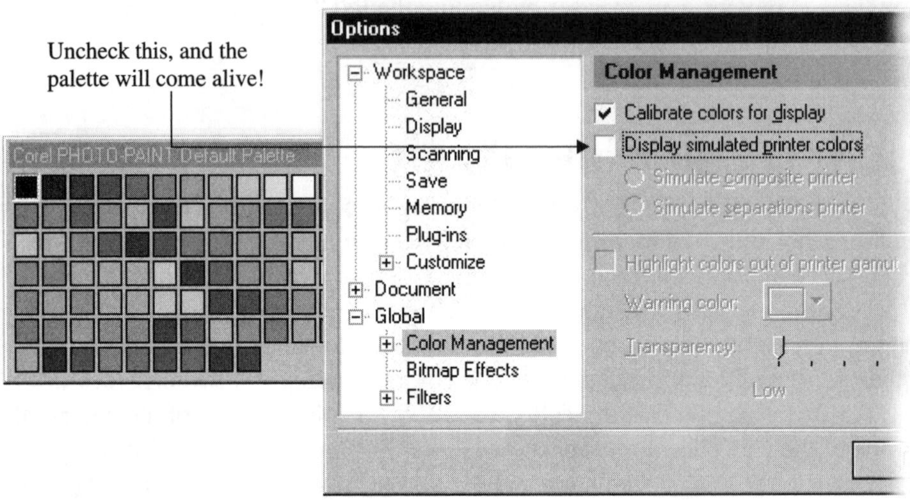

FIGURE 24-1 Set up PHOTO-PAINT to display colors as you and others are used to seeing them on a computer monitor

"padding" that slightly shrinks Navigator's preview area. In Figure 24-2, I've done the math for you: In the Create A New Image dialog box, create a template for Mr. UniFruit that is 637 pixels wide by 314 pixels high.

NOTE: *Visitors with a video card of 2MB—which is about as low as they come—can view your page in 24-bit, TrueColor mode, so you do not have to fool with your graphics to make a special, limited color palette (in case you've heard about Netscape Color Safe palettes). In fact, most computers sold in 1999 come with an 8MB video card, so visitors can easily view your site in 24-bit color at resolutions of 1024 × 768 or higher.*

Create a layout in PHOTO-PAINT similar to Figure 24-3, save it in PHOTO-PAINT's CPT format as TEMPLATE to your hard disk, and close the image now to conserve resources.

The embellished template, called TEMPLATE.TIF, is in the WEBTOOTS\ EXAMPLES folder in case you want to use this template instead of your own. Copy the file to hard disk, call it TEMPLATE, and save it in PHOTO-PAINT's native file format. Our next step is the creation of different types of background images, because simply knowing one technique is not going to get you rich!

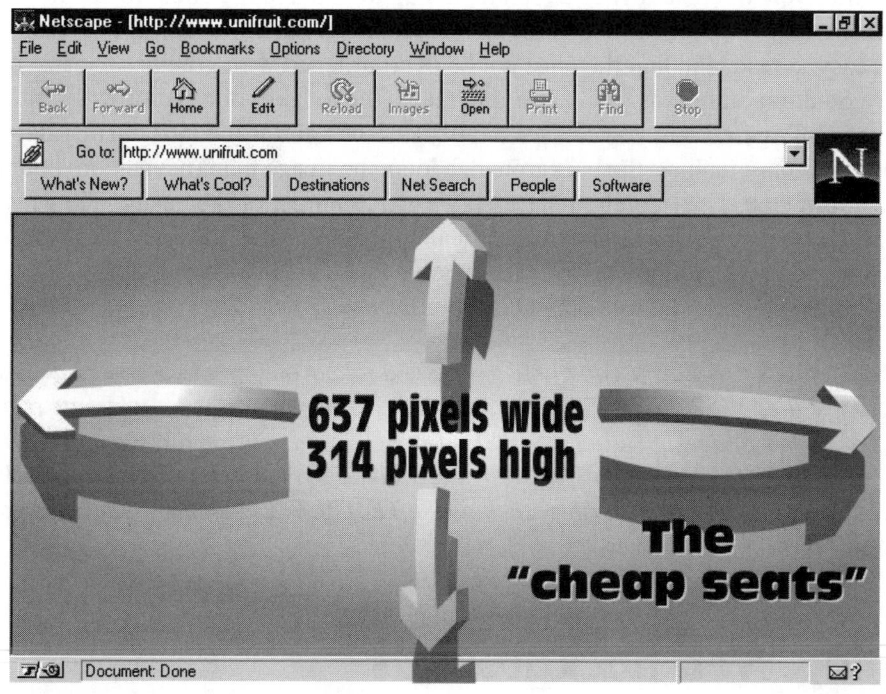

FIGURE 24-2 You are, quite literally, the host of your site. Make visitors feel welcome by accommodating the lowest common denominator of screen resolutions

FIGURE 24-3 A template is the key to taking accurate measurements for the elements that will be featured on the page

After you've created your template, it's up to you and the client to decide what elements will be featured first on the site. I recommend that the message(s) be clear and easy to read, and that the page not be overburdened with graphics the size of Shea Stadium billboards (the larger the image, the longer your visitor will wait . . . or not). In Figure 24-3, you can see a fairly neat design for the introductory page. There are four graphics: the background, a logo, the image map (navigation) buttons, and a fruit crate as a (largely unnecessary <g>) reminder of the business in which UniFruit operates. Also notice that vertically, the page is divided into three areas. This was done to put the elements into a table when HTML coding time comes around. We'll get into more detail on this a little later.

NOTE: *Now's a good time to create a folder on one of your hard drives called WEBSITE. Within the WEBSITE folder, you'll want to create two other folders: SITE and STASH. The SITE folder is for the elements that will actually make up the web site, and the STASH folder is where you'll keep resource materials, such as the TEMPLATE document, that will not be seen on the Web.*

Creating Web Backgrounds

As I mentioned earlier, it would be good to leverage the full capability of PHOTO-PAINT's features to come up with a number of techniques for creating web backgrounds. It's important to understand that you do *not* create a texture background image that's the size of the browser window. It would be much too large to download in less than several weeks. Instead, you create a seamless tiling pattern that today's browsers automatically tile in the background, thus conserving a good deal of bandwidth. Let's begin with creating an organic background—one that looks as natural as the UniFruit products are.

The Recipe for a "Ground Dirt" Background

PHOTO-PAINT's texture fill collection and the new bump-map feature can't be topped for creating images of any size that look like close-ups of trees, the ocean, stone, and other natural surfaces. The only trick you need to learn is how to make textures that tile *seamlessly*—that is, when you put several of them edge to edge, you cannot tell where one tile begins and the other leaves off. Because a web browser repeats an image that is designated as the background image, these next few steps are important to learn if you don't want seams showing in the background (hint: you don't).

Follow these steps to create a seamless-tiling, complex pattern that can be used as the background for UniFruit's web site:

1. In PHOTO-PAINT, press CTRL-N to open the Create A New Image dialog box. Specify in this dialog box that the new image should be in RGB Color mode with a white background. Set the unit of measure to pixels. Enter **200** for Width and Height and **72** for Resolution. Click OK to display the image in PHOTO-PAINT's workspace.
2. Choose the Fill tool (the paint bucket icon) on the Toolbox. On the Property Bar, click the Texture Fill icon (directly to the left of the Edit Fill command), and then click the Edit Fill button. The Texture Fill dialog box displays.
3. From the Texture list, choose Aerial Photography. You're free in your own assignments to begin with any texture you like, but Aerial Photography tends to work better with the other commands you'll use shortly for creating an organic, seamless tile.
4. To avoid creating a texture that looks like everyone else's, click the Preview button a few times to change the look. As you can see in Figure 24-4, I've got a texture that has about 50 percent of a corrosive look, and 50 percent smooth. This is going to work terrifically by the time we're done filtering and modifying it. Click OK when you've defined a similar texture to return to the workspace.
5. Make sure the transparency field to the right of the Edit Fill command is at 0% (totally opaque) and that the Color Tolerance Mode in the Property Bar shows Normal. Click in the image to apply the texture fill.
6. Let's complicate things a little, at least visually, by applying a different sort of texture to an object above the texture fill, using partial merging opacity. First, open the Objects palette by pressing CTRL-F7.
7. Click the New Object icon at the bottom of the Objects Docker. A new, empty object appears on the Objects list and is the current editing object. With the Fill tool active, right-click any color swatch to change the Fill color. It doesn't make any difference what the color is—the Canvas effect we will apply next needs to fill in an object that contains some pixels. Click the image window to fill the new object with color, as indicated in the Objects Docker.

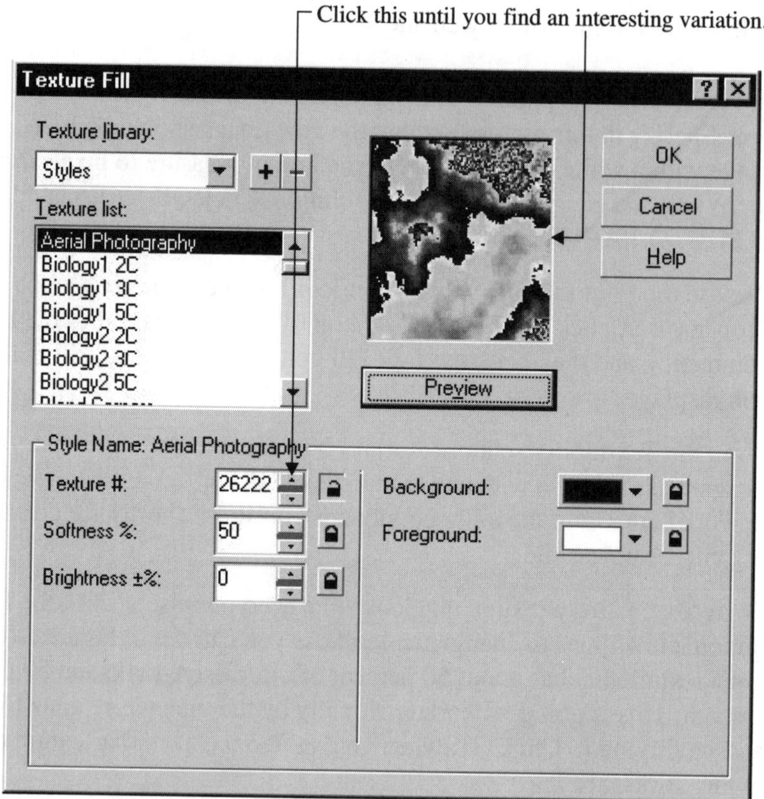

FIGURE 24-4 There are approximately 32,000 variations of the Aerial Photography texture. It's not hard to choose one that will serve as the base image for your web page background!

8. Choose Effects | Texture | Canvas and, in the Canvas dialog box, click the open folder icon on the bottom right. Choose Stucco from the CUSTOM\CANVAS folder on your hard drive, within the COREL main folder, and click OK to load it. In the Canvas dialog box, drag the Transparency slider to 0%, and click OK to apply the Canvas effect and to return to the workspace. On the Objects Docker, make the Opacity 50 percent so you can still see the aerial photography background.
9. Click the New Object icon again on the Objects Docker so you have an Object 2 in the composition. Fill the object using the Fill tool and any color.
10. Choose Effects | Custom | Alchemy. The Alchemy Effects dialog box appears. In the Style drop-down list, choose Ice Cubes, click the Preview

button to see what we're doing here, and then click OK to apply the ice to the new object in the image. Then set the Opacity to about 25 on the Objects Docker. You're on your way to making a visually intricate image to be used as a bump map for the background of the web site.

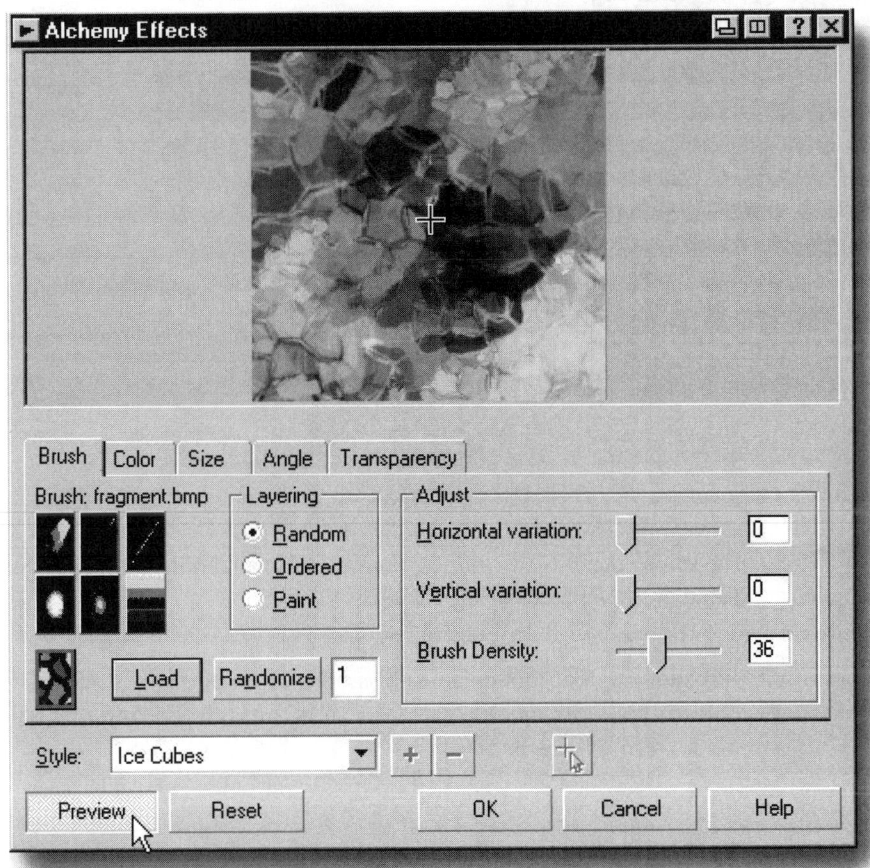

11. You should now have three objects in the image, as shown in Figure 24-5. When your document looks like this, proceed to step 12.

12. From the Object menu, choose Combine | Combine All Objects With Background to create a single image out of its components. You should now have only the Background listed in the Objects Docker. Save the file as ROUGH in PHOTO-PAINT's native format to your hard disk. Keep the image open and take a breather for a moment.

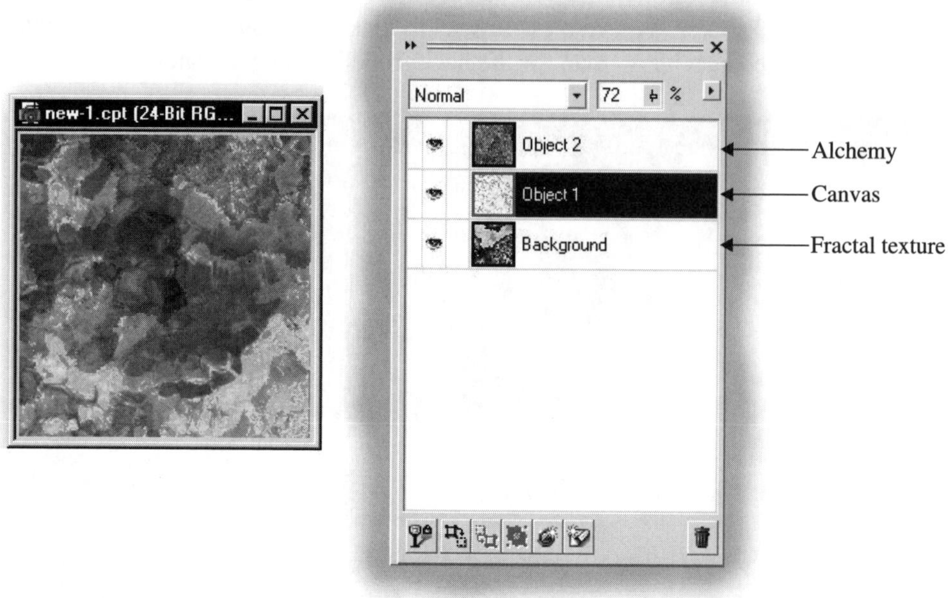

FIGURE 24-5 The source material for your tile consists of several objects, all at different strengths of opacity

You might well suppose that this meaningless blob of pixel tones is going nowhere, but we haven't *filtered* the piece yet, and it is through filtering that a wonderful, organic texture will be had.

Creating a Tiling Source Image

None of the three layers that you used to compose this ROUGH image was a tiling texture. In other words, every 200 pixels, the texture, when tiled, will leave a visible mark onscreen, both vertically and horizontally. The trick to fixing this is to use PHOTO-PAINT's Offset command in combination with the Clone (Brush) tool. Here are some easy steps that you can apply to any texture to make it a seamless-tiling texture:

1. Open ROUGH and choose Effects | Distort | Offset from the main Menu Bar. The Offset filter takes the edges of an image and places them somewhere near the center of the piece. Similarly, the center of the image is divided into four sections that represent the edges of the picture. You're essentially turning an image inside out.
2. Choose 50% for the Horizontal and Vertical Shift amounts, click the Wrap Around button, click the Preview button to see what's going to happen, and then click OK to apply the effect.

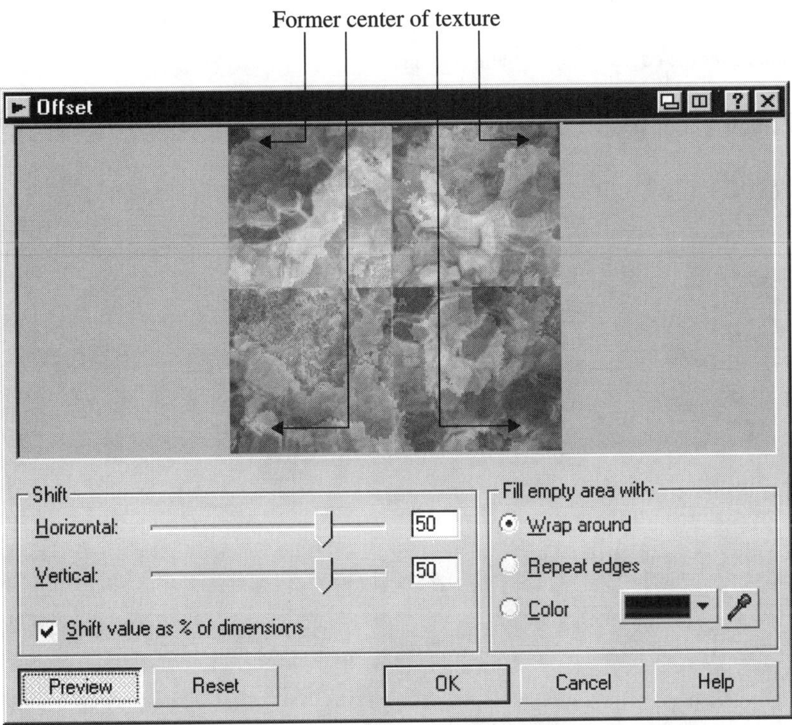

3. Open the Paint tool flyout and select the Clone tool. Double-click this tool to display the Stroke Style Docker. You might or might not want to increase the size or softness of the brush tip in this example—it depends on your style of work (I'm using the default settings shown in the illustration).

4. Right-click a point from which to sample in the upper right of the image, and then hold the primary mouse button and drag along the visible horizontal edge in the image, as shown in Figure 24-6.

5. When your sample cursor comes close to an edge in the image, it's time to redefine the beginning point for the sampling, in relation to the brush tip. Right-click in an area with no edges, and then stroke over any remaining

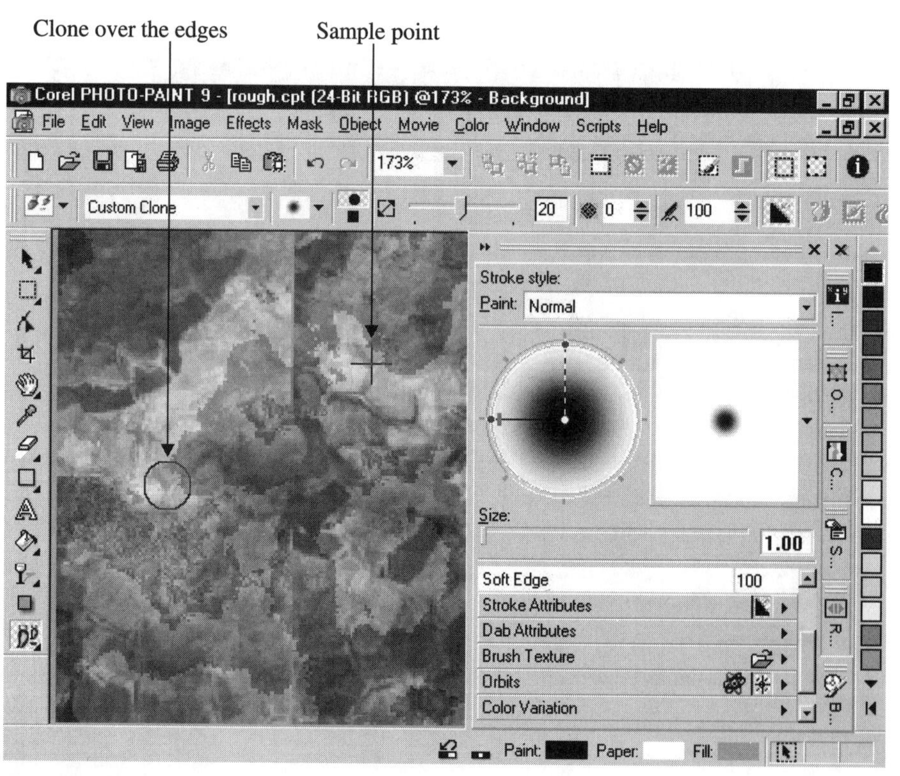

FIGURE 24-6 Use an unaltered area of the image as your sample point, and then stroke over an area that displays a hard edge

edges in the piece. Press CTRL-S to save your work up to this point—I recommend that you save it to your WEBSITE\STASH folder (you'll need to locate and call upon it shortly). You can close the file now.

In the section that follows, you'll finish creating a beautiful seamless tile of something that suggests dirt, a natural enough environment for fruit, and UniFruit's background image on their site.

Using the Bump-map Effect

Bump mapping, although you see it used all the time in computer graphics, is a little hard to describe. What will be happening shortly is that the ROUGH image you've created will be examined by PHOTO-PAINT for its lighter and darker areas. The Bump map filter translates visual information into elevation information and then casts shadows from the tall elements onto the shorter ones in the image. For example, if you were to create a black circle on a white canvas, declare black as being high in the target image, and then use this image as a bump map, the resulting image would be a column rising out of the background.

Fortunately, our bump map is a lot more intricate than a simple circle shape, and it will produce a very interesting yet subtle tiling texture. Just follow these steps:

1. Create a new document that is the same size as ROUGH (200 × 200 pixels), but has a pale, neutral paper color, such as H: 55, S: 9, and B: 94 (R: 240, G: 238, B: 218). To choose a custom color, click the down arrow and choose Other from the pop-up color swatch that appears. This opens the Select Color dialog box, where you can enter your own values.
2. Choose Effects | Custom | Bump-map to open the Bump-map dialog box. On the Bump-map tab, click the folder icon, and then choose ROUGH from your STASH folder on hard disk. Click OK to return to the dialog box.
3. Click the Surface tab. The author chose to invert the bump map, because the shadows looked better to him when they cast downward instead of upward. Set the Scale Factor to **5** (this creates either mild-looking or steep-looking topology in your image, depending on the Scale Factor amount). Drag the Floor slider to about **150**. The *floor* is the cutoff point at which tones in your image either produce bumps or are completely flat. It's sort of like

you're looking down at mountains and watching a plane rise in the area, until lower altitude mountains are covered by the plane.

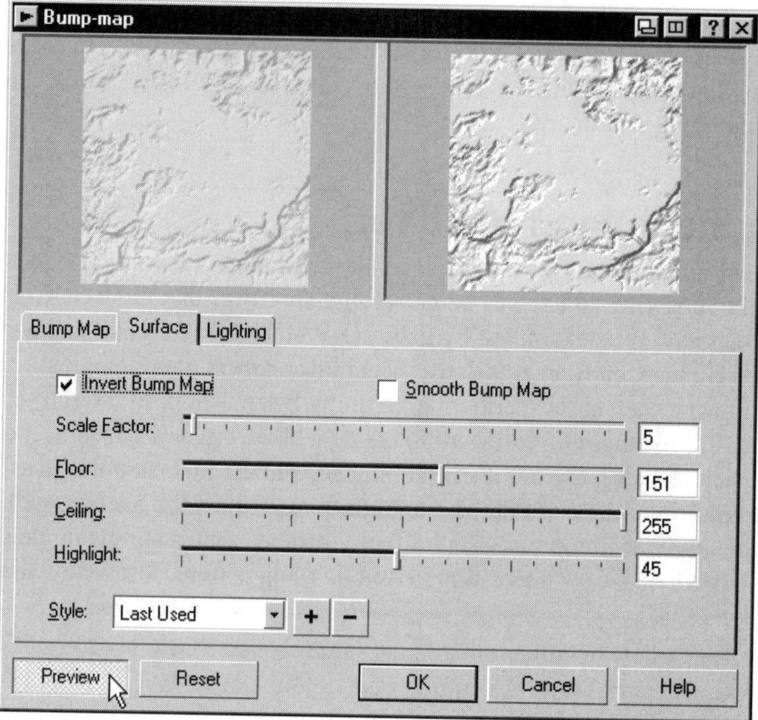

4. There are certainly more options to choose from in the Bump-map effect, but we've accomplished our specific task using only step 3. Click OK to apply the bump map to the pale neutral image.

5. Save the image to your WEBSITE\STASH folder as BACKGROUND in PHOTO-PAINT's native file format. Keep the image open for now.

If you recall, back in Figure 24-3 there is a column of text on the far right of the template image for this site. Text can be a graphic on web pages, but this is a wasteful practice when the Web supports text in many different sizes, styles, and colors. If you're on your own as a web designer, ask your partner who does the scripting to sit beside you for this next section. We're simply going to test how well text reads against this BACKGROUND image. All too often, a background pattern on someone's page is so dense that you can't read the text. But we're smarter than that, right?

Creating a Legibility Test

Our next procedure in PHOTO-PAINT is a simple one, and one we can correct and finish using a minimum of steps. You'll first create an object on top of BACKGROUND, and then apply black, 16-point Times Roman text to the object. This is the font style and size at which most browsers display default text. Let's see how text reads against the background, and what we need to do to ensure text legibility:

1. Choose the Text tool and then choose black as the Paint color from the color palette.
2. Type **Legibility Test** three times as shown in Figure 24-7, but turn off the Anti-aliasing feature on the Property Bar for the text, because web browsers do not support anti-aliased text. It's my opinion that the background needs to contain a little less contrast and can be slightly lighter to allow the text to be read.
3. Select the Object Picker tool to deselect the Text tool. Click the Background thumbnail on the Objects Docker to make it the current editing area. The specifics are your own call here, but the author chose Brightness-Contrast-Intensity from the Image | Adjust menu—CTRL-B gets you there the quickest.

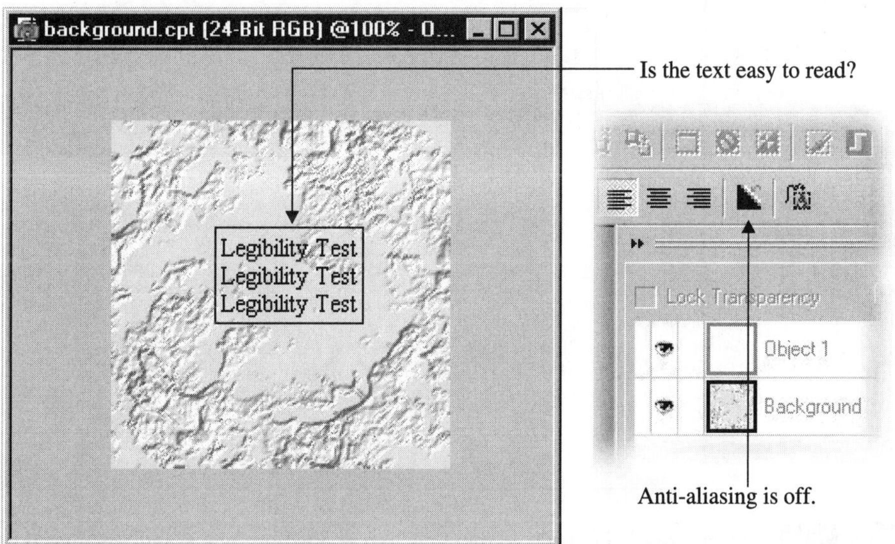

FIGURE 24-7 Type something on your texture and see how it reads

4. Set the Brightness to about **14** and the Contrast to **–31**, and see how you feel about this new tone of background image, as shown (poorly, because it's in black and white!) in Figure 24-8.

5. Click OK to apply the tone changes. Remove the text object by clicking on its title on the Objects Docker, and then click the trash icon. You can save and close the image at any time now.

There are other ways to create a background texture using PHOTO-PAINT, so let's digress. A background cannot work unless it *stays* in the background and is harmonious in color and mood with the other elements that populate the web page.

In Figure 24-9, I've sampled the ROUGH image as a fill and applied it to our template. I started by opening the TEMPLATE file and selecting the Fill tool in the Toolbox. Next I clicked the Bitmap Fill button and then the Edit Fill command on the Property Bar to open the Bitmap Fill dialog box. I then clicked the Load button in the dialog box and chose ROUGH in the Load Fill dialog box. I next created a new object on top of the background of TEMPLATE and filled the area using the Fill tool. This is also a good way to ensure that the tile resource image seamlessly tiles.

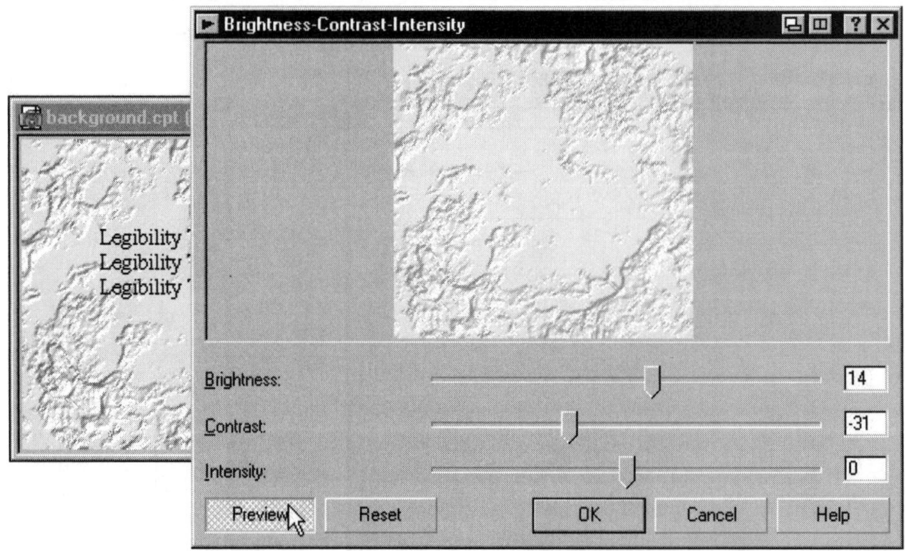

FIGURE 24-8 Decrease the contrast so there are fewer absolute black and absolute white areas in the image, and then heighten the Brightness to make the background contrast better against black text

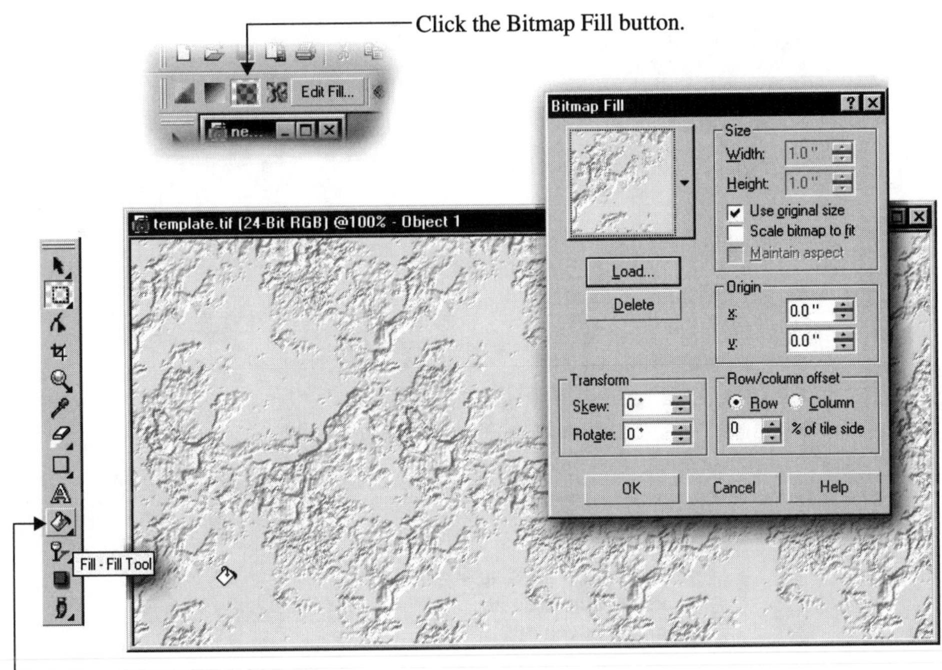

FIGURE 24-9 Load ROUGH as a fill, and then apply it to a new object on the TEMPLATE file to check out its lightness, color, and tiling property

Okay, the texture background looks fine from a tiling point of view and we've demonstrated that it supports text, but how does it look with one of the graphics that UniFruit has supplied us? Again, this is a simple one. Open the CRATE image from the WEBTOOTS\EXAMPLES folder on the Corel CD. This image has been conveniently presized for you to exactly fit the layout. Decrease the opacity of the Object 1 layer (the Rough texture) so you can see the template, and then CTRL-drag on the crate with the Object Picker tool into the template window, as shown in Figure 24-10. You then position the crate, close the original file, crank the opacity on Object 1 back up to 100%, and see whether this is the best, most harmonious background for the composition.

Okay, as far as the UniFruit web site goes, the ROUGH fill will work nicely. Close the TEMPLATE file and don't save the changes. Now let's explore other ways of creating fills. Our client, Mr. UniFruit, is out of town this week, so we can lay off his site design until later in this chapter.

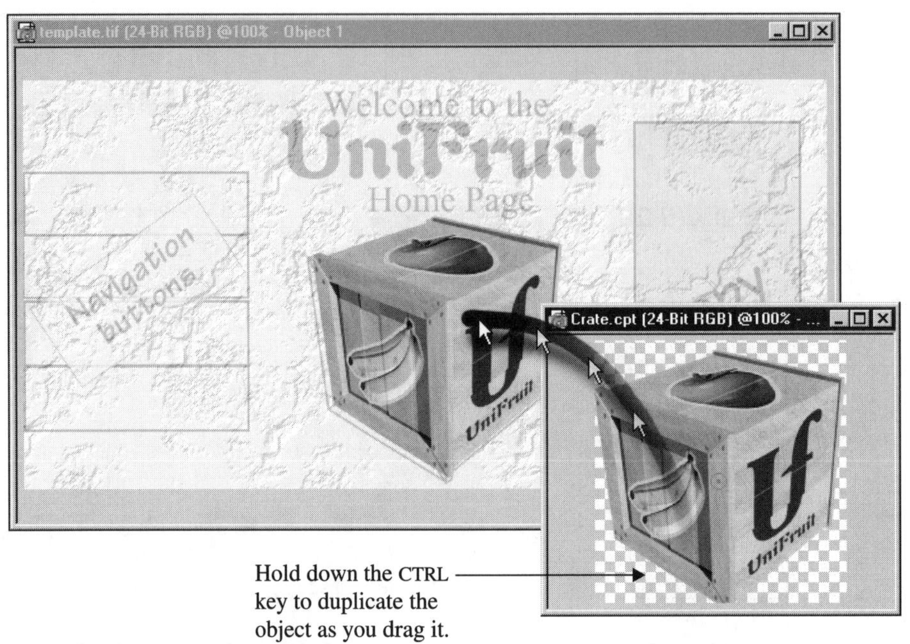

FIGURE 24-10 Check out how well the elements for the web page work together by adding fills and art to the template

Other Methods for Generating Background Tiles

PHOTO-PAINT 9 has a lot of different features that are indispensable for the web designer. The following is an "idea book," a gallery of techniques for creating subtle, yet visually rich and compelling, web page backgrounds.

Using the Bitmap Fill Presets

The Bitmap Fill option in PHOTO-PAINT contains a lot of preset textures, most of which need a little help from the Clone tool to make seamless tiling, and a few that need a *lot* of help to make them tile seamlessly. The only downside to using these presets is that the competition can produce the same thing, and this is why we walk through *custom* methods of creating elements in this chapter. To refine a preset texture:

1. Create a small image (2 inches or 150 pixels on a side is plenty of space within which to create a tile).
2. Click the Fill tool.
3. Click the Bitmap Fill button on the Property Bar, and then click the down arrow to the right of the preview window to scroll through the various images. Then apply the Offset effect after you fill the image, and use the Clone tool as described earlier in this chapter to make the image seamlessly tile.

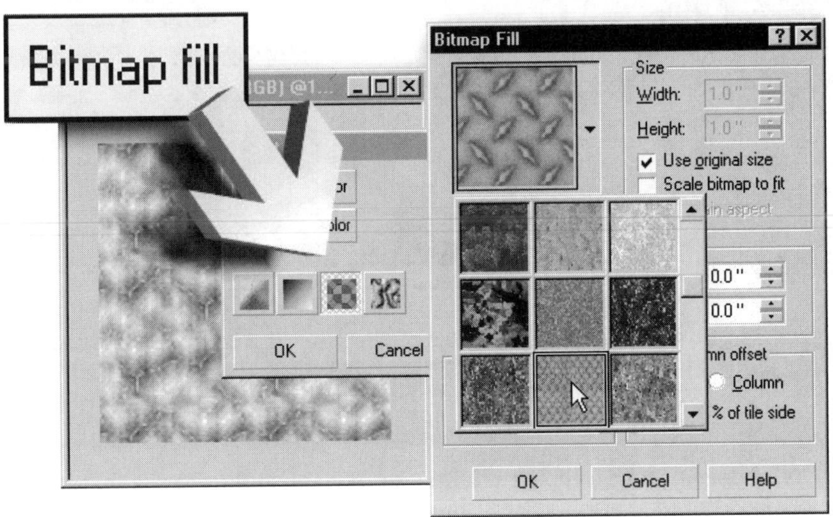

Inspiration from Windows' Desktop Patterns

Ever since Windows 3.0 (circa April 1991), we have had both Desktop patterns and images to choose from and to modify. Let's flash forward a little here to Windows 98, and take a peek at what's under the hood of the display properties. Right-click the Desktop and then choose Properties. On the Background tab of the Display Properties dialog box, there's a Pattern drop-down list. If you click a strange name on the list, such as Cargo Net, you're presented with an oversized picture of a single tile of the selected pattern, as shown in Figure 24-11.

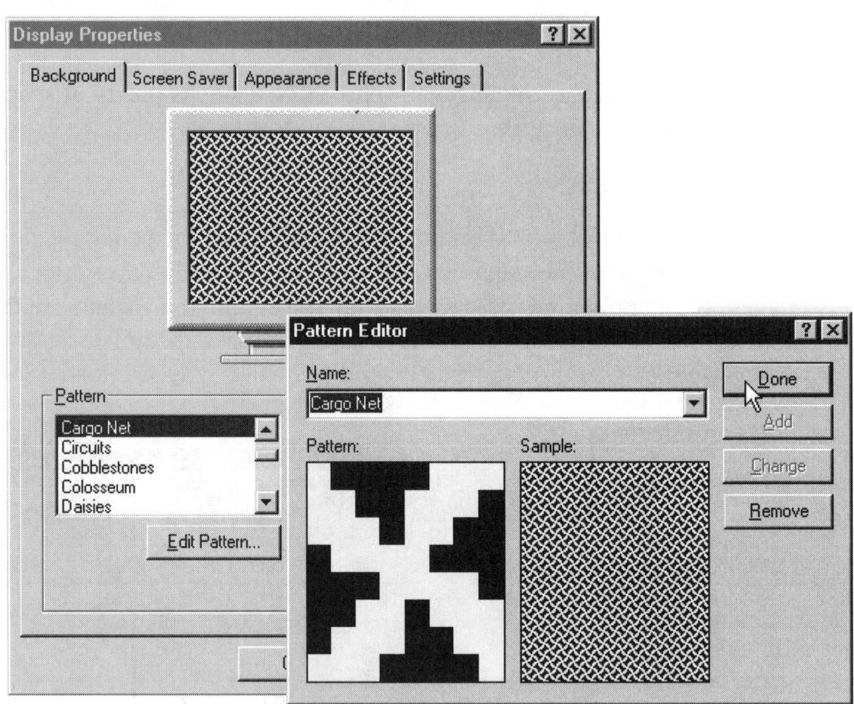

FIGURE 24-11 Click a name for a pattern and then choose the Edit Pattern button to see an 8 × 8 pixel close-up of the pattern

Okay, it doesn't take a rocket scientist or even an author to see that if you copy these designs, blow them up a little, and then use them as the bump-map source image, you've got tons of possibilities for creating finely woven, fabric-like backgrounds for your web site.

Tiling Background Resources from DRAW

Chances are pretty good that if you own PHOTO-PAINT, you also have CorelDRAW, as the two programs are sold in one bundle. And CorelDRAW sports a handsome collection of seamless tiling vector patterns that are *not* included in PHOTO-PAINT.

To copy and modify them:

1. Create a square in CorelDRAW that's two inches on each side.
2. Choose the Pattern Fill option from the Fills flyout on the Toolbox.
3. In the dialog box, choose Two-Pattern Fill and pick a tile from the drop-down list. Type **2** in the Width and Height fields, and then click OK to apply the pattern.
4. With the square selected, choose File | Export and check the Selected Only box. Export the square to CMX or CDR format, open it in PHOTO-PAINT, and add some objects as fills for the pattern.

Before you know it, you've got some ingenious fills, two of which are shown here (the files are also in the WEBTOOTS\EXAMPLES folder of the Corel CD as TILE01 and TILE02, if you'd like to play with them).

In the next illustration, I've applied the TILE01 pattern to a new object, and I'm erasing some of the top of the object so I can see how the pattern plays against both the UniFruit logo and the crate image. Next you can see how TILE02 works with the design. They're pretty good matches, but not as close as the original ground dirt pattern you created.

Using a Logo as Background

If you want to make instant friends with a client, propose that a subtle repetition of their logo be placed on the web page. On a scale of 1 to 10, this is about a 3 in terms of obnoxiousness on the Internet, but it certainly leaves the visitor remembering the company the next time they shop at a store!

To create such a background in PHOTO-PAINT, follow these steps:

1. Create a new file that is 200 pixels wide by 100 pixels high, and make the paper color a 30% black.
2. Apply the logo to the center of the image, using a 10 to 20% black fill, depending on how bold the logo is. Leave lots of empty space around the four corners of the image.
3. Choose Image | Duplicate from the main menu, press ENTER to create the new image, and then choose Effects | Distort | Offset from the main menu. Offset the duplicate, using the Wrap Around feature, by 50 percent of its height and width.
4. Once the duplicate has been offset, click the original's Title Bar to make it the current editing image, press CTRL-SHIFT-A to select all (or use the Property Bar's shortcuts), and then press CTRL-C to copy the original image.

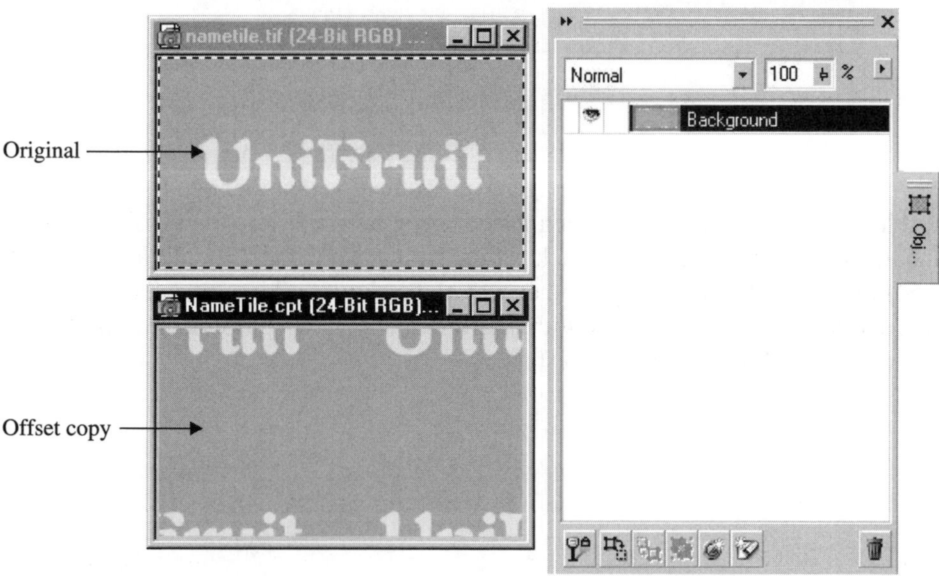

5. Select the duplicate image window and paste the Clipboard copy in the center of the duplicate image window as a new object using CTRL-V. On the Objects Docker, choose If Lighter from the Merge Mode drop-down list, so that only the logo will show through and the background will still have the offset logo. Then choose Object | Combine | Combine Object(s) With Background from the main menu.

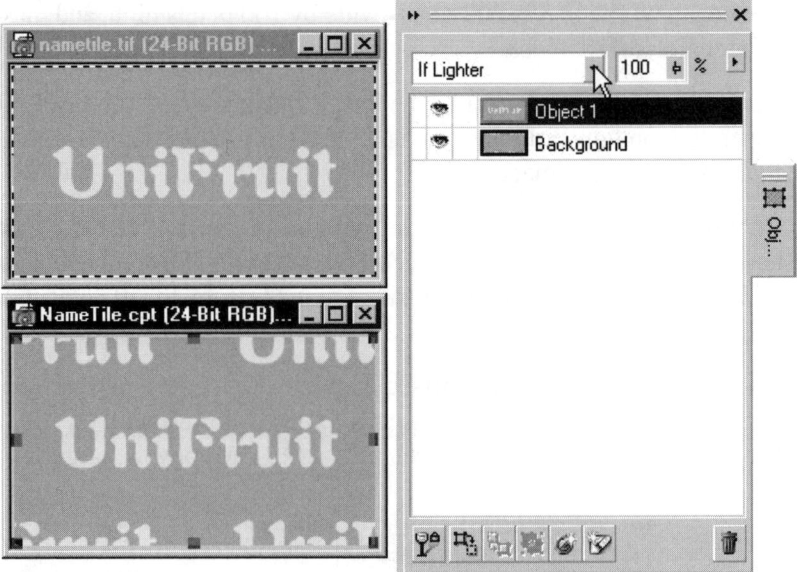

You can now see that this treatment of tiling patterns is completely grotesque when used on the UniFruit home page. The problem is that the logo itself is too striking, and the difference between the background shade and the logo shade should be much less (say 30% black for the background and 25% black for the logo). Ah, well, this is simply another way to go about building attention into a site, and it could certainly work with a different client. The important thing is that you now know how to create the effect.

Creating the "Impossible" Background

Here's a neat and simple trick that'll really command attention to your site. Pixels, those building blocks of larger images, are rectangular, so you'd expect to see a lot of designs on the Web that kowtow to these rectangular angles—and there will be a lot of horizontal and vertical background out there. But how about a *diagonal* background that repeats? Impossible? Hardly: it only took the author five minutes in PHOTO-PAINT and two years of geometry back in high school to figure this one out. Ready?

1. In PHOTO-PAINT, open a new image that's 50 × 50 pixels. Choose the Fill tool, click the Fountain Fill button on the Property Bar, and then click Edit Fill.
2. In the Type drop-down list, choose Linear, and in the Angle box, type **45** (degrees).

3. Click Custom in the Color Blend section of this dialog box, and then click the square marker over the fountain preview strip at the far left. Click the Others button and, in the Select Color dialog box, choose a pale, neutral color (H: 56, S: 5, and B: 96 is a good choice). Click OK to apply the settings, and you're back in the Fountain Fill dialog box.
4. Double-click the far left marker to get another marker with the same color settings, and position it at 50%.
5. Click the right square marker and make this marker a little darker than the first color (H: 52, S: 14, and B: 63). Double-click this marker to get another marker with the same color and position it at 50%.

See Figure 24-12. It's easier than it sounds!

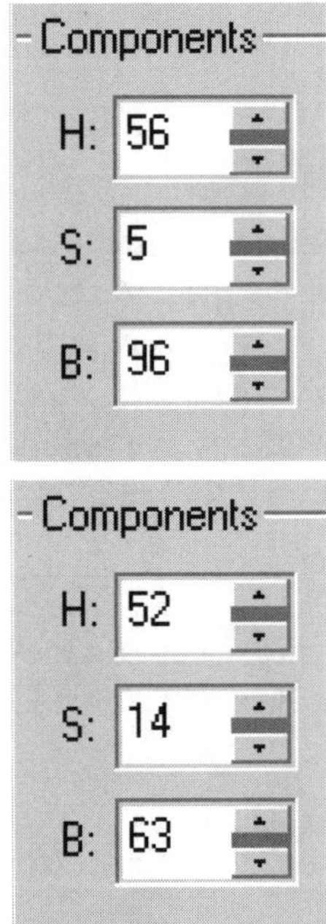

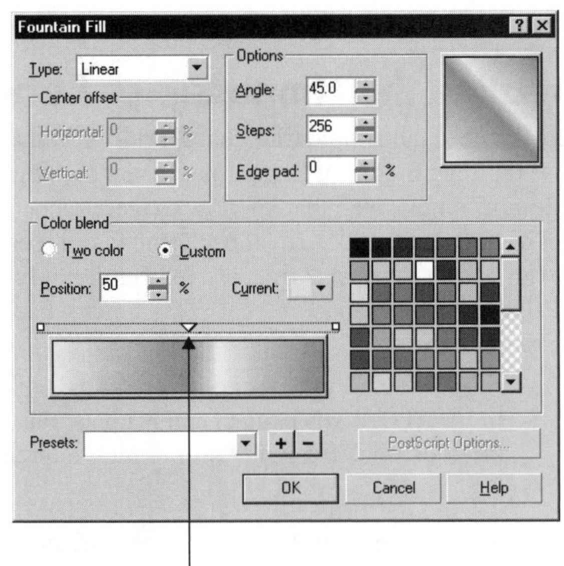

FIGURE 24-12 A "two-tone" fountain fill will repeat without showing a seam if you set up the fill to repeat an even number of times (such as twice)

6. You probably want to save this masterpiece, so click the plus button at the bottom of the dialog box, call it **web fill #1**, press ENTER, and then click OK to exit the Fountain Fill dialog box with your custom fountain fill loaded.
7. With the Fill tool, fill the image window. Save the image as BEIGE DIAGONAL TILE to your STASH folder. You're done creating the tile.

This tile will have to be converted to a file format such as JPEG or GIF for use on the Web, but the interesting thing about this tile technique is that you can make really small source files that load very quickly in the visitor's browser. Check out how the tiny tile looks in the UniFruit web site. See Figure 24-13. It's a little too intense, but again, here's another background-creation trick you've mastered.

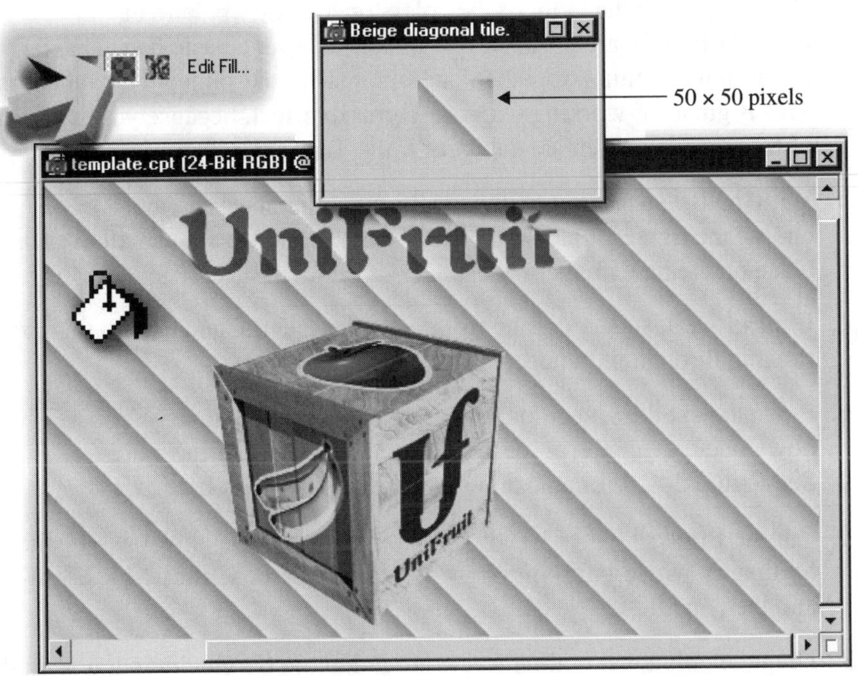

FIGURE 24-13 Diagonal tiles are not only possible, but can be very small and of visual interest in your web work

Before this chapter is through, I'll show you how to make this file take up 603 bytes (not even a kilobyte) when displayed on a web page. But all of this optimizing and compressing stuff can come later.

Let's Not Forget the Terrazzo Filter

The Terrazzo filter can provide you with an almost inexhaustible supply of *soft-shaded* backgrounds (for products that are soft and mushy, unlike UniFruit's offerings), so it's worth a little space here to show you how to set up the best-looking Terrazzo source information.

1. Create a small new image, no larger than 100 pixels on a side. The background color makes no difference here.
2. You will notice that a lot of the colors on the color palette in PHOTO-PAINT are grouped into tints of the same basic hue. That is, greens tend to clump together, and blues share the same locale on the strip. This is great for working with the Terrazzo effect, because you'll use tints of the same hue to create a target for the Terrazzo effect.
3. With the Brush tool set to about a 35-pixel diameter and a soft edge, choose the lightest blue on the color palette, and then brush all over the place on the new image.
4. Choose the next deeper tone from the color palette, and draw a fat line running through the image.
5. Pick the next deepest color, and paint a circle in the image. You're now done creating resource colors and shapes for Terrazzo to use. See Figure 24-14 for an example of the host artwork here.
6. Choose Effects | Fancy | Terrazzo. In the dialog box, click once on the Symmetry window. From the Symmetry dialog box, click Monkey Wrench and then on OK.
7. Drag the polygonal outline frame around in the Original window, and then drag on the handle of the frame to resize it. XAOS Tools calls this frame the *"motif,"* and I have no idea why, so we accept the nomenclature. Move and size the motif until you have an interesting pattern in the Result window. Drag the Feather slider to about 52 to really blend these different tones into a subtle, relaxing geometric tile. We are not going to apply this

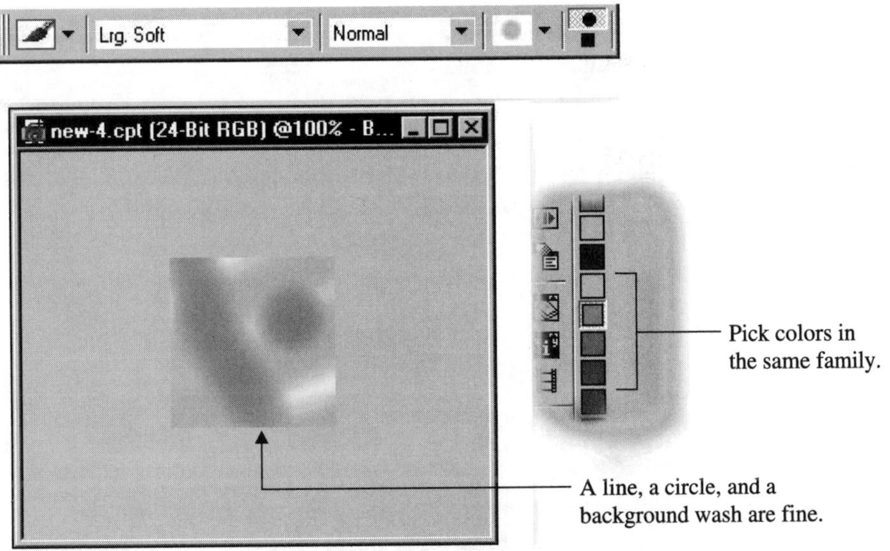
Lrg. Soft
Normal
new-4.cpt (24-Bit RGB) @100% - B...
Pick colors in the same family.
A line, a circle, and a background wash are fine.

FIGURE 24-14 What looks like a mish-mash of colors will turn into a beautiful geometric pattern when you apply the Terrazzo filter

pattern; instead, we will save a *tile* of it. Look at Figure 24-15—see the Save Tile button and the single pattern image below the Symmetry window? *This* is what we want to save—we couldn't care less about filling the new image window back in PHOTO-PAINT.

NOTE: *Okay, I'm not being exactly on the up and up when I say the Terrazzo filter is only good for pastel artwork. You can certainly use rich contrasting colors to create images that look like pinwheels that are having a bad hair day. However, it is our primary goal in web design to make the background attractive but subordinate to foreground graphics and text. And the only way I know of accomplishing this with the Terrazzo filter is by going "pastel."*

8. Click the Save Tile button, save the button file in BMP format to your STASH folder, and then choose Cancel to duck out of the dialog box.

You can see that by loading this Terrazzo tile file as a fill (try saying that twice quickly), you can accent just about any web page without overdoing it.

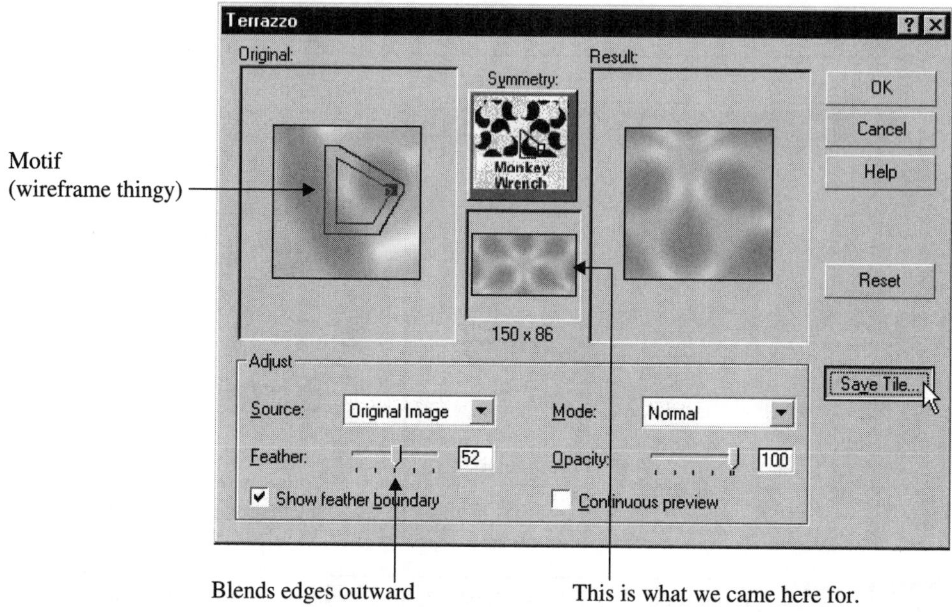

FIGURE 24-15 Snag an attractive seamless tile to use later by working with the Terrazzo filter's features

I've applied our tile to the UniFruit template. It's a little too bland to make an exciting presentation, but again, there are plenty of clients ahead for you if you learn this stuff.

The time has come, after all these techniques, to show you how to finish what you began. Follow along in this next section to learn the best way to export your work to a file format that can be used on the Web.

JPEG Versus GIF89a: When Do You Choose?

In 1999, sadly, we aren't all wearing rocket packs, we can't teleport to other planets, and 98 percent of the folks who browse the Internet use one of two programs. Both only natively support JPEG and GIF file formats for images. Microsoft Internet Explorer and Netscape Communicator require special plug-ins for a special file format such as PNG (Portable Network Graphic, a file format that still holds a lot of promise, if only the leaders in browser making would support it), and other file formats that you use every day.

The reason for the Web's use of GIF and JPEG graphics is a very simple one: they both compress files very well, so they appear on the visitor's monitor very quickly. But when should you use which format?

For background images on the Web, both JPEG and GIF formats are supported, so our ROUGH tile could be exported to either format and used. *Image integrity* is what the deciding issue here is. You lose a little of the original image quality when you save as a GIF or a JPEG, so the *content* of the picture really dictates which format to choose.

JPEG's strong point is that the format can contain up to 16.7 million unique colors, so your image looks brilliant in this format. Its weak point is that JPEG uses *lossy* compression—some of the original hues in the image are averaged to a single color to compress the file. You usually don't see what's missing from a JPEG when compared with the original except if the original is a *high-frequency* image, which our ROUGH image is. A *high-frequency* image is an image where there are sudden tonal changes as you "read" the image from left to right or from top to bottom. ROUGH will appear plain lousy as a JPEG—there will be noticeable distortion of image content.

GIF (the *89a* subformat) has one big shortcoming: it can only contain a maximum of 256 unique colors. Typically, there are tens of thousands of unique colors in a digital photograph or artwork. To create a GIF image, you must *downsample*—average a lot of colors down to a single common shade—for the image to qualify as a GIF candidate. Downsampling typically uses dithering to help disguise the fact that there aren't many unique colors in the image (see Chapter 2 for more information on dithering).

However, the GIF format is a very good choice for ROUGH. Although ROUGH is a high-frequency image, it only contains 289 unique shades—you almost don't need to dither down the image at all to preserve absolute image fidelity. (There's a command in PaintShop Pro that tells you how many unique colors are in an image—I'm not omniscient. <g>) Are you ready for the big trick, the secret of the pros? Here it comes.

You don't *need* to fill in all 256 "color slots" in a GIF image. For every tone under 256, you get a little more compression into the image. So I would suggest that you start at a number such as 100 unique tones in PHOTO-PAINT's Convert To Paletted dialog box, and work your way up as you see the need to preserve image integrity. Open the ROUGH image in PHOTO-PAINT, and play along with me here to demonstrate a point:

1. Choose File | Export, and then choose GIF-CompuServe Bitmap from the Save As Type drop-down list, choose your WEBSITE\SITE folder as the directory, and call the image ROUGH.GIF. Click the Save button, and the Convert To Paletted dialog box appears, shown next. PHOTO-PAINT knows that the image has to be color reduced to appear in GIF format.

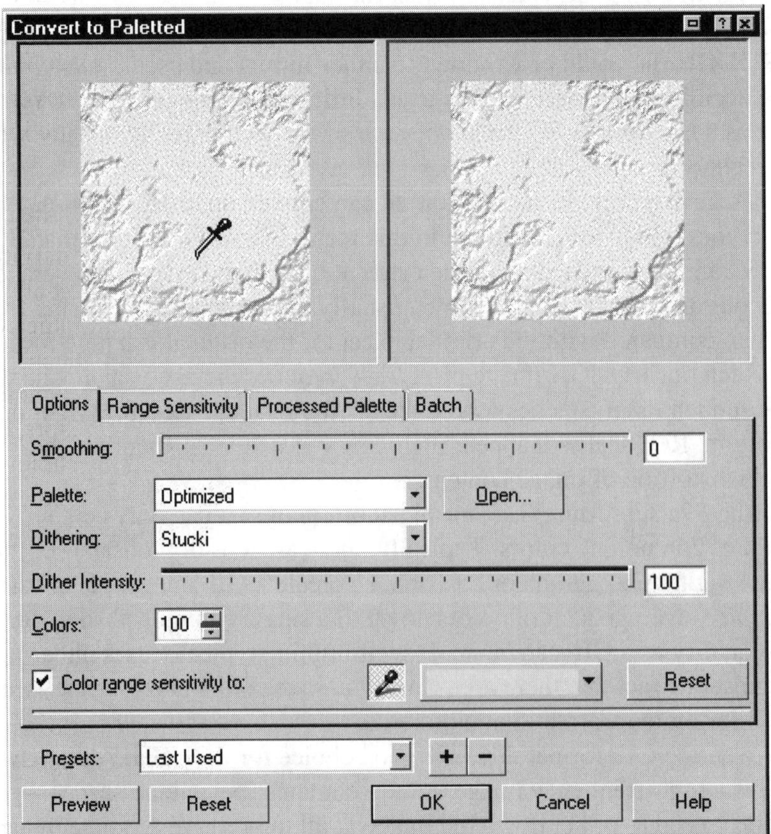

2. Choose Optimized from the Palette drop-down list. "Optimized" means that as many colors as possible within the original image will be written to the GIF file. If you use other methods here, PHOTO-PAINT will allocate some of the 256 available colors to tones that don't exist in the target image (but exist in the visible spectrum of light), and this wastes space and causes more dithering than is necessary.

3. For the type of Dithering, you might as well use Stucki from the drop-down list. None and Ordered are poor choices, and the rest refer to different types of error diffusion dithering. *None,* as the name suggests, simply reassigns unavailable colors to a close color that is available…and the resulting image looks posterized. *Ordered* dithering creates a pattern in the image, sort of like a weave. With small web images, this pattern overwhelms the visual content of the image.

4. Set the Dither Intensity to 100 (smaller values produce a larger saved file with a nominal difference in original image fidelity). Type **100** in the Colors box and then press TAB to move on. You've told PHOTO-PAINT that there should be no more than 100 unique tones in the image. That's less than half the colors in the native file, but trust me, you'll never miss the subtle nuances of tone variation in this fairly monochromatic image. What you'll gain is better compression with the image.

5. Check the Color Range Sensitivity To check box. Then click the Eyedropper tool, and click over a medium shade of beige in the left (Original) image. What you're doing here is telling PHOTO-PAINT, "Yo! I want all the 100 colors in this image to tend toward the area I clicked over. In other words, don't sweat about matching the darker and lighter tones too much." Why? Because most of the visual information in this image lies in its midtones, and no one will criticize you for weird highlights or shadows colors, because they will never see the original file, right? Seriously, color accuracy in the shadows and highlights here will not make a significant difference in the way the file is written, because as long as you *have* highlights and shadows in the image, the image will look correct.

6. Click OK and you'll be presented with the GIF Export dialog box. Here you should check the Interlace check box. By doing this, you make your image stream from the Internet server to the visitor's browser program, and almost no time is lost as the image begins to build itself on the visitor's screen. This is a lot better than having visitors wait until the entire image is

received—it tells them that the connection to your site is good, and stuff will happen momentarily.

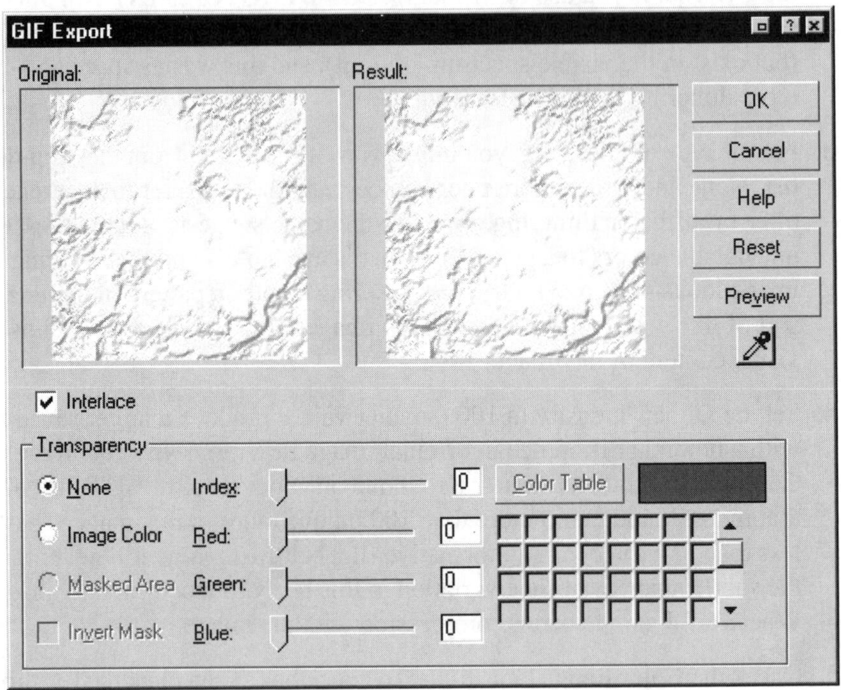

7. That's the end of the options needed for the image. Click OK and you now have a GIF version of the ROUGH image in the SITE folder on your hard disk, waiting for the other components you'll add to this site. Close ROUGH at any time without saving.

Until now everything we've been through on exporting might lead you to conclude that GIF is the file format of preference on the Web. Not true. GIF is simply more flexible. JPEG format images can look a million times better than an equivalent GIF, because of the format's color capability. We'll get into exporting JPEGs later in this chapter.

The next piece of the site you'll want to build is the lettering for the UniFruit logo. This can be done in a boring fashion—by simply typing the text in a unique color and exporting it—or we can flex our artistic muscles and see how we can make this UniFruit lettering pop out at the viewer.

Making Text Pop Out at the Viewer

CorelDEPTH (originally licensed to Corel Corp. as AddDepth by MetaCreations) is a largely misunderstood program, I think, because I don't see a lot of examples of CorelDEPTH work on the Web. This is a shame, because CorelDEPTH produces absolutely wonderful extruded (3-D) text in any color at any angle. PHOTO-PAINT imports a DEPTH file flawlessly, with anti-aliasing around the edges and a clear object background, so placement of the graphic is a snap. Unfortunately, version 9 of DRAW does not include CorelDEPTH. But earlier versions *do*; so get those version 6–8 CDs from the attic if you don't have CorelDEPTH installed. If you're new to CorelDRAW and its sister programs, you can always purchase AddDepth from MetaCreations for less than $50, or go all the way with Adobe Dimensions, a full-featured vector 3-D program for less than $150. You'll also need the Auriol Black font, the official typeface of the UniFruit Company, from the Corel CD(s), so install this font as you're installing CorelDEPTH. If you have absolutely no access to the product(s), use the UNIFRUIT.WMF file in the WEBTOOTS\EXAMPLES folder and skip to step 9.

Follow these steps needed to create an attention-getting 3-D logo:

1. Launch CorelDEPTH, and then click with the Text tool in the drawing window. This brings up the Text dialog box.
2. Choose Auriol Black from the font drop-down list, let the size be 72 points, and then type **UniFruit** in the text entry window. Because CorelDEPTH writes files to vector format, they can be scaled to any size without loss of focus or image detail when a bitmap program such as PHOTO-PAINT translates the vector data into a format it can use, like a bitmap format. So we do the scaling later in PHOTO-PAINT. For now, click OK to apply the text to the workspace.

3. The text appears in whatever the default color style is, and this probably won't be your choice of color schemes. Let's think about this a moment. UniFruit is a fruit company, so the lettering should probably be of a fruity motif. Green and pale cream are sort of reminiscent of bananas, and these colors will work well with the browns we've already decided upon for the background and the crate image. So do this: drag the left handle on the side of the picture of the lettering in the Geometry box a little toward the center of the palette (you can see this in Figure 24-16). This creates a bevel on the text that helps separate visually the sides from the front face of the text.

4. Once the letter has stopped redrawing, use the Zoom tool to fill the screen with your 3-D lettering, and then use the Rotate tool on the Toolbox to push the top of the lettering backward, ever so slightly, so you can see the bottom lip of the text. Hint: Three-dimensional text doesn't look like much unless you can see at least two of the three dimensions of the object.

5. Click the triangle on the top right of the Styles palette. This rolls out additional options, as shown in Figure 24-16. Click Duplicate while the

FIGURE 24-16 Expand the Styles palette so you can duplicate and edit a selected color combination for the extruded lettering

default Blue is highlighted, and then in the dialog box, type **UniFruit** as the name for the duplicate. Then, with "UniFruit" selected on the palette, choose Edit.

6. Click the Front Face button, choose Gradation from the Effect drop-down list, and then make the Starting Color R: 247, G: 194, and B: 0. For the Ending Color, you want white (R: 255, G: 255, B: 255). You then need to drag the line within the circle below the Gradation Precision slider, to set the direction and position of the gradation. Next click the Front Bevel button, and choose Shading from the Effect drop-down list. Specify a rich green, such as R: 0, G: 128, and B: 0. Finally, click the Side Surface button, and enter the values you see in Figure 24-17. As the callouts indicate, no one is ever going to see the backface of the 3-D lettering options, so you might as well leave them alone. Click OK to return to the workspace after setting the colors.

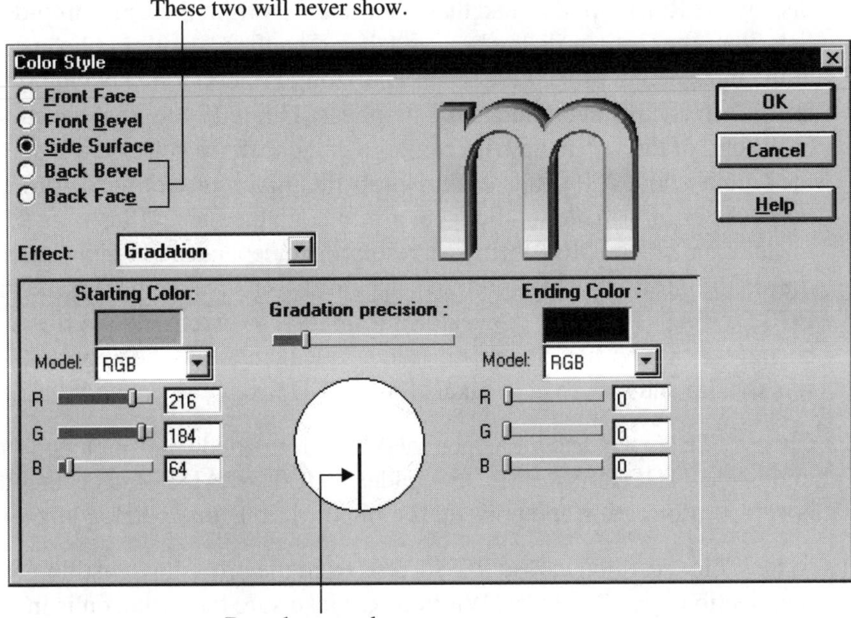

FIGURE 24-17 Specify fountain fills ("gradations") for the side and front of the lettering, and make the letters look like they were carved out of bananas or something

7. Close the extended palette on the Styles palette, click the text object in the editing window, and click the UniFruit style on the Styles palette. The 3-D text will take on the style (the combination of colors) you've defined. See the general tonal scheme of the finished 3-D text?

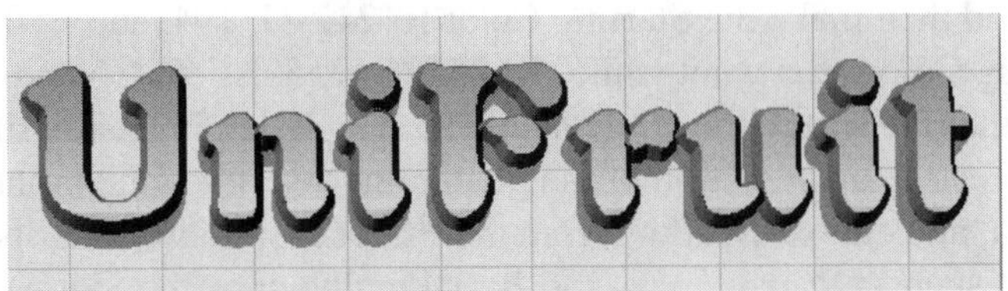

8. Save the lettering to CorelDEPTH's native file format, and then save it to your WEBSITE\STASH folder in the Windows Metafile (WMF) format: UNIFRUIT.WMF.

9. In PHOTO-PAINT, open the TEMPLATE file, and then press CTRL-R to display rulers around the image window. Double-click one of the rulers to display the Ruler Options, and then choose Pixels from the Units drop-down list. Close the Options dialog box, and then drag the zero origin (the marker at the intersection of the vertical and horizontal rulers) to the beginning of the "U" in "UniFruit" in the template image. Hmm. If you float the cursor to the end of the "t" in the UniFruit logo and check the ruler, you'll see that the logo is about 250 pixels wide. Here's the importance of measuring right now: vector information—the type of info contained in an Illustrator file, a metafile, or a CorelDRAW file—is resolution independent. In human terms, the vector information has no fixed size until you have a program such as PHOTO-PAINT convert the vector information to pixels and the file becomes a bitmap file. So we will add a little padding to the imported file's width and specify 275 pixels for the 3-D text.

10. Choose File | Open, and then open the WMF-formatted UniFruit logo found in the WEBTOOTS\EXAMPLES folder. PHOTO-PAINT detects that this is vector information and pops up the Import Into Bitmap dialog box.

11. In the Color section, choose RGB Color from the drop-down list. In the Size section, type **275** in the Width box. Make sure the lock icon is in its locked position (constrain aspect ratio). Press TAB to get to the Height box, and "52" should automatically appear. Check Transparent Background. Set the Resolution at 72 dots [pixels] per inch (dpi), and check the Anti-aliasing check box. When your dialog box looks like Figure 24-18, click OK to commence the conversion process.

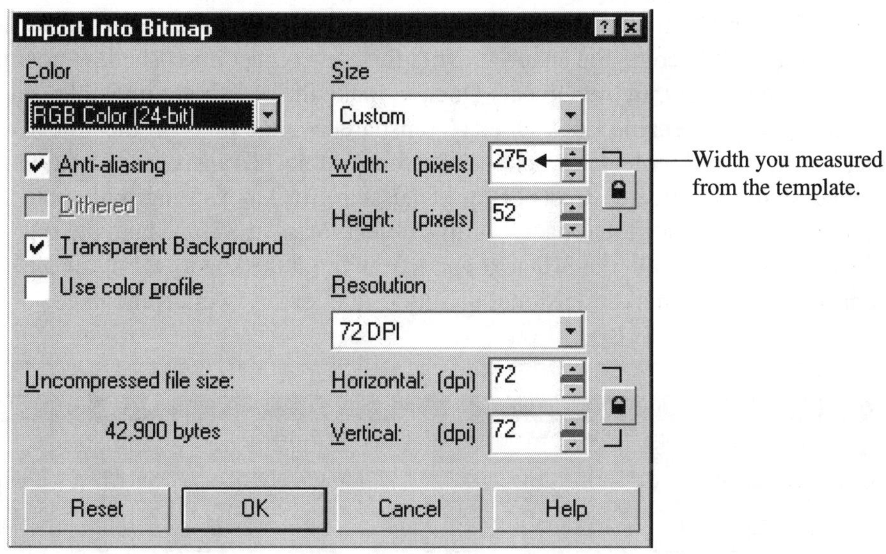

FIGURE 24-18 When an imported design is in vector format, you can specify the dimensions of it before PHOTO-PAINT converts the visual information to bitmap format

12. Save the file as UNIFRUIT in PHOTO-PAINT's native file format and keep it open. Let's take a break for a moment and make some observations.

NOTE: *Adobe Illustrator's file format is a special type of Encapsulated PostScript file. As such, the Illustrator file typically has a page description within the data. You might be surprised when you bring an Illustrator file into PHOTO-PAINT. The dimensions offered in the dialog box refer to the page (from CorelDEPTH) and not to the extremes of the actual object. Therefore your work will usually import much smaller than you want it. To solve this problem, you should save the DEPTH file in Illustrator format, open the image, and save it in CorelDRAW to CorelDRAW's CMX format, which PHOTO-PAINT reads accurately. The point here is to remove the header information from the file that DEPTH creates, and for us nonprogrammers, passing the data through an intermediate program provides the solution.*

First of all, if you look at Figure 24-19, you see I've included a drop shadow behind the 3-D text. That shadow hasn't been copied to the template image yet. I've done this for effect, and you can, too. With UNIFRUIT open, CTRL-drag the logo into the template image, choose Object | Duplicate, and then open the Objects Docker (CTRL-F7). There are two new objects: the one directly above the Background will become the shadow. Drag this new object into "shadow position" in the image window. In the Objects Docker, make the top object invisible, select the shadow object, enable Lock Object Transparency, and then fill the object with black using the Fill tool. Next, uncheck the Lock Object Transparency box, apply the Gaussian Blur effect (Effects | Blur | Gaussian Blur) at a strength of about 4 pixels, and then reduce the Opacity of this object to about 85%. Make the top object visible. Certainly, the 3-D text can live without the shadow, but the shadow seems to emphasize the dimensional quality of the text, as well as the page.

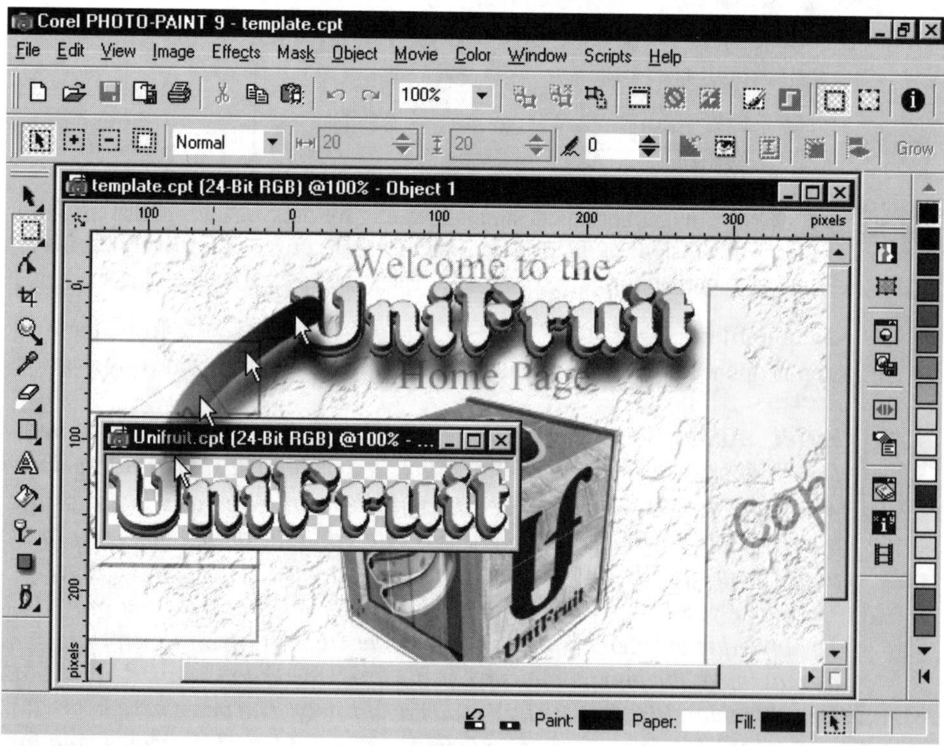

FIGURE 24-19 CTRL-drag the text from its window into the template window using the Object Move tool to place a duplicate in the template document

Two more things to notice: PHOTO-PAINT created a copy of the vector information to exactly the dimensions you asked for, so the layout is coming together perfectly. The second thing is that other applications such as CorelDEPTH and modeling programs frequently write information to a file to include masking information. Notice that the 3-D text is just touching the edges of the image window. This is good that the application crops the foreground content to the absolute minimum, because now you can add an object, fill it with background texture, and the file's ready to export to GIF or JPEG with no wasted pixels outside the foreground object. Always trim an object as small as possible to keep the saved file size down; when an application can do it for you, *let* it.

To save the 3-D text and the drop shadow you have placed in the TEMPLATE file to GIF format (or JPEG), this is how you should prepare the elements:

1. With the Object Picker tool, either marquee-select the lettering and the drop shadow, or SHIFT-click after choosing one, to add the other to the selection. You know you've got both objects picked when both their titles are highlighted on the Objects Docker.

2. Choose Object | Combine | Combine Objects Together from the main menu. Alternatively, you can click the third button on the Objects Docker to combine selected objects.

3. Choose Image | Crop | To Mask. Now the image window is as small as it can be, and the window edges are flush with the outer extremes of the combined lettering and shadow.

4. Press CTRL-SHIFT-R to remove the mask. Click the Background title on the Objects Docker to make it the current editing object.

5. Click the Fill tool to make it the current tool, and then click the Bitmap Fills button and then the Edit Fill button on the Property Bar. Load the ROUGH fill you created earlier and click OK. Click in the background to fill it with beige texture. Flatten the image by choosing Object | Combine | Combine All Objects With Background from the main menu.

From here, you probably want to export to JPEG and not GIF, because there are a lot of unique tones in the drop shadow and the face of the 3-D text. You'd lose this sort of subtle shading if you used the GIF format, with its 256 or fewer unique colors. Do this instead:

1. Choose File | Export, and then choose JPEG Bitmaps from the Save As Type drop-down list, call the file 3DLOGO.JPG, direct the file toward your WEBSITE\SITE folder, and then click Save.
2. In the Encoding field, click the Optimized, but *not* the Progressive check box, and click Preview. Note at the bottom of the dialog box that the saved file size has dropped from an estimated 41K (this is the author's figure; your file size might be a little different) to about 9K, using only 10 percent compression—and the image still looks pretty decent. Your image might not get the same compression, or even be exactly the same size, because we've been filtering and combining our images all over the place, and small differences in file sizes might add up in the end result. I've tried this step three times, and I can guarantee that with the settings shown here, you will get at least 10:1 compression.

You're not using Progressive JPEGs here because not all web browsers and not all HTML editing programs know how to handle (display) a Progressive JPEG (it's sort of like a streaming image that immediately begins to build once you hit a site). Click OK and you can save the UNIFRUIT image as UNI3DLOGO and then close the image at any time. We've just finished our tour of two of the four elements that make up an interesting web site—the 3-D logo and the tiling background texture.

The After-Class Special: Other Ways to Make 3-D Text

Assuming you bought the entire CorelDRAW 9 bundle, you have two other easy ways to make 3-D text. In PHOTO-PAINT, there's a filter under 3D Effects called *The Boss* that apparently pushes the masked area toward the viewer. I'd call this more like embossing than extruding, because the effect does not cast a shadow on the ground plane of the text, and you really have only one possible view to render using this effect—face forward. You can then put a drop shadow behind the "Bossed" text. Check out Chapter 15 for more details on embellishing a Bossed text object.

On a more sophisticated level, there is CorelDRAW's 3-D Extrude filter, which will put sides of any color on text. You can rotate the text, specify the amount of extrusion, and when you're done, you can detach the lettering from the sides and give the lettering a unique fill. Figure 24-20 shows both The Boss at its best and CorelDRAW's Extrude effect. I can't compare them to the wonderful renderings that CorelDEPTH does, but in the world, and particularly the world of art, it's each to his or her taste. As an author, I'm merely trying to show you the options in a non-partisan way. (Hint: Use CorelDEPTH.)

Ready for a mindblower? Our next stop is the creation of image maps. An *image map* is a single image that has multiple hot spots that link to different parts of a document, or a different part of the Web. You're not only going to design buttons, but you also will command PHOTO-PAINT to write you the HTML code to make this image map web-ready.

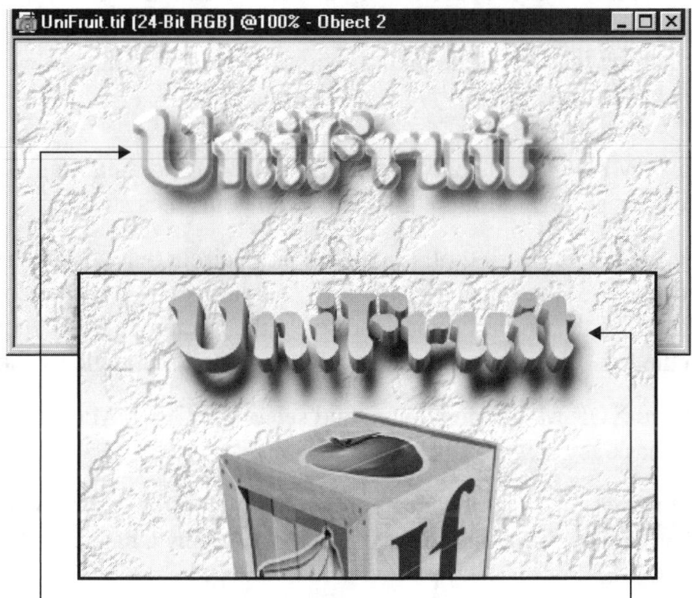

FIGURE 24-20 The Boss and CorelDRAW's extrude effects can both be used to create dimensional lettering and symbols

Image Mapping and Button Making

When the WWW started, there weren't a lot of talented artists providing graphics, so a link button or an image map collection of buttons looked exactly like buttons to be clicked. Today, *nothing* seems obvious on a web page—every element, whether or not it looks like a button—is prone to send you and your browser reeling into another part of cyberspace by clicking on it. So as conservative as it might sound, our discussions to follow show you how to go about button-making and displaying them on a web page so your visitors actually know that something is a button to be clicked and not simply a pretty graphic. Don't worry, we're going to be hip; we're simply not going to go "bleeding edge" here.

Picking the Shape of the Button

Because the template calls for four index buttons, we can design a single shape and then duplicate it and finally add text to the buttons. In Figure 24-21, I've designed something that looks like half a tongue depressor with a hole carved out of it. Let's make buttons:

1. Open TEMPLATE. Display the rulers (CTRL-R) and then drag guides out of the ruler as shown in Figure 24-21 to keep your lines straight.
2. Using the Circle Mask tool, drag out a large circle that will become the rounded end of the rectangle. Click the Additive Mask Mode icon (+ sign on the left of the Property Bar), and select the Rectangle Mask tool. Starting from the top center of the circle mask, drag out a rectangle as shown.
3. Click the XOR Mask Mode icon, and select the Circle Mask tool. Draw a circle mask as shown.
4. Save the mask to an alpha channel by clicking on the Channels tab on the Docker, and clicking on the Save Mask To A New Channel button on the Docker.
5. With the Rectangular Mask tool, drag a selection around the navigation buttons area, and then choose Image | Crop | To Mask. Using File | Save As, save the piece as IMAGE MAP BUTTONS to your STASH folder.

I've experimented with the The Boss filter and the saved mask, and this produces a pretty interesting image map button. But I think we can do far better

FIGURE 24-21 Create a mask for the index button by tracing over the template

than this button by designing it manually. It takes fewer steps than you'd think, and I believe you'll find the technique to be useful in a multitude of design situations.

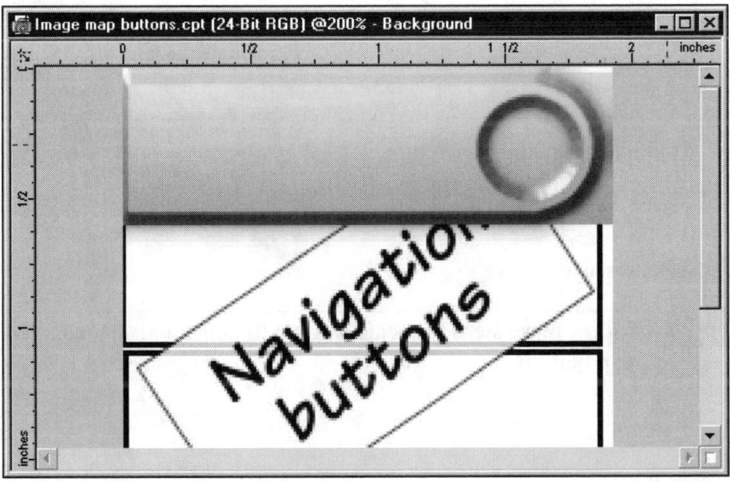

Here's how to produce a dimensional button for the image map. The procedure is laid out in Figure 24-22 (take a look at it right now). Once you've created one button, you can duplicate it to make up the four slots on the template.

1. Remove all masks from the IMAGE MAP BUTTONS file. Using the Objects Docker, create a new object, and while it is the active object, select Mask | Load | Alpha 1 from the main menu to load the mask you saved in this image earlier. If the mask outlines the outside of the button and not the inside, the mask is inverted and you'll need to press CTRL-SHIFT-I to make the selection correct.
2. Choose Mask | Shape | Expand, type **3** in the Width box, and then click OK. See Figure 24-22 (#1). This will be the shape of the "side" of the button. Trust me—you'll see.

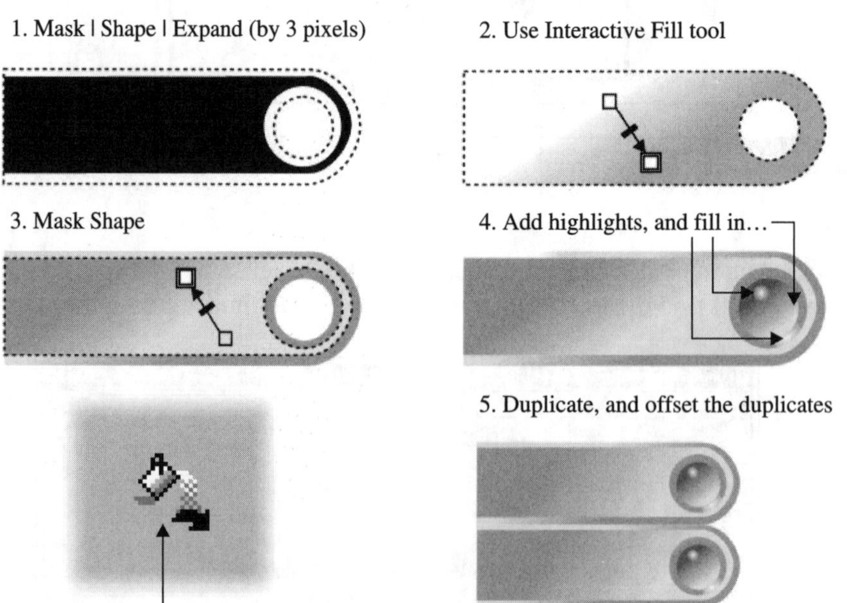
1. Mask | Shape | Expand (by 3 pixels)
2. Use Interactive Fill tool
3. Mask Shape
4. Add highlights, and fill in...
5. Duplicate, and offset the duplicates
The Interactive fill tool

FIGURE 24-22 Follow these steps to create a crisp, dimensional shape for your image map buttons

3. Open the Fill tool flyout, and choose the Interactive Fill tool. Drag the cursor from about 11 o'clock to about 4 o'clock in the selection. Double-click the top square (the *node)* that is part of the interactive onscreen marker. This leads to the Node Color dialog box. Choose R: 255, G: 116, and B: 69. You're working on the outside edge of the button. See Figure 24-22 (#2).

4. Double-click the bottom node, and in the Node color dialog box, specify R: 127, G: 32, and B: 0. This makes the button look sort of a burnt tangerine color, and our client *is* into fruit!

5. Select the Object Picker tool and load the original mask again. This time drag the Interactive Fill tool from 4 o'clock to 11 o'clock. See Figure 24-22 (#3). This creates the illusion that the button is dimensional and is responding to lighting. Press CTRL-SHIFT-R now to deselect the mask.

6. Use the Circle Mask tool to encompass the white circle within the button; remember to reset the masking property to Normal—you were using XOR mode last. Choose the Interactive fill tool, specify Radial as the fill type on the Property Bar, and then drag the Interactive Fill tool inside the circle from 4 to 11 o'clock. Press CTRL-SHIFT-R to remove the mask.

7. Add highlights to the button, as shown in Figure 24-22 (#4). Use the Airbrush tool, set to a Nib size of 10 pixels (use the slider on the Properties Toolbox). Set the Transparency to 90% (also from the Properties Toolbox) and the Paint to white, and then paint a few times in the same place on the button until you see an effect similar to that shown in Figure 24-22 (#4).

8. Choose Image | Paper Size, change the measurement to pixels, and then type **224** (pixels) in the Height box (the button's about 56 pixels high, times 4 buttons, equals 224 pixels). Right-click over the object thumbnail on the Objects browser, and choose Duplicate Selected from the shortcut menu. Do this three times, and then carefully align each button so they are vertically centered and aligned on the left and right. See Figure 24-22 (#5).

9. Click the Background title on the Objects Docker, choose the Fill tool, choose the ROUGH image as the Fill source, and then click the background in the image. Keep the image open.

We now have five objects in the image. Next, it's a good idea to give the button objects a name on the Objects palette so you can add text, and so that PHOTO-PAINT knows which button to link to when we get to the image mapping part of this assignment. First, let's add text to the buttons. I'd suggest using

Verdana or MS-Sans Serif in white, with a duplicate in black offset by one pixel left and to the top to accomplish the text. Why these odd fonts? Because small type is best viewed *without* anti-aliasing, and these fonts were specifically designed to be clean, attractive, and legible at small sizes with no anti-aliasing (so don't have the Anti-aliasing button clicked when you add the text). In general I think text that's smaller than 16 points that is anti-aliased produces fuzzy, hard-to-read content. Check out this illustration:

Using the illustration as a reference, we are going to add text to the buttons and combine the button and the text into one object. It is easier if you make only one button visible at a time using the Objects Docker. With the top button visible, select the Text tool, type **New Products**, and position it on the button. In the Objects Docker, a new Object will have appeared with the text as its title. Marquee-select both objects in the image window, and then click the Combine Objects Together button on the Objects Docker. This creates a new object. Repeat this process, making each button visible in turn, until you have four labeled buttons. Now we will give a title and an URL using the Objects Docker:

1. Right-click the object title on the Objects Docker, and then choose Properties. In the Name box on the General dialog box, type **New Products**. Click the WWW URL tab, and then in the URL box, type **products.htm**. You'll need to build a products page later so this button can link to it. But I've done most of the HTML work for this page, so rest easy and let's continue. Click OK to return to the image.

2. One by one, right-click on the other buttons, respectively name them "History," "Investor News," and "Contests," and in each WWW URL box, type **construct.htm** as the URL link. CONSTRUCT.HTM is a placeholder file I've created for you to link to. It's merely an under-construction sign, so you get the experience of creating links in PHOTO-PAINT without having to generate 15 million link pages.

3. Choose File | Publish To Internet. Don't worry; you're not exporting anything to the Internet. You're only creating HTML map coordinates and links to places in the image.

   Click each name in the Objects column of the Tag WWW URL dialog box, and make sure that the clicked name matches the part of the image that contains the correct button (at the right side of the dialog box) and that the URL that appears in the area beneath the images is correct. If it's not, now's the time to correct it.

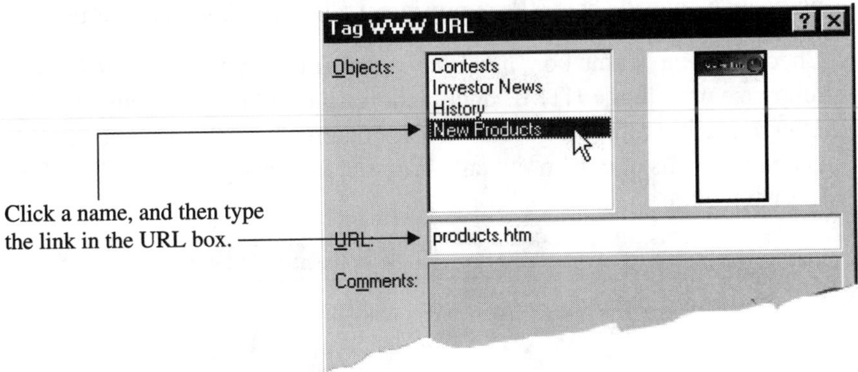

4. Click OK and the Export Image To Disk box pops up. You want to save both the HTML code and the image to your WEBSITE\SITE folder. The SITE folder is where all the elements of the UniFruit site need to reside. In the Save As Type box, choose JPEG Bitmaps. Why not choose a GIF? Because fountain fills are made of many different colors butted against each other, and a GIF cannot accurately display all the nuances you've created in the buttons. Besides, this image is a low-frequency image. Name the file **map.jpg** and then click OK. A warning pops up that objects will be merged in the finished file—this is okay. Click OK.

5. In the JPEG Export dialog box, check the Optimize check box, do *not* check the Progressive box, drag the Compression and Smoothing sliders to

around 10, and click Preview to see how well the compression value works here. When I did this, the saved size of the JPEG was down from 113K to a mere 5.4K—and the preview looks very nice—not a lot of corruption with the compression. Your compression amounts might differ from mine because you're using your own image, but the compression will be significant. Click OK to export a JPEG copy of your work.

6. After you close out of the JPEG Export dialog box, the Save Map File dialog box opens. This is the dialog box that tells PHOTO-PAINT where to store the (text) coordinates and link names you specified earlier for the image map. In the File Name box, type **buttons**. BUTTONS.HTM will be the file written to the STASH folder (the same folder where you saved the JPEG image map). In the Save As Type field, choose "Client-side (*.htm)." You're selecting the client side (in other words, *your* side instead of an Internet provider's side of the Internet "fence"), because image maps do not need any intervention by the server. They can work and reside on your site and work without any outside help (IPs appreciate it when you *don't* ask for their help).
7. Check the Map Name box, and type in **uni-info**. This will be the internal reference used in the HTML document for the MAP.JPG document. *Everything* is a reference in an HTML document; all the graphics are called from this document when a browser accesses your site. Click OK to save the file.

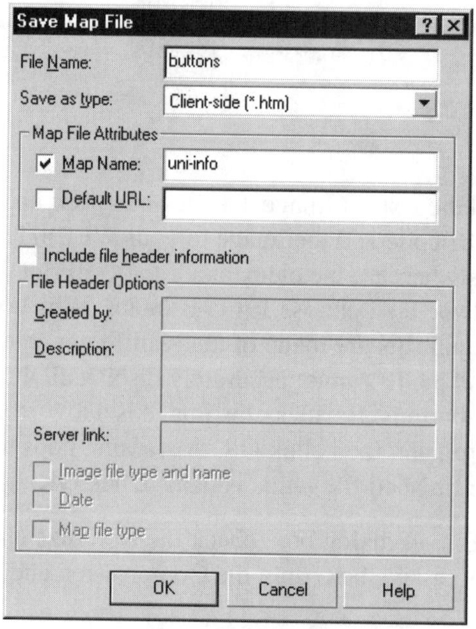

The composite screen figure, Figure 24-23, is intended to show you the "action/reaction" when you double-click BUTTON.HTM in your SITE folder, and then click one of the buttons that is linked to the CONSTRUCT.HTML document. Okay, you will not see the same effect, because although your PHOTO-PAINT work is done, you still need to copy some files to your site directory, and hack a line or two of HTML code to get exactly these results.

NOTE: *Want to know how to get these two pages up and running, and how to get the background image tiling? In a plain text editor (such as Windows' Notepad), open the BUTTONS.HTM document. Right after the* `</HEAD>` *(the closing of the header of the file), type* **`<BACKGROUND= "rough.gif">`**. *It is important that you use a lowercase filename; UNIX Internet servers use case-sensitive references. Save and close the file. Copy CONSTRUCT.HTM, SIGN.GIF, and BACK.HTM from the WEBTOOTS\SITE folder on the Corel CD to your SITE folder on your hard disk.*

FIGURE 24-23 It's not hard to get a hypothetical site up and running, if you know a little HTML

You're done and the image map will work as expected, except the New Products button will not work properly because you have not created this HTML page yet.

It's HTML Time!

Until now, you've done every step and understood every procedure it takes to get the top page of the UniFruit site up and working. What's missing is HTML language in the BUTTON.HTM document (or a new document that you copy the contents of the BUTTON.HTM document to). In Figure 24-24, let me explain what's been done, and if you'd like to see the end result on your screen and take apart this example, double-click the UNIFRUIT.HTM filename in the WEBTOOTS\DONE folder on the Corel CD.

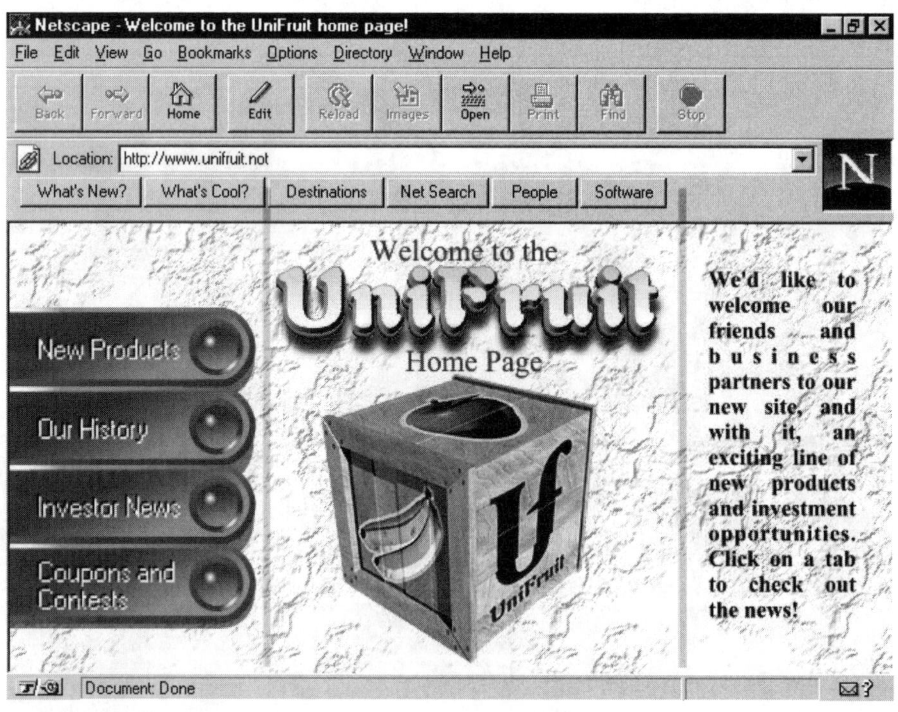

FIGURE 24-24 The finished top page (ignore the two, light, vertical guidelines here—I'll explain later)

First, a new document was created in an HTML editor. If you'd like to try your hand at HTML composition, Corel makes Web.SiteBuilder 8, Adobe's PageMill is very easy to use, and Microsoft's Front Page is full-featured with some fun add-ons. They're all around the same price.

Second, a table was created—one row and three columns. That's what the light vertical lines in Figure 24-24 are—the table edges. The code for the image map buttons and the graphic were copied to the new document, and the image is placed in the far left cell of the table. The UniFruit logo and the crate image were exported from PHOTO-PAINT as JPEG images, and they were both cropped tightly and have the background poured behind them, so the background visually melds with the actual HTML document background. You can find these images in the WEBTOOTS\EXAMPLES folder. This is a "killer trick": if you make your background image very loose and vague-looking (that is, no strong visual details), you can simply lay a GIF or JPEG graphic on top of the background, and no one will notice where the graphic's edges end and the background begins. Take a close look at Figure 24-24—can you honestly see the edges around the crate, the buttons, or the 3-D logo?

In the far right table cell, text was added. Our customer provided it, and to play it on the safe side in the legibility arena, I specified a bold typeface instead of a normal one, to really make the text stand up on its own.

Batch Editing and a New Web Page

Let's assume at this point that your relationship with the UniFruit group is a long-term one, and that you'll be constantly providing UniFruit's HTML person with new graphics in the future. Again, a template for pages whose contents change but whose overall layout remains the same can be a real time-saver.

As you can see in Figure 24-25, the product pictures are different sizes. Three pictures aren't too bad, but what if you need to downsample *50* of these a day?

Let's move on to the creation of a template, and see exactly what our needs are to complete the products page.

Setting Up Batch Processing in PHOTO-PAINT

Batch processing begins with creating a script. In other words, you walk through the steps you want PHOTO-PAINT to perform over and over (and over) again.

2.46 inches wide
@ 162 pixels/inch

3.74 inches wide
@ 93 pixels/inch

3.12 inches wide
@ 96 pixels/inch

FIGURE 24-25 Don't count on your client bringing you pictures that are all the same size. Getting them onto a web page so they look right is *your* responsibility as a designer

PHOTO-PAINT records these actions and saves them as a script you can play back on one or a hundred different images. Our needs in this assignment are fairly modest. All we need is for three images to be the same size. PHOTO-PAINT can resize images in "batch mode," but there's one catch: the images have to be of the same *aspect ratio.* The processed images will be distorted if the images don't all share the same proportions. This means that PHOTO-PAINT's most useful conversion capability would be with images that all came off a roll of film, sharing the same aspect ratio of 2:3.

TEMPLAT2.TIF is an image I created and is located in the WEBTOOTS\EXAMPLES folder on the Corel CD. I did the math for you (you'll do enough of it when your web career takes off!) and discovered that images that are 155 pixels wide and 233 pixels high will fill the page nicely, without the visitor having to scroll the window (the single biggest irritant on the Web). The way it's set up, this products page has room for link buttons, some text, and a fancy headline. Let's tackle the images first.

Here's how to record a custom batch file:

1. In PHOTO-PAINT, open the SODA.TIF image from the WEBTOOTS\EXAMPLES folder, and save it to your WEBSITE\STASH folder. Keep the image open.
2. Click the Recorder button on the Docker. It's the symbol that looks like a forward/backward toggle on a VCR.
3. Click the Record button at the bottom of the Docker—and *don't do anything else* yet. Any move you make at this point *will* be recorded.
4. As soon as you click Record, the first entry is automatically made in the script, which is to open an image of unique dimensions. Choose Image | Resample.
5. In the Resample dialog box, change the default unit of measurement to Pixels (in the drop-down box). In the Image Size Width box, type **155**, and then press TAB to move to the Height box. Surprise! PHOTO-PAINT's way ahead of you, and automatically scaled the height to be in proportion to the width. Ain't technology grand?

6. Click OK and PHOTO-PAINT scales down the soda image. The picture's less than picture-perfect right now, because anytime you remove or add pixels to an original image or design, the application has to "guess" how the image is redistributed with color pixels. This leads to loss of focus, which we'll correct in the batch script.

7. Choose Effects | Sharpen | Unsharp Mask. The Unsharp Mask is probably one of the top five tools you'll use in PHOTO-PAINT for web design work, so let's digress for a moment and look at the options in this dialog box, shown in Figure 24-26.

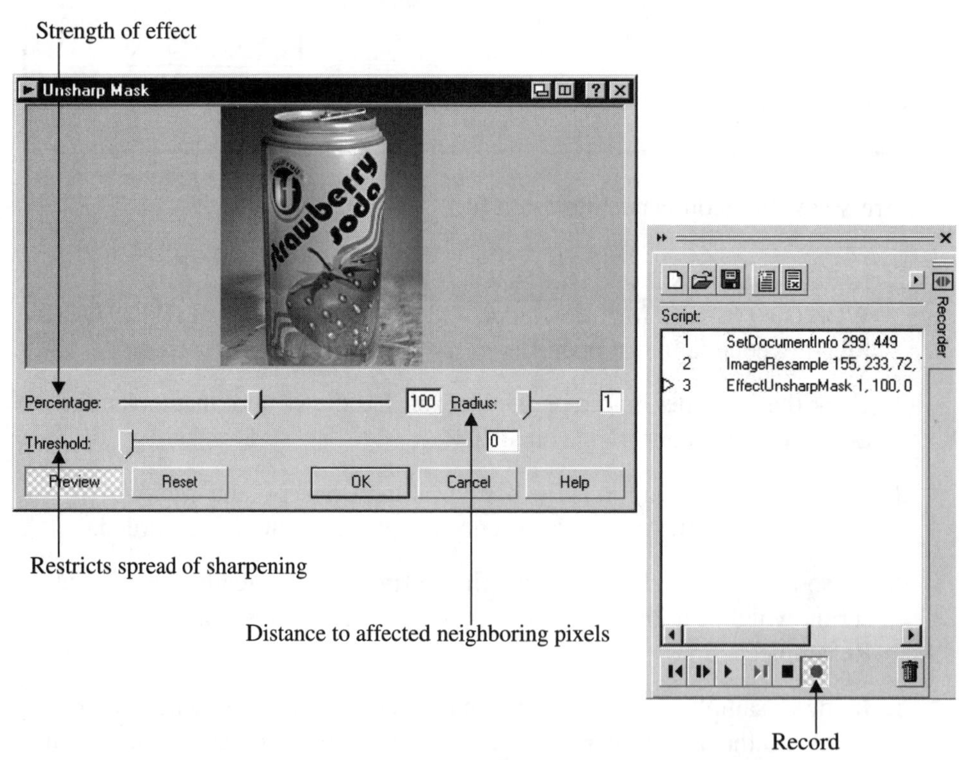

FIGURE 24-26 The Unsharp Mask, unlike the name implies, is actually the most sophisticated and subtle sharpening tool in any pixel-editing program today

8. Set the Percentage to 100%. This slider controls the intensity of the sharpening, from 0 to 500% (so you're using a mild amount of this filter). Too high of a percentage, and your images will look fried, or posterized. Set the Radius to 1 pixel. This control tells PHOTO-PAINT to scout only one pixel away from edge pixels in the image to increase their contrast. Higher amounts produce a harsh visual effect, but you'd use a higher amount on images that need sharpening that are 12MB and up in size. Set the Threshold to 0. This control sets the distance from target sharpening areas that are affected. At zero, we'll only be sharpening the edges within the image. Click OK to apply the filter.

9. Choose File | Export, and then choose JPEG Bitmaps from the Save As Type drop-down list in the Export An Image To Disk dialog box. Click Save. PHOTO-PAINT automatically appends "copy of" to the beginning of the original file's name (which is a lifesaver!), but you'll want to change these names to something more succinct before posting them on a web site. In the JPEG Export dialog box, click Preview and look below the right picture to see how much compression you're gaining by using the default values (which don't noticeably affect the quality of the soda can). Click OK to export the image and return to the workspace.

10. Click the Stop button on the Recorder, and then click the Save icon on the top of the Recorder Docker. Save the script as UNIFRUIT.CSC, and you might as well save it to PHOTO-PAINT's SCRIPTS folder (where factory preset scripts reside). This will make it much easier to find the script in a few moments. Click Save and take a breather for a moment.

As I mentioned earlier, a script will do anything you write into it by specifying commands, filters, making selections, and so on. All you really need to do now to get the PIES.TIF image and the PRESERVE.TIF image to the same size as the JPEG image of the soda is to set up the parameters of how the processing goes. Here's what you need to do:

1. Choose File | Batch Process. Click the Add File button at the top of this dialog box, and then choose PRESERVE.TIF (either off the CD or from your hard disk). Once the name of the file appears, click Add File again, and add PIES.TIF to the list. In practice, you could add a dozen or more images to this list, as long as they are 2:3 in proportion.

2. Click the Add Script button, and then go to the SCRIPTS folder on your hard drive and choose UNIFRUIT.CSC.

3. In the Options section, drop down the On Completion list, and choose Save To New Folder. Select the Close File After Batch Playback check box, and save the processed JPEG images to your WEBSITE\SITE folder on your hard disk. If your screen looks even vaguely like Figure 24-27, click Play and put the machinery in motion.

4. When the Script Recorder stops, your JPEG images have now been processed and saved. If you're working with someone who speaks HTML, now's your chance to turn half of the project over to him or her.

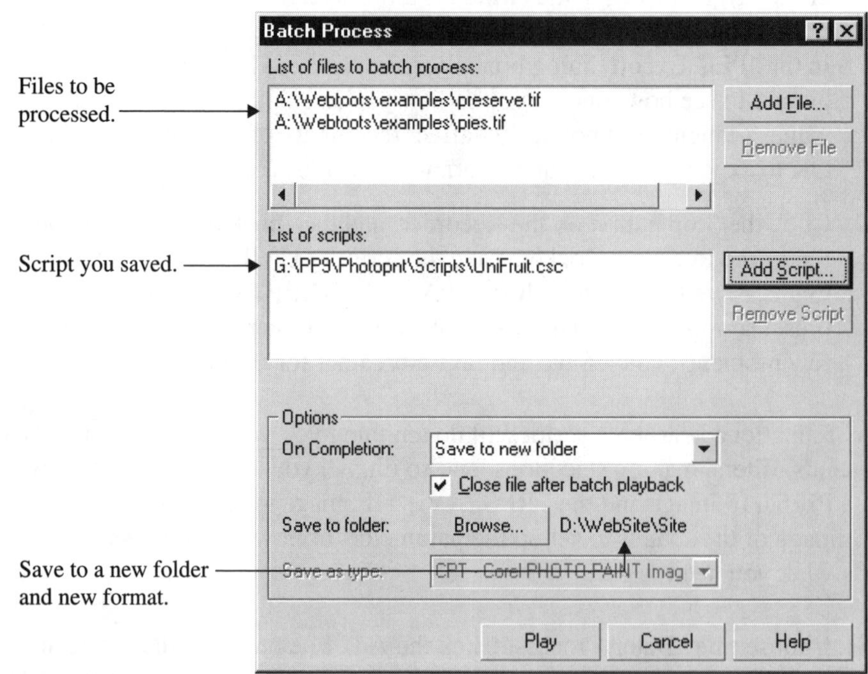

FIGURE 24-27 The Batch Process command can save you hours, or days, with complex image editing that needs to be applied to a number of images

Okay, what else did we see on this TEMPLAT2.TIF image that needs to be knocked down? There are three link buttons that will whisk the visitor off to a comprehensive sales sheet on each of the product lines. Let's turn our attention now to the art of making link buttons.

Single Buttons for a Single Purpose

Unlike the image map buttons you created earlier in this chapter, *link buttons* do not have associations with more than one location—you click a button, and it does one thing—usually taking you to another part of the document (and sometimes to a different site altogether).

It's my opinion in today's "hipper than hip" web design contest that buttons should still look like buttons. In this way, visitors know clearly that they are supposed to click the small piece of artwork. I've seen tubes of paint animate, and icons that look as though they were written in Sanskrit on web pages. Trust me, the more clearly you make the button look like a button, the more easily users will navigate and continue to visit the site you've designed.

In Figure 24-28, you can see what can be easily produced in CorelDEPTH, using different shading styles and a picture font such as Wingdings or Zapf Dingbats. On the right of this image, however, are buttons created by *moi*—and PHOTO-PAINT. Why not take a few extra moments and learn to design buttons by hand?

TIP: *You can put text on buttons you create yourself, and save on overall text on a web page.*

Here's how to get really familiar with the Interactive Fill tool and some of the other tools in PHOTO-PAINT, as you create a miniature masterpiece (buttons are supposed to be small):

1. Create a new image that is 0.5 inch on a side. You will have to work on this image at 500% viewing resolution or more, but how often do you get to do strange stuff like this and tell folks it's your profession?
2. Create a new object on the Objects Docker, and then zoom in to the image to about 600%. Select the Circle Mask tool, and while holding CTRL, drag a perfect circle that is one or two pixels smaller than the image window.

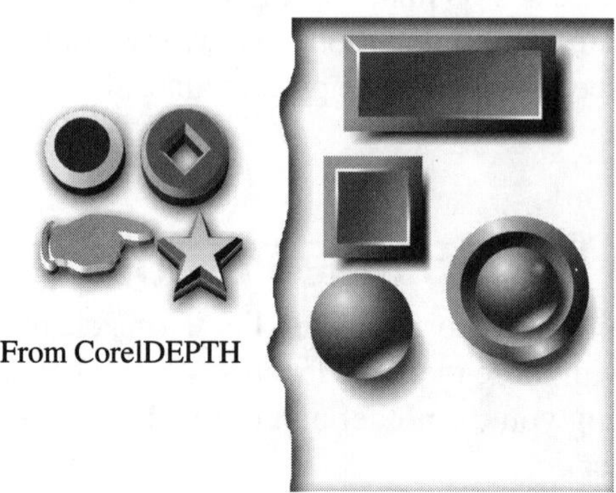

FIGURE 24-28 Buttons can be made by an application, or painted by yourself in PHOTO-PAINT. The only caveat is that the buttons should *look like* buttons

3. Click the Interactive Fill tool, and then drag it in the window from about 11 o'clock to 4 o'clock. Chances are either that the Interactive Fill tool has colors that are factory preset or that you used other colors before picking up this book. We need to get 20% black at the starting node and 80% black at the end node, and we need the fill to be linear, as shown in Figure 24-29. Click and drag on the 20% black swatch on the color palette, and drag it into the rectangular (beginning) node in the image window. Then drag the 80% black swatch off the color palette, and drop it in the ending node in the image. If you have intermediate nodes, right-click on them, and choose Delete from the pop-up list.

4. With the Object Pick tool selected, press CTRL-SHIFT-R to remove the mask from the filled circle. Press CTRL-R to display rulers around the image (this is the only way to drag guidelines into the image). Drag the zero origin to the upper left of the image canvas. Drag a horizontal, and then a vertical, guideline to +1/16th inch into the image. Click the New Object button on the Objects palette. This is all illustrated in Figure 24-30, so peek ahead if you need to.

5. With the Circle Mask tool, hold CTRL and then drag a circle from the vertex of the two guidelines to about 1/16th inch up and to the right of the bottom right of the original circle. Drag the Interactive Fill tool in the opposite direction, from 4 to 11 o'clock. Press CTRL-SHIFT-R to remove the mask.

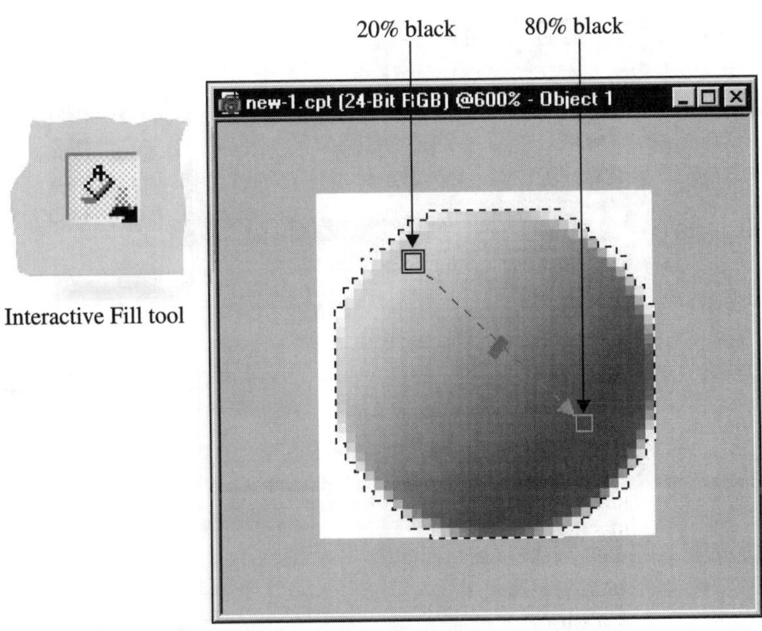

FIGURE 24-29 Use the Interactive Fill tool to suggest lighting on the button you'll create

6. Click the New Object icon on the Objects Docker. Drag a horizontal and a vertical guideline into 1/8th the upper left of the first circle you filled, and then with the Circle Mask tool, hold CTRL and drag a circle inside the two other filled circles.

7. Time for a change of pace. Select the Interactive Fill tool, but choose Radial from the Property Bar, and then drag from 11 to 4 o'clock, as shown in Figure 24-30. This is a pretty fancy button, considering you only have half an inch to work in, eh?

8. SHIFT-click all the Object titles on the Object Docker *except* the Background. Press CTRL-ALT-DOWN ARROW to combine all the selected objects. Save the image as BUTTON, in PHOTO-PAINT's format, to the STASH folder on your hard drive.

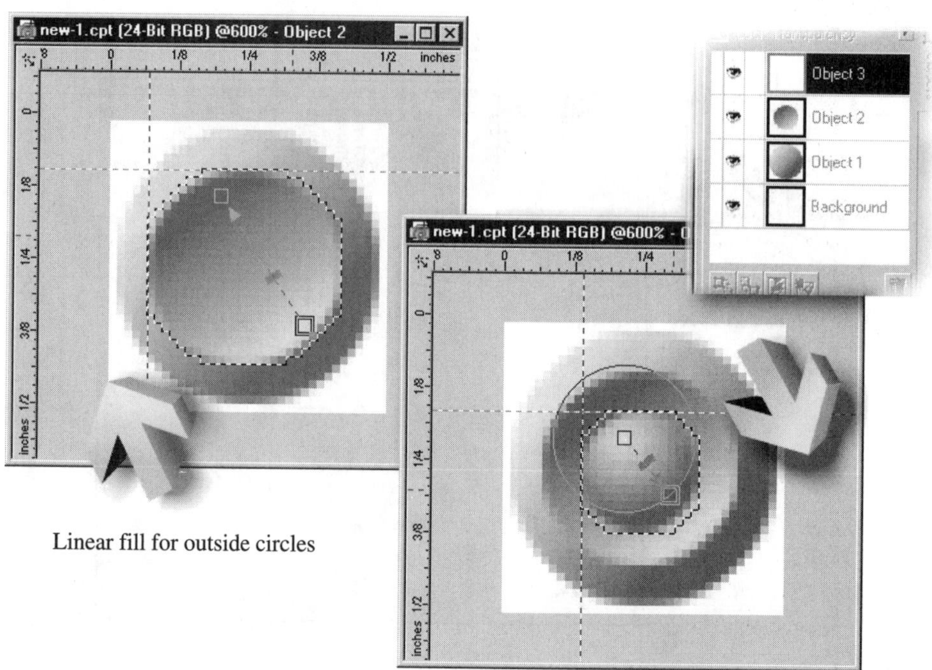

FIGURE 24-30 By changing the fill direction, you are specifying that areas of the button protrude while others recede

9. As a small embellishment, click the Brush tool and set the Paint to white. On the Objects Docker, click the Lock Transparency button for the object. From the drop-down list on the Property Bar, choose Airbrush, and then set the Nib size to 6, and the Transparency to 90. See Figure 24-31. Then click, don't drag, a number of times in the areas shown in Figure 24-31 to add subtle highlights to this button.
10. Press CTRL-S and keep the image open.

Scaling and Transparent GIFs

The button image you painted is small, but it's still too large to be placed on the products page, where it's indicated that the link buttons are only a little larger than the text.

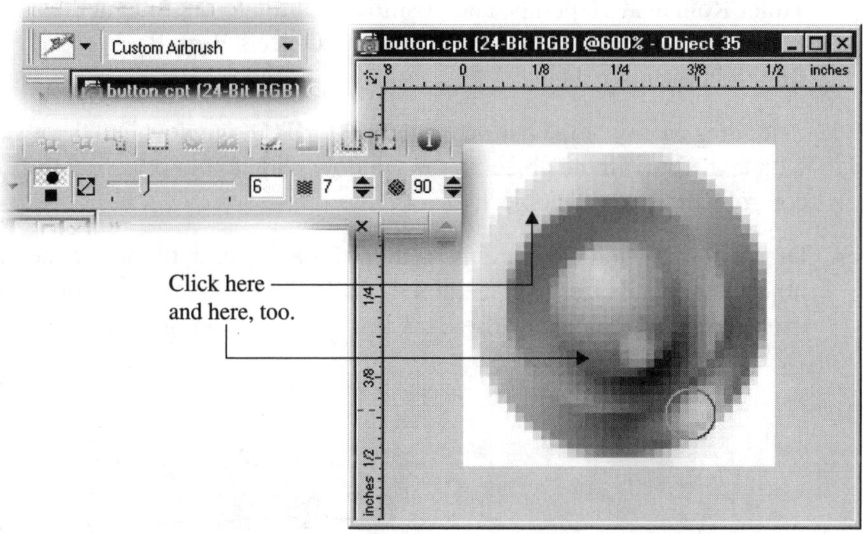

FIGURE 24-31 Although this button is made up of only a few pixels, it is rich in detail and realistic in its lighting

TIP: *Times Roman at 16 points, which is a browser's default font, is approximately 16 pixels high. Your half-inch button is about 36 pixels high, because there are 72 pixels to an inch—usually. This depends on whether you accept the PostScript equivalency of 72 points to an inch, or if you use the traditional, physical measurement of 72.27 points to the inch.*

One thing that I've not yet discussed, but will now, is the option to save GIF images with one transparent color in them, which will show the background through these areas. You'd choose a transparent GIF over one that's totally opaque when a background consists of a regular, repeating pattern. There's no way you could include some background with the GIF image and get it to align with the web page background. Although you can play a lot of tricks using HTML, precise graphics placement is not one of HTML's strong suits. So let's pretend that there is a pattern that you cannot match in the following steps, and you'll convert a copy of this button to GIF format with transparency:

1. Press CTRL-N and then in the New Image dialog box, make the new image 2 inches on a side. Click OK to put the image into the workspace.

2. With the Text tool selected and the Paint set to black, type **Click here**, in Times Roman at 16 points, and position it a little to one side in the new image. Click Object | Combine | Combine Objects With Background Button in the main menu.

3. CTRL-drag a copy of the button from the BUTTON window into the window with text. Drag on the object in the window with text to bring out the control handles on the object.

4. Drag a corner handle toward the center of the object until the outline of the object is a little larger than the text. Double-click inside the button to execute the size change. Close BUTTON without saving.

Drag handle toward the center to scale to text size.

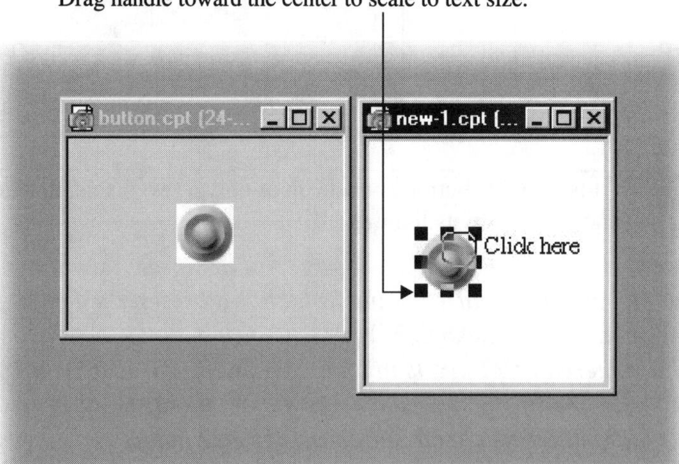

5. With the Rectangular Mask tool, draw a marquee around the button in the 2-inch image window onscreen. Choose Edit | Copy and then Edit | Paste | As A New Document from the main menu. We did this to give the button only the minimum necessary space to fill an image window—another way to keep file sizes down. Click the New Object button on the Objects Docker, and then drag the new object's title to below the button object so the clear object is behind the button. Select the button object on the Dockers panel and choose Effect | Sharpen | Sharpen. Accept the default settings and click OK to sharpen the button. Plain Sharpening works well with very small objects; the Unsharp Mask works best with larger pieces.

6. Open the ROUGH.GIF image you saved earlier to your SITE folder. Hold down the "E" key to get the Eyedropper tool, and right-click to sample a new Fill color from the image. Make sure the eyedropper is over the predominantly beige-colored areas, and not a deep ridge or such.

7. Click the clear object thumbnail on the Dockers panel to make it active. With the Fill tool, click in the new image window. This fills the new object with the fill color you sampled, as shown in Figure 24-32. Why are we giving the button a beige background when it's only going to have transparency in these areas? Good question, and the answer is, to prevent *fringing*. Most things have a soft edge in PHOTO-PAINT images, particularly around curves and diagonal lines. There are "in-between" colored pixels at the edge of objects whose color is comprised of a mixture of foreground and background color. To keep this button from displaying a white fringe when it's placed in the HTML document, you define the transparent color as the background color.

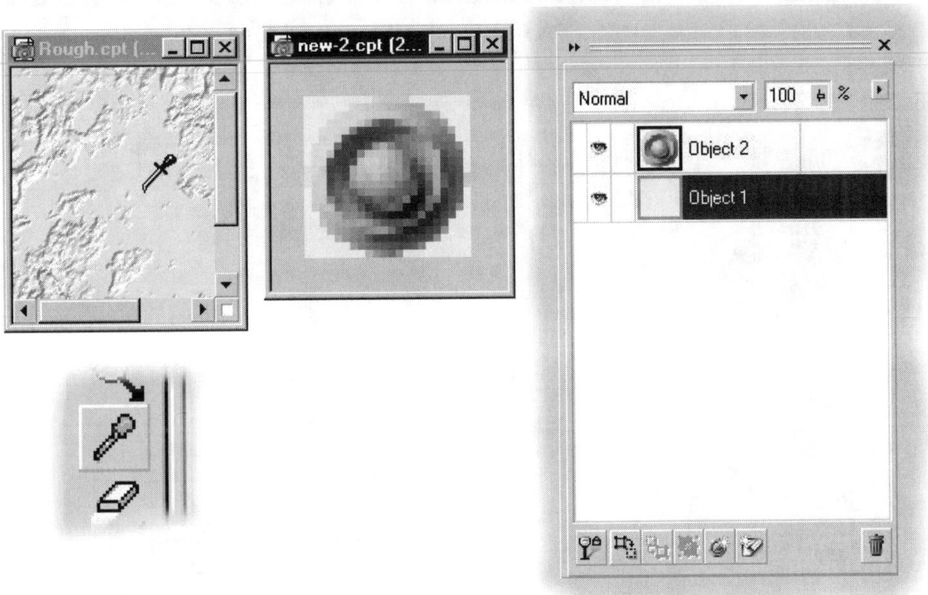

FIGURE 24-32 Sample an average color in the background tile, and then fill the object behind the button with the color

8. Click the button title on the Objects Docker, and then choose Object | Combine | Combine Objects With Background in the main menu.
9. Choose File | Export and then choose CompuServe GIF from the Save As Type drop-down list. Name the file BUTTON.GIF and direct the saved file to your SITE folder on hard disk. Click Save to continue.
10. In the Convert To Paletted dialog box, choose Optimized from the Palette drop-down list, set Colors to 50, Dither to Stucki, and Dither Intensity to 100. With the Color Range Sensitivity eyedropper, click over a medium shade on the button on the left, not the background. Click OK. In the GIF Export dialog box (shown here) check the Interlace box, click the Transparency Image Color button, and then click the eyedropper over the background of the button—the beige. Click Preview and you'll see the transparency checkerboard in the Result window pane. Click OK and you're finished.

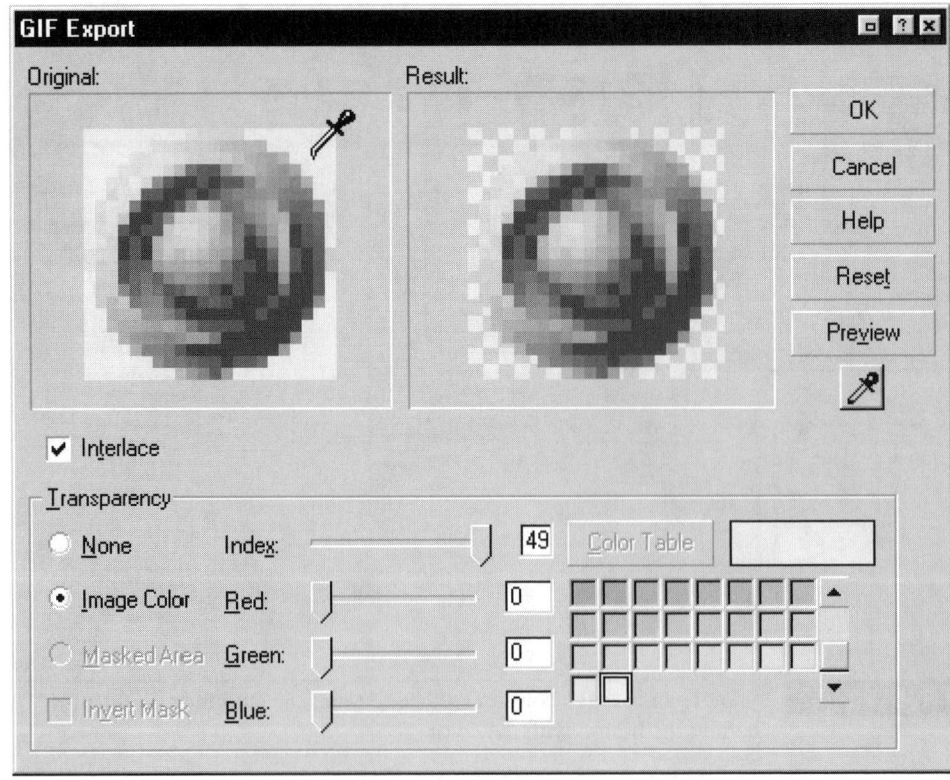

You can save and close the BUTTON file; the file with the text is no longer of use to you, so you can close it without saving.

A quick tally here: so far, you've learned how to create backgrounds and image map buttons, how to write a batch script, and how to make a transparent GIF. Let's put these skills together and create an animation to conclude this chapter.

Creating an Animated GIF

Animated GIFs were created by accident a few years ago when it was discovered that the combination of Netscape Navigator 2.0 and a GIF file that contains multiple images will play an animation when loaded in the browser. Microsoft quickly emulated the technology. It wasn't long before GIF animation kits were being offered all over the Internet. Fortunately, you have zero shopping to do to create your own animation, because the capability lies right inside PHOTO-PAINT's interface.

Now, there's animation and there's animation. A lot of the dancing baloney on the Web steals from this wonderful technical reality of creating tiny animations. Let's not go for the flashing, blinking marquee lights nonsense, okay? Let's play it low key. We'll take the UniFruit logo on the products page and make lights travel inside the lettering to subliminally push the viewer toward the product pictures.

Here's how to create the animation:

1. Open the TEMPLAT2.TIF image from the WEBTOOTS\EXAMPLES folder. With the Rectangular Mask tool, drag a marquee very tightly around the UniFruit logo, without actually touching any of the lettering.
2. Choose Image | Crop | To Mask, and then save the image as TEMPLAT2 and keep the file open. Convert this grayscale file to an RGB file by choosing Image | Mode | RGB Color (24-bit).
3. Remove the mask. With the Magic Wand Mask tool, click in a white area of the image, and then press CTRL-SHIFT-I to invert the selection. All the black lettering is selected now.
4. On the Channels Docker, click the Save Mask To A New Channel button, and then press CTRL-SHIFT-R to remove the mask.
5. With the Fill tool, click in the background of the image. The last color you used for a fill was the beige, so your image now is completely beige with an Alpha channel of the lettering.

6. Choose Movie | Create From Document, and then click the plus button on the bottom of the image window. In the Insert Frames dialog box, type **3** in the Insert box, and select the Copy Current Frame option.

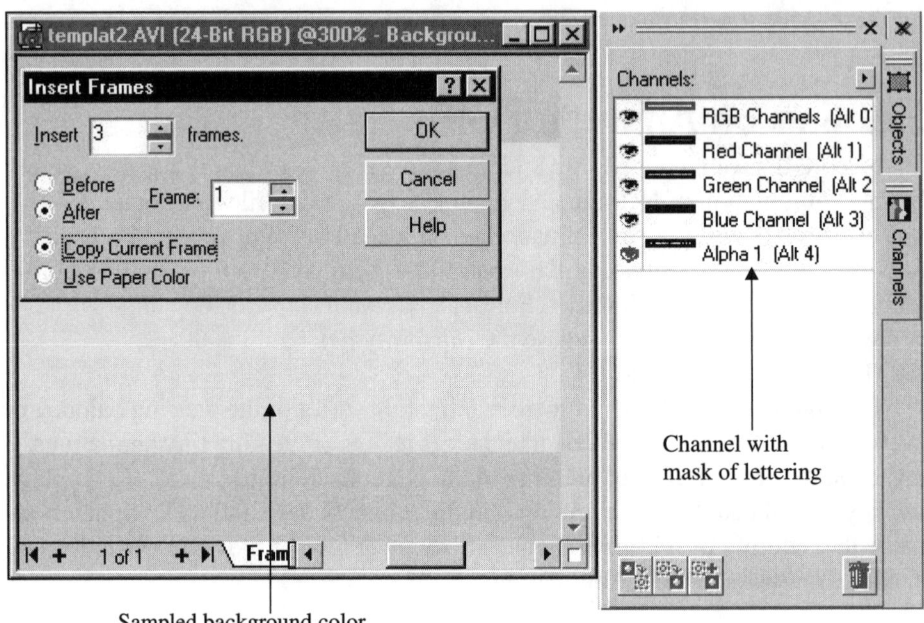

7. Click the arrow buttons to get to frame 1. Click the Alpha channel on the Channels Docker, and then click the Channel To Mask button. Click the RGB channel title to return to the color view of this frame. Click the Interactive Fill tool. Zoom in to the frame so you get a close-up view of the image and of the Interactive tool when you use it. (You're going to be doing some precision color selecting here.) Drag the cursor from top to bottom. Drag the black color swatch from the color palette to the beginning node. Drag the black color swatch to the end node. Click the chartreuse color swatch on the color palette, and then drag it to the arrowhead on the Interactive Fill tool cursor. Drag this new color so it's midway between the end and beginning nodes. Make sure that there's a lot of green at the top of the lettering by repositioning the Interactive cursor if necessary. Once you have a little green on the top and black on the bottom, click the Object Picker tool (see Figure 24-33), and then press CTRL-SHIFT-R to remove the mask. You're done with frame 1—click the forward button at the bottom of the document to move to frame 2.

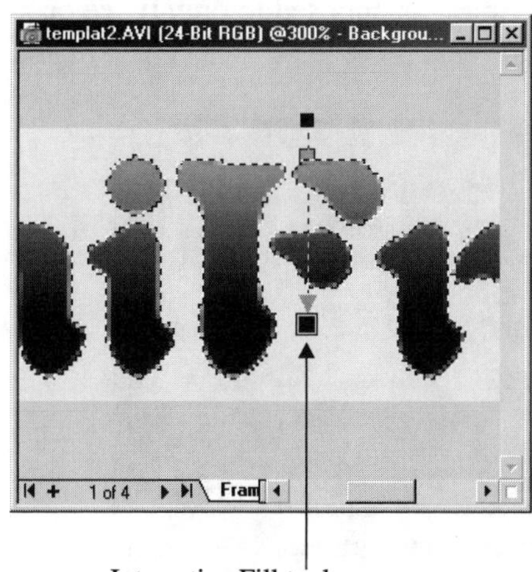

Interactive Fill tool

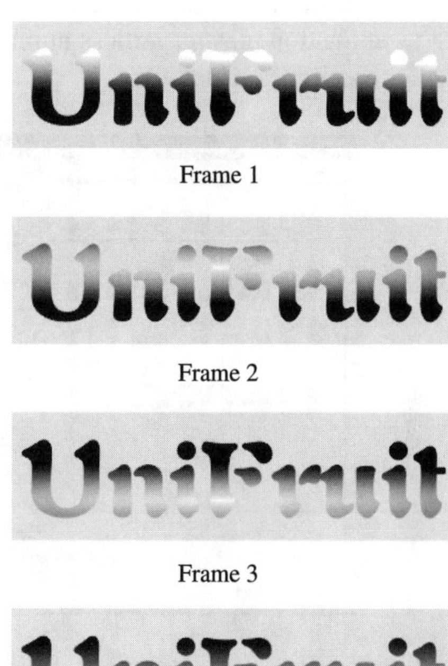

FIGURE 24-33 Keep advancing the frames, loading the mask, and moving the green downward in the progression of frames until at frame 4 the green is at the bottom of the lettering

8. Refer to Figure 24-33 as you repeat step 7 for the remaining three frames, making sure that the green "strip" between the black end and beginning nodes makes a downward transition in the four frames. This is going to be an eye-pleaser instead of an irritant to your audience, because there is a smooth transition between frames because of the fountain fill.

9. Choose File | Export, and then choose GIF Animation from the Save As Type drop-down list. Call the animation UNIFRUIT.GIF, and direct the dialog box to your SITE folder. Click Save.

10. In the GIF89 Animation Options dialog box, check the Automatic check box in the Page Size section; this ensures that your animation is only as large as the image window. Type **256** in the Convert To box of the Color Options section, and select the Loop Frames check box in the Frames

Repetition section. Also, choose the Forever button—this will make the animation play a limitless number of times, as opposed to only twice or three times. Click OK.

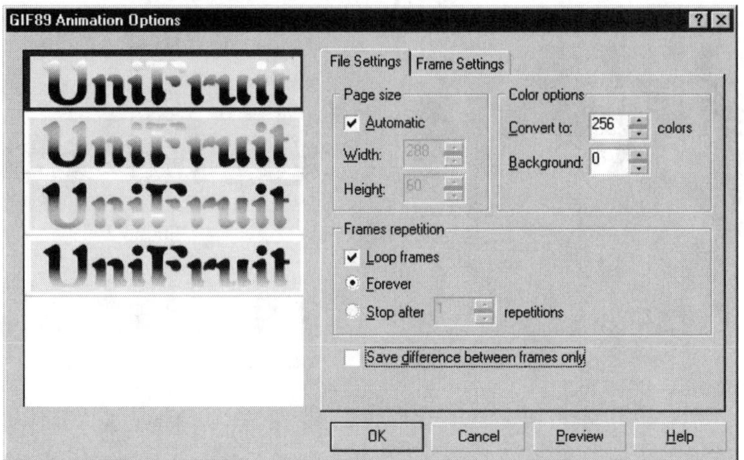

11. Click the Frame Settings tab, and click the Image Color button in the Transparency section. Then click the Select Color button. A subdialog box pops up and offers the Eyedropper tool for you to pick the one transparent color in this image. Click the beige background tone, and then click OK to return to Frame Settings. Click the Interlace Rows check box (this makes the animation begin to download to the visitor's browser almost immediately), type **20** in the Frame Delay box, and relax for a moment.

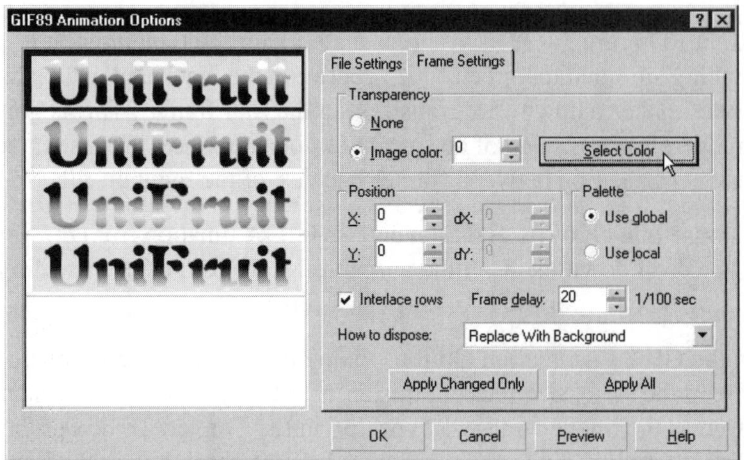

NOTE: *Simply because you typed 20 in this box does not mean that your animation frames will appear for 2/10ths of a second on the visitor's machine. Everything is relative, Albert said, and playback speeds of animations on the Web depend on the visitor's connection to your site (the quality and speed), how fast a machine he or she has, and a number of other factors. It's like those rows of TV sets at the appliance store. They're all playing the same program, but every one has a different color cast, right? My advice is to keep your frame delays as short as possible (but not ridiculous, like 1/100th of a second), play the animation back once it's on your web site, and then see if it needs further modification.*

12. In the How To Dispose drop-down list, choose Replace With Background. This means that once a frame has played its length, the background of the document is restored as the next frame loads. Oddly, this is the smoothest of the animation replacement types, and you should definitely invest in some quality time with PHOTO-PAINT's animation capabilities to see what other settings do for your work. Click OK.

That's it! That's the whole enchilada. Your animation is safely tucked away in the SITE folder, you can drag it into Explorer's or Navigator's window to see how it plays against a white background, or bone up on some HTML and actually create the pages we've only discussed from a graphics side throughout this chapter. By the way, the finished UniFruit site can be found in the WEBTOOTS\DONE folder on the Corel CD. Just double-click UNIFRUIT.HTML in the folder, and your browser will load with the finished site. Please take a moment to look at the source code of this site in a plain text editor. You'll learn some neat HTML tricks that this book cannot cover (hey, it's a book on *art,* not text).

Parting Gift

As a special going-away prize for being such a diligent and fast learner throughout this chapter, we'd like to send you home with a little surprise. It's a piece of JavaScript code that you can use in your own work to make a button light up when a visitor hovers his or her cursor over it, and it turns to a completely new image when you click it (and you're whisked away to a site on the Web). This is not the time or place to explain how this JavaScript works, so we've made it "cut and paste" for you to get visual results like those shown in Figure 24-34. If you open the JAVA.PDF Acrobat file in the WEBTOOTS\JAVA folder, you'll notice that there's a lot of typing, with some callouts that tell you what certain phrases do in this script. If you play the HTML document straight off the CD, you'll see three states for the button: default, what it looks like when you hover over it, and what it looks like when you click it. The whole page comes to 4K—how much smaller do you want for this little piece of magic? Follow these simple steps to make this document your own to modify for your purposes:

1. Copy the text from the Acrobat document into a plain text editor by highlighting the text in Acrobat Reader and then pressing CTRL-C.
2. Replace the names of the files in the text document with files of your own.
3. Change the dimensions of the three graphics that are stacked on one another, and you change the URL that this button points to.

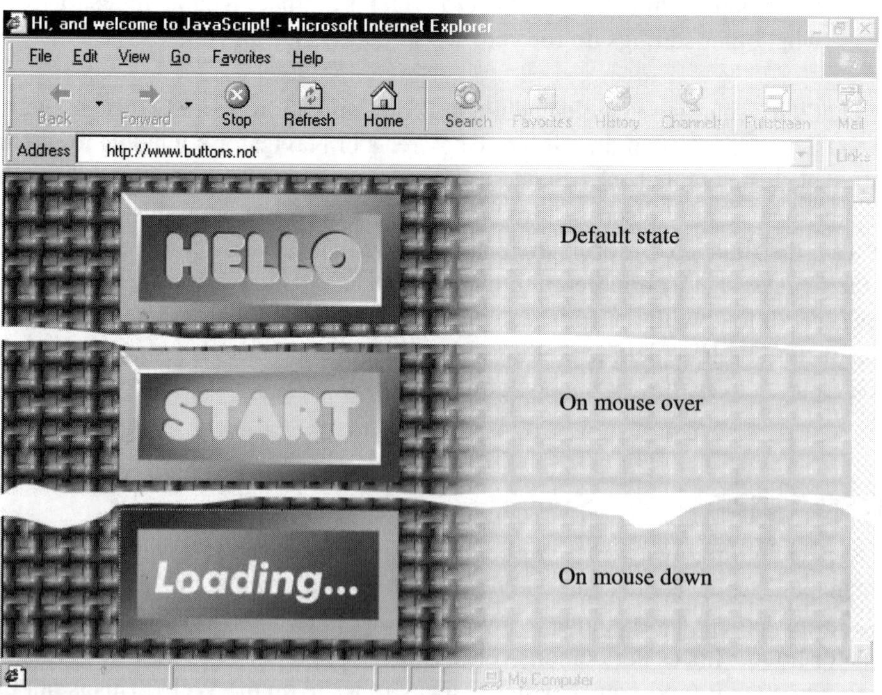

FIGURE 24-34 A JavaScript in an HTML document can create *rollover* buttons—buttons that change depending on your cursor action

Now you have the beginning of a glorious future as a PHOTO-PAINT web artist who knows more than the average designer about HTML code.

Conclusion

It's been a long, but hopefully inspiring, road from, "What's a web page?" at the beginning of this chapter to, "I'm hanging my shingle out tomorrow. The Web's where it's at!" Like any art form or communications medium, it takes a while for public acceptance to catch up, but if you ever doubt that web designing skills will increasingly become the topper in your bag of visual tricks, here's an interesting statistic for you. Communications devices like the telephone and television took 30 years to gain 25 percent acceptance in America. The Internet has taken *seven* years to do the same thing. Use the power of the medium and the talent to mix up those pixels to make your career anything you want it to be.

CHAPTER 25

Repairing and Restoring Photographs

Photographs seem to be coming at us from every direction these days. It wasn't that long ago that the key to good graphics in a publication was the effective use of drop caps or of some black-and-white clip art. With the cost of color reproduction getting cheaper by the minute, the placement of color photographs in a brochure or a newsletter is no longer extraordinary. It is expected.

The major sources of these photographs are two general groups: professional photos from stock photography houses, like Corel Professional CD-ROMs, and pictures (either digital or film) taken by ourselves or other equally gifted amateurs—or not gifted, as the case may be. In this chapter we will learn some techniques for correcting professional stock photography and for dealing with the latest craze—photos from digital cameras. We will begin with professional stock photography.

Touching Up a Stock Photo

Even when working with professional stock photographs, it is possible to have a photo that needs some touchup. This is especially true of the less expensive stock photos. The image shown in Figure 25-1 is a color photograph of a beloved lady that needs some work. In the following tutorial we are going to go through the process of correcting the image—including all of the missteps.

1. Open the image EXERCISE\PHOTOS\LADY DI. The photograph is shown in Figure 25-1. Although it is a stock (which is supposed to mean good) photograph, she looks as if she has been sunburned. Before we start, choose Edit | Checkpoint. Now you have a temporary copy of the image to return to.
2. Choose Image | Adjust | Auto-Equalize. This is the first command you should always apply, as it "levels the playing field." In my experience, in one of out 15 cases it actually corrects or, at the least, improves the image. Unfortunately, this photograph is one of the other 14. (No need to Undo.)
3. Another way to soften or tone down offending colors is to reduce the saturation of the image. To access the Hue/Saturation/Lightness, use the keyboard shortcut CTRL-SHIFT-U. Move the Saturation slider, as shown here, to the left until the bright red is gone from her face. This is a judgement call. I had to reduce the saturation 44% until the red was reduced, but the image looks almost like a tinted black-and-white photo. While this procedure might be acceptable if we were really pressed, we can

FIGURE 25-1 A less-than-lovely photo of a lovely lady needs some work

do better. So, I use the Undo command (CTRL-Z) to return to the starting point. When these "quick tricks" don't work satisfactorily, it is good to quit doing and start thinking. At this point we'll pause our step-by-step tutorial and plan our next move.

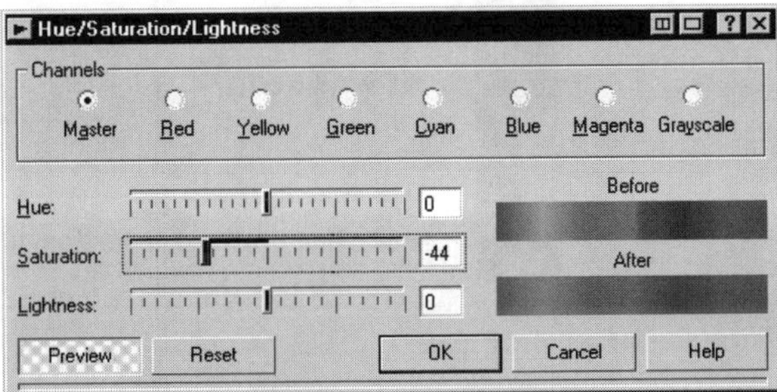

Revealing the Secrets of Color Channels

Looking at the photograph more closely, we can see a possible clue to the problem. It is seen in the bright red (almost purple) area of her face. The colors in this image have drifted toward the purple end of the spectrum, creating a slight color shift (or cast). Even though all of the colors in the image have shifted the same amount, only the colors that appear most predominately on her face exhibit the cast. This type of color shift cannot be corrected using the Image | Adjust | Color Hue controls. How do I know that? Experience! At this point we need to look deeper into this photograph. We need to look at the individual color channels.

If the thought of opening the color channels is intimidating, fear not. First of all, we need to know what the color channel is. The color channel represents one component of an image's color model. Corel PHOTO-PAINT automatically generates color channels when you create or open a color image file that has a 24-bit or 32-bit color depth. Individual channels are grayscale images that, when applied to their assigned color of red, green, and blue (or cyan, magenta, yellow, and black), produce the colors we see in the image. Combining all color channels displays the entire range of color present in the image. This photograph is an RGB image and so contains the channels red, green, and blue. Use the keyboard shortcut CTRL-F9 to open the Channels Docker window as shown next.

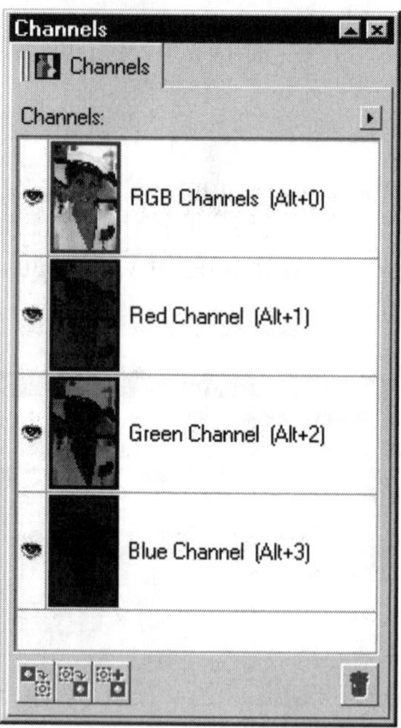

I have placed the three channels that make up the image in Figure 25-2(a), (b), and (c). While you have the option in PHOTO-PAINT of having each channel tinted the color it represents, I do not recommend it. It is hard enough to see image detail without the window dressing of the tint.

(a) 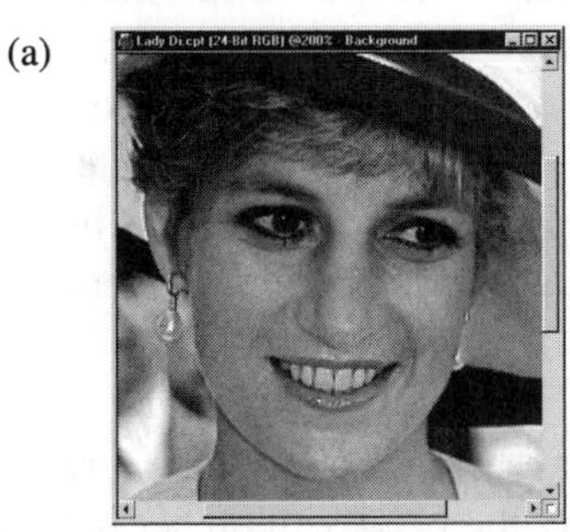

(b) 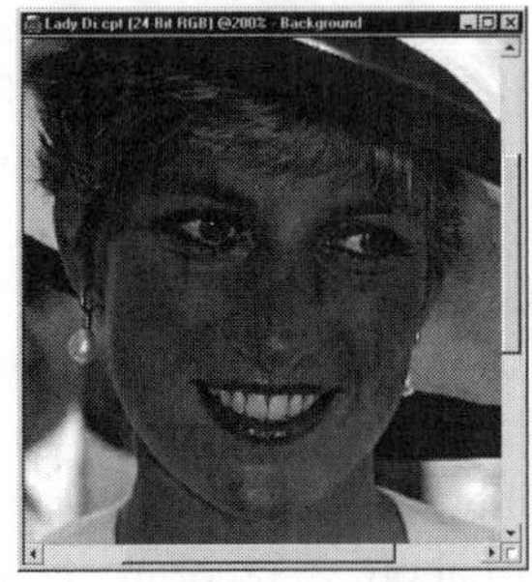

(c) 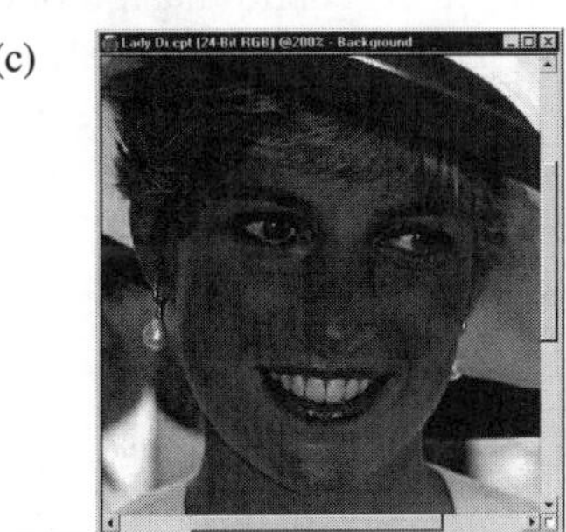

FIGURE 25-2 Close-ups of the (a) red channel (b) green channel (c) blue channel reveal some specific problems

Using the Channels Docker, click on the individual channels to get more information visually. The green and blue channels are quite a bit darker than the red. It is not unusual for the red to be a brighter channel. Of concern is how much brighter the red channel is than both the green and blue channels. This difference in the channels can be minimized. We now know that one channel (red) needs some attention. So now that the channels have revealed their secrets (so to speak), let's get back to the tutorial and fix the image.

Click on the RGB Channels title in the Channels Docker. Choose Image | Adjust | Hue/Saturation/Lightness. Shift the Hue +9 degrees in the Master channel. This moves all of the colors in the image away from the reds and toward the greens, just as the tint control does on a television. Shifting the hue in the Master channel applies the change equally to all three channels. While we have the dialog box open, reduce the Saturation 10% (–10) on all three channels.

We could call it quits at this point and tell ourselves what a wonderful job we have done. Look at the photo again and see what you notice. First, the rose she's wearing has an almost black leaf. Another issue is a slight blotching of red on her face, which looks almost like a mild rash. Both of these problems are related. You will remember that, when we looked at the channels, the red channel was brighter (by far) than either the green or the blue. While this is not uncommon, in this case we need to make some adjustments.

4. This step requires localized correction because, if we apply the correction I am about to recommend to the entire image, the black rim on her hat will begin to go weird. Select the Freehand mask tool (K) and make a rough mask outlining her, as in the image shown next. It isn't necessary to spend a lot of time to make a pretty mask because we are removing it in the next step. The one shown took all of 30 seconds to create.

5. Returning to Hue/Saturation/Lightness (CTRL-SHIFT-U), click the Reset button. First, select the Red channel at the top of the dialog box and reduce the Saturation of this channel by 5% (–5). This is enough reduction to remove the slight red discoloration from her face and keep the red of the rose. Next, select the Green channel (the settings we made to the Red channel remain). Increase the Lightness of the Green channel by 15% (15), and, to get a wee bit more blue in her eye, select the Blue channel and then add no more than 5% Lightness to the blue channel. We are not finished yet. Remove the mask, and next we'll correct the lighting.

The photographer who shot this photograph did not have the benefit of additional spots or reflectors or other studio gadgets to reduce and/or remove shadows. We have a wonderful tool in PHOTO-PAINT 9 (one that Photoshop users have always had) called the Dodge and Burn tool, shown next. *Dodge* and *burn* are traditional photographic terms describing processes used to lighten and darken areas of an image. In this case, we are going to use the Dodge (lighten) tool to lighten her face, which has a soft shadow made by the enormous hat.

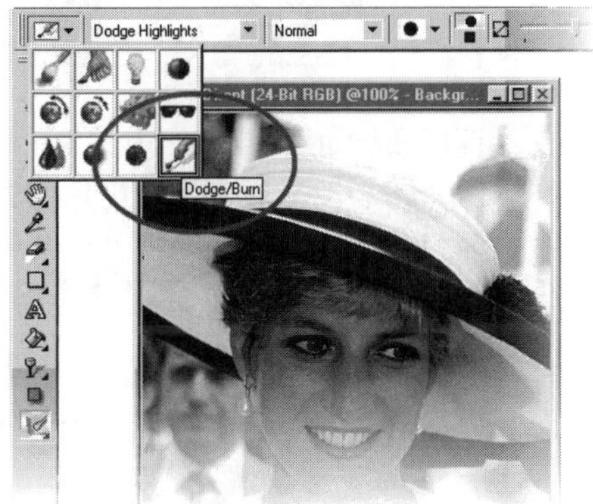

6. Open the Effects tools (V) and, from the Property Bar, select the Dodge and Burn tool. Change the Type to Dodge Highlights. There are two approaches to this technique. We can zoom in and use a very low setting (like 5 instead of the default 50); this way takes a lot of time, but it works the best. The other way (and the way I recommend that we use for this session) is to increase the Soft Edge to 100% and change the nib size to about 80. What we are trying to avoid is a line of demarcation that looks not unlike a tan line. Apply the Dodge Highlights setting to her face and to the rose bud. Just a thought—don't go wild on the rose bud. It will begin to get a neon glow if applied too much.

7. Two very small touchups remain. We need to remove the very slight pink coloration in the left (as you view the photo) eye with the Clone tool. Select the Clone tool from the Brush tool flyout. It should be in Normal clone. Change the Nib size to 5. Now zoom 400 percent and adjust the image window to fit both of her eyes, as shown below. Set the anchor and clone as shown next.

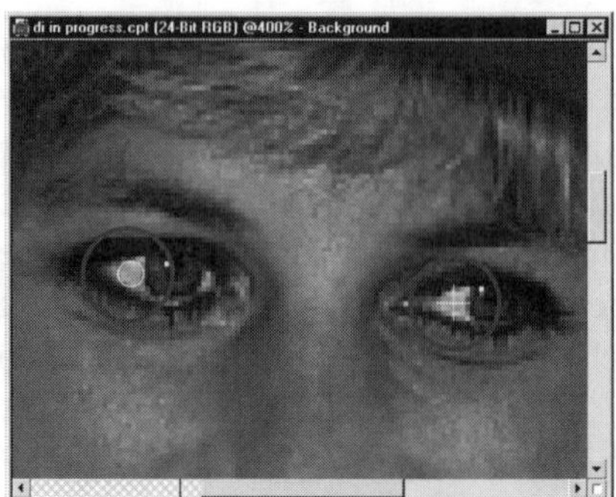

8. The remaining defect is at the far left in her hat. Remove the mask and fix the black defect in the upper-left edge of her hat with the Clone tool. The completed restoration is shown in Figure 25-3, to the right of the original. Go to page 7 of the color insert in this book to see the before and after photos in color.

FIGURE 25-3 Making the original stock photograph (left) look better is what PHOTO-PAINT is all about

In this session we have demonstrated that using a combination Hue and Saturation applied to individual channels along with the Dodge and Burn tools allows you an ability to color-correct most photographs. As you can see, tools in PHOTO-PAINT can change anything in this photograph to make it come out the way we want—except for bringing her back.

Hidden Treasure

Sometimes the camera records things that remain hidden until you use PHOTO-PAINT to locate what is hidden. In the photograph shown in Figure 25-4, it looks as though the happy waitperson (I remember when I could call them waitresses) stepped out of a black hole. This is a common occurrence with flash photography. The foreground is picked up and the background is lost, or at least it

FIGURE 25-4 This woman can sure hold her beer

seems lost. Here is a demonstration that will show you how to detect and then restore the background.

1. Open the image EXERCISE\PHOTOS\BEERHALL LADY. Our first step is to see if there is anything back there to recover. Choose Image | Histogram; the histogram, shown next, reveals some important information about the photograph.

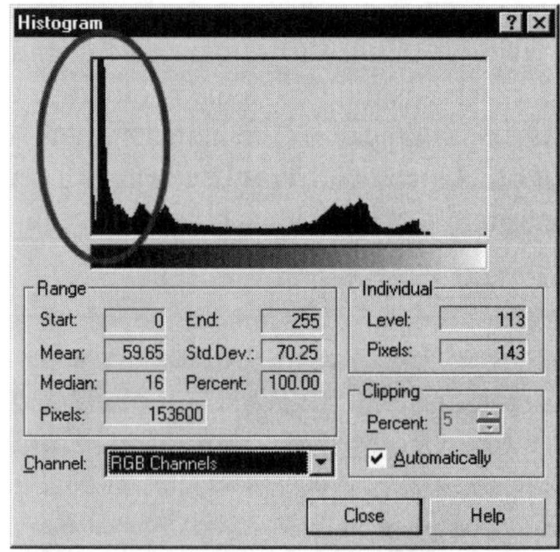

2. Don't let all of the numbers concern you, as we are only looking at the part of the graph that I have circled. This is the shadow region (sounds like the name of a daytime soap). If there were no recoverable information back there, a thin line would be flat up against the left side. Instead, there is some space between the last major spike and the left side. Our histogram has told us that there is image detail in the darkness. Click Close to close the histogram. Next, let's find out what's there.

3. To see what we have got back there, we will use a Lens. Choose Object | Create | New Lens. A list like the one shown next will appear. Select Gamma, and another dialog box appears. Change the setting to 3.0 and click OK.

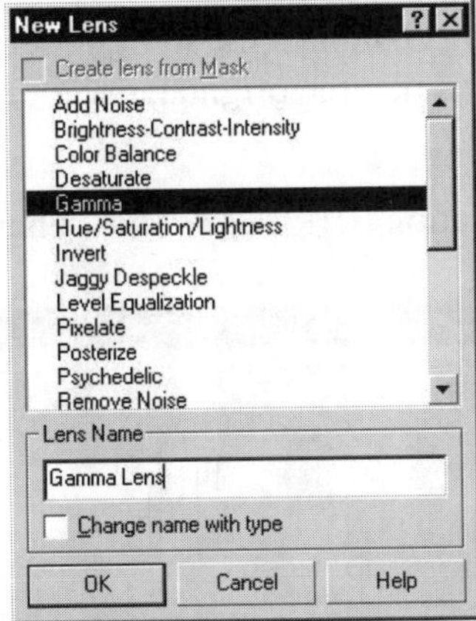

25

4. Now we can see what's in the background. It looks really washed out because we set the Gamma quite high. We did this because we must first mask the foreground to recover the background. Without the gamma being so high we would be unable to see where the foreground ends and the background begins. At this point you can select the Freehand mask tool and mask the beer lady and the man next to her, as shown next, or you can choose Mask | Load | Foreground and load the mask I saved with the image.

5. We are done with the Gamma lens, so right-click on it and choose Delete. The photograph looks like the original, except now it has a mask. Invert the mask (CTRL-SHIFT-I).

6. Open Level Equalization (CTRL-E), as shown here:

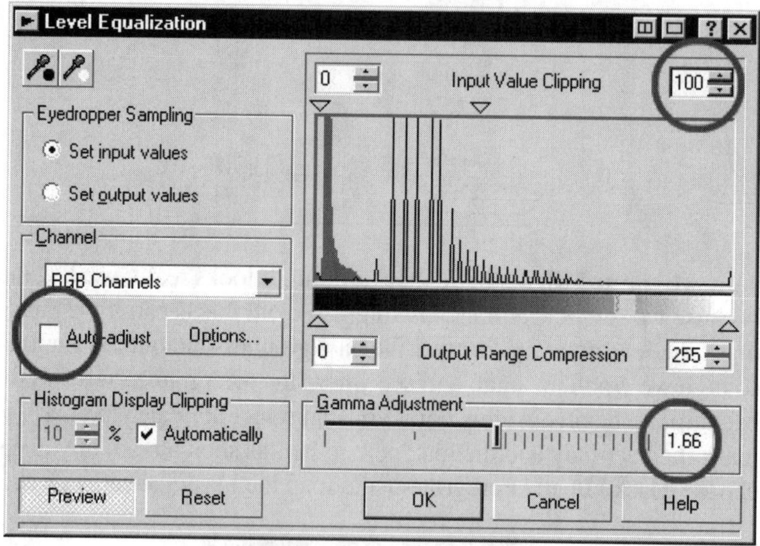

Uncheck the Auto-adjust in the Channel section of the dialog box. Change the white Input Value Clipping to 100 and the Gamma to around 1.6–1.7. The resulting brighter background is shown next.

7. Now we need to make some final adjustments to the background. Choose Image | Adjust | Color Hue and click the More Yellow box one time. We are doing this to compensate for blue being generally too strong in the shadow areas.

8. The background is still too soft (low contrast), so open Brightness | Contrast | Intensity (CTRL-B) and change both the Contrast and Intensity to 15, as shown next.

Brightness-Contrast-Intensity

Brightness: 0

Contrast: 15

Intensity: 15

Preview | Reset | OK | Cancel | Help

9. Next, apply a Gaussian blur (Effects | Blur | Gaussian Blur) of 1.5 to the background. A blur? Yes, for two reasons. First, as you can see, we have done some pretty drastic things to the background to recover it from the darkness, and it shows it in the form of graininess. Second, we expect the background to be slightly out of focus. The result is shown next.

10. To suit only my perfectionist nature, I use the Clone tool (after removing the mask) to remove the empty beer stein from the table (is their any sadder than an empty beer stein?) as well as the cigarette package. I also use the Clone tool (at a transparency of 80) to darken the poor individual behind the man in the foreground. His bald head and brightly colored clothes suffered greatly at the hands of our image correction. This mild darkening of head and clothes makes his fashion crimes less visible. The last thing I did was select the Effect tools and choose the Blend tool, set to the Blend a Lot brush type. I used this tool to soften the transition between the foreground and the background. The finished result is shown in Figure 25-5.

Now that we have learned a few things about image correction, let's learn how to improve images made with digital cameras.

FIGURE 25-5 PHOTO-PAINT allows us to reveal the hidden portions of photographs

Fixing Digital Camera Photographs

"You can't make a silk purse out of a sow's ear." That phrase, a favorite in Texas, seems fitting when working on photos created by the vast array of digital cameras that have recently flooded the market. The pictures produced by digital cameras tend to be grainy, the colors may be completely different from those of the original subject, and the image may exhibit a bluish cast. Yet, for all that's wrong with them, these new digital marvels represent the beginning of a new era. It seems that each day sees a newer and less expensive version of a digital camera that only six months ago represented the best of the best. I believe that digital photography will continue to expand and that it is therefore imperative that we, as publishers of these digital gems, learn how to repair the faulty images. So, we are about to learn the basics of making silk purses out of sow ears.

Some Digital Camera Basics

To help us understand the problems, it will help to know just a little bit about digital cameras. Digital cameras are scanners. While that is an oversimplification, the basic premise is valid. Sensors, usually using CCDs (Charged Couple Devices), capture digital images. Photosensitive pixels within these sensors respond to light, and their response is recorded digitally. Filters control the wavelengths of light recorded. In some digital cameras, the individual pixels are coated with color filters, while others use multiple CCDs to capture red, green, and blue values. The point to note is that CCDs are used in digital cameras to record the image and are almost identical to the ones used in scanners. Why is that important? Because from working with scanners, we know that CCDs have some limitations.

The CCD in the camera is least sensitive to the blues and has difficulty in interpreting those colors. Also, when you capture an image with a digital camera, it is often as not compressed with JPEG compression. The combination of these two factors introduces noise into an image that is already challenged. If all of that weren't bad enough, CCDs have poor ability to record subtle tonal differences in the shadow region (darker portions) of an image. So it shouldn't come as a big surprise that some digital images don't look great when we first get them. The first task, learning how to make general corrections, applies to images produced with a digital camera or a scanner.

In the next section we will look at an image taken with the HP PhotoSmart camera.

Fundamental Color Correction

The photo in Figure 25-6 was taken indoors with an HP PhotoSmart camera, which sold for around $400. You will find that most digital cameras that cost less than $900 produce images with hue shifts when photographs are taken indoors. I can see by examining the pug in the image that the colors are off in the direction of green and possibly cyan. I know this for two reasons. First, you don't see many pugs with fur that has a greenish-blue tinge. Second, that said same pug, Mr. Belvedere, is lying at my feet as I type, and I assure you there definitely isn't any green.

FIGURE 25-6 Two dogs who can't sleep because they need some attention regarding their color correction

Changing the Color Hue

Fortunately, PHOTO-PAINT offers an easy correction for minor shifts in color (which we already used earlier in the chapter): the Color Hue dialog box. Since the primary tinge we want to remove is green, we need only apply the complement (Magenta). To this image, I applied both Magenta and Red.

Softening the Image

After applying the color correction, I did a few other things to emphasize the dogs. This doesn't have anything to do with color correction and is more along the line of composition. First, although the sofa the two dogs are resting on is their favorite, it is distracting. So, I took the freehand mask tool and made a crude outline of their shape. Next, a Feather of 8 was applied to the mask so the transition boundary of any effects applied would be subtle. After inverting the mask (so the dogs would be protected), I applied a very light (1) Gaussian Blur. The sofa is still in focus, but the pattern is softened. Inverting the mask again (so the background is protected), I applied Contrast at a setting of 10. Normally, I do not advise using linear tone controls like contrast or brightness, but in the case of digital photographs, contrast really seems to help. This effect is especially apparent if the camera has compressed the image by making it into a JPEG image. My last step was to remove the mask and apply the Vignette filter to darken the edges. You can see the resulting image on page 7 of the color insert.

After all of this fancy work we have learned to do, let's now explore some basic non-color related issues.

Repairing Non-color Photographic Problems

I cannot deny that I enjoy using PHOTO-PAINT to create tantalizing text textures (try saying that after 2 pints of Guinness) and other exotic effects. Yet, for every wild and wonderful image I create with PHOTO-PAINT there are many more photographs that I manipulate to look good for publication.

Some of the material I cover in this section may be old hat for many of you, but I encourage you to review it nonetheless, as you still might find some little nugget you didn't know before.

Cropping—It's Quick and Easy

One of the most basic functions of PHOTO-PAINT is the cropping and resampling of images. Cropping is an easy way to improve the composition of an image and is often overlooked. Our subject is a photograph of a wine bottling facility in Argentina. In many ways it is a classic problem of composition. The photographer, my son, included the cardboard boxes on the left as well as most of the rear wall. Too many times, the photo appears in the company newsletter as shown in Figure 25-7. Although most page layout programs allow an image to be cropped with the frame, the original image is not actually cropped. I was always puzzled about this, so I asked Kelly Fraiser, Ventura Product Manager at Corel. Her answer: "Because Ventura doesn't have any way of knowing if the image is being used in another part of the publication, the original image is left unaltered." While the image appears cropped in the publication, the file remains at its original size. This is true of the other major page-layout programs as well.

The advantage of cropping the image in PHOTO-PAINT is that, after the photo is cropped, its file size is reduced. The original image in Figure 25-7 is over 2MBs. After cropping, the image shown in Figure 25-8 has a file size of 1.01MBs.

FIGURE 25-7 A poorly composed photograph is easily corrected in PHOTO-PAINT

In a publication with a lot of nonrecurring photos, this process can create a significant reduction in the size of a file sent to the bureau.

Figure 25-8 shows the same image after it has been cropped to center the viewer's attention on the subject. There have been several additional steps. For instance, the soft green cast of the fluorescent lamps was corrected by the addition of a small amount of magenta via the Color Hue dialog box. The dirty apron worn by the operator was cloned out and replaced with tiled background and then an Airbrush tool painted him a new pair of trousers. The Eyedropper tool was used to get a matching color from the cuff of the existing pants. Of course, I also made the bottling machine much larger. I don't recommend doing this with most clients. The white soft edges were produced using PHOTO-PAINT's Vignette filter.

Changing Image Size

When an image is too large or too small to fit into a frame and cropping is not an option, it must be scaled up or down. Back in the old days, we changed the size of

FIGURE 25-8 Now the picture looks better and the bottling machine is much bigger

pictures using PhotoMechanical Transfer. That process consisted of using a camera as large as a small car to take a picture of the image with the appropriate zoom factor. Now we can change the size of the image through resizing or resampling.

RESIZING *Resizing* is a process in which the pixels that make up the image get either squeezed together or stretched apart. The process of resizing distorts the image. If the amount of resizing is very small, you may not notice the distortion; however, if the image size is changed more than 10 to 15 percent, you will notice several types of distortion. With an image with an 8-bit color depth (256 color), expect to see posterization appear as the pixels are shifted. If a very small image is resized to fit a large frame, pixelization is the result.

RESAMPLING The best way to change the size of the image so it will fit in a publication is to resample it (we already covered resampling in Chapter 6, but it is worth recapping in this section). *Resampling* is the process of changing the resolution or size of an image to alter the number of pixels it contains. Making the image larger is called *upsampling,* and decreasing an image size is *downsampling*. The PHOTO-PAINT Resample command in the Image menu downsamples by either increasing the resolution of the image (thereby making it physically smaller while maintaining the same file size) or removing pixels from the image using a complex algorithm. Conversely, it upsamples by decreasing resolution or adding pixels to the image through a process called *interpolation*.

Going Up or Down?

Downsampling with PHOTO-PAINT is quite simple. Select the image and choose Resample from the Image menu to open the dialog box shown next. If you choose the Maintain Original Size option, PHOTO-PAINT will increase the resolution of the image to obtain the desired size. The image will remain unchanged as the resolution information settings of an image are maintained in its file header. If you do not choose this option, PHOTO-PAINT will keep the image at its current resolution and remove the pixels necessary to obtain the requested size. Upsampling is accomplished in the same manner, except the results will not be as satisfactory because, in order to increase the size of the image, PHOTO-PAINT must create pixels to make the image larger. Doing this always results in a slight blurring in the image. I have a simple rule regarding upsampling: don't do it if it can be avoided. The best alternative to upsampling is to rescan the image. If you can't rescan the image, then try my personal recipe for making images larger. Resample the image so it is about 50 percent larger than the desired size, apply the Unsharp Mask filter, downsample to the correct size, and then apply a small amount of Directional Sharpening.

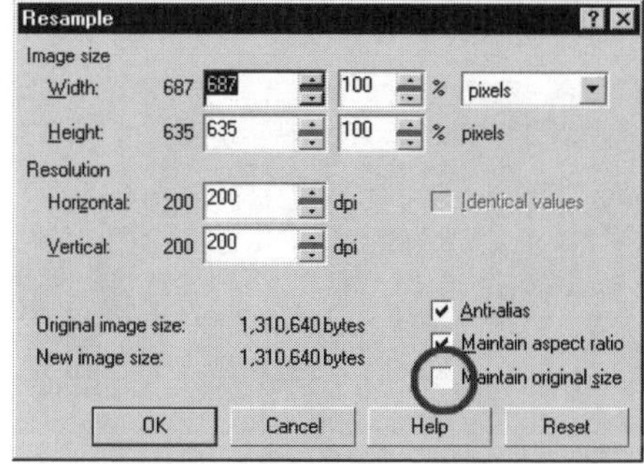

Keystone (Not the Cops) Magic

One of the obstacles of photography with wide-angle lenses is a phenomenon of distortion known as *keystoning*. An example of this is shown next. While this building may look familiar to those of you who saw the movie *Men in Black*, the apartment building on the left looks as though it is leaning over and the street looks as though it dips in the middle. This is not the type of image the local chambers of commerce want to use in their brochures.

We can correct this type of distortion with PHOTO-PAINT's Perspective Transform capability. It takes a little work, but it's not complicated—the following steps show you how.

1. Mask the entire image (CTRL-SHIFT-A) and make an object from the image (CTRL-SHIFT-UP ARROW).
2. Once it is an object, click on it until the object handles appear as small circles, indicating it is in Perspective mode. Now drag the lower-left handle in towards the center until the apartment building (or whatever subject in the image you wish to use for a reference point) appears vertical, as shown next.

3. In this image I used my genuine calibrated eyeball to determine when the apartment building was vertical, and I was just a tad off. (Note: a *tad* is a Texas unit of measurement. 1 tad = 0.2837 mm plus or minus a foot.) A more accurate way to have done this is to display the Rulers (CTRL-R) and drag a vertical guideline for reference. Regardless of how you get there, when you get your reference point so that it appears to be vertical, double-click the object to apply the Transform. Until you apply the Transform, you will find that hardly anything else in PHOTO-PAINT works.
4. The challenge we face now is the keystoned border of the photograph. The easy way to correct this is to crop the photo. The result is shown next.

While this process is simple, it does remove part of the original image. A different approach that maintains more of the original image requires the Clone tool to clone parts of the transformed image onto the original. (Note that this may be the only cloning that can be accomplished without sheep or controversy.)

1. For this technique, you need to make a copy of the original photograph (CTRL-UP ARROW) for the object to transform in step 1 in the previous exercise, leaving a copy of the original as the background.
2. Next, drag the transformed duplicate image off of the original so it becomes a separate image—it's just easier that way. Next, align the Clone tool so the source point on the transformed image is on the bottom-left corner, then place the Clone tool on the bottom-left corner. From this point, you drag the Clone tool straight up, replacing the buildings and the top half of the buildings, leaving the bottom half alone. I ended up with a white triangle on the right side but used the Clone tool to fill in the white area with pixels from the adjoining area. The finished image is shown next.

The are many more things in the area of correction and photo enhancement you can do with PHOTO-PAINT but it is time to move on to the last chapter, "Dazzling PAINT Projects."

CHAPTER 26

Dazzling PAINT Projects

If you have made it through the book up until this point, you have learned (or at least have read) a lot about how PHOTO-PAINT works. While we have had workshop sessions before now, this chapter is dedicated to showing you some fun things that can be created with PHOTO-PAINT. These projects that follow came into being as a result of work I needed to do for clients or articles written for magazines. Regardless of their origin, it is my hope that you try them out and learn first-hand how to create some dazzling PHOTO-PAINT effects. OK, maybe dazzling is a little over the top, but they *are* really cool. We will begin with a favorite of mine—twisted metal.

Twisted Metal

There is something intriguing about text that appears to be created from twisted or distorted metal. Do you think I need therapy? The creation of this effect requires some complex mask manipulation that is combined with The Boss filter, but it is not difficult to make. This technique has several variations and works well with most typefaces.

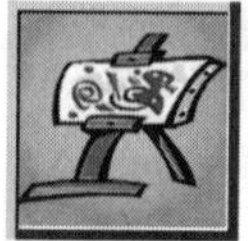

1. Create a new image that is 6 × 2 inches at 100 dpi. Next, select the Text tool in the Toolbox and, using the Property Bar, change the font to Staccato222 BT at a size of 150. Click inside of the Image Window and type **Metal**. Select the Object Picker tool and enter the text in the image (CTRL-A).

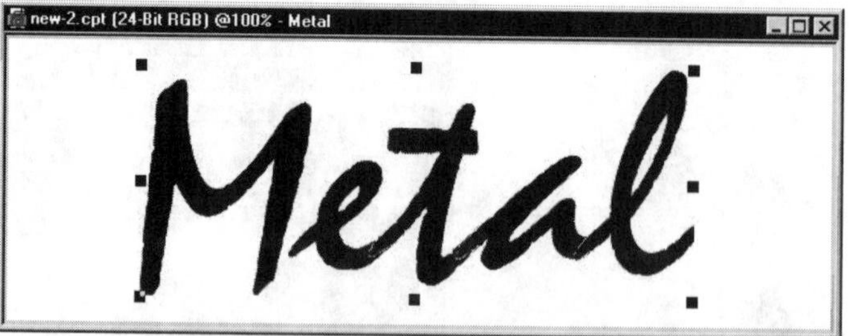

2. Create a mask (CTRL-M). Choose Edit | Fill and, from the dialog box, select the Bitmap fill button and click the Edit button. From the next dialog box click Load and locate the file EXERCISE\TILES\METAL. Click Open to select and then click OK again to apply the fill.

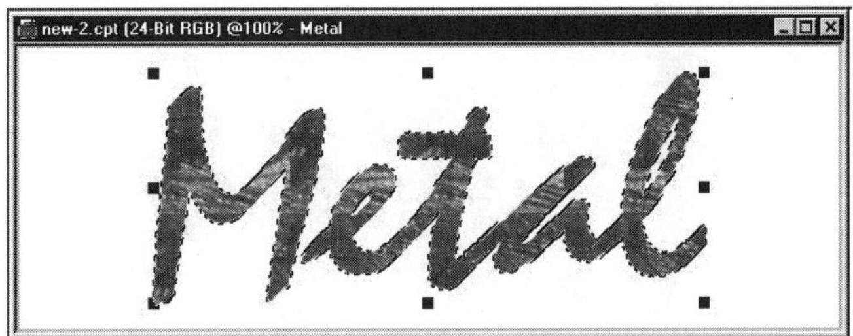

3. Enable Paint on Mask (POM) mode (CTRL-K). Choose Effects | Noise | Add Noise. Click Reset, change the Noise Type to Uniform, and click OK. Choose Effects | Distort | Whirlpool. Select Style: Default and change the Streak Detail to 100. Click OK.

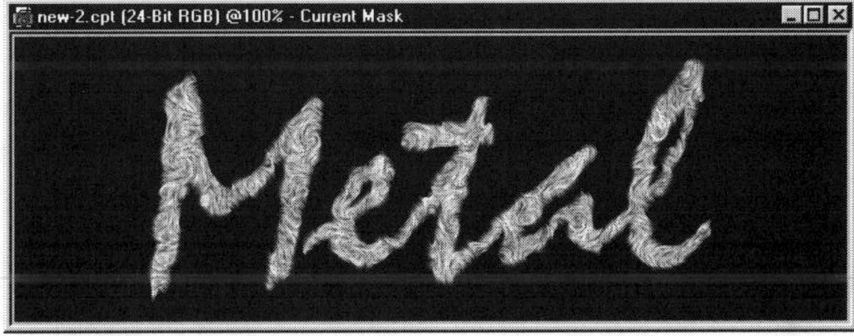

4. Close Paint on Mask (CTRL-K) and turn off the Mask marquee (CTRL-H). Choose Effects | 3D Effects | The Boss, change the settings as shown here, and click OK.

- Width: 3
- Height: 200
- Smoothness: 60
- Drop off: Mesa
- Brightness: 100
- Sharpness: 3
- Direction: 135
- Angle: 65

5. For the finishing touches, from the Toolbox select the Object Dropshadow tool and create a bottom drop shadow. Select the Object Picker tool and then remove the mask (CTRL-SHIFT-R). Select the Background in the Objects Docker Window before using Edit | Fill to apply a suitable background color or texture. In the final image, I choose a warm-colored wood from the Bitmap fill default selection.

In the next image, a Bitmap fill was again used but on a different typeface. The same technique was used except that the smoothness was adjusted. Please note that the settings shown in step 4 are for that specific image, and they serve as a good starting point for other images. I have these settings saved in my The Boss preset list as Twisted Metal so that I can open the filter, select Twisted Metal, and begin adjusting. When adjusting The Boss, you should concentrate on the Width, Angle, and Smoothness for controlling texture, while the Brightness and Sharpness define how shiny the object will appear.

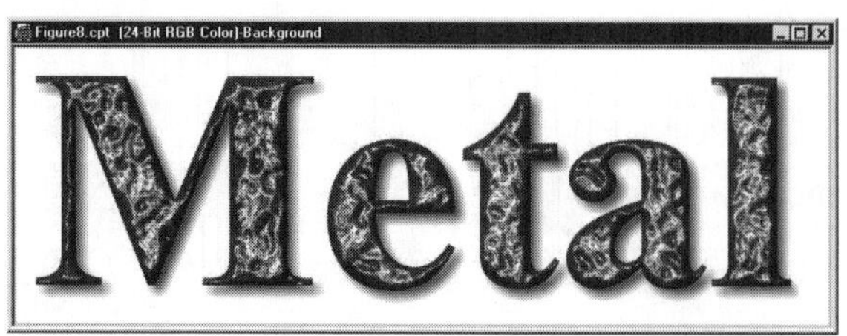

Old and Faded Type

This technique is simple but very effective in communicating the feeling of antiquity. It is designed to look like text printed on thick paper many eons ago.

1. Create a new image that is 6 × 4 inches at 100 dpi. Select the Text tool in the Toolbox and change the font in the Property Bar to AmerType Md BT at a size of 150. Place the cursor in the Image Window and click the mouse. To achieve the uneven effect that is so familiar to those of us who used manual typewriters, we need to make each character a separate object. Hold down the SHIFT key and type the letter "**T**". Now click at another part of the image and type a lower-case "**r**". Click another part of the image and type a lower-case "**i**". You get the idea. Repeat until all of the letters for "Tribal" have been entered, as shown next. As you can see, placement isn't critical.

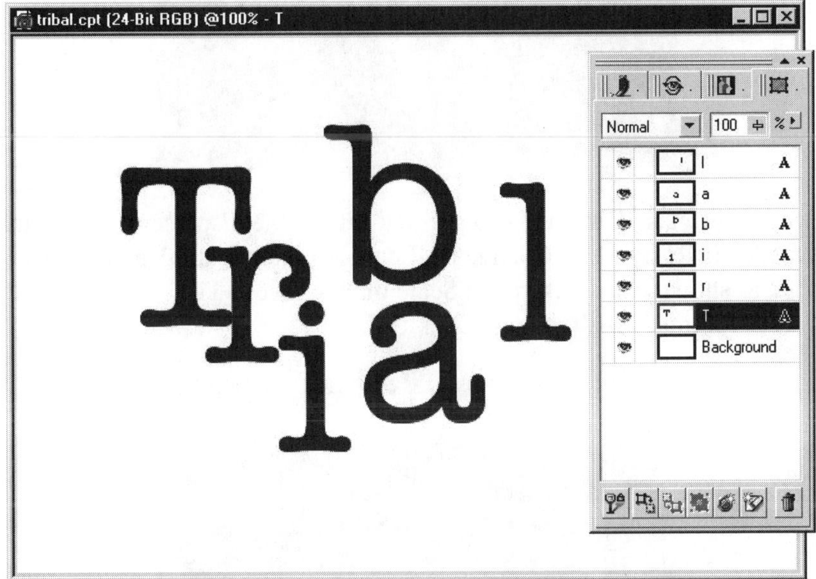

2. Select the Object Picker tool in the Toolbox and begin to place the letters as shown next. You can place the letters almost anywhere and have the effect work, but to make it look as though it was typed, it is good to keep the baseline of the text somewhat in line.

Tribal

3. Once you have the text where you want it, choose Object | Select All. Create a mask from the text (CTRL-M). Delete the text (DEL). Don't panic if your screen looks empty because your mask marquee is turned off. Enter Paint on Mask mode (CTRL-K).

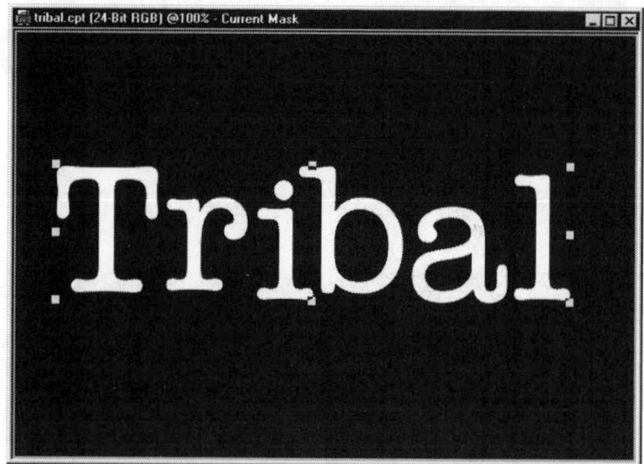

4. Select Effects | Distort | Displace. By default the displacement map that is loaded is Rusty.PCX. Change the Scale Horizontal and Vertical sliders to 50, as shown next. Ensure the Scale mode is set to Tile. The Undefined areas setting doesn't matter. Click OK.

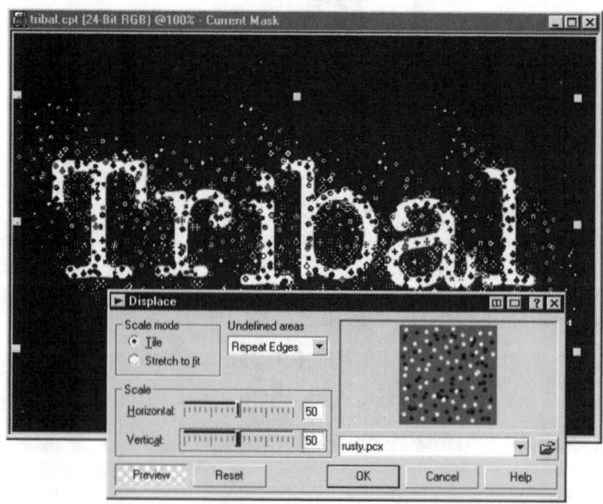

5. Now to achieve the effect we want, select Effects | Noise | Median. Change the slider to 6, as shown next. Click OK.

6. Exit Paint on Mask (CTRL-K). Select the Brush tool and, from the Property Bar, select the Artistic Brush and then change the brush style to Pointillism. Set the Paint to Black and scrub back and forth across the text mask until it is mostly filled. The object is not meant to completely fill the masked area. The result can be seen in the image shown next.

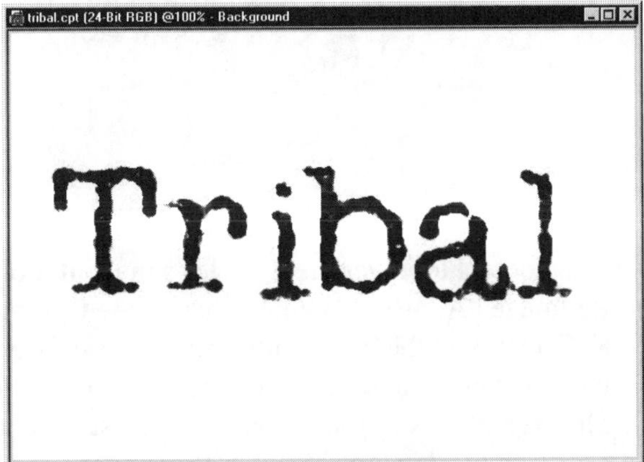

7. We could use it at this point, but it will look better with a background. First we must create an object from the masked area (CTRL-SHIFT-UP ARROW).

Select the Object Picker tool in the Toolbox. In the Objects Docker window, select the background by clicking on it. The black thumbnail of the background will become a red rectangle, indicating it is selected.

8. Choose Edit | Fill and from the dialog box click the Bitmap fill button. Click Edit and then click the color preview swatch in the Bitmap Fill dialog box. Scroll down the list until you see a tan-looking parchment in the left column. Click on it to select it, then click OK to select the Bitmap fill, and then click OK again to apply the fill to the background as shown next. (Note: As the final contents of the Bitmap pop-up menu have not been determined at the time of this writing, if there is not a parchment tile available, load the parchment tile in the COREL CD-ROM in EXECISE\TILES\PAPER03M.) In the Objects Docker, select the Object and change the Merge mode to Multiply. This makes the white invisible. Change the Opacity to 80%; the resulting image is shown next.

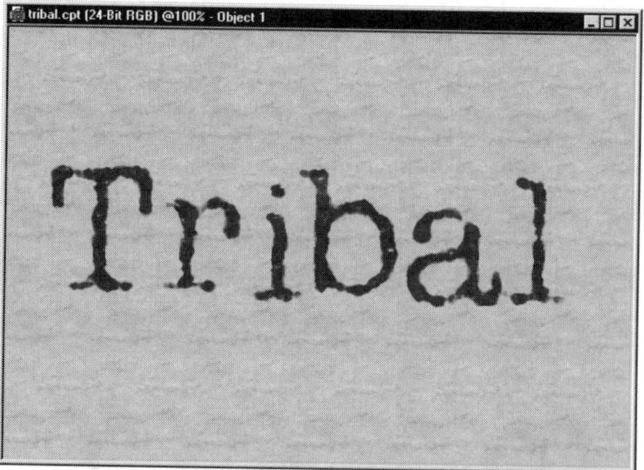

9. This bitmap tile doesn't look very real, so let's make it look more like old paper. Choose Image | Adjust | Gamma. Change the Gamma setting to 2 and click OK. Select only the background and choose Effects | 3D Effects | Emboss. Change the settings to Original Color, Direction 90, and Level 400. Click OK. It is still too perfect, so choose Effects | Noise | Add Noise. Use Gaussian at a level of 25 and a Density of 50. The result is shown next.

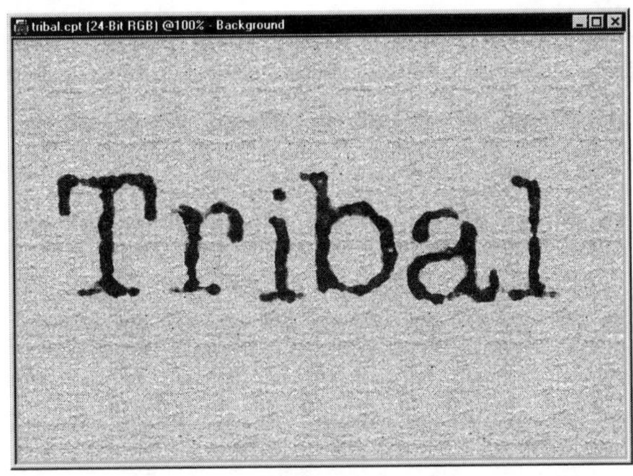

10. Choose Object | Combine | Combine Objects with Background. Save the file as TRIBAL.

Making the Parchment Look Real

It is one thing to make type look old and faded, now let's learn how to make the paper it's printed on appear real.

1. Open the file we just made—TRIBAL (it can also be found in EXERCISE\OBJECTS on the Corel CD.
2. Mask the entire image (CTRL-SHIFT-A) and make it into an object (CTRL-SHIFT-UP ARROW). Select Image | Paper Size and make the image 7.5 × 5 inches. Click OK. Select F4 to view the entire image.

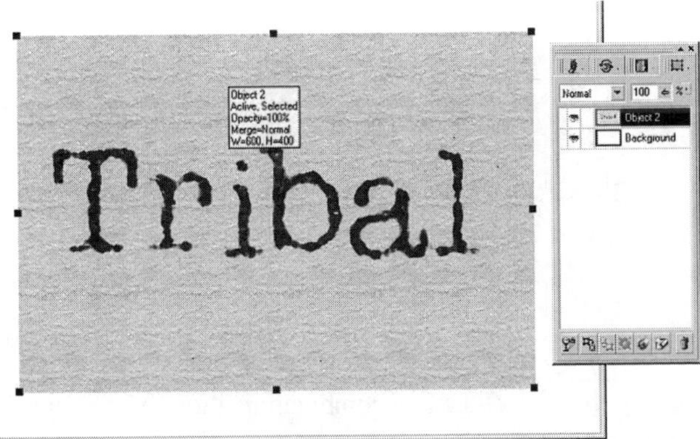

3. Select the Object Picker tool from the Toolbox—the object should be selected as just shown. Choose Effects | Distort | Ripple. Change the settings to Period: 35; Amplitude: 4; Angle: 55. Leave Perpendicular Wave unchecked. Click OK.

4. Well, we have ripples and distorted text but the mind still isn't buying it. It doesn't look real. That's because there are no shadows or highlights. Let's add some. Select the Brush tools in the Toolbox, pick the Air Brush tool, and change the style to Wide Cover and make the following changes: Nib size: 100; Amount: 5; Transparency: 96. Ensure that the Paint color is black and that Lock Object Transparency is enabled. Click at the point marked "A" in Figure 26-1 and then, while holding down the SHIFT-ALT key, click at the point marked "B." Repeat with "C" to "D" and "E" to "F."

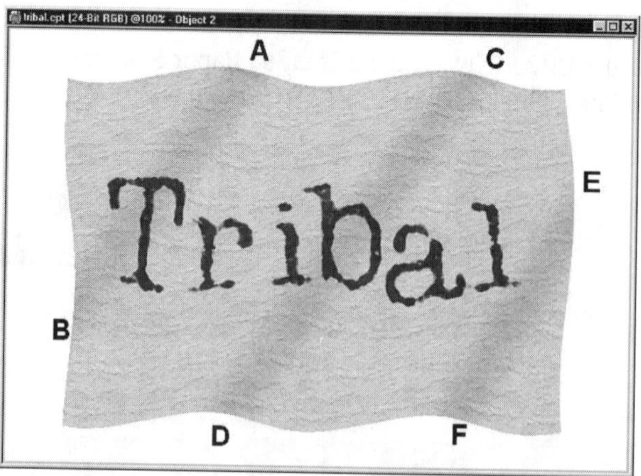

FIGURE 26-1 Using the SHIFT-ALT key combination allows us to paint straight lines to form shadows

5. Now go back and repeat the previous step except move the brush so the stroke is to the right of the first strokes. Change the Paint to white and repeat, except this time make the strokes to the left of the original black paint strokes. Apply light paint strokes near the edges:

6. Select the background in the Objects Docker window. Load the Bitmap fill Txtil23m located in the EXERCISE\TILES folder of the Corel CD-ROM. Choose 90 degrees rotation and click OK:

7. With the Parchment object selected in the Object Dockers windows, choose the Object Dropshadow tool in the Toolbox. Click and drag a down-to-the-right shadow:

8. Now for the finishing touches. The parchment is too perfect, so choose the Effects tools from the Brush Tools flyout and select the Hue Tool in the Property Bar. Change the settings to Nib 50, Amount –3, and Soft Edge 100. Paint randomly over the parchment object. Change the Amount to 4 and apply it again in other areas. The difference is subtle. Finally, select Level Equalization (CTRL-E) and change Black Input Value Clipping from 0 to 40. Click OK. Apply Effects | Sharpen | Adaptive Unsharp at the default value of 50%. The final image is shown in Figure 26-2.

Go Forth and Multiply (Create Cool Stuff)

Well, I could go on for another 200 pages, but the book wouldn't fit on the shelf. I hope that you have learned a lot about Corel PHOTO-PAINT 9 and, more importantly, that you will go beyond what we have explored. My favorite e-mail is from readers who have taken my techniques and gone beyond what I have done. Of course, I also like it when they tell me how they did it. So, until PHOTO-PAINT 10 (which I think is due next week—just kidding), as Red Skelton used to say, "Good-bye and God bless."

FIGURE 26-2 Now that we know how to make realistic looking parchment, let's learn how to forge passports—just kidding

Index

Note: Italicized page numbers indicate illustrations

A

B

C

D

E

F

G

H

I

J

K

L

M

N

O

P

T

U

V

W

X

Z

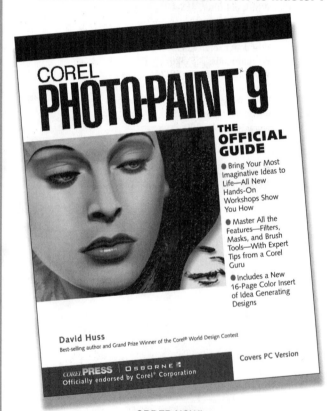